HISTORY

OF

MARYLAND

From the Earliest Period to the Present Day.

BY

J. THOMAS SCHARF,

Author of the "Chronicles of Baltimore," &c.—Member of the Maryland Historical Society and Academy of Sciences.—Member of the Historical Society of Pennsylvania.—Honorary Member of the Georgia Historical Society.—Corresponding Member of the Historical Societies of New York, Wisconsin, Minnesota, South Carolina and Virginia; of the Historical and Philosophical Society of Ohio; of the New England Historic-Genealogical Society, &c., &c.

IN THREE VOLUMES.

VOL. I.

1879

LAWS OF MARYLAND OF 1876, CHAPTER 346.

AN ACT PROVIDING FOR A STATE SUBSCRIPTION TO J. THOMAS SCHARF'S HISTORY OF MARYLAND:

SECTION 1. *Be it enacted by the General Assembly of Maryland*, That the State Librarian be and he is hereby authorized and directed to subscribe, in the name of the State, for three hundred copies of Scharf's History of Maryland, when published by J. Thomas Scharf; provided, any three Judges of the Court of Appeals shall certify under their hands that the said history is a faithful history of the State of Maryland and deserves the patronage of the State. * * *

SEC. 3. *And be it enacted*, That this Act shall take effect from the date of its passage. Approved, April 7th, 1876.

ANNAPOLIS, *July 24th, 1878.*

In accordance with the Act of the General Assembly of Maryland (Acts of 1876, Ch. 346,) and the certificate of the Honorable Judges of the Court of Appeals, I hereby subscribe in the name of the State for three hundred copies of J. Thomas Scharf's History of Maryland.

JOHN H. T. MAGRUDER, *State Librarian.*

PREFACE.

At a time like the present, when historical studies are pursued with a zeal and an acumen never before known, when, especially, local histories are the subjects of diligent and enthusiastic research, when counties and townships have their annalists, and historical societies are active in collecting the records of the past, it is somewhat surprising that Maryland, with a past so illustrious, so full of interest, and in many respects unique, should have no proper history.

We say this with all respect to the distinguished writers who have preceded us in this field, to two of whom we hasten to acknowledge our indebtedness. The work of Bozman is a master-piece of diligent research and deep reflection, and a treasury of materials for the study of our earliest colonial period; though important documents, not accessible in Bozman's time, have since been brought to light. But Bozman's work covers a space of only twenty-eight years of Maryland history, from the visit of George Calvert to the Chesapeake in 1629, to the restoration of the government to Cæcilius in 1657.

Of the *Historical View of the Government of Maryland*, by McMahon, it is scarcely possible to speak in terms of too high praise. But that acute and profound jurist has confined his labors strictly to his especial object. He has given a thorough and luminous view of the foundation of the government, its operation, and the changes it progressively underwent during one hundred and fifty years; but to give a continuous narrative of events was foreign to his purpose.

It remains, unfortunately, but a grand fragment, the proposed second volume never having seen the light.

The work of McSherry is pervaded by a warm feeling of patriotism which we cannot but respect, even when, as in some cases, it makes the author an advocate or a panegyrist rather than a historian. But Mr. McSherry, as his preface intimates, aimed rather at producing a popular narrative than a work of thorough research; and on many points he seems either not to have had access to, or not to have carefully examined, the original documents and records; and the errors and omissions thus occasioned render his work, which comes down to the year 1847, very far from satisfactory.

It has thus happened that not only aliens, but even her own sons, have been very imperfectly informed of Maryland's true history; and she has been denied her due meed of honor, both abroad and at home. Yet no land has a history more worthy of being studied and laid to heart by its children.

The relations of Maryland with the mother-country, of the people with the Proprietary, the policy and political questions of colonial times, the attitude assumed during the wars between Great Britain and France, her position just before and during the American Revolution, were all peculiar, and are in the highest degree instructive to the student of the present, as well as of the past.

In the preparation of this history no pains have been spared to verify the narrative by the study of original and contemporary documents. The records of the Province and State have been searched from the beginning in their various places of deposit: the files of the *Maryland Gazette* from 1745 to 1840, have been carefully examined, and every book, pamphlet or broadside, bearing on the subject that could be procured, has been read and collated. During the years that this work has been in preparation, the text has been again and again revised, whenever any new light seemed to have been thrown upon any point, the writer's sole object being to record the truth; and if the patient investigation of weeks resulted in fixing a single uncertain date, he has held that his labor was rewarded.

Fortunately for the historian of Maryland, there exists, in addition to her own records and archives, a mass of material for her colonial history, preserved in those various collections of documents and correspondence now united in the British State-Paper Office. The historical treasures here collected were formerly comparatively little known, and not easily accessible to a historian on this side the Atlantic; but by the kindness of the late Mr. Peabody, who felt a filial interest in the history of his adopted State, a full and descriptive catalogue of such papers as bore upon that history was made out and presented to the Maryland Historical Society. By the help of this catalogue, the present writer has been able to procure from London authentic copies of many important documents hitherto unknown, and of high historical value.

As a son of Maryland, the writer feels a natural pride in her honorable history; but he has never (to the best of his belief, at least,) allowed himself to be moved from the straight path of truth by any bias in her favor; nor has he, in treating the dissensions of parties, early or late, looked at the questions at issue in a partisan spirit, nor swerved, knowingly, from the exact truth, as far as it could be ascertained. As an offset to the many defects which, doubtless, the work contains, the author ventures to plead his entire independence and accuracy, if not absolute, as perfect as could be attained by the means at his command.

That the reader himself may judge the soundness of the conclusions arrived at, the citations from rare or MS. sources, especially in reference to matters obscure or controverted, will be found frequent and full. Among these may be particularized the correspondence about the Coode Rebellion, and the extracts from the correspondence of Governor Sharpe and others, during the French and Indian War, which latter shed a flood of light on the political history of the colony, and the causes which led her to declare her independence of Great Britain.

Frequent citations have been made from other writers and incorporated into the text, sometimes with, and sometimes without, a textual reference to the authority; but in all cases (it is believed) the source is indicated in the foot-notes. When documents are cited without reference, they are from the records of the Land Office, or, if published, from the files of the Maryland *Gazette*, the official journal, or other newspapers of the day.

It is greatly to be regretted that a large mass of documents, correspondence, etc., belonging to the pre-revolutionary history of the province, has been so imperfectly cared for as to cause irreparable loss. Many papers have disappeared altogether; still more are perishing from decay, careless handling and improper stowage. The papers which properly should be assembled at one point, are scattered in different places. It is much to be wished that the Legislature of the State would make some provision for collecting and arranging these archives, and depositing them in some place of security; also for publishing those of greatest historical value.

In conclusion, the writer begs to express his sincere thanks to the many friends who have been helpful to him in his task.

J. THOMAS SCHARF.

BALTIMORE, *December*, 1879.

VOL. I.

COLONIAL PERIOD—1600 TO 1770.

CHAPTER I.

ENGLISH DISCOVERIES AND SETTLEMENTS.

CHAPTER II.

THE STATE OF RELIGION IN EUROPE.

CHAPTER III.

THE SETTLEMENT OF MARYLAND.

CHAPTER IV.

THE ABORIGINES.

CHAPTER V.

CLAIBORNE'S REBELLION.

CHAPTER VI.

INGLE'S REBELLION.

PAGES.

CHAPTER VII.

RELIGIOUS TOLERATION.

CHAPTER VIII.

THE JESUIT MISSIONARIES.

CHAPTER IX.

DEPOSING THE PROPRIETARY.

CHAPTER X.

SETTLEMENTS ON THE DELAWARE.

CHAPTER XI.

THE PROPRIETARY GOVERNMENT.

CHAPRER XII.

PROTESTANT REVOLUTION.

CHAPTER XIII.

A ROYAL GOVERNMENT.

CHAPTER XIV.

THE PROPRIETARY GOVERNMENT RESTORED.

CHAPTER XV.

THE FRENCH AND INDIAN WAR.

CHAPTER XVI.

RESISTING THE ENCROACHMENTS OF ENGLAND.

CHAPTER XVII.

THE PASSAGE AND REPEAL OF THE STAMP ACT.

ILLUSTRATIONS.

HISTORY OF MARYLAND.

CHAPTER I.

When we look attentively at any period of history, we usually find some one fact striking deeper and wider roots than the rest. Concurrent events which do not directly spring from it, are yet shaped and guided by it, frequently to unexpected issues; and when such a cardinal fact is understood, it gives the key-note of the time. Such a fact, in the latter half of the sixteenth century, was the rivalry between England and Spain. Originating in the peculiar mental and physical temperament of Henry VIII., fostered by the virtues and foibles of Elizabeth, and stimulated by unhoped-for success and the most memorable deliverance recorded in history, this rivalry took a bolder flight as ambition and avarice allied themselves with patriotism. On the fields and dykes of the Low Countries the English had learned to hold their own against the first infantry of Europe; in Cadiz harbor, in the Southern Ocean and the narrow seas, English sailors had grown to despise the formidable Spanish navy; but there still remained the wondrous aggrandizement of Spain in the New World, and the tide of silver that every year flowed into the Spanish treasury from across the Atlantic. It was but natural that England, in her new sense of freedom and mastery, should seek to cope with her great rival on this new ground; to replace her lost provinces on the mainland by new acquisitions in another hemisphere; to grasp a share in the Eldorados of the West, and retrieve the lost opportunity of Henry VII.

The first attempts in this direction form no part of the special history of Maryland, and influence the latter only by their results; the chief of which was the decision of the question whether the North American continent was to be English or Spanish. The other question, whether it was to be English or French, did not receive its answer until a century and a half later.

Nor were these first attempts encouraging. The expedition sent out by Elizabeth under the lead of Sir Walter Raleigh had disastrously failed, and the consequent discouragement had rendered the English mind almost torpid upon the subject. Fifteen years passed, in which Elizabeth herself died, and no effort was made to rekindle the former enthusiasm. At last a single voice was heard—that of Bartholomew Gosnold, who had visited the coast in 1602—

1

urging the importance to England and the world of colonizing the country called Virginia after the Virgin Queen, and embracing the region lying between the 34th and 45th degrees of north latitude, with an undefined western boundary. Some attention was given to Gosnold's representations and urgent appeals; but the prospect of success was gloomy, until a man, the report of whose heroic daring and wild adventures in other lands had preceded him, made his appearance in London, and united with Gosnold in urging the enterprise. This man was Captain John Smith, an adventurer in whom the romantic and the practical were strangely blended; who, to a courage which no danger could appal, and a resolution which no difficulties could subdue, joined a shrewd policy, wise forethought, and an extraordinary faculty of extricating himself from situations of no common peril. These qualities marked him out as one specially fitted to direct an expedition of the kind proposed; and his wide and varied experience, combined with a peculiar romantic enthusiasm, gave his representations great force and persuasiveness. Others soon united with Gosnold and Smith in urging the enterprise, which was recommended to the pious by the prospect of an unlimited field for the spread of Christianity; to the covetous by the allurements of certain and enormous profit; to the daring and restless by the vision of wild adventures and glorious exploits; and to the patriot by the glory of extending the English name and dominion over rich and boundless regions.

CAPTAIN JOHN SMITH.

These arguments had the desired effect. A company was soon organized, at the head of which was placed Sir Thomas Smith (or Smyth), an eminent London merchant, who had been chief of Sir Walter Raleigh's assignees, was the first Governor of the East India Company chartered by Elizabeth, and had been ambassador to Russia.

A petition was presented to James I. for his sanction of the new company, and the support of the royal authority. Well pleased to resume a favorite speculation, and willing to encourage a scheme that opened a safe and peaceful career to the active genius of his new subjects, he listened readily to the application; and highly commending the plan, acceded to the wishes of its projectors. Letters patent were issued April 10, 1606, to Sir Thomas Gates, Sir George Somers, Richard Hakluyt, and their associates, granting to them those territories in America lying on the seacoast between the thirty-fourth and forty-fifth parallels of north latitude, together with all islands situated within a hundred miles of their shore. The design of the patentees was declared to be, "to make habitation and plantation, and to deduce a colony of sundry of our people into that part of America commonly called Virginia." The patentees were required to divide themselves into two distinct companies;

the one consisting of noblemen, gentlemen, and merchants in and about London, whose projected establishment was termed the first or southern colony; the second or northern colony being assigned to a company composed of knights, gentlemen and merchants in and about Bristol, Exeter, Plymouth, and elsewhere. The territory appropriated to the first or southern colony was generally called Virginia, and preserved that name after the region assigned to the second or northern colony obtained, in 1614, the name of New England.

The summer was spent by the patentees in preparations for planting a colony, for which the vain, pedantic king found a peculiarly congenial occupation in framing a code of laws. At length, on the 19th day of December, 1606, one hundred and nine years after the discovery of the American continent by Cabot, the little squadron of three vessels, one of twenty tons, one of forty, and the third of one hundred tons burthen, bearing one hundred and five colonists, set sail under the command of Captain Christopher Newport.

Captain Newport took the old West India route, and owing to a fortunate storm which drove the vessels past Roanoke, the place of destination, they entered Chesapeake Bay the 26th of April, 1607. The headlands at its mouth they named Cape Henry and Cape Charles, in honor of the Prince of Wales and his brother, the Duke of York, afterwards Charles I. The deep water for anchorage "putting the emigrants in good Comfort," gave a name to the point which terminates the Virginia peninsula.

A party of thirty landing on Cape Henry, were attacked by five of the natives, and had two of their number wounded. Thence coasting the southern shore, they entered a river which the natives called Powhatan, and explored its banks for the space of forty miles from its mouth. Impressed with the superior advantages of the coast and soil, after a search of seventeen days, during which they encountered the hostility of one small savage tribe, and at Hampton smoked the calumet of peace with another, they selected a spot on the peninsula about forty miles above the mouth of the river for the site of the colony. They gave to their infant settlement, as well as the neighboring river, the name of their king; and Jamestown retains the distinction of being the oldest existing habitation of the English in America.

The aspect of the new country seems to have charmed the colonists and completely fascinated Smith, for he declared that "heaven and earth seemed never to have agreed better to frame a place for man's commodious and delightful habitation!"[1]

It is not within our purpose to recite the hazards encountered by the early settlers of Virginia, or the narrow escapes of the colony from destruction. The red and white man stood face to face, and the latter was regarded by the former as an audacious intruder and deadly enemy. The contest between them was a contest of life and death. Unlike the Indians of Peru, who approached the Spaniards with awe and reverence, as superior beings,

[1] Smith's *History of Va.*, p. 114.

the Indians here looked upon the settlers with fearless hatred, and promptly made war upon them. But a still more formidable enemy assailed the colonists, born of their own improvidence. Famine, and its accompanying diseases, soon set in, and in one year from the time of their landing, their numbers were reduced from 100 to 38; and these, too, would have perished but for timely supplies of corn, which Smith had procured at great risk from the Indians. Among those who perished was Bartholomew Gosnold, the originator of the expedition; and we can but regret that he did not live long enough to see even the first glimmering success in that adventure he had been the earliest to advocate. The cause of this calamity lay partly in the provision of their charter, which required that the product of the united labor of the emigrants should be brought into the public stores, and that all should draw their supplies from thence. For nearly five years was this provision enforced; and during that time, with the exception of the short period of Smith's administration, the condition of the colony was most wretched. It is difficult to conceive a state of things more propitious to the theories of Communism or Socialism, and yet the failure was most signal. A productive soil invited cultivation, while rapidly diminishing stores admonished to industry and labor, and yet, in the face of certain ruin, the large majority wasted their time in idleness, relying for subsistence upon the stores provided by the industrious few. In this they were encouraged by the censurable course of their officers who controlled the supplies, and feasted abundantly, while others had doled out to them a pint of damaged wheat or barley. To aggravate their sufferings, a fire broke out and left them houseless in the depth of a severe winter. Smith's fortunate return from an exploring expedition, bringing supplies of corn, alone saved the poor remnant of the first settlers from perishing.

With his return a new spirit seemed to be aroused in the colonists; every one went steadily to work to repair the damages occasioned by the fire, and the town soon arose from its ashes. The church was substantially rebuilt, and better houses took the places of those destroyed. Smith had been denied a place in the council by the men who had borne sway, but the spirit of the many now broke into open revolt—the unwise and selfish councillors were expelled by the popular voice, and Smith installed in the presidency; the first instance of popular revolt against tyrannical misrule which occurred in America.

While the presidency was filled by Smith, "peace was firmly established with all the people of Powhatan." Plenty returned and discontent ceased; works of public utility progressed with rapidity, while the internal affairs of the colony were regulated by a spirit of discipline and integrity. Unhappily, on the retirement of Smith from the presidency, and his return to England, all fell again into disorder, and in a short time the numbers of the settlers which had risen to 500, fell to 60, and they half-starved and miserable. At last these wretched survivors resolved to abandon the country, and under the command of Sir Thomas Gates and Sir George Somers, who had been wrecked on the Bermudas, in the *Sea Vulture*—an incident which is supposed to have suggested Shakspeare's drama *The Tempest*—they took, as they thought, a final leave of Virginia, where they had buried so many of their comrades, and where they themselves had suffered so severely. Every sail was set, and every heart was filled with joy at what was considered an escape from death, when Lord Delaware, the first "governor" in America, with well-appointed ships, more than three hundred immigrants, and abundant supplies, met them in the river, off Mulberry Island, and prevailed on them to return to Jamestown.

A brighter morning was now to dawn upon the colony. A new charter had been granted by the king, and under Sir Thomas Dale, lands were assigned to every one who chose to cultivate them, and their profits inured to the industrious cultivator for his exclusive benefit under easy conditions. William Spencer and Thomas Barrett, two of the original settlers, were the first who undertook to cultivate land; and they were speedily followed by others. From this moment we hear no more of "the starving times," as the year succeeding Smith's departure for England had been termed. Peace prevailed with the Indians, who, for moderate wages, helped the settler to clear and cultivate his land. From this period the permanent existence of the colony may be dated. The golden dreams in which some had so wildly indulged, gave way to the safe and rational conclusion that substantial independence was to be acquired more readily by cultivating the land, than by pursuing delusive visions of mines of gold or mountains of precious stones. And now the woodman's axe awakened echoes in the primeval forest; simple but comfortable houses arose on the shores of the rivers, and in the bosom of the wilderness new plantations and hundreds were established.[1]

The explorations of the English settlers had not up to June, 1608, extended beyond the countries adjacent to the James river. Smith, who was disgusted at the follies which then agitated the colonists, formed the bold design of carrying his researches further, and of exploring the whole of the great bay of Chesapeake, for the purpose of ascertaining the qualities and resources of its territories, and establishing friendly intercourse with the remote tribes of its inhabitants. With his friend Dr. Walter Russell, six gentlemen and seven soldiers, whose fortitude and perseverance he was frequently obliged to revive, and over whom he possessed no other authority than the ascendant of a vigorous character and superior intelligence, he performed, in an open boat, two voyages of discovery, that occupied about three months, and embraced a navigation of above three thousand miles. With prodigious labor and extreme peril, he visited every inlet and bay on both sides of the Chesapeake, from Cape Charles to the river Susquehannah; he sailed up the Patapsco and probably entered the harbor of Baltimore;

[1] Tyler's *Jamestown*; Bancroft, i., p. 117; Hildreth, i., p. 99; Grahame, i., p. 48; Campbell's *Virginia*, p. 35; Sanford, p. 13.

ascended the Potomac to the falls above Georgetown, and diligently examined the territories into which he penetrated, and the various tribes that possessed them. He brought back with him an account so ample, and a plan so accurate of that great portion of the American continent now comprehended in the States of Maryland and Virginia, that all subsequent researches have only expanded and illustrated his original report; and his map has been made the groundwork of all delineations, with no other diversity than what has inevitably arisen from the varieties of appropriation and the progress of settlements. As this excursion appears to have been the first exploration of the Chesapeake that had been as yet attempted by any European, it forms as interesting a part of the History of Maryland as of that of Virginia; and from the only authentic record of it, that of Smith himself, we shall extract so much as properly belongs to the former.

"CHAPTER V." (*of Smith's General History of Virginia*, Volume I.)

"*The accidents that happened in the discovery of the bay of Chisapeack.*"

"The second of June, 1608, *Smith* left the fort to performe his discovery with this company:

"Walter Russell, *doctor of physicke*, Ralfe Morton, Thomas Momford, William Cantrill, Richard Fetherstone, James Burne, Michell Sicklemore, *Gentlemen*."

"Jonas Profit, Anas Todkill, Robert Small, James Watkins, John Powell, James Read, Richard Keale, *Souldiers*."

"These being in an open barge neare three tons burthen, leaving the Phœnix at Cape *Henry*, they crossed the bay to the eastern shore, and fell with the isles called *Smith's isles* after our captaine's name. The first people we saw were two grim and stout salvages upon Cape *Charles;* with long poles like jauelings, headed with bone, they boldly demanded what we were, and what we would; but after many circumstances they seemed very kinde, and directed us to *Accomack*, the habitation of their *Werowance*, where we were kindly intreated. This king was the comeliest, proper, civill salvage we incountered. His country is a pleasant fertile clay soyle, some small creekes; good harbours for small barks, but not for ships. They spake the language of *Powhatan*, wherein they made such descriptions of the bay, isles, and rivers, that often did us exceeding pleasure. Passing along the coast, searching every inlet and bay, fit for harbours and habitations. Seeing many isles in the midst of the bay we bore up for them, but ere we could obtaine them, such an extreame gust of wind, rayne, thunder, and lightening happened, that with great danger we escaped the unmerciful raging of the ocean-like water. The highest land on the mayne, yet it was but low, we called *Keale's* hill, and these uninhabited isles, *Russell's* isles. The next day, searching them for fresh water, we could find none; the defect whereof forced us to follow the next eastern channel, which brought us to the river of *Wighcocomico*. The people at first with great fury seemed to assault us yet at last with songs and dances and much mirth, became very tractable, but searching their habitations for water, we could fill but three barricoes, and that such puddle, that never till then we ever knew the want of good water. We digged and searched in many places, but before two daies had expired, we would have refused two barricoes of gold for one of that puddle water of *Wighcocomoco*. Being past these isles, which are many in number, but all naught for habitation, falling with a high land upon the mayne, found a great pond of fresh water, but so exceedingly hot, wee supposed it some bath; that place we called poynt *Ployer*, in honour of that most honourable house of *Monsay* in *Britaine* that in an extreame extremitie once relieved our captaine. From *Wighcocomico* to this place, all the coast is low broken isles of morass, growne a myle or two in breadth, and ten or twelve in length, good to cut for hay in summer, and to catch fish and foule in winter; but the land beyond them is all covered with wood, as is the rest of the country.

"Being thus refreshed in crossing over from the maine to other isles, we discovered the wind and waters so much increased with thunder, lightning and raine, that our mast and sayle blew overboard, and such mighty waves overracked us in that small barge, that with great labour we kept her from sinking, by freeing out the water. Two days we were inforced to inhabite these uninhabited isles, which for the extremitie of gusts, thunder, raine, stormes, and ill wether we called *Limbo*. Repairing our saile with our shirts, we set sayle for the maine and fell with a pretty convenient river on the East called *Cuskarawaock*, the people ran as amazed in troups from place to place, and divers got into the tops of trees, they were not sparing of their arrowes, nor the greatest passion they could expresse of their anger. Long they shot, we still ryding at an anchor without their reatch making all the signes of friendship we could. The next day they came unarmed, with every one a basket, dancing in a ring to draw us on shore, but seeing there was nothing in them but villany, we discharged a volley of muskets charged with pistoll shott, whereat they all lay tumbling on the ground, creeping some one way, some another into a great cluster of reedes hard by, where thare companies lay in ambuscade. Towards the evening we wayed, and approaching the shoare, discharging five or six shot among the reedes, we landed where there lay a many of baskets and much bloud, but saw not a salvage. A smoake appearing on the other side the river, we rowed thither, there we left some peeces of copper, beads, bells and looking-glasses, and then went into the bay, but when it was darke we came back againe. Early in the morning four salvages came to us in their canoes, whom we used with such courtesie, not knowing what we were, nor had done, having beene in the bay a fishing, bade us stay and ere long they would returne, which they did and some twentie more with them; with whom, after a little conference, two or three thousand men, women and children, came clustering about us, every one presenting us with something, which a little bead would so well requite, that we became such friends they would contend who should fetch us water, stay with us for hostage, conduct our men any whither, and give us the best content. Here doth inhabite the people of *Sarapinagh*, *Nause*, *Aroeck*, and *Nantaquak*, the best marchants of all other salvages. They much extolled a great nation called *Massawomekes*, in search of whom we returned by *Limbo;* this river but onely at the entrance is very narrow, and the people of small stature as them of *Wighcomoco*, the land but low, yet it may prove very commodious, because it is but a ridge of land betwixt the bay and the maine ocean. Finding this eastern shore, shallow broken isles, and for most part without fresh water, we passed by the straites of *Limbo*[1] for the westerne shore; so broad is the bay here, we could scarce perceive the great high clifts on the other side: by them we anchored that night and called them *Riccards* Cliftes. 30 leagues we sayled more northwarde not finding any inhabitants, leaving all the eastern shore, lowe islandes, but ouergrowne with wood, as all the coast beyond them so farre as we could see; the westerne shore by which we sayled we found all along well watered, but very mountainous and barren, the valleys very fertile, but extreame thicke of small wood as well as trees, and much frequented with wolves, beares, deere, and other wild beasts. Wee passed many shallow creekes, but the first we found navigable for a ship, we called *Bolus*,[2] for that the clay in many places under the clifts by the high water marke, did grow up in red and white knots as gum out of trees; and in some places so participated together as though they were all of one nature, excepting the

[1] Now called Hooper's Straits.

[2] Now called the Patapsco river.

colour, the rest of the earth on both sides being hard sandy grauell, which made vs thinke it *bole-armoniack* and *terra sigillata.* When we first set sayle some our gallants doubted nothing but that our captaine would make too much haste home, but having lien in this small barge not above twelve or fourteen dayes, oft tyred at the oares, our bread spoyled with wet so much that it was rotten, (yet so good were their stomachs that they could digest it,) they did with continuall complaints so importune him now to returne, as caused him bespeake them in this manner.

"*Gentlemen, if you would remember the memorable history of Sir* Ralph Layne, *how his company importuned him to proceed in the discovery of* Moratico, *alledging that they had yet a dog, that being boiled with sassafras leaues, would richly feed them in their returnes; then what a shame would it be for you (that have bin so suspitious of my tendernesse,) to force me returne, with so much provision as we have, and scarce able to say where we have beene, nor yet heard of that we were sent to seeke! You cannot say but I have shared with you in the worst which is past; and for what is to come, of lodging, dyet, or whatsoever, I am contented you allot the worst part to myselfe. As for your feares that I will lose myselfe in these unknowne large waters or be swallowed up in some stormie gust, abandon these childish feares, for worse than is past is not likely to happen, and there is as much danger to returne as to proceede. Regain, therefore, your old spirits, for returne I will not (if God please) till I have seene the* Massawomeks, *found* Patawomek, *or the head of this water you conceit to be endlesse.* Two or three dayes we expected winde and wether, whose aduerse extremities added such discouragement, that three or foure fell sicke, whose pitiful complaints caused vs to returne, leaving the bay some nine miles broad, at nine and ten fadome water.

"The 16th of *June* we fell with the river *Patawomek*,[1] feare being gone, and our men recovered, we were all content to take some paines, to know the name of that seven-mile broad riuer: for thirtie myles sayle, we could see no inhabitants: then we were conducted by two savages up a little bayed creeke, towards *Onawmanient*, where all the woods were layd with ambuscados to the number of three or foure thousand salvages, so strangely paynted, grimed and disguised, shouting, yelling and crying as so many spirits from hell could not have shewed more terrible. Many bravados they made, but to appease their fury, our captaine prepared with as seeming a willingnesse as they to incounter them. But the grazing of our bullets upon the water (many being shot on purpose they might see them), with ecco of the woods so amazed them, as downe went their bowes and arrowes; (and exchanging hostage), *James Watkins* was sent six myles up the woods to their king's habitation. We were kindly used of those salvages, of whom we understood, they were commanded to betray us, by the direction of *Powhatan*, and he so directed from the discontents at *James*-towne, because our captaine did cause them stay in their country against their wills.

"The like incounters we found at *Patawomek*, *Cecocawanee*, and diuers other places: but at *Moyaonees*, *Nacochtant*, and *Toags*,[2] the people did their best to content us. Hauing gone so high as we could with the bote, we met diuers salvages in canowes, well loaden with the flesh of beares, deere and other beasts, whereof we had part, here we found mighty rocks, growing in some places above the ground as high as the shrubby tree, and diuers other solid quarries of diuers tinctures: and diuers places where the waters had falne from the high mountaines they had left a tinctured spangled shurfe, that made many bare places seeme as guilded. Digging the growne above in the highest clifts of rocks, we saw it was a claie sand so mingled with yellow spangles as if it had beene half pin-dust. In our returne inquiring still for this *Matchqueon*, the king of *Patawomeke* gaue us guides to conduct us up a little river called *Quiyough*,[3] up which we rowed so high as

[1] The Potomac river.

[2] An Indian tribe inhabiting Charles county near Indian or Maryland Point, afterwards called the *Doages*.

[3] Now called Aquia creek, on the Virginia side of the Potomac.

we could. Leauing the bote, with six shot, and divers salvages, he marched seuen or eight myle before they came to the mine: leading his hostages in a small chaine they were to have for their paines, being proud to be so richly adorned. The mine is a great Rocky mountaine like *Antimony;* wherein they digged a great hole with shells and hatchets: and hard by it, runneth a fayre brooke of *christal*-like water, where they wash away the drosse and keepe the remainder, which they put in little baggs and sell it all over the country to paint there bodyes, faces, or idolls; which makes them looke like Blackmoores dusted over with silver. With so much as we could carry we returned to our bote, kindely requiting this kinde king and all his kinde people. The cause of this discovery was to search this mine, of wkich *Newport* did assure us that those small baggs (we had given him) in *England* he had tryed to hold half silver; but all we got proved of no value; also to search what furr, the best whereof is at *Cuscarawaocke*, where is made so much *Rawranoke* or white beads that occasion as much dissention among the salvages, as gold and silver amongst Christians; and what other minerals, rivers, rocks, nations, woods, fishings, fruites, victuall, and what other commodities the land afforded; and whether the bay were endlesse or how farre it extended; of mines we were all ignorant, but a few beauers, otters, beares, martins and minkes we found, and in divers places that aboundance of fish, lying so thicke with their heads above the water, as for want of nets (our barge driuing amongst them) we attempted to catch them with a frying pan; but we found it a bad instrument to catch fish with; neither better fish, more plenty, nor more variety for small fish, had any of vs euer seene in any place so swimming in the water, but they are not to be caught with frying pans; some small cod also we did see swim close by the shore by *Smith's* isles, and some as high as *Riccard's* cliffs. And some we have found dead upon the shore.

"To express all our quarrels, trecheries, and encounters amongst those salvages, I should be too tedious; but in breefe, at all times we so incountred them and curbed their insolencies, that they concluded with presants to purchase peace; yet we lost not a man: at our first meeting our captaine euer observed this order to demand their bowes and arrowes, swordes, mantalls and furrs, with some childe or two for hostage, whereby we could quickly perceive, when they intended any villany. Having finished this discovery (though our victuall was neere spent), he intended to see his imprisonment acquaintances upon the river of Rappahanock, by many called *Toppahanock*, but our bote by reason of the ebbe, chansing to grounde upon a many shoules lying in the entrance, we spyed many fishes lurking in the reedes: our captaine sporting himself by nayling them to the grownd with his sword, set vs all a fishing in that manner: thus we tooke more in one houer than we could eate in a day. But it chansed our captaine taking a fish from his sword (not knowing her condition) being much of the fashion of a Thornback, but a long tayle like a riding rodde, whereon the middest is a most poysoned sting, of two or three inches long, bearded like a saw on each side, which she strucke into the wrist of his arme neare an inch and a halfe; no bloud nor wound was seene, but a little blew spot, but the torment was instantly so extreame, that in foure houres had so swollen his hand, arme, and shoulder, we all with much sorrow concluded his funerall and prepared his graue in an island by, as himselfe directed; yet it pleased God by a precious oyle Doctor *Russell* at the first applyed to it with a probe, (ere night) his tormenting paine was so well asswaged, that he eate of the fish to his supper, which gaue no less joy and contant to vs than ease to himselfe, for which we called the island *Stingray* isle after the name of the fish."

It would be unnecessary to insert here the remaining part of this account of *Smith's* "first voyage" for a discovery of the Chesapeake, inasmuch as it relates principally to their return from the mouth of the Rappahannock to

Jamestown, where they arrived on the 21st of July, after an absence of nineteen days. They did not, however, remain long, for within three days Smith "embarked himself to finish his discovery."

"CHAPTER VI." (*of "The General Historie of Virginia."*)

"*What happened the second voyage in discovering the Bay.*"

"The 24th of July, captaine *Smith* set forward to finish the discovery with twelve men: their names were Nathaniel Powell, Thomas Momford, Richard Fetherstone, Michell Sicklemore, James Bourne, Anthony Bagnell, *Chir., Gentlemen.*

"Jonas Profit, Anas Todkill, Edward Pising, Richard Keale, James Watkins, William Ward, *Souldiers.*

"The wind being contrary caused our stay two or three dayes at *Kecoughtan* [now called *Hampton* in Virginia]: the king feasted vs with much mirth, his people were perswaded we went purposely to be revenged of the *Massawomeks*. In the evening we fired a few rackets, which flying in the ayre so terrified the poor salvages, they supposed nothing impossible we attempted; and desired to assist us. The first night we anchred at *Stingray* isle. The next day crossed *Patawomeks* river, and hastened to the river *Bolus*. We went not much further beffore we might see the bay to divide in two heads, and arriving there we found it divided into foure, all which we searched so farre as we could sayle them. Two of them we found inhabited, but in crossing the bay we encountred 7 or 8 canowes full of *Massawomeks*, we seeing them prepare to assault us, left our oares and made way with our sayle to incounter them, yet were we but fiue with our captaine that could stand, for within two days after we left *Kecoughtan*, the rest (being all of the last supply,) were sicke almost to death, until they were seasoned to the country. Having shut them under our tarpawling, we put their hats upon stickes by the barges side, and betwixt two hats a man with two peeces, to make us seeme many, and so we thinke the *Indians* supposed these hats to be men, for they fled with all possible speed to the shore, and there stayed, staring at the sayling of our barge till we anchored right against them. Long it was ere we could draw them to come unto us. At last they sent two of their company unarmed in a canow, the rest all followed to second them if neede required. These two being but each presented with a bell, brought aboord all their fellowes; presenting our captaine with venison, beares flesh, fish, bowes, arrowes, clubs, targets, and beare skinnes. We understood them nothing at all, but by signes, whereby they signified unto vs they had beene at warres with the *Tockwoghes*, the which they confirmed by shewing us their greene wounds, but the night parting us, we imagined they appointed the next morning to mete, but after that we never saw them.

"Entering the river *Tockwogh*,[1] the salvages all armed, in a fleete of boats, after their barbarous manner, round environed vs; so it chanced one of them could speake the language of *Powhatan*, who perswaded the rest to friendly parley. But when they saw vs furnished with the *Massawomeks* weapons, and we faining the invention of *Kecoughtan*, to have taken them perforce; they conducted us to their pallizadoed towne, mantelled with the barkes of trees, with scaffolds like mounts, brested about with brests very formally. Their men, women and children, with daunces, songs, fruits, furres, and what they had, kindly welcomed vs, spreading mats for vs to sit on, stretching their best abilities to expresse their loves.

"Many hatchets, knives, peeces of iron and brasse, we saw amongst them, which they reported to have from the *Sasquesahanocks*, a mightie people and mortall enemies with the *Massawomeks*. The *Sasquesahanocks* inhabit upon the chiefe spring of these four branches of the bayes head, two dayes journey higher than our barge could passe for rocks, yet we

[1] Sassafras river.

prevailed with the interpreter to take with him another interpreter, to perswade the *Sasquesahanocks* to come visit us, for their language are different. Three or four dayes we expected their returne, then sixty of those gyant-like people came downe, with presents of venison, tobacco pipes three foot in length, baskets, targets, bowes and arrowes. Five of their chiefe *Werowances* came boldly aboard vs to crosse the bay for *Tockwhogh*, leaving their men and canowes; the winde being so high they durst not passe.

"Our order was daily to haue prayer, with a psalme, at which solemnitie the poore salvages much wondered, our prayers being done, a while they were busied with a consultation till they had contrived their businesse. Then they began in a most passionate manner to hold up their hands to the sunne, with a most fearful song, then embracing our captaine, they began to adore him in like manner: though he rebuked them, yet they proceeded till their song was finished: which done with a most strange furious action, and a hellish voyce; began an oration of their loues; that ended, with a great painted beares-skin they covered him: then one ready with a great chayne of white beads, weighing at least six or seaven pounds hung it about his necke, the others had 18 mantels, made of diuers sorts of skinnes sowed together; all these with many other toyes they layd at his feete, stroking their ceremonious hands about his necke for his creation to be their governour and protector, promising their aydes, victualls, or what they had to be his, if he would stay with them, to defend and revenge them of the *Massawomeks*.—But we left them at *Tockwhogh*, sorrowing for our departure, yet we promised the next yeare againe to visit them. Many descriptions and discourses they made vs, of *Atquanachack*, *Massawomek*, and other people, signifying they inhabit upon a great water beyond the mountaines, which we vnderstood to be some great lake, or the river of *Canada*: and from the French to haue their hatchets and commodities by trade. These know no more of the territories of *Powhatan*, than his name, and he as little of them, but the *Aquanachucks* are on th oceane sea.

"The highest mountaine we saw northward we called Peregrine's mount, and a rocky river, where the *Massawomeks* went vp, *Willowbyes* river,[1] in honor of the towne our captaine was born in; and that honorable house the Lord Willowby, his most honored good friend. The *Susquesahanocks* was called *Smith's* falles; the next poynt to *Tockwhogh*, *Pising's* poynt; the next poynt *Bourne*.[2] *Powell's* and *Smal's* poynt is by the river *Bolus*; and the little bay at the head—*Profit's* poole; *Watkins*, *Reads*, and *Mumford's* poynts are on each side Limbo; Ward, Cantrell, and Sicklemore, betwixt *Patawomek* and *Pamaunkee*, after the names of the discoverers. In all those places and the furthest we came vp the rivers, we cut in trees so many crosses as we would, and in many places crosses of brasse, to signifie to any, Englishmen had been there.

"Thus having sought all the inlets and rivers worth noting, we returned to discover the river of *Pawtuxunt*, these people we found very tractable, and more civill than any, we promised them, as also the Patawomeks, to revenge them of the *Massawomeks*, but our purposes were crossed."

Here ends all that is said in Chapter VI. of Smith's History, as to "what happened the second voyage in discovering the bay," that has immediate relation to Maryland. In his "Second Book" of his General History of Virginia, he gives a kind of summary account and description of the country bordering on the Chesapeake, in which he says:

"The fourth river is called *Patawomeke*, 6 or 7 myles in breadth. *It is navigable 140 myles*, and fed as the rest with many sweet rivers and springs, which fall from the bordering hils. These hils, many of them are planted, and yield no lesse plentie and varietie of fruit, then the river exceedeth with abundance of fish. It is inhabited on both sides.

[1] Bush river.

[2] Swan Point in Kent county.

First on the south side at the very entrance is *Wighcocomoco*, and hath some 130 men, beyond them *Sakacawone* with 30. The *Anawmanient* with 100. And the *Patawomekes* more than 200. Here doth the river divide itselfe into 3 or 4 convenient branches. The greatest of the least is called *Quiyough*, trending northwest, but the river itselfe turneth northeast, and is still a navigable streame. On the westerne side of this bought is *Tauxenent* with 40 men. On the north of this river is *Secowocomoco* with 40. Somewhat further *Potopaco*[1] with 20. In the east part is *Pamacacack* with 60. After *Moyowance* with 100. And lastly, *Nacotchtanks* with 80. The river above this place maketh his passage downe a low pleasant valley overshaddowed in many places with high rocky mountaines; from whence distill innumerable sweet and pleasant springs.

"The fift river is called *Pawtuxunt*, of a lesse proportion than the rest; but the channell is sixteen fadome deepe in some places. Here are infinit skuls of divers kinds of fish more than elsewhere. Upon this river dwell the people called *Acquintanacksuah*, *Pawtuxunt* and *Mattapanient*. Two hundred men was the greatest strength that could be perceived. But they inhabit together, and not so dispersed as the rest. These of all other we found most civil to give entertainment.

"Thirtie leagues northward is a river not inhabited, yet navigable: for the red clay resembling *bole armoniack* we called it *bolus*. At the end of the bay where it is 6 or 7 myles in breadth, it divides itselfe into 4 branches, the best commeth north-west from among the mountaines, but though canows may go a dayes journey or two up it, we could not get two myles up it with our boat for rockes. Upon it is seated the *Susquesahanocks*, neare it north and by west runneth a creeke a myle and a halfe: at the head whereof the Ebbe left us on shore, where we found many trees cut with hatchets. The next tyde keeping the shore to seeke for some salvages; (for within thirtie leagues sayling we saw not any, being a barren country,) we went up another small river like a creeke, 6 or 7 myle. From thence returning we met 7 canows of the *Massawomeks*, with whom we had conference by signes, for we understood one another scarce a word: the next day we discovered the small river and people of *Tockwhogh* trending eastward.

"Having lost our grapnell among the rocks of *Susquesahanocks*, we were then neare 200 myles from home, and our barge about two tuns, and had in it but twelve men to performe this discovery, wherein we lay about 12 weeks upon those great waters in those unknowne countries, having nothing but a little meale, oatmeale and water to feed us, and scarce halfe sufficient of that for halfe that time, but what provision we got among the salvages, and such rootes and fish as we caught by accident, and God's direction; nor had we a mariner nor any hand skill to trim the sayles but two saylers and myselfe, the rest being gentlemen, or them were as ignorant in such toyle and labour. Yet necessitie in a short time by good words and examples made them doe that that caused them ever after to feare no colours. What I did with this small meanes I leave to the reader to judge, and the mappe I made of the country, which is but a small matter in regard of the magnitude thereof. But to proceed, 60 of these *Susquesahanocks* came to us with skins, bowes, arrows, targets, beads, swords, and tobacco pipes for presents. Such great and well-proportioned men are seldom seene, for they seemed like giants to the English, yea and to the neighbours, yet seemed of an honest and simple disposition, with much adoe restrained from adoring us as Gods. These are the strangest people of all these countries, both in language and attire; for their language it may well become their proportions, sounding from them as a voyce in a vault. Their attire is the skinnes of beares, and wolves, some have cossacks made of beares heads and skinnes, that a mans head goes through the skinnes neck, and the eares of the beare fastened to his shoulders, the nose and teeth hanging downe his breast, another beares face split behind him, and at the end of the nose hung a pawe, the halfe sleeves coming to the elbowes were the necks of

[1] Now called Port Tobacco.

beares, and the armes through the mouth with pawes hanging at their noses. One had the head of a wolfe hanging in a chaine for a jewell, his tobacco-pipe three quarters of a yard long, prettily carved with a bird, a deare, or some such devise at the great end, sufficient to beat out ones braines: with bowes, arrowes, and clubs, sutable to their greatnesse. These are scarce knowne to *Powhatan*. They can make neare 600 able men, and are pallisadoed in their townes to defend them from the *Massawomekes* their mortall enemies. Five of their chiefe *Werowances* came aboord vs and crossed the *bay* in their barge. The picture of the greatest of them is signified in the mappe. The calfe of whose leg was three quarters of a yard about, and all the rest of his limbs so answerable to that proportion that he seemed the goodliest man we ever beheld. His hayre, the one side was long, the other shore close with a ridge over his crowne like a cocks combe. His arrowes were five quarters long, headed with the splinters of a white christall-like stone, in forme of a heart, an inch broad, an inch and a halfe or more long. These he wore in a woolues skinne at his backe for his quiver, his bow in the one hand and his clubbe in the other, as is described.

"On the east side of the bay is the river *Tockwhogh*,[1] and upon it a people that can make 100 men, seated some seaven myles within the river: where they have a fort very well pallisadoed and mantelled with barkes of trees. Next them is *Ozinies* with sixty men. More to the south of that east side of the bay, the river *Rapahanock*, neere vnto which is the river *Kuscarawaock*. Upon which is seated a people with 200 men. After that, is the river *Tanto Wighcomoco*, and on it a people with 100 men. The people of these rivers are of little stature, of another language from the rest and very rude. But they are on the river Acohanock with 40 men, and they of *Accomack* 80 men doth equalize any of the territories of *Powhatan*, and speake his language, who over all these doth rule as king.

"Southward we went to some parts of *Chowanock* and the *Mangoags* to search for them left by Mr. *White*. Amongst those people are thus many severall nations of sundry languages, that environ Powhatan's Territories. The *Chowanocks*, the *Mangoags*, the *Monacans*, the *Mannahokes*, the *Massawomekes*, the *Powhatans*, the *Sasquesahanocks*, the *Atquanachukes*, the *Tockwoghes*, and the *Kuscarawaocks*. All these not any one understandeth another but by interpreters."[2]

In further illustration of what may be termed the primeval state of the country bordering on the Chesapeake Bay and its tributary waters, we will now add "A brief Journal of a voyage made in the bark *Virginia*, to Virginia and other parts of the continent of America," by Captain Henry Fleet.[3]

[1] Sassafras river.

[2] See Bozman, Vol. I., for further information on these interesting voyages, and his valuable historical notes.

[3] About the year 1621 the pinnace *Tiger*, with twenty-six men, was sent from Jamestown, under the direction of an experienced trader named Spilman, to trade for corn with the Indians near the head of navigation on the Potomac. Arriving opposite the present site of Washington city, Spilman left five men on board of his vessel, and with the remainder landed among the Anacostan Indians. Soon after he was attacked by the Indians, and all of his party were either killed or taken prisoners, and among the latter was Captain Henry Fleet. Remaining in captivity for several years, Fleet returned to England, where a contemporary writer thus mentions him:

"Here is one, whose name is Fleet, newly come from Virginia, who being lately ransomed from the Indians, with whom he hath long lived, till he hath left his own language, reporteth that he hath oftentimes been within sight of the South Seas, that he hath seen Indians besprinkle their paintings with powder of gold, that he had likewise seen rare precious stones among them, and plenty of black fox, which of all others is the richest fur."

By his flattering representations he induced, in September, 1627, William Cloberry, a prominent merchant of London, to place the pinnace *Paramour*, of one hundred tons burden, under his charge.—Bruce's *British State Papers*.

He returned to the Indian town of Yowaccomoco (afterwards St. Mary's City), where he had lived with the Indians and traded largely with them for their fur skins. He made a number of voyages across the Atlantic with cargoes of furs, and when Governor Leonard Calvert, before landing his company, made a reconnoissance of the Potomac as far as

"The 4th of July 1631, we weighed anchor from the Downs, and sailed for New England, where we arrived in the harbor of Pascattouaie, the 9th of September, making some stay upon the coast of New England. From thence, on Monday the 19th of September, we sailed directly for Virginia, where we came to anchor in the bay there, the 21st of October, but made little stay. From thence we set sail for the river of Potomack, where we arrived the 26th of October at an Indian town called Yowaccomoco, being at the mouth of the river, where I found that, by reason of my absence, the Indians had not preserved their beaver, but burned it, as the custom is, whereupon I endeavoured by persuasion to alter that custom, and to preserve it for me against the next spring, promising to come there with commodities in exchange by the first of April. Here I was tempted to run up the river to the heads, there to trade with a strange populous nation, called Mowhaks, man-eaters, but after good deliberation, I conceived many inconveniences that might fall out. First, I considered that I was engaged to pay a quantity of Indian corn in New England, the neglect whereof might be prejudicial both to them that should have it, and to me that promised payment. And when I observed that winter was very forward, and that if I should proceed and be frozen in, it might be a great hindrance to my proceedings; therefore I did forbear, and making all the convenient haste I could, I took into the barque her lading of Indian corn as I supposed, being persuaded and overruled by John Dunton, whom I entertained as master. But upon the delivery of our lading found not above 800 bushels to our great hindrance.

"The 6th of December we weighed anchor, shaping our course directly for New England, but the wind being contrary, ending with a fearful storm, we were forced into the inhabited river of James Town. There were divers envious people, who would have executed their malice upon us had it not been for a rumour of a commission they supposed I had, which I took great pains to procure, but (time being precious and my charge great) I came away only with the copy. Divers that seemed to be my friends advised me to visit the Governor. I showed myself willing, yet watched an opportunity that might be convenient for my purpose, being not minded to adventure my fortunes at the disposing of the Governor.

"Then we did a little replenish our provisions. But at this time I was much troubled with the seamen, all of them resolving not to stir until the spring, alleging that it was impossible to gain a passage in winter, and that the load being corn, was the more dangerous. But the master and his mate, who were engaged for the delivery of the corn, laboured to persuade and encourage them to proceed, showing that it would be for their benefit; so that, with threats and fair persuasions, at last I prevailed.

"On Tuesday, the 10th of January, we set sail from Point Comfort and arrived at Pascattoway, in New England, on Tuesday the 7th of February, where we delivered our corn, the quantity being 700 bushels.

Piscattaway. Father White, in his Journal [*Relatio Itineris in Marylandiam*], says:

"The Governor had taken with him, as a companion on his voyage, Henry Fleet, a captain from the Virginia colony, a man especially acceptable to the savages, well versed in their language, and acquainted with the country. This man was at first very intimate with us, afterwards, being misled by the evil counsels of one Clayborne, he became very hostile to us, and excited the natives to anger against us by all the means in his power.

"In the meantime, however, while he was still on friendly terms with us, he pointed out to the Governor a spot so charming in its situation that Europe can scarcely show one to surpass it."—[This was the site of St. Mary's.]

A short time after Governor Calvert landed, Captain Fleet received a patent for 2,000 acres of land on St. George river, St. George Hundred. He was a member of the Assembly of 1638, together with his brothers Edward, John and Reynold. In 1645 he was trading with the Indians on the Rappahannock river, and in December, 1652, sat as a member from Lancaster county in the Virginia House of Burgesses. In 1654 he is last mentioned as an interpreter to a proposed expedition against the Indians.—Rev. E. D. Neill's *Founders of Maryland.*

"On Tuesday, the 16th of March, we weighed anchor and sailed to the Isle of Shoals, where we furnished ourselves with provisions of victual. Sunday, the 11th of March, we sailed for the Massachusetts Bay, and arrived there on the 19th day. I wanted commodities to trade with the Indians, and here I endeavoured to fit myself if I could. I did obtain some, but it proved of little value, and was the overthrow of my voyage.

"From the Massachusetts, was sent with me a small pinnace of the burthen of twenty tons, the which I was to freight with Indian corn for trucking stuff, which proved to me like that I had before from the Bay, and Pascattoway, from whence I had some likewise. Yet this was not the greatest wrong I received by this barque, as shall hereafter be related.

"On Monday, the 9th of April, 1632, we both weighed anchor, and shaped our course for Virginia, but the sixth day being stormy weather we lost our pinnace. Contrary winds and gusty weather, with the insufficiency of the master, made our return to Virginia tedious, to the overthrow of the voyage. But it so pleased God that we anchored against the English colony the 13th of May, when, for want of wind, being a flat calm, we came to an anchor at Acomack. Having some English commodities I sold them for tobacco. Wednesday, the 16th of May, we shaped our course for the river of Potomack, with the company of Captain Claybourne, being in a small vessel. By the relation of him and others of the plantation of Acomack, the Governor of Virginia was much displeased with me, unto whom complaints had been made by divers of the country, and it had been discovered by one of my company that was run away, how that I had but the copy of my commission. Friday, the 17th of May, we might discern a sail making toward us about two o'clock in the afternoon. She came up to us, and we found that it was the pinnace that came out with us, which having had a short passage, had been up the river of Patomack, at Yowocomaco, an Indian town, where she had stayed three weeks, and then I was certified, that he who had usually been in those parts with me, after my last departure, came there and went up the river to truck, where he found good store of beaver, and being furnished with commodities such as Virginia affords, did beat about from town to town for beaver, but prevailed not. And in the end, coming where my barque had been, that town having 300 weight of beaver, he then reported that I was dead, they supposing his vessel to be the same that I was to come in, desired them to bring me dead or alive, and this report caused some distraction for the present, who supposed that by reason of my long absence, past my appointed time, some mischance had befallen me. And the Indians there disposed of their beaver to Charles Harman, being 300 weight, who departed but three days before I came there.

"This relation did much trouble me, fearing (having contrary winds) that the Indians might be persuaded to dispose of all their beaver before they could have notice of my being in safety, they themselves having no use at all for it, being not accustomed to take pains to dress it and make coats of it. Monday, the 21st of May, we came to an anchor at the mouth of the river, where hastening ashore, I sent two Indians, in company with my brother Edward, to the Emperor, being three days' journey towards the Falls. And so sailing to the other side of the river, I sent two Indians more, giving express orders to all of them not to miss an Indian town and to certify them of my arrival. But it so happened that he (Harman) had cleared both sides of the river, so far as the Emperor's where these Indians, when they came, certified him of my being well, and of my brother's being there, so that afterwards he could not get a skin, but he made a very hand of it, and an unexpected trade for the time, at a small charge, having gotten 1500 weight of beaver, and cleared fourteen towns. There were yet three that were at the disposing of the Emperor, so the barque and myself passing by divers towns, came to the town of Patomack on Saturday, the 26th of May.[1] There I gave the pinnace her lading of Indian corn, and

[1] Potomac town supposed to be at the mouth of Potomac creek in Virginia.

sent her away the 1st of June, with letters from our company to their friends in London, and elsewhere in England, which were safely conveyed from New England. The same day, with a north-west wind (Charles Harman staying no longer), we set sail, and the third we arrived at the Emperor's, but before we could come to the town he was paddled aboard, by a petty king, in a canoe.

"When he came he used divers speeches, and alleged many circumstances for the excuse of the beaver which Charles Harman had of his men in that river, and after compliments used, he presented me with one hundred and fourteen beaver skins, which put me into a little comfort after so much ill success. Yet this was nothing, in regard to the great change at his town, and at a little town by him called the Nacostines, where I had almost 800 weight of beaver. There is but little friendship between the Emperor and the Nacostines,[1] he being fearful to punish them, because they are protected by the Massomacks or Cannyda Indians, who have used to convey all such English truck as cometh into the river to the Massomacks.

"The Nacostines before, here occasioned the killing of twenty men of our English, myself then being taken prisoner and detained five years, which was in the time of Sir Francis Wyatt, he being the Governor of Virginia. The 13th of June I had some conference with an interpreter of Massomack, and of divers other Indians that had been lately with them, whose relation was very strange in regard of the abundance of people there, compared to all the other poor number of natives which are in Patomack and places adjacent, where are not above five thousand persons, and also of the infinite store of beaver they use in coats. Divers were the imaginations that I did conceive about this discovery, and understanding that the river was not for shipping, where the people were, not yet for boats to pass, but for canoes only. I found all my neighbor Indians to be against my design, the Pascattowies having had a great slaughter formerly by them to the number of one thousand persons in my time. They coming in their birchen canoes, did seek to withdraw me from having any commerce with the other Indians, and the Nacostines were earnest in the matter, because they knew that our trade might hinder their benefit. Yet I endeavored to prosecute my trade with them nevertheless, and therefore made choice of two trusty Indians to be sent along with my brother, who could travel well.

"I find the Indians of that populous place are governed by four kings, whose towns are of several names, Tonhoga, Mosticum, Shaunetowa, and Usserahak, reported above thirty thousand persons, and that they have palisades about the towns made with great trees, and with scaffolds upon the walls. Unto these four kings I sent four presents in beads, bells, hatchets, knives, and coats, to the value of £8 sterling.

"The 14th of June they set forth, and I entreated them to bring these Indians down to the water to the Falls, where they should find me with the ship. On Monday, the 25th of June, we set sail for the town of Tohoga, when we came to an anchor two leagues short of the Falls,[2] being in the latitude of 41, on the 26th of June. This place, without all question, is the most pleasant and healthful place in all this country, and most convenient for habitation, the air temperate in summer and not violent in winter. It aboundeth with all manner of fish. The Indians, in one night commonly, will catch thirty sturgeons in a place where the river is not above twelve fathom broad. And as for deer, buffaloes, bears, turkeys, the woods do swarm with them, and the soil is exceedingly fertile, but above this place the country is rocky and mountainous like Cannida.

"The 27th of June I manned my shallop, and went up with the flood, the tide rising about four feet in height at this place. We had not rowed above three miles, but we might hear the Falls to roar about six miles distant, by which it appears that the river is

[1] The Nacostines or Anacostans lived near the site of the city of Washington. The suburb opposite the Navy Yard is now called Anacostia, and Mason's Island is often called Analostan.—*Neill.*

[2] Nine miles above Washington.

separated with rocks, but only in that one place, for beyond is a fair river. The 3d of July my brother, with the two Indians, came thither, in which journey they were seven days going, and five days coming back to this place. They all did affirm that in one palisado, and that being the last of thirty, there were three hundred houses, and in every house forty skins at least, in bundles and piles. To this king was delivered the four presents, who dispersed them to the rest. The entertainment they had I omit as tedious to relate. There came with them, one-half of the way, one hundred and ten Indians, laden with beaver, which could not be less than 4000 weight. These Indians were made choice of by the whole nation, to see what we were, what was our intent, and whether friends or foes, and what commodities we had, but they were met with by the way by the Nacostines, who told them we purposed to destroy those that came in our way, in revenge of the Pascattowaies, being hired to do so for 114 skins, which were delivered aforesaid, for a present, as a preparative.

"But see the inventions of devils; the life of my brother, by this tale of the Nacostines, was much endangered. The next morning I went to the Nacostines to know the reason of this business, who answered, they did know no otherwise, but that if I would make a firm league with them, and give their king a present, then they would undertake to bring those other Indians down. The refusal of this offer was the greatest folly that I have ever committed, in mine opinion.

"The 10th of July, about one o'clock, we discerned an Indian on the other side of the river, who with a shrill sound, cried, "Quo! Quo! Quo!" holding up a beaver skin upon a pole. I went ashore to him, who then gave me the beaver skin, with his hatchet, and laid down his head with a strange kind of behavior, using some few words, which I learned, but to me it was a foreign language. I cheered him, told him he was a good man, and clapped him on the breast with my hands. Whereupon he started up, and used some complimental speech, leaving his things with me ran up the hill.

"Within the space of half an hour, he returned, with five more, one being a woman, and an interpreter, at which I rejoiced, and so I expressed myself to them, showing them courtesies. These were laden with beaver, and came from a town called Usserahak, where were seven thousand Indians. I carried these Indians aboard, and traded with them for their skins. They drew a plot of their country, and told me there came with them sixty canoes, but were interrupted by the Nacostines, who always do wait for them, and were hindered by them. Yet these, it would seem, were resolute, not fearing death, and would adventure to come down. These promised me if I would show them my truck, to get great store of canoes to come down with one thousand Indians that should trade with me. I had but little, not worth above one hundred pound sterling, and such as was not fit for these Indians to trade with, who delight in hatchets, and knives of large size, broad-cloth, and coats, shirts, and Scottish stockings. The women desire bells, and some kind of beads.

"The 11th of July there came from another place seven lusty men, with strange attire; they had red fringe, and two of them had beaver coats, which they gave me. Their language was haughty, and they seemed to ask me what I did there, and demanded to see my truck, which, upon view, they scorned. They had two axes, such as Captain Kirk traded in Cannida, which he bought at Whits of Wapping, and there I bought mine, and think I had as good as he. But these Indians, after they came aboard, seemed to be fair conditioned, and one of them, taking a piece of chalk, made a plain demonstration of their country, which was nothing different from the former plot drawn by the other Indians. These called themselves Mostikums, but afterwards I found they were of a people three days' journey from these, and were called Herecheenes,[1] who, with

[1] Iroquois?

their own beaver, and what they get of those that do adjoin upon them, do drive a trade in Cannida, at the plantation, which is fifteen days' journey from this place. These people delight not in toys, but in useful commodities.

"There was one William Elderton very desirous to go with them, but being cannibals I advised him rather to go with the others, whither I had sent a present, telling him they had no good intentions, yet upon his earnest entreaty, though unwilling, I licensed him to proceed, and sent a present with him to their king, one of them affirming that they were a people of one of the four aforenamed nations. But I advised my man to carry no truck along, lest it might be a means to endanger his life. Nevertheless, as I was afterwards informed, he carried a coat, and other things to the value of ten shillings more, and on the 14th of July departed.

"The 15th of July the Indians were returned with the interpreter, according to promise, and being come, looked about for William our interpreter, to whom I made relation whither he was gone, and they seemed to lament for him, as if he were lost, saying, that the men with whom he went would eat him, that these people were not their friends, but that they were Herecheenes. At the departure of these Indians, they told me that two hundred were come to the place from whence they came with store of English truck to trade for beaver, and told us they had a purpose to come down and visit us, and take a view of our commodities, and they inquired after divers kinds of commodities, of which I had some very good, part of which I gave them, and sent them away, desiring them to follow after the other Indians, and to get away my man. All this time did my truck spend not so much upon beaver as upon victuals, having nothing but what we bought of the Indians, of whom we had fish, beans, and boiled corn. The seamen, nevertheless, hoped to sell away all their clothes for beaver.

"The 18th of July I went to the Pascattowaies, and there excused myself for trading with those that were enemies, and from thence I hired sixteen Indians, and brought them to the ship, and made one of them my merchant, and delivered to them, equally divided, the best part of my truck, which they carried up for me, to trade with their countrymen; and I gave charge to the factor to find out my man, and to bring him along with them when they came back.

"The 7th of August these Indians returned, and the Tohogaes sent me eighty skins with the truck again, who showed these Indians great packs of beaver, saying there were nine hundred of them coming down by winter, after they had received assurance of our love by the Usserahaks, although the Nacostines had much labored the contrary. And yet they were all at a stand for a time, by reason of two rumors that had raised, the one that I had no good truck, neither for quantity, nor for quality; the other that one of our men was slain by the Herecheenes, three days' journey beyond them, and that they had beguiled us with the name of Mostikums, one of their confederate nations. Nevertheless, they being desirous to have some trial of us, had sent us these skins, minding to have an answer whether we would be so satisfied of this deceit or no, and that they would come all four nations and trade with us upon their guard.

"I liked this motion very well, but was unwilling to protract time, because I had but little victuals, and small store of trucking stuff, and therefore I sailed down to Pascattowie, and so to a town on this side of it called Moyumpse. Here came three cannibals of Usserahak, Tohoga, and Mostikum; these used many complimenting speeches and rude orations, showing that they desired us to stay fifteen days, and they would come with a great number of people that should trade with us as formerly they had spoken. I gave them all courteous entertainment, and so sent them back again.

"At this time I had certain news of a small pinnace with eight men, that made inquiry in all places for me, with whom was Charles Harman. The Indians would willingly have put them by for me, or I could have shifted them in the night, or taken them, as I pleased; but, knowing my designs to be fair and honest, I feared nothing that might happen by this means. And now, after much toil and some misery, I was desirous of variety of company.

"The 28th of August, in the morning, I discerned the barque, and having the shallop which I built amongst the Indians, I manned her with ten men and all manner of munition, with a full resolution to (discover) what they were, and what were their intentions. Being come near them, I judged what they were and went aboard, where I found Captain John Utye, one of the Council of Virginia. In which barque I stayed with them by the space of two hours, and then invited them aboard my ship, where, being entered into my cabin, after a civil pause, this salutation was used:—

"'Captain Fleet, I am sorry to bring ill news, and to trouble you in these courses, being so good; but as I am an instrument, so I pray you to excuse me, for, in the King's name I arrest you, your ship, and goods, and likewise your company, to answer such things as the Governor and Council shall object.'

"I obeyed; yet I conceived that I might use my own discretion and most of his company being servants, and ill-used, were willing to have followed me, yea, though it had been to have gone for England.

"The 29th of August we came to Patomack; here was I tempted to take in corn, and then to proceed for New England; but wanting truck, and having much tobacco due to me in Virginia, I was unwilling to take any irregular course, especially in that I conceived all my hopes and future fortunes depended upon the trade and traffic that was to be had out of this river.

"I took in some provisions, and came down to a town called Patobanos,[1] where I found that all the Indians below the cannibals, which are in number five thousand persons in the river of Patomack, will take pains this winter in the killing of beavers and preserve the furs for me now that they begin to find what benefit may accrue to them thereby. By this means I shall have in readiness at least five or six thousand weight against my next coming to trade there. Thursday, the 6th of September 1632, we came to the river of James Town, and on the 7th day anchored at James Town, and I went ashore the same night.

"The Governor, bearing himself like a noble gentleman, showed me very much favor, and used me with unexpected courtesy. Captain Utye did acquaint the Council with the success of the voyage, and every man seemed to be desirous to be a partner with me in these employments. I made as fair weather as might be with them, to the end I might know what would be the business in question and what they would or could object, that I might see what issue it would come to.

"The Court was called the 14th of September, where an order was made, which I have here enclosed, and I find that the Governor hath favored me therein. After this day, I had free power to dispose of myself. Whereupon I took into consideration my business, and what course would be most for mine advantage, and what was fittest for me to resolve upon. I conceived it would be prejudicial to my designs to lose the advantage of the spring, because of the infancy of this project, considering how needful it was to settle this course of trade with the Indians so newly begun, and now that I had gotten £200 worth of (beaver) in readiness, and some of it very good.

"And I having now built a new barque of sixteen tons, and fitted myself with a partner that joineth with me for a moiety in that vessel, which we have sent to the Cannadies with provisions, and such merchandize, are there good commodities, and so to the Medeiras and Tenariffe. The loading is corn, meal, beef, pork, and clapboards. For myself, I hope to be gone up the river within the six days.

[1] Also called Fotopaco and Potobatto, now Port Tobacco.

"And so, beloved friends, that shall have the perusal of this journal, I hope that you will hold me excused in the method of this relation, and bear with my weakness in penning the same. And consider that time would not permit me to use any rhetoric in the form of this discourse, which, to say truly, I am but a stranger unto as yet, considering that in my infancy and prime time of youth, which might have advantaged my study that way, and enabled me with more learning, I was for many years together compelled to live amongst these people, whose prisoner I was, and by that means am a better proficient in the Indian language than mine own, and am made more able that way.

"The thing that I have endeavored herein is, in plain phrase, to make such relation of my voyage as may give some satisfaction to my good friends, whose longing thoughts may hereby have a little content, by perusing this discourse, wherein it will appear how I proceeded, and what success I have had, and how I am like to speed if God permit. All which particulars, the whole ship's company are ready to testify on behalf of this Journal."[1]

An allusion to the Chesapeake Bay appears in the narrative by Ralph Lane of the proceedings of the colonists sent by Sir Walter Raleigh in 1585, to occupy the country then first named Virginia, bordering upon the two bays now known as Albemarle and Pamlico Sound. He there relates that an exploring party of English had penetrated northward from their settlements on Roanoke Island, between the two sounds, one hundred and thirty five miles to the country of the Chesepians, or of Chesepiook; and he had been at the same time told by an Indian king, "that going three days' journey in a canoe, up his river of Chawanock (the Chowan) and then descending to the land, you are within four days' journey to pass overland north-east, to a certain king's country whose province lieth upon the sea; but his place of greatest strength is an island, situated, as he described unto me, in a bay, the water about the island very deep." The country of the Chesepiooks, here mentioned, we afterwards learn, from Smith's *History of Virginia*, to have been on Elizabeth's River, near the southernmost shore of Chesapeake Bay, as its position and distance with reference to Roanoke Island plainly indicate. The bay described by the King of Chawanock could have been no other than the Chesapeake. Lane laments that he has not been able to explore it by way of the river, as well as by vessels sent along the coast to its entrance, particularly as he was assured that it yielded "great store of pearls," and that it received a large river called Moratuc, running from the west.

Oldmixon, in his *British Empire in America*,[2] speaking of Captain Bartholomew Gilbert's arrival off the mouth of the Chesapeake Bay, July 25th, 1603, says: "Gilbert proceeded from the Carribee Islands to the bay of Chesapeake in Virginia, being the first that sailed up into it and landed there. The Indians set upon him and his company in the woods; and Captain Gilbert and four or five of his men were killed by their arrows, upon which his crew returned home."

This is all that appears on record concerning the bay in any English authority earlier than 1607; nor is any indication of its existence given

[1] Rev. E. D. Neill, *Founders of Maryland*.

[2] Vol. i., p. 354.

in any map, anterior to that date, except in that of the New World, attached to the sixth part of De Bry's celebrated collection in 1596, containing Lane's narrative, on which a bay is represented extending westward from the Atlantic under the thirty-seventh degree of latitude, with a river called Moratuc entering its upper extremity.

When and by whom the name "Chesapeake" was given to the bay, is not directly stated. Stith in his *History of Virginia*[1] had been informed "that Chesapeake signifies in the Indian language the *mother of waters*, implying that it was the parent and grand reservoir of all the great rivers within it." But this, he properly observes in continuation, "was a dark and uncertain guess; especially considering the unstableness and vast mutability of the Indian tongues, and that nobody at present can pretend to understand their language at that time." "The best authority," adds Stith, "that I have met with for this derivation, is what a gentleman of credit once assured me, that in a very old Spanish map which he had seen, our bay was laid down under the name of *Madre de aguas*, or some expression to the like purpose." More probably, however, the Chesapeake Indians, inhabiting the country on the southernmost side of the bay between Cape Henry and Hampton Roads, were the first people met by the English in 1607, and their name may have been transferred to the bay as those of Pamunkey, Potomac and Susquehannock were subsequently assigned to the rivers on which the Indian nations, so called, respectively dwelt.

It would, however, have been strange that this great basin should have remained thus long unknown to the Spaniards, who, as early as 1526, had not only explored the whole coast from the Mexican Gulf northward, to and beyond the thirty-fifth degree of latitude, but had even attempted to form a settlement about that parallel; considering moreover that their vessels on the way from Mexico and the West Indies to Europe kept close to the mainland nearly as far as Cape Hatteras before striking across the Atlantic, and must often have been driven much farther in the same direction; but without dwelling on these probabilities, there is evidence apparently incontrovertible that the Chesapeake was known to the Spaniards, and that an expedition had been made by them for the occupation of its coasts at least twenty years before any attempt of the English to establish themselves in any part of the American continent.

The evidence here mentioned is contained in the Chronological History, or, Annals of Florida, published at Madrid in 1723, under the title of "*Ensayo Cronologico para la Historia de la Florida. Por Don Gabriel de Cardenas y Cano.*" The name thus given on the title page of the work is fictitious, being an anagram of that of its real author, Don Andres Gonzales Barcia, who did such good service in the cause of American history by the republication of Herrera, Torquemada and many other

[1] Page 13.

narratives of the early discoveries and proceedings of his countrymen in the New World, then nearly out of print. The work now in question was composed in great part from original documents in the archives of the council of the Indies, and of the Franciscan order in Spain, to which he had access; and its extreme minuteness on all points, with little regard to their importance, while rendering the book intolerable to the general reader, gives it at the same time the highest value as evidence where accuracy is required. On the point now under consideration, he says indeed but little; so little as entirely to dispel the idea that he could have fabricated, or exaggerated in any respect; yet, that little is sufficiently clear for the establishment of the fact asserted in the preceding paragraph.

While lying with his squadron in the river of San Matheo, now the St. John's in Florida, in the summer of 1556, "he dispatched," writes Barcia,[1] "a captain with thirty soldiers and two monks of the order of St. Dominick, to the bay of Santa Maria, which is in the latitude of thirty-seven degrees, together with the Indian, brother to the cacique of Axacan (who had been brought by the Dominicans from that province, and baptized at Mexico, by the name of the Viceroy Don Luis de Velasco), to settle in that region, and to endeavour to convert its inhabitants to Christianity." The result of the Spanish expedition is thus related by Barcia:[2] "The captain, who went with the Indian Luis de Velasco to the bay of Santa Maria, was overcome by his crew, acting under the influence of the two monks, who, accustomed to the delights of Peru and Spain, were not inclined to enter upon a life of labor, privation and dangers; and the soldiers, needing little persuasion to induce them to turn back, made false depositions to the effect that they had been prevented by storms from reaching the bay of Santa Maria. So they sailed with a fair wind for Seville, abusing the King and the Adelantado for attempting to settle in that country, of which they spread the worst accounts, though none of them had seen it." Thus it appears that the bay of Santa Maria, joining the Atlantic ocean, in the latitude of thirty-seven degrees, in which the entrance of the Chesapeake is situated—the thirty-seventh parallel running just midway between Cape Henry and Cape Charles—was so well known to the Spaniards in 1556 that an expedition was made for the purpose of taking possession of the surrounding country. We do not know that the attempt was repeated. It appears, however, from Barcia[3] that "in 1573 Pedro Menendez Morquez, Governor of Florida for his uncle, the Adelantado, reduced many Indian nations to obedience, and took possession of their provinces, for the King, in presence of Rodrigo de Carnon, the notary of the government of Santa Helena. Being, moreover, himself a good seaman—he had been admiral of the fleet, according to Francisco Cano—he, by order of the Adelantado, examined the coasts from the cape of Martyrs [Cape Sable] and the peninsula of Tequesta [the southern portion of Florida], where it begins to run north and south, at

[1] Page 110. [2] Page 123. [3] Page 146.

the outlet of the Bahama channel, along the land, to and beyond the port and bay of Santa Maria, which is three leagues wide, and is entered towards the northwest. In this bay are many rivers and harbors, on both sides, in which vessels may anchor. Within its entrance, on the south, the depth is from nine to thirteen fathoms, and on the north side from five to seven; at two leagues from it, in the sea, the depth is the same on the north and the south, but there is more sand within. In the channel there are from nine to thirteen fathoms; in the bay, fifteen, ten and six fathoms; and in some places the bottom cannot be reached with the lead."

Furthermore, after relating the particulars of the governor's voyage from the Cape of Martyrs to Santa Helena, Barcia proceeds thus[1] with regard to the course from the latter place "to the bay of Santa Maria, in the latitude of thirty-seven degrees and a half. He steered northeastward, and after sailing a hundred and ten leagues in water of from sixteen to twenty fathoms deep, he passed over the edge of a shoal running directly northward, the point of which is in thirty-four degrees and three-quarters, having between it and the land a passage two fathoms deep, but of little width. Continuing towards the east, one-quarter northeast, he found another shoal, with a good passage on the land side; it is in thirty-five degrees, and runs six leagues in the sea, northwest and southeast, to the distance of thirty leagues from the bay of Santa Maria. The coast is thereabout very clear, so that you may sail near to the land, and anchor at some distance from it. There are on it three or four rivers, one of them very good, and three sand islets like turtle shells or shields, about six leagues from the bay of Santa Maria, all three being within the space of a league. And he [the governor] thus went, as I have said, beyond the port and bay of Santa Maria."

This is all that Barcia says of the bay of Santa Maria; and nothing has been found with regard to it elsewhere. Those who are familiar with the old historians of America will admit that the descriptions thus given are more than usually clear and definite, and correspond in a remarkable degree with the true state of the places to which they refer. The shoal mentioned in the last-quoted paragraph, in latitude of thirty-four degrees and three-quarters, is evidently the same which runs out from Cape Lookout in North Carolina; and the other shoals, twenty-two leagues farther northeast and thirty leagues from the bay of Santa Maria, may be at once identified with that which renders the passage around Cape Hatteras so much dreaded by our mariners. Cape Hatteras is thirty-four leagues from Cape Henry, the southern point of the entrance to the Chesapeake. That entrance is four leagues in width; the depth of its channel varies from six to thirteen fathoms on the south side, being much shallower towards the northern point, Cape Charles; and as the thirty-seventh parallel runs through the middle of this entrance, it appears unnecessary to adduce any farther arguments to show that the bay of Santa Maria could have been none other than the Chesapeake.[2]

[1] Page 148.

[2] Robinson's *Early Voyages*, p. 483.

CHAPTER II.

At the accession of James I., in 1603, Europe was still in the heat of that terrible religious war which, beginning with the arming of the Schmalkaldic League, in 1546, lasted, with brief intermissions, until terminated by the Peace of Westphalia, in 1648. Down to the time referred to, England had never fairly been drawn into war, but was perpetually threatened by it; and had stood, as it were, with sword half-unsheathed, and with eyes now fixed on the movements of fleets and armies without, now watching the intrigues of conspirators within. Elizabeth's long reign had still left in England a large body of adherents to the ancient faith, the great majority of whom, it is true, were loyal subjects, as they abundantly proved; but among whom were many discontented and intriguing spirits, stimulated by French, Spanish and Italian influence, who had cherished the hope of placing a Catholic sovereign on the throne, and were familiar with the webs of those conspiracies in which the assassination of the queen and of her most faithful counsellors too often formed the soul of the plot. Thus politics and religion went hand in hand: one side was bent on dethroning, not only the heretic, but the usurper; the other, on resisting, not only the papist, but the foreigner. It is no wonder then that religious animosities were bitter, and that the nation was composed of bigoted Catholics and bigoted Protestants.

JAMES I.

We shall err if we attempt to judge those times by the standard of our own. An enthusiastic faith is apt to be a narrow and persecuting faith, even when not interwoven with politics; and in the sixteenth century a change of religion in the sovereign naturally meant the axe, the cord, or the stake for those of opposite belief. None save a few rare spirits had risen to the height of either intellectual or religious toleration. Opinions or creeds other than our own were to be suppressed, if not by argument and exhortation, then by steel and fire. The true Church, by her head, whether seated in the chair of St. Peter or that of Edward the Confessor, had the power to cut off such offenders; and to spare them was a culpable lenity, to punish them an act well-pleasing to God. Even the pious and gentle Bishop Latimer—himself foredoomed to the martyr's death—speaks of the burning of Anabaptists, and their fortitude at the stake, without sympathy and almost with a scoff.[1] Faiths that found themselves on the losing side, it is true, lauded

[1] Sermon before King Edward VI., March 20th, 1549.

toleration—to themselves—but they were equally ready to persecute when they found themselves in power. It was the spirit and temper of the age; and while we, their descendants, may congratulate ourselves that we live in more liberal times, we should not forget that to indulge in recrimination on account of the persecution of our forefathers, not only shows our ignorance of history, but proves the presence in ourselves of the very spirit which we condemn.

At the coronation of James, the first monarch who united under one crown the three kingdoms of the British empire, the people were divided under three forms of belief, each of which was predominant in one of those three great divisions, and each of which hoped, under the new sovereign, to assume the protectorate of faith and reason. The Catholics regarded the event as auspicious, for James had before endeavored to enlist them in his favor by holding out hopes of relief from the cruel laws then in force against them. Their attachment to the house of Stuart, and their sufferings in the cause of his unfortunate mother, gave them claims upon his gratitude. He had bound himself to grant them indulgence, by his promises to their envoys and the Catholic princes. He even invited some of them to court, and promised to protect them from the penalties of recusancy.

The Puritans had still higher expectations. As the king had been educated in the Kirk of Scotland, and had hitherto professed that faith, they flattered themselves that he would reform the English Church and regulate its discipline by their standard. But both parties soon discovered their mistake. Neither the Catholic nor the Puritan system suited the policy and ambition of James. The one looked to the Pope as the supreme head of the Church, and the other admitted no earthly but only a heavenly Head; while the Church of England not only offered him the title, but, in the persons of too many of its prelates, prostrated itself before him in degrading servility. With all his folly, pedantry and absurdity, which brought upon him the epigrams of statesmen,[1] and have made him the mark for the derision of historians, James had no common measure of shrewdness. He clearly saw in what direction his interest lay, and from the moment of his accession resolved to conform to the Established Church.

Having thus chosen his faith, he began to persecute the others, though his persecution seems at first to have been inspired rather by avarice and policy than bigotry. On February 22d, 1604, he required all priests to depart the realm before the 19th March, under the pain of having the sanguinary laws of Elizabeth put in force against them; and many of them were shipped off. In that year and the next, one priest and five laymen were executed for their religion.[2] To the dismay of those Catholics who had relied upon assurances of the king's lenity, the legal fine for recusancy, £20 per lunar month, was again exacted, and not only for the time to come, but

[1] Sully, who had been ambassador to the court, pronounced him "the wisest fool in Europe."

[2] Challoner, i., 12.

for *the whole period of the suspension.* This atrocious exaction, by crowding thirteen payments into one, reduced many families to beggary. To satisfy the wants of his needy countrymen, whose importunities were incessant, he transferred to them the claims on his more opulent recusants, with authority to proceed against them by law in his name, unless the sufferers should submit to compound by granting an annuity for life or the immediate payment of a large sum.[1]

But when James began to desire a marriage between his son and the Infanta of Spain, it became necessary, in order to obtain a favorable answer from Philip III., to relax the severity of the laws against Catholics. The prisons had been crowded with priests, yet from 1607 to 1618 only sixteen had been put to death for the exercise of their functions.[2] From the fines of lay Catholics the king derived a net income of £36,000 per annum,[3] equivalent to more than twice that sum at the present day. "When the king," says Dr. Lingard, "in 1616, preparatory to the Spanish match, granted liberty to the Catholics confined under the penal laws, four thousand prisoners obtained their discharge."[4] In 1620 he promised the King of Spain relaxation of the laws against Catholics; in July, 1622, to reconcile the Pope to the match, this relaxation took place, and in 1623 James bound himself by the word of a king that the English Catholics should no longer suffer restraint, provided they confined the exercise of their worship to private houses.[5]

The Spanish match was broken off in the last days of 1623, and when the king met the Parliament in February, 1624, he declared that although he had connived at a less rigorous execution of the penal laws, yet to dispense with, to forbid, or alter any that concerned religion, "he had never promised or yielded—never thought it with his heart, nor spoke it with his mouth."[6]

Hated and persecuted by Puritan, Independent and Churchman, the Catholics of England now drained the bitter chalice of oppression. They were deprived even of incidental protection; for to pardon a single Catholic was to give mortal offence to a Puritan, who was conciliated even when persecuted.[7] Yet they were guilty of no treasonable designs; nor had the plots of a few fanatics tainted the body of English Catholics. Lord Montague, under the stern reign of Elizabeth, had borne fearless and unquestioned testimony to their loyalty. "They dispute not, they preach not, they disobey not the Queen," he exclaims in his powerful appeal to the Lords.[8] They had seen their proudest hopes wither on the scaffold of Mary of Scotland, and gave vent to no open murmur.[9] In that memorable year, when Europe watched in fearful suspense to see the result of that great cast

[1] Lingard, ix., 31.

[2] Challoner, ii.

[3] *Hardwick Papers*, i., 446.

[4] Vol. ix., 128.

[5] Lingard, ix., p. 163.

[6] *Ibid.*, ix., p. 175; authorities stated. B. U. Campbell's Review of Kennedy's Discourse on the Life and Character of George Calvert.—*U. S. Cath. Magazine*, 1846.

[7] Hallam, *Const. Hist.*, i., p. 221.

[8] *Ibid.*, 156.

[9] *Ibid.*, 219.

in the game of human politics, what the craft of Rome, the power of Philip, the genius of Farnese could achieve against the island-queen with her Drakes and her Cecils—in that agony of the Protestant faith and English name they stood the trial of their spirits without swerving from their allegiance. "They flew from every country to the standard of the Lord Lieutenant; and the venerable Lord Montague brought a troop of horse to the Queen at Tilbury, commanded by himself, his son and grandson."[1] But neither uncomplaining submission, nor courage, nor patriotism that, superior to the "scavenger's daughter" and the dungeon, to insult and wanton spoliation, had rushed to the shore when the terrible Armada came on, could soften the cruelty that demanded their lives and the avarice that lusted for their fortunes. There was not one generous pulse to stay the hand that crushed them; and the work of death and confiscation went on more mercilessly than before.

Archbishop Whitgift's Court of High Commission, clothed with almost unlimited powers, studied to entrap the unwary dissenter, and employed every artifice to hush forever the uncouth voice of liberty of conscience. The cruelty of this tribunal must have been excessive, since Strype and Burleigh, employing terms by which they meant to express the height of fiendish malice, stamped it as worse than the Spanish Inquisition.[2]

As the oath of supremacy denied the spiritual power of the Pope,[3] the Catholic found that perjury or apostasy were conditions precedent to his enjoyment of civil privileges. On the other hand, it was not until the Puritan became the Independent, that he refused to concede what the monarch claimed in the oath. There was a wide difference between persecuting the Catholic and persecuting the Independent. In the first case, it was unprovoked oppression; in the last partly defensive. The Catholic, as we have seen, guilty of no political offence, could not expiate his sin by any political virtue. A deep-rooted antipathy to his faith sealed his doom, though his behavior as a citizen was unquestioned. But the Independent had long displayed that restless and determined opposition which ultimately triumphed at Naseby. The Catholic suffered because he obeyed the Pope as the head of the Church; the Independent because he was a political agitator. The acts of Parliament and the State Trials mark this distinction.

Mayne was hanged with no charge against him but papistry; but it was necessary to convict the Brownists under the statute against the spreading of seditious writings.[4] The statute[5] was an expedient to bring the Independent within the pale of persecution; for the temper of the nation required a political offence to justify severity to the Protestant dissenter. In the year 1581, we find the Commons condemning the castigation of Puritans, and in the next breath declaring their willingness to assist in the extirpation of

[1] Hallam, *Const. Hist.*, i., p. 219.

[2] Bancroft, i., p. 289.; Hallam, *Const. Hist. of England*, i., p. 220.

[3] 1st Eliz., c. i.; Hallam, *Const. Hist.*, p. 150, n. 1.

[4] Hallam, *Const. Hist.*, i., p. 296, 289.

[5] 23d Eliz.

Popery.[1] The insolence of the court was inflamed by the stubbornness of the Commons, and every fresh stretch of power awakened a corresponding burst of opposition. Zeal for prerogative had reached an alarming height under Elizabeth, when Heyle and Cecil insisted that her ability to convert her subjects' property to her own use was as clear and perfect as her right to any revenue of the Crown;[2] but it fell far short of the madness for despotism that raged under James. Then the Barons of the Exchequer tore down, with insane joy, the fundamental liberties which neither Henry VII. nor his less scrupulous son had dared to invade. "The seaports are the King's gates, he may open and shut them to whom he pleases!"[3] was the argument by which the inability of the king to impose a duty without the assent of Parliament was answered. Even Raleigh was infected with the mania, unless we suppose that he stooped to conquer, and flattered the king to induce him to call a Parliament. It seems the very irony of history when we find this bold and lofty spirit writing: "The bonds of subjects, to their Kings, should always be wrought out of iron; the bonds of Kings unto subjects, but with cobwebs!"[4]

Still more alarming to the patriot, and more dangerous to liberty, were the doctrines promulgated by the bishops and high churchmen. The canons of 1616 prescribe passive obedience in all cases to the established monarch.[5] "Civil power is God's ordinance!" exclaims the second canon. The logic of Cowel, supported by the archbishop and approved by the king, enjoins that "the King is above law by his absolute power, and may disregard his coronation oath. He may break all laws, inasmuch as they were not made to bind him, but to benefit the people; and to fetter the King, is to injure the people."[6] To give the crowning touch to this Asiatic servility, we have the Star Chamber, in 1616, listening with complacent approval to the king as he declares, "It is atheism and blasphemy to dispute what God can do; good Christians content themselves with His will as revealed in His Word. So it is presumption and high contempt in a subject to dispute what a King can do, or say that a King cannot do this and cannot do that."[7] Spiritual supremacy, therefore, was made to issue from the throne; and thus the authority claimed by the Roman Pontiff became a mere corollary to the omnipotence of the King of England. Thus, with a clergy straining every nerve to sanctify the person of their head, and claiming infallibility, not only for his dogmas, but for his policy, England had well nigh forfeited forever the name of a limited monarchy.

Such was the state of things in England; while in Ireland, if possible, they were worse. Nor was religious persecution idle in either France, Germany or Holland. There, acting upon the same illiberal principle, but with a different object in view, the Huguenots and Puritans were harshly pursued

[1] Hallam, *Const. Hist.*, i., p. 195.
[2] *Ibid.*, 355, n. 1.
[3] *Ibid.*, 427, 431.
[4] *Ibid.*, p. 374, n. 1.
[5] *Ibid.*, 435.
[6] *Ibid.*, 439.
[7] *Ibid.*, 448.

by the politic rulers of the land. The feeble and effeminate Louis XIII., relying for the stability of his kingdom upon the vast abilities of his great minister, busied himself only in the pursuit of those who held a different faith from his own. Although there were no churches to confiscate, because his was the established religion of the kingdom, disqualifications and annoyances were nevertheless heaped upon all dissentients. And here, as everywhere, the weight of persecution fell precisely upon the noblest spirits. While the timid, the indifferent and the time-serving crouched and let the storm pass by, those whose lofty conscientiousness could condone no temporizing, those whose fervent piety counted earthly sufferings but light when weighed with their duty to God, and those whose manly patriotism could ill brook the encroachments of tyranny—these, by standing erect, offered themselves as the fairest mark for cruelty and oppression. But the kings of that day could not see these things. A servile people, ruled by an irresponsible sovereign whose lightest wish was law, seemed to them to realize on earth the pattern of the Divine government.

Irritated to the acutest suffering by the unremitting oppressions to which they were exposed, the Huguenots of France, the Catholics of England and Ireland, and the Puritans of England joyously contemplated the possibility of escape from a thralldom so oppressive. Those who had found in Holland, under the liberal government of the Estates, an asylum where they might enjoy their belief and worship without molestation, were discontented with their residence among a people of different manners and unknown tongue. To all, imagination pictured a far-off land where, amid the grandeur of nature, they might pursue their way undisturbed, and regulate matters, both spiritual and temporal, according to their faith and conscience; and many had long turned their eyes to the vast forests and boundless fields of the New World, whither Providence was directing them, to sow the seed that was to ripen into a mighty people.

To George Calvert, the first Baron of Baltimore, and his son, Cæcilius Calvert, belongs the glory of providing a shelter from Anglican intolerance, not only for their brethren in faith, but for the oppressed of every Christian denomination. The one projected, and was prevented only by death from executing, the plan which the other accomplished, of opening an asylum for conscience. Of these great and good men we will say what is due to their fame and necessary to the elucidation of our subject. All his contemporaries and all unprejudiced historians agree in ascribing to Sir George Calvert extensive learning as a statesman, the most enlarged and just views respecting colonization, a bold and chivalrous spirit of adventure, and a character of stainless purity.

George Calvert, afterwards created the first Baron of Baltimore, and the founder of the Province of Maryland, descended from a noble family in Flanders, and was born at a place called Kipling, in Yorkshire, England, in the year 1582. His father, Leonard Calvert, married Alicia Crossland, and

GEORGE CALVERT, FIRST LORD BALTIMORE.

lived at Danbywiske. When only eleven years old, in 1593, he entered All Saints' College at Oxford, took the degree of Bachelor of Arts in 1597, and was created Master of Arts August 30th, 1605. As a student he displayed a fondness for literature, and at the early age of fifteen he published a Latin poem on the death of his friend, Henry Unton, a brave and much esteemed soldier, and English ambassador at the court of France. Leaving college, he made a tour of Europe and returned to England in 1602 or 1603. In 1604-5 he married Anne, the daughter of George Wynne, of Hertfordshire, and grand-daughter of Sir Thomas Wroth, of Durance, in Enfield, Middlesex,—a gentleman of some distinction in his time. He was appointed, September 3d, 1606, prothonotary and keeper of the writs, bills, files, records and rolls within the Province of Connaught and Thomand, Ireland. He was also appointed Clerk to the Crown and of the Peace, and of the Assizes and Nisi Prius for life, but resigned this office April 1st, 1616. Previous to this he had been frequently sent abroad on public business, and was appointed one of the commissioners sent to Ireland to examine the condition of affairs and hear and adjust grievances. His abilities were such that Sir Robert Cecil, who had been one of the principal secretaries of State under Queen Elizabeth, and who, by his great services in securing James' succession, was continued in that office by the king, appointed young Calvert his chief clerk, and when he was himself advanced to the office of Lord High Treasurer, as Earl of Salisbury, he still retained Calvert in his service, and afterwards procured for him the position of a clerk of the Privy Council. In 1617 Calvert received the honor of knighthood, and upon the dismissal of Sir Thomas Lake, in 1618 or 1619, the king appointed him one of the secretaries of State. Calvert professed some hesitation in regard to assuming so important a station, and particularly objected his unworthiness to hold an office "so recently filled by his noble lord and master;" but he did not decline the proffered honor. Buckingham reported his replies to the king, who was so much pleased with his modesty and frankness, that he called him into his presence, and, among other queries, inquired what kind of a woman his wife was. "She is a good woman," answered Calvert, "and has brought me ten children; and, I can assure your majesty, she is not a wife with a witness." Which reply, it is stated, gave the king great satisfaction, as it was an assurance that Lady Calvert was by no means a second Lady Lake. The king bestowed not only honors upon him, but rewards more substantial. In 1620 he received a grant of the increased customs on silk for twenty-one years, and an annual pension of £1000. In 1620–21 the University of Oxford chose him their representative in Parliament. Soon after he repaired to Ireland to reside, where the king had given him a large grant of land.[1]

VISCOUNT FALKLAND.

In the earlier part of his official career, it seems that Calvert's attention had been directed to America, for we find that in 1609 he was a member of the Virginia Company of Planters. He was still a member in 1620, and on July 15, 1624, he was one of the provisional council in England, appointed for the temporary government of that province. Like most of the public-spirited men of the age, he determined to establish a colony in some far-off land, and in 1620 purchased of Sir William Vaughan, a former fellow-student at Oxford, who had an interest in a patent for the southern part of Newfoundland as early as 1617, the whole south-eastern peninsula of that island. Vaughan, it appears, was disappointed in his expectations of his colony, and so assigned a portion of his grant to Viscount Falkland and to "Sir George Calvert, Knight, then principal Secretary of State to King James."[2]

[1] John G. Morris, D.D., Md. Hist. Society, *Lords Baltimore*; Burnap's *Calvert*; Neill, *Terra Mariæ*.

[2] MS. Md. Hist. Society.

Attention had been drawn to Newfoundland[1] as a site for a colony a number of years before. Mr. John Grey, a merchant, afterwards Mayor of Bristol, published several treatises on the subject of colonization, about the year 1609, which revived the public interest in the matter. He had the chief agency in procuring the patent to Henry Howard, Earl of Southampton and others, and in 1610 fitted out, at his own expense, an expedition on a large scale with a view of establishing permanent intercourse with Newfoundland. A patent was granted to the Earl of Southampton, Keeper of the Privy Seal, Sir Lawrence Tanfield, Lord Chief Baron of the Exchequer, Sir Francis Bacon, Solicitor General, Sir John Dodderidge, King's Sergeant, and more than forty associates, incorporating them under the name of "The Treasurer and Company of Adventurers and Planters of the Cities of London and Bristoll, for the Colony and Plantation in Newfoundland." This document recites that the English had resorted for more than fifty years in no small numbers to that island for the purpose of fishing, and it was hereby intended to protect them in the pursuit of their trade. Supplies were sent yearly from Bristol to the settlers until 1614, after which period we find no trace of the active operations of the company. But intercourse with the island was kept up, and other parties undertook to plant colonies there.

In 1621, the year following his purchase from Vaughan, and a year after the landing of the pilgrims of Massachusetts at Plymouth, Sir George Calvert sent over Captain Edward Wynne with a commission as governor, and a small colony. Among those "who wintered and stayed with Captain Wynne in 1622" were "Captain Daniel Powel, John Hickson, salt maker, Nicholas Hoskins, Robert Stoning, Sybill Dee, maid, Elizabeth Kerne, Joan Jackson, girls, Thomas Wilson, John Praler, smiths, John Bevell, stone-layer, Ben Hacker, quarryman, Nic. Hinckson, Robert Bennett, Will Hatch, carpenters, Henry Duke, boatmaster, William Sharpus, tailor, Rob. Fleshman, surgeon, Henry Dring, husbandman, Owen Evans, Mary Russel, Eliz. Sharpus, John Bayley, Ann Bayley his wife, Widow Bayley, Joseph Pauser, Robert Row, fisherman, Philip Lane, cooper, Will Bond, Peter Wolton, boatmaster, Ellis Hinkson, Gregory Fleshman, Richard Higgins, boys; in all thirty-two."[2]

They settled at Ferryland, one of the chief promontories upon the eastern coast, where Calvert expended of his private fortune not less than £25,000 in building granaries and store-houses, and in erecting a handsome house for his own residence. "His public spirit," says Fuller, "consulted not his

[1] In 1578 Sir Humphrey Gilbert obtained a patent for a colony in that region, and made two expeditions, in both of which his half-brother, Sir Walter Raleigh, was interested, and one of which he accompanied. After the failure of Gilbert's enterprise, Raleigh himself obtained a patent from the queen, but more wisely selected a region of milder climate. Yet the abundant fisheries of Newfoundland and the Grand Banks kept up the attraction. It is possible that Calvert, the friend of James may have wished to show that he could succeed where Raleigh, whom that sovereign detested—and Calvert, probably did not love—had failed.

[2] Oldmixon, i., p. 11.

private profit, but the enlargement of Christianity and the King's dominions." In May, 1622, the colony was reinforced by an additional number of colonists, and a supply of provisions brought over by Captain Daniel Powel, who, in a letter to Calvert, dated July 28, says: "The land whereon our Governor hath planted is so good and commodious that for the quantity I think there is no better in many parts of England. His house, which is strong and well contrived, stands very warm at the foot of an easy ascending hill on the southeast, and defended with a hill standing on the further side of the haven on the northwest, the beach on the north and south sides of the land lock it, and the seas on both sides are so near that one may shoot a bird-bolt in either sea. No cold can offend it, though it be accounted the coldest harbor in the land; and the seas do make the land behind it to the southeast—being near 1,000 acres of good ground for hay, feeding of cattle, and plenty of wood—almost an island, safe to keep anything from ravenous beasts. . . . If a plantation be there this next spring settled, and your Honor will let me be furnished with charters and give me leave to work, I make no doubt but to give your Honor and the rest of the undertakers such content that you shall have good encouragement to proceed."[1]

The report of Powel was so satisfactory that on April 7, 1623, Calvert received a patent from the king, constituting him and his heirs absolute proprietors of the whole southeastern peninsula of Newfoundland. He gave his new settlement the name, which it still retains, of Avalon, the ancient name of Glastonbury, in Somersetshire, England. Tradition reports that Joseph of Arimathea, having come to Britain, received from King Arviragus twelve hydes of land at Avalon as a dwelling-place for himself and his companions, and here he preached the gospel for the first time to the Britons, and built an abbey, in which he was afterwards buried, and which long remained the most renowned and venerated monastic establishment in the island. Calvert may, or may not, have believed the story—historical criticism was not the strong point of his age—but the selection of the name was a happy one. As Avalon had been the starting-point of Christianity for ancient Britain, in pious legend, at all events, so he hoped that his own settlement might be a similar starting-point from which the gospel should spread to the heathen of the Western World; and he spared neither labor nor expense in his efforts to carry out this noble and devout purpose.[2]

As most of the historians of America vary in the dates which they assign to Sir George Calvert's patent for the province of Avalon, and it appears that none of them have seen a copy of that document, we here give it in full, from *Sloane MS.*, No. 170, in the British Museum:

[1] Oldmixon, i., p. 10.

[2] "The Right Hon. Sir George Calvert, Secretary to the King's most excellent Majesty, hath undertaken to plant a Colony of his Majesty's subjects in this country, and hath already most worthily sent thither in these last two years, a number of persons with all means for their livelihood, and they are building houses, clearing off lands and making salt."—Whitborne's *Description of Newfoundland*, 1622.

CHARTER OF AVALON.

I. JAMES, by the grace of God, King of England, Scotland, France and Ireland, Defender of the Faith, &c. To all to whome these presents shall come, greeting.

II. WHEREAS our right trusty and well beloved Counsellor Sr. George Calvert Knight, our Principall Secretary of State, being excited with a Laudable and pious Zeale to enlarge the extents of the Christian world, and therewithall of our Empire and dominion, hath heretofore to his greate cost purchased a certain Region or Territory hereafter described, in a Country of ours scituate in the West part of the World, commonly called Newfound Land, not yet husbanded or planted, though in some parts thereof inhabited by certaine barbarous People wanting the Knowledge of Almighty God; And intending now to transport thither a very greate and ample Colony of the English Nation, hath humbly besought our Kingly Maiesty to give, grant, and confirme all the said Region with certaine Privileges and Jurisdictions requisite for the good Government and State of the said Colony and Territory to him, his heires, and Assignes for ever.

III. Know yee therefore, that wee favoring the Godly and Laudable purpose of our said Counsellor, of our speciall grace, certaine knowledge, and meere motion, have given, granted, and confirmed, and by this our present Charter for us, our heires and successors, doe give, grant, and confirme unto the said Sr George Calvert Knight, his heires and assignes; for ever, All that entire portion of Land situated within our Country of New-found Land aforesaid, beginning Southerly from the middle part of a certaine neck of Land or Promontory scituate betweene the two harbours of Hermose and Aquafort, and from thence following the shore towards the North, unto the middle part or halfe way over a little harbour (called in that regard Petit Port) which boundeth upon the South part of the Plantation of St. Johns, including the one halfe of a certaine fresh river that falleth into the said Port of Petit Harbour, and so trending all along the south border of the said Colonye of St. Johns, extendeth itselfe to a certain little bay comonly called Salmon Cove lying on the South side of the Bay of Conception including the one halfe of the River that falleth into the said Cove, as also the one halfe of the said Cove it selfe. From whence passing along the shore of the said Bay towards the South, and reaching unto the bottom thereof where it meets with the Lands of John Guy Citizen of Bristoll, named Sea-forest, is bounded with a certaine River or Brooke wich there falls into the Sea, and from the mouth of the said Brooke ascendeth unto the furthest spring or head thereof; From thence passeth towards the South, for five Miles together alongst the borders of the said John Guies Plantation, and there crossing over Westward in a right line reacheth unto the Bay of Placentia; and the space of one League within the said Bay from the Shore thereof hence turning againe towards the South passeth along the harbour Placentia with the like distance from the shore, and descending unto New Falkland towards the North and West part thereof stretcheth itself in a righte Line Eastward, continuing the whole Southerly length upon the bounders of the sayd New-Falkland, unto the middle part or point of the Promontory or neck of Land aforementioned between the said Ports of Fermose and Aquafort, at which place is described and finished the perambulation of the whole precinct.

IV. Wee doe further give, and by this present Charter for us our heirs and successors, wee doe grante and confirme unto the said Sr George Calvert his heires and Assignes all and singular the Islands and Iletts that are or shall be within Tenne Leagues from the Easterrne Shoare of the said Region towards the East with all and singular Ports, harbours and Creekes of the Sea belonging unto the said Region or the Islands aforesaid, And all the Soile, Landes, Woods, Lakes, and Rivers scituate or being within the Region Isles or Limitts aforesaid, with the Fishings of all sortes of Fishe, Whales, Sturgions, and other Royall Fishes in the Sea or Rivers; and moreover all Veines, Mines and delues as well discovered as not discovered, of Gold, Silver, Gemmes and precious Stones, and all other whatsoever be it of Stones, Metalls, or of any other thing or matter whatsoever found and to be found within the Region Iles and Limitts aforesaid. And furthermore the Patronages and Advowsons of all Churches which as Christian Religion shall increase within the said Region Isles and Limitts shall happen hereafter to be erected, Together with all and singular the like and as ample Right jurisdictions privileges prerogatives Royaltyes, Liberties, Imunityes and Franchises whatsoever as well by Sea as by Land within the Region, Iles and Limitts aforesaid, To have exercise use and enjoy the same, as any Bishop of Durham within the Bishopprick or County Palatine of Durham in our Kingdome of England hath at any time heretofore had, held, used, or enjoyed, or of right ought or might have had, held, used, or enjoyed.

V. And him the sayd Sr George Calvert his heires and Assignes wee doo by these presents for us our heires and successors make Create and constitute the true and absolute Lords and Proprietaryes of the Region aforesaid, and of all other the Premisses, saving allwayes unto us our heirs and successors the faith and Allegiance due unto us, To have holde possesse and enjoy the said Region Isles and other the premisses unto the said Sr George Calvert his heires and assignes to the sole and proper use and behoofe of him the said Sr George Calvert his heirs and assignes for ever, To be holden of us our heirs and successors Kings of England in Capite by Knights service, And yielding therefor to us our heirs and successors, a white horse whensoever and as often as it shall happen that wee, our heirs or successors, shall come into the said Territory or Region; And moreover the fift part of all Gold and Silver Oare which within the Limitts aforesaid shall from time to time happen to be found.

VI. Now that the sayd Region thus by us granted and described may be eminent above all other parts of the sayd Country of Newfound-Land, and graced with larger Titles, knowe yee that we of our further grace certayne knowledge and meere motion have thought fitt to erect the same Territory and Ilands into a Province, as out of the fulness of our Royall power and prerogative wee doe for us our heirs and successors erect and incorporate them into a Province and doe call it Avalon or the Province of Avalon, and soe hereafter will have it called.

VII. And forasmuch as wee have hereby made and ordeyned the sayd Sr George Calvert the true Lord and Proprietary of all the Province aforesayd, knowe yee therefore moreover, that wee for us, our heirs and successors, reposing especiall trust and confidence in the fidelity, wisedome, justice and provident circumspection of the sayd Sr George Calvert, doe grant free, full and absolute power by vertue of these presents to him and his heires for the good and happy government of the sayd Province, to ordaine, make, enact, and under his or their seales to publish any Lawes whatsoever apperteyning either unto the publick state of the sayd Province, or unto the private utility of particular persons, according unto their best discretions, of and with the advice assent and approbation of the Freeholders of the sayd Province, or the greater parte of them, whome for the enacting of the sayd Lawes when and as often as need shall require, wee will that the sayd Sr George Calvert and his heires shall assemble in such sort or forme as to him shall seeme best; And the same Lawes upon all men and people within the sayd Province and Limitts thereof for the time being or that shall be constituted under the government and power of him the sayd Sr George Calvert or his heires either sayling towards Avalon from our Kingdom of England or any other our dominions or Contryes, or returning from thence to our Kingdome of England or any other our dominions or Contryes, by the sayd Sr George Calvert and his heires, or by his or their deputies Lieutenants, Judges, Justicers, Magistrats, Officers and Ministers to be ordayned and appointed according to the tenor and true intentions of these presents, by imposition of penaltyes, imprisonment and any other coertion, yea if it be needfull and that the quality of the Offence require it, by taking away member or life, duly to execute; As likewise to appoint and establish Judges and Justicers,

Magistrats and Officers, whatsoever by Sea and by Land for what causes soever, and with what power and authority soever, and in such forme as to the sayd Sr George Calvert and his heires shall seeme most convenient: Also to remitt, release, pardon, and abolishe whether before judgement or after, all crimes and offences whatsoever against the said Lawes, and to doe all and every other things which unto the establishment of Justice, Courts and Tribunalls, formes of Judicature and manners of proceeding doe belong, although in these presents expresse mention be not made thereof. Which Lawes, so as aforesayed to be published, our pleasure is and so wee enjoynd require and command shall be most absolute and available in Law, and that all the liege people and subjects of us, our heires and successors, do observe and keepe the same inviolably so farre as they concerne them under the penaltyes therein contained or to be contained. Provided nevertheless that the sayd Lawes doe stand with reason, and be not repugnant nor contrary, but as near as conveniently may be, agreeable to the Lawes, statutes and Customes of this our Kingdome of England.

VIII. And forasmuch as in the government of soe greate a Province suddeine accidents doe often happen whereunto it will be necessary to apply a Remedy before the Freeholders of the sayd Province can be assembled to the making of Lawes, neither will it be convenient that instantly upon every such emergent occasion so greate a multitude should be called together, Therefore, for the better government of the sayd Province wee will and ordaine, and by these presents for us, our heires and successors, do grant unto the sayd Sr George Calvert and his heirs, that he, the sayd Sr George Calvert and his heirs, by himself and his Magistrats and Officers in that behalfe duly to be ordayned as aforesayed, may make and constitute fitt and wholsome ordinances from time to time within the sayd Province, to be kept and observed as well for the preservation of the peace, as for the better government of the people there inhabiting, and publickly to notify the same to all persons whom the same doth or may any way concern. Which ordinances our pleasure is shall be observed inviolably within the said Province, under the paines therein to be expressed. So as the sayd ordinances be consonant to reason, and not repugnant, nor contrary, but so farre as conveniently may be agreeable with the Lawes and Statutes of our Kingdome of Englande, and so far as the sayd ordinances be not extended in any sort to binde, charge, or to take away the right or interest of any person or persons, of or in their freeholde, goods or chattells.

IX. Furthermore, that this new Colony may the more happily increase by the multitude of people resorting thither, and likewise may be the more strongly defended from the incursions of Salvages or other enemies, Piratts and Robbers, Therefore, we, for us, our heirs and successors, doe give and grant by these presents power, License and Liberty unto all the liege people and subjects, both present and future, of us our heirs and successors (excepting those who shall be specially forbidden) to transport themselves and Familyes unto the sayd Province of Avalon with convenient shipping and necessary Provisions, and there to settle themselves dwell and inhabite, and to buyld and fortify Castles, Forts and other places of strength for the publick and their own private defence, at the appointment of the sayd Sr George Calvert, Knight, his heires and assignes. The Statute of Fugitives or any other Statutes whatever to the contrary of the premises in any thing notwithstanding.

X. And we will also, and of our more especiall grace for us our heires and successors we do straightly enjoyne, constitute, ordaine and command, that the sayd Province shall be of our Allegiance and that all and singular the subjects and Liege people of us, our heires and Successors transported or to be transported into the sayd Province, and their Children there already borne, or hereafter to be borne, be and shall be denizens and Lieges of us, our heires and Successors and be in all things held, treated, reputed and esteemed as the Liege faithfull people of us, our heires and Successors borne within our Kingdome of England; and likewise any Landes, Tenements, Revenues, Services and other hereditaments whatsoever Within our Kingdome of England, and other our dominions may purchase, receive, take, have, hold, buy and possesse, and them to occupie and enjoy, give, sell, alien and bequeath, as likewise all Liberties, Franchises and Privileges of this our Kingdome freely, quietly and peaceably have and possesse, occupy and enjoy as our Liege people borne or to be borne within our saide Kingdome of Englande, without the Lett, molestation, vexation, trouble or offence of us, our heires, or Successors whomsoever, any Statute, Act, Ordinance, or Provision to the contrary hereof notwithstanding.

XI. And furthermore, that our Subjects may be the rather incouraged to undertake this expedition with ready and cheerful mindes, through the hope of gaine and comfort of Privileges, Know yee that wee of our especiall grace certaine knowledge and meere motion doe give and grant free License and Liberty by virtue of these presents, as well unto the sayd Sr George Calvert his heires and assignes, as to all other that shall from time to time repaire unto Avalon with a purpose to inhabite, to lade and fraiget, and into the sayd Province of Avalon by them their servants or Assignes from any Ports whatsoever of us our heires and successors to transport all and singular their goods, moveable or unmoveable wares and merchandise, as likewise Armes and warlike instruments offensive and defensive, without any Imposition, Subsidy, Custome or any other thing to be paid therefor unto us our heires or successors, and without the impediment or molestation of us our heires or successors, or of any officer whatsoever or Farmo of us our heires or successors, any Statute, Act, Ordinance or any other thing to the contrary notwithstanding. Provided alwayes that before the sayd Goods and Merchandises be carried or Laden aboorde the Shippes, leave be first asked and obtained of the highe Treasurer of us our heires and successors of our Kingdome of England, or of the Comissioners for our Treasury, or of sixe or more of the Privy Counsell to us our heires and successors under their handes in writing. To which highe Treasurer, Comissioners and Privy Counsell of us our heires and successors, or to any sixe or more of them, Wee have for us our heires and successors given and granted, as wee doe by these presents give and grant, power to grante such Licenses in forme aforesayd.

XII. And because in so remote a Country and scituate amongst so many barbarous Nations, the incursions as well of the Salvages themselves as of other Enimies Piratts and Robbers may probably be feared, Therefore wee have given, and for us our heires and successors by these presents doe give power unto the sayd Sr George Calvert Knight his heires and assignes, by himselfe or his Captaines or other of his Officers, to Levy, Muster and Trayne all sorts of men whatsoever, or wheresoever borne, in the Province of Avalon for the time being, and to make warre and to prosecute the enemies and Robbers aforesayd as well by Sea as by Land, yea even without the Limitts of the sayd Province, and by God's assistance to vanquish and take them, and being taken to putt them to death by the Lawe of warre, or to save them, as the sayd Sr George Calvert and his heires and assignes shall think fitt, and to doe all and every other thing which unto the Charge and office of a Captaine generall belongeth or hath accustomed to belong, as fully and freely as any other Captaine generall hath ever had the same.

XIII. Also our will and pleasure is, and by this our Charter wee do give to the sayd Sr George Calvert Knight his heires and assignes in case of Rebellion, Suddaine Tumult or sedition if any should happen (which God forbidd) either upon the Land within the Province aforesayd or upon the Maine Sea in making a voyage thither, or returning from thence, power, liberty and authority by himselfe or his Captaines, deputies or other Officers to be authorized under his Seale to that purpose (to whom wee also for us our heires and successors doe give and grante by these presents full power and authority) to exercise the Lawe military against mutinous and seditious persons, such as shall refuse to submitt themselves to his or their Government, or shall refuse to serve in the Warres, or shall flye to the Enemy or forsake their Ensignes, or be Loyterers or straglers, or otherwise howsoever offending against the Lawe, Custome, [and] discipline Military, as freely and in as ample a manner and forme as any Captaine Generall by virtue of his Office might or hath accustomed to use the same.

XIV. Furthermore that the way to honors and dignityes may not seem to be altogether precluded and shutt up to men well borne and such as shall prepare themselves unto this present Plantation, and shall deserve well of us and our Kingdomes both in peace and warre in so farre distant and remote a Country, Therefore we, for us our heires and successors, doe give free and absolute power unto the sayd Sr George Calvert Knight, his heires and assignes, to conferre favors, Rewardes and honors upon such inhabitants within the Province aforesayd, as shall deserve the same, and to invest them with what Titles and dignityes soever as hee shall think fitt, so as they be not such as are at this present used in our Kingdome of England; As likewise to erect and incorporate Townes into Burroughes, and Burroughes into Cittyes, with convenient privileges and imunityes according to the meritt of the Inhabitants, and the fittness of the places, and to doe all and every other things touching the premises, which to him or them shall seeme meete and requisite, albeit they be such as of their owne nature might otherwise require a more speciall comandment and warrant than in these presents is expressed.

XV. And forasmuch as the beginnings of all Colonyes and Commonwealths are incumbred with sundry inconveniences and difficulties, wee therefore favouring the growth of this present Collonye and providing out of our Royall care, that those who are burdened one way may be eased another, of our especiall grace and meere motion doe by this our Charter give and grant to the sayd Sr George Calvert his heires and assignes and to all the Inhabitants and dwellers whomsoever present and to come in Avalon aforesayd, License to import and unlade by themselves or their servants, Factors, or assigns, all whatsoever Marchandize and Goods that shall arise of the fruits and Comodityes of the sayd Province either by Land or Sea into any of the Ports of us, our heires and successors in our Kingdomes of England or Ireland, or otherwise to dispose of the sayd Goodes in the sayd Ports, and if neede be within one yeare after the discharge of the same, to Lade the sayd Marchandise and Goods again into the same shippes, or others, and to export the same into any other Countryes either of our dominion or forraigne without paying in any sort any manner of subsidy, Custome, Taxe, or imposition whatsoever unto us, our heires or successors, or to the Customers, Farmors and Lessees of us, our heires or successors in any manner wise. Provided allways, and it is our meaning and intention that this our grace and immunity from Customes, impositions, subsidies shall continue and be of force for Tenne yeares onely to be reckoned from the date of these presents, and no longer, which Tenne yeares being expired and ended, Our will and pleasure is, and wee doe, for us, our heires and successors grante, and ordaine, that the sayd Sr George Calvert, Knight, his heires and assignes, and all and every other Inhabitant and dweller present and to come within the Province of Avalon aforesayd, may by themselves or their Factors and servants import and unlade, and within the time aforesayd if they will relade and export all manner of Marchandises, wares and goods whatsoever arising from the fruites and comodities of Avalon into and out of any the Ports whatsoever of us, our heires and successors, Provided allwayes that they doe pay for the same unto us, our heires and successors such customes and Impositions subsidies and duties as other our subjects, for the time are bound to pay, beyond which we do not intend that the sayd Inhabitants of Avalon bee any way charged.

XVI. And furthermore of our more ample and speciall grace certaine knowledge and meere motion wee doe for us our heires and successors grante unto the sayd Sr George Calvert Knight, his heires and assignes full and absolute power and authority to make erect and constitute within the Province of Avalon and Islands aforesaid, such and so many Sea Ports, harbours, Creekes and other places of charge and discharge for Shippes Boats and other Vessells, and in such and so many places and with such

Rightes, jurisdictions, freedomes and Privileges unto the sayd Ports belonging, as to him or them shall seeme most expedient; And that all and singular the Shippes Boats and other Vessells which shall come for Marchandise and trade unto the sayd Province, or out of the same shall depart shall be Laden and Unladen only at such Ports and no other, as the sayd Sr George Calvert his heires and assignes shall erect and constitute, any use, custome, or other thing to the contrary notwithstanding. Saving allwaies and ever reserved unto all our subjects, and the subjects of our heires and successors of our Kingdome of England free liberty of Fishing as well in the Sea as in the Ports and Creekes of the Province aforesayed, and the privilege of salting and drying their Fishe upon the Shoares of the sayd Province, as heretofore they have reasonably used and enjoyed the same, any thing in these presents to the contrary notwithstanding. Which Liberties and Previleges nevertheless the subjects aforesayd of us our heires and successors shall enjoy without doing any injury or notable losse and detriment unto the sayd Sr George Calvert his heires and assignes, or to the dwellers and Inhabitants of the sayd Province in the Ports Creekes and shoares aforesayd and especially in the Woodes growing within the sayd Province. And if any shall presume to offer any such injury or spoile, hee shall thereby incurre the heavy displeasure of us our heires and successors, together with the danger and penalty which by the Lawes shall be unto the same.

XVII. Wee doe furthermore will, appoint, and ordayne, and by these presents for us our heires and successors wee doe grante unto the sayd Sr George Calvert, his heires and assignes, that hee his heires and assignes may from time to time for ever have and enjoy all and singular the Subsidies, Customes and Impositions payable or accruing within the Ports, harbours and other places aforesayd within the Province aforesayd for all goods and Merchandises there to be laden and unladen.

XVIII. And further our pleasure is and by these presents for us our heires and successors wee doe covenant and grant to and with the sayd Sr George Calvert Knight, his heirs and Assignes, That we our heires and successors shall at no time hereafter sett or make, or cause to be sett any Imposition, Custome or other Taxation whatsoever in or upon the dwellers or inhabitants of the Province aforesayd, or upon any of the Landes Tenements goods or Chattells within the sayd Province, or in or upon any of the goods or Merchandises within the sayd Province to be Laden or unladen within the Ports or harbours of the sayd Province. And our pleasure is, and for us our heirs and successors wee charge and command that this our declaration and grante shall be received and allowed from time to time in all Courts, and before any the Judges of us our heires and successors for a sufficient and Lawfull discharge, payment and acquittance, Commanding all and singular our Officers and ministers of us our heires and successors, and enjoyning them upon paine of our highe displeasure, that they doe not presume at any time to attempt anything to the contrary of the premisses, or that they doe in any sorte withstand the same, but that they be at all times aiding and assisting, as is fitting, unto the sayd Sr George Calvert Knight, and to the Inhabitants and Marchants of Avalon aforesayd, their servants, Ministers factors and Assignes, to the full fruition and enjoying of the benefitt of this our Charter.

XIX. And if perchance hereafter it should happen that any doubtes or questions should arise concerning the true sense and understanding of any words clause or sentence contained in this our present Charter, Wee will, ordaine and command, that at all times and in all things such interpretation bee made thereof and allowed in any of our Courts whatsoever, as shall be judged most advantageous and favorable unto the sayd Sr George Calvert his heires and assignes. Provided allways that no interpretations bee admitted thereof whereby Gods holy and truly Christian Religion or Allegiance due unto us our heires and successors may in any thing suffer any prejudice or diminution. Although express mention be not made in these presents of the true yearly value or certainty of the premises or of any part thereof, or of other gifts or grantes made by us heretofore or by any of our Progenitors or predecessors unto the sayd Sr George Calvert Knight, or any

Statute, act, ordinance, provision, proclamation or Restraint heretofore had made published ordained or provided, or any other thing cause or matter whatsoever to the contrary thereof in any wise notwithstanding.

XX. In witnesse whereof we have caused these our Letters to be made patents. Witnesse ourself at Westminister the seventh day of Aprill in the one and twentith yeare of our Raigne of England, France and Ireland, and of Scotland the sixe and fifteth.

This grant was apparently in direct repugnance, not only to that previously made by the king in 1610 to the Earl of Northampton and others, as before mentioned, but also to the grant then recently made to the Duke of Lennox and others in 1620, under the denomination of New England; which latter grant, extending as high up as the forty-eighth degree of north latitude, must have comprehended the whole of Sir George Calvert's province of Avalon. As the settlement attempted by Guy under the first mentioned patent of 1610 totally failed, and the patentees had, to all appearance, entirely relinquished their intention of making any further use of their patent, Sir George might perhaps see no impropriety in accepting a re-grant of the same territory. Whether the collision between his grant and that of New England in 1620 produced any dispute, we are not informed. The surrender of the New England patent in the year 1635 must have relieved him from such interference. Notwithstanding these prior grants, Sir George prepared to execute the purposes and intention of his patent.[1]

Up to this period Calvert had been a member of the established Church of England, in which faith he had been baptized.[2] But early in 1624 he announced to the king that he had joined the Roman Catholic communion, and therefore resigned his office of Secretary of State, which he could no longer conscientiously hold. This change of religion, however, wrought no change in the confidence and regard of his royal master. James, though far from liberal in religious matters, was a man of warm personal attachments, and his friendship for Calvert was not diminished, nor did his marks of favor cease. He retained him in the Privy Council, and in 1625 raised him to the Irish peerage as Baron of Baltimore in the county of Longford, Ireland. His release from his secretaryship, Sir George "obtained from the King with some difficulty, His Majesty having a particular affection to him by reason of his great abilities and integrity."[3]

After the death of King James, which occurred on the 27th of March, 1625, King Charles I. "desired his lordship to be continued a Privy Counsellor to him, resolving to dispense with him taking the oath of supremacy, but, at his request, gave him leave, at length, to retire from Court."[4]

Thus we see that while high in favor at the court of James and Charles, holding the station of Secretary of State, and respected and trusted above all others, he resigned an office of great importance and large emoluments, and with it his brilliant hopes of higher political distinction, in obedience to the

[1] Bozman.

[2] Anderson, *Colonial Church*, i., p. 326.

[3] MS. Maryland Historical Society.

[4] *Ibid.*

dictates of his conscience; and voluntarily associated his fortunes with a church in the minority, laboring under disabilities, and the object of popular odium. Few recorded changes of faith bear more convincing marks of sincerity.

Calvert was consistent and reasonable, his opinions moderate, the tenor of his life such that he had few enemies, and was entangled but little with parties in his latter years. Before his conversion he had been a successful aspirant to political station and had filled every position with honor and ability. His services to King James were considered of high value by that monarch, who relied upon him in his hours of need to retrace the evil steps he had taken, and defend him before his unruly Parliament, and this favor of the king towards the man who had served him so faithfully throughout the troubles of the Spanish negotiation did not forsake him after his change of religion. But there was another feeling which may have tended to secure Calvert in his continuance of the king's favor. It was necessary to obtain the aid of the Catholics in resisting the progress of the Independents, who were becoming daily more powerful; and the conversion of Calvert presented a favorable opportunity of impressing upon a leading man the grateful recollection of his kindness.

CHARLES I.

After Lord Baltimore's resignation of the secretaryship, he proposed to visit his colony in Newfoundland, as we learn from a letter of April 9th, 1625, which says: "It is sajd the Lord Baltimore is now a professed Papist; was going to Newfoundland and is stayed."[1] Blackstone in his *Commentaries* upon the law, "Of the Rights of Persons," Book I., chapter 7, section 265, says, the king has the right "whenever he sees proper, of confining his subjects to stay within the realm, or of recalling them when beyond the seas."

Lord Baltimore, however, was still in favor with Charles I., and was the next year called from his retirement in Ireland, to be employed at Brussels in a treaty of peace. It was announced by a London correspondent, under date of March 2d, 1626, that "the talk of divers great commissioners to go over about a treaty of peace, still holds, and Sir George Calvert, sent for out of Ireland for that service, is now come, and on Tuesday rode with the Duke's grace toward the Court." He did not, for some reason, go to Brussels, and being disengaged from his many previous duties, he had now leisure to mature his project of visiting his colony. On the 7th of April, 1627, he wrote from his lodgings in the Surrey to Edward Nicholas, secretary of the Duke of Buckingham, for the speedy despatch of the warrant for his ships, the *Ark*, of Avalon, one hundred and sixty tons burden, and the *George*, of Plymouth, one hundred and forty tons, to be exempted from

[1] *Terra Mariæ*, p. 36.

the general stay, as Sir Arthur Aston was waiting to sail to his "young plantation."[1] Having obtained the long desired permission to visit his possessions in Newfoundland, Lord Baltimore, on May 21st, 1627, writes to his intimate friend, Sir Thomas Wentworth:

"I am heartily sorry, that I am farther from my hopes of seeing you, before my leaving this town, which will be now within these three or four days, being bound for a long journey, to a place which I have had a long desire to visit, and have now the opportunity and leave to do it.

"It is Newfoundland I mean, which it imports me more than in curiosity, only to see, for I must either go and settle it in better order or else give it over, and lose all the charges I have been at hitherto, for other men to build their fortunes upon. And I had rather be esteemed a fool by some, for the hazard of one month's journey, than to prove myself one certainly for six years by past, if the business be now lost for the want of a little pains and care."[2]

He embarked in a ship of three hundred tons, and twenty-four guns, and arrived at the settlement of Ferryland about the 23d of July, the same year. The companions of his journey were Longvyll and Anthony Smith, two seminary priests. After remaining a short time, Lord Baltimore returned with Longvyll to England and soon after to his family, which was then in Ireland.

THOMAS EARL ARUNDEL.

Late in the spring of 1628, he made a second voyage to his colony, taking with him his wife[3] and all his children excepting his eldest son, including his sons-in-law, Sir Robert Talbot and Mr. William Peasley, also a priest named Hacket and about forty colonists. His eldest son, who married Anna, daughter of Thomas Earl Arundel, one of the most influential noblemen of the Roman Catholic faith, was left in charge of his estate in Ireland. During the summer he was obliged to contend with many difficulties, and in the following letter addressed to the Duke of Buckingham, he pours forth his troubles:

"MAY IT PLEASE YOUR GRACE:[4]

"I Remember that his Matie once told me that I writt as faire a hand to looke upon a farre of as any man in England, but that when any one came neare it, they weare not able to read a word: wherevppon I gott a dispensation both from his Matie and yor Grace to vse another mans pen when I write to eyther of you, and I humblye thanke you for it: for Writting is a greate payne to mee nowe:

"I owe yor Grace an accompte of my actions and proceedings in this Plantation, since vnder yor patronage and by yor favourable mediation to his Matie I haue transported my selfe hither: I came to builde, and sett, and sowe, but I am falne to fighting wth Frenchmen who haue heere disquieted mee and many other of his Maties subiects fishing in this Land: One de la Rade of Deepe [Dieppe] wth three shipps and 400 men, many of them Gentlemen of qualitie and La fleur de la Jeunesse de Normandye (as some frenchmen heare

[1] State Paper Office, *American, West India and Md. Colonial Papers.*

[2] Strafford's *Letters*, i., p. 39.

[3] His second wife, his first died in 1622.

[4] Public Record Office in London, *Colonial Papers*, iv., p. 57.

haue told vs) came first into a harbor of myne called Capebroile not aboue a League from the place where I am planted, and there surprising divers of the fishermen in their shallops att the harbors mouth, w^th^in a short tyme after possest themselues of two English shipps w^th^in the harbour, wth all their fishe & provitions, and had donne the like to the rest in that place had I not sent them assistance wth two shipps of myne one of 360 tonnes and 24 peces of Ordnance and thother a barke of 60 tonnes wth 3 or 4 small gunnes in her, & about 100 men abord vs in all: These Shipps being discou'ed to moue by a skowt whom the french kepte at the harbors mouth they staid not waying Anchor, but let slip their Cables and awaye to sea as faste as they coulde Leaving their bootie and 67 of their owne men behinde them on shore for hast: wee gaue them chase but coulde not ou'take them: and that nighte I sent a Companye to fech the 67 men out of the woods, fearing that being well armed as wee vnderstood they weare, and then in despiration, they mighte force some boatt or weake shippe, or do other Mischeife, and the nexte morning they were broughte vnto mee hither, where I haue been troubled and charged wth them all this sommer. Within a fewe dayes after, advertisement was given me that De la Rade was gonne into the Bay of Conception some 20 leages to the Northward of this Place and their Committed more spoile, wherypon I sent forth the greate shippe agayne wth all the seamen I had heere and one of my sonnes, wth some gent and others that attend mee in this Plantation, but before they came neere him he was againe freighted by the *Vnicorne* of London, having first taken divers English Prisoners and Caryed them with him: from thence my shipp and Companye by my directions Consorting wth Captayne Fearnes a man of Warre, retourned backe to the Southward and in a harbor called Trepasse where De la Rade first toucht in the beginninge of the sommer, and came from thence to vs, they found 6 French shipps 5 of Bayonne and one of St. Jan de luz: who had almost made their Voyage and weare neere Readie to retourne homewards: Them wee tooke for the hurte they haue donne vs, and haue sent them now for England, where they shall arive safelye I hope w^th^in yor Grace's Admirall Jurisdiction and I p^r^sume soe much of yor wonted fauour as in any p^te^ of this busynes that hath relation to my intrest yor Grace will bee pleased, I shall bee respected as one of your sarvants and that you will pardon all errors of formalitye in the proceedings: Whether this French gent may retourne agayne when the shipps are gonne I know not: if he doe, wee shall defende this place as well as we are able: but for the tyme to come, it much concernes his Maties service and the good of that Kingdome in my poor judgement that two men of warre att the least mighte bee continued all the yeare, excepte it bee the winter tyme, vppon this coast for p^r^servinge of soe many of his subjects being all bred seamen and their shipping and goods, wch maye easilye bee done by a contribution vppon the fisherye it selfe and it may verye well beare it w^th^out any sensibell burthen to particular men, if yor Grace will be pleased to intercede vnto his Matie in that behalfe and that some principall Owners of the west countrey may be conferd w^th^all to that purpose before the nexte Spring and the contribution Imposed heere by his Maties Authoritye. I have desired this bearer Mr Peaslye, sometymes a servant to our late Soueraigne, whose company I have had heere this sommer, to attend yor Grace on my behalfe and I humblye beseech you to vouchsafe him accesse to yor person as there shall bee occasion wth favour and I shall alwayes rest the same now and for ever.

DUKE OF BUCKINGHAM.

"Yo^r^ Graces most faithfull and humble servant

"FERRYLAND, 25 Aug: 1628: "GEO: BALTIMORE."

This "fighting with Frenchmen," was an interesting episode in the brief history of the colony. War was then progressing between England and France—that war so insignificant in its immediate results, and so momentous in its ultimate consequences—and the colonies were sometimes the scenes of hostilities.

In the autumn of 1628, Leonard Calvert and his brother-in-law, William Peasley, returned to England to look after the interests of the colony; and Leonard Calvert humbly petitions that Lord Baltimore may have a share in the prizes that had been taken from the French by the ships *Benediction* and *Victory*, and that a letter of marque might be issued, antedated so that he might receive his proportion. In December, William Peasley also presented a petition to the Lords Commissioners of the Admiralty on behalf of Lord Baltimore, asking for the use of the ship *St. Claude* in lieu of the *Esperance*, for the defence of his plantation and the English fishermen in Newfoundland against the inroads of the French. On the 13th of December, his majesty, through Sir Francis Cottington, addressed an order to the Lord High Treasurer "that one of the six prize ships is to be lent to the Lord Baltimore that he might be the better able to defend himself against the French; and requesting that it may be a good one." And a few days afterwards the prize ship *St. Claude* was delivered to Leonard Calvert "for one year," "in consideration of Lord Baltimore's good services last year in Newfoundland against the French." The Rev. Erasmus Sturton, who had been the resident Protestant minister at Ferryland, left there on the 26th of August, 1628, and in October complained to the authorities in England that in violation of law, mass was publicly celebrated in Newfoundland.

SIR FRANCIS COTTINGTON.

Soon after Leonard Calvert obtained the *St. Claude*, he sailed in her as supercargo for his father's province, and on the 19th of August, 1629, Lord Baltimore, in the following letter to the king, "gives thanks upon his knees for the loan of a fair ship":

"MOST GRACIOUS AND DREAD SOVERAIGNE:

"Small benefits and favors can speake and give thanks, but such as are high, invalerable, cause astonishment and silence. I am obliged unto yo'r ma'ty for the latter in such a measure, As reflecting upon my weakness and want of merit, I know not what to say. God Almighty knowes, who is the searcher of hearts, how myne carnes to sacrifice myself for yo'r ma'ty's service. Yf I do but know how to employ my endeavors worthy of that greate goodness and benignity, which your ma'ty is pleased to extend towards me upon all occasions, not only by reaching yo'r gracious and royall hand to my assistance in lending me a faire shipp (for w'ch upon my knees I render yo'r ma'ty most humble thankes), but by protecting me also against calumny and malice, w'ch hath already sought to make me seeme fowle in yo'r ma't's eyes. Whereas I am so much the more confident of God's blessing upon my labor in these plantations (notwithstanding the many crosses and disasters I have found hitherto), in that a prince so eminently virtuous hath vouchsafed to take it into the armes of his protection; and that those who go about to supplant and destroy me, are persons notoriously lewd and wicked. Such a one is that audacious man, who being banished the colony for his misdeeds, did the last wynter (as I understand) raise a false and slanderous report of me at Plymouth, w'ch comming from thence to yo'r ma'ty's knowledge, you were pleased to referre to some of my lords of the councell, by whose hon'ble hands (for avoyding the ill manners of drawing this letter to too much length) I have presumed to returne my just appologie to yo'r ma'ty.

"But as those rubbs have been layed to stumble me there (w'ch discourage me not, because I am confident of yo'r ma'ty's singular judgment and justice); so have I mett with greater difficultyes and incumbrances here, w'ch in this place are no longer to be resisted, but enforce me presently to quitt my residence and to shift to some other warmer climate of this new world, where the wynter be shorter and less rigourous. For here yo'r ma'ty may please to understand that I have found by too deare bought experience, w'ch other men for their private interests always concealed from me, that from the middlest of October to the middlest of May there is a sadd fare of wynter upon all this land; both sea and land so frozen for the greater part of the tyme, as they are not penetrable, no plant or vegetable thing appearing out of the earth, untill about the beginning of May, nor fish in the sea, besides the ayre so intolerable cold, as it is hardly to be endured. By means whereof and of much salt meate, my house hath been an hospitall all this wynter; of 100 persons, 50 sick at a time, myself being one; and nyne or ten of them dyed. Hereupon I have had strong temptations to leave all proceedings in plantations, and being much decayed in my strength, to retire myselfe to my former quiett; but my inclination carrying me naturally to these kynd of workes, and not knowing how better to employ the poore remaynder of my dayes, that, with other good subjects, to further, the best I may, the enlarging yo'r ma'ty's empire in this part of the world, I am determined to committ this place to fishermen that are able to encounter stormes and hard weather, and to remove myselfe with some 40 persons to yo'r ma'ty's dominion Virginia; where, if yo'r ma'ty will please to grant me a precinct of land with such priveleges as the k. yo'r father, my gracious master, was pleased to grante me here, I shall endeavor, to the utmost of my power, to deserve it and pray for yo'r ma'ty's long and happy raigne as

"Your ma'ty's most humble and faithful subject and servant,

"FERRYLAND, 19 August, 1629. "GEO. BALTIMORE."

In his new home he seems to have been totally disappointed. The climate on the north-eastern coast of America was found to differ greatly from that of the same latitude in western Europe. The summers were brief and hot, the winters long and excessively severe, and the soil unfavorable to agriculture. The colonists, accustomed to the mild climate of England, suffered greatly in health and grew disheartened. Baltimore could not avoid seeing that the colony was a failure; and he had to choose either the total abandonment of his designs, returning to England with injured health and impaired fortune, or the removal of his settlement to some more genial region.

In reply to Lord Baltimore's letter of the 19th of August, 1629, King Charles said:

"Right trustie and well-beloved, we greete you well. Such is and ever hath been the estimation we make of the persons of our loving subjects who employ themselves in publick actions that tend to the good and glorie of their countrie, and the advancem't of our service, as we cannot but take notice of them, though of the meanest condition; but much more of a person of yo'r qualitie, who have been so neare a servant to our late deare father of blessed memorie. And seeing your plantation in Newfoundland (as we understand by yo'r letters) hath not answered your expectation, which we are informed you take so much to heart (having therein spent a great part of yo'r meanes) as that you are now in pursute of new countries, We, out of our princely care of you, well weighing that men of yo'r condition and breeding are fitter for other employments than the framing of new plantations, which commonly have rugged and laborious beginnings, and require much greater meanes in managing them than usually the power of one private subject can reach unto, have thought fit hereby to advise you to desist from further prosecuting yo'r dessigns that way, and with your first conveniency to returne backe to yo'r native countrie, where you shall be sure to enjoy both the libertie of a subject and such respect from us as yo'r former services and late endeavors doe so justly deserve.

"Given at o'r pallace of Whitehall, this 22nd of Novemb'r in the 5th year of our raigne.

"*Endorsed:*

"Copie of his ma'tie's letters to L'd Baltimore as (two equall copies) were brought to the L'd Viscount Dorchester by the Earl Marshall and the l'd president of the North, and by my lord sealed with the signet, the day of the date 22 of November, '29."

Lord Baltimore had doubtless received full information of the flourishing condition of the Virginia colony, and favorable accounts of the climate and soil of the country bordering on the Chesapeake, for in the year 1629 we find him visiting that colony in search of some more desirable situation for his colonists. Speaking of this event, Rev. Mr. Mead, of Christ Church, England, in a letter written to Sir Martin Stutville, says: "My Lord Baltimore, alias Sir George Calvert, being weary of his intolerable plantation at Newfoundland where he hath found between eight and nine months winter, and upon the land nothing but rocks, lakes, or morasses like bogs, which one might thrust a pike down to the butt-head, for so Mr. James, Sir Robert Cotton's library keeper, who was sent minister thither some nine years ago describes the place; his lordship this last summer sent home all his children into England, and went with his lady into Virginia."[1]

"Whether a jealousy of his colonial views, or those general prejudices against the Catholics, which were now more prevalent than ever, even in the mother country, operated with the Virginians, his visit was received by them most ungraciously indeed. What renders this reception of him somewhat more surprising, is, that the colonists of Virginia had not emigrated from England to evade religious persecution, as those of New England are supposed to have done, but seem to have been allured to it originally by the prospect of a sudden accumulation of wealth, by means of the discovery of mines as the Spaniards had done, or a shorter route to the Indies. The Church of England was then the established religion in Virginia, and Puritanism had not been hitherto encouraged among them. It is true that those in England, who were denominated high churchmen, as Archbishop Laud and others, were accused by the Puritans of being inclined to Popery; but it is to be remembered, that King Charles constantly professed, and apparently with sincerity, to be alike opposed to Popery and Puritanism. He was evidently less inclined to favour the Papists than his father had been. It is clearly perceptible throughout the early part of his reign, that the churchmen considered themselves as standing upon a ground quite distinct from either the Papists or the Puritans. Taking the tone from the sovereign, the officers of justice began to put in execution the laws against both more

[1] Neill's *Terra Mariæ*, p. 46. Mr. James erred in saying that he "sent home all his children," as we shall see.

frequently than in the former reign, though the emptiness of the royal coffers induced the monarch to connive at the frequent practice of compounding for the penalties. It is not impossible, but that this disposition of the minds of churchmen towards the Catholics had passed by this time across the Atlantic to Virginia."[1]

Lord Baltimore arrived at Jamestown, Virginia, on the first of October, 1629,[2] accompanied by his wife and several of their children.[3]

Immediately on the arrival of Lord Baltimore in Virginia, Governor Dr. John Pott and his council, composed of Captain Roger Smyth, Captain Samuel Matthews, Secretary William Claiborne and others, called him before them and tendered him the oath of allegiance and supremacy which he refused to take, as will be seen by the following statement, signed by the Virginia Council and forwarded to the King's Privy Council on the 30th of November, 1629:

"RIGHT HON'BLE,

"May it please yo'r lordshps to understand that about the beginninge of October last, there arrived in this colony, the Lord Baltimore from his plantation in Newfoundland, w'th an intention, as we are informed, rather to plant himself to the Southward then settle here, although since he hath seemed well affected to this place, and willing to make his residence therein, w'th his whole family. We were readyly inclined to render unto his lordsh'p all those respects w'ch were due unto the honor of his person or w'ch might testifie w'th how much gladness we desired to receive and entertain him, as being of that eminence and degree; whose presence and affection might give greate advancem'ts to this plantation. Whereupon, according to the instructions from yo'r lordsh'pps, and the usual course held in this place, wee tendered the oaths of supremacie and aleidgeance to his lordsh'p, and some of his followers, who making profession of the Romish religion, utterly refused to take the same, a thing w'ch we could not have doubted in him, whose former employm'ts under his late ma'ty, might have indeared to us a privation, he would not have made denyall of that in poynt, whereof consisteth the legalitie and fidelitie w'ch evry true subject oweth unto his soveraigne. His lord'hp then offerred to take this oath, a copy whereof is included, but in true discharge of the trust imposed in us by his ma'tie, wee could not imagine that soe much latitude was left for us to decline from the prescribed forme, so strictly exacted and soe well justified and defended by the pen of our late soveraigne, Lord King James, of happy memory. And among the many blessings and favors for w'ch wee are bound to blesse God, and w'ch the colony has received from his most gratious ma'tie, there is none whereby it hath beene made more happy than in the freedome of our religion, w'ch wee have enjoyed, and that no Papists have beene suffered to settle *their* abroad amongst us. The continuance wherof wee most humbly implore from his most sacred ma'tie, and earnestly beseech yo'r lord'hps that by your mediations and councells the same may be established, and confirmed

[1] Bozman, i., p. 254.

[2] *Va. H. Report*, 1870.

[3] This lady was his second wife, his first wife having died seven years before. Her death is thus mentioned by a correspondent of Sir Dudley Carleton, in a letter of August 10, 1622:—"Two days since Secretary Calvert's lady went away in childbirth, leaving many little ones behind her."—*MS. Maryland Historical Society.* By his first wife he had eleven children: 1. Cæcilius, the heir to the title; 2. Leonard, who in 1633 was appointed by his brother first Governor of Maryland; 3. George; 4. Francis; 5. Henry; 6. John; 7. Anne, married to William Peasely, Esq.; 8. Dorothy; 9. Elizabeth, who, with Dorothy, died unmarried; 10. Grace, married to Sir Robert Talbot, of Cartown, County Kildare, Ireland; 11. Helen.—*Irish Compendium*, 1756; *London Magazine*, 1768. Philip Calvert, who in 1656 was made secretary of the province of Maryland, afterwards chancellor, and then governor, was son of the second wife.

unto us. And wee, as our duety is, w'th the whole colony, shall always pray for his ma'tie's long life and eternall felicity: from his royal hands this plantation must expect her establishment and for whose honor God hath reserved so glorious a worke as the p'fection thereof. Wee humbly take our leaves.

"Yo'r lord'shp's very humble serv'ts,

"SAM. MATHEWE,
"JOHN POTT,
"ROGER SMYTH,
"W. CLAYBOURNE."

As a loyal subject of the King of England, Lord Baltimore certainly did not refuse to take the oath of "allegiance" to his benefactor, in return for the many favors he had received from his hands. It was simply a promise "to be true and faithful to the king and his heirs, and truth and faith to bear of life and limb and terrene honor, and not to know or hear of any ill or damage intended him, without defending him therefrom." The authorities of Virginia knew, of course, that Lord Baltimore, as a conscientious Roman Catholic, and believing the Pope to be the supreme head of the Church on earth, "in all spiritual or ecclesiastical things or causes," could not take the oath of "supremacy" which was tendered him; and probably when they did so, they trusted that it would deter him from his proposed settlement among them. Only three years before, in 1626, Pope Urban VIII. had issued a bull to the Irish Catholics—and Baltimore was an Irish peer—in which "he exhorted them rather to lose their lives than take that wicked and pestilent oath of supremacy, whereby the sceptre of the Catholic Church was wrested from the hand of the Vicar of God Almighty."[1]

The following is the "Oath of Supremacy," as prescribed by the statute of 1st Elizabeth, chapter 1, section 19, which was tendered him:[2]

"I —— do utterly testify and declare in my conscience, that the Queen's [King's] Highness is the only Supreme Governor of this realm, and of all other her [his] highness' dominions and countries, as well *in all spiritual or ecclesiastical things or causes*, as temporal; and that no foreign prince, person, prelate, State or potentate hath or ought to have any jurisdiction, power, superiority, preheminence or authority, ecclesiastical or spiritual, within this realm; and therefore I do utterly renounce and forsake all foreign jurisdictions, powers, superiorities and authorities, and do promise, that from henceforth I shall bear faith and true allegiance to the Queen's [King's] highness, her [his] heirs and lawful successors, and to my power shall assist and defend all jurisdiction, preheminences, privileges and authorities granted or belonging to the Queen's [King's] highness, her [his] heirs and successors, or united and annexed to the Imperial crown of this realm. So help me God and by the contents of this book."

Upon Lord Baltimore's refusal to take the oath of supremacy, the Virginia Council told him that they dared not admit any man into their settlement

[1] Bozman, p. 250.

[2] That the oaths of supremacy and allegiance were distinct, is further shown by the *Brieffe Note* of John Robinson and Wm. Brewster (1617), in which they say, "The oath of supremacy wee shall willingly take, if it be required of us, if that convenient satisfaction be not given by our takeing the oath of allegiance."—*Hazard*, i., 365.

who would not acknowledge all the prerogatives of his majesty, and asked him to depart in the next ship. Before his departure he must have been treated rather rudely, for we find that in the beginning of the next year, some persons who had insulted him were brought to justice. A record of March 25th, 1630, (O. S.), reads: "Thomas Tindall to be pilloried two hours for giving my Lord Baltimore the lie and threatening to knock him down."[1]

Disappointed in finding a residence among the Virginians, but not discouraged, Lord Baltimore turned his attention and his hopes to the neighboring territory. Then it was that his eyes were cast upon the region along the Chesapeake Bay, as yet unsettled, and by the amenity of its situation and the fertility of its resources, inviting him to its inspection. Here, if he could but obtain a grant from the crown, he might retreat to his own territory, and, under his own government, build up in the wilderness a home for religious freedom. Having determined on his course, Lord Baltimore left his wife and some of his children by her in Virginia, and embarked for England. Arriving there, he found that the king had written the letter of November 22d, 1629, advising him to "desist from further prosecuting his designs and to return to his native country," and, for the first time, he also heard of the remonstrance of the Virginia commissioners.

The king's friendship for Baltimore was not impaired by any reports from Virginia, as appears from the application of his Lordship, in December, 1629, to the Privy Council:

> "That your Lordship would be pleased to procure me a letter from my Lords of the Council to the Governor of Virginia in favor of my wife now there, that he would afford her his best assistance upon her return into England in all things reasonable for her accommodation, in her passage and for recovery of any debts due unto me in Virginia, or for disposing of her servants according to the custom of the country[2] if she shall think fit to leave any behind her or upon any other occasion, wherein she may have use of his lawful favor.
>
> "Moreover that your Lordship would be pleased to move his Majesty that whereas upon my humble suit unto him from Newfoundland for a proportion to be granted unto me in Virginia, he was graciously pleased to signify by Sir Francis Cottington that I should have any part not already granted, that his Majesty would give me leave to choose such a part now, and to pass it unto me, with the like power and privileges as the King his father of happy memory did grant me that precinct in Newfoundland, and I shall contribute my best endeavors, with the rest of his loyal subjects, to enlarge his Empire in that part of the world, by such gentlemen and others, as will adventure to join with me, though I go not myself in person."

[1] Henning's *Virginia Statutes*, i., p. 552. Mr. Bozman, (Vol. i., p. 255), argues, with considerable force, that the charter of Virginia having been annulled, and the assembly itself being an uncommissioned, self-constituted body, it had no legal right to tender these oaths to Baltimore.

[2] This phrase, "according to the custom of the country," would seem to show that Baltimore took his idea of the "redemptioner" system from Virginia. The phrase constantly occurs in the laws of the province, and seems to have become a legal technicality.

Although the king would not permit Lord Baltimore to return,[1] yet he granted him permission to send for his wife and children left with her, who embarked for England, but unfortunately the bark on its return voyage was cast away, and they were all lost together with "a great deal of plate and other goods of great value."[2]

In a letter of condolence written to his intimate friend Wentworth, Earl of Strafford, on the loss of the latters second wife, Arabella, dated Lincoln's Inn Fields, October 11th, 1631, he thus touchingly refers to his own affliction:

"There are few perhaps can judge of it better than I, who have been myself a long time a man of sorrows. But all things, my Lord, in this world pass away; *Statutum est*, wife, children, honor, wealth, friends, and what else is dear to flesh and blood; they are but lent us till God please to call for them back again, that we may not esteem anything our own, or set our hearts upon anything but Him alone, who only remains forever."[3]

Lord Baltimore, on his arrival in England, made application for a grant of territory "lying to the southward of James River in Virginia, between that river and the bounds of Carolana," now called Carolina, and sustained, as was his application, by his past services, his unimpeachable reputation, and above all, by the favor with which King Charles and his father, James I., had invariably regarded him, notwithstanding his religious sentiments, his petition was successful. The territory fixed upon was that which now constitutes the northern portion of North Carolina and southern portion of Virginia, as far north as the James River. It was described and bounded according to the existing knowledge of the geography of the country.[4] This charter was prepared and signed in February, 1631. During the spring of this year Francis West, who had been governor; William Claiborne, secretary; and William Tucker, one of the Council of Virginia, were in London endeavoring "to obstruct" the planting of a new colony within the limits of Virginia. To avoid any difficulty with "the old dissolved Company of Virginia," who "endeavored to obstruct, and to comply with them, his Lordship desired his Majesty to grant him in lieu thereof some part of that continent to the northward, which was accordingly granted, and a bill prepared and brought to his Majesty to sign."[5]

EARL OF STRAFFORD.

[1] Joseph Mead, Chaplain of Archbishop Laud, on February 12, 1629-30, writes:—"Though his Lordship [Baltimore] is extolling that country to the skies, yet he is preparing a bark to send to fetch his Lady and servants from thence, because the King will not permit him to go back again."—*Neill's Founders of Maryland*, p. 49.

[2] *Ayscough MS.*, in the British Museum.

[3] *Terra Mariæ*, p. 51.

[4] Mr. Neill says: "In October, 1629, Sir Robert Heath, the Attorney General of England, obtained a grant of land in America, between the degrees of 31 and 36 of north latitude, under the name of the 'Province of Carolana,' and two days before Mead wrote, an association of gentlemen asked for two degrees of land, to be held under Heath, as lord paramount, with liberty to appoint all officers, both civil and ecclesiastical. On April 30, 1630, the Privy Council ordered that no aliens should be settled in Carolana, without special direction, nor any but Protestants."—*Founders of Maryland*, p. 47.

[5] *Ayscough MSS.*, in the British Museum, and *Sloane MSS.*, No. 3662, p. 24.

HENRIETTA MARIA.

Lord Baltimore, it is said, drew up the charter with his own hand and left a blank in it for the name "which he designed should be *Crescentia*, or, the land of Crescence, but leaving it to his majesty to insert."[1] "The King, before he signed the charter, put the question to his Lordship, what he should call it, who replied that he desired to have it called something in honor of his majesty's name, but that he was deprived of that happiness, there being already a province in those parts called Carolina." "Let us therefore," says the king, "give it a name in honor of the Queen; what

[1] It seems to have been modelled on the Charter of Avalon, free socage having been substituted for knight's tenure. The clause which has so surprised historians, providing that in cases of doubt, that interpretation should be chosen which was most favorable to the grantee, also occurs in the Avalon charter. The charter of Avalon also disposes of the supposition of some historians that the Maryland charter was modelled upon that of Carolana, granted in 1629. It is probable that the charters of Maryland, Carolina and Pennsylvania were copied after that of Avalon.

think you of *Mariana?*" To this his lordship expressed his dissent, it being the name of a Jesuit, who had written against monarchy. "Whereupon the King proposed *Terra Mariæ*, in English, Maryland, which was concluded on and inserted in the bill.[1] And thus the proposed colony was named in honor of Henrietta Maria, daughter of Henry IV., king of France and Navarre, and sister of Louis XIII., who was usually called Queen Mary by writers of the day. Thus Laud writes in his *Diary* (p. 6): "An. 1625, June 12, Queen Mary crossing the sea, landed upon our shores about seven o'clock in the evening." Similar instances are to be found in Fuller's *Church History*.

The grant passed the privy seal a few days after the name was inserted, but owing to the objections made by the old Virginia Company, William Noy, the attorney general, advised Lord Baltimore to delay the passing of it under the great seal "for some time." Before the patent could be finally adjusted and pass the seals, Lord Baltimore fell sick, and after sending a farewell message to his long-tried friend, Wentworth, died on April 15th, 1632, in the fifty-third year of his age, at his lodgings in Lincoln's Inn Fields in London. He was buried in the chancel of St. Dunstan's Church, Fleet street, London.

Thus George Calvert was gathered to his fathers, but his works have survived him. He had projected a scheme for the happiness of his fellow man which was carried into execution by his son and successor, Cæcilius, with results with which the world is familiar. "Sir George Calvert died," says Bancroft, "leaving a name against which the breath of calumny has hardly dared whisper a reproach."[2] His personal character is thus given in the *Biographia Britannica:*

> "Though he was a Roman Catholic, yet he kept himself sincere and disengaged from all interests, and was the only statesman that, being engaged to a decried party, managed his business with that great respect for all sides, that all who knew him applauded him, and none that had anything to do with him complained of him. He was a man of great sense, but not obstinate in his sentiments, taking as great pleasure in hearing others' opinions as in delivering his own. Judge Popham and he agreed in the public design of foreign plantations, but differed in the manner of managing them. The first was for extirpating the original inhabitants; the second for converting them; the former sent the lewdest people to those places, the latter was for the soberest; the one was for making present profit, the other for a reasonable expectation; liking to have few governors, and those not interested merchants, but unconcerned gentlemen; granting liberties with great caution; and leaving every one to provide for himself by his own industry, and not out of a common stock."

We should like to dwell upon his fame and memory, if our space permitted; for calumny has not shrunk from attacking his honored name. Detraction has been busy; and as the facts could not be denied, Calvert's motives have been assailed; but empty assertion, conjecture, surmises, however ingeniously malevolent, have happily exercised very little influence over the minds of intelligent and candid men.

[1] *Ayscough MSS.*, and *Sloane MSS.*, in the British Museum, No. 3000, p. 24.

[2] Bancroft, i., p. 214.

On the death of Lord Baltimore, his eldest son, Cecil[1] Calvert, succeeded to his honors, his fortunes and his spirit. "Treading in the steps of his father," the phrase used by the king, is not here the language of empty compliment. For him, as heir of his father's intentions, the following Charter of Maryland was published and confirmed on June 20, 1632.

CHARTER OF MARYLAND.

CHARLES, by the grace of GOD, of England, Scotland, France, and Ireland, KING, Defender of the Faith, &c. To ALL to whom these presents shall come, GREETING.

II. WHEREAS our well beloved and right trusty subject CECILIUS CALVERT, Baron of BALTIMORE, in our kingdom of Ireland, son and heir of GEORGE CALVERT, knight, late Baron of BALTIMORE, in our said kingdom of Ireland, treading in the steps of his father, being animated with a laudable and pious zeal for extending the Christian religion, and also the territories of our empire, hath humbly besought leave of US, that he may transport, by his own industry and expense, a numerous colony of the English nation, to a certain region, herein after described, in a country hitherto uncultivated, in the parts of America, and partly occupied by savages, having no knowledge of the Divine Being, and that all that region, with some certain privileges and jurisdictions appertaining unto the wholesome government and state of his colony and region aforesaid, may by our royal highness be given, granted, and confirmed unto him, and his heirs.

III. KNOW YE, therefore, that WE, encouraging with our royal favour the pious and noble purpose of the aforesaid Barons of BALTIMORE, of our special grace, certain knowledge, and mere motion, have GIVEN, GRANTED and CONFIRMED, and by this our present CHARTER, for US, our heirs and successors, do GIVE, GRANT and CONFIRM unto the aforesaid CECILIUS, now Baron of Baltimore, his heirs and assigns, all that part of the Peninsula, or Chersonese, lying in the parts of America between the ocean on the east and the bay of Chesapeake on the west; divided from the residue thereof by a right line drawn from the promontory, or head-land, called Watkin's Point, situate upon the bay aforesaid, near the river Wighco on the west, unto the main ocean on the east; and between that boundary on the south, unto that part of the bay of Delaware on the north, which lyeth under the fortieth degree of north latitude from the æquinoctial, where New England is terminated; and all the tract of that land within the metes underwritten—(that is to say,) passing from the said bay, called Delaware bay, in a right line, by the degree aforesaid, unto the true meridian of the first fountain of the river of Pattowmack, thence verging towards the south, unto the farther bank of the said river, and following the same on the west and south, unto a certain place called Cinquack, situate near the mouth of the said river, where it disembogues into the aforesaid bay of Chesapeake, and thence by the shortest line unto the aforesaid promontory, or place, called Watkin's Point. So that the whole tract of land, divided by the line aforesaid, between the main ocean and Watkin's Point, unto the promontory called Cape Charles, and every the appendages thereof, may entirely remain excepted for ever to US, our heirs and successors.

IV. Also We do GRANT, and likewise CONFIRM unto the said Baron of BALTIMORE, his heirs and assigns, all islands and islets within the limits aforesaid, all and singular the islands and islets, from the eastern shore of the aforesaid region, towards the east, which have been, or shall be formed in the sea, situate within ten marine leagues from the said shore; with all and singular the ports, harbors, bays, rivers and straits belonging to the region or islands aforesaid, and all the soil, plains, woods, mountains, marshes, lakes, rivers, bays and straits, situate, or being within the metes, bounds and limits

[1] So baptized, but confirmed under the name of Cæcilius.

aforesaid, with the fishings of every kind of fish, as well of whales, sturgeons, or other royal fish, as of other fish in the sea, bays, straits or rivers, within the premises, and the fish there taken; and moreover, all veins, mines and quarries, as well opened as hidden, already found, or that shall be found within the region, islands or limits aforesaid, of gold, silver, gems and precious stones, and any other whatsoever, whether they be of stones, or metals, or of any other thing, or matter whatsoever; and furthermore, the PATRONAGES and ADVOWSONS of all churches which (with the increasing worship and religion of CHRIST), within the said region, islands, islets and limits aforesaid, hereafter shall happen to be built; together with license and faculty of erecting and founding churches, chapels and places of worship, in convenient and suitable places, within the premises, and of causing the same to be dedicated and consecrated according to the ecclesiastical laws of our kingdom of ENGLAND; with all and singular such, and as ample rights, jurisdictions, privileges, prerogatives, royalties, liberties, immunities and royal rights, and temporal franchises whatsoever, as well by sea as by land, within the region, islands, islets and limits aforesaid, to be had, exercised, used and enjoyed, as any bishop of Durham, within the bishoprick or county palatine of Durham, in our kingdom of England, ever heretofore hath had, held, used or enjoyed, or of right could, or ought to have, held, use or enjoy.

V. And WE do by these presents, for US, our heirs and successors, MAKE, CREATE and CONSTITUTE HIM, the now Baron of BALTIMORE, and his heirs, the TRUE and ABSOLUTE LORDS and PROPRIETARIES of the region aforesaid, and of all other the premises (except the before excepted) saving always the faith and allegiance and sovereign dominion due to US, our heirs and successors; to HAVE, HOLD, POSSESS and ENJOY the aforesaid region, islands, islets, and other the premises, unto the aforesaid now Baron of BALTIMORE, and to his heirs and assigns, to the sole and proper behoof and use of him, the now Baron of BALTIMORE, his heirs and assigns, for ever. To HOLD of US, our heirs and successors, kings of England, as of our castle of Windsor, in our county of Berks, in free and common SOCCAGE, by fealty only for all services, and not *in capite*, nor by knight's service, YIELDING therefore unto US, our heirs and successors, TWO INDIAN ARROWS of those parts, to be delivered at the said castle of Windsor, every year, on Tuesday in Easter-week; and also the fifth part of all gold and silver ore, which shall happen from time to time, to be found within the aforesaid limits.

VI. Now, that the aforesaid region, thus by us granted and described, may be eminently distinguished above all other regions of that territory, and decorated with more ample titles, KNOW YE, that WE, of our more special grace, certain knowledge, and mere motion, have thought fit that the said region and islands be erected into a PROVINCE, as out of the plenitude of our royal power and prerogative, WE do, for US, our heirs and successors, ERECT and INCORPORATE the same into a PROVINCE, and nominate the same MARYLAND, by which name WE will that it shall from henceforth be called.

VII. And forasmuch as WE have above made and ordained the aforesaid now Baron of BALTIMORE, the true LORD and PROPRIETARY of the whole PROVINCE aforesaid, KNOW YE therefore further, that WE, for US, our heirs and successors, do grant unto the said now baron, (in whose fidelity, prudence, justice, and provident circumspection of mind, WE repose the greatest confidence) and to his heirs, for the good and happy government of the said PROVINCE, free, full, and absolute power, by the tenor of these presents, to ordain, make, and enact LAWS, of what kind soever, according to their sound discretions, whether relating to the public state of the said PROVINCE, or the private utility of individuals, of and with the advice, assent, and approbation of the free men of the same PROVINCE, or of the greater part of them, or of their delegates or deputies, whom WE will shall be called together for the framing of LAWS, when, and as often as need shall require, by the aforesaid now Baron of BALTIMORE, and his heirs, and in the form which shall seem best to him or them, and the same to publish under the seal of the aforesaid now Baron of BALTIMORE and his heirs, and duly to execute the same upon all persons, for the time being, within the aforesaid PROVINCE, and the limits thereof, or under his or their government and power, in sailing towards MARYLAND, or thence returning, outward-bound, either to England, or elsewhere, whether to any other part of our, or of any foreign dominions, wheresoever established, by the imposition of fines, imprisonment, and other punishment whatsoever; even if it be necessary, and the guilty of the offence require it, by privation of member, or life, by him the aforesaid now Baron of BALTIMORE, and his heirs, or by his or their deputy, lieutenant, judges, justices, magistrates, officers, and ministers, to be constituted and appointed according to the tenor and true intent of these presents, and to constitute and ordain judges, justices, magistrates and officers, of what kind, for what cause, and with what power soever, within that land, and the sea of those parts, and in such form as to the said now Baron of BALTIMORE, or his heirs, shall seem most fitting: and also to remit, release, pardon, and abolish, all crimes and offences whatsoever against such laws, whether before or after judgment passed; and to do all and singular other things belonging to the completion of justice, and to courts, prætorian judicatories, and tribunals, judicial forms and modes of proceeding, although express mention thereof in these presents be not made; and, by judges by them delegated, to award process, hold pleas, and determine in those courts, prætorian judicatories, and tribunals, in all actions, suits, causes, and matters whatsoever, as well criminal as personal, real and mixed, and prætorian: Which said laws, so to be published as abovesaid, WE will, enjoin, charge, and command, to be most absolute and firm in law, and to be kept in those parts by all the subjects and liege-men of US, our heirs and successors, so far as they concern them, and to be inviolably observed under the penalties therein expressed, or to be expressed. SO NEVERTHELESS, that the laws aforesaid be consonant to reason, and be not repugnant or contrary, but (so far as conveniently may be) agreeable to the laws, statutes, customs and rights of this our kingdom of England.

VIII. And forasmuch as, in the government of so great a PROVINCE, sudden accidents may frequently happen, to which it will be necessary to apply a remedy, before the freeholders of the said PROVINCE, their delegates, or deputies, can be called together for the framing of laws; neither will it be fit that so great a number of people should immediately on such emergent occasion, be called together. WE, therefore, for the better government of so great a PROVINCE, do will and ordain, and by these presents, for US, our heirs and successors, do grant unto the said now Baron of Baltimore; and his heirs, by themselves, or by their magistrates and officers, thereunto duly to be constituted as aforesaid, may, and can make and constitute fit and wholesome ordinances from time to time, to be kept and observed within the PROVINCE aforesaid, as well for the conservation of the peace, as for the better government of the people inhabiting therein, and publicly to notify the same to all persons whom the same in any wise do or may affect. Which ordinances, WE will to be inviolably observed within the said PROVINCE, under the pains to be expressed in the same. So that the said ordinances be consonant to reason, and be not repugnant nor contrary, but (so far as conveniently may be done) agreeably to the laws, statutes, or rights of our kingdom of England; and so that the same ordinances do not, in any sort, extend to oblige, bind, charge, or take away the right or interest of any person or persons, of, or in member, life, freehold, goods or chattels.

IX. Furthermore, that the new colony may more happily increase by a multitude of people resorting thither, and at the same time may be more firmly secured from the incursions of savages, or of other enemies, pirates, and ravagers: WE, therefore, for US, our heirs and successors, do by these presents give and grant power, license and liberty, to all the liege-men and subjects, present and future, of US, our heirs and successors, except such to whom it shall be expressly forbidden, to transport themselves and their families to the said PROVINCE, with fitting vessels, and suitable provisions, and therein to settle, dwell, and inhabit; and to build and fortify castles, forts, and other places of strength, at the appointment of the aforesaid now Baron of BALTIMORE, and his heirs, for the public and their own defence; the statute of fugitives, or any other whatsoever to the contrary of the premises in any wise notwithstanding.

X. We will also, out of our more abundant grace, for US, our heirs and successors, do firmly charge, constitute, ordain and command, that the said PROVINCE be of our allegiance; and that all and singular the subjects and liege-men of US, our heirs and successors, transplanted, or hereafter to be transplanted into the PROVINCE aforesaid, and the children of them, and of others their descendants, whether already born there, or hereafter to be born, be and shall be natives and liege-men of US, our heirs and successors, of our kingdom of England and Ireland; and in all things shall be held, treated, reputed, and esteemed as the faithful liege-men of US, and our heirs and successors, born within our kingdom of England; also lands, tenements, revenues, services, and other hereditaments whatsoever, within our kingdom of England, and other our dominions, to inherit, or otherwise purchase, receive, take, have, hold, buy, and possess, and the same to use and enjoy, and the same to give, sell, alien, and bequeath: and likewise all privileges, franchises and liberties of this our kingdom of England, freely, quietly, and peaceably to have and possess, and the same may use and enjoy in the same manner as our liege-men born, or to be born within our said kingdom of England, without impediment, molestation, vexation, impeachment, or grievance of US, or any of our heirs or successors; any statute, act, ordinance, or provision to the contrary thereof, notwithstanding.

XI. Furthermore, that our subjects may be incited to undertake this expedition with a ready and cheerful mind: KNOW YE, that WE, of our especial grace, certain knowledge, and mere motion, do, by the tenor of these presents, give and grant, as well to the aforesaid Baron of BALTIMORE, and to his heirs, as to all other persons who shall from time to time repair to the said province, either for the sake of inhabiting, or of trading with the inhabitants of the province aforesaid, full license to ship and lade in any the ports of US, our heirs and successors, all and singular their goods, as well moveable as immovable, wares and merchandises, likewise grain of what sort soever, and other things whatsoever necessary for food and clothing, by the laws and statutes of our kingdoms and dominions, not prohibited to be transported out of the said kingdoms; and the same to transport by themselves, or their servants or assigns, into the said PROVINCE, without the impediment or molestation of US, our heirs or successors, or of any officers of US, our heirs or successors, (SAVING unto US, our heirs and successors, the impositions, subsidies, customs, and other dues payable for the same goods and merchandizes,) any statute, act, ordinance, or other thing whatsoever to the contrary notwithstanding.

XII. But because, that in so remote a region, placed among so many barbarous nations, the incursions as well of the barbarians themselves, as of other enemies, pirates and ravagers, probably will be feared, therefore WE have given, and for US, our heirs and successors, do give by these presents, as full and unrestrained power, as any captain-general of an army ever hath had, unto the aforesaid now Baron of BALTIMORE, and to his heirs and assigns, by themselves, or by their captains, or other officers, to summon to their standards, or to array all men, of whatsoever condition, or wheresoever born, for the time being, in the said province of MARYLAND, to wage war, and to pursue, even beyond the limits of their province, the enemies and ravagers aforesaid, infesting those parts by land and by sea, and (if God shall grant it) to vanquish and captivate them, and the captives to put to death, or, according to their discretion, to save, and to do all other and singular the things which appertain, or have been accustomed to appertain unto the authority and office of a captain-general of an army.

XIII. We also will, and by this our CHARTER, do give unto the aforesaid now Baron of BALTIMORE, and to his heirs and assigns, power, liberty, and authority, that in case of rebellion, sudden tumult, or sedition, if any (which GOD forbid) should happen to arise, whether upon land within the province aforesaid, or upon the high sea in making a voyage to the said province of MARYLAND, or in returning thence, they may, by themselves, or by their captains, or other officers, thereunto deputed under their seals (to whom WE, for US, our heirs and successors, by these presents, do give and grant the fullest power and authority) exercise martial law as freely, and in as ample manner and form, as any captain-general of an army, by virtue of his office may, or hath accustomsd to use the same, against the seditious authors of innovations in those parts, withdrawing themselves from the government of him or them, refusing to serve in war, flying over to the enemy, exceeding their leave of absence, deserters, or otherwise, howsoever offending against the rule, law, or discipline of war.

XIV. Moreover, lest in so remote and far distant a region, every access to honours and dignities may seem to be precluded, and utterly barred, to men well born, who are preparing to engage in the present expedition, and desirous of deserving well, both in peace and war, of US, and our kingdoms; for this cause, WE, for US, and heirs and successors, do give free and plenary power to the aforesaid now Baron of Baltimore, and to his heirs and assigns, to confer favours, rewards and honours, upon such subjects, inhabiting within the province aforesaid, as shall be well deserving, and to adorn them with whatsoever titles and dignities they shall appoint; (so that they be not such as are now used in England,) also to erect and incorporate towns into boroughs, and boroughs into cities, with suitable privileges and immunities, according to the merits of the inhabitants, and convenience of the places; and do all and singular other things in the premises, which to him or them shall seem fitting and convenient; even although they shall be such as, in their own nature, require a more special commandment and warrant than in these presents may be expressed.

XV. We will also, and by these presents do, for US, our heirs and successors, give and grant license by this our CHARTER, unto the aforesaid now Baron of BALTIMORE, his heirs and assigns, and to all persons whatsoever, who are, or shall be, residents and inhabitants of the province aforesaid, freely to import and unlade, by themselves, their servants, factors or assigns, all wares and merchandizes whatsoever, which shall be collected out of the fruits and commodities of the said province, whether the product of the land or the sea, into any of the ports whatsoever of us, our heirs and successors, of England or Ireland, or otherwise to dispose of the same there; and, if need be, within one year, to be computed immediately from the time of unlading thereof, to lade the same merchandizes again, in the same, or other ships, and to export the same to any other countries they shall think proper, whether belonging to US, or any foreign power, which shall be in amity with us, our heirs or successors: Provided always, that they be bound to pay for the same to US, our heirs and successors, such customs and impositions, subsidies and taxes, as our other subjects of the kingdom of ENGLAND, for the time being, shall be bound to pay, beyond which we will that the inhabitants of the aforesaid province of the said land, called MARYLAND, shall not be burdened.

XVI. And furthermore, of our more ample special grace, and of our certain knowledge, and mere motion, We do, for us, our heirs and successors, grant unto the aforesaid now Baron of BALTIMORE, his heirs and assigns, full and absolute power and authority to make, erect, and constitute, within the province of MARYLAND, and the islands and islets aforesaid, such, and so many sea ports, harbours, creeks, and other places of unlading and discarge of goods and merchandizes out of ships, boats, and other vessels, and of lading in the same, and in so many, and such places, and with such rights, jurisdictions, liberties, and privileges, unto such ports respecting, as to him or them shall seem most expedient. And, that all and every the ships, boats and other vessels whatsoever, coming to, or going from the province aforesaid, for the sake of merchandizing, shall be laden and unladen at such ports only as shall be so erected and constituted by the said now Baron of BALTIMORE, his heirs and assigns, any usage, custom, or any other thing whatsoever to the contrary notwithstanding. Saving always to us, our heir and successors, and to all the subjects of our kingdoms of England and Ireland, of us, our heirs and successors, the liberty of fishing for sea-fish, as well in the seas, bays, straits and navigable rivers, as in the harbours, bays and creeks of the province aforesaid; and the privilege of salting and drying fish on the shores of the same province; and, for that cause, to cut down and take hedging-wood and twigs there growing, and to build huts and cabins, necessary in this behalf, in the same manner as heretofore they reasonably might, or have used to do. Which liberties and privileges, the said subjects of us, our heirs and successors, shall enjoy without notable damage or injury in any wise to be done to the aforesaid now Baron of Baltimore, his heirs or assigns, or to the residents and inhabitants of the same province in the ports, creeks, and shores aforesaid, and especially in the woods and trees there growing. And if any person shall do damage or injury of this kind, he shall incur the peril and pain of the heavy displeasure of us, our heirs and successors, and of the due chastisement of the laws, besides making satisfaction.

XVII. Moreover, We will, appoint, and ordain, and by these presents, for us, our heirs and successors, do grant unto the aforesaid now Baron of BALTIMORE, his heirs and assigns, from time to time, for ever, shall have, and enjoy the taxes and subsidies payable, or arriving within the ports, harbours, and other creeks and places aforesaid, within the province aforesaid, for wares bought and sold, and things there to be laden, or unladen, to be reasonably assessed by them, and the people there as aforesaid, on emergent occasion; to whom we grant power by these presents, for us, our heirs and successors, to assess and impose the said taxes and subsidies there, upon just cause, and in due proportion.

XVIII. And furthermore, of our special grace, and certain knowledge, and mere motion, We have given, granted, and confirmed, and by these presents, for us, our heirs, and successors, do give, grant, and confirm, unto the aforesaid now Baron of BALTIMORE, his heirs and assigns, full and absolute license, power and authority, that he, the aforesaid now Baron of BALTIMORE, his heirs and assigns, from time to time hereafter, for ever, may and can, at his or their will and pleasure, assign, alien, grant, demise, or enfeoff so many, such and proportionate parts and parcels of the premises, to any person or persons willing to purchase the same, as they shall think convenient, to have and to hold to the same person or persons willing to take or purchase the same, and his and their heirs and assigns, in fee simple, or fee tail, or for term of life, lives, or years; to hold of the aforesaid now Baron of BALTIMORE, his heirs and assigns, by so many, such, and so great services, customs and rents OF THIS KIND, as to the same now Baron of BALTIMORE, his heirs and assigns, shall seem fit and agreeable, and not immediately of us, our heirs or successors. And we do give, and by these presents, for us, our heirs and successors, do grant to the same person and persons, and to each and every of them, license, authority, and power, that such person and persons, may take the premises, or any parcel thereof, of the aforesaid now Baron of BALTIMORE, his heirs and assigns, and hold the same to them and their assigns, or their heirs, of the aforesaid Baron of BALTIMORE, his heirs and assigns, of what estate of inheritance soever, in fee simple or fee tail, or otherwise, as to them and the now Baron of BALTIMORE, his heirs and assigns, shall seem expedient; the statute made in the parliament of lord EDWARD, son of king HENRY, late king of England, our progenitor, commonly called the "STATUTE QUIA EMPTORES TERRARUM," heretofore published in our kingdom of England, or any other statute, act, ordinance, usage, law, or custom, or any other thing, cause or matter, to the contrary thereof, heretofore had, done, published, ordained or provided to the contrary thereof notwithstanding.

XIX. We, also, by these presents, do give and grant license to the same Baron of BALTIMORE, and to his heirs, to erect any parcels of land within the province aforesaid, into manors, and in every of those manors, to have and to hold a court-baron, and all things which to a court-baron do belong; and to have and to keep view of frank-pledge, for the conservation of the peace and better government of those parts, by themselves and their stewards, or by the lords, for the time being to be deputed, of other of those manors when they shall be constituted, and in the same to exercise all things to the view of frank-pledge belonging.

XX. And further We will, and do, by these presents, for us, our heirs and successors, covenant and grant to, and with the aforesaid now Baron of BALTIMORE, his heirs and assigns, that we, our heirs and successors, at no time hereafter, will impose, or make or cause to be imposed, any impositions, customs, or other taxations, quotas or contributions whatsoever, in or upon the residents or inhabitants of the province aforesaid, for their goods, lands, or tenements within the same province, or upon any tenements, lands, goods or chattels within the province aforesaid, or in or upon any goods or merchandizes within the province aforesaid, or within the ports or harbours of the said province, to be laden or unladen: And we will and do, for us our heirs and successors, enjoin and command that this our declaration shall, from time to time, be received and allowed in all our courts and pretorian judicatories, and before all the judges whatsoever of us, our heirs and successors, for a sufficient and lawful discharge, payment, and acquittance thereof, charging all and singular the officers and ministers of us, our heirs and successors, and enjoining them, under our heavy displeasure, that they do not at any time presume to attempt anything to the contrary of the premises, or that may in any wise contravene the same, but that they, at all times, as is fitting, do aid and assist the aforesaid now Baron of BALTIMORE, and his heirs, and the aforesaid inhabitants and merchants of the province of MARYLAND aforesaid, and their servants and ministers, factors and assigns, in the fullest use and enjoyment of this our CHARTER.

XXI. And furthermore We will, and by these presents, for us, our heirs and successors, do grant unto the aforesaid now Baron of BALTIMORE, his heirs and assigns, and to the freeholders and inhabitants of the said province, both present and to come, and to every of them, that the said province and the freeholders or inhabitants of the said colony or country, shall not henceforth be held or reputed a member or part of the land of Virginia, or of any other colony already transported, or hereafter to be transported, or be dependent on the same, or subordinate in any kind of government, from which we do separate both the said province and inhabitants thereof, and by these presents do will to be distinct, and that they may be immediately subject to our crown of England, and dependent on the same for ever.

XXII. And if, peradventure, hereafter it may happen that any doubts or questions should arise concerning the true sense and meaning of any word, clause, or sentence, contained in this our present CHARTER, we will, charge and command THAT interpretation to be applied, always, and in all things, and in all our courts and judicatories whatsoever, to obtain which shall be judged to be the more beneficial, profitable and favourable to the aforesaid now Baron of BALTIMORE, his heirs and assigns: provided, always, that no interpretation thereof be made, whereby GOD'S holy and true Christian religion, or the allegiance due to us, our heirs and successors, may in any wise suffer by change, prejudice or diminution; although express mention [1] be not made in these presents

[1] Mr. Bacon, in his edition of the charter, and the translation as above, has here subjoined the following note: "The remainder from this mark * is copied from the old translation, published (together with some assembly proceedings) by order of the lower house, in the year 1725." To the same sentence, (to wit, *Ea quod expressa Mentio, etc.*) of the original Latin, in the opposite page, he has subjoined another note, as follows: "So endeth the attested copy, taken in the year 1758, from the original record remaining in the Chapel of the Rolls, and signed by *Henry Rooke*, clerk of the rolls, which was lent me by his excellency *Horatio Sharpe*, esqr., from whence the above" (the charter in the original Latin, which is here omitted,) "is transcribed. The said copy is entitled at the head, *Tertia Pars Patentium de Anno Regni* CAROLI *Octavo;* and at the end is written as in sect. xxiii."

N. B.—A copy of the charter of Maryland, in the original Latin, (taken from Bacon's Collection of the Laws of Maryland,) is inserted in Hazard's *Collections*, i., p. 327.

of the true yearly value or certainty of the premises, or of any part thereof, or of other gifts and grants made by us, our heirs and predecessors, unto the said now Lord BALTIMORE, or any statute, act, ordinance, provision, proclamation or restraint, heretofore had, made, published, ordained or provided, or any other thing, cause, or matter whatsoever, to the contrary thereof in any wise notwithstanding.

XXIII. In witness whereof WE have caused these our letters to be made patent. Witness ourself at Westminster, the twentieth day of June, in the eighth year of our reign.

Thus it will be seen that the province of Maryland was in fact a palatinate, and enjoyed the peculiar immunities attached to that species of government.

The origin of the term *palatine* is usually ascribed to the Merovingian Kings of France, who delegated a quasi-royal power in judicial matters to an officer called "count of the palace," (*comes palatii*, or *palatinus*). The title and extensive powers were afterwards bestowed upon great vassals, who were entrusted with almost kingly powers in their fiefs. It was a part of the feudal system that the sovereign could annex to any grants of land to his feudatories such share of the *jura regalia* as he saw fit, even to the extent of royal power, provided he reserved the suzerainty to himself. These dignities were known as kingdoms, principalities, dukedoms, seignories, etc., outside of England, but when granted within the limits of England, were usually designated *counties palatine*. Thus, Chester and Durham were counties palatine in the reign of William I.; Edward III. erected Lancaster into a palatinate; Henry IV. granted the Isle of Man as a kingdom to the Earls of Northumberland, and after their attainder, Henry VII. granted it in the same form to the house of Stanley, to whom, in large part, he owed his crown. The heads of these palatinate governments were invested with powers and prerogatives which fell little short of those of royalty itself. They appointed all officers within the counties. The courts of justice were emphatically their courts: for all process which was issued out of them ran in their names, instead of that of the king's; and all offences were held and charged in indictments, as offences against them, and not against the king. They had power to pardon all offences whatsoever committed within their respective jurisdictions. The lands lying within their provinces were deemed to be holden of them, and they were, therefore, entitled to escheats, wardships, and the other fruits of the feudal tenures, which fell to the lord of the fee. They had the right of levying forces and waging war for the defence of their provinces, and of pursuing invaders even beyond the limits of the kingdom.[1]

The sovereign, however, could grant no powers of which he was not himself possessed; so that if he was bound to govern a certain territory by peculiar laws, or to respect ancient customs, the count palatine was under the same obligation. But in a newly-discovered country, such as America, there

[1] McMahon, p. 152. For the nature and extent of these palatinate jurisdictions, see 6th Viners' *Abridgment*, 573 to 583; 2d Bacon, 188 to 192, and the case of Russell's Lessee *vs.* Baker, in which the extent of those jurisdictions was much discussed.

were no such limitations: the power of the sovereign over the land and the original inhabitants was absolute; and hence a palatinate there could approach much nearer to absolute sovereignty than it could in Europe; and this is shown in the charter of Maryland.

In condensed form the Charter of Maryland invested the proprietary with the following rights:

Territorial.—All the land and water within the boundaries of the province, and islands within ten marine leagues of the shore, with mines and fisheries, in perpetual possession to himself and his heirs.

Legislative.—The right to make all laws, public or private, with the assent of the freemen of the province; and ordinances (not impairing life, limb or property,) without their assent.

Judicial.—To establish courts of justice of various kinds, and appoint all judges, magistrates and civil officers; also to execute the laws, even to the extent of taking life.

Regal.—To confer titles and dignities; to erect towns, boroughs and cities, and make ports of entry and departure. Also to pardon all offences.

Ecclesiastical.—To erect and found churches and chapels, and cause them to be consecrated according to the ecclesiastical laws of England; and to have the patronage and advowsons thereof.

Military.—To call out and arm the whole fighting population, wage war, take prisoners, and slay alien enemies; also to exercise martial law in case of insurrection.

Financial.—To alienate, sell, or rent the land. To levy duties and tolls on ships and merchandise.

To the people it gave the right to remain English subjects, and as such to inherit, purchase, or possess land or other property in England. Also, freedom of trade to English ports; participation in making the laws, and exemption from taxation by the crown. They had also the right of trade to Holland and elsewhere, which Virginia had not; and hence Maryland could always undersell Virginia in the staple of tobacco; and the various laws for keeping down the crop, etc., could never be enforced.

Mr. McMahon has treated so learnedly and exhaustively of the legal and political aspects of the Maryland charter, that it would be superfluous for us to go into any extensive comments upon it. He, however, not having seen the charter of Avalon, has fallen, with most historians, into the minor error of supposing that the extreme liberality of the charter of Maryland was due to the partiality of Charles I., whereas we can see that the Maryland charter was entirely framed upon that of Avalon, granted by James. In nearly all the provisions the two are identical: Avalon, however, was held by knight's service (binding the grantee to assist his lord in war), and Maryland in free and common socage, as if it had been an English manor. Avalon was more favored than Maryland in the license to import merchandise from England free of all impositions and duties to the crown, and to export merchandise to England free of duty for ten years. The proprietary of Maryland could make grants of land, to be held of himself directly, and not immediately of the crown, and enjoy the annual quit-rents.

On the whole, the charter of Maryland was more favorable to the proprietary than that of Avalon, and was, in McMahon's words, "the most ample and sovereign in its character that ever emanated from the English Crown." In addition to the great feudal privileges of the old palatinates, it conveyed the modern right of calling assemblies and of making laws; and exempted the grantee from the heavy feudal burden of military service. The proprietary was, in his own province, little less than a king; and that, too, a king whose interests were identical with those of his lieges. Under the mild and just rule of the earlier Calverts, we can discover no attempt to infringe the liberties of the people; and all aggressions seem to have been on the popular side. For nearly two generations the heavy hand of royal government was unfelt. And we can not be far wrong in ascribing the peculiar independence of Marylanders, their unflinching maintenance of their rights, their stubborn resistance to wrong, their Spartan courage and endurance, and their ardent patriotism, to the extraordinary liberties of the charter, and the singularly excellent administration of a government under which they felt themselves to be truly freemen.

CHAPTER III.

Cæcilius Calvert, the second Lord Baltimore, having obtained the charter of Maryland, hastened to avail himself of his grant, and began his preparations for assembling and transporting a colony.[1] It was his original design to accompany the expedition in person, but he abandoned this intention, and confided the settlement to his younger brothers, Leonard and George, constituting the former lieutenant-governor, or general. As the great object perhaps was to provide a refuge from persecution for those of the faith then proscribed in England, a great part of the original emigrants were Roman Catholics. They had been for years the objects of increased dread and antipathy to all classes of their fellow subjects, and had experienced from the English government a progressive severity of persecution. Upon every side in England, at this time, men's minds were disturbed by notes of alarm. Among the loudest and most vehement of these was the clamour which the Puritans were raising against the policy of the English court toward the Roman church. The extreme dread and hatred of this church for which they were always conspicuous, had been exacerbated by the proceedings connected with the proposed marriage of Charles, when Prince of Wales, with the Infanta of Spain, and afterwards by those which attended his actual marriage with Henrietta Maria, of France. The union of a Protestant king of Protestant England, with a Catholic princess, daughter of a powerful monarch, who was actively hostile to the form of Protestantism which existed in his own dominions, seemed to their minds ominous of mischief, and these feelings of mistrust and apprehension, over which they had long been brooding, were quickened by the extraordinary grant to a Catholic proprietor of an important territory in America, investing him at the same time with the amplest powers which a royal charter could confer.

Yet their apprehensions were unfounded. If, at any time, from motives of humanity or a regard for the feelings of the queen, Charles seemed inclined to a less rigorous execution of the statutes against recusants and nonconformists, such seeming moderation was usually but the precursor of some public and signal proof of his orthodoxy and of his subserviency to the intolerant spirit in which the disabling statutes had been enacted. He knew that he

[1] After Lord Baltimore obtained the charter for Maryland he still retained his property at Avalon, and governed his little colony by deputies. About the year 1654 Sir David Kirk, an English nobleman, determined to remove to Newfoundland, and made an effort to purchase from Cæcilius, Lord Baltimore, his interests there, which he refused to part with. Notwithstanding this, Sir David Kirk lived there until his death, and gave his name to a sound a short distance from Cape Breton.—Oldmixon, i., p. 11.

CÆCILIUS CALVERT, SECOND LORD BALTIMORE.

had been accused by the Puritans of harboring a secret design to restore the Roman Catholic worship; and doubtless, conforming to the suggestions of his adviser, Laud, he resolved so to act that this groundless charge should not be used as a weapon by those who were hostile, on political grounds, to his government.

It had been expressly stipulated in the marriage treaty that the queen should not be hindered or interfered with in the exercise of her religion; and the king had also bound himself to grant to the English Catholics all the indulgence in his power. Yet he had let loose the pursuivants, and had rigidly enforced the penal laws against them; and when Louis complained of this manifest breach of the treaty, Charles excused himself with the shallow pretext that the treaty was "one of State, not of religion," and that the promise of indulgence was introduced "simply as a matter of form to satisfy the Pope and the Catholics of France," but without any expectation on either side that it was to be carried into execution. To the envoy of France, however, he expressed his willingness to forbid the employment of pursuivants, and to deliver up to him—as he did—all priests confined in the prisons of

London. With these promises the court of France professed itself satisfied. But the popular sentiment would not allow their fulfillment; and as a concession to the public clamor, he strictly excluded all English Catholics from the queen's chapel, issued successive proclamations offering heavy rewards for the apprehension of their bishops and priests, and repeatedly commanded the judges and magistrates to enforce the penal statutes against them. Many were arrested and condemned: some died by the hands of the executioner, others perished in prison; some went into voluntary exile, while others again obtained a temporary respite by giving bond for their appearance when summoned.

Charles, having thus thrown the unfortunate clergy as a sop to the popular ferocity, felt himself free to show more lenity to the lay recusants, especially as the articles of the marriage treaty had been ratified for the third time. The law, as we have stated, left it to the king's option to exact from these a fine of twenty pounds per lunar month, or to take two-thirds of their personal estate. But instead of these penalties, he permitted them to compound by a fixed annual payment to the exchequer, the amount to be determined by commissioners appointed for the purpose. Thus, by a sacrifice of sometimes a tenth, and sometimes a third of his yearly income, the English Catholic bought the liberty, not indeed of the open exercise of his worship, but of absenting himself from a rite of which he did not approve. Severe as these exactions were, they were so much milder than the barbarous penalties of the law, that the Catholics gladly submitted to them, as almost a privilege rather than an oppression.[1]

Thus, exposed to persecution from the authorities, and apprehending still greater severity from the predominance of a party gradually advancing in strength and hardening in sternness of spirit, many of the English Catholics began to meditate a retreat from a land of persecution to some vacant corner of the British dominions, where, as their presence would no longer minister offence, they might enjoy their worship free from molestation. Among these were the leaders of the first Maryland emigrants.

But the fitting-out of a band of colonists was a task not to be accomplished in a day. Estates had to be sold, money collected, affairs settled, implements and supplies necessary for the founding a new home in the wilderness had to be procured. Lord Baltimore generously defrayed, from his private property—which, in consideration of the services of his father, had been spared—the entire cost of the first emigration, amounting to about £40,000. Two vessels were to transport the colonists to their new home: the larger, the *Ark*, of about three hundred tons, and the *Dove* of about fifty tons. The names were, doubtless, of Calvert's conferring, and symbolized his aims and his hopes; for these ships bore religious freedom and the olive branch of peace to the new world.

[1] John C. Legrand, *Pilgrims of Maryland*, p. 13.

In them embarked nearly two hundred "gentlemen adventurers and their servants." Many of them were persons of wealth and consideration at home. Some of the names of the "gentlemen" which have been preserved, are: Leonard Calvert, the governor, and George Calvert,[1] his brother. Two persons were joined with them in the commission, as counsellors, Jerome Hawley and Thomas Cornwallys. There also accompanied them Richard Gerard, son to Sir Thomas Gerard, knight and baronet; Edward Wintour and Frederick Wintour, sons of Lady Anne Wintour; Henry Wiseman, son of Sir Thomas Wiseman, knight; John Saunders, Edward Cranfield, Henry Greene, Nicholas Fairfax, John Baxter, Thomas Dorrell, Captain John Hill, John Medcalfe and William Saire. Among those who, it is supposed, came with the first colonists, were: Thomas Wills, Robert Simpson, Mary Jennings, John Hilliord, Robert Shorly, Rogers, John Hill, Christopher Carnock, John Bryant, William Ashmore, Richard Lusthead, Nicholas Hardy, Robert Edwards, Thomas Charinton, William Edwyn, Thomas Grigsta, Richard Duke, Henry Bishop, Thomas Heath, John Tomson, James Thornton, Lewis Fremond, Richard Nevill, John Hollis, Richard Cole, John Eckin, Thomas Hodges, Thomas Green, Anam Bonam, Thomas Cooper, John Hallowos, John Holder, Roger Walter, Roger Morgan, Josias Walter; and two Jesuit priests, Andrew White and John Altham. Richard Thompson at the same time brought into the colony Mathias Tousa, a "mulato," whom he no doubt brought from the Island of Barbadoes, where the *Ark* and the *Dove* stopped on their voyage to Maryland.

After the objections raised by the Virginia Commissioners had been heard by the Privy Council (of which we shall speak more fully hereafter), and determined, the following order was issued by that body:

"Whereas the good ship called the *Ark* of Maryland of the burthen of about 350 tons, whereof one Lowe is Master, is set forth by our very good Lord, the Lord Baltimore for his Lordship's plantation at Maryland in America and manned with about 40 men. For as much as his Lordship hath desired, that the men belonging to his said ship, may be free from press or interruption, these are to will and require you, to forbear to take up, or press any, the officers, seamen, mariners or others belonging to his Lordship's said ship either in her voyage to Maryland, or in her return for England, and that you permit and suffer her quietly to pass and return without any let or hindrance, stay or interruption whatsoever."[2]

On the 19th of October Lord Coke, the British Secretary of State informed Admiral Pennington "that the *Ark*, Richard Lowe, master, carrying men for Lord Baltimore to his new plantation in or about New England, had sailed from Gravesend contrary to orders, the company in charge of Capt. Winter not having taken the oath of allegiance,"[3] and instructed him

[1] George Calvert went to Virginia and, it is stated, acted in the interest of Claiborne, and died before the year 1653.

[2] MSS. in London State Paper Office.

[3] In consequence of the bull issued by Pope Pius V., freeing all English subjects from allegiance to the King of England, after the Gun-Powder Plot, all persons sailing to the British colonies were required to take the oath of allegiance.—*Neill.*

to have the *Ark*, and the pinnace of twenty tons, commanded by Captain Winter, called the *Dove*, brought back. After the vessels were anchored "near Gravesend, they were visited by Edward Watkins, the London Searcher," who administered the following oath to all whom he found on board the *Ark* and the *Dove*:

"I do truly and sincerely acknowledge, profess, testify, and declare in my conscience, before God and the world;

"That our Sovereign Lord, King Charles, is lawful and rightful King of this realm, and of all other his Majesty's dominions, and countrie, and that the Pope neither of himself, nor by any authority by the Church, or See of Rome, or by any other means with any other, hath any power or authority to depose the King, or to dispose of any of his Majesty's Kingdoms or dominions; or to authorize any foreign Prince to invade or annoy him or his countries; or to discharge any of his subjects of their allegiance, and obedience to his Majesty; or to give license or leave to any of them to bear arms, raise tumults, or to offer any violence or hurt, to his Majesty's royal person, state, or government, or to any of his Majesty's subjects within his Majesty's domains.

"And I do swear from my heart, that notwithstanding any declaration, or sentence of excommunication, or deprivation, made or granted by the Pope, or his successors, or by any authority derived, or pretended to be derived from him, or his See, against the said King, his heir or successors, or any absolution of the said subjects from their obedience, I will bear faith and true allegiance to his Majesty, his heirs and successors, and him and them will defend to the uttermost of my power, against all conspiracies and attempts whatsoever, which shall be made against his or their persons, their crown and dignity, by reason or color of any such sentence, or declaration, or otherwise; and will do my best endeavor to disclose and make known unto his Majesty, his heirs and successors, all treasons, or traitorous conspiracies, which I shall know or hear of, to be against him or any of them.

"And I do further swear, that I do from my heart, abhor, detest, and abjure, as impious and heretical, this damnable doctrine and position; that, Princes which be excommunicated or deprived by the Pope, may be deposed or murthered by their subjects, or any other whatsoever.

"And I do believe, and in conscience am resolved, that neither the Pope, nor any person whatsoever, hath power to absolve me of this Oath, or any part thereof, which I acknowledge by good and full authority to be lawfully ministered unto me, and do renounce all pardons, and dispensations to the contrary. And all these things I do plainly and sincerely acknowledge and swear, according to these express words by me spoke, and according to the plain, and common sense and understanding of the same words, without any equivocation or mental evasion, or secret reservation whatsoever. And I do make this recognition and acknowledgment heartily, willingly, and truly upon the true faith of a Christian: So help me God." [1]

Upon his return from this duty the "London Searcher" made to the Privy Council the following report:

"According to your Lordship's order of the 25th day of this instant month of October, I have been at Tillbury Hope where I found a ship and pinnace belonging to the Right Honorable Cecil Lord Baltimore, where I offered the oath of allegiance to all and every the persons aboard, to the number of about 128, who took the same, and inquiring

[1] *Founders of Maryland*, p. 89.

of the master of the ship whether any more persons were to go the said voyage, he answered that some few others were shipped who had forsaken the ship and given over the voyage, by reason of the stay of said ships."

On their passage out the vessels stopped at the Isle of Wight, where Father White and others, who "had forsaken the ships," were received on board. They sailed from this Isle on the 22d of November, and Father White writes, "yet we were not without apprehension, for the sailors were murmuring among themselves, saying that they were expecting a messenger with letters from London, and from this it seemed as if they were ever contriving to delay us." On the departure of the ships, Lord Baltimore, on the 10th of January, 1633 (O.S.), wrote to his father's constant friend, Lord Wentworth (Earl of Strafford), the following statement of the difficulties he encountered in fitting out the colonists for his province:

"After many difficulties since your Lordship's departure from hence, in the proceedings of my Plantation wherein I felt your Lordship's absence, I have at last sent away my ships, and have deferred my going till another time, and indeed my Lord, my ships are gone; after having been so many ways troubled by my adversaries, after they had endeavored to overthrow my business at the Council Board, after they had informed by several means some of the Lords of the Council that I intended to carry over nuns into Spain, and soldiers to serve that King, which I believe your Lordship will laugh at, as well they did, after they had gotten Mr. Attorney General to make an information in the Star-Chamber that my ships were departed from Gravesend without any cockets from the Custom House, and in contempt of all authority, my people abusing the King's officers, and refusing to take the oath of allegiance; whereupon their Lordships sent present order to several captains of the King's ships who lay in the Downs, to search for my ships in the river, and to follow them into the narrow seas, if they were gone out, and to bring them back to Gravesend, which they did, and all this done before I knew anything of it, but imagined all the while that my ships were well advanced on their voyage; but not to trouble your Lordship with too many circumstances, I, as soon as I had notice of it, made it plainly appear unto their Lordships, that Mr. Attorney was abused and misinformed, and that there was not any just cause of complaint in any of the former accusations, and that every one of them was most notoriously and maliciously false, whereupon they were pleased to restore my ships to their former liberty.

"After they had likewise corrupted and seduced my mariners, and defamed the business all they could by their scandalous reports, I have as I said, at last, by the help of some of your Lordship's good friends and mine, overcome these difficulties, and sent a hopeful colony into Maryland with a fair and probable expectation of good success, however without any danger of any great prejudice unto myself, in respect that others are joined with me in the adventure. There are two of my brothers gone, with very near twenty other gentlemen of very good fashion, and three hundred laboring men well provided in all things."[1]

Of the "twenty other gentlemen and three hundred laboring men,"[2] who composed that company, many perhaps had more to leave behind, but none had certainly less to hope. Many had bidden adieu to the fields which had

[1] Strafford's *Letters*.

[2] Virginia, on the contrary, was settled by more "gentlemen adventurers" than laborers. This difference of origin may, perhaps, be the source of some of the differences of character of the two colonies.

been in the possession of their families for generations, but they sought for more extensive possessions in the New World. There they hoped to plant their name and their posterity forever.

The time first intended for the embarkation was as early as the month of September, 1633; but it was delayed for two months. It has been suggested that the delay was for the purpose of arriving at the place of their destination at a more favorable season of the year, at the opening of the spring, rather than in the autumn or winter. It is certain that they made no haste to leave the mild climate of the tropics, for which they immediately steered on leaving England.

We have a narrative of the voyage from the pen of Father White, in his official report to his religious superiors at Rome; and from which we append a full extract, as one of the most precious and interesting records of the early days of the Maryland colony.[1]

This volume, with the *Relation of Maryland*, contains a brief account of the first settlement, in the points upon which they touch and agree almost entirely with Father White's narrative, which is as follows:

NARRATIVE OF A VOYAGE TO MARYLAND.

Written towards the end of April, 1634, to the Very Rev. Father, General Mutius Vitellesetis.

On the Twenty Second of the month of November, in the year 1633, being St. Cecilia's day, we set sail from Cowes, in the Isle of Wight, with a gentle east wind blowing. And, after committing the principal parts of the ship to the protection of God especially, and of His most Holy Mother, and St. Ignatius, and all the guardian angels of Maryland, we sailed on a little way between the two shores, and the wind failing us, we stopped opposite Yarmouth Castle, which is near the southern end of the same Island (Isle of Wight). Here we were received with a cheerful salute of artillery. Yet we were not without apprehension; for the sailors were murmuring among themselves, saying that they were expecting a messenger with letters from London, and from this it seemed as if they were even contriving to delay us. But God brought their plans to confusion. For that very night, a favorable but strong wind, arose; and a French cutter, which had put into the same harbor with us, being forced to set sail, came near running into our pinnace. The latter, therefore, to avoid being run down, having cut away and lost an anchor, set sail without delay; and since it was dangerous to drift about in that place, made haste to get farther out to sea. And so that we might not lose sight of our pinnace, we determined to follow. Thus the designs of the sailors, who were plotting against us, were frustrated. This happened on the 23d of November,

[1] About the year 1832, the Rev. William McSherry, S.J., of Baltimore, discovered in the archives of the "*Domus Professa*" of the Jesuits' society in Rome, the original MSS. of "*Relatio Itineris in Marylandiam; Declaratio Coloniæ Domini Baronis de Baltimoro; Excerpta ex Diversis Litteris Missionariorum, Ab Anno 1635 ad Annum 1638*," which was ably edited by the Rev. E. A. Dalrymple, and published by the Maryland Historical Society in February, 1874. There are also two curious and rare little volumes, each entitled *A Relation of Maryland*, one of which was published in 1634, and the other in 1635. The former was edited by Colonel Brantz Mayer, of Baltimore, and republished in 1865 as No. 1 of Shea's *Early Southern Tracts*. The latter was edited by Francis L. Hawks, D.D., LL.D., and republished with *Map of the Country* in the same year by Joseph Sabin, of New York.

St. Clement's day, who, because he had been tied to an anchor and thrown into the sea, obtained the crown of martyrdom.' 'And showed the inhabitants of the earth, how to declare the wonderful things of God.'

Now on that day, we were again greeted with a cheerful salute, about ten o'clock in the morning, from Hurst Castle, and then sailed past a number of rocks near the end of the Isle of Wight, which, from their shape, are called the Needles. These also are a terror to sailors, on account of the double tide of the sea, which whirls away the ships, dashing them against the rocks on the one side, or the neighboring shore on the other; to say nothing, meanwhile, of the other risk we ran near Yarmouth Castle. For while we were waiting there, before we had weighed anchor, the wind and tide pressing hard upon us, the ship came near being driven on shore. And this would have happened, unless we had been suddenly turned away with great force; and driving out to sea, had evaded the danger, by the mercy of God, who deigned to give us this additional pledge of his protection, through the merits of St. Clement. On that day, which fell on the Sabbath, and the following night, we had such favorable winds, that early on the next day, about nine o'clock, we left behind us the western promontory of England and the Scilly Isles, and sailing easily on, we directed our course more towards the west, passing over the British channel. Yet we did not hasten as much as we could have done, fearing, if we left the pinnace too far behind us, that it would become the prey of the Turks and Pirates, who generally infest that sea.

Hence it came to pass, that a fine merchant ship of six hundred tons, named the *Dragon*, while on her way to Angola, having sailed from London, overtook us, about three o'clock in the afternoon. And as we now had time to enjoy a little pleasure, after getting out of danger, it was delightful to see these two ships, with fair weather and a favorable wind, trying for a whole hour to outstrip each other, with a great noise of trumpets. And our ship would have beaten the other, though we did not use our top-sail, if we had not been obliged to stop on account of the pinnace, which was slower; and so we yielded the palm to the merchant ship, and she sailed by us before evening, and passed out of sight.

Now on Sunday the 24th, and Monday the 25th of November, we had fair sailing all the time until evening. But presently, the wind getting round to the north, such a terrible storm arose, that the merchant ship I spoke of from London, being driven back on her course, returned to England, and reached a harbor much resorted to, among the Paumonians. Those on board our pinnace also, since she was a vessel of only 40 tons, began to lose confidence in her strength, and sailing near, they warned us, that if they apprehended shipwreck, they would notify us by hanging out lights from the mast-head. We meanwhile sailed on in our strong ship of four hundred tons—a better could not be built of wood and iron. We had a very skilful captain, and so he was given his choice, whether he would return to England, or keep on struggling with the winds: if he yielded to these, the Irish shore close by awaited us, which is noted for its hidden rocks and frequent shipwrecks. Nevertheless his bold spirit, and his desire to test the strength of the new ship, which he then managed for the first time, prevailed with the captain. He resolved to try the sea, although he confessed that it was the more dangerous, on account of being so narrow.

And the danger was near at hand; for the winds increasing, and the sea growing more boisterous, we could see the pinnace in the distance, showing two lights at her masthead. Then indeed we thought it was all over with her, and that she had been swallowed up in the deep whirlpools; for in a moment she had passed out of sight, and no news of her reached us for six months afterwards. Accordingly we were all of us certain the pinnace had been lost; yet God had better things in store for us, for the fact

[1] The Church, in the office for St. Clement's Day.

was, that finding herself no match for the violence of the waves, she had avoided the Virginian ocean, with which we were already contending, by returning to England, to the Scilly Isles. And making a fresh start from thence, in company with the *Dragon*, she overtook us, as we shall relate, at a large harbor in the Antilles. And thus God, who oversees the smallest things, guided, protected, and took care of the little vessel.

We, however, being ignorant of the event, were distressed with grief and anxiety, which the gloomy night, filled with manifold terrors, increased. When the day dawned, although the wind was against us, being from the south-west, yet, as it did not blow very hard, we sailed on gradually by making frequent tacks. So Tuesday, Wednesday, and Thursday passed with variable winds, and we made small progress. On Friday, a south-east wind prevailing, and driving before it thick and dark clouds, so fierce a tempest broke forth towards evening, that it seemed every minute as if we must be swallowed up by the waves. Nor was the weather more promising on the next day, which was the festival of Andrew the Apostle. The clouds, accumulating in a frightful manner, were fearful to behold, before they separated, and excited the belief that all the malicious spirits of the storm, and all the evil genii of Maryland had come forth to battle against us. Towards evening, the captain saw a *Sunfish* swimming, with great efforts, against the course of the sun, which is a very sure sign of a terrible storm; nor did the omen prove a false one. For about ten o'clock at night a dark cloud poured forth a violent shower. And such a furious hurricane followed close upon it, that it was necessary to run with all speed to take in sail; and this could not be done quickly enough to prevent the mainsail, the only one we were carrying, from being torn in the middle from top to bottom. A part of it was blown over into the sea, and was recovered with difficulty.

At this juncture, the minds of the bravest among us, both passengers and sailors, were struck with terror; for they acknowledged that they had seen other ships wrecked in a less severe storm; but now, this hurricane called forth the prayers and vows of the Catholics in honor of the Blessed Virgin Mary and Her immaculate Conception, of Saint Ignatius, the Patron Saint of Maryland, Saint Michael, and all the guardian angels of the same country. And each one hastened to purge his soul by the Sacrament of penance. For all control over the rudder being lost, the ship now drifted about like a dish in the water, at the mercy of the winds and the waves, until God showed us a way of safety. At first, I confess, I had been engrossed with the apprehension of the ship's being lost, and of losing my own life; but after I had spent some time, in praying more fervently than was my usual custom, and had set forth to Christ the Lord, to the Blessed Virgin, St. Ignatius, and the angels of Maryland, that the purpose of this journey was to glorify the Blood of Our Redeemer in the salvation of barbarians, and also to raise up a kingdom for the Saviour (if he would condescend to prosper our poor efforts), to consecrate another gift to the Immaculate Virgin, His Mother, and many things to the same effect; great comfort shone in upon my soul, and at the same time so firm a conviction that we should be delivered, not only from this storm, but from every other during that voyage, that with me there could be no room left for doubt. I had betaken myself to prayer, when the sea was raging its worst, and (may this be to the glory of God,) I had scarcely finished, when they observed that the storm was abating. That indeed brought me to a new frame of mind, and filled me at the same time with great joy and admiration, since I understood much more clearly the greatness of God's love towards the people of Maryland, to whom your Reverence has sent us. Eternal praises to the most sweet graciousness of the Redeemer!!

When the sea had thus immediately abated, we had delightful weather for three months, so that the captain and his men declared they had never seen it calmer or pleasanter; for we suffered no inconvenience, not even for a single hour. However, when I speak of three months, I do not mean to say we were that long at sea, but I include the whole voyage, and also the time we stopped at the Antilles. For the actual voyage occupied only seven weeks and two days; and that is considered a quick passage.

After that time then, while we were sailing along the shore of Spain, the winds were not against us, nor were they very favorable. We feared that we might meet with the Turks, yet we fell in with none of them; they had gone home, perhaps to celebrate a solemn fast, which they call , for it took place at that season of the year. But when we had sailed past the Strait of Gibraltar, and the Madeiras, with favorable winds, which were no longer variable, but blew steadily towards the south and the south-west, the direction we were sailing; three ships came in sight, one of which was larger than ours; moreover, they appeared to be about three leagues (nine miles) off, towards the west, and to be trying to come up with us; now and then, also, they would send messengers to and fro and communicate with each other. As we suspected that they were Turkish pirates, we made all the necessary preparations for fighting. And there were some among our men, who inconsiderately urged the captain to approach and attack them without provocation. But since he had a Master, to whom he had to render an account, he doubted whether he could give a plausible reason for fighting, and indeed I think the contest would have been an arduous one, though, perhaps they feared us as much as we did them; and they were, as I conjecture, merchants who were on their way to the Fortunate Islands, not far distant, and either could not overtake us, or did not wish to.

Sailing hence to the Fortunate Isles, we were received in a large bay, where there is nothing to be feared excepting the calms, but since these last fifteen days and sometimes three weeks, the supplies of the navigators give out. But this rarely happens, scarcely once or twice in a century. Nevertheless very frequent delays are unavoidable, on account of the wind's failing, which, when it blows, is always one and the same, being favorable to this voyage of ours. When we arrived at this bay, we had sailed three thousand Italian miles under full sail, passing over a milk-white sea, without being delayed at all by calms, except occasionally, for a single hour about mid-day.

I cannot easily discover the cause of such a constant wind, unless, perchance, one should say it arises from the sun's being so near, as it passes between the tropics, and from the fact that it draws from the sea, by the power of its heat, two kinds of vapor, the one dry from the saltness of the sea, the other moist by reason of the water: the wind proceeds from the former, and from the latter are produced the rains; and so the sun drawing both towards itself, is the cause of their always keeping the same obliqe course. with the sun, and constantly following it. And this, too, may have been the reason, why we met with great heat and an abundance of rain, between the tropics at the same time, and that regularly, at morning, noon and evening; or at any rate the winds were stronger then. From this also can be drawn the reason why the bay was at this time free from calms. For the sun in the tropic of Capricorn going beyond the Equinoctial Line, and passing down to the extreme southern point of the same line (as happened to us between the 13th and 17th degrees of longitude, the heat there being as great in our winter months as it is in the summer months in Europe), draws the wind and rain obliquely towards the Equinoctial Line; and for this reason, the winds are more certain during those months, especially in this Bay, and blow towards the tropic of Cancer. But the calms are more frequent in the summer time, when the sun crosses the equator towards us, and draws up the salt and watery vapors, not obliquely, but almost perpendicularly.

And here also I cannot pass on, without praising the Divine Goodness, which brings it to pass, that all things work together for good to them that love God. For if, meeting no delay, we had been allowed to sail at the time we had appointed, namely, on the twentieth of the month of August, the sun being on this side of the equator, and striking down vertically, the intense heat would not only have ruined our provisions, but would have brought disease and death upon almost all of us. We were saved by the delay, for by embarking in the winter time, we escaped misfortunes of this kind; and if you except the usual sea-sickness, no one was attacked by any disease, until the Festival of the Nativity of our Lord. In order that that day might be better kept, wine was given out; and those who drank of it too freely, were seized the next day with a fever; and of these, not long afterwards, about twelve died, among whom were two Catholics. The loss of Nicholas Fairfax and James Barefote was deeply felt among us.

While continuing our voyage (after having seen the Sunfish, which swims with difficulty against the course of the sun, and is a sign of storms, and indeed after more than one storm), we met with many curious things. Especially Flying fish, which sometimes swim in the sea, and sometimes fly up in the air. They are about the size of flounders or the larger giltheads, and very much resemble these in their delicious flavor. A hundred of them rise into the air at once, when flying from the Dolphins which pursue them. Some of them fell into our ship, their wings failing them; for in one flight they do not fly over a greater space than two or three acres, then, because their fins are dried by the air, they plunge into the water again, and venture a second time into the air. When we were twenty-one degrees and some minutes from the equator, where the tropic begins, we could see the birds which are called, from the place where they are found, the tropic birds, hovering in the air. These are as large as falcons, and are remarkable for having two very long, white feathers in their tails; it is uncertain whether they always stay in the air, or sometimes rest on the water. The other things I omit, as being already known from the letters of others.

When we had sailed beyond the Fortunate Islands, Lord Leonard Calvert, the commander of the enterprise, began to consider where he could get any merchandise to load the ship with, on its return, in order to defray the expenses of his brother, the Baron of Baltimore. For he, having originated the whole expedition, had to bear all the expense. No profit was expected from our countrymen in Virginia: for they are hostile to this new settlement; accordingly we were directing our course to the Island of St. Christopher, when, after holding a council, apprehending that at that late season of the year others had been before us, we turned our prows to the south to go to Bonavista. This island, situated near Angola on the African coast, 14 degrees from the equator, is a post of the Hollanders, where they collect salt, which they afterwards carry home, or take to cure fish with in Greenland. The abundance of salt, and also the number of goats which are found on the island, were inducements for us to go there; for it has no other inhabitants. Only a few Portuguese, transported for crime, drag out their lives the best way they can. We had gone barely 200 miles when, changing our plans a second time, at the suggestion of some among us, lest provisions should fail us, in going so far out of our way, we turned aside into Barbadoes which we reached on the third of January. * * * * * *

On the twenty-fourth of January, we weighed anchor in the night, and passing the Island of St. Lucia on our left, about noon of the following day, we reached Matalina towards evening. At this place two canoes full of naked men appeared, who, keeping at a distance from apprehension, of our huge ship, held up (Pumpkins,) gourds, the fruit of the Plane tree, and Parrots, offering to exchange them. They were a savage race, fat, shining with red paint, who knew no God, and devoured the flesh of human beings; and they had before made away with several English interpreters. They inhabit a country which is especially fertile, but is entirely covered with woods, having no open plains. Hanging out a white flag, as a sign of peace, we invited those who were displaying themselves in the distance, to trade with us, but objecting to this sign they made their usual signals.

After we repeated these, when they understood who we were, they took courage and came up nearer, but not trusting too much to so powerful a ship, they took only a few little bells and knives, and went to the pinnace, promising that if we should decide to stay until the next day, they would bring better wares. Some one, I hope, will hereafter have compassion on this forsaken people. A rumor spread among the sailors (started by certain Frenchmen who had been shipwrecked), that an *animal* is found on this island, in whose forehead is a stone of extraordinary lustre, like a live coal or burning candle. They named this animal *Carbunca*. Let the author of this story answer for its truth.

At length, sailing from this place, we reached the *cape*, which they call *Point Comfort*, in Virginia, on the 27th of February, full of apprehension, lest the English inhabitants, who were much displeased at our settling, should be plotting something against us. Nevertheless the letters we carried from the King, and from the high treasurer of England, served to allay their anger, and to procure those things which would afterwards be useful to us. For the Governor of Virginia hoped, that by this kindness towards us, he would more easily recover from the Royal treasury a large sum of money which was due him. They only told us that a rumor prevailed, that six ships were coming to reduce everything under the power of the Spaniards, and that for this reason, all the natives were in arms; this we afterwards found to be true. Yet I fear the rumor had its origin with the English.

After being kindly treated for eight or nine days, we set sail on the third of March, and entering the Chesapeak Bay, we turned our course to the north to reach the *Potomeack* River. The Chesopeacke Bay, ten leagues (30 Italian miles) wide, flows gently between its shores: it is four, five and six fathoms deep, and abounds in fish when the season is favorable; you will scarcely find a more beautiful body of water. Yet it yields the palm to the Potomeack River, which we named after St. Gregory.

Having now arrived at the wished-for country, we allotted names according to circumstances. And indeed the Promontory, which is toward the south, we consecrated with the name of St. Gregory (now Smith Point), naming the northern one (now Point Lookout,) St. Michael's, in honor of all the angels. Never have I beheld a larger or more beautiful river. The Thames seems a mere rivulet in comparison with it; it is not disfigured with any swamps, but has firm land on each side. Fine groves of trees appear, not choked with briers or bushes and undergrowth, but growing at intervals as if planted by the hand of man, so that you can drive a four-horse carriage, wherever you choose, through the midst of the trees. Just at the mouth of the river, we observed the natives in arms. That night, fires blazed through the whole country, and since they had never seen such a large ship, messengers were sent in all directions, who reported that a *Canoe*, like an island had come with as many men as there were trees in the woods. We went on, however, to Herons' Islands, so called from the immense number of these birds. The first island we came to, [we called] St, Clement's Island,[1] and as it has a sloping shore, there is no way of getting to it except by wading. Here the women, who had left the ship, to do the washing, upset the boat and came near being drowned, losing also a large part of my linen clothes, no small loss in these parts.

This island abounds in cedar and sassafras trees, and flowers and herbs, for making all kinds of salads, and it also produces a wild nut tree, which bears a very hard walnut with a thick shell and a small but delicious kernel. Since, however, the island contains only four hundred acres, we saw that it would not afford room enough for the new

[1] "St. Clement's. . . . The name has disappeared; and almost the whole of the island, as it seems, has been washed away by the river. It was situated at the mouth of the bay, which is now called *St. Clement's Bay*. All that is left of it is a sand bank of about ten acres, which can hardly be cultivated. It has kept the name of Heron's Island. It was the first you met in sailing between those islands which are now called *Blackstone Islands*; at that time, however, they were probably called *Herons' Islands*. A tradition prevailing among the people of the neighbourhood, in the year 1835 was, that they had seen the island more extensive in length and breadth; but that within the memory of the older inhabitants it had been gradually washed away by the waters."—*E. A. Dalrymple*.

settlement. Yet we looked for a suitable place to build only a Fort (perhaps on the island itself) to keep off strangers, and to protect the trade of the river and our boundaries; for this was the narrowest crossing-place on the river.[1]

On the day of *the Annunciation of the Most Holy Virgin Mary* in the year 1634 we celebrated the mass for the first time, on this island. This had never been done before in this part of the world. After we had completed the sacrifice, we took upon our shoulders a great cross, which we had hewn out of a tree, and advancing in order to the appointed place, with the assistance of the Governor and his associates and the other Catholics, we erected a trophy to Christ the Saviour, humbly reciting, on our bended knees, the Litanies of the Sacred Cross, with great emotion.

Now when the Governor had understood that many Princes were subject to the Emperor of Pascatawaye, he determined to visit him, in order that, after explaining the reason of our voyage, and gaining his good will, he might secure an easier access to the others. Accordingly, putting with our pinnace (the *Dove*) another, which he had procured in Virginia, and leaving the ship (the *Ark*) at anchor, he sailed round and landed on the southern side of the river. And when he had learned that the Savages had fled inland, he went on to a city which takes its name from the river, being also called Potomeack.[2] Here the young King's uncle named *Archihu* was his guardian, and took his place in the kingdom; a sober and discreet man. He willingly listened to Father (John) Altham (altam, that is Oliver), who had been selected to accompany the Governor (for he (the Governor) kept me still with the ship's cargo). And when the Father explained, as far as he could through the interpreter, Henry Fleet, the errors of the heathen, he would, every little while, acknowledge his own: and when he was informed that we had come thither, not to make war, but out of good will towards them, in order to impart civilized instruction to his ignorant race, and show them the way to heaven, and at the same time with the intention of communicating to them the advantages of distant countries, he gave us to understand that he was pleased at our coming. The interpreter was one of the Protestants of Virginia. And so, as the Father could not stop for further discourse at the time, he promised that he would return before very long. "That is just what I wish," said Archihu, "we will eat at the same table; my followers too shall go to hunt for you, and we will have all things in common."

They went on from this place to *Piscataway*, where all the inhabitants flew to arms. About five hundred, equipped with bows, had stationed themselves on the shore with their Emperor. But after signals of peace were made, the Emperor, laying aside all apprehension, came on board the pinnace, and when he heard of our friendly disposition towards those nations, he gave us permission to dwell wherever we pleased in his dominions.

[1] "The narrowest. . . . At the present time also, as is seen to-day, this crossing is shorter than any other in the whole course of the river. It is easy, then, to infer from this, that the fleet sailed to the island in question, but not to St. George's Island or elsewhere; for there is no other narrower crossing place anywhere on the river.

"In addition to this, the island was nine leagues (or twenty-seven miles) from the mouth of the river, which is now called St. Mary's, as will appear in this letter. Now, indeed, this is the exact distance between *Heron's Island* and the mouth of St. Mary's River or bay, which the pilgrims then called St. George's. Moreover, St. George's Island, which goes by the same name to-day, is situated just at the mouth of the river, and from the western extremity of this island, by making a circuit of only three miles, you can enter the main stream of the river."—*E. A. Dalrymple.*

[2] ". . . This place appears in the recent Maps, under the name of *New Marlborough* or *Marlborough Point*. So Bernard Ulysses Campbell, Esq., states in the Metropolitan Catholic Almanac for the year 1841; and this is confirmed by good authorities."—*Ibid.*

In the meantime, while the Governor was with the Emperor on this voyage, the savages at St. Clements, growing bolder, began to mingle more freely with our sentinels. For we kept watch by day and night, to guard, from sudden attacks, our men, who were cutting wood, as well as the vessel which we were building, having brought with us the separate planks and ribs. It was pleasant to hear them admiring everything, especially wondering, where in the world a tree had grown large enough to be carved into a ship of such huge size; for they supposed it had been cut out from a single trunk of a tree, like an Indian canoe. Our cannon filled them all with astonishment, as indeed they were not a little louder than their own twanging bows, and sounded like thunder.

The Governor had taken with him as a companion, on his voyage to the Emperor, *Henry Fleet*, a Captain from the Virginia colony, a man especially acceptable to the Savages, well versed in their language, and acquainted with the country. This man was, at first, very intimate with us, afterwards, being misled by the evil counsels of one *Clayborne*, he became very hostile to us, and excited the natives to anger against us, by all the means in his power. In the meantime, however, while he was still on friendly terms with us, he pointed out to the Governor, a spot so charming in its situation, that Europe itself can scarcely show one to surpass it.

Going about nine leagues (that is about 27 miles) from St. Clement, we sailed into the mouth of a river, on the north side of the Potomac,[1] which we named after St. George. This river (or rather, arm of the sea), like the Thames, runs from south to north about twenty miles before you come to fresh water. At its mouth are two harbors, capable of containing three hundred ships of the largest size. We consecrated one of these[2] to St. George: the other, which is more inland, to the Blessed Virgin Mary.

The left side of the river[3] was the abode of King *Yaocomico*. We landed[4] on the right hand side[5] and going in about a mile from the shore, we laid out the plan of a city, naming it after St. Mary. And, in order to avoid every appearance of injustice, and afford no opportunity for hostility, we bought from the King thirty miles of that land,

[1] That is, the mouth of the St. George; it is, and was situated, on the north side of the Potomack river.

[2] "Two harbors . . . one of these . . . within these 200 years, since 1634, the force of the current has washed away certain portions of the banks of the river. This is evident, from an examination of the place called *Fort Point*, on an estate near Saint Inigoes, where Leonard Calvert had built a fort, which was swallowed up, together with ten or twelve of the very cannon he had placed there. But Father Joseph Carbery drew out seven, which were sunk in the sand and covered by the advancing tide, more than a hundred fathoms (or 200 yards) from the shore, and which were easier to reach, though one or two lay at about the depth of 20 feet. If in only one place the water swallowed up so many fathoms of solid land, why could not the same thing have happened around *Herons' Island*, at St. Clements? Why not around *Piney Point*, and along the channel between the present island of St. George and the whole shore, clear to *Cherry Point*—the shore being extended by deposits of earth brought down from other places? Perhaps at this time the mouth of the *Bay*, which the writer calls *St. George's*, could be entered directly from *Piney Point*, and the above mentioned channel, now impassable for large ships, at that time afforded them a passage. The fact that the smaller Bay—the first one to the left of *Piney Point*—still bears the name of St. George, is in favor of this supposition, and also the channel which is mentioned above.

"From this there is an entrance to the larger Bay, which the travellers also called St. George's, but which has now changed its name, being called *St. Mary's*, as well as the inner bay of St. Mary's towards the north and beyond the channel of St. Ignatius. Moreover, what if the present island of St. George was small at that time, having grown by deposits of mud and sand? For on this island are seen to-day no doubtful proofs that the land was formerly sunk [below the water?]; that it has recently been thrown up and is not yet completely formed."—*E. A. Dalrymple.*

[3] The eastern bank of St. Mary's river which flows from the north.

[4] On the right-hand side of the Bay of St. Ignatius, leaving the ship there until they went, either on foot or in the pinnace, and found a place for a permanent settlement, and this indeed they found about a mile from the left bank of St. Mary's river.

[5] Perhaps near the promontory called *Chancelor Point*.

delivering in exchange, axes, hatchets, rakes, and several yards of cloth. This district is already named Augusta Carolina.[1] The Susquehanocs, a tribe inured to war, the bitterest enemies of King Yaocomico, making repeated inroads, ravage his whole territory, and have driven the inhabitants, from their apprehension of danger, to seek homes elsewhere. This is the reason why we so easily secured a part of his kingdom: God by this means opening a way for His own Everlasting Law and Light. They move away every day, first one party and then another, and leave us their houses, lands and cultivated fields. Surely this is like a miracle, that barbarous men, a few days before arrayed in arms against us, should so willingly surrender themselves to us like lambs, and deliver up to us themselves and their property. The finger of God is in this, and He purposes some great benefit to this nation. Some few, however, are allowed to dwell among us until next year. But then the land is to be left entirely to us.

The *Relation of Maryland* gives the following details relative to the settlement of the colony:

"On the 3d of *March*, 1634, they left *Point Comfort*, and two days after they came to Patowmeck river, which is about 24 leagues distant, there they began to give names to places, and called the *Southerne* point of that River, Saint Gregories; and the *Northerne* point Saint Michaels.

"They sayled up the River till they came to Heron Island, which is about 14 leagues, and there came to an anchor under an Island neere unto it, which they called S. Clements, where they set up a Crosse, and took possession of this country for our *Saviour*, and for our Soveraigne Lord the king of *England*.

"Here the Governor thought fit for the ship to stay, vntill hee had discovered more of the Countrey; and so hee tooke two Pinnaces, and went up the River some 4 leagues, and landed on the South side, where he found the Indians fled for feare, from thence hee sayled some 9 leagues higher to Patowmeck Town, where the *Werowance* being a child, *Archihau* his vnckle (who governed him and his countrey for him) gave all the company good wellcome, and one of the company having entered into a little discourse with him, touching the errours of their religion, hee seemed well pleased therewith; and at his going away, desired him to return thither againe, saying he should live with him, his men should hunt for him, and hee would divide all with him.

"From hence the Governor went to Paschatoway, about 20 leagues higher, where he found many *Indians* assembled, and heere he met with one Captain *Henry Fleete*, an *English-man*, who had lived many years among the *Indians*, and by that meanes spake the Countrey language very well, and was much esteemed of by the natives. Him our Governour sent a shore to invite the Werowance to a parley, who thereupon came with him aboard privatley, where he was courteously entertained, and after some parley being demanded by the Governour, whether hee would be content that he and his people should set downe in his Countrey, in case he should find a place convenient for him, his answere was, *that he would not bid him goe, neither would hee bid him stay, but that he might use his owne discretion.*

"While this *Werowance* was aboard, many of his people came to the water side, fearing that he might be surprised, whereupon the *Werowance* commanded two Indians that came with him to goe on shore, to quit them of this feare, but they answered, they feared they would kill them; the *Werowance* therefore shewed himselfe upon the decke and told them hee was in safety, wherewith they were satisfied.

"Whilst the Governour was aboard, the neighbouring *Indians*, where the ship lay[2] began to cast off feare, and come to their Court of guard, which they kept night and day upon Saint Clements Ile, partly to defend their barge, which was brought in pieces

[1] It is now called St. Mary's county.

[2] At St. Clements.

out of *England*, and there made up; and partly to defend their men which were imployed in felling of trees, and cleaving pales for a Palizado, and at last they ventured to come aboard the ship.

"The Governour finding it not fit, for many reasons to seate himselfe as yet so high in the River, resolved to returne backe againe, and to take a more exact view of the lower part and so leaving the Ship and Pinnaces there, he tooke his Barge (as most fit to search the Creekes, and small rivers) and was conducted by Captaine *Fleete* (who knew well the Countrey) to a River on the North-side of *Patomeck* river, within 4 or 5, leagues from the mouth thereof, which they called, Saint Georges River.[1] They went up this river about 4 Leagues, and anchored at the Towne of *Yoacomaco;* from whence the *Indians* of that part of the Countrey, are called *Yoacomacoes.*[2]

"At their coming to this place, the Governour went on shore, and treated friendly with the *Werowance* there, and acquainted him with the intent of his coming thither, to which hee made little answere (as it is their manner, to any new or suddaine question) but entertained him, and his company that night in his house, and gave him his owne bed to lie on (which is a matt layd on boords) and the next day, went to shew him the countrey, and that day being spent in viewing the places about that towne, and the fresh waters, which there are very plentifull and excellent good (but the maine rivers are salt) the Governour determined to make the first Colony there, and so gave order for the ship and Pinnaces to come thither. * * *

"To make his entry peaceable and safe, hee thought fit to present the *Werowance* and the *Wisoes* of the Towne with some English Cloth (such as is used in trade with the Indians), Axes, Howes, and Knives, which they accepted very kindly, and freely gave consent that hee and his company should dwell in one part of their Towne, and reserved the other for themselves; and those *Indians* that dwelt in that part of the Towne, which was alloted for the *English*, freely left them in their houses, and some corne that they had begun to plant: It was also agreed between them, that at the end of harvest they should leave the whole towne; which they did accordingly: and they made mutuall promises to each other, to live friendly and peaceably together, and if any injury should happen to be done on any part, that satisfaction should be made for the same, and thus upon the 27th day of *March, Anno Domini*, 1634 the Governour tooke possession of the place, and named the Towne Saint *Maries.*"

The site of this town, the improvements already made around it by the Indians, and the depth and security of the navigation from the Potomac to that point, presented every facility which the governor could desire for the settlement of his colony. His first act was one of justice and humanity towards the aborigines, which presents a striking contrast to the first establishment of the other colonies.

The disposition to misrepresent Calvert's conduct has even attempted to throw a coloring of injustice over his dealing with the Indians, truly styled "an act of justice and humanity." Instead of treating the aborigines as

[1] This river, upon which they bestowed the name of St. George's, is known at this day by the name of St. Mary's river. It flows into the Potomac between ten and twelve miles above its mouth; and alike most of the other rivers arising in the champaign country adjacent to the bay, at its mouth, and for several miles above it, it is a bold, deep and wide stream.

[2] Powhatan's territories, over which he had been emperor or grand chief, was said to extend along the lowlands upon the Chesapeake, from Cape Henry to the mouth of Patuxent, in Maryland, and that his empire consisted of at least forty different tribes. As Governor Calvert, in his present explorement of the Potomac, found, it seems, several distinct independent chiefs, called "Werowances," it is probable, that they were the chiefs of so many distinct tribes, who formerly composed a part of that grand confederacy, which had existed under Powhatan.

wild beasts, or savages toward whom no moral law was binding, and laying the foundation of his colony in violence and wrong, he dealt with them as with men whose rights had a claim to respect. He raised no sophistical question whether savages could acquire or transfer any rights in the soil, or whether it was worth while to pay them any price for what they were preparing to abandon. The quantity of goods given them is not known; but the compensation was satisfactory, and there is no reason for alleging that it was not ample. The land ceded was mostly forest hunting-grounds; and the former possessors left them only to remove to others chosen in the boundless wilderness. The articles given in exchange were not trinkets and cheap gewgaws to pamper savage vanity, nor the maddening draught that has been the bane of the race, nor the arms that would render their internal wars more deadly, and hasten their extermination; they were not merely of intrinsic worth, but of absolutely inestimable value to the Indian, who could procure nothing comparable to them, and was at once raised a degree in civilization by their acquisition. The possession of an axe of steel instead of his rude tool of stone, multiplied his strength and efficiency an hundred-fold. If the whites occupied his fields, they gave him, in improved implements, the means of raising larger crops with less labor, in his new abode; if they restricted his hunting-grounds, they taught him to dispense with his rude garment of skin, and clothed him in the warmer fabric of the loom.

The Indians, on their side, faithfully performed their part of the contract. They shared at once their cabins with the strangers and prepared to abandon them and the cultivated fields as soon as the corn was harvested. In the meantime they mingled freely with the colonists, who employed many of their women and children in their families. From them the wives and daughters of the settlers learned the modes of preparing maize and other products of the soil. While the colonist of New England ploughed his field with his musket on his back, or was aroused from his slumber by the hideous war-whoop to find his dwelling in flames, the settler of St. Mary's accompanied the red warriors to the chase and learned his arts of woodcraft; and the Indian coming to the settlement with wild turkeys or venison, found a friendly reception and an honest market; and if belated, wrapped himself in his mantle of skins or duffield cloth, and lay down to sleep by the white man's fireside, unsuspecting and unsuspected.

Such were the happy results of the truly Christian spirit that animated the first Maryland colonists; and their descendants may be proud in their knowledge of the fact that whatever wrongs the Indian suffered in laying the foundations of the great republic, or in extending its power and influence, no portion of them can be ascribed to their forefathers. Let them, then, jealously guard this memory and the reputation of their ancestors as a precious heritage.

The first thing the colonists did on landing was to build a guard-house for their defence, and a storehouse for the reception of the various articles of

CHAPTER IV.

When the first European discoverers landed on the shores of the Western World, they found these peopled by a race of men, whose appearance and habits confirmed them in their too hasty belief that they had reached the goal of their voyagings; the farther coast of Asia, the dusky complexions, straight black hair, high cheekbones, and partly nomadic habits of the inhabitants, agreed sufficiently with what they had heard of the people of the Great Khan and distant Cathay to justify their calling them *Indios*, or Indians. Later discoveries, correcting the first misconception, also corrected the second, though the name has survived the error in which it originated. It was soon apparent that not only were these red men not Asiatics, but that, however great the differences of the various nations from each other, they differed still more strongly and in more essential particulars from all other peoples of the known world; and science has since shown that all the aborigines of the western hemisphere—at least all who have survived to historic times—belong to a distinct race of mankind, which, whether spreading from one centre or from many, had peopled all the land from ocean to ocean, and from the Arctic Circle to Tierra del Fuego.

But while this unity of origin or of race may be conceded, there were among these various nations remarkable differences in manners, character, intelligence, and degrees of barbarism. The tribes inhabiting the extreme north and south of the continent, where they suffered continually from the rigor of the climate and the scarcity of nutritious food, remained in a low grade of savagery; while the peoples inhabiting the table-land of Mexico, and still more markedly those dwelling on the western slope of the Peruvian Andes, had attained what by comparison may be called a high degree of civilization. Those tribes who lived in the mountain and hilly regions of the temperate zone, were for the most part fierce and warlike hunters, while those in the tidewater country gave more attention to agriculture. These latter, being of necessity less nomadic than the hunter-tribes, and living in villages surrounded with their plantations, were more social, more civilized, and of gentler nature and manners.

Unfortunately for our knowledge, and probably still more unfortunately for themselves, none of these peoples possessed anything that can properly be called a written language; their nearest approach to writing being rude pictorial representations of things, with a few conventional signs of ideas; and of this picture-writing, made only for temporary purpose, but few ancient specimens are preserved. The antiquarian, therefore, who would study their history before it came into contact with that of the European settlers, has to draw his conclusions from legends and traditions of uncertain meaning and very doubtful authenticity, from relics of the past, and, chiefly, from the study of their various tongues; so that much confusion and uncertainty rest upon the whole subject. Such, however, of the conclusions of science as relate to the Indian tribes in and adjacent to Maryland and have any bearing upon its history, may be here set down.

The Indians anciently occupying the vast expanse of country lying between the Atlantic and the Mississippi, and reaching from the Saint Lawrence to the Gulf, have been classified by ethnologists, according to the affinities of language, into three great stocks. These were, first, the ALGONQUIN STOCK, the most numerous and wide-spread of all, whose territories extended north as far as Hudson's Bay, and south to Pamlico Sound, and from the coast to the Mississippi, and in the northwest as far as Lake Winnipeg. The tribes of this stock were numerous. Among the most important were the great nation of Lenni Lenape or Delawares, the Chippewas, Ottawas, Pottawatomies, Mohegans and Shawnees. To them also belonged all the New England tribes, and most of those of Maryland and Virginia. South of the Algonquins, occupying part of North Carolina, South Carolina, Georgia and the Gulf region, was the MUSCOGEE STOCK, comprising the Natchez, Uchees and Creeks, forming the Muscogee Confederacy, and the Yamassees, Cherokees, Choctaws, Chickasaws and Seminoles. In the midst of the Algonquin territories, thrust in like a wedge, its base resting on the Saint Lawrence and Lake Huron, and its apex reaching North Carolina, was the powerful IROQUOIS STOCK, comprising the famous Confederacy of the Five Nations, the Mohawks, Oneidas, Onondagoes, Cayugas and Senecas. To the same stock, though not confederate with them, belonged the Hurons, the Susquehannoughs and the Tuscaroras, which last tribe, in 1712, joined the confederacy, which was thenceforth known as the Six Nations.

A convenient and rational classification of all these tribes is their division into hunting Indians and fishing Indians. The former were necessarily nomadic—within certain limits at least—moving about as game grew scarce, and scattering themselves over a large extent of country. This life was necessarily unfavorable to the formation of regular communities, with the consequent advance in the scale of civilization, though it favored courage, craft, endurance, strength, and all the arts and aptitudes of war. As a rule, therefore, the hunting Indians were better fighters than the fishing Indians, and when the two came into contact, either conquered, expelled or destroyed the latter. The Susquehannoughs and Iroquois were hunting Indians. They lived always on streams of fresh water, but in the spring and summer would make visits to the salt water for fish and oysters; and these visits were usually attended with inroads upon the fishing tribes.

The Powhatanic tribes, and other Algonquin races of Maryland and Virginia, were fishing Indians. They had permanent settlements or villages near the waterside, where they cultivated the soil and raised maize, beans, tobacco and other crops, and enjoyed a kind of civil government. All down the bay, from the mouth of the Sassafras River to Dorchester, we find shell-banks, "kitchen-middens," and sites of old villages. These relics are not the remains of hunters' camps but of permanent settlements long kept up. Deposits of this kind, from six to fifteen feet deep, with great trees growing on them, often in from three to five feet of soil of later accumulation, are found at the mouth of Fairlee Creek and at Swann Point, in Kent, up the Chester, on both sides of the river, on Wye Island, Spaniard's Neck, and other places.

The tribes whom Smith found at and near the site of Jamestown, were of the Algonquin stock, as were the various Maryland tribes, except the Susquehannoughs. These Virginia Indians were formed into a loose confederacy, under the supremacy of Powhatan, who seems to have had a decided talent for government. His personal ascendancy was great, and he increased his power by many marriages, until he was the acknowledged head of thirty tribes, comprising about 24,000 souls. The southern Maryland tribes, on the western shore of the Chesapeake Bay, as far east as the Patuxent River, and those on the eastern shore of Virginia, yielded some slight allegiance to the Powhatanic confederacy. Of many of these Maryland Algonquins little more than the names remain; that mysterious influence which seems to blight a savage race when brought into contact with civilization, having rapidly swept them away. Within fifty years after Calvert's arrival, they had dwindled into insignificance, and with the exception of the Nanticokes, the Piscataways, and, perhaps, one or two more, their names scarcely appear in the pages of history, though perpetuated in many a mountain, valley and stream.

The Iroquois, although less numerous, were the bravest, the fiercest, and most intelligent of all, and were the terror of the surrounding tribes. It is these who have furnished the typical Indian of romance; grave, taciturn, patient of suffering and death; faithful to a friend, remorseless to a foe; adroit in all the arts of the chase; cunning in strategy, surprises and ambuscades; fierce and vindictively cruel in war. They possessed a higher degree of political and military genius than the rest; and their famous league or confederacy of the Five Nations was more firmly organized than the loose Algonquin federations, and carried dismay as far west as Lake Superior, and as far south as North Carolina. The Iroquois were of a more noble and martial appearance than their neighbors; and all early travellers are struck with the tall, sinewy forms, harsh but not ignoble features, and majestic demeanor of their warriors. Those whose personal knowledge of the Indian is confined to the degraded remnants still lingering in the North, or the wretched savages of the far West, can form no idea of a Mohawk or Cayuga chief as he was seen two hundred years ago.

Native tradition assigns the origin of this people to the far North-west, whence they removed to the upper waters of the Saint Lawrence, and the mountainous region about the Saranac Lakes. As they increased in numbers they spread over the high forest country in northern and middle New York, where game was abundant, and a fertile soil and a milder climate yielded them an ample supply of maize. Skillful boatmen, their war fleets descended the Hudson, the Delaware and the Susquehanna, and carried fire and slaughter among the coast tribes, many of whom they subjugated, and among the rest the once powerful Delawares, whom—probably in mockery of their proud name of Lenni Lenape, or "Manly Men,"—they reduced to the condition of "women," that is, forbidding them to undertake wars, meddle with military matters, or to alienate the soil. Some confusion has arisen from the various names they bore; they were called Mingoes in some regions, and in others Nadoues, Nottoways, or Nadowassies, a name said to signify "cruel." Smith mentions one of their nations, probably the Mohawks, under the name of Massawomekes.

"Beyond the mountains from whence is the head of the river Patawomeke [Potomac] the Salvages report in habit their most mortall enemies, the Massawomekes, upon a great salt water which by all likelihood is either some part of Cannada, some great lake, or some inlet of some sea that falleth into the South Sea. These Massawomekes are a great nation and very populous. For the heads of all those rivers, especially the Pattowomekes, the Pautuxuntes, the Susquesahanocks, the Tockwoughes, are continually tormented by them; of whose crueltie they generally complained, and very importunate they were with me and my company to free them from those tormentors. To this purpose they offered food, conduct, assistance, and continnall subjection."

The charge of cruelty brought against the Iroquois by the other Indians is justified if, as is alleged, they were the first to introduce the practice of scalping and torturing prisoners, which, however, was adopted by most of the other tribes. Their importance was so great, that in all the early treaties made by the white colonists, they are included. During the English and French wars, they were almost constantly allied with the English, who sought their friendship to use them against the Chippewas, Ottawas, Shawnees, and other tribes of Algonquin stock, who were the firm allies of the French.

To this great stock, as shown by connection of language, as well as by similarity in other respects, belonged the Susquehannoughs, the most powerful tribe in the province of Maryland. They were not, however, members of the Iroquois confederacy, but, on the contrary, were among their fiercest enemies; and it is probable that they separated from the Iroquois at a time not much later than the eastern migration formerly mentioned, and coming south, established themselves on the fertile and well-wooded shores of the great river that still bears their name. Their warlike appearance, grave and haughty carriage, and sonorous speech, seem to have strongly impressed the early voyagers. Smith's description of some whom he saw near the mouth of the Susquehanna River, has already been cited.

The gallant Captain's imagination, here as in some other points, casts some discredit upon his veracity, since, as Bozman (who seems rather disposed to believe the statement) remarks, a man the calf of whose leg was "three-quarters of a yard about, and all the rest of his limbs answerable to that proportion," must have been about ten feet high; and we know from abundant later evidence of persons familiar with these Indians, that though stately men, they were not of gigantic stature.

The fullest early account of the Susquehannoughs is given by George Alsop in his *Character of the Province of Maryland*, published in 1666. He says:

"Those Indians that I have conversed withal here in this Province of Maryland . . . are called by the name of Susquehanocks, being a people lookt upon by the Christian Inhabitants as the most Noble and Heroick Nation of Indians that dwell upon the confines of America; also are so allowed and lookt upon by the rest of the Indians, by a submissive and tributary acknowledgement; being a people cast into the mould of a most large and Warlike deportment, the men being for the most part seven foot high in latitude, and in magnitude and bulk suitable to so high a pitch; their voyce large and hollow as ascending out of a Cave, their gate and behavior strait, stately, and majestick, treading on the Earth with as much pride, contempt, and disdain to so sordid a Center as can be imagined from a creature derived from the same mould and Earth. * * *

"These Susquehanock Indians are for the most part great Warriours, and seldom sleep one Summer in the quiet armes of a peaceable Rest, but keep (by their present Power, as well as by their former Conquest) the several Nations of Indians round about them in a forceable obedience and subjection. * * * * * * * *

"When they desire to go upon some Design that will and doth require a Consideration, some six of them get into a corner and sit in Juncto; and if thought fit, their business is made popular and immediately put into action; if not, they make a full stop to it, and are silently reserved.

"The warlike Equipage they put themselves in when they prepare for Belona's March, is with their faces, arms and breasts confusedly painted, their hair greased with Bears oyl, and stuck thick with Swans Feathers, with a wreath or Diadem of black and white Beads upon their heads, a small Hatchet instead of a Cymetre stuck in their girts behind them, and either with Guns, or Bows and Arrows. In this posture and dress they march out from the Fort or dwelling to the number of Forty in a Troop, singing (or rather howling out) the Decades or warlike exploits of their ancestors, ranging the wide woods untill their fury has met with an enemy worthy of their revenge. What Prisoners fall into their hands by the destiny of War, they treat them very civilly while they remain with them abroad, but when they once return homewards, they then begin to dress them in the habit for death, putting on their heads and arms wreaths of Beads, greazing their hair with fat, some going before and the rest behind, at equal distance from the Prisoners, bellowing in a strange and confused manner, which is a true presage and forerunner of destruction to their then conquered Enemy.

"In this manner of march they continue till they have brought them to their Berken City, where they deliver them to those that in cruelty will execute them, without either the legal Judgement of a Council of War, or the benefit of their Clergy at the Common Law. The common and usual deaths they put their Prisoners to, is to bind them to stakes, making a fire some distance from them: then one or other of them, whose Genius delights in the art of Paganish dissection, with a sharp knife or flint cut the Cutis or outmost skin of the brow so deep, untill their nails, or rather Talons, can fasten themselves firm and secure in, then (with a most rigid jerk) disrobeth the head of skin and hair at one pull, leaving the skull almost as bare as those Monumental Skelitons at Chyrurgions-Hall; but for fear they should get cold by leaving so warm and customary a Cap off, they immediately apply to the skull a Cataplasm of hot Embers to keep their Pericranium warm. While they are thus acting this cruelty on their heads, several others are preparing pieces of Iron, and barrels of old Guns, which they make red hot, to sear each part and lineament of their bodies, which they perform and act in a most cruel and barbarous manner. And while they are thus in the midst of their torments and execrable usage, some tearing their skin and hair of their head off by violence, others searing their bodies with hot irons, some are cutting their flesh off and eating it before their eyes raw while they are alive; yet all this and much more never makes them lower the Top-gallant sail of their Heroick courage, to beg with a submissive Repentance any indulgent favour from their persecuting Enemies, but with an undaunted contempt to their cruelty, eye it with so slight and mean a respect, as it were below them to value what they did, they courageously (while breath doth libertize them) sing the summary of their Warlike Atchievements.

"Now after this cruelty has brought their tormented lives to a period, they immediately fall to butchering of them into parts, distributing the several pieces amongst the Sons of War, to intomb the ruines of their deceased conquest in no other Sepulchre then their unsanctified maws; which they with more appetite and desire do eat and digest, them if the best of food should count their stomachs to participate of the most restorative Banquet. Yet though they now and then feed upon the Carkesses of their Enemies, this is not a common dyet but only a particular dish for the better sort. * * * *

"When any among them depart this life, they give him no other intombment then to set him upright upon his breech in a hole dug in the Earth some five foot long and three foot deep, covered over with the Bark of Trees Archwise, his face Du-West only leaving a hole half a foot square open. They dress him in the same Equipage and Gallantry that he used to be trim'd in when he was alive, and so bury him (if a Soldier) with his Bows, Arrows and Target, together with all the rest of his impliments and weapons of War, with a kettle of Broth, and Corn standing before him lest he should meet with bad quarters in his way. His Kinred and Relations follow him to the Grave, sheath'd in Bear skins for close mourning, with the tayl dragling on the ground in imitation of our English Solemners. . . . They bury all within the wall or Pallisado'd impalement of their City or Connadago, as they call it. Their houses are low and long, built with the Bark of Trees Arch-wise, standing thick and confusedly together. They are situated a hundred and odd miles distant from the Christian Plantations of Maryland, at the head of a River that runs into the Bay of Choesapike, called by their own name the Susquehanock River, where they remain and inhabit most part of the Summer time, and seldom remove far from it, unless it be to subdue any Foreign Rebellion.

"About November the best Hunters draw off to several remote places of the woods, where they know the Deer, Bear, and Elk useth; there they build them several cottages, which they call their Winter-quarters, where they remain for the space of three months, untill they have killed up a sufficiency of Provisions to supply their Families with in the Summer.

"The Women are the Butchers, Cooks, and Tillers of the ground, the men think it below the honour of a Masculine to stoop to any thing but that which their Gun, or Bow and Arrows can command. The men kill the several Beasts which they meet with all in the woods, and the women are the Pack horses to fetch it in upon their backs, fleying and dressing the hydes (as well as the flesh for provision) to make them fit for Trading, and which are brought down to the English at several seasons in the year to truck and dispose of them for course Blankets, Guns, Powder and lead, Beads, small Looking-glasses, knives, and Razors.

"I never observed all the while I was amongst these naked Indians, that even the women wore the Breeches, or dared either in look or action predominated over the men. They are very constant to their wives; and let this be spoken to their Heathenish praise, that did they not alter their bodies by their dyings, paintings, and cutting themselves, marring those Excellencies that Nature bestowed upon them in their original conceptions and birth, these would be as amiable beauties amongst them as any Alexandria could afford, when Mark Anthony and Cleopatra dwelt there together. Their marriages are short and authentique, for after 'tis resolved upon by both parties, the woman sends her intended Husband a kettle of boyl'd Venison or Bear; and he returns in lieu thereof Beaver or Otter's skins, and so their Nuptial Rights are concluded without other Ceremony."

The principal other Indian settlements in Maryland mentioned by Smith are as follows: Between the Potomac and Patuxent rivers, Secowocomoco, Potopaco (now Port Tobacco), Pamacacack (Pomokey?), Moyowance (Piscataways?), and Nocotchtauke. These were all members of the Powhatanic confederacy. On the Patuxent he found "the people called Acquintanacksuak, Pawtuxunt, and Mattapanient. Two hundred men was the greatest strength that could be their perceived; but they inhabit together and not so dispersed as the rest. These of all others, we found most civil to give entertainment." Between the Bolus or Patapsco and the Susquehanna, he places the Susquehannoughs, and to the north of these (by report only,) the Atquanackukes, who may have been the Delawares. To the far west, on the borders of a great water, which perhaps was meant for Lake Ontario, he locates by report the headquarters of the Massawomekes, that is the Iroquois, or some nation of their league.

On the eastern shore of the bay, about the present site of Cecil County, he places the Tockwhoghs, with a fort and stockade on a river of the same name; then the Ozinies, then the Kuscarawaocks on a river so-called, and then the Wighcocomicos (Wicomicos) on the river Tants Wighcocomico. He reports the people of these rivers as small of stature and very rude.

Some uncertainty seems to rest upon the identity of the two considerable nations mentioned by Smith as the Tockwhoghs and Kuscarawaocks, names that do not appear (except as borrowed from Smith) in later history. That one of these nations was the Nanticokes, there can be no doubt; and Bozman's reasons for identifying these with the Kuscarawaocks, and the river of the same name with the present Nanticoke River, seem conclusive, though other authorities have argued in favor of their identification with the Tockwhoghs. Smith's map places the mouth of the Kuscarawaock River opposite to and a little south of the mouth of the Patuxent, and just off its mouth he places a group of islands; which exactly corresponds with the position of the Nanticoke and the islands west of Tangier Sound. Hooper's Strait, between Bloodworth's Island and the southern point of Dorchester County seems to be the passage which Smith calls "Limbo." The name "Nantaquack" assigned by Smith to an Indian settlement on the north shore of the river, also confirms this opinion. And finally, in a memorial addressed by the survivors of the Nanticokes, then residing on Grand River in Canada, to the Maryland Assembly in 1852, they state that their forefathers occupied a district of country in the province of Maryland "lying on the banks of a noble river which still bears their name."

Smith's map, although astonishingly accurate, considering the circumstances under which it was made, fails to mark either the Chester or the Choptank rivers, unless two slight indentations and breaks in the shore-line be meant to indicate their mouths. It is evident that he did not land on the thickly wooded coast which he marks as "Brooke's Forest," reaching from near Swan Point in Kent County to James Point in Dorchester County; and he clearly mistook the deeply indented peninsulas of Dorchester and Talbot counties for islands, which, with Kent Island, form the three great islands he calls "Winstone's Isles."[1]

About the identity of the nation whom Smith calls the Tockwhoghs, there seems much doubt. Some writers identify them with the Nanticokes of later authors; but, as we have seen, the position of Smith's Kuscarawaocks more accurately corresponds with that of the Nanticokes, and the Tockwhoghs dwelt north of these, with their fort (as Bozman shows) on the Sassafras River. They there had a hundred warriors, and were enemies of the Massawomekes or Iroquois, some of whom showed Smith the wounds they had received in an encounter with the Tockwhoghs. As they were evidently a considerable people, both in numbers and ability to hold their own, there can be little doubt that their apparent disappearance is merely due to confusion of names. Heckewelder, in his *Historical Account*, makes no mention of the Tockwhoghs, but gives a long account of the Nanticokes, taken from a chief of that nation, long after their emigration from Maryland. These, according to the tradition preserved by the chief, were an off-shoot of the Lenni Lenape or Delawares, which nation they called their "grandfather." But they had many names. *Nentego*, meaning "tide-water," or "sea-side" people, and *Tayachquans*, meaning "bridge-builders." Now Nentego is almost certainly the origin of the name Nanticoke; and Tayachquan, pronounced with the Indian guttural, resembles Smith's Tockwhoghs. Both the Tockwhoghs and Kuscarawaocks may have been off-shoots from the Delaware stock, and both, as sea-side or bay-side peoples, have called them-

[1] How the careful Bozman, with Smith's map before him, could say that "the Isle of Kent must have been entirely unknown to him," is surprising. The most northern of "Winstone's Isles" exactly corresponds to it in situation, lying southeast of the mouth of the Bolus, or Patapsco, opposite the mouth of the Severn, which is indicated, though not named, and nearly south of Swan's Point, which he calls Borne's Point. An indentation and break in the coast-line also mark the mouth of the Wye, which Smith did not explore. Nothing could be more natural than that he should mistake the peninsulas of Talbot and Dorchester for islands, as they are connected with the main land by narrow necks, and deeply indented with bays, and the errors could only have been avoided by coasting all along their shores. The position of "Rickard's Cliffs," or high lands, just north of the Patuxent, on his map, relatively to the most southern of "Winstone's Isles," confirms this view. On an earlier page (p. 115) Bozman has suggested that Winstone's Isles were Kent, Poplar, and Tilghman's islands, "most inaccurately designed;" but an examination of the map will show, we think, our opinion to be correct. It is inconceivable that Smith, from whatever point his view was taken, could have drawn Poplar Island, whose small dimensions are everywhere apparent, as larger than Kent: whereas, on our hypothesis, he has preserved the relative proportions very accurately, making the middle island (the peninsula of Talbot) the largest of the three, Kent Island the next in size, and the most southern island (the peninsula of Dorchester) the least.

selves by the common name of Nentego or Nanticokes, and so been known to the whites. As the two tribes together, according to Smith's account, could muster three hundred warriors, indicating an aggregate population of about fifteen hundred, we can understand the considerable importance of the Nanticokes in subsequent history, and the survival of a remnant of them to our own time. This conclusion, it is frankly admitted, is but a conjecture; but it is not discordant with the known facts, and explains what otherwise must be the inexplicable disappearance, within a few years, of a powerful tribe.

The customs of the Maryland Indians were almost identical with those of the Virginia tribes. Each tribe had its chief and its town, while beyond the town were outlying villages or scattered huts. The town was an aggregation of cabins or wigwams, constructed by fixing saplings in the ground in a circle, and tying the flexible ends together at the top, so as to form a conical cage or framework, which they covered with sheets of bark. A better style of house, such as the chiefs used, was constructed by inclosing an oblong space in the same manner. Holes were cut in the sides for windows, and an opening left at the top to let out the smoke from the fire, which was made in the centre of the floor. Mats of grass or rushes were sometimes used to partition off an apartment. Their mode of fortification was by inclosing the whole town, or a part of it, including the chief's house, with a strong and close stockade. Within this stockade was the council-fire, around which they gathered to discuss public matters, or for religious ceremonials.

The land about the village was held in common, but to each family a portion was allotted for cultivation, which work was done by the women. Each family delivered a part of the crop to the chief; which was placed in a general store-house to be used for the chief's subsistence, for the entertainment of guests, and as a reserve in case of scarcity or siege. They cultivated maize, beans, tobacco and several varieties of the melon and gourd. The confederate tribes exercised common rights of forestry over the surrounding wilderness; but certain natural boundaries, such as rivers and streams, distinguished the territory of each from its neighbor's.

The tribe was subject to its chief, who had absolute power over his people, and whose authority descended in the female line. When the chief died, he was succeeded by his brother of the same mother, or failing a brother, by his sister's son; the alleged reason being that descent derived through the mother is certain, while that through the father is uncertain. This custom would seem to point to a time when conjugal fidelity was rarer among the women than the early writers represent it. Next to the chief or "king" of the tribe was the *werowance* or general, who had command of all expeditions, whether peaceful or hostile. Such warriors as had distinguished themselves in council or battle were honored with a tittle which the early travellers and historians give as *cockarouse*, and there, with the chief, the werowance, and "medicine-man" or conjuror, formed the ordinary council of the tribe.[1]

This medicine-man was a person of great importance, combining in himself the functions of physician and magician, as is generally the case among savage tribes who look upon disease as the result of a hostile incantation, or the anger of a malignant or offended spirit. They were usually initiated into their profession by a long period of preparation, including protracted fasting, solitude, severe penances, and frequently the administration of narcotic drugs. This regimen produced hallucinations, in which "medicines" or charms were revealed to them by spirits, and a hysterical or epileptic tendency superinduced, which, under nervous excitement, readily gave rise to paroxysms. Their modes of *pow-wowing* were various, but usually began with drum-beating, shaking of rattles, and chanting by the assistants, and furious dancing or gesticulation on the part of the conjuror, until he was seized with convulsions, real or simulated, and rolled upon the ground with face distorted and mouth foaming. Sometimes he howled forth his oracle in this condition, and then it was understood to be a spirit that possessed him speaking with his voice; at other times he fell prostrate and apparently lifeless, and did not deliver his oracle until he recovered his senses; when he announced that his soul had quitted his body and journeyed to the world of spirits, whence it brought the desired answer. In their medical practice they combined these conjurations with treatment of a more orthodox sort, administering drugs, using scarification, cauterization, and other remedies; and in both capacities they were regarded with great veneration.

These medicine-men also took a prominent part in the religious ceremonies, solemn feasts, and other rites. These had mostly reference to the change of seasons and their events, the chief feast being at the maize-harvest; while others signalized the return of certain kinds of migratory game, the ripening of certain fruits, etc. Their festivals were celebrated with various ceremonies of a symbolical character, with singing, dancing and a grand banquet. Neither at these, nor in their ordinary life, did these Indians use any beverage but water, sometimes sweetened with the sap of the sugar-maple, until after they had learned the use of spirituous liquors from the whites; and to these, Father White[2] tells us, the Maryland Indians had at first a great repugnance, though afterwards drunkenness became a prevalent vice with them.

[1] The *Relation of Maryland* (1635) says that "he that governs in chief is called the *werowance*, and is assisted by some that consult with him of the common affairs, who are called *wisoes* . . . The *wisoes* are chosen at the pleasure of the *werowance*, yet commonly they are chosen of the same family . . . They have also *cockorooses* that are their captains in time of war" (p. 32). The statement in the text is from Beverly, who, having known the Indians for years, was perhaps more accurately informed than the author of the *Relation*.

[2] *Relatio Itineris in Marylandiam*, p. 40.

Father White[1] gives an account of a ceremony witnessed by some of his party, probably among the Yaocomicos, "in a temple":

"On an appointed day, men and women of all ages from several districts, gathered around a great fire, the younger ones standing nearest the fire, and the older behind them. Deer's fat was then thrown on the fire, and raising their hands to heaven they cried in a loud voice, *Yaho! Yaho!* A space is then cleared and some one brings foward a large bag, in which are a pipe and powder which they call *Potu.* The pipe is like that which is used among us for smoking tobacco, but much larger. The bag is then carried around the fire, the boys and girls following it, chanting alternately, in not unpleasant voices, *Yaho! Yaho!* When they have made the circuit, the pipe is taken from the bag and the powder *Potu* distributed to the bystanders, who, each in turn, light the pipe and blow the smoke over the several members of their body, thus consecrating them."

The custom of smoking tobacco was universal among the tribes at the time of the first arrival of the whites. It was regarded, however, in a far different light from the same practice among ourselves. Tobacco was a sacred herb, a precious gift of the Great Spirit to his children; and the act of smoking had always something of a ceremonial, or even religious character. In some tribes the chief, standing at the entrance of his cabin at sunrise, saluted the first appearance of the solar disk with solemn wafts of smoke from his pipe. In councils and other ceremonies, the *calumet* (a French, not an Indian word, as is sometimes supposed,) played an important part. It was solemnly lighted by the chief, who gave a few whiffs, sometimes directing these to the four cardinal points, and then opened the matter for consideration; the pipe was next handed to the second in rank, who in his turn took two or three whiffs and then delivered his opinion, and thus the pipe made the circuit of the assembly. A large and ornamented pipe was kept in each village for the ceremonious reception of strangers, whose peaceful or hostile intentions were known by their reception of it. The chief of the village filled and lighted the peace-pipe in the presence of the visitors, and after smoking a little, handed it to their principal man. If he refused to smoke, it meant that their intentions were hostile; but if he received and smoked it, it was a sign of peace, and it was passed alternately according to rank, between hosts and guests. These pipes were adorned with feathers and wings of birds, and whatever other ornaments their fancy could devise; and served also as credentials to travelling ambassadors, and like the herald's tabard of feudal times, was a safe-conduct ever among foes. Father Hennepin gives the following description of one that he saw among the Iroquois:

"This Calumet is the most mysterious thing in the World among the savages of the Continent of the Northern America: for it is used in all their important Transactions. It is nothing else but a large Tobacco Pipe, made of red, black or white marble; the Head is finely polished, and the Stem which is commonly two feet and a half long, is made of a pretty strong Reed, or Cane, adorned with Feathers of all Colours, interlaced with Socks of Women's Hair. They tie to it two Wings of the most curious Birds they

[1] *Relatio Itineris in Marylandiam*, p. 40.

can find, which makes their Calumet not much unlike Mercury's Wand, or that Staff Ambassadors did formerly carry when they went to treat of Peace. They sheathe that Reed in the neck of Birds they call *Huars*, which are as big as our Geese, and spotted with black and white; or else of a sort of Ducks which make their nests upon trees . . and whose Feathers be of many different Colours. However, every Nation adorns their Calumet as they like, according to their own Genius and the Birds they have in their country. Such a Pipe is a Pass and Safe-Conduct among all the Allies of the Nation who had given it. And in all Embasses, the Ambassador carries that Calumet as the Symbol of Peace, which is always respected; for the Savages are generally persuaded that a great Misfortune would befall them if they violated the public faith of the Calumet."

At the time of the arrival of the first colonists, the Virginia and Maryland Indians clothed themselves in skins, mostly of the deer, which the women had the art of dressing extremely soft and pliant. Some, according to Smith, used ingeniously woven mantels of turkey feathers. Their weapons were bows and arrows, pointed with pieces of deer-horn, the spurs of the wild turkey, or flints skillfully chipped to the requisite shape and keenness; hatchets of hard grit-stone ground to an edge and grooved for the attachment of a handle; and war-clubs of hard wood, sometimes edged with flints. As defensive armor they had shields of bark; and Smith mentions a kind of light targets used by the Massawomekes, made of small sticks woven between strings of hemp and silk grass, and proof against arrow shots. The introduction of fire-arms, however, rendering these simple contrivances useless, they were gradually abandoned.

They soon learned to buy improved arms, implements, and clothing from the Europeans, giving in exchange furs and peltries, and getting course heavy cloths of which they made mantels and leggings, hatchets and knives of steel, guns and ammunition, and pieces of iron, out of which they cut lighter and better heads for their arrows. Though iron ore was abundant, none of the Indians had the art of smelting it; their skill in metallurgy being limited to the manufacture of rude ornaments out of native copper, and occasionally gold. They had a medium of exchange, or kind of currency called *peak* and *roenoke*, which was afterwards used to some extent by the whites in dealings with them. *Peak* consisted of small polished cylinders about a third of an inch long and a quarter of an inch in diameter, wrought out of the clam, or mussel shell, and drilled longitudinally for the passage of a string. It was of two colors, dark purple and white, the former, which was called *wampum-peak*, being twice the value of the latter. *Roenoke* was of much less value, being rough bits of shell rudely shaped and pierced for stringing. As currency these were used in strings and valued according to measure; the yard of white peak being valued by the traders of Beverley's time at nine-pence, and that of wampum peak at eighteen. The strings of wampum were also woven into broad belts for convenience in transactions involving considerable payments.

Their mode of warfare was altogether of the guerilla sort, consisting chiefly of surprises and ambuscades, in which they displayed great skill and cunning. Such a thing as a pitched battle between two armies in the open field, was contrary to all their notions of good strategy. When a hostile expedition had been determined on by the chief and leading warriors in council, it was made known to the tribe, who celebrated the occasion by a solemn dance, in which the warriors, bedizened in paint and feathers, chanted their past or prospective exploits, and imitated in expressive pantomime, the shooting, tomahawking and scalping of their foes. On the appointed day they set out, in one or more parties, moving, as they approached their destination, with extreme wariness to prevent discovery, marching often by night in single file, slipping from shadow to shadow, or gliding through the forest so stealthily that hardly a twig snapped or leaf rustled under the tread of a moccasioned foot, until at a given signal that burst upon the village with terrific war-whoops. Those of their foes who survived after the rage of slaughter was glutted, they made prisoners and reserved for death by the most cruel tortures their ingenuity could devise; in inventing and enduring which, the Iroquois—who indeed have the credit of introducing the custom—seem to have surpassed all others. Instances are recorded of the tortures of distinguished warriors lasting for days, a sort of contest arising between the power of cruelty to inflict and that of fortitude to endure. In the intervals of torment the victim would sometimes smoke his pipe and talk on indifferent matters with his tormentors; while amid his suffering, he sang his own exploits or derided the unskillfulness of his tortures, and taught them devices for inflicting more exquisite pain. Women were sometimes tortured, but usually they were tomahawked or shot, unless the captors wanted women, in which case they were adopted into the tribe. The Susquehannoughs made frequent incursions on the more southern Maryland tribes for the purpose of carrying off women.

The policy of the early governors of Maryland was to treat the Indians with justice, moderation and kindness, and to acquire land by purchase. The settlement of St. Mary's was bought by Leonard Calvert for a quantity of axes, hoes and broadcloth,[1] articles of real and inestimable value to the Indians, who, indeed, were the more ready to part with the territory from the fact that they were suffering from the continued inroads of the fierce Susquehannoughs, who had harrassed them so cruelly that they had already determined to abandon their lands and seek safer homes elsewhere.[2] Some were allowed to remain on part of the purchased territory, and their wives and children were employed as servants in the settlers' families; others were

[1] *Relatio Itineris in Marylandiam*, p. 36.

[2] "The Susquehanoes, a warlike nation, and the fiercest enemies of King Yaocomico, ravage the whole territory with frequent invasions, and have forced the inhabitants by the dread of the danger to look for other homes. This is the reason of our so readily obtaining a portion of this kingdom. . . . Day by day they move off in parties, and leave us their houses, lands and plantations. . . . Some few are allowed to live among us until next year, and then the land is to be given up entirely to us."—*Ibid.*, p. 37.

allotted reservations, with full rights of hunting and fishing in the woods and streams. They very cheerfully submitted to the dominion of the whites for the sake of that protection against the Susquehannoughs which their ancestors had tried to purchase from Smith with the offer of perpetual subjection. The records of the first few years of the colony are very defective, but enough remains to show that this just and humane policy was carried out as far as possible; that the friendly Indians were protected against their enemies and secured in the enjoyment of their rights; and many of them, such as the Yaocomicos, Piscataways, Patuxents, and others, never, or scarcely, wavered from their amicable relations. With the exception of the fierce Susquehannoughs and Nanticokes, whose hostility to the whites it took long years to overcome, it is probable that no serious troubles would have arisen between the aborigines and the settlers, had it not been for the intrigues of parties hostile to the proprietary and the colony, as will be mentioned in the proper place.

Of the final fate of the southern tribes little need be said beyond the brief notices that will appear on subsequent pages. Those of the western shore remained in feudal subjection to the lord proprietary, who, when some of the tribes were crowded out by the increase of the white population, allotted them lands and erected courts for the administration of justice among them. The Piscataways and their confederates, the Doags, Mattawomans, Chapticos, and others, vested in the lord proprietary the right of appointing the "Emperor of Piscataway," and in 1666 we find them petitioning the governor to appoint, as his lordship's representative, a successor to "Wahacasso the Second, late deceased." A treaty made this year with these tribes provides that none of their people shall enter any English settlement with his face painted, as it was difficult to distinguish friendly Indians from foes; that the visiting Indian should call out to announce his approach and lay down his arms; and if under these circumstances he was killed by an Englishman, it should be punished as murder; but if he refused to take these precautions, he should be deemed an enemy. The governor was also to appoint a place of security and refuge for the wives and children of friendly Indians in case of their invasion by hostile tribes; and they bound themselves neither to make peace nor war with other tribes, without the consent of the lord proprietary or the governor.

Still, with all the protection afforded them, these friendly Indians dwindled away. The neighborhood of civilization seemed to have a blighting influence upon them. They wandered from their reservations: many, no doubt, left the province for the western wilderness; others lost their tribal organization and identity. Perhaps with them, as with other savage races in similar circumstances—such as the Maories and Tasmanians—fertility was impaired, and the race died out.

The two strong and warlike tribes of Nanticokes and Susquehannoughs, however, preserved an independent existence longer, and it will not be inappropriate to give here a brief sketch of their final fate.

At the time of the first settlement of Maryland there was a feud between the Nanticokes and the Susquehannoughs, and the former, as well as the latter, were often invaded by the Iroquois. As if this was not enough, the warlike Nanticokes were frequently embroiled with the whites, and war was several times declared against them. Under this double pressure they yielded at last, and requested to be put on the same footing as the Piscataways. The Iroquois, however, continued to harrass them, and finally brought them under subjection. About the middle of the eighteenth century, by advice or command of the Six Nations (who stipulated in a treaty with the province that the Nanticokes should be permitted to leave Maryland and settle where the Six Nations should appoint), a portion of the tribe left the province, carrying with them the bones of their ancestors, and removed to Otsiningo (now Binghampton, N. Y.), where they joined some fragments of the Shawnees and Mohickanders, and made a league under the name of the Three Nations. Others seem to have settled in Wyoming, Pennsylvania; and others again—if the theory be correct which identifies the Conoys or Kanawhas with the Nanticokes—to have removed to the vicinity of those rivers which now bear their name.

In 1767 ambassadors came from the Nanticokes, at Otsiningo, to Governor Sharpe, for the purpose of selling the lands of their tribe in Dorchester, Somerset and Worcester counties. Sir William Johnson, the chief agent of the English government in its dealings with the Indians, assisted by letter in the negotiation, and the sum offered by Governor Sharpe being considered far too small by the Indians, who seemed disposed to hostilities, Sir William—who was exceedingly anxious to secure the wavering friendship of the Iroquois and their confederates to the British—made up the difference at the expense of the crown. As late as 1852, a remnant of the tribe (about one hundred) was living on Grand River, north of Lake Erie, in Canada West; and their chiefs and headmen petitioned the Assembly of Maryland for compensation for certain annuities which a tradition current among them represented to have once been paid to their nation in consideration of the cession of their lands to the province. As their traditions, however, according to the terms of the petition, represented that "there had never been any war or hostile feeling" between their ancestors and the whites, from the time of the first arrival of the latter, they may have been equally faulty in other particulars. At all events the claim was not allowed by the Assembly.

The history of the Susquehannoughs is a little more more eventful. In 1661 they were engaged in fierce war with the Five Nations, especially the Cayugas and Senecas, and being helped by the Maryland authorities, were the victors. For nearly twelve years this war was kept up, success being mostly on the side of the Susquehannoughs; but a more terrible enemy than even the Iroquois had by this time invaded them—the small-pox, which first appeared among them in 1661, and whose ravages became terrible. In 1673 they could only number about 300 warriors, while ten years before they had been able to turn out 700; and probably the mortality was even greater among the women and children. In the next year they were utterly defeated by the Senecas, and driven from their abode, at the head of the Chesapeake, to a position near the border of Maryland and Virginia, below the territory formerly occupied by the Piscataways, who had been removed by the assembly to grounds near the head of navigation on the Potomac. Here they took refuge in an old fortification. The Senecas pursued, and while on the war-path did some damage to the plantations of the whites on both sides of the Potomac, and committed several murders, which, being attributed to the Susquehannoughs by the Virginians and Marylanders, and cruelly revenged, gave rise to a tragical series of events, which will be chronicled in a future chapter.

After the Susquehannoughs had been crushed by the Virginia militia under Bacon, the remnant of the tribe submitted to the Five Nations, and were allowed to remain in their ancient territories on the Susquehanna River, where they lived, a weak and dwindling people, for near a hundred years.

In 1763, the massacres committed on the borders by the Indians under Pontiac, having excited in the breasts of the whites an undiscriminating rage and hatred against all Indians, the few survivors of the tribe, perceiving their danger, took refuge in Lancaster jail, where they were cruelly butchered by a mob, thus ending this brave and high-spirited people.

The last interest attaching to this tribe centres in the celebrated Logan, whose pathetic story and more pathetic speech, or rather letter, the work of some unknown fabulist, have not been able to stand the strain of historical criticism.[1] Yet Logan, in his double aspect of romance and reality, is no inapt type of the race to which he belonged, whose better and whose worse qualities furnish an admirable figure for the poet or novelist, but are alike incompatible with the new social order which was destined to prevail in the Western World. His part, whatever that was, has been performed; and his longer continuance on the stage is a solecism in the world's history. Sentimentalists may lament in plaintive tones that there is "no one to mourn for Logan," but in truth we can see no rational cause for grief that he has vanished before the advance of a civilization that he was powerless to resist and impotent to share.

[1] *Tah-gah-jute*. By Brantz Mayer. Albany, 1867.

CHAPTER V.

THE colony of Maryland, thus happily founded, and governed with wisdom, justice, and humanity, seemed destined to a long career of prosperity and peace. Unfortunately, this period of quiet and harmony was not of long duration. Both private and public jealousies had been aroused against the colony, in the adjacent provinces, which soon gave evidence of their unfriendly feeling.

Virginia held herself aggrieved by the invasion of her ancient charter rights in the grant to Lord Baltimore. But it will be shown that, so far as the rights of this colony were concerned, it was perfectly justifiable for Baltimore to apply for, and no breach of law for the king to grant, all the territory included within the lines of his patent.

We have seen, that under the first charter from King James, the first or southern company, which was called the London Company, was permitted to make its settlements anywhere between the 38th and 45th degrees, subject to certain restrictions as to the contiguity of their respective settlements. In 1609, this company obtained from King James a new charter, which severed it from the northern company, and incorporated its members and others, whom they had received as associates, under the name of "*The Treasurer and Company of Adventurers of the City of London, for the first Colony of Virginia*," and to them were granted the rights of soil and government, in all the lands north and south of Cape Comfort, to the extent of two hundred miles, in both directions. A third charter was granted in 1611, which did not vary these limits on the main land. Under these charter governments, the colony of Virginia remained until the year 1623, when, in consequence of the refusal of the company to surrender their charters, and to accept in their stead such a charter as the king might be pleased to grant, a *Quo Warranto* was issued out of the King's Bench, on which judgment was given in Trinity term, 1624, against the company, its charter was annulled, and the rights granted by it revested in the crown. "From that period," says the late eminent lawyer and historian of Maryland, John V. L. McMahon, "Virginia became what was termed 'a royal government,' and as such, there was an inherent right in the crown to alter and contract its boundaries, or to carve new and distinct territories or governments out of it, at pleasure." In this view he is sustained, after a careful analysis of the question, by Chief Justice Story, who affirms that the whole effect of the judgment was to revest the powers of government, and the title to the lands, in the crown.[1]

[1] Story on *Constitution*, i., p. 22. "George Calvert, Knighte, one of our principal Secretaries of State," was one of a commission appointed by the king to direct the affairs of Virginia after the revocation of the charter.

Thus it will be seen that by this judgment (from which they did not appeal,) all political rights of the Virginia colonists (as distinct from their individual holdings of land,) were taken away, and the king had a legal right to grant any part or the whole to Calvert, or any other, at his pleasure.

But the most formidable objection raised against the grant to Lord Baltimore, seems to have been founded on a circumstance, apparently immaterial to the public, however it might interfere with the private rights of some individuals. It has been alleged, on a variety of occasions, that settlements had been established by the Virginians, under the authority of William Claiborne, within the country afterwards denominated Maryland, prior to the date of his lordship's charter or grant for the same, and that as it was suggested therein, that the country was *hitherto unsettled*, "*hactenus inculta*," his grant became thereby void. But it seems to be extraordinary, that although history recognizes this objection as being frequently made, yet it furnishes no authentic proof of the fact on which it is founded.[1]

In little more than two years from the time in which Virginia had become the exclusive property of the British Crown, she was twice exposed to the evil of a change of governors; an evil at all times great, but fraught with especial mischief to a colony beset with difficulties such as hers. She could ill spare, at such a moment, the head that could devise, or the hand that could execute, measures needful for her welfare. Nor was the loss of such faithful friends as Wyat and Yeardley had proved themselves to be, her only misery. A further punishment was inflicted upon her by another commission, issued before the death of Yeardley, appointing Sir John Harvey to the office of governor, whensoever it might become vacant, and William Claiborne to that of secretary.[2]

Harvey was not in Virginia at the time of Yeardley's death; and, until his arrival, Francis West, brother of Lord De la Warr, who had been a distinguished member of the colony from its earliest settlement, was entrusted with the government. Upon his death, soon afterwards, Dr. John Pott, another member of the council, was appointed governor, whose career was quickly ended by his having been found guilty of stealing cattle.[3] A repetition, therefore, of the evils incident to a frequent succession of governors took place; and Claiborne, who, amid all these changes, remained secretary, had the better opportunity of effecting his sinister purposes.[4]

As it seems to have been a practice with many of the first colonists of Virginia, especially those of note and influence, to endeavor to derive some emolument to themselves, by carrying on a traffic or bartering with the Indian natives, particularly those inhabiting the shores of the Chesapeake, for their peltry and such other commodities as would afford a profit, when sold in the province or exported to Europe, we find that Mr. Claiborne was

[1] Bozman, i., p. 263.

[2] Claiborne had first gone out to Virginia with Wyat, in 1621, "to survey the planters' lands, and make a map of the country."—Henning, i., p. 116. He was admitted to the council in 1629. —*Ibid.*, p. 138.

[3] *Ibid.*, p. 145.

[4] Anderson, *Colonial Church.*, i., p. 457.

one of those, who, availing himself of his station and influence, early sought to better his fortunes in this way. It appears also that during the years 1627, '28 and '29, the governors of Virginia gave authority to William Claiborne, "the Secretary of State of this Kingdom," to explore the Chesapeake Bay, or any other part of the Virginia territory from the 34th to the 41st degree of north latitude. Under this authority or commission for making discoveries in the Chesapeake, it would appear that Mr. Claiborne first availed himself of the opportunity of establishing a system of traffic with the natives on the shores of the upper parts of that bay, and most probably first fixed some trading-houses, for that purpose, on the Isle of Kent. But it seems that this species of traffic could not lawfully be carried on without a special license either from the king himself or the governor of the province, for reasons founded, without doubt, in the personal danger to the colonists in general, by too indiscriminate an intercourse with the natives, especially in furnishing them with fire-arms and teaching the use of them.[1]

Just at this time, 1629, Lord Baltimore made his visit to Virginia, and, in all probability, made known his intention of obtaining a grant of territory bordering upon the Chesapeake Bay. This must have alarmed Claiborne, who had a station on the island of Kent, situated nearly in the centre of the province of Maryland, and had likewise established a post for trade with the Indians on Palmer's Island, near the mouth of the Susquehanna. Claiborne had considered his settlements, wherever made, to belong to Virginia, and "the Isle of Kent" had been represented as such, by sending Captain Nicholas Matian to the House of Burgesses of that province as early as 1631–2. To secure himself still further, or to anticipate Lord Baltimore, it is not now known which, he insinuated himself into the good graces of Sir William Alexander, the king's Secretary of State for Scotland, who had lately obtained a sub-grant of Nova Scotia, under a pretence of promoting an interchange of trade between the colonies of New England, Nova Scotia and Virginia, and through him obtained a license, under the hand of King Charles (and, as it seems, under his signet for Scotland), bearing date May 16th, 1631, "to *trade* in all seas, etc., in or near *about those parts of America.*" For the more effectual execution of this license, it will be seen command was also given to the governor of Virginia, Sir John Harvey, to permit the said Claiborne and his company "freely to repair and *trade* to and again *in all the aforesaid parts*, as they should think fit and their occasion should require."

The following copy of the license is taken from Chalmers' *Annals* (chapter ix., note 13), with this prefatory remark:

"The following royal license is subjoined; because it is the most ancient state paper of Maryland; it laid a train of numerous woes to that province, by giving an interested man a pretence to claim a large part of it.

[1] Bozman, i., p. 265.

"'CHARLES REX.

"Whereas, our trusty and well beloved William Claiborne, one of the council and secretary of state for our colony of Virginia, and some other adventurers, which with him have condescended, with our trusty and well beloved councellor, Sir William Alexander, knight, our principal secretary of state for our kingdom of Scotland, and others of our loving subjects, who have charge over our colonies of New England and Nova Scotia, to keep a course for interchange of trade among them as they shall have occasion, as also to make discoveries for increase of trade in those parts; and because we do very much approve of all such worthy intentions, and are desirous to give encouragement to their proceedings therein, being for the relief and comfort of those our subjects, and enlargement of our dominions: These are to license and authorise you, the said William Claiborne, his associates, and company, freely, without interruption, from time to time, to trade for corn, furs, or any other commodity whatsoever, with their ships, boats, men and merchandize, in all seas, coasts, harbours, lands or territories, in or near about those parts of America, for which there is not already a patent granted to others for sole trade; and, to that effect, we command you and every one of you, and particularly our trusty and well beloved Sir John Harvey, knight, governor, and the rest of our council of our colony of Virginia, to permit him and them, with their ships, mariners, merchandize, servants, and such as shall willingly accompany or be employed by them from time to time, freely to repair and trade to and again in all the aforesaid parts as they shall think fit and their occasions shall require, without any hindrance whatsoever, as you and every of you will answer the contrary at your perils; Giving, and by these presents granting, unto the said William Claiborne, full power to direct and govern, correct and punish, such of our subjects as shall be under his command in his voyages and discoveries; and for his so doing these presents shall be a sufficient warrant. Given at our manor of East Greenwich, the 16th of May, in the seventh year of our reign, 1631.

"'To our trusty and well beloved our governor and council of Virginia, and to all our lieutenants of provinces and countries in America, governors and others having charge of colonies of any of our subjects, captains and masters of ships, and, generally to all our subjects whatsoever, whom these presents do or may concern.'"

On this license Chalmers has subjoined a further remark:

"This paper was evidently drawn by Sir William Alexander, and afterwards passed under the privy signet of Scotland: what right within an English colony could that convey?"[1]

In about ten months afterwards Claiborne applied to Sir John Harvey, the governor of Virginia, for a commission "to sail and traffic unto the adjoining plantations *of the Dutch* seated upon this territory of America." A commission was accordingly granted to him by the governor, bearing date the 8th of March, 1631 (the 19th of March, 1632, N. S.), "authorizing him to go unto the said plantations of *the Dutch*, or unto any *English* plantation, or to such other harbours, rivers, and places, as he shall find occasions; praying all governors, captains and commanders to afford to him all lawful favour and respect."

This commission from Sir John Harvey is also published in Chalmers' *Annals* (chapter ix, note 14), as "the second State paper of Maryland;" for which he cites *Virginia Papers*, bundle 75, page 130; and is as follows:

[1] Bozman, i., p. 266.

"'To all to whom these presents shall come. I, Sir John Harvey, knight, governor and captain-general of Virginia, send greeting, in our Lord God everlasting. Whereas my trusty and well beloved friend, William Claiborne, esquire, and one of the council of state for this colony, hath desired, for increase of trade, to obtain this my commission to sail and traffic unto the adjoining plantations of the Dutch seated upon this territory of America; which may tend to an intermutual benefit, wherein we may be useful to one another: Now know ye, that I, the said Sir John Harvey, out of the good opinion I conceive of the discretion and understanding of the said capt. William Claiborne, do, by these presents, with the consent of the council of state, authorise him, with the first convenience of wind and weather, to set sail from hence, in such barques and pinnaces, and with such companies of men as shall willingly accompany him to go unto the said plantations of the Dutch, or unto any English plantation, or to such other harbours, rivers, and places as he shall find occasions; praying all governors, captains and commanders to afford to him and them all lawful favour and respect, they behaving themselves fairly and honestly in all things: Giving and by these presents granting, unto him, the said captain William Claiborne, full power and authority to direct and govern such persons as shall accompany him in his said voyage. Given at James city, the 8th March, A. D. after the computation of the Church of England, 1631; and in five and twentieth year of this southern colony of Virginia.

"'JOHN HARVEY.'

"Now it is very obvious, from a perusal of these two several commissions and a fair construction of them, that neither of them mentions or apparently refers in the slightest degree to any plantations or settlements, or indeed to any traffic in the Chesapeake. It is evident that, first—the king's license was intended only to promote a trade between the colonies of Virginia, New England, and Nova Scotia; in the last of which Sir William Alexander, without doubt, felt himself somewhat interested, although he had, the year before, sold the greatest part of that territory to Sir Claude St. Estienne; upon the express condition, however, that he (Sir Claude), and those claiming under him, should continue to be faithful subjects of the King of Scotland. The other commission from the governor of Virginia does not appear to have been granted in pursuance of or in obedience to the command expressed in that of the king, no reference thereto being mentioned in it; but as stated in the preamble, and apparently understood by the governor and council of Virginia, it appears to have been granted solely in contemplation of *a trade with the Dutch;* which meant, most probably, the Dutch colony at Manhattan. The recommendation of Claiborne also, in the commission, to "all governors," etc., shews, that it could not have been meant as a license to trade in the Chesapeake. But supposing these licenses or commissions for trade extended everywhere throughout America, "for which there was not already a patent granted to others for sole trade," it is impossible, by any subtlety of interpretation, to construe either of them as *a grant of territory* in any part of the soil of America; and so the lords commissioners of plantations thought in the year 1639, when the matter came before them, as will be hereafter seen at large in their proceedings upon it. Upon the whole view of the subject, then, it appears, that if Claiborne had, prior to these licenses of 1631 and 1632, formed any settlements either on the isle of Kent or at the mouth of the Susquehannah, they must have been unauthorized settlements made under the exploring instructions before mentioned for discoveries in the Chesapeake, or special licenses by the governor of Virginia for trafficking with the natives. It could not possibly have entered into the head of Lord Baltimore, at the time of his visit to Virginia, even if he had been then apprised of such unauthorised settlements within the territories for which he afterwards prayed a grant, that these settlements could ever have been raised up as objections of any validity against his charter.

"It has been deemed necessary to state the preceding circumstances relative to the objections against Lord Baltimore's grant, in order to show what was the real situation of the country thereby granted to him, at the time of his visit to Virginia; in the year 1628 [1629]. From all which, it would seem, that his lordship might have returned to England, with the intention of soliciting a grant of all that country which he subsequently denominated Maryland; and with a thorough conviction in his own mind, that it was then, in the year 1628 [1629], uninhabited by any but savages, and with the most perfect honesty and integrity of conduct, suggested to the king, that the country for which he desired a patent, was, as that instrument expresses it, '*hactenus inculta*,' hitherto unsettled."[1]

In this connection Chief Justice Marshall, in delivering his opinion in the celebrated case of Johnson *vs.* McIntosh,[2] says:

"The power now possessed by the government of the United States to grant lands, resided, while we were colonies, in the crown or its grantees. The validity of the titles given by either has never been questioned in our courts. It has been exercised uniformly over territory in possession of the Indians. The existence of this power must negative the existence of any right which may conflict with and control it. An absolute title to lands cannot exist at the same time in different persons, or in different governments. An absolute must be an exclusive title, or at least a title which excludes all others not compatible with it. All our institutions recognize the absolute title of the crown, subject only to the Indian right of occupancy, and recognize the absolute title of the crown to extinguish that right. This is incompatible with an absolute and complete title in the Indians. . . . Thus has our whole country been granted by the crown while in the occupation of the Indians. These grants purport to convey the soil, as well as the right of dominion, to the grantees. In those governments which were denominated royal, where the right to the soil was not vested in individuals, but remained in the crown, or was vested in the colonial government, the king claimed and exercised the right of granting lands, and of dismembering the government at his will. The grants made out of the two original colonies, after the resumption of their charters by the crown, are examples of this. The governments of New England, New York, New Jersey, Pennsylvania, Maryland, and part of Carolina were thus created. In all of them the soil, at the time the grants were made, was occupied by Indians. Yet almost every title within those governments is dependent on these grants."

Such were the origin, extent and condition of the English settlements on Kent Island when it was granted to Lord Baltimore. Shortly after the grant of Maryland a petition was preferred to the king by the planters of Virginia, which was finally acted upon in the Star Chamber, July 3d, 1633, when it was adjudged by the Privy Council, that Lord Baltimore should be left in possession of this grant, and the petitioners to their remedies at law, if they had any such. The following report of proceedings is copied from Chalmers' *Annals* (chapter ix, note 18), who publishes it as—"From *Maryland Papers*, volume i., bundle C;"—which purports to be from *papers* still extant in the Plantation Office, England:

"*At the Star Chamber: 3d July, 1633.*

"PRESENT—Lord Keeper, Lord Privy Seal, Lord High Chamberlain, Earl Dorset, Earl Bridgewater, Earl Danby, Lord Viscount Wentworth, Lord Viscount Falkland, Lord Cottington, Mr. Secretary Windebank.

[1] Bozman, i., p. 267, etc.

[2] 8 Wheaton, 543.

"Whereas an humble petition of the planters of Virginia was presented to his majesty, in which they remonstrate, that some grants have lately been obtained of a great portion of lands and territories of the colony there, being the places of their traffic, and so near to their habitations, as will give a general disheartening to the planters, if they be divided into several governments, and a bar put to that trade which they have long since exercised toward their supportation and relief, under the confidence of his majesty's royal and gracious intentions towards them, as by the said petition more largely appeareth: Forasmuch as his majesty was pleased, on the 12th of May last, to refer to this board the consideration of this petition, that, upon the advice and report of their lordships such orders might be taken as to his majesty might seem best; It was thereupon ordered, on the 4th of June last, that the business should be heard on the second Friday in this term, which was the 28th of the last month, and that all parties interested should then attend; which was accordingly performed; and their lordships, having heard the cause, did then order, that the lord Baltimore, being one of the parties, and the adventurers and planters of Virginia, should meet together betwixt that time and this day, and accommodate their controversy in a friendly manner, if it might be, and likewise set down in writing the propositions made by either party, with their several answers and reasons, to be presented to the board this day; which was likewise accordingly done. Now, their lordships, having heard and maturely considered the said propositions, answers, and reasons, and whatever else was alledged on either side, did think fit to leave lord Baltimore to his patent, and the other parties to the course of law, according to their desire. But, for the preventing of farther questions and differences, their lordships did also think fit and order, that, things standing as they do, the planters on either side shall have free traffic and commerce each with the other, and that neither party shall receive any fugitive persons belonging to the other, nor do any act which may draw on a war from the natives upon either of them: And, lastly, that they shall sincerely entertain all good correspondence, and assist each other on all occasions, in such manner as becometh fellow subjects and members of the same state."

What part William Claiborne had acted in getting up the petition to the king against Lord Baltimore's charter is not now known; but it is probable that it had been an active one, for there was no other person to whom the phrase "being the places of their traffic," could apply but to him, there being at that time no places of traffic but his own. The right of traffic, as we have stated, however, gave him no permanent right to the soil, or claim to jurisdiction over it. Nor could he rest his title on the ground of prior occupancy, for we have shown that as his license from the king went no further than a permission to trade, which might have been granted to a citizen of a foreign State, the instant that the territory, now Maryland, was granted by King Charles to Lord Baltimore, Kent Island and Claiborne (if he was a resident there, as is asserted, although he was at this time secretary of the colony of Virginia, and therefore more likely to be a resident of that colony), became subject to his jurisdiction and authority. The resistance, therefore, of Claiborne to the authority of Lord Baltimore "was unjustifiable, seditious, and subversive of all just government."[1]

A proceeding of the governor and council of Virginia very recently afterwards, is quite irreconcilable with the injunctions of the Privy Council, and forces upon us the conclusion either that they were not then apprised of

[1] Burnap's *Calvert*, p. 105.

these injunctions, or were determined not to respect them. In March, 1634, a few days after the Maryland colony had sailed up the Chesapeake, the governor and council of Virginia held a consultation as to the manner in which they were to treat their new neighbors. The record is as follows:

"PRESENT—Sir John Harvey, governor, Capt. Claiborne, Capt. Tho. Purfry, Capt. John West, Mr. Wm. Farrer, Capt. Jos. Bullock, Capt. Sam. Matthews, Capt. John Uty, Capt. Wm. Perry.

"Captain William Claiborne requested the opinion of the board, how he should demean himself in respect of lord Baltimore's patent, and his deputies now seated in the bay; for that they had signified to captain Claiborne, that he was now a member of that plantation, and therefore should relinquish all relation and dependence on this colony. It was answered by the board, that they wonder why any such question was made; that they knew no reason why they should render up the rights of that place of the isle of Kent, more than any other formerly given to this colony by his majesty's patent; and that, the right of my lord's grant being yet undetermined in England, we are bound in duty and by our oaths to maintain the rights and privileges of this colony. Nevertheless, in all humble submission to his majesty's pleasure, we resolve to keep and observe all good correspondence with them, no way doubting that they on their parts will not entrench upon the interests of this his majesty's plantation."[1]

Here is certainly expressed a determination on the part of the council of Virginia to withhold, for the time at least, from Governor Calvert and the authorities of Maryland the surrender of the jurisdiction of Kent Island; though they give no sanction for the violent measures which Claiborne, on his own responsibility, it would seem, afterwards ventured to take.

There is extant, also, the following rescript from a committee of the king's council in England, which must have been seen by Claiborne, and perhaps emboldened him still further to attempt resistance to the Maryland charter, although it only shows that the grant to Baltimore was not meant to invade *private* rights.

"After our hearty commendations: we have thought fit to let you know, that his majesty, of his royal favour, and for the better encouragement of the planters there, doth let you know, that 'tis not intended that interests which men have settled when you were a corporation, should be impeached: that for the present they may enjoy their estates with the same freedom and privilege as they did before the recalling of their patents; to which purpose also, in pursuance of his majesty's gracious intention, we do hereby authorise yǒu to dispose of such proportions of lands to all those planters, being freemen, as you had power to do, before the year 1625. Whitehall, 22d July, 1634.

"MANCHESTER, KELLEY, E. NEWBURG, T. COVENTRY,
"F. COTTINGTON, T. GERMAINE, F. WINDEBANK.

"To our loving friends, the governor and council in Virginia."[2]

Not long after the landing of the "Pilgrims of Maryland," while they were building habitations for the coming winter, still occupying the old Indian town jointly with the natives, they perceived in these an entire change of demeanor. The supply of provisions was suddenly stopped,

[1] Chalmers.

[2] *Ibid.*

familiarity ceased, and their previous open bearing was changed to suspicion and distrust. The English became alarmed, abandoned their building, and set about providing for their defence.

To guard against sudden surprise, they built a fort, and then resumed their former occupations. Gradually the Indians renewed their intercourse, and soon treated them with the same confidence as before. This singular change in the behavior of the Indians was afterwards explained; and it was found that Claiborne had persuaded them that the colonists were Spaniards, come to rob and destroy them; in proof of which assertion, he had referred to the similarity of their religious rites. The writer of the *Relation of Maryland* says:

"One Captain Claiborne, who had a desire to appropriate the trade of those parts unto himself, began to cast out words amongst the Indians, saying, that those of Yaocomaco were Spaniards and his enemies, and by this means endeavored to alienate the minds of the natives from them, so that they did not receive them so friendly as formerly they had done. This caused them to lay aside all other works, and to finish their fort, which they did within the space of one month."

Captain Thomas Young, who was a friend of Lord Baltimore, and who was in Jamestown in July, 1634, in a letter to Secretary Windebank, upon this subject, says:

"This, so far as I can learn, is the true state, wherein my Lord of Baltimore's Plantation stands with those of Virginia, which perhaps may prove dangerous enough for them, if there be not some present order taken in England for suppressing the insolence of Claiborne and his accomplices, and for disjointing this faction, which is so fast linked and united, as I am persuaded will not by the governor be easily dissevered or overruled, without some strong and powerful addition to his present authority, by some new powers from England. And it will be to little purpose, for my Lord to proceed in his colony, against which they have so exasperated and incensed all the English colony of Virginia: as here it is accounted a crime almost as heinous as treason to favor, nay, to speak well of that colony of my Lord's.

"And I have observed myself a palpable kind of strangeness and distance between those of the best sort in the country which have formerly been very familiar and loving to one another, only because the one hath been suspected to have been a well-wisher to the plantation of Maryland."[1]

By one of his vessels returning from Maryland, Baltimore had news of Claiborne's hostility, and on the 4th of September he instructed Leonard Calvert, if Claiborne would not recognize his authority, to seize and detain him a close prisoner, at Saint Mary's, and if they could, "take possession of his plantation on the Isle of Kent." At the same time recognizing the many favors which his colony had received from Sir John Harvey, governor of Virginia, he, on the 15th of September, 1634, addressed the following letter to Secretary Windebank, which speaks for itself:

[1] Young, in *Aspinwall Papers*. Mass. Hist. Soc. Publications, 4th series, vol. ix.

A Patuxent chief at a conference denied that Claiborne had prejudiced his tribe against the Marylanders, and said that Fleet "was a liar, and that if he were present he would tell him so to his face."—*Streeter Papers*. Neill, *Founders of Maryland*, p. 50.

"Right Hono[ble]

"Since the returne of my shipp from my Maryland plantation, I was seuerall times to waite vpon yo[r] honor at yo[r] house in London, to haue acquainted you how readily S[r] John Haruie complyed wth his Ma[ties] commandes in assisting, all he could, my plantation; w[ch] he receiued in a letter from his Ma[tis] procured for me by yo[r] honor. Indeed he hath obserued them in a very dutifull manner to the King and a very noble and friendly manner vnto me, and therefore, (seeing it was not my good fortune to find you in Towne, and my Wiue's lying in Child bedd detayning me heere for some time) I have intreated my Bro: Peaseley to waite vpon yo[r] honor on my behalf & to be a sutor to you to procure a letter of thankes from the King to S[r] John Haruie, for that w[ch] he hath done and command to continue his care of my plantation: my Bro: Peaseley will likewise shew yo[r] honor some papers w[ch] I lately received from those parts concerning one Clayborne's malicious behauiour to me and my plantation there. If yo[r] honor be at leisure to peruse them, and that a letter from the King may be had, you may please to take notice & insert what you thinke fitt of that buisiness, in it, for S[r] John Haruie's encouragem[t] in assisting me against Clayborne's vnlawfull proceedings there. If a letter from the King may not be gotten so suddainly, before the departure of this shipp, by w[ch] I would send it, w[ch] is already (as I heare) fallen downe into the Downes, and will sett sayle from thence w[th]in a few dayes; howsoeuer I humbly beseech you S[r] to honor S[r] John Haruie w[th] a few lines from yo[r] self, to the aforesaid purpose; as much as yo[r] honor shall thinke conuenient: necessity obliges me to trouble you in this manner, for my plantation wilbe in greate danger of being ouerthrowne now in the infancy of it; if it be not strengthened sometime by such fauorable and lawfull protection as I now desire. I beseech you present my humble seruice to my Lady; and pardon this vnciuill importunity of mine: for you have not in the world one that honors you more then does

"Yo[r] honors most affectionate & humble seruant

"WARDER CASTLE, 15 Septem: 1634. "CECILIUS BALTEMORE."[1]

In response to this letter, Secretary Windebank, on the 18th of September forwarded the following letter to Governor Harvey in Virginia:

"S[r], I vnderstand from the Lord Baltimore of the fauorable assistance, that you (in obedience to his Ma[ty] commaundm[t]) haue giuen to his people, at their first arriuall to plant in those parts by vertue of his Ma[ty] graunt; And as I doubt not, but the King will take in good part this yo[r] present conformity to his will and pleasure, as you will perhaps most particularly vnderstand shortly by his owne Royall Letters, taking notice thereof to yo[r] contentm[t], so I am assured his Ma[tie] wilbee very sensible of any disobedience, or vndutifull interpretacion that shalbee giuen to his commaund, by any there, when it proceeds eyther from faction, or pride, presuming of importunity, by their farre distance from hence, or some other silly hopes heere; who should knowe, (if any such there bee) that it is the duty of good subjects to obey, and not to dispute their Soueraignes Commaundm[t], espetially if they bee of the Number of those that are trusted wth place and gouerm[t], from whom his Ma[tie] hath reason to expect a more ready conformity, then from others; And therefore you haue done well to assist the sayd Lo. Baltimores proceedings in his plantacion there, wherein yo[r] humanity to them no lesse appeared, then yo[r] judgm[t], in conceiuing that both plantacions may well subsist together to the benefitt of both. And I do earnestly desire you to continue yo[r] assistance to his Gouverno[r] and Planters against the malitious practises of Clayborne, and as they shall haue occasion otherwise for their benefitt and protection, and shall not be justly prejudiciall to the good of

[1] Public Record Office, London—*Colonial Papers*, viii., No. 25.

Virginia; In wch you shall much oblige the Lo: Baltimore, and mee for his sake, who will not fayle to acknowledge the courtisies you shall do his Lop in those parts at my request, in any thing w^{th}in the power of

"Dated: 18°: Sept: 1634.

"To Sr John Harvy Knt Gouernor of his Maty Plantation in Virginia."[1]

On the 29th of September, the king wrote the following to Governor Harvey from Hampton Court:

"Trusty and welbeloued wee greete you well. So desirous wee are of the planting and civilizing of those parts of our dominions by our good subjects, as wee neither haue nor will leaue any due meanes vnattempted for the encouragemt of such as shalbee contented for the publique benefitt and honor of our kingdomes & for their particular commodity to transport themselues thither, and inhabitt that part of the world and they shall finde our continuall care of them in all occasions; The consideracion whereof was a powerfull motiue to vs, to graunt to the Lo: Baltimore a part of that our territory of Virginia, vpon the devoluing of the old Companies right therein justly to vs, As also in respect of the vastnesse of that country, there being land and profitt enough for the entertainment of many thowsands, and allso for that wee conceiued the difficulties of the worke would easily be ouercome by multitude of hands and assistance, though of different bodies and societies, yet all deriuing their Interest from vs. And being now informed that the sayd Lo: Baltimore to his greate charges hath accordingly begunne a Plantacion in Mariland, and that you haue readily assisted his Planters (in conformity to our Commaund) at their first descent in those wilde parts, wherein, wee obserue yor dutifull obedience to vs and do take in in good part, giuing you thanks for the same, we haue thought good by these our speciall letters to require you to continue yor assistance to them, by sufferring them quietly to enjoy the Country and profitt thereof wch wee haue graunted vnto the said L: Balt: w^{th}out disturbance or interrupcion, and by protecting his planters from the malice and injury of the Indians, or any other, As also by giuing them leaue to buy and transport such necessaries from yor Colonies, as you may conueniently spare, and they haue occasion to vse; Wherein, you shall do vs acceptable seruice, and giue them such releefe in their commendable endeavors, as may both much incourage them and produce benefitt to yor gouermt and plantacion. The due perfourmance whereof wee expect from you and the rest of our councell and people there, as becometh good and dutifull subjects, and as you will answere the contrary.

"Dated at Hampton Court: 29° Sept: 1634.

"To Sr John Haruey Gouernor of Virginia."[2]

In response to the letters he had received, Governor Harvey, on the 16th of December, 1634, wrote to Secretary Windebank as follows:

"Sr I shall put the daye wherein I did that seruice to my Lord Baltimore wch deserued thankes from yr Honor into the accompt of my happie dayes, next vnto that day wherein I was designed to doe his ma^{tie} seruice in this place; and for the respect I owe to yor Honor and for the Noblenes I know to be in my Lord Baltimore and his designes I do promise yor Honor to do him and his all the seruice I am able: but I must sincerely let yor Honor know that my powre heere is not great, it being limited by my Commission to the greater number of voyces at the Councell table, and there I haue almost all against me in whateuer I can propose, especially if it concerne Maryland; and these proceedings of the Councell do so embolden others that notwithstanding the obligation of Christianity and his ma^{ties} commands to be assisting to them in their first beginning, many are so

[1] Pub. Record Office, London—*Colonial Papers*, viii., No. 26.

[2] *Ibid.*, No. 27.

auerse as that they crye, and make it their familiar talke that they would rather knock their cattell on the heads then sell them to Maryland; I am sorry its not in my power to rule these exorbitant courses, but for their p'sent accomodation I sent vnto them some Cowes of myne owne, and will do my best to procure them more, or anything else they stand in need of. This Faction I finde great cause to suspect is nourished from England, for this Summer came Letters to Capt: Mathewes who is the Patron of disorder as yo[r] Honor will vnderstand by the bearer hereof Lieftenant Euelin (and by his comportment in other matters as yo[r] Honor will finde in these papers) vpon the reading whereof hee threw his hatt upon the ground scratching his head and in a fury stamping cryed, 'a pox vpon Maryland.' Many letters and secrett intelligences he and the rest of the Councell haue and especially Cleyborne and many meetings and consultations, for w[ch] Letters if I had power to search, and to examine their consultations I doubt not but to finde notable combinations. I haue written at large of the estate of this Colonie in my letters to the Lords in generall to w[ch] I remitt yo[r] Honor, humbly crauing pardon for my breuity w[ch] is enforced by my indisposition of health at this tyme; so humbly p'senting to yo[r] Honor my best seruice and respects I take my leaue and still will rest

"Yo[r] Hono[rs] very affectionate seruant

"Virginia 16th of Decemb: 1634. "JOHN HARVEY."[1]

Claiborne, however, was not content with the friendly course of Governor Harvey towards the Marylanders, and his underhand mode of annoying the colony by exciting the Indians to rebel, was but the preparation for a formidable resistance to Lord Baltimore's claim. The attempt was rash—almost desperate—and was probably stimulated by exasperated feelings, encouraged by the remoteness of the mother-country, and his associates in the Virginia council, and supported, perhaps, by some slight hope that early and vigorous opposition might induce Governor Calvert and his colonists to abandon their enterprise, depending, as it did, mainly on the resolution and perseverance of one man. If such were his calculations, he had altogether mistaken Calvert's character and the temper of the colony.

Early in the year 1635, a pinnace called the *Long Tail*, belonging to Claiborne, was captured by Captain Thomas Cornwaleys, one of the Maryland commissioners, for being a Virginia vessel trading in the waters of the Chesapeake without a Maryland license.

To retaliate for this offence, Claiborne immediately granted his special warrant or commission, under his hand, to Lieutenant Ratcliffe Warren, "to seize and capture any of the pinnaces or other vessels belonging to the government of St. Mary's," and fitting out an armed boat, manned with about thirty men from Kent Island, placed it under Warren's command. Upon this, Governor Calvert immediately fitted out, manned, and placed under the command of Captain Thomas Cornwaleys, two pinnaces called the *St. Margaret* and *St. Helen*, with orders to proceed to the island of Kent to put down the rising rebellion. The hostile vessels met, it seems, on the 23d of April, 1635, in the Pocomoke River, on the eastern shore of the bay, and fought the first naval battle upon the inland waters of America. In the proceedings of the assembly in this case, it is alleged that Claiborne's men

[1] Public Record Office, London—*Colonial Papers*, viii., No. 37.

fired upon Cornwaleys' boats first and killed William Ashmore of the Maryland force. The fire was returned by Cornwaleys' men, killing Lieutenant Warren, the commander, John Bellson and William Dawson; upon which the insurgent pinnace surrendered and her crew were made prisoners. "Again on the 10th of May, in the harbor of Great Wighcomoco, Cornwaleys met Thomas Smith of Kent Island, who was arrested for piracy."[1]

The prisoners must have created almost as much embarrassment as the war itself. There was no prison into which they could be put, there was no court constituted to try them, and no law by which they could be tried. It was three years before Thomas Smith was brought to trial; and then the legislative assembly acted as a court of justice. He was convicted of felony and piracy, and condemned to death, with but one dissenting voice.

The Virginians, upon learning the treatment of Claiborne and his followers, became very indignant, and hearing that their governor, Sir John Harvey, approved of Governor Calvert's course, and incited by that "patron of disorder," Samuel Matthews, one of the Virginia council, they rebelled against their governor and refused to acknowledge his authority. Four days after Warren was killed, a public meeting was held at Yorktown, at the house of William Warren, perhaps a relative, speaker of the Virginia assembly, to consider the conduct of Harvey. The next day the governor called a meeting of his council. On the 25th of May, 1635, Samuel Matthews from "Newport Neewes" writes the following very interesting letter to Sir John Wolstenholme, in which he gives full particulars of their transactions:

"Honoured Sir

"I haue made bold to present you wth diuers passages concerning our late Gou'nor by the hands of my worthy friend Sr John Zouch. But such was the miserable condition wee liued in that it dayly giues iust occasion of new complaints wch I doe hereby presume to acquaint you withall wch I beseech you to creditt as they are true in euery particular. Sr you may please to take notice that since Sr John Harvie his deteyning of the Letters to his Matie the Lords & others concerning a Contract, of wch Sr John Zouch had only bare copies such as the Secretary would giue without either his or the Clarkes hand. Notwithstanding he promised me to certifie them vnder his hand wherevpon Sr John Zouch declared before his departure that it was not safe for him to deale as Agent in the Cuntreyes affaires as they had desired him to doe hauing no warrant for his proceedings. And therefore desired that if the Colony would haue him deale therein for them They should giue him further authority vnder their hands. To that purpose when a Letter was drawen and carried to the Burgesses to subscribe, The Consideracion of the wrong done by the Gou'nor to the whole Colony in detayning the foresaid Letters to his Matie did exceedingly perplex them whereby they were made sensible of the miserable condicion of the present Gouernor wherein the Gou'nor vsurped the whole power in all causes without any respect to the votes of the Councell whereby iustice was now done but soe farr as suited wth his will to the great losse of many mens estates and a generall feare in all. They had heard him in open Court reuile all the Councell

[1] Neill's *Founders of Maryland*, p. 52.

and tell them they were to giue their attendance as assistants onely to aduise wth him wch if liked of should pass otherwise the power lay in himselfe to dispose of all matters as his Maties Substitute. Next that he had reduced the Collony to a great straight by complying wth the Marylanders soe farr that betweene them and himselfe all places of trade for Corne were shutt vp from them and no meanes left to releiue their wants without transgressing his Commands wch was very daungerous for any to attempt. This want came vpon vs by the increase of aboue 2000 persons this yeare to the Colony as alsoe by an vnusuall kind of wevell that last yeare eate our Corne. Againe they saw a dangerous peace made by him wth the Indians against the Councells and Cuntreyes aduice that although the Indian had offered any insolent injuries, yet he witheld vs from revenging ourselues and had taken of them satisfaccion for many Hoggs, of wch in one place a Lyst was brought in of aboue 500: which satisfaccion the Interpreter iustefies he had receiued for the Gouerno^rs^ owne vse. The Inhabitants also vnderstood wth Indignacion that the Marylanders had taken Captain Claybornes pinnasses and men with the goods in them whereof they had made prize and shared the goods amongst them wch action of theirs Sr John Harvey vpheld contrary to his Maties express commands in his Royall Letters and the Letters of the Lords, wch Letter from his Matie he did not communicate to the rest of the Councell though Capt Clayborne in his Peticion had directed them to the whole Board, But said they were surreptitiously gotten. S^r^ these and infinite number of perticular mens iniuries were the grounds of their greife and the occasion of the Peticion and letter that they exhibited to the Councell for some speedy redress of these euills wch would otherwise ruine the Colony. These generall greiuances made some of the people meete in some numbers and in an vnlawfull manner yet without any manifestacion of bad intents only desires to exhibitt their complaints as did appeare vpon strict examinacion though Capt Purfrey had in a Letter accused them in a neare sence to rebellion, wch since he denyed vnder his owne hand, being vsuall wth him to affirme and deny often the same things. The Gouerno^r^ having intelligence of this Peticion grew inraged and sent out his warrants to apprehend the complaynants wch some of the Councell accordingly executed, vpon these appearances he himselfe only constituted a new Sheriff at James Citty a defamed fellow to whom he committed the keeping of the Prisoners in Irons, Some of them desiring the cause of their committm^t^ to whom he answered that they should at the Gallowes, presently the Councell being called together he declared it necessary that Marshall law should be executed vpon the Prisoners But it was desired they might haue legall tryall soe growing into extreame Coller and passion after many passings & repassings to and fro at length sate downe in the Chayre and wth a frowning Countenance bid all the Councell sitt. After a long pawse he drew a Paper out of his Pockett and reading it to himselfe said to the Councell I am to propound a question vnto you. I require eu^r^y man in his Maties name to deliu^r^ his opinion in writing vnder his hand and no man to advise or Councell wth the other but to make a direct answer vnto this proposicion (wch is this) What doe you thinke they deserue that haue gone about to persuade the people from their obedience to his Maties Substitute? And to this I doe require you to make yor present Answer and no man to aduise or interrupt wth other. And I begin wth you Mr Menefie; who answered I am but a young Lawyer and dare not vpon the suddain deliu^r^ my opinion. The Gouerno^r^ required that should be his Answer vnder his hand. Mr Farrar begann to complaine of that strong command, the Gou^r^no^r^ cutt of his speech saying in his Maties name I command you not to speake till yor turne; Then myselfe replyed I conceiue this a strang kind of proceeding, instantly in his Maties name he commanded me silence, I said further there was no President [precedent] for such a Command wherevpon he gaue me leaue to speake further. But it was by a Tyrant, meaning that passage of Richard the Third against the Lord Hastings, after wch relacion the rest of the Councell begann to speake and refused that course. Then followed many bitter Languages from him till the sitting ended. The next meeting in a most sterne manner he demanded the reason that wee conceiued of the Cuntreyes Peticion against him. Mr Menefie made Answere the cheifest cause was the detayning of the Letters to his Matie and the Lords. Then he rising in a great rage sayd to Mr Menefie & doe you say soe? he replyed yes; presently the Gou'nor in a fury went and striking him on the shoulder as hard as I can imagine he could said I arrest you of suspicion of Treason to his Matie Then Capt Vtie being neare said and wee the like to you Sr. Wherevpon I seeing him in a rage tooke him in my armes and said, Sr there is no harme intended against you saue only to acquaint you wth the greiuances of the Inhabitants and to that end I desire you to sitt downe in yor Chayre. And soe I related to him the aforesaid greiuances of the Colony desiring him that their iust complaints might receiue some satisfaccion wch he altogether denyed soe that sitting ended. After wee were parted the secretary shewed a letter sent vp by Capt Purfrey to the Gou'nor wch spake of daungerous times that to his knowledge the wayes were layd, wch when wee had considered wth the things before specified wee much doubted least the Inhabitants would not be kept in due obedience if the Gou'nor continued as formerly and soe acquainted him therewth. The wch opinion of ours he desired vnder our hands the wch being granted him he was requested the sight of his Maties Commission; and the same being publiquely read, (notwithstanding any former passages) wee of the Councell tendred the Continuance of our assistance, prouided that he would be pleased to conforme himselfe to his Maties pleasure expressed by his Commission and Instruccions, the wch request was in no part satisfied, wherevpon being doubtfull of some Tyrannicall p'ceedings wee requested the Secretary to take charge of the Commission and Instruccions vntill wee had some time to consider of a safe course for the satisfying of the Inhabitants Peticion and the safety of the Gou'nors Person wch by reason of Capt Purfreyes Letter wee conceiued to be in some danger whereupon wee appointed an Assembly of all the late Burgesses whereby they might acquaint vs wth their greiuances as may appeare by their Peticion wee looke vp for that meeting wth a resolucion to returne againe within six dayes hauing according to Sr John Harveyes desire appointed a sufficient gard for the safety of his Person, within three dayes after he departed from James Citty and went vnto the Mills to the house of one William Brockas whose wife was generally suspected to have more familiarity wth him than befitted a modest woman, where he thought himselfe soe secure that he dismissed his guard. Soone after the Councell and Burgesses according to the time prefixed mett at James Citty. But before wee entred vpon any business the Secretary showed vs a Letter wch he had receiued that morning from Sr John Harvie (the true Coppie whereof I haue hereinclosed) And notwithstanding his threats therein the assembly proceeded according to their former Intentions. The next morning the Secretary shewed vs another Letter from Sr John Harvie wherein he had required him to redeliver him his Maties Commission and Instruccions charging him vpon his Allegiance to keepe secresie therein. But the Councell had before thought of his late practises wth the Secretary concerning the detayning of the former proceedings had committed the charge of the Commission and Instruccions to Mr George Menefie vntill all differences were settled. And for the effecting of this wee proceeded to giue a hearing vnto the greiuances of the Inhabitants wch were innumerable; and therefore it was thought fitt that their generall greiuances only should be presented vnto the Right hoble the Lords Commissioners for Plantacions omitting particular complaints wch would haue beene over tedious vntill a fitter opportunity. Sr wee were once resolued not to proceed to the Eleccion of a new Gou'nor but finding his Maties Commands to the Contrary that vpon the death or absence of any Gouernor to make a new Eleccion. Therefore vntill wee heare of his Maties further pleasure wee haue made choice of Capt John West an auntient Inhabitant who is a very honest Gentleman of a noble family being brother to the Lord Laward sometimes Gouernor of Virginia. I beseech God to direct his Matie in appointing of some worthy religious Gentleman for to take charge of this his Colony and I doubt not by Gods assistance and the industry of the people but Virginia in few years will flourish. You may please to take notice that Capt Clayborne two dayes since repayred vnto vs for redress against the oppressions of the Marylanders who haue slaine three and hurt others of the Inhabitants of the Isle of Kent. Notwithstanding their knowledge of his Maties late express Letter to command freedome of trade (the true Copie whereof I haue hereinclosed) I doe believe that they would not haue committed such Outrages without Sr John Harvies instigation howeuer in conformity to his Maties command wee haue entreated Capt Vtie and Capt Pierce to sayle for Maryland wth Instruccions and Letters from the Gouerno^r and Councell desiring them to desist their violent proceedings promising them all fayre correspondence on the behalfe of the Inhabitants of the Isle of Kent vntill we vnderstood his Maties further pleasure In the meane time wee rest in expectation of their Answer acording to wch wee intend to proceed. In the wch I beseech God to direct vs for the best. I conclude wth an assured hope that Sr John Harvies returne will be acceptable to God not displeasing to his Matie and an assured happiness vnto this Colony wherein whilst I liue I shall be ready to doe you all the true Offices of a faythfull friend and Seruant

"From NEWPORT NEEWES this 25th May, 1635. "SAM: MATHEWS."[1]

The council demanded that Governor Harvey should depart for England, to which he reluctantly consented, as they would no longer obey his authority, and on the 7th of May, John West, a brother of Lord Delaware, was chosen temporary governor, and Messrs. Utie and Pearce, of the council, were sent as commissioners to effect a settlement of the difficulties with Governor Calvert.

Upon the arrival of Governor Harvey at Plymouth, England, he immediately addressed a letter, dated the 14th of July, 1635, to Secretary Windebank, of which the following is a copy:

"Right Honble

"I doubt not but that your Honnor will admire at my comming from my Charge without any licence or other directions from his Matie or the Lords; But it may please your Honnor to calle to mynde howe that in my last letter concerning the affayres of Virginia, I signified that the Assemblies being composed of a Rude, Ignorante, and an Ill conditionde people, were more likelye to effect mutinye, then good lawes and orders, especiallie whilest ye Councell gaue them such examples; what I then feared I soone after founde; but I must confess theyr exorbitances haue by much exceeded my expectation; for presently after the departure of the ships, hauing receiued an Information of sum mutinous Assemblies I sent for the Councell, as also warrants for the Apprehending of the chieff mutineers; The Councell I called for their Aduice in so daungerous a business; But I found them so farre from intending any good, that they came Armed with a strength to surprise mee; And laying violent hands vpon mee, charged mee with Treason, for going about (as they sayde) to betray theyr Forte into the hands of theyr Enemies of Marylande, telling mee that I must resolue my self to goe presently into Englande, theare to make Answer to the Countries Complaints agaynst mee, forthwith setting at libertie such of the mutiney whome I had caused to bee layd fast in Irons. In the next place they called an Assembly of the Burgisses—And sum few dayes after made a new Governor, my self being yet resident in the countrie; a large account of all theyr proceeds, I shall with all conuenient speed in person tender vnto

[1] Public Record Office, London—*Colonial Papers*, viii., No. 65.

yo[r] Honnor; In the meane tyme I thought these but of Dutye, As also to signifie to your Honnor, that landing at Plimmouth the 14th of this month I haue made vse of the Authoritie of the Mayor of the Place, to fasten vpon two persons which came in the ship wth mee, The one a person principally employd vp and downe the Collonie to perswade the Inhabitants to subscribe to a rabbell of pretended greivances agaynst mee, The other expresly sent with letters from the Councel and theyr vnlawfull Assemblie to theyr Agents and Abettors in Englande; I haue also vsed the same meanes to fasten vpon theyr Letters, w[ch] being brought to view no doubt but thearby the malice of theyr Rebellious Actions and Intentions may be truely discerned, And it is to bee feared that they intend no less then the subuersion of Marylande; for whilest I was aboorde the ship, and readie to departe the Collonie, theare arrived Captin Claborne from the Isle of Kent, with the newes of of an hostile encounter twixt sum of his people and those of Marylande; And Captin Francis Hooke tould mee that by the relation of sum of Captin Clabornes owne companye it was they that sought out the Marylande Boates w[ch] were trading among the Indians and twice assaulted them, And that there were sum hurte and slayne on bothe sydes. And at Captin Clabornes request two of the Councell were dispatchd for Marylande, wth a message, vnto w[ch] if those of Marylande condiscend not, they intende to supplant them, and to send them home as they haue don mee; I presume M[r] Kemps letter will more fully Informe your Honnor the[reof] After many troubles and a wearisom passage I am boulde to repose a day or two I will hasten vp to render an account to your Honnors of all matters concerning my Trust, in the meane tyme I rest

Most readie to obey your Honnors Commands

"PLIMOUTH the 14th of July 1635. "JOHN HARVEY."[1]

A correspondent of the Earl of Strafford, under date of August 19th, 1635, alludes to Governor Harvey's arrival in England and his difficulties in these words:

"Sir John Harvey Governor of Virginia being invited on board of a ship, was suddenly carried away and is now brought into England. The company allege he was a Marylander, that is, one that favored too much my Lord Baltimore's Plantation, to their prejudice; but it is ill taken, that the Company of their own authority, should hurry him away in that manner."[2]

The issue of the engagement in the Pocomoke ended for a time Claiborne's resistance to the authority of Lord Baltimore on Kent Island. He was not himself present in the action, and soon after took refuge in Virginia. His settlement, as he stated in a petition to the king, was reduced, by the loss of their pinnace, to great distress for want of provisions: an additional proof that his was merely a trading post and not a plantation.

Learning of Claiborne's flight to Virginia, it is said that Governor Calvert made a requisition on the Virginia authorities for his delivery, as a fugitive from justice. With this requisition, however, we know that they did not comply, for in 1637 Claiborne went to England to have his affairs adjusted there; Mr. William Cloberry, his London partner, in the meantime having sent out Mr. George Evelyn, who took charge of his affairs on Kent and Palmer's Islands, and acknowledged the jurisdiction of Maryland.

[1] Pub. Record Office, London—*Colonial Papers*, viii., No. 73.

[2] Strafford's *Letters*.

Soon after Claiborne's arrival in England, he presented a petition to the king to obtain redress of the "wrongs and injuries" which he alleged he had sustained.

The following imperfect copy of this petition now remaining on our records at Annapolis has no date, but from the proceedings of the Privy Council thereon, it would appear to have been presented on or about the 26th of February, 1637, O. S. (1638, N. S.)

"The petition of captain William Claiborne on the behalf of himself and partners to the king shewing;

"That the petitioners by virtue of a commission under his majesty's hand, &c., divers years past, discovered and did then plant upon an island in the great bay of Chesapeake in Virginia by them named the isle of Kent, which they bought of the kings of that country, and built houses, transported cattle, and settled people thereon, to their very great costs and charges, which the lord Baltimore taking notice thereof, and the great hopes for trade of beavers and other commodities like to ensue by the petitioners' discoveries, hath since obtained a patent from your majesty comprehending the said island within the limits thereof, and sought thereby to dispossess the petitioners thereof, and debar them of their discovery, &c. Complaint thereof being made, your majesty was pleased to signify your royal pleasure by letter, intimating that it was contrary to justice and the true intent of your majesty's grant, to the said lord ——, that notwithstanding the said patent the petitioners should have freedom of trade, requiring the governor and all others in Virginia to be aiding and assisting unto them, prohibiting the lord Baltimore and all other pretenders —— him to offer them any violence, or to disturb or molest them in their —— plantation, as by your majesty's letter annexed appeareth; since which —— be it your —— majesty's said royal pleasure hath been made known to Sr. —— governor of Virginia, (who slighted the same,) as also to the lord Baltimore —— agents there, yet they have in a most wilful and contemptuous manner disobeyed the same and violently set upon your petitioner's pinnaces and boats —— goods to trade, and seized them, and do still detain the same by the ——, of which pinnaces and goods the inhabitants within the said isle were —— so great famine and misery as they became utterly destitute of any corn —— sustain themselves, which enforced them to send a small boat —— why they obeyed not your majesty's said royal letters and commands —— the said pinnace and goods to enable them to trade for corn —— boat approaching near unto some vessel of the said lord Baltimore's —— agents, they shot among the petitioner's men and slew three of them and —— more, and not content with these great injuries the said lord Baltimore and his agents have openly defamed and unjustly accused the petitioners of —— crimes, to his exceeding great grief, which hath caused him purposely —— pair into this kingdom, and humbly prostrates himself and his cause —— majesty's feet to be relieved therein.

"And the petitioners having likewise discovered —— plantation and factory upon a small island in the mouth of a river at the bottom of the said bay in the Susquehannock's country, at the Indians' desire and purchased the same of them, by means whereof, they are in great hopes to draw thither the trade of beavers and fur, which the French now wholly enjoy in the Grand Lake of Canada, which may prove very beneficial to your majesty and the commonwealth, but by letter now from thenceforth your petitioner is advised, that the lord Baltimore's agents are gone with 40 men to supplant the petitioner's said plantations, and to take possession thereof, and seat themselves thereon.

"And the petitioner being desirous to propose a way, whereby your majesty may receive to the crown for plantations an annual benefit—be certain to enjoy the same with the fruits of their labours, they offer unto your majesty £100 per ann. viz. £50 for the said isle of Kent, and £50 for the said plantation in the Susquehannock's country, to have there 12 leagues of land, &c., from the mouth of the said river on each side thereof down the said bay southerly to the seaward and so to the head of the said river and to the Grand Lake of Canada, to be held in fee from the crown of England, and to be yearly paid unto your majesty's exchequer, to be governed according to the laws of England, with such privileges as your majesty shall please to grant, by which means your majesty may raise a great revenue annually, and all planters will be encouraged to proceed cheerfully in their designs.

"And the petitioners having now a ship ready to depart with goods and people for the prosecution and managing of their said discoveries and trade, which without speedy supply and your majesty's favour, &c., is like to come to ruin.

"May it therefore please your majesty to grant a confirmation of your majesty's said commission and letter under your majesty's broad seal for the quiet enjoyment of the said plantations, &c., to send now with the said ship, and to refer the speedy examination of the said wrongs and injuries unto whom your majesty shall please to think fit, to certify to your majesty thereof, and that your petitioners may proceed without interruption of the lord Baltimore's agents."

Immediately following the foregoing petition, there appears on our provincial records the following entry, which is a copy from the proceedings of the Privy Council in England:

"*At the court at New-market, the 26th of February, 1637.*

"His majesty approving the proposals made in this petition for the advancement of those plantations and the hopeful trade of furs, is graciously pleased to confirm what was contained in his former commission and letter under the broad seal, and to that end referreth to the lord archbishop of Canterbury, lord keeper, lord privy seal, and any other the commissioners for plantations, who shall be near at hand and whom they please to call, the consideration of all the contents of this petition, and with Mr. Attorney's advice to settle such a grant of the things herein desired, as they shall think fit to be prepared by him for his majesty's signature. Their lordships are also to examine the wrongs complained of, and certify his majesty what they think fit to be done for redress thereof.

"JOHN COOKE,
"*Ext.* T. MEAUTYS."

"We appoint the first council day after Easther for the hearing of this business at the council board, and do hereby will and require, that present notice be given to the lord Baltimore or any else whom it may concern, together with a true copy of this petition and reference, and that they, by themselves or counsel, fail not to attend accordingly.

"WM. CANT.,
"THOS. COVENTRY,
"W. MANCHESTER."

The king referred this petition to the commissioners of plantations, who soon after made the following report:

"*At Whitehall, 4th of April, 1638.*

"PRESENT—Lord Archbishop of Canterbury, Lord Keeper, Lord Treasurer, Lord Privy Seal, Earl Marshall, Earl of Dorset, Lord Cottington, Mr. Treasurer, Mr. Comptroller, Mr. Secretary Cooke, Mr. Windebank.

"Whereas a petition was presented to his majesty by captain William Claiborne, on the behalf of himself and partners, shewing, that, by virtue of a commission under his majesty's hand and signet, they, divers years past, discovered and planted upon an island in the great bay of Chesapeake, in Virginia, named by them the Isle of Kent, whereupon, as they pretended, they had bestowed great charges; and that the lord Baltimore, as they alleged, taking notice of the great benefit that was likely to arise to them thereby, obtained a patent from his majesty, comprehending the said island within the limits thereof; and that they had likewise settled another plantation upon the mouth of a river in the bottom of the said bay, in the Susquehanough's country, which the said lord Baltimore's agents there, as they allege, sought to dispossess them of, pretending likewise great injuries and violence offered to them in their trade and possessions in those parts by the said agents, in killing some of the said captain Claiborne's men and taking their boats, contrary to the said commission and the express words of a letter from his majesty under his hand and signet; and therefore besought his majesty to grant to the petitioners a confirmation, under the great seal of his majesty's said commission and letter for the quiet keeping, enjoying, and governing of the said island, plantation and people, with other additaments of lands and immunities in those parts; and likewise that his majesty would refer the examination of the said wrongs and injuries to such as his majesty should think fit, as by the said petition more at large appeareth. Forasmuch as his majesty was pleased, at New Market, on the 26th of February, 1637, to refer the consideration of the petitioner's request unto the lord archbishop of Canterbury, the lord keeper, the lord privy seal, and any other the commissioners for plantations, who should be near at hand, and whom they pleased to call, and with all to advise with Mr. Attorney General, for preparing and settling the grant desired for his majesty's signature, and to examine the wrongs complained of, and to certify his majesty what they thought fit to be done for redress thereof. Whereupon all parties attending their lordships this day, with their counsel learned, and being fully heard, the said commission and letters being likewise read, it appeared clearly to their lordships, and was confessed by the said Claiborne himself then present, that the said isle of Kent is within the bounds and limits of the lord Baltimore's patent, and that the said captain Claiborne's commission, (as it likewise appeared,) was only a license, under the signet of Scotland, to trade with the Indians of America, in such places where the said trade had not formerly been granted by his majesty to any other; which commission, their lordships declared, did not extend nor give any warrant to the said Claiborne or any other, nor had they any right or title thereby to the said island of Kent, or to plant or trade there, or in any other parts or places with the Indians or savages within the precincts of the lord Baltimore's patent. And their lordships did likewise declare, that the aforesaid letter, under his majesty's signature, which had reference to the said commission under the signet of Scotland, was grounded upon misinformation, by supposing that the said commission warranted the plantation in the isle of Kent, which (as now appears) it did not. Whereupon, as also upon consideration of a former order of this board, of the third of July, 1633, wherein it appeared, that the differences now in question being then controverted, the lord Baltimore was left to the right of his patent, and the petitioners to the course of law; their lordships having resolved and declared as above said the right and title to the isle of Kent and other places in question to be absolutely belonging to the said lord Baltimore; and that no plantation or trade with the Indians ought to be within the precincts of his patent without license from him; did, therefore, think fit and declare, that no grant from his majesty should pass to the said Claiborne or any others, of the said isle of Kent or other places within the said patent; whereof his majesty's attorney and solicitor general are hereby prayed to take notice. And, concerning the violences and wrongs by the said Claiborne and the rest complained of, in the said petition to his majesty, their lordships did now also declare, that they found no cause at all to relieve them, but do leave both sides therein to the ordinary course of justice.

"*Ext.* T. MEAUTYS."

Within a few months after the decision of the lords commissioners of plantations, but, as we may fairly conjecture from circumstances, *before* the lords commissioners had "certified his majesty what they had thought fit to be done," agreeably to the terms of the reference before stated, and therefore, *before* the king knew the result of their adjudication, Claiborne, assisted by Sir William Alexander, his patron in the business, "partly by misrepresentation," as Mr. Chalmers observes, procured in July, 1638, the following order or letter to Lord Baltimore, commanding him to allow Claiborne and his agents or partners to enjoy their possessions, and be safe in their persons and goods, till the cause referred, as mentioned, should be decided:[1]

"CHARLES REX.

Right, trusty, &c. Whereas formerly, by our royal letters to our governor and council of Virginia, and to others, our officers and subjects, in these parts, we signified our pleasure, that William Claiborne, David Morehead, and other planters in the island near Virginia, which they have nominated Kentish island, should in no sort be interrupted in their trade or plantation by you, or any other in your right, but rather be encouraged to proceed cheerfully in so good a work; we do now understand, that though your agents had notice of our said pleasure, signified by our letters, yet, contrary thereto, they have slain three of our subjects there, and by force possessed themselves by right of that island, and seized and carried away both the persons and estates of the said planters. Now, out of our royal care to prevent such disorders, as we have referred to our commissioners of plantations the examination of the truth of these complaints, and required them to proceed therein according to justice; so now, by these particular letters to yourself, we strictly require and command you to perform what our former general letter did enjoin, and that the aboved named planters and their agents may enjoy, in the mean time, their possessions, and be safe in their persons and goods there, without disturbance or farther trouble by you or any of yours, till that cause be decided. And herein we expect your ready conformity, that we may have no cause of any farther mislike. Given under our signet, at our manor of Greenwich, the 14th day of July, in the 14th year of our reign, 1638."

Lord Baltimore, on receiving the order, "with an attention which he deemed due to the commands of his prince, though founded on misinformation, said, that he would wait on the king and give him perfect satisfaction."[2] Subsequent events justify us in inferring that when the king came to be fully informed of all the circumstances relative to Claiborne's claims and Lord Baltimore's rights, the adjudication of the lords commissioners was finally ratified by his majesty, and in the terms of that decision, "both sides were left to the ordinary course of justice."

Pursuant to this judgment, and most probably in pursuance of some special order from the king to that purpose, the governor and council of Virginia issued the following proclamation, forbidding any person belonging to their jurisdiction from trading within the limits of Lord Baltimore's charter without license first obtained of him or his agents:

[1] Bozman, ii., p. 72.

[2] Chalmers' *Annals*.

"By the governor and captain general of Virginia, with the advice and consent of the council of state,

A PROCLAMATION.

"*Whereas* the king's most excellent majesty was pleased, by his letters-patent, to grant unto the right honourable the lord Baltimore, a territory or tract of land therein nominated and now known by the name of the province of Maryland, with divers franchises and immunities thereunto belonging as in and by the said letters-patent more at large appeareth; notwithstanding which said royal grant and publication thereof in this colony, divers persons, ill-affected to the government established by his majesty both here and in the said province, have by pretence of a former commission, factiously combined to disturb the said lord Baltimore in the possession of part of his said territory, as also to infringe the privilege of trade, in express terms solely granted to the said lord Baltimore within the said province, and, after many violent and disorderly courses, the said pretenders have so far proceeded as to petition his majesty, that part of the said province, now known by the name of the island of Kent and Palmer's island, with the trades thereof, might be confirmed to them; the consideration of which, their said petition, his majesty was pleased to refer to the most reverend and right honourable the archbishop of Canterbury, the lord keeper, the lord privy seal, and any others, the commissioners for plantations, who should be near at hand, and whom their lordships were pleased to call: Whereupon, their lordships meeting, after a full hearing of both sides, the said pretender's commissions being likewise read, their lordships did declare, the right and title to the isle of Kent and other places in question to be absolutely belonging to the lord Baltimore, and that no plantation or trade with the Indians ought to be within the precincts of his patent without licence from him, as in and by the order of their lordships more at large appeareth: These are, therefore, for the future preventing of further mischiefs and injuries, which may arise from ignorant mistakes or presumptions and pretences as formerly, in his majesty's name to prohibit all persons being or inhabiting, or which shall hereafter be and inhabit within the government of this colony, by themselves or others, either directly or indirectly, from the date of these presents, to use, exercise, or entertain any trade or commerce, for any kind of commodity whatsoever, with the Indians or savages inhabiting within the said province of Maryland, viz. northward from the river Wiconowe, commonly known by the name of Onancock on the eastern side of the grand bay of Chesapeake, and northward from the river *Chinquack* called great Wicocomico, on the western side of the said bay; and for the better regulating of all trades within the said colony, it is further hereby commanded, that no person shall resort unto the habitations of the aforesaid Indians, without license first obtained for their so doing from the lord Baltimore or his substitute, upon forfeiture of the goods and vessels, or the full value of them, which shall be lawfully evicted to be traded or employed contrary to the premises, with such further punishment by imprisonment of the party or parties, offending against the true intent and meaning of the said proclamation, as shall be thought fit by the government and council.—Given at James city, the 4th of October, *Anno Regni Regis Caroli decimo quarto, Anno Domi, 1638.* God save the king.

"*Vera Copia.*—RICHARD KEMP, *Secretary.*"

Baffled in his attempts to obtain redress, Claiborne returned to Virginia;[1] and now that force, fraud and complaint had all failed in effecting his purpose, there remained to him but the spirit of deadly animosity

[1] "In the year 1644, between October and Christmas, with a party of men from Chicacoan in Virginia, Clayborne took possession of Kent Isle, but did not remain; and in 1640 came again with forty persons, under a commission from Governor Berkeley of Virginia, but in the next year was compelled to retire."—Neill's *Founders of Maryland*, p. 56.

towards the colony, waiting only the opportunity of revenge. During his absence, one of the first acts of legislation in the Provincial Assembly of 1637 had been to declare his property forfeited to the government,[1] and in 1640 he is found petitioning for its restoration, and otherwise biding his time.

[1] The act of attainder was to the following effect:

"Saint Maries. In the house of generall Assembly, on the 24th Marth, Anno Domini, 1637, was read the fourth time, a Bill of the tenor and effect following, viz.:

An act for the attainder of William Cleyborne, gent.

WHEREAS, William Cleyborne, gent., is notoriously knowen to have committed sondry contempts, insolencies, and seditious acts against the dignity, government, and domination of the Lord Proprietarie of this Province, and to have conspired and contrived sondry mischeivous machinations and practices with the Indians of those parts, to the subversion and destruction of this Colony, and the people thereof: and to have used and exequuted sondry magistraticall and regall powers and jurisdictions, within this Province, and upon the inhabitants of the same, by levying of souldiers, appointing Leutenants and other Officers, imprisoning and otherwise punishing of offenders, and by granting lettres of reprisall and Commissions for the exequution of justice upon the vessells and goods of the Leutenant generall of this Province, and of the people inhabiting this colony of St Maries, without any authority or Commission for the same, from our Soveraigne Lord the King, or from the Lord Proprietary of this Province, or from any other Prince or State whatsoever: And whereas, by an Act of generall Assemblie held at St Maries on the six and twentieth day of February, 1634 [1635 N. S.], among other wholesome lawes and ordinances then made and provided for the welfare of this Province, it was enacted, that the offenders in all murthers and felonies should suffer such paines, losses, and forfeitures as they should or ought to have suffered in the like crimes in England. Since the making of which Act, that is to say, on the three and twentieth day of Aprill, 1635, the said William Cleyborne hath not onely continued his said insolences, mutinies, and contempts against the Lord Proprietary and the government of this place, but hath instigated and commanded sundry persons to committ the greivous crimes of pyracie and murther, [which—the manuscript illegible here,] pyracie and murther is lawfully indicted by a grand Enquest of foure and twenty freemen of this Province; and since, and after the committing of the same pyracie and murther, hath fledd and withdrawen himself out of the Province, whereby he cannot be attainted of the said crimes by any ordinary course of justice;—We the freemen assembled in this present generall Assembly, considering the premises and the necessity of exemplary justice to be inflicted on such notorious and insolent rebells and disturbers of the peace and safety of the inhabitants of this Province, and for the terror of like offenders in time to come, doe request your Lordship that it may be enacted, and be it enacted by the Lord Proprietary with the advice of the Freemen of this present generall Assembly, that the said William Cleyborne be attainted of the crimes aforesaid, and that he forfeite to the Lord Proprietarie all his lands and tenements which he was seized of on the said three and twentieth day of April, in the year 1635. And that he forfeite to the said Lord Proprietary all his goods and chattells, which he hath within this Province at this present.

And the aforesaid Bill, being engrossed in parchment, was approved and signed by the Leutenant generall, and all the Freemen assembled."

CHAPTER VI.

So soon as the colonists were well established in their new homes, lands marked out, cleared and planted, the abandoned Indian cabins improved in conformity with the needs of civilized life, and means of defence in an emergency provided, they set about framing a system of laws for their government. On the 26th of February, 1634, O.S. (1635 N.S.), the first assembly, composed, probably, of all the freemen in the colony, was convened. The record of their transactions has unfortunately perished; and it is only known that, "among other wholesome laws," they enacted that "all felonies shall be punished with the same pains as for the same crimes in England."[1] The proceeding, though doubtless it had the governor's approval, seems to have been a little irregular, as the charter of the colony gave to the Lord Proprietary the right of propounding or initiating all laws to be enacted by the provincial legislature; so they transmitted their code, when framed, to Baltimore for his assent, without which it could have no validity. He disapproved of it; so the colony remained under the common law of England for two years, at the end of which time Baltimore had drawn up and sent them a code of his own framing.

In 1636 the proprietary transmitted to the colony a series of instructions relative to the grants of land to be made to the various "adventurers" or settlers of the province, giving, as was equitable, the greatest advantages to the first colonists. As this letter of instructions contains the outline of his plan for parcelling out the lands of the province among the settlers, in conformity with his charter, and thus develops the mode of colonization afterwards pursued, we append it in full.

"To our dear brother Leonard Calvert, esqr., and our lieutenant-generall of the province of Maryland, or to any other our lieutenant-generall there for the time being.

"Whereas the adventurers to plant that our province of Maryland have made suit unto us, that we would be pleased to grant unto them under our great seal of our said province such proportions and quantities of land there upon such considerations and agreements as we have heretofore propounded and promised to grant the same unto all such adventurers; forasmuch as we are bound in honour really to perform the same in all points, these are, therefore, to will and authorize you, that presently upon receipt hereof you make or cause to be made under our great seal of that our said province unto every first adventurer for every five men aged between sixteen and fifty years, which such adventurer did bring into our said province to inhabitt and plant there in the year of our Lord 1633, and unto his heirs for ever, a grant of two thousand acres of land of English measure, for the yearly rent of 400 ℔. of good wheat, and to every adventurer which in that year did bring a less number than five men into that our said province of

[1] Chalmers' *Revolt of the Colonies*, i., 64.

the ages aforesaid to inhabitt and plant there and unto his heirs for ever a grant of one hundred acres of land of like measure for himself, and one hundred acres more for his wife, (if he brought any,) and for and in respect to every servant, and fifty acres for every child under the age of sixteen years, for the rent of 10 lb. of wheat yearly for every fifty acres.

"And to every other adventurer which hath adventured to transport men into our said province of the age aforesaid in the years of our Lord 1634 and 1635, for every ten men which such adventurer did bring into our said province in either of the said years, and to his heirs for ever a grant of two thousand acres of land of the like measure for the yearly rent of 600 lb. weight of good wheat, and to every other adventurer which in either of the said years did bring a less number than ten men as aforesaid, and to his heirs forever, a grant of one hundred acres of land (of like measure) for himself, and one hundred acres for his wife, (if he brought any,) and for and in respect of every such servant one hundred acres, and for every child under the age of sixteen years fifty acres, for the yearly rent of 70 lb. weight of wheat for every fifty acres.

"And to every other adventurer which hath adventured to plant and transport any men into our said province, since the year of our Lord 1635, or which at any time hereafter shall transport any men of the age aforesaid, to inhabit and plant there until some other or further condition of plantation shall by us be propounded and published to adventurers, and an authentic copy of such conditions by us signed and transmitted into our said province for every five men which he or they shall so transport thither, and to his or her heirs for ever, a grant of one thousand acres of English measure for the yearly rent of twenty shillings to be paid in the commodities of the country, for every such thousand acres, and to every other adventurer which within the time next aforementioned, hath or shall transport any number of persons less than five a grant of one hundred acres of land for him or herself, and one hundred more for and in respect of his wife, (if he brought any,) and as much for and in respect of every man servant, and fifty acres more for and in respect of every child under the age of sixteen years, and for in respect of every maid under the age of forty years which he or she hath or shall so transport thither, and to his or her heirs for ever, for the yearly rent of twelve pence for every fifty acres.

"And we do further will and authorize you, that every two thousand acres, and every three thousand acres, and every one thousand acres of land so to be passed or granted as aforesaid unto any adventurer or adventurers, be erected, and created into a manor to be called by such name as the adventurer or adventurers shall desire.

"And we do hereby further authorize you, that you cause to be granted unto every of the said adventurers within every of their said manors respectively, and to his or their heirs a court-baron and court-leet, to be from time to time held within every such manor respectively. And to the end you may the better be informed in what manner to pass every such grant, court and courts as aforesaid, according to our intention, We have sent unto you under our hand and seal a draught of a grant of a manor court-leet and court-baron, and a grant of a freehold, which precedents you are to follow, changing only the adventurers' names, the rents and conditions of plantation as the case shall require; for doing whereof this shall be your sufficient warrant. So we bid you heartily farewell. Given at Portsmouth, the eighth of August, 1636. Signed "C. BALTIMORE."

Baltimore evidently hoped, by these favorable conditions, to attract men of means, who, by bringing with them parties of tenants or dependants, at their own expense, might thus acquire large manorial rights. He may have entertained at the time the idea of establishing an upper house of the great landed proprietors, who would strengthen his position and authority. He certainly sought to lay the foundation for a landed aristocracy, the most powerful and enduring of any that can be created.

"In pursuance of these instructions and correspondent also with the charter, manors of lands were, in process of time, laid off in different parts of the province; and some of them appropriated or reserved for the lord proprietor's own particular use; others again were erected by the special orders of the lord proprietor for the benefit of his relations or particular friends, with special conditions and privileges; and others also so denominated and granted to individuals, according to the terms of those instructions or conditions of plantation, as they so became entitled, for the transportation of colonists or settlers into the province. But, although the power and right of holding courts-baron and courts-leet might have been inserted in some or all of these grants of manors, yet we are told [by Mr. Kilty, in his *Landholders' Assistant*, p. 93,] that no memorial appears on the records of the province, of any practical use of either of those kinds of courts."[1]

For the first five years no considerable settlements were made beyond the precinct of the town of St. Mary's. The lands within these limits were divided among the first colonists in a liberal and equitable manner, as is shown by the directions received by Governor Calvert from his brother, and dated August 29, 1636. He was to "pass in freehold, to every of the first adventurers that shall claim or desire it, and to their heirs, ten acres of land within the plots assigned or to be assigned for the town and fields of St. Mary's, for every person that any of the said adventurers transported or brought into Maryland, according to their conditions first published; and five acres of land to every other adventurer for every other person which he hath or shall transport thither since that time of the first plantation until the thirteenth day of August which shall be in the year of our Lord 1638."

Somewhere about this time, or a little later, the settlement of St. Mary's was erected into a county, as we find notice of a commission issued in 1637 to John Lewger, to be a "conservator of the peace within the county of St. Mary's."

By the 15th of April, 1637, Lord Baltimore, having completed his arrangements for reorganizing the government of the province, executed a new commission to his brother, explicitly defining his powers, and stating fully the official functions which he was to discharge. After specifying the various offices which he intended his brother to fill, and among the rest, giving him the power of chancellor and chief justice, he grants him special authority to call an assembly in the following winter, to make known to them the proprietary's dissent from the laws passed in 1635, and to propose for their adoption a body of laws of his own preparation, which he would send over before the time fixed for the session.

Here, within four years of the first settlement of the Maryland colony, began between the colonists and the authorities in the mother country that controversy concerning the rights of legislation which was waged at intervals

[1] Bozman, ii, p. 39.

for a hundred and fifty years, and ended only by the Declaration of Independence in 1776.[1] Lord Baltimore, however, saw fit, afterwards, to recede from the position here taken, and empowered his brother to adjourn and to dissolve the assembly, to summon and dissolve other assemblies as he should think fit, and to prepare and propound other wholesome laws and ordinances for the government and well-ordering of the people, to be assented to and confirmed by himself, if they met his approval.

In pursuance of the instructions of the commission, Governor Calvert proceeded to make arrangements for a legislative assembly to meet on the 25th of January, 1638.

The constitution of this assembly is one of the most interesting facts in the history of the country, and it is easy to see in it the germ of all subsequent political organization. It consisted of but one branch, composed of all the freemen of the colony, each of whom was present, in person or by proxy, and the governor presided in the double capacity of chief executive and speaker of the house.

The governor's commission contained also the appointment of three councillors, Jerome Hawley, Thomas Cornwaleys and John Lewger, with whom he was to advise, as he should see cause, upon all occasions touching the good of the province and the people. These councillors took their seats in the assembly as simple members without any distinction of power or dignity, while they formed what we may call the ministry. Thus, singularly enough, the infant colonial government, though subject to a monarch and under him to a feudal suzerain, was very nearly an example of a pure democracy, in which the whole people met to devise laws for their own government. The model of it was, of course, the British House of Commons, which at the time was almost annihilated in England by the encroachments of the royal prerogative. The British House had grown up almost imperceptibly, through the crystallization, during centuries, of ancient customs, rights, privileges and necessities; but this was complete and definite from the beginning, and maintained its independence and preponderance through all Maryland's history. The form in which it at first existed was rendered practicable at the time by the smallness of the colony, which did not as yet extend much beyond the town of St. Mary's and, including the people on Kent Island, probably did not number more than seven hundred inhabitants.

Toward the latter part of the year 1637, the Isle of Kent had been in some measure reduced to obedience, and measures seem now to have been taken to extend the civil authority over that part of the province. A commission, dated December 30, 1637, was issued by Governor Calvert to Captain George Evelyn, appointing him "commander" of the island. The gradual growth of the colony is also marked by another commission bearing date January 5, 1637, O.S. (1638 N.S.), appointing Robert Vaughan constable of St. George's Hundred, on the west side of St. George's River. The following

[1] Burnap, p. 146.

warrant was addressed to Captain Evelyn, which we copy as not only showing the form of the summons and the principle on which the governor proposed to organize the legislature, but also as evidence that the full privilege of freemen as members of the colony was offered to the people of the Isle of Kent:

"Whereas my dear brother, the Lord Proprietor of this province, hath, by his commission to me directed, in that behalf, bearing date at London, in the realm of England, the 15th day of April, 1637, appointed a general assembly of all the freemen of this province, to be held at his town of St. Mary's, on the 25th of January next; these are therefore, in his lordship's name, to will and require you, all excuses set apart, to make your personal repair to the fort of St. Mary's, on the said 25th day of January, then and there to consult and advise of the affairs of this province; and further, to will and require you at some convenient time, when you shall think fit, within six days after the receipt hereof at the farthest, to assemble all the freemen inhabiting within any part of your jurisdiction, and then and there to publish and proclaim the said general assembly, and to endeavour to persuade such and so many of the said freemen as you shall think fit, to repair personally to the said assembly, at the time and place prefixed, and to give free power and liberty to all the rest of the said freemen, either to be present at the said assembly, if they so please, or otherwise to elect and nominate such and so many persons, as they or the major part of them, so assembled, shall agree upon, to be the deputies or burgesses for the said freemen, in their name and stead, to advise and consult of such things as shall be brought into deliberation in the said assembly; and to enter all the several votes and suffrages upon record, and the record thereof, and whatsoever you shall do in any of the premises, to bring along with you, and exhibit it at the day and place prefixed, to the secretary of the province for the time being; and for so doing, this shall be your warrant."

It is not easy to determine whether the Isle of Kent was at this time considered as a county by itself, or a distinct territorial government, within the Lord Baltimore's jurisdiction, subordinate to the general government of the province. From the circumstance of Captain Evelyn's having a council assigned him of six persons, as mentioned in his commission of the 30th of December, 1637, it would seem to have been the latter.

By one of the bills of this session of 1638–9, it was to be erected into a hundred, and called Kent Hundred, which hundred was to be considered as being *within the county of St. Mary's*, until another county should be erected on the eastern shore.[1]

According to the above writ of summons, the assembly was evidently intended to be purely democratic, that is, an assembly of the whole people. The only ambiguity, as to the right of suffrage and representation contained in it, is in the word "freeman." It has been supposed by some that by this term some property qualification is intended, that none could vote who had no real or at least personal estate; so that the word "freeman" would be synonymous with the word "freeholder." But a vote of the assembly of 1642 seems to prove that the term "freeman," in the first years of the colony, designated a citizen above the age of majority and not held to personal service.

[1] No. 13, Bacon's *Laws*.

In the journal of the assembly of that year it is said that "Mr. Thomas Weston, being called, stated that he was no freeman, because he had no land nor certain dwelling-house here; but being put to the question, it was voted that he was a freeman, and as such bound to make his appearance, by himself or proxy; whereupon he took place in the house." Beverly, in his *History of Virginia*, has shown that the same meaning was attached to the term in that colony. "Every freeman," says he, "by which denomination they call all but indented or bought servants, from sixteen to sixty years of age, is listed in the militia." If we may judge from the record, any one who could not, or did not, choose to attend, had the right of being represented and voting by proxy.

The assembly met, in pursuance of the summons, on the 25th of January, 1638, N.S. It was probably in the fort that the members convened, for no town-hall or state-house had at that time been erected; nor was it, indeed, until after some years that the colony was able to provide a building for the purpose, and even then a portion of it was leased out as an ordinary or tavern. In this respect, however, her neighbor, Virginia, was no better off; for, several years after this date, the legislators of that colony complained that they had "too long made their laws in an ale-house." Our legislators at this time did not, it seems, need a very spacious apartment, as eleven members constituted a quorum.

Among their first proceedings was the adoption of the following rules:

"*Imprimis*—The lieutenant general, as president of the assembly, shall appoint and direct all things that concern form and decency, to be observed in the same; and shall command the observance thereof, as he shall see cause, upon pain of imprisonment or fine, as the house shall adjudge.

"*Item*—Every one that is to speak to any matter shall stand up, and be uncovered, and direct his speech to the lieutenant general, as president of the assembly; and if two or more stand up to speak together, the lieutenant general shall appoint which shall speak.

"*Item*—No man shall stand up to speak to any matter, until the party that spoke last before, have sat down; nor shall any one speak above once to one bill or matter at one reading, nor shall refute the speech of any other with any reviling or contentious terms, nor shall name him but by some circumlocution; and if any one offend to the contrary, the lieutenant geneial shall command him to silence.

"*Item*—The house shall sit every day at eight o'clock in the morning and at two o'clock in the afternoon.

"*Item*—The freemen assembled at any time, to any number above ten persons, at the hours aforesaid, or within one hour after, shall be a house to all purposes.

"*Item*—Every one, propounding any matter to the house, shall digest it at first into writing, and deliver it to the secretary, to be read unto the house.

"And it was ordered by the house, that these orders should be set up in some public place of the house, to the end all might take notice of them."

The house met again on the next day, the 26th of January, at eight o'clock, according to regulation, with Governor Calvert as speaker; John Lewger, clerk, and the two other councillors, Jerome Hawley and Thomas Cornwaleys, sitting as private members.

The first official business after the organization of the assembly, was the consideration of the laws sent over by the lord proprietary for their assent, as all laws under the charter were to be enacted by the proprietary, "by and with the advice, assent and approbation of the majority of the freemen of the province or of their delegates or deputies." And as the lord proprietary had rejected the laws passed by the colonists at their first assembly, the colonists now, considering their power "of advising, assenting to, and approving laws," as conferring upon them equal and co-ordinate rights with the proprietary, returned the compliment by rejecting in bulk all the laws which he had propounded.

"It is somewhat remarkable that throughout the whole colonial existence of Maryland, the history of its legislation does not exhibit a single instance of treacherous or timid abandonment, by this House, of the rights and interests of the colony. Pursuing, in the general tenor of their conduct, the happy medium between the arrogance of power and the servility of submission, they were the vestal preservers of liberty in every age of the colony. The consequence was, that this uniform yet temperate adherence to their rights, even whilst it encountered the resistance, seldom provoked the serious indignation of the proprietary: and the good correspondence between the government and the people being thus preserved, the colonial history of Maryland exhibits one of the finest specimens of colonial administration.

"The freemen were successful in their opposition to the exclusive right claimed by the proprietary; for from this period their right to originate laws does not appear to have been seriously contested. But notwithstanding this concession, the proprietary in the early years of the province, still claimed, and occasionally exercised similar rights, as a co-ordinate branch of the legislature; but these occasions were very rare, and in the ordinary course of the legislation of the province, his powers were in practice limited to his veto upon the acts of the assembly. Throughout the proprietary government, the full veto power was always retained in the person of the proprietary. The commissions and instructions to the governors of the province, gave them, in general, the right of assenting to or rejecting laws; but this assent, when given, never concluded the proprietary, except in cases where he had specially authorised the governor to assent in his name to a particular law. The only effect of the governor's assent was to give efficacy to the laws so assented to, until the proprietary's dissent was declared, and when this was declared, they ceased to operate. The governor had the general power of giving to laws this partially operative assent, subject only to such modifications and restrictions as were specially imposed by his commission and instructions.

"The charter having referred to the proprietary the exclusive right to convene assemblies, and to determine the time and manner of convention, the power of convening, adjourning, proroguing, and dissolving the assemblies at his pleasure, always belonged to the proprietary, and was delegated to, and excercised by the governors of the province, throughout the whole period of the government. This general right carried with it another power, the improper exercise of which might have been attended with very dangerous consequences to the co-ordinate rights of the people. The proprietary under it posesessed, and for a long time exercised, the exclusive right of determining the manner in which the assembly should be constituted. The warrants for convening the assemblies issued by the governors during this period, determined whether they should be convened in person or by deputies; or, if by deputies, the number of deputies to which they should be entitled, and the manner in which these should be elected. If vacancies occurred, the propriety and mode of filling them up were determined by the same discretion. The people's participation in legislation might have been rendered of but little avail by this unlimited discretion on the part of the proprietary and his governors, to regulate the manner in which the assembly should be constituted. But the usage of the governors and the legislation of the province soon restrained this discretion, or corrected its tendencies. From the convention of the first assembly of the province until the government passed into the hands of Cromwell's commissioners, there was no determinate and uniform mode of convening assemblies. The freemen were summoned to attend, sometimes in person, or by proxy or by deputies, sometimes by delegates or deputies only, and sometimes by a general direction to attend, prescribing the mode of appearance. These were the various modes of convening the freemen generally; but throughout this period there were always writs of summons, which were specially directed, in the discretion of the governor, to the councillors and other high officers of the province, and also on some occasions to other persons of trust and distinction.

"Yet although there was no uniform mode of convening assemblies generally, the manner adopted for the formation of any particular assembly, was uniform, and impartial in its operation. The particular form adopted for the organization of any assembly, applied to the inhabitants of the province generally, who were thus placed upon an equal footing in point of privilege. After the restoration of the government to the proprietary, in 1658, by the protector's commissioners, the right of appearing in person or by proxy wholly ceased. From that period the distinct organization, and independent existence of the Upper and Lower Houses of Assembly, which had been established *pro hac vice* at the session of 1650, became permanent: and under this permanent establishment, which endured by usage or law until the American revolution, the Upper House consisted of the councillors to the governor, and the Lower House of delegates, elected by the people of the several counties. Under this system of county representation for the Lower House, which superseded the old system of representation by hundreds, the manner of election, and the number of delegates to be elected by each county, continued to be regulated from 1658 until 1681, by the warrants of election issued for each assembly. But throughout this period, with a single exception, the warrants uniformly authorized each county to elect two, three, or four delegates; and after such election notified to the governor, it was usual to summon the persons elected by special writ. The proprietary's ordinance of 6th September, 1681, reduced the number of delegates to two for each county; and prescribed a permanent and uniform rule as to the qualification of the voters and the manner of election. The proprietary having been divested of the government of the province in 1689, (which shortly afterwards fell directly under the immediate administration of the crown, as other royal governments) the organization of the Lower House was settled by the act of 1692, chap. 76, and continued to be regulated by law, until the adoption of our present government, by the succeeding acts of 1704, chap. 35; 1708, chap. 5; 1715, chap. 42, and 1716, chap. 11. Under these acts, (which all agree in this respect), the same equal and uniform right of county representation was permanently established. Each county was entitled to elect four delegates; and the qualifications of voters and delegates were established by a permanent and uniform rule."[1]

During this session of the assembly, it seems that the inhabitants of the Isle of Kent were far from being quiet and obedient to the lord proprietary's government. The authority of the provincial government was yet so openly contemned and resisted by many of the inhabitants of that island, as to render it necessary for the governor to proceed thither with an armed force,

[1] McMahon, p. 145 to 149.

to quell and punish the refractory and disobedient. We find in the records of the "Council Proceedings" of this period, an entry explanatory of the reasons and causes of this measure of the government.

"By the governor and council, this 12th of February, 1637 (1638, N.S.), the governor and council, taking into consideration the many piracies, insolencies, mutinies, and contempts of the government of this province, formerly committed by divers of the inhabitants of the isle of Kent, and that the warrants sent lately into the said island, under the great seal of the province, for apprehending some malefactors, and to compel others to answer their creditors in their lawful suits of debt or accompt, were disobeyed and contemned, and the prisoners rescued out of the officers' hands, by open force and arms; and being now newly informed, that divers of them do maintain and protect themselves in their said unlawful and rebellious acts, did practice and conspire with the Susquihanoughs and other Indians, against the inhabitants of this colony, have thought it fit, that the governor should sail, in person, to the said isle of Kent, and take along with him a sufficient number of freemen, well armed, and there, by *martial law*, (if it shall be necessary,) reduce the inhabitants of the said island to their due obedience to the lord proprietor, and by death, (if need be,) correct mutinous and seditious offenders, who shall not, (after proclamation made,) submit themselves to a due course of justice; and for his better assistance herein, it was thought fit, and so ordered, that captain Thomas Cornwaleys, esquire, and one of the council of this province, should go along with the governor, and be aiding and assisting to him, to the uttermost of his power, for the command of the forces, according to such directions as he shall receive from the governor during the expedition.

"LEONARD CALVERT,
"JEROME HAWLEY,
"JOHN LEWGER."

To provide for accidents, and to prevent any suspension of legislative proceedings, the governor deputed the secretary, John Lewger, to preside over the house in his absence, and to use his proxy if need occurred.

No record remains of what was done by the governor on the island, nor whether the proclamation of martial law was resorted to. As any summary or violent proceedings would, almost certainly, have been referred to in later debates in the assembly or in public documents, we may reasonably infer that the islanders offered no resistance, and that an amicable arrangement was effected. On the appointed day the House met, pursuant to adjournment, but the governor not having returned, it adjourned to the 5th of March, and on that day again adjourned to the 12th. The governor having now returned, they proceeded to business, and the twenty bills originated by the committee were read a second time. On the next day, fourteen new bills were read, and three on the succeeding day. Whether these seventeen bills embraced any of those sent over by Lord Baltimore we are not informed. In all, forty-two bills were passed this session, of which the titles now only remain. They were sent over to the lord proprietary, and upon them he chose, as before, to exercise his veto power. Thus the colony was left for another year without proper and sufficient laws. This want of legislation, from the peculiar structure of the charter, might have continued indefinitely, had both parties been equally obstinate in insisting upon the right of originating laws; but Lord Baltimore, with magnanimity which did him honor, not only overlooked the indignity offered him, but waived his claim in favor of the assembly, reserving to himself only the right of veto.

This determination was communicated to the governor in the following letter:

"DEAR BROTHER,—I do hereby give you full power and authority from time to time in every general assembly summoned by you in the province of Maryland, in my name to give assent unto such laws as you shall think fit and necessary for the good government of the said province of Maryland, and which shall be consented unto and approved of by the freemen of that province or the major part of them, or their deputies assembled by you there from time to time for the enacting of laws within that province; Provided that the said laws, so to be assented unto, be, as near as conveniently may be, agreeable and not contrary to the laws of England; every which law, so to be assented unto by you in my name, and consented unto and approved of by the freemen aforesaid, I do hereby declare shall be in force within the said province, till I or my heirs shall signify mine or their dissassent thereto, under the great seal of the said province, and no longer, unless, after the transmission thereof unto us, and due consideration had thereupon, I or my heirs shall think fit to confirm the same. Given under my hand and seal at London in the realm of England, the 21st of August, 1638.

"C. BALTIMORE.

"To my dear brother Mr. LEONARD CALVERT esq.
"my lieutenant general of the province of Maryland."

Although this letter does not in *express words* concede to every member of the assembly a right of propounding any law, which he may deem proper to be passed by the house, yet the expressions therein, which authorize the governor "to *give assent* unto such laws as he should think fit and necessary," strongly imply that laws might be proposed in the house by other persons than the governor himself.

The difficulties in the way of legislation being now happily removed, no time was lost by Governor Calvert in availing himself of the permission extended by his brother to the colonists of legislating for themselves. In December he issued orders for summoning an assembly to meet at St. Mary's in the following February; and on the 25th of that month, 1639 (N.S.), the session was opened. This body seems to have been composed partly of representatives chosen by the people (a change which naturally followed on the system of proxies), and partly of gentlemen selected at will by the governor and constituted members by special writ.

At the opening there were present:—The Lieutenant General, Captain Thomas Cornwaleys, Mr. Fulk Brent, Mr. Giles Brent, Mr. Secretary (Lewger), Mr. Thomas Greene, and the following "delegates," viz.: Mr. Gerard and Mr. Gray, for St. Mary's Hundred, Mr. Wickliff and Mr. Revell for St. George's, Mr. Canther and Mr. Price for St. Michael's, Mr. Bishop for Mattapanient, and Mr. Thomas and Mr. Browne for the Isle of Kent.

It appears that immediately after their assembling, "they removed the assembly to be held at St. John's," which was probably the mansion house of the manor of St. John's near the town of St. Mary's, reserved for the use of the Lord Baltimore or his lieutenant general.

The members being reassembled, and the governor and council, together with the gentlemen specially summoned, having taken their seats with the burgesses or delegates, the lord proprietary's letter, herein before inserted, was read.

The first business, which appears to have been transacted in the house, (after reading the foregoing letter), even prior to the formation of rules and orders, was the passing an act entitled, "An act for establishing the house of assembly, and the laws to be made therein;"—which was done "by the general consent of all the freemen and of the lieutenant general for the lord proprietary." The substance of this act was, that "the several persons elected and returned (pursuant to the writs issued), shall be called burgesses, and supply the place of all the freemen consenting to such election, in the same manner and to all the same intents and purposes as the burgesses in any borough in England, in the parliament of England, use to supply the place of the inhabitants of their respective boroughs. And that the gentlemen summoned by his lordship's special writ, to each of them directed, the said burgesses, and such other freemen who have not consented to any of the elections as aforesaid, as shall be at any time assembled, or any twelve or more of them (whereof the lieutenant general and secretary to be always two), shall be called *the house of assembly.* And all acts, etc., assented unto and approved by the said house, or a major part thereof, and afterwards assented unto by the lieutenant general, in the name of the lord proprietary, shall be adjudged and established for laws, to the same force, etc., as if his lordship and all the freemen of this province were personally present and did assent," etc.

In the course of the session a law was passed, providing for the calling together of the legislature once in three years. Thus, in five years after the landing of the first company of emigrants, the colony was established with a settled form of government, and prepared to enjoy all the rights and privileges of an organized and individual community.

The legislation of this session related to the simplest rights of person and property, and the establishment of a judiciary to carry the laws into effect. As a sort of declaration, or bill of rights of the citizen, they adopted the great charter of England. They confirmed to the lord proprietary all his chartered rights. They established a species of county court, a court of chancery, a court of admiralty, and a special court, which they called "pretorial," for the summary trial and punishment of enormous offences.[1]

A bill, passed at this session, displays forcibly the condition of the infant province. A mill for the use of the community was much needed, and the governor and council were authorized to contract for its erection,

[1] Burnap, 106.

provided the cost should not exceed ten thousand pounds of tobacco—the early currency of Maryland, equal, according to the rates of a later period, to the sum of three hundred and thirty-three dollars and thirty-three cents—which was to be raised by general taxation in two years. A similar provision was made for building a "towne-house," by which it was provided, that "every housekeeper should contribute to the said building, either in stuff, workmanship, labour, or tobacco, in such manner and after such rates proportionally to each man's personal estate." Both these laws, while they display the past weakness of the colony, also prove its growing extent and population, which rendered such improvements necessary. Heretofore hand mills had sufficed to grind the wheat and Indian corn in sufficient quantities for the sparse settlements, and the house of the governor was large enough to accommodate their delegates. But with the necessity came the improvement; and the erection of the first water mill and the first state house may be considered no unmomentous epoch in the history of the province.

Such was Maryland at the opening of her career. But this peaceful time was not to be of long endurance, and however wise her rulers, however equitable her government, and however fortunate her circumstances, she was to be allowed no exemption from the common lot. Here, as elsewhere, discontent, envy and ambition were to bear their evil fruit.

The wise and just policy which Governor Calvert pursued toward the Indians, assisted by the labors of the Jesuit missionaries, who either resided at the headquarters of the principal tribes, or made frequent visits to the large towns and villages throughout the province, had hitherto surrounded the infancy of the colony with peace. But as the white settlements extended more and more, and the Indian hunting-grounds were more and more encroached upon, the latter at length, with alarm, perceived the approaching danger in the increase and permanence of the intruding colonists. Symptoms of general discontent were now plainly to be seen among all the tribes inhabiting the shores of the Chesapeake, stirred up, we have no doubt, by the intrigues and false representations of Claiborne.

The Susquehannoughs, who, as we have shown, were one of the boldest and most warlike tribes of Indians found in the province of Maryland, seem to have been now (1639) engaged in hostilities against our colonists. It would appear from facts on record that this state of things was brought about by the interposition of the settlers in behalf of the peaceable and friendly tribes of Piscataway and Patuxent, and probably the Yoamacoes, whom, it would seem, the Susquehannoughs had never ceased to harass since the first settlement of the colony.

As early as 1638, it was found necessary to pass a militia law, which provided that "the captain of the military band," at the direction of the lieutenant general, should "use all power necessary, or conducing, in his discretion, to the safety or defence of the province. And the commander of Kent to do the like within that island." In pursuance of the "Act for

Military Discipline," a commission was issued to Giles Brent, Esq., one of the council, bearing date the 29th of May, 1639, "appointing him to be captain of the military band next under our lieutenant general, requiring him to train and instruct *all the inhabitants of our said colony* able to bear arms (those of our council excepted), in the art and discipline of war on holy-days and at any other time when there should be need; and by himself or his sergeant or other officer, once a month if he should find it needful, to view at every dwelling house within the said colony the provision of necessary arms and ammunition, and where he found any defect to amerce the party failing at his discretion, so that it exceed not 30 lb. tobacco for one default, and further to punish any delinquent in any kind offending against the discipline military." We may suppose that in virtue of these laws and this commission, the inhabitants of the colony were immediately formed into a regular militia, and trained and disciplined accordingly.

Of the details of this year, relating to the military or other transactions of the colony, little now remains. That their wars were not conducted upon a very extensive scale would appear from the following general orders, issued under nearly the same date with the preceding, and signed by Governor Calvert and his council:

"By the lieutenant general and council, 28th May, 1639.

"Whereas it is found necessary forthwith to make an expedition upon the Indians of the eastern shore upon the public charge of the province, it is to that end thought fit that a shallop be sent to Virginia for to provide 20 corsletts, a barrel of powder, four roundlets of shot, a barrel of oat-meal, 3 firkins of butter, and 4 cases of hot waters; and that 5 able persons be pressed to go with the said shallop; and necessary provisions of victuals be made for them; and that a pinnace be pressed to go for Kent[1] sufficiently victualled and manned, and there provide 4 hhds. of meal; and likewise that a pinnace be sent to the Susquehanocks[2] sufficiently victualled and manned, and 30 or more good shotts with necessary officers, be pressed out of the province, and that each of the shott be allowed after the rate of 100 lb of tobacco per month, or another man in his room to tend his plantation, and 2 sergeants double the said rate; and that victuals and other necessary accommodations for the said soldiers and for all others, which shall go as volunteers, be made and provided, and 2 pinnaces and 1 skiff, (if there be need,) shall be pressed and fitted for the transporting and landing of the said companies, and that good labouring hands be pressed to supply the places of such planters as shall be pressed upon the service, and be allowed after the same rate of 100 lb per month.

"LEO. CALVERT,
"GILES BRENT,
"JOHN LEWGER."

What was the result of this expedition no record is left to show. But the order is curious, as exhibiting the resources of the colony at that time, their connections with the Virginians, and their mode of carrying on military operations.

[1] The Isle of Kent.

[2] By this expression, of course, "*against* the Susquehannoughs" is meant.

The next year a commission was issued to Nicholas Hervey, bearing date the 3d of January, 1639 (1640, N.S.), from which it appears that certain Indians of the nation or tribe called the *Maquantequats*, had "committed sundry insolencies and rapines upon the English inhabiting within this province;" for which they had refused to make any satisfaction, as demanded of them. The government was therefore "compelled to enforce them thereto by the justice of a war." This commission, therefore, authorized Hervey, "with any company of English as should be willing to go along with him, so they exceed the number of twelve men sufficiently provided with arms, to invade the said Maquantequats *only*, and against them and their lands and goods to execute and inflict what may be inflicted by the law of war; and the pillage and booty therein gotten to part and divide among the company that shall perform the service." From the express direction above, to make war *only* upon the Maquantequats, it is to be inferred that the colonists were at peace with all other Indians; at least with such as lived in the neighborhood of the Maquantequats. Correspondent with this supposition, a proclamation was issued not long afterwards, bearing date, January 24th 1639 (1640, N.S.), declaring, "that we are in peace and amity with the Patuxent Indians our neighbours, and have taken them into our protection, and therefore do by these presents prohibit all English whatsoever within our province of Maryland for the time being, that they do not offer any injury or outrage whatsoever to any of the said Indians, upon pain of such punishment as the offence shall deserve." It may be here remembered that these Indians of Patuxent seem to have been hitherto uniformly friendly to the colony in conformity to the remarkable sentiment expressed by their king on the first landing of the colonists, as before mentioned.[1]

In the latter end of the year 1638, William Brainthwayte had been appointed captain and commander of the Isle of Kent, in military as well as civil matters, and he appears to have acted as such until the period under review, when a commission was issued to "Captain Giles Brent, Esq., one of the council of our said province," bearing date February 3d, 1639 (1640, N.S.), constituting and appointing him "to be commander of our Isle of Kent within our said province, to rule and govern the inhabitants and all other persons within our said island, according to the powers herein committed to him."

He did not remain long in command, for we find in August of this year Captain Brainthwayte again as commander of the Isle of Kent. In this year also William Claiborne, who then resided in Kecoughton, Virginia, made application through an attorney for the restoration of his property left by him in the Isle of Kent at his departure.

By a letter of attorney, bearing date the 8th of August, 1640, he appointed "George Scovell of Nancimim, in Virginia, his true and lawful attorney to ask, demand, recover, and receive for him, in his name and to his

[1] Bozman, p. 164.

use, all sums of money, debts, cattle, and tobacco debts, and everything whatsoever to him due or payable from any inhabitant of the province of Maryland." In virtue of this authority, Scovell presented a petition to the governor and council of the following purport:

"That captain William Claiborne, at his departure from the isle of Kent, left an estate within your province, as your petitioner is informed, amounting to a good value; since which time divers inhabitants within your province, are possessed of the said estate, but by what right your petitioner knoweth not. Your petitioner's humble request therefore is, the premises considered, that your worships would be pleased not only to allow of your petitioner's letter of attorney, but also to grant unto him free power and liberty, together with your worship's furtherance therein, for the recovery of the aforesaid estate in the hands of any, in whom it shall be found."

The answer thereto is not long, but pithy, as follows:—

"What estate captain William Claiborne left with this province at his departure, undisposed of, on the 24th of March, 1637, the petitioner may know, that it is possessed by right of forfeiture to the lord proprietary for certain crimes of piracy and murder, whereof the said William Claiborne was attainted the day aforesaid by judgment of the house of general assembly. If the petitioner can find out any of the said estate not possessed or held by that right, he shall do well to inform his lordship's attorney of it, that it may be recovered to his lordship's use; but if the said Claiborne, or any other to his use, have since the said day acquired any estate within the province, the law of the province, without any grant or furtherance of governor or commissioners, gives the petitioner or any other attorney of the said Claiborne, free power and authority to recover it, and, when it is recovered, such order shall be taken with it, as justice shall require."

In August another assembly was summoned, and met on the 12th of October, at St. John's, where it remained in session but a short time, and after passing several laws was prorogued until the 5th day of August, 1641. At this latter session the principle of a representative legislature seems to have been fully established, the freemen of the province no longer appeared, as hitherto, in person or by proxy, but by burgesses, chosen, of course, electively, and doubtless in rude imitation of the county and borough representation which the British Parliament rests upon.

Some of the more powerful Indian tribes seem now, in 1641, to have grown confirmed in their discontent with the intrusion of the colonists. The region around the Piscataway settlements was still too much of a frontier, and exposed to the assaults of hostile bands of the natives, to be a safe or attractive spot for peaceful settlers. The fierce Susquehannoughs, who had ever been foes to the colony, took occasion, as they followed the war-path against their savage enemies of the south, or the back settlers of Virginia, to strike a blow at the unprotected Marylanders; and at times they organized expeditions with the express purpose of surprising the frontier plantations, murdering their occupants and plundering their dwellings. Even the devoted and fearless missionaries began seriously to think of abandoning their station, and establishing themselves at Potupaco (Port Tobacco), which was less exposed to the ravages of this cruel and warlike tribe. On the east, also, a number of colonists had been killed, and their dwellings burned; while even the peaceful Patuxents, so long the friends of the colony, showed signs of a hostile disposition.[1] In the latter part of 1640 the governor had authorized, by commission, the high constable of St. Clement's Hundred, in St. Mary's County, to attend Mr. William Britton, gentleman, of that hundred, in demanding of the king or great men of some Indians, who had done him considerable injury in his swine, to make reparation to him, and warning them that if such reparation be refused or delayed, that free liberty should be given to Mr. Britton "to right himself upon any the persons or goods belonging to that town, by all means that he may." Such petty plunders might be considered, indeed, as a natural result from the habits and customs of the American savages; but the inhabitants of the Isle of Kent were threatened with more determined acts of hostility, insomuch that the governor was induced to issue (on the 10th of July, 1641,) a proclamation to the inhabitants of that island of the following tenor: "Whereas it is necessary at this present to stand upon our guard against the Indians, these are therefore to publish, and strictly to prohibit all persons whatsoever, that no man presume to harbour or entertain any Indian whatsoever after notice hereof, upon pain of such punishment as by *martial law* may be inflicted; and I do hereby authorize and declare it lawful to any inhabitant whatsoever of the Isle of Kent, to shoot, wound, or kill any Indian whatsoever coming upon the said island, until further order be given herein."

We see by this proclamation that a state of feeling had arisen between the natives and the colonists in violent contrast with the amity which at first prevailed, the fruit, doubtless, of mutual injuries and aggressions, but above all, of the irreconcileable hostility of their position; a state of things which has never failed to take place where the Indians have long been in close contact with the whites. The Indian feels himself wronged by the very presence of the whites upon his hunting-grounds, and he does not stint himself when the opportunity occurs for vengeance; and the white man finds no safety but in the destruction of his foe.[2]

On the state of things indicated by this proclamation, Bozman remarks: "The Indians thus in hostility to the inhabitants of the Isle of Kent were, most probably, those denominated the *Ozinies*, whose principal residence or town seems to have been, according to Smith, at or near the confluence of the Corsica Creek with the Chester River, in Queen Ann's County, and within fifteen miles from the Narrows or Strait, which separates the Isle of Kent from the main. This tribe of Indians, according to Smith, in his *History of Virginia*, could then turn out, as he was informed, sixty warriors. Had these warriors been armed with fire-arms, they would have been a most formidable enemy, indeed, to the English inhabitants of the Isle of Kent at

[1] Streeter's *Early Papers on Maryland*, p. 167. Md. Hist. Soc. Publications.
[2] Burnap, p. 190.

that time, whose militia or fighting-men did not probably exceed twenty-five in number, as appears from the number of voters thereon in the year preceding."[1]

It is also known that the Susquehannoughs had dominion over a considerable part of the eastern and of the western shore—were the lords of some, the allies of other tribes and confederacies—and in their treaty with the commissioners of Maryland, in 1652, they ceded the territory, including the site of Chestertown, Centreville and Easton.

It will not be out of place to introduce here some facts relating to Kent Island, which, as we have seen, was occupied first by Captain Claiborne about the year 1629. The island at this time was inhabited by the Matapeake Indians, whose village was situated on the southeast side of the island. The site of this village was included in a tract of one hundred acres surveyed for Henry Morgan in 1650, and sold by him the following year to Edward Coppedge, in whose family it remained for several generations.[2] With regard to Claiborne's station, Mr. Davis says:

"The seat of Clayborne's settlement was at Kent Point. There also was the 'Mill,' several of which (that is, windmills) can still be seen. There is not a single waterfall upon the island, and the records mention the 'vane,' and other things, which prove that wind was the motive power.

"Near the 'Mill' was Fort Kent. Fort Crayford stood near Craney Creek, now a pond, and is frequently noticed upon the old records at Chestertown, especially in the deeds containing the boundary lines to tracts of land. It is not named in any of our histories; but the recorded evidence is as strong as that relating to the site of the other fort.

"Kent Fort Manor included Kent Mill and Kent Fort. It was given by the proprietary to Governor Calvert as a reward for his services in the conquest of the island; but assigned to Capt. Giles Brent, whose family, for many generations, held the title."

There was also a court house upon the island, the first on the east side of the Chesapeake. "The Virginians," says Chalmers, "boasted, with their wonted pride, that the colonists of Kent sent burgesses to their assembly, and were subjected to their jurisdiction, before Maryland had a name." And in fact the records show that in 1631–2 the island was represented by Captain Nicholas Martin.

In 1652, Francis Hunt, who lived near the Matapeakes, was "slain by the Indians on the Isle of Kent."[3] After this, we find no other record of any collision or act of violence; from which we may infer that the peaceful rela-

[1] Page 183. The number of voters is, however, no guide to the number of fighting-men, which included servants as well as freemen, and probably young men under the voting age. From the position of the Susquehannoughs in reference to the island, they would seem to have been the invaders. What tribe the Ozinies of Smith composed is very uncertain.

[2] This tract was owned by the late General Emory, and is now a part of Captain Legg's estate. On the rent-roll of a later date it was called "Indian Spring," which name it still bears.

[3] *Kent Records*, 1647-1653, fol. 56.

tions between the Indians and the settlers were not disturbed. A remnant of the tribe, about fifteen in number, were still surviving on the island about a hundred years ago.[1]

This is, however, a tradition, that an atrocious massacre was once perpetrated upon these Indians by the colonists, who invited them to an interview, and while they were performing their humble salutations, slaughtered them without warning. The legend associates this cruel deed with a barren spot, still called "Bloody Point," a little northwest of Kent Point, the southern extremity of the island. At a later day, another tragedy was enacted at Bloody Point in the execution of a French pirate. This pirate had taken a small vessel, and murdered the captain and two boys, who formed the crew Not long after he was seen in Norfolk, wearing the silver knee and shoe-buckles of his victim, marked with the initials of their former owner, and was arrested, taken to Easton, tried and condemned to be hung in chains at Bloody Point, as a terror to all similar offenders that might pass that way. The sentence was executed, and the pirate's skeleton swung from its chain for several years.[2]

On March 2, 1642 (N.S.), Governor Calvert issued a proclamation, summoning an assembly "of all the freemen of the province" to meet at St. Mary's on the 21st of the month. It met on the day appointed, with the unusual number of forty-eight members, six of whom held proxies for thirty more; and two gentlemen, Mr. Lodington and Mr. Thompson, "were admitted for the proxies of *all* the inhabitants of Kent." It seems, therefore, that this was not a meeting of delegates or representatives of the people chosen by the freemen of each hundred, according to the plan adopted at a former session, but an assembly of all the freemen of the province. One object of the meeting seems to have been to provide against anticipated trouble from the Indians, as a bill for an expedition against them was introduced, though it does not appear to have passed.

In the summer of this year the Indians were very troublesome, and kept the planters in perpetual uneasiness. These savages had lately become more formidable by acquiring the possession and use of fire-arms. The sale of either arms or ammunition to them by the colonists had been made penal; but the Swedes and Dutch, who had settled on the Delaware, had no scruples in supplying the Indians with those dangerous articles of merchandise, and it was said, even taught them military discipline. Claiborne, too, was not free from suspicion of stimulating the discontent of his old neighbors and associates.

[1] Mr. James Bryan, a soldier of the Revolution, and born about 1755, says, in a letter to Mr. George Lynn Lachlan Davis:

"I remember the Indians; their last dwelling place was upon the northwest side of the island, near the mouth of Broad Creek; and they lived in their cabins of bark upon a small tract of woodland near the gate which opens upon the estate now owned by General O'Donnell, of Baltimore. I was then a well-grown boy. They always seemed friendly. . . . I also remember the very time of their departure. They left the island near the mouth of the creek, and turned their faces westward. They were the last of the Indians upon the island."

[2] MSS. of Mr. G. L. L. Davis, kindly lent to the author by the Hon. John and Albert Ritchie, administrators of his estate.

This was, indeed, a trying time for Leonard Calvert. In addition to savage hostility without, there was dissatisfaction and discontent within; but he manfully faced the difficulties of his position, and prepared to meet the coming storm. The following "orders" were "proclaimed on the 23d of June, 1642, upon pain of death or other penalties as by severity of martial law may be inflicted:"

"That no inhabitant or housekeeper entertain any Indian upon any colour of license, nor do permit to any Indian any gun, powder and shot. That all housekeepers provide fixed guns and sufficient powder and shot for each person able to bear arms. No man to discharge three guns within the space of one quarter of an hour, nor concur to the discharging so many, except to give or answer alarm. Upon the hearing of an alarm every housekeeper to answer it, and continue it so far as he may. No man able to bear arms to go to church or chapel or any considerable distance from home without fixed gun, and a charge at least of powder and shot. Of these every one required to take notice upon pain of contempt; for better execution the serjeant to inform the lieutenant general or captain."

On the same day the governor commissioned William Blunt, Esq., to be a "captain of the soldiers of St. Mary's County," and sent orders to Robert Evelyn "to take the charge and command of all or any the English in or near about Piscataway, and to levy, train, and muster them," etc. And on July 11th he sent Father Roger Rigby "to repair to the great men of Patuxent and of the nations adjoined to them, and of them to demand in my name" (the lieutenant general,) "to deliver without delay unto Simon Demibiel or Henry Bishop, or any other the bearer or bearers hereof, the persons of such Indians of any of those nations, as shall be named to you by the said Simon or Henry to have done unto them and other English, injury in their swine and otherwise, to the end the said Simon or Henry may bring the said Indians before me to answer such complaints as shall be objected against them by the said Simon or Henry or any others, and certify me what you have done herein, as soon as you may, and this shall be your warrant." He then summoned an assembly to meet on the 18th of July, and to consist of burgesses from each hundred, besides delegates specially called. It was at the opening of this session that Robert Vaughan, a member from Kent Island, proposed that the burgesses should form a separate body by themselves and have a distinct vote, for which there was a good reason, in the fact that the governor, council, and special delegates outnumbered the burgesses, and if they acted in unison, could always control the vote of the house; but the governor would not allow Mr. Vaughan's motion to pass. This important measure became the law of the province, however, at a later day, and was the ground work of that system of "checks and balances," which, in Maryland, as in all other States of English origin, constitutes along with the principle of representation, the peculiar excellence of our scheme of government.

The essential business of the session having been concluded, an expedition against the Indians was then brought forward, but met with the most decided opposition from the members; whereupon the governor informed them that it was not his purpose to ask their advice or consent that an expedition should be organized, for that power, by the provisions of the charter, rested with him alone; he merely wished to know what assistance they would give in case he should think fit to go against the savages. Secretary Lewger moved that a levy of twenty pounds of tobacco per head be laid to defray the charges of "a march," as it was called, but the subject was postponed to the next day, and was not acted upon during the session. Other matters of public interest engaged their attention, and the session closed on the 1st of August.[1]

Father White relates an incident among the events of this year, which serves to show the dangers to which the colonists were constantly exposed:

"An attack having been recently made on a place of ours, they slew the men whom we had there, and carried away our goods, with great loss. And unless they be restrained by force of arms, which we little expect from the counsels of the English, who disagree among themselves, we will not be safe there.

" . . . A certain Indian, called an Anacostan from his country, but now a christian, whilst he was making his way with others through a wood, fell behind his companions a little ahead, when some savages of the tribe of Susquehannoes, which I have mentioned before, attacked him suddenly from an ambuscade, and with a strong and light spear of locust wood, (from which they make their bows), with an iron point oblong at the sides, pierced him through from the right side to the left, at a hand's breath below the armpit near the heart itself with a wound two fingers broad at each side. From the effect of this when the man had fallen, his enemies fly with the utmost precipitation; but his friends who had gone on before, recalled by the sudden noise and shout, return and carry the man from the land to the boat, which was not far distant, and thence to his home at Pascataway, and leave him speechless and out of his senses."[2]

These outrages of the Susquehannoughs were perpetrated, it is probable, within the dominions of the Tayac. Had he been alive, no such thing could have happened. But he had now been dead a year, and his two sons and a daughter were receiving a Christian education at St. Mary's. One hundred and thirty of his people had already been baptized. This fact accounts for the neutrality of the large and powerful tribe of the Piscataways during the Indian wars.

The backwardness of the burgesses did not change the determination of Calvert to punish and subdue the hostile Indians. On the 18th of August, 1642, a commission was issued to Captain Cornwaleys, who is justly characterized by Bozman as "the guardian genius of the colony," to levy men for an expedition, and command them. The following letter was next addressed to Sir William Berkeley, who had become governor of Virginia in January or February of this year, detailing the aggressions of the savages:

"Honoured Sir,

The knowledge I have of your most diligent and provident care of the general good and safety of all his majesty's subjects committed to your charge, and the affection you have to ours of this province your neighbors and fellow subjects, makes me confident to present unto you the necessity, which the barbarous massacres

[1] Streeter's *Maryland Papers*, p. 169. [2] *Relatio Itineris*, p. 85.

committed formerly upon John Angood and four others of his majesty's subjects in his company belonging to your colony, and now lately again upon eight more belonging to this province, together with the burning and robbing of their houses, hath drawn both upon yourself and me [the necessity] of setting forth an expedition against the said Indians, for the vindicating of the honour of our nation, and also to deter the like outrages upon us for the future. For which purpose I have desired this gentleman, colonel Trafford, to present my requests unto you for the aid of one hundred men, furnished and set forth, fitting for the service, from you out of your colony, to be with me at the isle of Kent, where I have appointed our rendezvous on the first of October next, where I will have in readiness one hundred more, if this province will be able to afford them with the safety of those that must be left at home in their houses. Sir, the first harm was yours from the foresaid Indians, which I was desirous to have revenged, had I been able, being nearest to the habitations of them, (as I formerly have done upon the Nanticoke Indians, for the death of one Rowland Williams of Accomack, before the joint expedition made by both colonies). Since we have received this last mischief, by reason yours by Angood's death and his company was no sooner punished, therefore I doubt not, but you will apprehend the necessity, which our general safety for the future requires, that it be no longer deferred, but put in execution with all the speed that may be, to which I will not fail to add what help I can from hence. This gentleman, colonel Trafford, will be able to inform you of all things, that you shall desire to know concerning it from hence. His worth and abilities are known unto you, wherefore give me leave to refer you to him, and rest your faithful friend to serve you,

"From St. Mary's, 23d August, 1642. "LEONARD CALVERT."

"From an expression in the foregoing letter," says Mr. Bozman, "we might infer that a 'joint expedition' against the Indians had been made on a former occasion by both colonies before the one now proposed;[1] but our records afford no other evidence of it; nor do they inform us, whether the aid now asked of Virginia was ever rendered. The government of Maryland continued to make exertions for its own defence. A fort had been erected at or near the Patuxent, in the neighborhood of which, it seems, were several scattered settlements of the English. As a further precaution, Mr. Henry Bishop, who had before this received injury from the Indians of Patuxent in plundering his live stock, was authorized to take command of the fort in that quarter, which was to form a rendezvous of the inhabitants in case of danger; and the following proclamation was issued August 28th, 1642, 'For the purpose of reducing the inhabitants living weakly dispersed in several plantations to some places of better strength, in case of any sudden inroad of Indian robbers and pillagers.'" It was therefore commanded,

"That no inhabitant of this colony presume (until further order or liberty in that behalf,) to discharge, or concur to the discharging of, three guns within the space of one-quarter of an hour upon any occasion whatsoever, unless upon mustering days, except there be reasonable occasion to make an alarm, and that every one, upon the sight of any Indians in any suspicious manner, without delay, use the best means he may to make an

[1] The caution of the excellent Bozman, (from whom we are quoting) is sometimes amusing. When the governor of one province, in an official letter to the governor of another, refers to a joint expedition formerly made by both, certainly we are justified in something more than a mere *inference* that such an expedition had taken place, be the records never so silent.

alarm by the discharging of three guns, and that every house-keeper, upon the hearing of an alarm, answer it by shooting off three guns, and that every house-keeper inhabiting in St. Michael's hundred, between St. Inigoe's creek and Trinity church, immediately upon the knowledge thereof, carry such women and children as are belonging to his family unto St. Inigoe's fort; there to abide for one month from the date hereof, unless liberty be sooner given to the contrary, and I do hereby command and authorise the sheriff of this county to take charge and command of all the persons able to bear arms within the division aforesaid, and to appoint six able men to keep guard in the said fort day and night during the time aforesaid, and I do further appoint and command, that the house-keepers of the other part of St. Michael's hundred, from Trinity creek southward, do carry their women and children to the house of Thomas Steerman, and that lieutenant Thomas Baldridge take charge of the said southern part, and keep guard in like manner as is afore appointed for St. Inigoe's, and further that the house-keepers of St. George's hundred do carry their women and children to the house of Mr. Weston, and that George Pye take charge and command of the said hundred, and appoint and keep guard in like manner as is afore appointed for St. Michael's hundred, and that all several persons of the said several hundreds, able to bear arms, be obedient and assistant unto the said several persons respectively appointed to take charge and command thereof as aforesaid, as they will answer the contrary at their peril, and of all the several commands aforesaid I do hereby require every one to take notice so far as it may or shall concern them, upon the several pains as by martial law may be inflicted upon the contemners of an ordinance so much importing to the common safety."

Finally, the governor publicly proclaimed, on the 13th September, the Susquehanoughs, Wicomeses and Nanticokes "enemies to the province, and as such to be reputed and proceeded against by all persons."

In the midst of these warlike preparations, the attention of the governor was temporarily occupied with the reorganization of the government, made necessary by the arrival of a new commission and new conditions of plantation prepared in England in November of the preceding year. A session of the assembly was deemed expedient, and on the 22d of August, the day before he wrote his letter to Sir William Berkeley, Calvert issued a proclamation to that effect, again adopting the democratic principle, and requiring every freeman inhabiting within the province to be present at St. Mary's, on Monday, the 5th of September, either in person or by proxy. The time of rendezvous at Kent Island was fixed for the 1st of October, on the supposition that before that date the session would be ended, and there would be time sufficient to organize and concentrate the Maryland forces.

The day before the opening of the session (September 4th), the new commission was passed under the great seal of the province, and publicly proclaimed at the fort of St. Mary's; and the next day the same formality was gone through with in regard to a special commission, appointing Colonel Francis Trafford, Thomas Cornwaleys, John Lewger, William Blount, and John Langford, Esqs., members of the privy council of the province.[1]

Among the first bills passed, was one empowering the governor, or any captains under him, "to make an expedition against the Susquehannahs or other Indians as have committed the late outrages upon the English, at such

[1] Streeter's *Maryland Papers*, p. 171.

time and in such manner as he or they shall think fit, to take out of every county or hundred within the province, the third man able to bear arms, such as he or they shall think fit to go upon the said expedition, except that the lieutenant general and his apprentices are not to be reckoned in any hundred to any purpose of this act."

The letter addressed by Calvert to Governor Berkeley, late in August, did not reach James City until the 5th of October, when it was at once laid before the council. That body, on mature consideration, decided to return answer that it was "impossible to comply with this request, as many of the inhabitants were about to remove to new plantations, and were hardly able to get arms and ammunition to defend themselves; and those remaining upon the old plantations, not having a supply of military provisions, besides the heavy hand of God's visitation upon the plantations generally, of which few were recovered."[1]

Except some petty plundering committed by the Indians on the inhabitants of St. Clement's Hundred, some time in October of this year, for which Mr. Gerard and Mr. Neale were authorized, by commission from the lieutenant general, to threaten and punish them, if necessary, our materials furnish no other occurrence of the present year than the appointment of Mr. Giles Brent, by commission of the 16th of December, "to be commander of our isle and *county* of Kent; to be chief captain in all matters of warfare; and to be chief judge in all matters and things civil and criminal, happening within the said island, not extending to life, or member, or freehold." In the same commission also, "William Ludington, Richard Thompson and Robert Vaughan, gentlemen, were appointed to be commissioners within our said island to all powers and effects as to commissioners of a *county* by the law of the province do or shall belong." Commissioners of a county appear to have been then considered as having, not only the powers of conservators of the peace at common law, but as thereby authorized to hold a county court. These gentlemen seem, therefore, to have been now first authorized to hold a county court in the Isle of Kent. Mr. Bozman says:

"This seems to be the first passage, which occurs in the records, wherein the *isle of Kent* was considered as a *county*. By the bill of 1638-9, entitled, 'an act for the government of the isle of Kent,' the island was erected into a *hundred*, to be considered as within the *county* of St. Mary's, 'until another county should be erected of the eastern shore, and no longer.' It appears to have been the sense of those who administered the provincial government in its earliest period, that no *legislative* interposition was neccessary for the erection of a county within the province. Nor is any act of assembly to be found for the original erection of any of the counties in this province (except that of 1650, ch. 8, 'for the erecting of *Providence* into a county, by the name of *Ann Arundel*'), until the year 1695, when by an act of that year (ch. 13), a county was 'constituted' by the name of *Prince George's* county, and the *bounds* of the several counties of St. Mary's, Charles, Prince George's, Talbot, Kent, and Cecil were therein 'regulated;' and, by a distinct clause therein, the *isle of Kent* was 'made part of Talbot county.'—We may, therefore,

[1] Streeter's *Maryland Papers*, p. 178.

suppose that the power of erecting a county within the province was considered as a part of the palatinate *regalia*, and a personal prerogative of the lord Baltimore as lord proprietary of the province; but no proclamation or other *executive* document for the erection of any county within the province in the earliest period of the settlement of the province, or prior to the restoration of the lord proprietary in the year 1658, appears on the records."

After the refusal of the Virginians to join in the expedition against the Indians, it seemed an act of folly to attempt the organization of an expedition with means so limited. Calvert determined, however, to put a bold face on the matter, and on the 16th of January, 1643, issued his proclamation, avowing his determination, "by all possible care and diligence to provide that the colony be put in safety, not only from all danger of the Indians, but from fear of any," and authorized the inhabitants to "shoot" or kill any Indian who should show himself, on land or water, without a white flag, within a district bounded by a straight line drawn from the Patuxent to the Potomac. Ten days after the issuing of this proclamation, it was revoked, except as to the Susquehannoughs and Wicomeses; and public notice was given that a treaty of peace was in negotiation between the authorities and the Nanticokes, formerly declared enemies of the province, for perfecting which, a truce of six weeks had been agreed upon, during which time they were to be under his lordship's protection. Of all the tribes or nations of Maryland, except the Susquehannoughs and Wicomeses, the Nanticokes appear to have been the most warlike, and they were frequently so bold as to carry their hostilities across the bay against the inhabitants of St. Mary's.

The governor now formed a resolution to go to England, and on the 15th April, 1643, he appointed Mr. Giles Brent to act with full powers as governor during his absence. Before his departure from St. Mary's, the oath was administered to Mr. Brent, in which he declared that he would "do equal right and justice to the poor and to the rich after his cunning, wit and power, according to the laws of the province, and to delay nor to deny to any man right or justice."

The departure of Leonard Calvert caused no interruption in the design to chastise the savage invaders of the province. Scarcely had he lost sight of its shores, when a commission was issued by Brent to Cornwaleys (April 17th), appointing him captain general of a force to be led against "the Susquehannoughs or other Indians," who had been concerned in the late outrages, to take, if necessary, every third man to make up the number required, and to lead forth the expedition at such time and in such manner as he should deem fit. And yet, the very next day the council, on the plea of the difficulty, and indeed the impossibility of organizing an expedition for the present, determined to raise a company of ten good marksmen, and post them, as a garrison, fully armed and equipped, upon Palmer's Island, in the mouth of the Susquehannah, to keep an eye on the movements of the formidable tribe, whose fort was a few miles above the falls of that river, on the eastern bank, and prevent their war parties from coming down the bay to assault and ravage the unprotected frontiers of the colony.

The outrages of the Susquehannoughs aroused the martial spirit of the gallant Captain Cornwaleys, who applied to Governor Brent for authority to raise a band of volunteers and make an expedition against them. The authority was readily granted, and the expedition, no doubt, made, though the scanty colonial records have preserved no account of it. Some facts, however, are preserved in Plantagenet's *New Albion*,[1] which throw a faint light upon his proceedings. The author, after stating that the Swedes, then settled on the Delaware, had sold arms and ammunition to the Indians, asserts "that they had hired out their soldiers to the Susquehannoughs, who, training the tribe to the use of arms and to European tactics, had led them into Maryland and Virginia, and assisted them to take the chief of the Potomacks prisoner, and to subdue eight Indian tribes in Maryland that had been civilized and subjected to the English crown." He then goes on to say, that "of the Susquehannoughs, there are not now of the naturals left above one hundred and ten, though, with their forced auxiliaries, the *Ihonadoes* [Oneidas, perhaps,] and *Wicomeses*, they can make two hundred and fifty," and, after some disparaging but unjust expressions in relation to their courage, adds—"these two hundred and fifty, having surprised in the reeds and killed three Englishmen, with the losse of one of theirs, Capt. Cornwallis, that noble, right valiant and politic soldier, losing but one man more, killed with fifty-three of his, and but raw and tired Marylanders, twenty-nine Indians, as they confessed, though compassed round with two hundred and fifty." Yet this severe chastisement did not, it seems, suffice; for on July 18th, another commission was issued to the captain to lead an expedition "against the Susquihanowes or any their aiders and confederates," the result of which expedition, if ever made, is not upon record. Either that or a subsequent expedition must have ended disastrously, for in a set of instructions issued in June of the next year to Captain Fleete, who was to go up to Piscataway fort with a strong party to negotiate with a deputation of the Susquehannoughs who were to be there, one article especially directed him to obtain the restitution of "as much as he could get of the arms and other goods lost or left in the last march upon them, at least the two field pieces."

While these warlike Indians were threatening the colony on the north, Captain Richard Ingle, an associate of Claiborne, and a pirate and rebel, was discovered hovering about the settlement with an armed ship, holding communications with, and endeavoring to strengthen the numbers of the disaffected. Governor Brent immediately issued the following proclamation ordering his arrest and the seizure of his ship:

[1] Printed in 1648. The passage is quoted in Streeter's *Papers*.

"*26th January, 1643.*

"PROCLAMATION AGAINST RICHARD INGLE.

"I do hereby require, in his majesty's name, Richard Ingle, mariner, to yield his body to Robert Ellyson sheriff of this county, before the first day of February next, to answer to such crimes of treason, as on his majesty's behalf shall be objected against him, upon his utmost peril of the law in that behalf; and I do further require all persons, that can say or disclose any matter of treason against the said Richard Ingle to inform his lordship's attorney of it at some time before the said court to the end it may be then and there prosecuted.

"G. BRENT."

Ingle was taken, but soon succeeded in making his escape, to join Claiborne and concoct fresh designs against the peace of the province.

Some idea of the disagreeable situation of the frontier settlements of St. Mary's at this time may be derived from the following proclamation, issued by Governor Brent, on the 4th of May, 1644:

"I authorize the inhabitants upon Patuxent River (being they are so far from other plantations, and so weakly peopled, and continually exposed thereby to danger and outrage from the Indians as well friends as enemies, by whom they received an assault to their very near cutting off one of their plantations last year, besides the eminent losses they have otherwise received), that upon approach of any Indian whatsoever, unto them in the woods, their plantations or houses, they may (after having bid the said Indian depart, and declared that if they do not depart they will shoot them) shoot them whatsoever Indians they are; which bidding them depart I do enjoin the inhabitants unto, in case the Indians shall be of our friends, until the 25th of May next, in which time all the said Indian friends shall have notice not to approach the said plantations, and after the said 25th of May, I do license the said inhabitants to shoot and kill any Indians, coming about their woods, plantations, or dwellings, without the foresaid warning given. Witness my hand.

"GILES BRENT.

"The same authority I do give them against any Indians upon the water between the back river of Patuxent and the mouth of Patuxent river."

We find, about a month afterwards, a protection or "pass" under the great seal, issued by the governor, bearing date the 8th of June, 1644, declaring:

"That the bearer hereof, Peter Mimascave, alias Nicoatmen, an Indian of Patuxent, and all other Indians of that town and nation are within our protection, peace and amity, to be treated and used with all humanity as our friends and confederates, until they shall give cause to the contrary; and therefore we do hereby require all and every of you (inhabitants of the county of St. Mary's), upon the utmost peril that may be by law inflicted upon the transgressors hereof, that you commit not any hostile act or outrage upon him, the said Peter, or any other of his town and nation, unless it be such as shall put you in fear of your lives by repairing to any of your houses or plantations in numbers lurking or other suspicious manner, without shewing or holding forth this or some other instrument or pass under our great seal, but that you suffer him and them quietly to pass and repass to or from the houses of our lieutenant-general and council or any of them, according to the full intent and effect of this our safe-conduct."

About ten days later, Secretary Lewger received information that the Susquehannoughs were expected at Piscataway, either with the intention of negotiating a peace or with designs of inveigling the friendly Indians of Piscataway into a confederacy with them. He immediately issued a commission to Captain Henry Fleete—the same who was found by the first colonists living among the Indians at Piscataway, and highly esteemed by them—dated June 18th, 1644, empowering him to treat with them for the conclusion of a stable peace. He was instructed to stipulate for the inclusion of the Patowmacks and other friendly Indians in the peace; for the return of arms lost by the whites, including the two field-pieces before mentioned; for satisfaction for certain acts of plunder, and for an exchange of hostages. In case they would agree to a peace, he was to promise them the assistance of the colonists in their wars. In case, however, they proved intractable, or he should see reason to deem such a treaty impolitic, he was authorized to make war upon them, and, as far as possible, detach them from the less hostile tribes.

The conduct of Mr. Lewger in issuing this commission gave offence to Governor Brent, who deemed it an overstepping of his powers, and on the 26th August, 1644, suspended him from his office and revoked all commissions granted by him. The differences between them were, however, put an end to by the return of Leonard Calvert in September, and his resumption of his office. He brought new commissions from the lord proprietary for himself and others, and among the rest, one for Mr. Lewger, re-appointing him secretary of the province, and constituting him attorney-general, judge of causes testamentary and matrimonial, register of the land office, and councillor, so that his latter state was greater than his former.

Governor Calvert found the province much disturbed. The Indians were still threatening, Ingle was at large, and Claiborne was preparing, if he had not already begun, hostilities in the island of Kent. Without taking much time to repose himself after his long voyage, Calvert made a brief visit to the governor of Virginia, probably to counteract Claiborne's machinations in that province, and on his return issued a proclamation on November 16th, convening the assembly. He also issued a commision to Mark Pheypo and John Genalles to take command of a shallop and eight men, and repair secretly to the Isle of Kent, where they were to deliver dispatches to Captain Brent, and find out whether Claiborne was upon the island or not, and if so, with what force, and whether he had committed any outrage there. On January 1st, 1645, we find notice of a proclamation to be published on the island declaring Claiborne and one Richard Thompson enemies of the province, and prohibiting trade with the island, the command of which is given in a commission of the same date to Captain William Brainthwayte.

One of the most disastrous results of Claiborne's rebellion was the destruction or loss of most of the records of the province, so that we are left much in the dark as to the means used by that leader and his associate Ingle to win followers to his plans and foment disaffection to the proprietary and his government. The last that was heard of Claiborne previous to his invasion of Maryland, was in 1642. It appears by the records that he applied to the assembly to restore his property forfeited eight years before, and that his petition was refused. About this time he received from the king the appointment of treasurer of Virginia for life. As the king's cause waned, Claiborne sought favor with the winning side, and became a zealous partisan of parliament. All things now seemed favorable for his plans. Parties arose in the colonies corresponding to those which were contending in the mother country, and their influence rose and fell with the fortunes of war across the Atlantic. On July 2d, 1644, was fought the battle of Marston Moor, which nearly prostrated the royal cause, and increased the boldness of its adversaries.

Lord Baltimore had naturally taken side, at an early period of the quarrel, with the king, who had given him such signal proofs of friendship and favor; and as he was not the man to forsake his sovereign in the hour of his adversity, the preponderating power of parliament and their animosity against "malignants" rendered his possessions in Maryland very insecure, and weakened his authority with his colonists.

Of these favorable circumstances Claiborne was not slow to avail himself. He seized Kent Island without difficulty, and in conjunction with Ingle invaded the western shore. We have no account of his movements, nor what resistance was offered; but the expedition was completely successful. The proprietary government was overthrown, Governor Calvert compelled to take refuge in Virginia, and for nearly two years Claiborne and his faction maintained themselves in power. During this period those who had remained faithful to the proprietary suffered severely. Some were stripped of all their possessions and driven into exile; while those who were allowed to remain were ruined by fines and confiscations. Even the pious missionaries among the Indians, who had abstained from any mingling with the political questions of the day, were seized, their stations broken up, and they themselves, with the venerable Father White, the apostle of Maryland, sent in chains to England, where long imprisonment awaited them.

In an address of the assembly of Maryland to Lord Baltimore, in the year 1649, these two years of usurpation are thus described:

"Right Hon'ble:

"Great and many have been the miseries calamities and other sufferings which your poor distressed people inhabitants of this province have sustained and undergone here since the beginning of the heinous rebellion first put in practice by that pirate Ingle and afterwards almost for two years continued by his accomplices and confederates in which time most of your lordship's loyal friends here were spoiled of their whole estate and sent away as banished persons out of the province those few that remained were plundered and deprived in a manner of all livelyhood and subsistence only breathing under that intolerable yoke which they were forced to bear under those rebels which then assumed the govt. of your lordship's province unto themselves ever endeavouring by oaths and what other inventions and practices they might to withdraw the ears and affections of the inhabitants here from their wonted obedience to your lordship and to assure themselves of the province so wrongfully taken and unjustly possessed by them which our sufferings we hope your honour apprehends and is sensible and which tho' they were ever violent even like a tempest for the time yet now (thanks be to God) all is past and calm and the whole province in perfect subjection again under your lawful government and authority during all which time your honour cannot be ignorant what pains and travail your friends underwent in aiding your dear brother for the subduing of those rebels and after again in conserving the province for your lordship never sparing labour cost or estate which they were or could be possessed of until they had accomplished their intended purpose and desires in regaining it again and settled it under your lordship's protection and dominion."

Thus, even from the meagre and imperfect records which remain, we can see how Maryland, meant to be the abode of peace, was drawn into the vortex of the unhappy contentions which were convulsing the mother-country, and here, as well as there, religious differences embittered political controversies. Discordant elements had found their way into the province; and the "calm" for which the assembly was piously thankful, was but a brief and deceitful lull in the tempest.

After his rebellion in Maryland, Ingle returned to England, and while there, Captain Cornwaleys entered suit against him for the recovery of about £3000, for damages which he had suffered in the destruction of his property during the rebellion. Cornwaleys, who appears to have lived in considerable affluence, in his declaration[1] alleged that Ingle, in February, 1645, had incited his servants to rebellion, and led by a certain John Sturman, his son Thomas, and William Hardwick, they took possession of his mansion, burned his fences, killed his swine, carried off his cattle, wrenched off the locks of his doors, and damaged his estate to the amount of about £3000.

In response to this suit, Ingle appealed, in February, 1646, in the following memorial to the lords in parliament assembled:

"The humble petition of Richard Ingle showing: That whereas the petitioner, having taken the covenant, and going out with letters of marque, as Captain of the ship *Reformation*, of London, and sailing to Maryland, where finding the Governor of that province to have received a commission from Oxford to seize upon all ships belonging to London, and to execute a tyrannical power against the Protestants, and such as adhered to the Parliament, and to press wicked oaths upon them, and to endeavor their extirpation, the petitioner, conceiving himself, not only by his warrant, but in his fidelity to the Parliament, to be conscientiously obliged to come to their assistance, did venture his life and fortune in landing his men and assisting the said well affected Protestants against the said tyrannical government and the Papists and malignants. It pleased God to enable him to take divers places from them, and to make him a support to the said well affected. But since his return to England, the said Papists and malignants, conspiring together, have brought fictitious acts against him, at the common law, in the name of Thomas Cornwallis and others, for pretended trespass in taking away their goods, in the parish of St. Christopher's, London, which are the very goods that were by force of war

[1] He represents himself as possessing "a comfortable dwelling-house, furnished with plate, linen hangings, bedding, brass, pewter, and all manner of household stuff, worth at least a thousand pounds, about twenty servants, at least a hundred breed cattle, a great stock of swine and goats, some sheep and horses, a new pinnace about twenty tons, well rigged and fitted, besides a new shallop and other small boats."

justly and lawfully taken from these wicked Papists and malignants in Maryland, and with which he relieved the poor distressed Protestants there, who otherwise must have starved, and been rooted out.

"Now, forasmuch as your Lordships in Parliament of State, by the order annexed, were pleased to direct an ordinance to be framed for the settlement of the said province of Maryland, under the Committee of Plantations, and for the indemnity of the actors in it, and for that such false and feigned actions for matters of war acted in foreign parts, are not tryable at common law, but, if at all, before the Court and Marshal; and for that it would be a dangerous example to permit Papists and malignants to bring actions of trespass or otherwise against the well affected for fighting and standing for the Parliament:

"The petitioner most humbly beseecheth your Lordships to be pleased to direct that this business may be heard before your Lordships at the bar, or to refer it to a committee to report the true state of the case, and to order that the said suits against the petitioner at the common law may be stayed, and no further proceeded in."

CHAPTER VII.

In studying the rise of Claiborne's rebellion, the difficult question to answer is, how came he to be so strongly supported? His own feelings in the matter are easy to understand: as a Virginian of position and influence, and a Protestant, he objected to being brought under another jurisdiction administered by Catholics. Moreover, at his far-away station, with authority little less than supreme over all around him, he occupied an almost princely position; and he was now to be reduced to the rank of an ordinary planter or trader, and subject to the same control. But for him to obtain so large a following that he was able to overthrow the proprietary government, it would seem as if there had been no small amount of discontent in the colony.

Yet, in vain do we search in the public records for evidence of any misrule or oppression on the part of the governor which could arouse any general dissatisfaction. So far as the Protestant religion was concerned, the course of the laws and the administration up to the time of the governor's departure for England had been one of entire neutrality. Neither the proprietary nor the governor is anywhere charged by the assembly with any act or intention aiming at the exclusive establishment of his own church or the injury of the Protestant; nor can we discover such by the most diligent search. If Claiborne succeeded in arousing Protestant apprehensions, they were apprehensions of a merely chimerical nature for which no just cause was ever given.

As we have already shown, the evidence leads to the conclusion that the colony, though containing many non-Catholics, was a Roman Catholic settlement originally, and so continued until 1649, when the great Toleration Act was passed. But this act introduced no new principle nor policy into the government of the colony; it was but the legislative sanction and declaration of a principle and policy practised from the beginning. And these facts, that Maryland thus took the lead in religious freedom, and was the first community in modern times in which the civil was effectually separated from the ecclesiastical power, not only do high honor to its founders, but are of deep importance in the history of the world.

Various attempts have been made, either to deny the facts, or to detract from the honor of the founders; and to these we shall give some attention.

It has been asserted that Calvert, so far from being desirous to found an asylum for the persecuted of his own faith, was indifferent about religion, and solicited the grant for ambitious and mercenary objects alone. To this his acts furnish a sufficient answer. We have seen him embracing and making open profession of a faith which was in the minority, and subject to disabilities and persecution. This does not look like indifferentism. And we have seen him, for the sake of his faith, resigning offices of great power and influence and of opulent revenue. Do ambitious and mercenary men so act? Nor can these charges be brought against Cæcilius. From the time of his embracing the Roman Catholic faith, he cherished the idea of founding an asylum where its professors might exercise their worship unmolested. The charter of Maryland—prepared, as is generally admitted, either by his father, or under his direction—gave him the desired opportunity. His first movement was to collect a band of Catholic gentlemen and their retainers, to associate with them Catholic priests willing to brave the hardships and perils of the new world; and these he sent out, under the direction of his brother, to his new domain. No sooner do they touch the shores than they engage in solemn thanksgiving with all the forms of Roman Catholic worship; an altar and a cross are erected; litanies sung, and mass celebrated. Next, they name capes and islands, bays, rivers, and their new city after saints; showing not only the religious feeling that inspired them, but their eagerness to enjoy their new freedom. These facts, and a host of others in the early history of the colony, show the motives and intentions of the founders and first settlers in a light so clear that misty speculations and *a priori* inferences vanish before it.

The early writers on Maryland history confirm our views, not argumentatively, but as facts undenied and unquestioned.

Robert Beverly, in his *History of Virginia*, published in London in 1722, says: In 1628 [1629], five years before the settlement of Maryland, "Calvert (Lord Baltimore), a Roman Catholic, thought, for the more quiet exercise of his religion, to retire from his family into the new world. For this purpose he went to Virginia to try how he liked the place, but the people there looked upon him with an evil eye on account of his religion, for which alone he sought this retreat, and by their ill-treatment discouraged him from settling in that country."

Wynne, in his history of America published in London in 1776, says: "His Lordship (Sir George Calvert,) was a Catholic, and had formed his design of making this settlement in order to enjoy a liberty of conscience which, though the government of England was by no means disposed to deny, yet the rigor of the laws threatened in a great measure to deprive him, the severity of which it was not in the power of the court to relax. This settlement of the colony cost Lord Baltimore a large sum. It was made under his auspices, by his brother, and about 200 persons, Roman Catholics, and most of them of good families. No people could live in greater ease and security; and his lordship, willing that as many as possible should enjoy the benefits of his mild and equitable administration, gave his consent to an Act of Assembly, which he had before promoted in his province, for allowing a free and unlimited toleration to all who professed the Christian religion, of whatever denominations. This liberty, which was never in the least violated, encouraged a great number, not only of the Church of England, of Presbyterians, Quakers, and all kinds of dissenters, to settle in Maryland, which before that time, was almost wholly in the hands of Roman Catholics. When, upon the revolution, power changed hands in the province, the new men made but an indifferent requital for the liberties and indulgences they had enjoyed under the old administration. They not only deprived the harmless Catholics of all share in government, and of all the rights of freemen, but they even adopted the whole body of the penal laws of England against them."

Douglass, in his *Summary*, vol. ii, London, 1760, says: "Upon a new royal regulation in Virginia, several families went over from England to settle there; amongst them was Lord Baltimore, a rigid Roman Catholic; for the advantage of a more full exercise of his religion he retired thither."

The article "Maryland" in the *Modern Universal History*, published in London in 1780, has the following account of the motives and objects of our colonists: "The Lord Baltimore, who was of the Roman Catholic religion, and had obtained the grant to be an asylum to himself and those of his persuasion from the persecutions of the times, appointed his brother Lionel [Leonard,] Calvert, governor of his new colony, etc. The first plantations, consisting of about two hundred colonists, were sent thither in 1633, chiefly, if not wholly Roman Catholics, many of them gentlemen of fortune; and, like the Protestants of New England, their settlement was founded upon a strong desire for the unmolested practice of their own religion."

In addition to this testimony, we have public documents which prove that these motives were admitted in Maryland.

About the year 1751 the policy of requiring Catholics to pay on their lands double the amount of taxes exacted from the Protestant inhabitants, was first introduced. On this occasion, among other efforts to protect themselves from this unreasonable and unjust imposition, they addressed a petition to the governor, which contains the following passage:

"Many Roman Catholic gentlemen, of good and ancient families in the kingdoms of England and Ireland, and many others of lesser note, to avoid the penal laws in force in their native countries, and other vexations to which they were liable at home, quitted their countries, their friends and relations, and everything dear to them, to enjoy these privileges, that freedom, liberty, and equality in everything here, especially a full liberty of conscience, and to that end only transported themselves into this province." And in another place, in the same petition, they say: "For the province being granted to a Roman Catholic, the act concerning religion having passed, etc., the Roman Catholics looked upon Maryland as an asylum and place of rest for themselves and their posterity."

At a later date, 1758, the Upper House of Assembly refused to require the double tax from Catholics, and among other reasons gave the following:

"'The first settlement of this province was made by the Roman Catholics who had been driven from their native country by the severity of its laws, and an Act for an unlimited toleration of all Christians passed in 1649, after they had been promised and allowed an asylum here," etc. The Lower House, in reply, says: "As we have never discovered anything in history, or otherwise, that will justify or even countenance your assertion that the Papists were promised and allowed an asylum here, we should be glad to have it explained to us," etc. This explanation is furnished very amply in the rejoinder of the Upper House, of which the following is a part: "You have been pleased to remark, upon the passage of our message, that you have not been able to discover anything in history or otherwise to justify or countenance our assertions that the Papists were promised and allowed an asylum here. It may be so, but it is not our fault that you have not, and to be plain with you, we should have restrained from telling you what you have been pleased to acknowledge, by the apprehension of its offence. However, as you have desired to have this matter explained and we flatter ourselves it may have some effect, we shall undertake to do it in as full a manner as the shortness of the time will admit." After quoting some introductory passages of the charter, the explanation proceeds: "After the charter was thus granted to Lord Baltimore, who was then a Roman Catholic, his lordship emitted his proclamation to encourage the settlement of his province, promising therein, among other things, liberty of conscience, and any equal exercise of religion to every denomination of Christians who would transport themselves and reside in his province, and that he would procure a law to be passed for that purpose afterwards. The first or second assembly that met after the colonists arrived here, some time in the year 1638, a perpetual law was passed, in pursuance of his lordship's promise, and, indeed, such a law was easily obtained from those who were the first settlers. This act was confirmed in 1649 and again in 1650." Then follows the act: "The grant to Lord Baltimore, who was a Papist, his lordship's promises and declarations, the confirmations of them by acts of assembly, and the oaths we have recited, we hope will amply justify our assertion that the Roman Catholics were promised and allowed an asylum here."

"As you have been pleased to say that you have not discovered anything in history, or otherwise, to countenance our assertion, we shall mention some passages from books for your satisfaction, though we must observe to you that writers may be mistaken or misrepresented; but the evidence we have produced can't mislead. Mr. Bowen, speaking of Maryland, says: 'The first colony sent to Maryland was in 1633, and consisted of two hundred people. The chief of these adventurers were gentlemen of good families, and Roman Catholics; for persons of that religion being made uneasy as well as Protestant dissenters, they transported themselves to this province, hoping to enjoy there the liberty of their consciences, under a proprietary of their own profession, as the then Lord Baltimore was.'" The same paper contains numerous extracts from various other historians to the same purpose, and concludes this branch of the subject with remarking: "Many other passages from books to the like effect might be cited, but we presume they would be unnecessary."

In Governor Sharpe's MS. Letterbook, in the Maryland State library, there is a letter written by him, December 15, 1758, to the lord proprietary in England, in which he says: "It might, perhaps, be unknown, if not to the authors, at least to some of the propagators of the above mentioned report, that the people who first settled in this province were, for the most part, Roman Catholics, and that, although every other sect was tolerated, a majority of the inhabitants continued Papists till the revolution, soon after which event an act was made here for the support of a clergyman of the Church of England in every parish, which is still in force; and the Papists, as well as Protestants, are thereby obliged to pay annually very considerable sums for that purpose." "Upon the whole, my lord, I must say that, if I was asked whether the conduct of the Protestants or Papists in the province hath been most unexceptionable since I have had the honor to serve your lordship, I should not hesitate to give an answer in favor of the latter."

And now, with such evidence as the early Protestant writers on Maryland furnish, sustained by the testimony of a Protestant legislature of 1758—for no Catholic was then eligible as a member, or even entitled to vote for members—it is hard to give any charitable explanation of the conduct of writers who seize upon the facts of history and deduce therefrom arguments against the motives of Calvert and his colonists, which these facts in no way sustain—which they scarcely suggest.

As for those who attribute to Sir George Calvert mere mercenary motives, and look upon his attempts at colonization as so many commercial speculations, they, as we have already shown, are sufficiently answered by his public conduct. That he trusted his colony would flourish and prosper, is a matter of course; and that, in the course of time, when it was populous and prosperous, his heirs would reap a return for all his labor and expense, was a natural and laudable hope; but this was not the nearest motive with him. His contemporary, Fuller, judged him truly, when he said: "Indeed his public spirit consulted not his private profit, but the enlargement of Christianity and the king's domains." Power, wealth, and high position were already within his grasp; and to attain his utmost desires in either, he had nothing to do but to avoid open profession of his faith, and retain his assured place in the affection of the king.

There are other objectors who, admitting the existence of toleration in Maryland, endeavor to deprive the proprietary and the founders of the colony of the honor of introducing it, on the ground that it was in the charter, and that they were hindered by that instrument from displaying the same persecuting spirit that was active elsewhere—in the other colonies, for instance. Even if the facts were as stated, it is but a weak charge to impute to a man things which he did not do, on the ground that if circumstances had been altogether otherwise, he might, or would, have done them. And if the credit of Maryland toleration be due to the charter, to whom does the charter owe it but to Calvert, its inspiring spirit? The facts, however, are not as alleged; and this we shall attempt to show.

The composition of the charter was a matter of some delicacy. To extend the disabling laws of England to the colony would have been an insult and injury to the grantee, and have frustrated the very purpose for which he asked the grant. To offer open protection to the Catholics, and proclaim general toleration throughout the empire—even had Charles been so inclined—would have brought down upon the king the vengeance of parliament, and shaken the very pillars of his throne. Even to establish toleration and equality of rights to the disfranchised church in far-off Maryland, would have been an experiment too hazardous. But the charter is so constructed as to provide for both the repose of the king and the freedom of the colonists; to secure the rights of Charles without wounding the conscience of Calvert. The proviso concerning religion reads:

"Provided always that no interpretation thereof [of the charter] be made whereby *God's holy and true Christian religion*, or the allegiance due to us," etc., "may in any wise suffer by change, prejudice, or diminution."—"*Sacrosancta et vera Christiana religio.*"[1] If these words mean the Church of England, then there is no toleration in the charter, and freedom for Catholics and dissenters was no more secured in Maryland than in England; for a connivance—much more a toleration—was looked upon in those days as a

[1] Col. Brantz Mayer, commenting upon this phrase of the charter: "*Sacrosancta Dei et vera Christiana religio,*" argues that it should be rendered, "God's holy *rights* and the true Christian religion." This version would then require us to dissociate the adjective *sacrosancta* from the noun with which it agrees in both grammar and sense, and regard it as used absolutely, with the meaning "holy rights." The phrase, however, is not peculiar to the charter of Maryland, occurring in that of Avalon, with the difference of *vere* for *vera*.

It is admitted that the cancellary style was not precisely that of the Augustan age: but still these charters are in grammatical Latin, and subject to the ordinary rules of grammatical interpretation, which certainly require the adjective to be referred to the nearest noun with which it agrees, unless either the context or the idiom of the language compels us to a different construction. In this way the phrase has been construed by all who have cited it, at various periods of Maryland's history, down to Col. Mayer. To establish a version so constrained and unusual, and opposed to all preceding interpretation, Col. Mayer should have shown that *sacrosancta* is ever used in Latin for "holy rights"; or at least some instance of its use absolutely, without the noun qualified. This he has not done, and we believe—a belief in which we are confirmed by a gentleman who is probably the first Latinist in the country—that he can produce no such instance.

But the most conclusive proof that the natural construction, as given by Bacon, is the correct one, is found in the contemporary version of Commissioners Bennet and Mathews, men who were thoroughly qualified to understand not only the Latin text, but the spirit and meaning of the charter, which they vehemently attacked, and who would certainly not have neglected the opening that such a reading, if correct, would have given them. They say:

"By the patent it is provided that no construction be made thereof whereby God's holy and truly Christian religion, or the heirs and successors of the crown of England, should receive any prejudice or diminution."—*Objections against Lord Baltimore's Patent*, A.D. 1656.

"Another clause in his patent is that no construction be made thereof whereby God's holy and true Christian religion . . . shall receive any prejudice or diminution."—*A Paper relating to Maryland*, A.D. 1656.

Both these extracts are from Thurloe's *State Papers* in Hazard, i., pp. 621, 624.

diminution of the rights of the established church. But there is a positive as well as a negative reference to religion in the charter. The preamble recites that Lord Baltimore has solicited this grant, "treading in the footsteps of his father, and being animated with a laudable and pious zeal for extending the Christian religion"—"*patris inhaerens vestigiis, laudabili quodam et pio Christianam religionem dilatandi studio.*" Here we have the intention of spreading the Christian religion plainly expressed. This was not establishing the English church, for that Calvert could not have done, nor was it looked for of him; it was not to establish the Catholic church, for that, as we have shown, the king could not have granted consistently with his own security, and such a grant would have been a "diminution" of the rights of the Church of England. But the words here, as in the proviso, simply refer to Christianity at large; they provide that the colony shall be a Christian and not a heathen or infidel colony, and with this provision leave the particular form of Christian worship that was to be observed by the colonists, to be determined by the colonists themselves.[1]

Under their charter, therefore, the proprietary and the colonists could have passed laws prohibiting the exercise of a special form of worship, or excluding certain persons under pains and penalties, or laying a tax upon their admission, as was indeed done after the Protestant revolution, and continued under this very charter down to the war of Independence, for the purpose of preventing the increase of Catholics. So long as the colony was professedly Christian the letter of the charter was not broken. Further evidence is found in the form of the power to make laws, etc., which required them to be in accordance with the laws of England, "as far as conveniently may be." It would certainly have been very inconvenient for the Catholic proprietary, his Catholic governor and settlers to re-enact the English laws against their faith, to escape which was the great inducement that drew them across the ocean and into the wilderness.

Contemporary expositions of these sections will throw a still clearer light upon them. Lord Baltimore was also authorized to hold "the patronages and advowsons of all churches which (with the increasing worship and religion of CHRIST) happen to be built, together *with license and faculty* of erecting and founding churches and chapels, etc., and of causing them to be dedicated and consecrated according to the ecclesiastical laws of our kingdom of England." A mere power to do so, not an obligation on the part of Lord Baltimore to comply with it. For in England, a Catholic could hold the advowson of a parish of the established church. Now, when some forty-four years after the settlement, the Episcopal clergy of the province petitioned the government against the proprietary, and demanded a *provision* for themselves, because the Catholic clergy held lands for their support, Lord Baltimore replied that the Catholic clergy had obtained their lands as other settlers had done, under "the conditions of

[1] Col. Brantz Mayer's *Calvert and Penn.* Pa. Hist. Soc.

plantations." He was advised by the Board of Trade and Plantations to provide the Episcopal clergy with a public support. He refused to do so, for no other clergy in the province had received it, and so the matter ended. Now if the English church in Maryland had secured the rights it possessed under the English law, it would have had its tithes and its glebes, and Lord Baltimore could not have protected himself from the claim as he did, under the royal charter to his ancestor. This was changed afterwards, and under Protestant rule the English church was established by act of assembly, glebe lands provided, and tithes levied upon men of all religions or none, to support its clergy.

Thus we see that the charter neither enforced toleration nor forbade it. It left the whole matter under the control of the colonists and the proprietary, while, by its general phrases, the king was protected and Calvert shielded. Indeed, there is evidence of a constant care to secure the proprietary in the use of the word "allegiance," and the omission of the word "supremacy." Allegiance every Catholic was bound to give to his sovereign or his country; spiritual supremacy of the king no Catholic could hold and remain a Catholic. Calvert yielded nothing which his fidelity to the faith he had just adopted prohibited—he gave nothing which he could not conscientiously give. He was true and faithful in his legitimate duty to his king, and equally true and faithful in the duty which he owed to his God. So far, this charter from Charles to Calvert is worthy of much honor, for to be *negatively* tolerant—not to be a persecutor—was much, in that day, for a king of England. There is nothing in that instrument which might not have been equally appropriate in a grant to a Protestant nobleman. All the clauses of the charter, about the advancement of the Christian religion, were to be found in every charter. They existed in the Virginia charter, yet in Virginia there was no toleration. It was the cant of charters—it was one of the reasons why grants were supposed to be lawful; and English, French and Spanish grants were alike made for the extension of the Christian religion and the conversion of the natives.

If it be contended that the charter secured general toleration, how is it that after the Protestant ascendancy, the authorities, Protestants, *sworn to administer the government of the province according to its charter and laws*, could pass and execute laws which disfranchised and more or less persecuted, not only Catholics, but Protestants, who dissented from the form of worship established in England—the Episcopalian? The truth is, the men who lived under the charter, like those who framed it, never conceived that it did more than to prohibit the toleration of infidelity, leaving legislation upon religious subjects open to the judgment and discretion of the colony itself. It was left for sciolists, in later times, to make this discovery, which was never dreamed of in the principal workings of the charter—the constitution, in modern phrase, of the colony of Maryland. If the charter did not prohibit nor prevent the Puritans in their ascendency from passing persecuting laws, and did not interfere with the established Episcopalian church throughout its long supremacy, in enacting and enforcing persecuting laws, it is difficult to understand how—being granted, as we have stated, to a Catholic for a Catholic settlement—it could have prevented those Catholics from such legislation as would have kept out of the province men, who, when they had found there an asylum from the persecution of their fellow Protestants and become sufficiently numerous, turned upon the Catholic settlers, disfranchised and persecuted them.

It is clear that the Catholics had the power to pass these exclusive laws under the charter: would they have been permitted to do so by the government at home, if they had been disposed? This is in fact, the only point. But they who make this point, when they look at the history of that period, should blush for doing so. It admits neccessarily, that the early Catholic settlers of Maryland were in fact tolerant and liberal; and, while it attempts to rob them of every honor for being so, takes away the necessity of dwelling upon the second point before alluded to. Now as the Catholics or first settlers of Maryland never were intolerant or persecutors, we can only judge of what would have been the consequences to them from such acts, by the consequences that befel other denominations in the English colonies who really did persecute, when they were no more supreme in England and had less favor from the government than the Catholics. We demand that each colony be judged by its own acts without any reference to the imaginary wishes of the parent government; and we do this the more earnestly because we know that whenever it suits the purpose of certain writers they will make the state of the British government and the British king, during the early part of the seventeenth century, the means and the motive for conduct exactly opposite to that imputed to the respective Catholic and Protestant colonies. It is just to all parties to allow to each that amount of credit for motives which is fairly deducible from their acts; and if in a period of much religious intolerance a colony hedges itself about with edicts of the most persecuting character, and inflicts penalties, pains and death on those whose views of Christian requirements differ from those of the majority, it is but just to suppose that they left the parent country with no disrelish for intolerance in itself, but only as it affected their non-conformity; and it is no less fair to believe that a colony which leaving an intolerant country, gives freedom to religious creeds and makes it criminal to interfere with the differences of men's belief, nay, that not only admits to equality all that are within its borders, but invites to itself, as to an asylum for the oppressed, the sufferers in other colonies—it is fair, we say, to conclude that such a colony has in itself a better appreciation of human rights and Christian freedom than exists among its intolerant neighbors.

It is undeniable that James and his successor, Charles, hated the Puritans even more than they feared them; for they opposed the government while the Catholics then sustained it, and in many a later struggle loyally and truly, forgetting their past persecutions, fought and bled in the royal cause. But to these Puritans the king granted New England for an asylum, as he granted to Lord Baltimore Maryland as an asylum for the Catholics. He permitted them to erect their own form of government, as he permitted Lord Baltimore; and when the Episcopalian, the Catholic, and all others but those of their own peculiar sect, were disfranchised by the Puritans of Massachusetts, when the inoffensive Friends were lashed, their ears slit, their tongues bored and their blood shed upon the scaffold, when Roger Williams was exiled, the Lion of England slumbered over the fearful wrong. The Puritans of the North were not dearer to the Church of England and the king, than the Catholics, nor were they less feared. "It is insulting to common sense," says the Protestant historian, Oliver, in his history of the *Puritan Commonwealth*, "to assert that the spirit of Puritanism was not hostile to the principles of liberty on the shores of Massachusetts bay." For at the general court held in May, 1631, the freemen declared that: "To the end that the body of freemen may be preserved of honest and good men, none shall hereafter be admitted to the liberties of this commonwealth, but such persons as shall be members of some of the churches within its jurisdiction." And so harsh was the operation of this relentless law that, so late as the year 1676, says Judge Story, "five-sixths of the people were disfranchised." Mr. Oliver adds: "The statute book of the commonwealth, during this period, [1638,] groaned under the severity of laws against error, heresy and schism. Deaths, banishments, whippings, imprisonments and fines, are scattered throughout its leaves, and meet the eye at every turn. And this was liberty of conscience. . . . There is 'no room in Christ's army for tolerationists,' boldly declared Johnson, one of the earliest and sturdiest in the Puritan pilgrimage. 'Toleration,' said Cotton, 'made the world anti-Christian. The church never took hurt from the punishment of heretics.' 'Tis Satan's policy,' echoed Shepard in 1672, 'to plead for an indefinite and boundless toleration.' 'Poly-piety is the greatest impiety in the world,' said the Simple Cobbler of Agawam. 'My heart hath naturally detested toleration of divers religions, or of one religion in segregant shapes. He that is willing to tolerate will, for a need, hang God's Bible at the devil's girdle.' And, in like manner, thundered President Oakes, in 1673, 'I look upon toleration as the first-born of all abominations.' Such were the principles avowed by the Puritan Pilgrim. He abhorred the Church of Rome, disliked the Church of England, and despised the low rabble of schismatics. . . . In their eyes, the Quakers were a 'pernicious sect of heretics,' and were treated accordingly. They were 'made the subjects of reproach, scorn, buffeting, scourges, torture and death.' They were 'stripped of the clothes they wore, and robbed of the beds whereon they lay. The vessels in which they ate were forced from them, and their food itself reduced to almost nothing.'" In conclusion, Mr. Oliver adds: "I have exhibited those great principles of intolerance which our ancestors recorded in their histories and enrolled among their laws. And, regarded simply in a legal view, it is a startling fact, that every execution was a murder; every mutilation, a maiming; every whipping a battery; every fine, an extortion; every disfranchisement, an outrage; and all were *breaches of the charter.* There were no laws in England for hanging, or mutilating, or flogging the king's subjects, because they did not profess the Puritan faith; while, to disfranchise a member of the corporation for any cause unconnected with the objects for which the charter was given, was a clear violation of justice and authority. Unless, then, we lay aside abstract right and wrong, and disregard the nature of the charter, the liberty of the subject, the supremacy of parliament, the jurisdiction of the royal courts, the authority of the law, and the prerogative of the king, we cannot consider the persecutions of the elders of Massachusetts merely as acts of intolerance. They were, in any proper legal sense, violations of, and crimes against, the laws of England. For the king did not bestow upon the grantees of the charter the power of removing from the kingdom his 'loving subjects,' in order that they might deprive them of their ears, or their liberties, for refusing to conform to a certain sectarian religion."

But it may be said that the Puritan party in England was too strong for the government to act. A poor defence, indeed, for the old persecuting spirit of New England! But, at the same time, Virginia, which may be called the Episcopalian settlement, the settlement of the established religion of England in America, drove out from its borders those powerful Puritans, and would not tolerate them. As an evidence of this fact, Mr. Jefferson, in his *Notes of Virginia*, speaking of "the first settlers in this country," says that they "were emigrants from England, of the English Church, just at a point of time when it was flushed with victory over the religions of all other persuasions. Possessed, as they became, of the powers of making, administering and executing the laws, they showed equal intolerance in this country with their Presbyterian brethren, who had emigrated to the northern government." In this connection, Mr. Hening, in his *Virginia Statutes*[1] says:

"From the settlement of the colony to the death of Charles I., and the commencement of the commonwealth thereupon, an uniformity to the doctrines and discipline of the church of England was strictly enjoined; all non-conformists were compelled to leave the colony, with all convenience; popish recusants were disabled from holding any office, and their priests not suffered to remain more than five days in the country. During the commonwealth, the affairs of the church were left to the discretion of the parishioners; but no sooner did the Quakers, who had fled from the persecutions in England, arrive on our shores than they were met by the terrors of an act 'for suppressing them;' masters of vessels were subjected to a penalty of one hundred pounds sterling for each Quaker brought into the colony; all Quakers were imprisoned without bail or mainprize, till they found sufficient security to depart the colony; for returning, they were directed to be proceeded against as contemners of the laws and magistracy, and punished accordingly; and if they should come in a third time they were to be prosecuted as felons. All

[1] Vol. I., p. 14.

persons were prohibited, under the penalty of one hundred pounds sterling, from entertaining them, or permitting their assemblies in or near their houses; and no person was permitted to dispose of or publish any books or pamphlets containing the tenets of their religion."[1]

Thus it will be seen the members of the established church in Virginia were meting out a like measure of injustice to the Puritans and Quakers who ventured within their borders. Indeed, but little did king, or parliament, or people, heed the state of colonies not rich enough to plunder and not strong enough to fear. Men's minds in England were then too much occupied with that upheaving of the popular ocean, whose rising surges were already menacing the church and the throne, to care much what was doing in the forest settlements across the Atlantic. Had it been the will of the early settlers of Maryland, they could have done, with equal facility, impunity and completeness, what was done in the northern colonies. When parliament triumphed, it brought them all alike under its control; but when the royal authority was restored, the Marylander was again tolerant, the Virginian again exclusive, and the Puritan again a persecutor.

Another class of objectors take the ground that from the earliest years the Catholics of Maryland fell into a minority, and therefore were disabled from passing exclusive or persecuting laws. Even if this were admitted, the proof of their tolerant spirit is only strengthened. It is beyond all question that, whatever may have been the proportion of non-Catholics among the earliest settlers, the legislative and administrative powers were in the hands of the Catholics. No clause of the charter prevented them from prohibiting the admission of any colonists whom they did not wish, and thus closing the colony to all but those of their own faith; or admitting so few that their own supremacy could not be assailed. Again, Lord Baltimore, under the provisions of his charter, might refuse to sell, lease, or grant lands to any whose presence he did not desire. If this policy had been followed, how could Protestants have obtained a footing in Maryland? Could Claiborne's men on Kent Island have claimed the rights of citizens of the colony? They utterly repudiated it, refused to submit to its government, and took up arms against it; and when, defeated, they appealed to the king and council, the acts of the governor were sustained.

On the contrary, the Catholic rulers and settlers, so far from excluding, invited the persecuted from other colonies and from the mother-country, to share the asylum they had made for themselves, not dreaming that their generous confidence would ever be betrayed. And the time soon came when the settlers of St. Mary's and those of their faith began to be outnumbered by those whom they had invited to the "land of the sanctuary;" when they not

[1] See the discourses of Geo. H. Miles, James McSherry, Enoch Louis Lowe, Wm. Geo. Read, John C. Legrand, Jos. R. Chandler, Rev. P. Corry and Rev. John McCaffrey upon the commemoration of the landing of the pilgrims of Maryland.

merely had no further power to prosecute or exclude, but were unable to protect themselves from oppression. That time marked the beginning of the persecution of Catholics in Maryland.

To Calvert, then, and to his Catholic followers, and not to the king, or the charter, belongs the glory of Maryland toleration.

The character of George Calvert has been often drawn, and in some few cases by prejudiced or unfriendly hands. But such is its native beauty and simplicity, and the power of truth, that it must ever stand forth in bright relief from the shadows of that age, unharmed by the petty shafts of envy, or the fictions and surmises of those writers with whom truth is a secondary, not a primary object. The whole history of Calvert's life, both before and after he embraced the Catholic faith, bears testimony to the singleness of his mind, his inflexible integrity, and his entire disregard of personal interest when weighed with the dictates of his conscience. "He was the first," says Bancroft, "in the history of the Christian world, to seek for religious security and peace by the practice of justice, and not by the exercise of power; to plan the establishment of popular institutions with the enjoyment of liberty of conscience, to advance the career of civilization by recognizing the rightful equality of all Christian sects." The character of Cæcilius, his successor, and the founder of the colony, has come down to us identified in his acts and in the language of historians, with religious liberty and respect for the rights of the people. "Never," says Dr. Ramsay, "did a people enjoy more happiness than the people of Maryland under Cæcilius, the father of the province;" and on his tomb, says the more accurate Chalmers, ought to be engraven, "That, while fanaticism deluged the empire, he refused his assent to the repeal of a law which, in the true spirit of Christianity, gave liberty of conscience to all."

The true scope and character of the charter of Maryland has been well illustrated by the Hon. George William Brown, Chief Justice of the Supreme Bench of Baltimore. He says:

"It was a compact between the sovereign and the proprietary, in which the latter undoubtedly had the best of the bargain, but as the former voluntarily parted with that which to him was of little value, and to which, at best, he had but small right, he certainly had no cause to complain," in conveying "a certain region in a country hitherto uncultivated in the parts of America." The grantee and his heirs were made true and absolute lords and proprietors of the soil, and all that the sovereign reserved to himself was two Indian arrows of the country, to be delivered at the castle of Windsor every year, on Tuesday, of Easter week, in token of allegiance, and the fifth part of the gold and silver—the latter, as it proved, a barren right.

"The laws and institutions of the province were not required to be submitted to the crown for his approbation, and the right of taxation by it was expressly and forever abandoned. . . . Thus a government almost independent of the parent country, was created in the charter itself. . . . Express provision was made for manors, lords of manors, and manorial courts. The proprietary had the power of creating ports of entry, of erecting towns into boroughs, and boroughs into cities, with such privileges and immunities as he might deem expedient, of pardoning offences, of taking command in chief of the forces, with as full and unrestrained power as any captain general of any army ever had, of declaring martial law, and of granting lands on such terms and tenure as he thought proper.

"He was the source of justice. He had the power of establishing courts, of abolishing them at will, and of determining their jurisdiction and manner of proceeding; and all process from them ran in his name, and not in that of the king. He was not only the head of the executive branch of the government, but he had the power of appointing officers of every description, and of creating and abolishing the offices themselves at his own pleasure. He was the head of the church. That is, he had the power of erecting and founding churches, and was entitled to the patronage and advowsons appertaining to them. He had also in certain cases and to a limited extent, the dangerous power of promulgating ordinances which were to have the force of laws; and he also claimed as a part of his prerogative, and occasionally practiced, the equally dangerous power of dispensing with laws actually existing. He was invested with all the royal rights which the Bishop of Durham enjoyed within the County Palatine of Durham,[1] and this among other things gave him the right to all the game within the province. In the end of the instrument, there is a sweeping clause, that in case any doubt shall arise as to the true meaning of any word of the charter, an interpretation was to be put upon it most *beneficial*, *profitable* and *favorable* to Lord Baltimore, his heirs and assigns.

"Amid this imposing array of powers conferred on the proprietary, those granted to the people were neither numerous nor explicit. The most important right secured to them, was that the laws were to be enacted by the proprietary, with the advice and approbation of the freemen of the province, or of their deputies. The proprietary understood this clause to mean that *he* had the right of originating all laws, and that the people had nothing to do but *accept* or *reject* those which *he* might choose to propose. But whatever may be the true meaning of the charter in this respect, it is clear that the legislative assemblies were to be called together at such times only as the proprietary might prescribe, and in such form as he might think best; and he had the power of adjourning and dissolving them at pleasure. Thus their organization was left as indefinite as their functions. . . . If the view of the charter which I have given be correct, the people of Maryland are not mainly indebted to it for the freedom which they have always enjoyed. We must look elsewhere for an explanation of the fact, and we find it in the character of the men who planted the colony, and the circumstances by which they were surrounded. The colonists consisted of some two hundred, for the most part Roman Catholics. They brought with them stout English hearts, in which were cherished fundamental principles of liberty, learned in a land where, four hundred years before, *Magna Charta* had been extorted by the sturdy barons from the fears of King John, where parliament met, and where trial by jury was established."[2]

In corroboration of the opinion of this distinguished counsellor, Chalmers observes "that in this patent there is no clause which obliges the proprietary to transmit the acts of assembly to the king, for approbation or dissent, nor any saving of the royal interference in the government of the province. These essential omissions induced the commissioners of plantations to represent to the commons in 1633 (*Historical Register*, vol. xviii., p. 39,) 'that Maryland is under no obligations by its constitution to return authentic copies of its laws to the sovereign for confirmation or disallowance, or to give

[1] "Counties palatine are so called *a palatio*, because the owners thereof, the Earl of Chester, the Bishop of Durham and the Duke of Lancaster had in those counties *jura regalia* as fully as the king hath in his palace."—Blackstone, i., sec. iv., p. 117.

[2] Origin and growth of civil liberty in Maryland. Md. Historical Society Publication.

any account of its proceedings.'" In Thurloe's *State Papers,* vol. v., p. 482, published in 1656, we find the following objections made to "Lord Baltimore's patent:" "By the patent is provided that he makes laws with the advice and consent of the inhabitants and freemen; and by the practice of the Lord Baltimore and his officers there, the people have no law but what he allows and consents unto. . . . The covenant, laws and platform of government established in England declare the suppression and extirpation of Popery, to which his highness' oath tends; but the Lord Baltimore's government declares and swears the upholding and countenancing thereof, both by the officers and people. The Lord Baltimore exercised an arbitrary and tyrannical government, undertook a princely jurisdiction, styles himself absolute lord and proprietor, constituted a Privy Council, mostly of Papists, and the rest sworn thereto. This Privy Council must be the legislative power that is to put in execution such laws which the Lord Baltimore himself makes and imposeth; and he makes what laws he pleaseth. The people are, indeed, called to assemblies, but have neither legislative power nor of judicature, that being appropriated to the Privy Council, or Upper House, so that what is determined by them admits of no reference or appeal."

The interpretation of the charter by Justices Story, Marshall and Kent, sustains the views of Chief Justice Brown. We may, therefore, consider the point established, that the whole control of ecclesiastical affairs in the province was granted to the lord proprietary. The power over all church matters was vested in him, and was to emanate from him, and not from the people, as it does where religion is left free. The pastors were to be chosen, not by popular election, nor were the hearers to have any voice in their election, but by the appointment of the owner of the soil. The proprietary might prevent the erection of any church which he chose to forbid, and, by the exclusive power of appointment, dictate the faith of the province. The proprietary might renounce all these rights if he choose, and proclaim entire religious freedom; but there is no provision made for the exercise of that freedom in the charter. That instrument makes provision for the support of the clergy, not by the people, but by the rent of lands, or other property bestowed upon each individual church by the proprietary, or those to whom he might convey landed estates. Moreover, the fourth section of the charter confers "the patronage and advowsons of all churches" to be built, on the lord proprietary and his heirs.

The assertion, be it remembered, which we are combating, is—not that Protestants were persecuted in Maryland by the Catholics: that has never been alleged—but that the toleration which here existed under the proprietary goverment cannot be credited to the Calverts or the Catholics, inasmuch as (say some) the charter compelled toleration; or rather (say others) a Protestant majority in the colony compelled it. The former point we have answered at length, showing that the charter no more enforced toleration than it did exclusiveness; that it gave full control, in matters ecclesiastical, to the lord proprietary. The second point we have answered in part, but will answer it more fully by showing that in the earlier period of its history—the period of general toleration—Maryland was not a Protestant settlement, tolerating Catholics, but a Catholic palatinate, tolerating all Christians, and under which all Christians might live in peace and brotherhood.

When Cæcilius Calvert was planning his colonial expedition, in 1633, one of his earliest cares was to apply to the Superior of the Jesuits for priests to attend the planters and settlers, and to extend the Christian faith among the Indians. Under the sanction of the Superior, Father Andrew White—at that time under a sentence of perpetual banishment from England, under penalty of death—was selected for the service, and, accompanied by Father John Altham and two lay brothers, John Knowles and Thomas Gervase, joined the first expedition, and were active, as the journal shows, in their religious offices; celebrating worship after the rites of their church, consecrating the possession of the soil, and converting Protestant immigrants as well as heathen savages. The colony, therefore, whose only spiritual guides were Catholics, whose only public worship was according to Catholic rites, was a Catholic colony. Of the labors of these missionaries we shall speak further on, and of their success in diffusing their faith; but for the present we keep to the main topic, which is certainly not second in interest to any other in the history of Maryland.

Nothing happened to disturb the peaceful relations between Protestants and Catholics until the year 1638, when an incident occurred, small in itself, but admirably illustrating the liberality, impartiality and magnanimity of the governor and his council. A proclamation had been issued by the governor, which had the force of law, forbidding "all unreasonable disputations on points of religion, tending to the disturbance of the public peace and quiet of the colony, and to the opening of faction in religion." Now, Captain Cornwaleys, one of the council, and a Catholic, had two Protestant servants, Francis Gray and Robert Sedgrave, who lodged in the same house with William Lewis, a Catholic, who seems to have been a sort of overseer or steward in the service of Cornwaleys. These two servants were one day reading "Smith's Sermons," a Protestant book, when Lewis came into the room. Either by accident or design, they read loudly enough for him to hear some offensive passages in it, such as "that the Pope was anti-Christ, and the Jesuits anti-Christian ministers." Lewis told them "it was a falsehood, and came from the devil, as all lies did, and he that writ it was an instrument of the devil, and he would prove it; and that all Protestant ministers were the ministers of the devil," and forbade their reading that book any more. The men were irritated by this outbreak of temper, and, according to Lewis's statement, drew a petition to be presented to Sir John Hawley, governor of Virginia, as soon as they could obtain the signatures of all the Protestants in the colony. The servants denied this allegation, but admitted the intention of presenting a petition to the governor of Maryland, or rather a complaint against Lewis for his abuse of Protestant ministers, and his forbidding them to read books relating to their religion. But before they had an opportunity of either procuring the signatures of the Protestants or presenting the petition, William Lewis (on the first of July, 1638,) gave information thereof to Captain Cornwaleys, who, immediately calling in Mr. Secretary Lewger to his assistance, ordered the several parties, together with the witnesses, to be brought before them. The petition was delivered up to the captain, and after an examination of the parties, they were bound in recognizance with two surities to answer the matter at the next court. The *court*, (composed, as it appears, of the governor, Captain Cornwaleys, and Mr. Secretary Lewger), meeting on the third of July, the sheriff was commanded by warrant from the governor, to bring William Lewis, Robert Sedgrave, Francis Gray, Christopher Carnoll, and Ellis Beach, before the court. After an examination of the parties and one witness, (a Protestant,) the governor thought it proper, on account of the absence of another material witness to defer the trial and "censure" of the servants, till the witness could be produced in court; but desired the secretary to deliver his "censure" touching the complaint against William Lewis.

Governor Calvert called on Secretary Lewger for his opinion as to the proper punishment of Lewis for his "offensive speeches and unseasonable disputations in point of religion, contrary to public proclamation to prohibit all such disputes." He gave it as his opinion, that Lewis should be fined five hundred pounds of tobacco, and remain in the sheriff's custody till he should find sufficient security for his good behavior in time to come. Captain Cornwaleys was for the fine, but not for binding him over for his good behavior. But Governor Calvert concurred wholly in the sentence of the secretary, and it was carried into effect. The following is a copy of the bond:

"3 July, 1638.—William Lewis, John Medcalfe, and Richard Browne, acknowledged themselves to owe unto the lord proprietary 3000 lb. weight of tobacco to be paid unto the said lord proprietary, or his heirs, or officers, on the 10th of November next, in case the said William Lewis shall offend the peace of this colony, or of the inhabitants thereof, by incautious and unnecessary arguments or disputations in matter of religion; or shall use any ignominious words or speeches touching the books or ministers authorized by the State of England.

"WILLIAM LEWIS,
"JOHN MEDCALFE,
"RICHARD BROWNE.

"*Recogn. coram me*, JOHN LEWGER, Secretary."

Thus, four years only after the settlement, the liberty of conscience was vindicated by a recorded judicial sentence; and Lewis, the Catholic, on the complaint of Protestants inferior in position to himself, over whom he was the overseer, was, by Catholic judges, fined and committed to the custody of the sheriff until he could find bondsmen for his "unseasonable disputations in point of religion, tending to the disturbance of the peace and quiet of the colony."

While the proprietary and the people of Maryland were thus establishing the colony on a basis in which the rights of each should be distinctly recognized and fairly adjusted, the people of England, and the adjoining colonies of America, under the stimulus of political and religious excitement, were taking rapid strides in that career of revolution, which was to end in the subversion of the established church and the overthrow of the monarchy. From this time forward, we must look for an increasing sympathy on the part of the Protestant colonists with the movement in the mother country, and the introduction of a new element, calculated to change their social and political relations, in the sympathy felt by different portions of the people according to their education, prejudices and religious faith, with the royal party on the one hand or the party of the opposition on the other. In the reign of Charles I., theology was for the first time merged in politics. It was no longer a struggle of creeds and dogmas, but it was a struggle between those who favored the crown and those who supported the parliament. James I. had already seen that the Puritans were more dangerous to the State than to the church. "They do not," he said, "so far differ from us in points of religion, as in their confused view of policy and parity; being ever discontented with the present government, and impatient to suffer any superiority; which maketh their sects insufferable in any well governed commonwealth."[1]

This state of things in England, engendering a restive and factious spirit among the people, made the position of Governor Calvert one of great delicacy, anxiety and responsibility. The assembly, apprehensive of some danger to the freedom of their worship, from the great number of Protestants who were now entering the province, secured to their church its rights and liberties by an act passed March 19th, 1638, (O.S.,) entitled "Act for Church Liberties."

The first section ran in the following words: "Holy church, within this province, shall have all her rights, liberties and immunities, safe, whole and inviolable in all things." This section is a copy of the first clause of the great charter, which provides that "the Church of England shall be free and enjoy her whole rights and liberties inviolable;" and in these words it was confirmed again and again by John's successors. We may fairly suppose, then, that it was the intention of this act, passed by an assembly, the majority of whom were Catholics, and to be approved by the proprietary of the soil, himself a Catholic, to place the Catholic religion in the same position with regard to the government of Maryland, that it had occupied in John's time toward the government of England. The rights secured to the church related chiefly to the holding of property, freedom from taxation, and the exemption of the clergy from certain civil duties and burdens. Such, in the main, were probably the "rights and liberties" intended to be secured to the Catholic church in Maryland. At the next session of the assembly this law was made perpetual.

[1] Speech of James in *Parl. Hist.*, i, 982.

By a fundamental law, passed at this session, entitled "An Act for the Liberties of the People," it was made a part of the constitution, "that all the inhabitants of this province being Christians, (slaves excepted,) shall have and enjoy all such rights, liberties, immunities, privileges and free customs, within this province, as any natural born subject of England hath, or ought to have or enjoy in the realm of England, by force or virtue of the common law or statute law of England, saving in such cases as the same are or may be altered or changed by the laws and ordinances of this province; and shall not be imprisoned or disseized or dispossessed of their freehold, goods or chattels, or be outlawed, exiled, or otherwise destroyed, forejudged or punished, than according to the laws of this province: saving to the lord proprietary and his heirs all his rights and prerogatives by reason of his domination and seigniory over this province, and the people of the same."

Bozman remarks: "This bill appears to have been intended, not only as a recognition of the extent of the common and statute law of England to this province, but also as a specification of those particular clauses of *Magna Charta* by which the 'rights and liberties' of the inhabitants were to be secured to them. But the act, more properly perhaps, by a general clause, recognizes the whole of such parts of *Magna Charta* as relate to the 'rights and liberties' of the people."

There is another incident among the records of 1642 which goes to show that the rights of Protestant churches were as safe in the hands of the Catholics as the rights of Protestant individuals.

"22d of March,—in the afternoon.—Then was a petition presented by David Wickliff in the name of the *Protestant Catholics* of Maryland, and respited till the next morning.

"23d of March. The petition of the *Protestants* was read, complaining against Mr. Thomas Gerard for taking away the key of the chapel, and carrying away the books out of the chapel, and such proceedings desired against him for it, as to justice appertaineth. Mr. Gerard being charged to make answer, the house, upon hearing of the prosecutors and his defence, found that Mr. Gerard was guilty of a misdemeanor, and that he should bring the books and key taken away to the place where he had them, and relinquish all title to them or the house, and should pay for a fine 500 lb tobacco towards the maintenance of the first minister as should arrive."

Such is the scantiness of the records, that it is impossible now to ascertain who these "Protestant Catholics" were, or "Protestants," as they are called in the minutes of the second days' proceedings. We may conjecture, however, with some degree of probability, that they were Episcopalians, from "the carrying away of the books." From the form of expression near the close, that the fine should be appropriated "to the maintenance of the first minister who should arrive," it seems not unlikely that this was the first Protestant church erected in the colony; and that Gerard, an ardent Catholic, in his zeal to suppress the enterprise at the outset, was led to do an act, which, though consonant with the spirit of the times, was not borne out by the leading men of his own party in religion.[1] Mr. Davis says:

[1] Burnap, p. 177.

"The little chapel also, near the Fort at St. Mary's, the place for the worship of the Anglo-Catholic colonists before the arrival of any of their ministers, and given by most writers to the Protestants, was probably not their property exclusively, but erected with the joint funds or contributions of the Roman and of the Anglican Catholics. The key to it was seized in 1642 by Doctor Gerrard, a prominent Roman Catholic, and upon the ground of *some claim*, if we may judge from an expression in the decision against him. In the proposal, about the same year, for a transfer of the premises to Lord Baltimore (an arrangement not immediately, if ever at all, effected), another Roman Catholic gentleman was the ostensible owner or representative of the title. And there is evidence to show that, at a very early period, the graveyard was the usual burial-place of the Roman Catholics. Some, also, of the colonists, who held land under Doctor Gerrard, as the lord of St. Clement's Manor, as well as the Doctor's wife, were Protestants."[1]

Such were the relations which at this time prevailed between men of different creeds in the province, and such the dealings of the government in matters of religion.

Calvert, who was desirous of increasing the population of his colony by the immigration of men of worth and enterprise, did not limit his invitations to those of his own faith. In 1643 we find him writing to Captain Gibbons, of Boston, and sending him a commission with an offer of land in Maryland, and free liberty of religion, to any of the colonists of Massachusetts who would come with him; "but," says Winthrop, "our captain had no mind to further his desire herein, nor had any of our people temptation that way."[2]

"Their 'temptation' was then taking them in another way less innocent than would have been the way to Maryland. This letter to Gibbons reached Boston about the time of a transaction which, it were to be wished, could not be written upon the records of New England's history. The inhabitants of Massachusetts had but just been thrown into a pious consternation by the stupid and unintelligible ravings of Gorton and his followers, which merited nothing but contempt; and were now settling down into the repose produced by a sentence upon the poor sufferers, which purposed to cure heresy with fetters. At such a time, to offer 'liberty of religion' to men who were congratulating themselves upon the successful application of their iron preservative of orthodoxy, doubtless provoked a sneer at the stupidity which could present *toleration* merely as a temptation to removal. Human ingenuity could not have devised a better-timed or keener rebuke than is contained in this offer of religious freedom from the persecuted Papist to his Protestant fellow sufferer: human wit could not have made the memory of that rebuke more lasting than it is made by the scornful rejection of the offer.

"He had carried out in good faith the principle which he had professed on the subject of religion. The course of the government has been truly described as one 'which tolerated all Christian churches and established none.' To one conversant with the history of the times, and therefore but too familiar with many a bloody enactment, elsewhere made, by which persecution was elevated into piety, it is refreshing to find in the bosom of a little colony, scarce known by name even to the natives of the old world, the blessed influence of a holier principle, proving its goodness by its effects, and presenting a picture from which the legislators of ancient empires might have caught a lesson of wisdom, and learned, if not to condemn the wickedness of persecution, at least to avoid its folly. There is no prouder tribute to the memory of Cecil Calvert than is to be found

[1] *Day Star*, p. 33.

[2] Savage's *Winthrop*, II., p. 148-9.

in the oath of office which, from 1636 onward, he prescribed for his governors: 'I will not, by myself or any other, directly or indirectly, trouble, molest, or discountenance any person professing to believe in Jesus Christ, for, or in respect of religion. I will make no difference of persons in conferring offices, favors, or rewards, for, or in respect of religion; but merely as they shall be found faithful and well deserving, and endued with moral virtues and abilities: my aim shall be public unity, and if any person or officer shall molest any person professing to believe in Jesus Christ, on account of his religion, I will protect the person molested and punish the offender.'"[1]

The language of this oath, which was doubtless framed by the lord proprietary, "was taken," Chalmers tells us, "by the governor and council, *between* the years 1637 and 1657."[2] Doubt has arisen whether it was meant that this oath was taken *from* 1637 to 1657, or only in some year or years between those dates; but this latter surmise does violence to the plain meaning of the language, for if the historian did not mean to say that it was administered first in 1637, and continued afterwards to 1657, he would have named the year in which it began and that in which it ceased to be used. Chalmers was too accurate a writer to use dates so loosely; and as he was not only an experienced lawyer, but the custodian of the Maryland provincial papers, and had free access afterwards to all documents relating to the colony in the British state paper office, he could not have been in doubt as to the precise date, or ignorant of the exact language. That it was not, however, continued without change for these twenty years is evident from the oath prepared for Governor Stone, in 1648, which appears to have been amplified from the one quoted from Chalmers and Hawks, and so differs, both in phraseology and in specific obligations from the former, that the two cannot have been confounded by the learned annalist.

The circumstances under which Governor Stone was appointed may have prompted the framing of a more specific oath, as they differed greatly from those under which his predecessors had taken office.

While the little colony was laying a broad and enduring claim to the admiration of the world, public affairs in England were becoming more and more disturbed by the dissensions between the king and parliament. The spirit of discontent and turbulence was unhappily introduced into Maryland by a body of Puritans, who, expelled from Virginia, had been welcomed by her more hospitable sister colony, where they repaid the kindness that sheltered and protected them with discord and civil war. The success of the parliamentary party in England gave them confidence and audacity, and they aimed at nothing less than the control of the government. Governor Calvert, foreseeing trouble, resolved to make a voyage to England, to consult in person with his brother, the lord proprietary; so having appointed Mr. Giles Brent "lieutenant general, admiral, chief captain, magistrate, and commander," he sailed for England early in 1643.

[1] Hawk's *Rise and Progress of the Protestant Episcopal Church in Maryland*, pp. 27-30; Chalmers, p. 210; McMahon, p. 226.

[2] *Political Annals*, p. 235.

In the fall of the following year the cause of the parliament having finally triumphed, the governor returned to look after affairs in the colony. Here he found everything in disorder, in consequence of the rebellion of Claiborne and Ingle. So rapid were their movements, and so advanced their preparations, that Calvert was unable to oppose any effective resistance, and was forced to seek refuge in Virginia. Not until 1646 were the well-disposed able to make head against the usurped authority of the insurgents; but in August of that year the proprietary government was restored, the governor resumed his office and authority, and peace and prosperity returned to the province.

Governor Leonard Calvert did not long survive to enjoy the fruits of his success. He died at St. Mary's, on the 9th of June, 1647. The circumstances of his death are unknown, except that he was attended in his last moments by his kinswomen, Margaret and Mary Brent, and by Francis Anketill and James Linsey, and that he was buried at St. Mary's, though the spot where his remains repose is now unknown. After his death Margaret and Mary Brent made affidavit that on his death-bed he had, by virtue of the powers conferred on him, appointed Thomas Green his successor, who was accordingly acknowledged.

The last throes of the civil convulsions in England could not fail to fill the Maryland colonists with uneasiness and apprehension; and when it became evident that the royal cause was hopeless, it was felt that the peace and liberties of the province were in extreme peril. Lord Baltimore saw that while concessions to the Puritans might be neccessary to maintain his province, new safeguards were neccessary to prevent the destruction of that sanctuary which he had created at such heavy cost of care and treasure. So, on the 6th of August, 1648, he appointed William Stone, a resident of Northampton county, Virginia, governor of the province, and prescribed the following oath of office:

"*The Oath of the Lieutenant or Chief Governor of the Province of Maryland.*

"I, A B do swear that I will be true and faithful to the right hon'ble Cecilius lord baron of Baltimore the true and absolute lord and proprietary of this province of Maryland and his heirs, and him and them, and his and their rights, royal jurisdiction and seignory, all and every of them into and over the said province and islands thereunto belonging will at all times defend and maintain to the utmost of my power, and will never accept of nor execute any place, office or employment within the said province any way concerning or relating to the government of the said province, from any person or authority, but by, from, or under a lawful authority derived or to be derived from time to time under the hand and seal at arms of his said lordship or his heirs and assigns, lords and proprietaries of the said province; I will faithfully serve his said lordship as his lieutenant of the said province and in all other offices committed to my charge by his said lordship's commission or commissions to me, and will willingly yield up the said commission and commissions again, and all offices powers and authorities granted or to be granted by them or any of them into the hands of his said lordship and his heirs and assigns or to such person or persons as he or they shall appoint, whensoever he or they shall appoint me so to do, and shall signify the same unto me in any writing under his or their hand and seal at arms, and will not presume to put in execution or attempt to execute any office, power, or authority granted unto me by any of the said commission or commissions after that his said lordship or his heirs or assigns lords and proprietaries of the said province shall repeal them or any of them respectively by any writing under his or their respective hand and seal at arms, and that the said repeal be published within this province; I will do equal right and justice to the poor and to the rich within the said province to my best skill, judgment, and power according to the laws and ordinances of the said province, and in default thereof according to my conscience and best discretion and the power granted or to be granted to me by his said lordship's commission or commissions; I will not for fear, favour, or affection, or any other cause let, hinder, or delay justice to any; but shall truly execute the said office and offices respectively, according to his said lordship's commissions to me in that behalf, and to the true intent and meaning thereof, and not otherwise, to the best of my understanding and judgment; I will not know of any attempt against his said lordship's person or his right or dominion into or over the said province and the people therein, but I will prevent, resist, and oppose it with the utmost of my power and make the same known with all convenient speed to his said lordship, and I will in all things from time to time as occasion shall require faithfully counsel and advise his said lordship according to my heart and conscience, and do further swear that I will not by myself, nor any person directly or indirectly, trouble, molest, or discountenance any person whatsoever in the said province professing to believe in Jesus Christ, and in particular no Roman Catholick, for or in respect of his or her religion, nor in his or her free exercise thereof within the said province, so as they be not unfaithful to his said lordship, or molest or conspire against the civil government established here under him, nor will I make any difference of persons in conferring of offices, rewards, or favors proceeding from the authority which his said lordship hath conferred upon me as his lieutenant here, for or in respect of their said religion respectively, but merely as I shall find them faithful and well deserving of his said lordship, and to the best of my understanding endowed with moral virtues and abilities fitting for such rewards, offices, or favours, wherein my prime aim and end from time to time shall sincerely be the advancement of his said lordship's service here and the public unity and good of the province, without partiality to any or any other sinister end whatsoever, and if any other officer or person whatsoever shall, during the time of my being his said lordship's lieutenant here, without my consent or privity molest or disturb any person within this province professing to believe in Jesus Christ merely for or in respect of his or her religion or the free exercise thereof, upon notice or complaint thereof made unto me I will apply my power and authority to relieve and protect any person so molested or troubled, whereby he may have right done him for any damage which he shall suffer in that kind, and to the utmost of my power will cause all and every such person or persons as shall molest or trouble any other person or persons in that manner to be punished; I will faithfully serve his lordship as his chancellor and keeper of his great seal of this province committed to my charge and custody by his said lordship's commission to me to the best of my skill and understanding; I will cause the impression in wax of the said seal to be affixed to all such things as I have, or shall from time to time receive commission or warrant for so doing from his said lordship under his hand and seal at arms, and that it shall not be affixed to any other writing or thing whatsoever directly or indirectly with my privity, consent, or knowledge; I will do my best endeavour lawfully to preserve the said great seal in my custody so long as it shall please his said lordship to continue me in the charge and keeping thereof, to the end that it may not be lost, stolen, or unlawfully taken from me, and whereby any other person may affix the impression thereof unto any writing or thing whatsoever without authority for so doing lawfully derived or to be derived from by or under his said lordship's hand and seal at arms, and that I will truly and faithfully deliver up again the said great seal into the hands of such person or persons as his said lordship or his heirs shall appoint when his or their pleasure for that purpose shall be signified unto me under his or their hand and seal at arms. So help me God and by the contents of this book."

It is supposed Lord Baltimore was induced to appoint William Stone governor of Maryland, from the reason referred to in his commission, which says he "had undertaken in some short time to procure five hundred people of British or Irish descent to come from other places and plant and reside within our said province of Maryland."

With the commission to Governor Stone, his lordship also sent a new commission, appointing Thomas Greene, Esq., Captain John Price, Thomas Hatton, "our secretary," John Pile, and Captain Robert Vaughan, his "privy council of state." In this new commission, also, was inserted a proviso, that before any of the councillors therein mentioned should presume to act as such, they should take the oath annexed to the said commission; in which oath was inserted a clause similar to that of the lieutenant general before stated, relative to the religious liberty of all sects of the Christian religion, and particularly of that of the Roman Catholics. Heretofore the most of those appointed to office by the lord proprietary were Catholics, as were the majority of the settlers; but now, the Puritans being triumphant at home, he hoped by this measure to propitiate them, at the same time that, by the oath of office, he secured to all Christians the full toleration which had hitherto most scrupulously been observed. Governor Stone entered upon his duties towards the close of the year 1648, or the opening of the ensuing year.

On the 2d of April, 1649, the general assembly was convened at St. Mary's, when the doctrine of religious freedom was emphatically laid down in the memorable "Act concerning Religion." It is true that this act only gives legal form and expression to the principle on which the colony had all along been governed; none the less did its enactment place Maryland in advance of every community in this hemisphere, and Lord Baltimore among the first law reformers of history. The law reads thus:

"*An Act concerning Religion.*

"Forasmuch as in a well governed and christian commonwealth matters concerning religion and the honour of God ought in the first place to bee taken into serious consideration and indevoured to be settled, Bee it therefore ordayned and enacted by the right honourable Cecilius lord baron of Baltimore, absolute lord and proprietary of this province, with the advice and consent of the upper and lower house of this general assembly, that whatsoever person or persons within this province and the islands thereunto belonging, shall from henceforth blaspheame God, that is, curse him, or shall deny our Saviour Jesus Christ to be the Son of God, or shall deny the Holy Trinity, the Father, Son, and Holy Ghost, or the Godhead of any of the sayd Three Persons of the Trinity, or the Unity of the Godhead, or shall use or utter any reproachfull speeches, words, or language, concerning the Holy Trinity, or any of the sayd three persons thereof, shall be punished with death, and confiscation or forfeiture of all his or her land and goods to the lord proprietary and his heires.

"And bee it also enacted by the authority and with the advice and assent aforesaid, That whatsoever person or persons shall from henceforth use or utter any reproachfull words or speeches concerning the blessed Virgin *Mary*, the mother of our Saviour, or the holy apostles or Evangelists, or any of them, shall in such case for the first offence forfeit to the sayd lord proprietary and his heires lords and proprietaries of this province, the sum cf £5 sterling, or the value thereof, to bee levied on the goods and chattels of every such person so offending; but in case such offender or offenders shall not then have goods and chattels sufficient for the satisfying of such forfeiture, or that the same be not otherwise speedily satisfied, that then such offender or offenders shall be publickly whipt, and be imprisoned during the pleasure of the lord proprietary or the lieutenant or chiefe governor of this province for the time being; and that every such offender and offenders for every second offence shall forfeit £10 sterling, or the value thereof to be levied as aforesayd, or in case such offender or offenders shall not then have goods and chattels within this province sufficient for that purpose, then to be publickly and severely whipt and imprisoned as before is expressed; and that every person or persons before mentioned offending herein the third time, shall for such third offence forfeit all his lands and goods and be for ever banisht and expelled out of this province.

"And be it also further enacted by the same authority, advice and assent, that whatsoever person or persons shall from henceforth upon any occasion of offence or otherwise in a reproachful manner or way, declare, call, or denominate any person or persons whatsoever inhabiting, residing, trafficking, trading, or commercing, within this province or within any the ports, harbours, creeks, or havens to the same belonging, an Heretick, Schismatick, Idolator, Puritan, Presbyterean, Independent, Popish Priest, Jesuit, Jesuited Papist, Lutheran, Calvinist, Anabaptist, Brownist, Antinomian, Barrowist, Roundhead, Separatist, or other name or terme in a reproachful manner, relating to matter of religion, shall for every such offence forfeit and lose the sum of 10s. sterling or the value thereof to be levied on the goods and chattels of every such offender and offenders the one halfe thereof to be forfeited and paid unto the person or persons of whom such reproachful words are or shall be spoken or uttered, and the other halfe thereof to the lord proprietary and his heirs, lords and proprietaries of this province; but if such person or persons, who shall at any time utter or speak any such reproachful words or language, shall not have goods or chattels sufficient and overt within this province to be taken to satisfy the penalty aforesayd, or that the same bee not otherwise speedily satisfied, that then the person or persons so offending shall be publickly whipt and shall suffer imprisonment without bayle or mainprise until he, she, or they respectively shall satisfie the party offended or grieved by such reproachful language, by asking him or her respectively forgiveness publickly for such his offence before the magistrate or chiefe officer or officers of the towne or place where such offence shall be given.

"And be it further likewise enacted by the authority and consent aforesayd, that every person and persons, within this province, that shall at any time hereafter prophane the Sabaath or Lord's day called Sunday, by frequent swearing, drunkennesse, or by any unciville or disorderly recreation, or by working on that day, when absolute necessity doth not require, shall for every such first offence forfeit 2s. 6d. sterling or the value thereof; and for the second offence 5s. sterling or the value thereof; and for the third offence and for every time he shall offend in like manner afterwards 10s. sterling or the value thereof; and in case such offender or offenders shall not have sufficient goods or chattells within this province to satisfie any of the aforesayd penalties respectively hereby imposed for prophaning the Sabaath or Lord's day called Sunday as aforesaid, then in every such case the party so offending shall for the first and second offence in that kind be imprisoned till hee or she shall publickly in open court before the chief commander, judge, or magistrate of that county, towne, or precinct wherein such offence shall be committed, acknowledge the scandall and offence hee hath in that respect given against God, and the good and civil government of this province; and for the third offence and for every time after shall also be publickly whipt.

"And whereas the inforcing of the conscience in matters of religion hath frequently fallen out to bee of dangerous consequence in those commonwealths where it hath beene practised, and for the more quiet and peaceable government of this province, and the better to preserve mutuall love and unity amongst the inhabitants here, Bee it, therefore, also by the lord proprietary, with the advice and assent of this assembly, ordained and enacted, except as in this present act is before declared and set forth, that no person or persons whatsoever within this province or the islands, ports, harbours, creeks, or havens thereunto belonging, professing to believe in Jesus Christ, shall from henceforth be any waies troubled, molested, or discountenanced, for or in respect of his or her religion, nor in the free exercise thereof within this province or the islands thereunto belonging, nor any way compelled to the beleefe or exercise of any other religion against his or her consent, so as they be not unfaithfull to the lord proprietary, or molest or conspire against the civill government, estabblished or to be estabblished in this province under him and his heyres; and that all and every person or persons that shall presume contrary to this act and the true intent and meaning thereof, directly or indirectly, eyther in person or estate, wilfully to wrong, disturbe, or trouble, or molest any person or persons whatsoever within this province, professing to believe in Jesus Christ, for or in respect of his or her religion, or the free exercise thereof within this province, otherwise than is provided for in this act, that such person or persons so offending shall be compelled to pay treble damages to the party so wronged or molested, and for every such offence shall also forfeit 20s. sterling in money or the value thereof, half thereof for the use of the lord proprietary and his heires, lords and proprietaries of this province, and the other halfe thereof for the use of the partie so wronged or molested as aforesayd; or if the party so offending as aforesaid, shall refuse or bee unable to recompence the party so wronged or to satisfie such fine or forfeiture, then such offender shall be severely punished by publick whipping and imprisonment during the pleasure of the lord proprietary or his lieutenant or chiefe governour of this province for the time being, without baile or mainprise.

"And be it further also enacted by the authority and consent aforesayd, that the sheriffe or other officer or officers from time to time to be appointed and authorised for that purpose of the county, town, or precinct where every particular offence, in this present act contained, shall happen at any time to be committed, and whereupon there is heereby a forfeiture, fine, or penalty imposed, shall from time to time distrain, and seise the goods and estate of every such person so offending as aforesayd against this present act or any part thereof and sell the same or any part thereof for the full satisfaction of such forfeiture, fine, or penalty as aforesayd, restoring to the party so offending the remainder or overplus of the sayd goods and estate after such satisfaction so made as aforesayd."[1]

The passage of this act, the oath of the governor, and the consequent freedom of conscience which the colony enjoyed; their subsequent repeal by the laws establishing the Church of England in the province and disabling the Catholics, and the intolerance and persecutions which ensued, prove conclusively that, to the legislation of Lord Baltimore and his colonists, the credit is due for the early toleration in Maryland, and to the legislation of the faction that in a later day came to power, was owing the intolerance

[1] The foregoing act is recorded in *Lib.* C. and WH. p. 106;—*Lib.* WH. p. 111, and *Lib.* WH. and L. p. 1,—books in the office of the present Court of Appeals, and also in the book entitled "Assembly Proceedings from 1637 to 1658," p. 354, in the Land Office, Annapolis.

which stains the annals of the province. Here, too, we have more proof, if more were neccessary, that the charter had nothing to do with religion or church establishment. If it had secured toleration in the first instance, it would have been equally valid to prevent its overthrow in the second. No legislative action could destroy a constitutional sanction. In later days the Stamp Act, passed by the English Parliament, was declared unconstitutional by the judge of the Frederick county court in this State, because it infringed rights secured by the charter; and the people of Maryland solemnly planted themselves upon those provisions framed by the foresight of George Calvert, which protected them from taxation by the crown. The Jew, and perhaps a few others, were not covered by the protecting mantle of the law. But he who studies well the history of the times will find more reason to eulogize the Maryland colonists because they went so far than to blame them because they went no further. Assuredly the founders of Maryland were in advance of their times, and soared far above the spirit which animated the government of the mother country and the sister colonies.

It was a bigoted and persecuting age, and Catholics and Protestants alike were guilty of intolerance and persecution. But let honor be given where it is due; and the honor of passing the "Act concerning Religion" belongs to an assembly, the majority of whom were Roman Catholics.

For, in the first place, the Toleration Act of 1649 could not, under the charter, become a law, without the consent of the proprietary; for the law-making power was vested in him and the assembly, and this act in particular states that it was "enacted by the right honorable Cæcilius, etc., with the advice and consent of the Upper and Lower House of the General Assembly." He was a Catholic, and therefore this department of the law-making power was Roman Catholic.

It was for some years a matter of contest between them which possessed the right to initiate laws; the lord proprietary, however, finally conceded this privilege to the assembly. It was not uncommon for that body to reject the laws sent over by the proprietary, and afterwards to bring them forward themselves and pass them. But in 1648, when Governor William Stone was appointed, the "Act concerning Religion" was among the measures sent by Lord Baltimore for the action of the assembly.

Governor Stone and his council, consisting of Thomas Greene, John Pile, Robert Clarke, John Price, Robert Vaughan and Thomas Hatton, constituting the Upper House, were appointed by commissions from Cæcilius Calvert bearing date the 12th of August, 1648. The governor, and the three latter of his Privy Council, were Protestants; the three others were Catholics. The law also passed this body; but these were the Lord Proprietary's special representatives, appointed by him, removable at his pleasure, acquainted with his wishes, and, with the governor, charged to guard his interests and carry out his policy. They, as well as the governor were bound by a special pledge (as may be seen by the official oath before cited) to do nothing to interfere with the religious freedom of any believer in Christianity,[1] "and in particular no Roman Catholic."

This second department of the legislature, if not composed entirely of Catholics, was virtually a Catholic body, as it represented a Catholic proprietary, and acted in conformity with an oath touching this special subject, prescribed to them by him.

The lower house of the legislature consisted of nine burgesses, representing Kent and St. Mary's. Their names were Cuthbert Fenwick, Philip Conner, William Bretton, Richard Browne, George Manners, Richard Banks, John Maunsell, Thomas Thornborough and Walter Burke. Of these Philip Conner represented the freemen of Kent; which county also furnished one of the six councillors, Robert Vaughan.

Mr. Davis, in his *Day Star of American Freedom*, has very carefully investigated the records to determine the faith of each of these members, and gives in detail, from public acts, deeds of conveyance, last wills, etc., the proofs by which he has arrived at his conclusions. He says:

"As the result of the strictest historical criticism—of the most careful and exhausting analysis of the whole evidence—it is but right to say, the proof is not discoverable, that more than two members of the whole House of Burgesses (or representatives of the people) were either Protestants, or in direct sympathy with the Protestant class of colonists. That Mr. Conner and Captain Banks belonged to that class, is a matter of evidence. And there is some degree of probability that Mr. Browne also held the faith of the English Church. But it is certain, that five of the burgesses (Messrs, Fenwick, Bretton, Manners, Maunsell, and Peake) cherished a faith in the Roman church; and we have the basis of very strong presumption, that Mr. Thornborough, (a sixth member of this House) was also a Roman Catholic.

"Including the proprietary and Mr. Thornborough, ten of the law-givers of 1649 held the faith of the Roman Catholic Church. If we count the governor and the two burgesses; six, it will appear, belonged to some branch of the Protestant—probably the Anglo-Catholic. Adding Mr. Browne, we have a seventh. But this is a superficial view of the question, and refers only to the time they all sat in one House.

"All we have from the remaining parts of the journal is, that on the 'last day' of the Assembly the representatives of the freemen, with the governor, and with the privy councillors (excepting Messrs. Pile and Hatton), assembled in one 'House;' and that, on the same day, was passed the 'Act concerning Religion.' It can be proved from the records, that of the fourteen, eight (including Mr. Thornborough) were Roman Catholics; and six (with Mr. Browne) were Protestants. But this estimate does not render strict historical justice to the claim of the former. The privy councillors were, all of them, as well as the governor, the special representatives of the Roman Catholic proprietary. . . . It would be fairer, therefore, to place the governor and the four privy councillors on the same side as the six Roman Catholic burgesses. Giving Mr. Browne to the other side, we have eleven Roman Catholic against three Protestant votes.

"But there is the strongest evidence to show that, at a previous stage of the session, the Assembly sat in two Houses. This is the opinion of Bozman, who is by no means partial towards the Roman Catholics—an opinion sustained also by Chalmers, by Bacon, and by Bancroft. It is evident that Mr. Fenwick received an extra allowance. May we

[1] Davis' *Day Star*.

not suppose he was the chief officer, or speaker, of the Lower House? But the best argument is drawn from the analogy furnished by the Assembly of the following year, and by the very phraseology in the Act relating to religion. We know the Legislature of 1650, although expressly divided into two distinct chambers, sat near the end of the session in one House. And, in the Act of which we are speaking, there is a clear reference to an Upper and Lower House. If we suppose, therefore, (what cannot admit of a reasonable doubt), that the Act passed each House before its final adoption by the whole Assembly in one body—and still give Mr. Browne to the Protestants—we will find there were six Roman Catholics (including Mr. Thornborough), against three only of the other class of delegates.

"If we take the religious elements of the population represented in this assembly, the difference will again be in favor of the Roman Catholics.

"In 1648 the burgesses appeared either as individual freemen, or as the representatives, each of a definite number. And, in 1650, the six hundreds of St. Mary's county, as distinct integers, sent their own respective delegates. Assuming the constitution of either year, for the sake of the argument; the result, in 1649, would be substantially the same.

"The settlement upon Kent Island was an off-shoot of the Anglo-Catholic colony at Jamestown. Col. Clayborne was undoubtedly an Episcopalian. There, also, have we the traces of the life and labors of the Rev. Richard James, and of one or more other ministers of the Anglican church. It is but just to admit, that most of the Islanders were Protestants. But the population of Kent was small. In 1639, *if not many years later*, she was but a hundred of St. Mary's county. In 1648, she paid a fifth part only of the tax; and did not hold in the Assembly of that year, a larger ratio of political power. That also was before the return, we may suppose, of all the Roman Catholics, who had been expelled or exported from St. Mary's, by Captain Ingle, and the other enemies of the proprietary. In 1649, she had but one delegate; while St. Mary's was represented by eight. And this year, she paid but a sixth part of the tax. And for many years after, as well as before this Assembly, there is no evidence whatever of a division of the island, or the county, even into hundreds. Its population did not, in 1648, exceed the fifth; nor in 1649, the sixth part of the whole number of free white persons in the province.

"In no hundred of St. Mary's county, was there a majority of Protestants, unless in St. George's. It is not altogether certain that the Protestants outnumbered the Roman Catholics even in that hundred. . . . Conceding, what must remain a matter of considerable doubt, that St. George's was a Protestant hundred as early as 1649, and adding the county of Kent, on the eastern shore, the Protestants would hold two-sixths, or one-third of the whole political power, substantially, if not formally, represented during this year, in the Lower House of the Assembly—an estimate which also accords with the ratio of the Protestant to the Roman Catholic delegates—assuming that Mr. Browne was one of the former. But it is not improbable that the Protestants constituted a fourth only of the population of Maryland. * * * * * * * *

"St. Mary's was the home—the chosen home—of the disciples of the Roman church. The fact has been generally received. It is sustained by the tradition of two hundred years, and by volumes of written testimony; by the records of the courts; by the proceedings of the privy council; by the trial of law-cases; by the wills and inventories; by the land-records, and rent-rolls; and by the very names originally given to the towns and hundreds; to the creeks and rivulets; to the tracts and manors of the county. The State itself bears the name of a Roman Catholic queen. Of the six hundreds of this small county, in 1650, five had the prefix of *St.* Sixty tracts and manors, most of them taken up at a very early period, bear the same Roman Catholic mark. The villages and creeks, to this day, attest the wide-spread prevalence of the same tastes, sentiments, and sympathies."

Mr. Davis' very careful and thorough investigations lead him to the conclusion that for twenty years after the first settlement—that is until the year 1654—the Catholic population of Maryland was in the majority. He concludes his chapter on this subject with the following passage:

"Looking, then, at the question under both its aspects—regarding the faith either of the delegates or of those whom they substantially represented—we cannot but award the chief honor to the members of the Roman church. To the Roman Catholic freemen of Maryland is justly due the main credit arising from the establishment, by a solemn legislative act, of religious freedom for all believers in Christianity."

Another Protestant historian, Mr. Irving Spence, who diligently searched the records of our State for material for his *Early History of the Presbyterian Church*, states his conclusions in a manner at once so emphatic and so candid, that we cannot forbear reciting the passage in a note.[1] Would that all who have discussed the subject had done so in a like frank and honorable spirit.

Again the Rev. J. S. M. Anderson, the eminent Protestant historian in his *History of the Church of England in the Colonies*, vol. ii, page 28, says: "The mild and equitable rule, indeed, of the Roman Catholic Lord Baltimore would have shielded the members of our church (Protestant Episcopal) as others, from persecution; but the mere fact that powers so vast as those conveyed under the charter of Maryland were entrusted to a Roman Catholic proprietor, was sufficient under any circumstances to deter most of the members of our communion, whether in England or America, from selecting that province for their abode; and the jealousy with which the Virginians naturally regarded a colony planted in lands once belonging to themselves, was an additional reason why the churchmen of their body should not have wished to fraternize with their neighbors beyond the Potomac."

Fortunately, we have another document at hand signed in the most solemn manner by those who certainly must have known the truth of the case, as they were the contemporaries, witnesses of, and participators in, the

[1] "I doubt whether there be older Presbyterian blood in America than flows in my veins at this moment; but let us do justice. The government of Maryland was one of the first organized in christendom which made religious toleration a corner-stone. From its institution until the expulsion of the unfortunate James II. from the British throne, indeed until his Protestant successor laid violent hands upon it, the principle was not only recognized, but carried out in practice, that 'error of opinion in religion may be tolerated while reason is left free to combat it.' . . . The first lord proprietary and his successors, carried out the purposes of their benevolent ancestor, and whilst their chartered rights were undisturbed, the inhabitants of Maryland were as carefully protected in worshipping God according to the dictates of conscience as they are at this time. A man might live in peace, whether Jew, Mohammedan or Pagan; whether atheist, deist, or polytheist: provided he neither molested his neighbor, nor endangered the public morals. Religious opinions wrought no civil disqualifications; and no one could be vexed with religious tests, or legally taxed to support any church of any name. Never was any government more indulgent to persons of all religious persuasions, than was that of Maryland, whilst the Roman Catholic Lords Baron's of Baltimore controlled it; and they had powers, more ample in fact, as to the matter under consideration, than could have been exercised by the first James or his successor, in the kingdom of Great Britain."

very events of which we are treating. This what is usually known as the *Protestant Declaration*, made the year after the passage of the Toleration Act, and shortly after it was known that Lord Baltimore had signed the act and made it the law of the land. This important document is signed by Governor Stone, the councillors Price, Vaughan, and Hatton, all of whom were members of the assembly that passed the Toleration Act; by all the Protestant burgesses in the assembly of 1650, and by a number of the leading Protestants of the colony. Its evident object was to refute the calumnies of Claiborne's partisans who were endeavoring to undermine Lord Baltimore's tenure of his province by representing in England and to the parliament that Maryland Protestants did not enjoy the free exercise of their religion under a Catholic proprietary. It runs as follows:

"DECLARATION.

"The declaration and certificate of William Stone, esquire, lieutenant of the province of Maryland, by commission from the right honourable the lord Baltimore, lord proprietary thereof, and of captaine John Price, Mr. Thomas Hatton, and captain Robert Vaughan of his sayd lordship's councell there, and of divers of the burgesses now met in an assembly there, and other *protestant* inhabitants of the sayd province, made the 17 day of April, anno dom. one thousand six hundred and fifty.

"We the sayd lieutenant, council, burgesses, and other *Protestant* inhabitants above mentioned, whose names are hereunto subscribed, doe declare and certifie to all persons whom it may concern, That according to an act of assembly heer, and several other strict injunctions and declarations by his sayd lordship for that purpose made and provided, we doe heere enjoy all fitting and convenient freedome and liberty in the exercise of our religion, under his lordship's government and interest; And that none of us are any ways troubled or molested, for or by reason thereof within his lordship's sayd province.

"William Stone, *Governor;* Jo. Price, Robert Vaughan, Tho. Hatton, *Councell;* James Cox, George Puddington,[1] Tho. Steerman, John Hatche, Robert Robines, Walter Bain, William Brough, Francis Poesy, *Burgesses;* William Durand,[2] Anthony Rawlins, Thomas Maydwell, Marke Bloomefield, Thomas Bushell, William Hungerford, William Stumpson, Thomas Dinyard, John Grinsdith, William Edwin, Richard Browne, Stanhop Roberts, William Browne, John Halfhead, William Hardwick, Elias Beech, George Sawyer, William Edis, John Gage, Robert Ward, William Marshall, Richard Smith, Arthur Turner, William Pell, William Warren, Edward Williams, Raph Beane, John Slingsby, James Morphen, Francis Martin, John Walker, William Hawley, William Smoot, John Sturman, John Nichols, Hugh Crage, George Whitacre, Daniel Clocker, John Perin, Patrick Forrest, George Beckwith, Thomas Warr, Walter Waterling.[3]

This declaration proves that the religious toleration they enjoyed was not due alone to the act of 1649, but to the uniform policy of Lord Baltimore and his government.

It is said by some that the act of 1649, notwithstanding the broad liberality of its provisions, was in reality meant to protect Catholics only. Undoubtedly, Lord Baltimore intended to secure by it freedom of worship to

[1] James Cox and George Puddington were then burgesses for the people at Ann Arundel.

[2] This is the same man who attests Mr. Strong's pamphlet.

[3] Langford's "Refutation of Leonard Strong's *Babylon's Fall.*"

those of his own faith; and it was the more incumbent on him to do, since he had appointed a Protestant governor, and must have foreseen that the time was at hand when, under his liberal policy, the majority in the Lower House would be Protestant. It was well for him to secure, in this contingency, so far as it was possible for him to do so by legal enactments, that the policy of toleration which had been maintained hitherto should suffer no change, and that whatever faith or faiths might happen to fall into a minority, should be equally the subjects of its protection. And the provincial government responded to his confidence in a like spirit, as we see by the act and the subsequent declaration, the Protestant governor and members of both houses joining hand in hand with the members of the Catholic faith, in pledging themselves to maintain liberty of conscience.

The assertion that this act was passed under fear of the triumphant party in England scarcely needs reply. The law was sent over in the fall or winter of 1648, having been drawn up in England by Lord Baltimore. The protection it afforded to "Prelatists" and "Papists," must have been obnoxious to Presbyterians and Independents. But as conclusive proof that no intimidation, no pusillanimity, no abject truckling to the party in power dictated the provisions of this act, we have but to point to the fact that in face of the enactment of parliament in February, 1649, that those who should call Charles the Second, king, should be guilty of high treason, on the 15th of November of the same year he was publicly proclaimed in Maryland "the undoubted rightful heir to all his father's dominions;" and in furtherance of the public rejoicing, a general pardon was announced.

To conclude this subject—the most important in the early history of Maryland—we sum up our results as follows: Toleration in Maryland first arose in the breast of George Calvert, First Lord Baltimore,—

"clarum et venerabile nomen,"

and was embraced with equal nobility and generosity of soul by Cæcilius, the father of the province. The peculiar provisions of the charter, while they by no means prescribed toleration, yet, by making the province a palatinate, placed it in the power of the proprietary to carry out his liberal policy without molestation. The proprietary's spirit was caught by the first colonists, and the beneficent working of the policy was felt by all. When dissensions and civil war in the mother-country and at home seemed to threaten the overthrow of what had proved so great a blessing, the proprietary and the legislature, in which both faiths were represented, did what they could to secure toleration by making it the law of the land. The time was to come when narrower counsels were to prevail, and the ancient glory of Maryland to grow dim for a season, but nothing can rob Calvert and his band of colonists of the fame of founding the first settlement where conscience was free, and where, while persecution was raging around them, a sanctuary was established in which even Protestants found a refuge from Protestant intolerance.

CHAPTER VIII.

We have adverted on an earlier page to the labors of the missionaries that accompanied the colony, among the Indians, and of these we shall now give some account. So little information on the subject has been at the command of the earlier historians of Maryland, that the labors of these devoted men have received but slight notice, nor has the importance of the services they rendered the colony been properly understood. Fortunately, in comparatively recent times, the late Rev. W. McSherry, a native of Virginia, discovered in the archives of the Society of Jesus at Rome, the original narrative of Father White, giving an account of the voyage and landing of the first settlers, and a description of the country, written within a month of his arrival, and addressed to Father Mutius Vitelleschi, general of the order. Mr. McSherry also found various annual letters, written in subsequent years to the superiors of the society, giving account of the progress of their work, extracts from which have been published in connection with Father White's narrative.[1]

The records show that up to the time when the revolution trampled down the power of the Catholics, and banished the priests, these missionaries pursued their work with great zeal, fortitude and success. The dispositions of the Maryland Indians were specially favorable to their endeavors. They described them as generous, amiable, and grateful; temperate and chaste in their lives; not moved by sudden impulse, but grave, deliberate, and firm of purpose. The missionaries, fearing nothing, went at once among them, and shared their wild forest life. They followed them on their hunts, they launched the frail canoe on the bosom of unknown streams, they bivouacked with them in the depths of the primeval forest, and after chanting matins and lauds, slept fearlessly and peacefully among these dusky warriors, beneath the starry canopy of heaven. Hardships and privations they cheerfully endured: they patiently learned the barbarous tongue, that they might win the confidence and affection of the untutored savage, and raise his untaught mind to the height of Christian faith and Christian morals. Death itself sometimes stared them in the face—not only death from fatigue, from exposure, from fevers and other diseases, and the lack of proper medicines and attention, but death in more terrible forms of the tomahawk, the scalping-knife, and the torturing stake, in the many inroads which the fierce and cruel tribes of the north made upon the weaker Indians of southern Maryland. "But when," as Bancroft well asks, "did a Jesuit missionary seek to save his own life at what be believed to be the risk of a soul?"

[1] This work, published in 1874 by the Maryland Historical Society, is cited by us under the title of *Relatio Itineris*.

Upon the arrival of the colonists, the gentle disposition of the Indians, and the ready welcome extended to the whites, encouraged the missionaries to hope for a speedy conversion of all the natives to Christianity. The two priests, Fathers White and Altham, obtained, by consent of its owner, one of the Indian huts for their own use, and having fitted it up as well as their means allowed, they called it "the first chapel in Maryland." Here they applied themselves to the study of the Indian language, in which the diversity of dialects among the various tribes greatly added to their difficulties. A third priest arrived from Europe in 1635, at which period the missionaries state in their letters that:

"On account of the very many difficulties that present themselves in this mission, which has been lately undertaken, there has been thus far but little fruit from it, especially among the savages, whose language is slowly acquired by our countrymen, and can hardly be written at all. There are employed in it five associates, three priests, and two assistants, who, in hope of future results, endure their present toils with great cheerfulness."[1]

In the year 1636, the Maryland mission numbered four priests and one lay coadjutor. No extract from the annual letter for 1637 has been made public; so we know not what happened, or whether their numbers were increased in that year. In 1638, we have an account of their proceedings. The letter goes on to say:

"Though the rulers of this colony have not yet allowed us to dwell among the savages, both on account of the prevailing sickness, and also, because of the hostile disposition which the barbarians evince towards the English, they having slain a man from this colony, who was staying among them for the sake of trading, and having also entered into a conspiracy against our whole nation; yet we hope that one of us will shortly secure a station among the barbarians. Meanwhile, we devote ourselves more zealously to the English; and since there are Protestants as well as Catholics in the colony, we have labored for both, and God has blessed our labors.

"For, among the Protestants, nearly all who have come from England, in this year, 1638, and many others, have been converted to the faith, together with four servants, whom we purchased in Virginia, (another colony of our kingdom,) for necessary services, and five mechanics, whom we hired for a month, and have in the meantime won to God. * * *

"As for the Catholics, the attendance on the sacraments here is so large, that it is not greater among the Europeans, in proportion to the number of Catholics. The more ignorant have been catechised, and Catechetical Lectures have been delivered for the more advanced every Sunday; but on feast days sermons have been rarely neglected. The sick and the dying, who have been very numerous this year, and who dwelt far apart, we have assisted in every way, so that not even a single one has died without the sacraments. We have buried very many, and baptized various persons. And, although there are not wanting frequent occasions of dissension, yet none of any importance has arisen here in the last nine months, which we have not immediately allayed. By the blessing of God, we have this consolation, that no vices spring up among the new Catholics, although settlements of this kind are not usually supplied from the best class of men.

[1] *Relatio Itineris*, p. 54.

"We bought off in Virginia, two Catholics, who had sold themselves into bondage, nor was the money ill-spent, for both showed themselves good Christians: one, indeed, surpasses the ordinary standard. Some others have performed the same duty of Charity, buying thence Catholic servants, who are very numerous in that country. For every year, very many sell themselves thither into bondage, and living among men of the worst example, and, being destitute of all spiritual aid, they generally make shipwreck of their souls."[1]

The king of the Patuxents, whose name was Maquacomen, had shown the most friendly disposition towards the Maryland colonists from their first arrival. Indeed, the people dwelling upon the Patuxent were described by Captain Smith as more civil and hospitable than any other Indians seen by him, when he first visited that river, in 1608. It would also appear, by his account, that the Patuxent country was more thickly inhabited than any other portion of Maryland which he visited. The nations or tribes of Indians named Acquintanacksuah, Patuxent, and Mattapanient, dwelt there in Smith's time. Maquacomen is stated to have been possessed of great influence and authority among the savages. It was, therefore, considered of importance by the missionaries to attempt the conversion of this prince and the numerous people on the banks of the Patuxent.

With this view Father White took up his residence there, and employed himself diligently among the Indians near the mouth of that river. He had succeeded in the conversion of only six of these people, when Governor Calvert, discovering some indications of hostile or unfriendly feeling on the part of Maquacomen towards the colonists, recalled Father White to St. Mary's, lest his life or liberty should be endangered among the savages, in case of war.[2] Friendly relations having been re-established in the beginning of 1639, the missionaries immediately improved the favorable circumstance by dispersing themselves among the Indians, in such places as seemed to be most favorable for the general diffusion of Christianity. The annual letter of 1639 says:

"There are in this mission four priests and one coadjutor. All are in places far distant—thus, doubtless, that so they expect to obtain an earlier acquaintance with the barbarian language, and propagate more widely the sacred faith of the gospel. Father John Brock, the Superior, with a coadjutor brother, remains in the plantation. Metapawnien, which was given us by Maquacomen, the king of Patuxent, is a certain storehouse of this mission, whence most of our bodily supplies are obtained. Father Philip Fisher lives in the principal town of the colony, to which the name of St. Mary's is given. Father John Gravener lives in Kent Island, sixty miles distant. Father Andrew White is distant still farther, one hundred and twenty miles, to wit: at Kittamaquindi, the metropolis of Pascatoe, having lived in the palace with the king himself of the place, whom they call Tayac, from the month of June, 1639. * * * * * * *

"The salvation of Maquacomen being despaired of, father Andrew betook himself to him, [the Tayac], and being treated by him very kindly at the first interview, so attached the man to him, that he was afterwards held by him in the greatest love and veneration;

[1] *Relatio Itineris.*

[2] *Early Maryland Missions.* U. S. Cath. Magazine, 1846.

of which thing this is the strongest proof, that he was unwilling that the father should use any other hospitality than of his palace. Nor was the queen inferior to her husband in benevolence to their guest, for with her own hands, (which thing the wife of our treasurer also does willingly) she is accustomed to prepare meat for him and bake bread, with no less care than labor.

"So, not long after the coming of father White to his palace, the Tayac was in danger from a severe disease; and when forty conjurers had, in vain, tried every remedy, the father, by permission of the sick man, administered medicine, to wit:—a certain powder of known efficacy mixed with holy water, and took care, the day after, by the assistance of the boy whom he had with him, to open one of his veins for blood letting. After this, the sick man began daily to grow better, nor long after became altogether well. Restored from the disease entirely, of himself he resolved, as soon as possible, to be initiated in the Christian rites; nor himself only, but his wife also and two daughters: for, as yet, he has no male offspring. Father White is now diligently engaged in their instruction; nor do they slothfully receive the heavenly doctrine, for, by the light of heaven poured upon them, they have long since found out the errors of their former life. The king has exchanged the skins, with which he was heretofore clothed, for a garment made in our fashion; he makes also a little endeavor to learn our language.

"Having put away his concubines from him, he lives content with one wife, that he may the more freely (as he says) have leisure to pray to God. He abstains from meat on the days in which it is forbidden by the Christian laws; and men that are heretics who do otherwise, or are of that name, he thinks ought to be called bad Christians. He is greatly delighted with spiritual conversation, and, indeed, seems to esteem earthly wealth as nothing, in comparison with heavenly, as he told the Governor, when explaining to him what great advantages from the English could be enjoyed by a mutual exchange of wares—'Verily, I consider these trifling when compared with this one advantage—that through these, as authors, I have arrived at the true knowledge of the one God; than which there is nothing greater to me among you, or which ought to be greater.' So, not long since, when he held a convention of the empire, in a crowded assembly of the chiefs and a circle of the common people, father White and some of the English being present, he publicly attested it was his advice, together with that of his wife and children, that the superstition of the country being abjured, to give their names to Christ; for that no other true deity is any where else had, other than among the Christians, nor otherwise can the immortal soul of man be saved from death—but that stones and herbs, to which, through blindness of mind, he and they had hitherto given divine honors, are the humblest things created by the Almighty God for the use and relief of human life. Which being spoken, he cast from him a stone which he held in his hand, and spurned it with his foot. A murmur of applause from the people sufficiently indicated that they did not hear these things with unfavorable ears. But the greatest hope is, that when the family of the king is purified by baptism, the conversion of the whole empire will speedily take place. In the meantime, we heartily thank God for the joyful commencement of affairs; and are especially encouraged, when we daily behold those idols to be the contempt of the natives, which were lately reckoned in the number of deities."

The writer then proceeds to describe the execution of an Indian convicted of the murder of an Englishman. The culprit was converted to Christianity before his death, which he met with fortitude, and his remains were buried with the solemn rites of the church. The writer continues:

"No one, however, was more vehemently moved at the sight of the dying *neophyte* than the Tayac, who afterwards earnestly insisted that he too should receive the gift of baptism. The thing being considered in council, it appeared that it would be for the greater glory of God, if it be deferred a little, until it could be performed with splendid display, in the greatest solemnity, and in the sight of his countrymen; his wife also, and his children coming to a participation of his joy and gladness. The king, at length, won over by the attentions of the Catholics, and greatly delighted with their prolonged hospitality, returned home, the same father White being his attendant; whither as soon as he came, he gave command to his people to prepare the church by next Pentecost, the time appointed for the next baptism. On that day, at Kittamaquindi, the governor and other distinguished men of the colony contemplate honoring, by their presence, and by whatever other means they can, the Christian sacraments and the second better birth of the Tayac, a merciful God causing this thing to turn out to the good of all—to his glory, to our reward, and to the salvation of the whole tribe."

Father John Brock who is mentioned in the foregoing letter, took the station previously occupied by Father White, near the mouth of the Patuxent river, upon land which had been given to the missionaries by the Indians. The station was called Mattapany. This land was afterwards relinquished to Lord Baltimore, and is probably the same on which he built his mansion near the mouth of the Patuxent, the ruins of which are still to be seen. At Mattapany was the store house of the mission, from which supplies were furnished to the other stations.

The Tayac, mentioned in the last letter as king or emperor of Piscataway, was also called Chitomacon, or Chitomachen. The latter appears to have been his proper name, and Tayac an appellation expressing his rank or dignity. He had been represented as a chief of great power, exercising authority over several of the neighboring tribes. His capital, called Kittamaquindi, was probably at or near the present village of Piscataway, about fifteen miles south of Washington city.

The annual letter of 1640, gives an account of the baptism and marriage of this barbaric prince. So important was the event considered, that we find Governor Calvert and other of the principal men in the colony, making a journey into the wilderness to be present at it. As an incident in history it may be placed beside the baptism of Pocahontas, which has so often inspired the artist's pencil. As that ceremony secured for Virginia the friendship of the great chief Powhatan, so the baptism of the Tayac gained for the infant colony of Maryland the good will and alliance of the most powerful of the neighboring chieftains, without whose friendship its existence would probably have been seriously imperilled. The letter runs:

"In this mission this year have been four priests and one coadjutor. We stated last year what hope we had conceived of converting the Tayac, or the emperor of what they call Pascatoe. From that time, such is the kindness of God, the event has not disappointed the expectation; for he has joined our faith, some others also being brought over with him; and on the 5th of July 1640, when he was sufficiently instructed in the mysteries of the faith, in a solemn manner he received the sacramental waters in a little chapel, which, for that purpose and for divine worship, he had erected out of bark, after the manner of the Indians. At the same time the queen, with an infant at the breast, and others of the principal men, whom he especially admitted to his councels, together with his little son, were regenerated in the baptismal font. To the emperor, who was called Chitomachen before, was given the name of Charles; to his wife that of Mary. The others, in receiving the Christian faith, had Christian names alloted to them. The governor was present at the ceremony, together with his secretary and many others; nor was anything wanting in display which our means could supply.

"In the afternoon, the king and queen were united in matrimony in the Christian manner; then the great holy cross was erected, in carrying which to its destined place the king, governor, secretary and others, lent their shoulders and hands; two of us in the meantime chanting before them the litany in honor of the Blessed Virgin.

"When famine prevailed among the Indians, on account of the great drought of the past summer, that we might not appear to neglect their bodies, for the care of whose souls we had made so great a voyage, though corn was sold at a great price, nevertheless we considered it necessary to relieve their want of bread by assisting them. Amidst these cares, intent also on settling the affairs of the mission, we passed the greater part of the winter.

"On the 15th of February we came to Pascatoe, not without the great gratulation and joy of the inhabitants, who indeed seem well inclined to receive the Christian faith. So that not long after, the king bronght his daughter, seven years old, (whom he loves with great affection), to be educated among the English at St. Mary's; and when she shall well understand the Christian mysteries, to be washed in the sacred font of baptism. His counsellor, also, of whom we have spoken above, desiring the goodness of God, which he had experienced in his own case, to be brought also to his people, has nothing more earnest in his prayers, than that his wife and children may be brought to the waters of salvation; which most proper desire, after suitable instruction, by the favor of God, shall be gratified.

"But the king also of the Anacostans, whose territory is not far distant, is anxious to live among us, as one of us: from which it is plainly evident that a harvest will by no means be wanting to us, on which we may bestow labor with advantage; but rather it is to be feared that there will not be laborers for gathering so abundant a harvest. There are other villages lying near, which I doubt not, would run promptly and joyfully to the light of gospel truth, if any one would impart to them the word of eternal life. But it is not right for us here to be too anxious for bringing the others to the truth, lest we may seem to abandon prematurely our present tender flock. Nor need those who are sent for assisting us fear lest the means of life be wanting, when he who clothes the lilies and feeds the fowls of the air, will not suffer those, who are laboring to extend his kingdom, to be destitute of necessary sustenance."[1]

Father White continued to reside at Piscataway until 1642, occasionally visiting St. Mary's. Returning from one of these visits in the winter, he was detained by the ice, nearly opposite Potomac town, (then called Patemeak) in Virginia—the place visited by the governor and Father Altham, in their first exploring voyage. By walking over the ice, Father White reached the town, where he remained several weeks, preaching and instructing the natives. Owing to the destruction of the vessel in which he came, "the father was detained longer in his visit, to wit: seven weeks; for he found it necessary to bring another ship from St. Mary's. But the spiritual advantage of souls readily compensated for that delay; for, during that time, was added to the church the ruler of that little village, with the other principal men of its inhabitants, who received the faith of Christ and

[1] *Relatio Itineris.*

baptism. Besides these, also another, with many of his friends; a third likewise, with his wife, his son, and a friend; a fourth, in like manner, with another of no ignoble standing among his people. By their example, the people are prepared to receive the faith, whenever we will have leisure to instruct them by catechism. Not long after, the young empress (as they call her at Pascataway) was baptized in the town of St. Mary's and is being educated there, and is now a proficient in the English language."[1]

The missionaries were very successful in another quarter, of great importance. This was the Indian town of Potopaco, the site of Port Tobacco, the county seat of Charles county. This fertile district, embraced by the great bend of the Potomac river, being favorably situated for intercourse with the neighboring Indians, who were very numerous, the missionaries determined on establishing a residence there. This they were more inclined to do, because of interruptions at Piscataway from the Susquehannough Indians. In consequence of hostilities from the Nanticokes, the Wicomeses, and the Susquehannoughs, these tribes, as we have before mentioned, were declared to be enemies to the province, and great apprehensions were felt by the colonists. The Susquehannoughs about this time it seems, had taken up their residence upon the banks of the Potomac near Piscataway.[2] This fierce and truculent tribe made an attack upon one of the settlements, murdered the men, and carried off the property they found there. As the colony was feeble in numbers, and some internal dissensions amongst the English settlers prevented the prosecution of vigorous measures against the Indians, it was deemed most prudent to withdraw Father White from Piscataway.

In 1642 the missionaries made many excursions up the Patuxent river, as they saw occasion in the disturbed state of the country. Among their converts were the young queen of Patuxent town, and her mother, also the young queen of Potopaco, and the wife and two sons of "the great Tayac," who died the year before, as well as the greater part of the natives, to the number of one hundred and thirty. In their letter of 1642 they thus describe their excursion:

"We are carried in a pinnace, or galley, to wit: the father, the interpreter, and a servant—for we use an interpreter, as will be stated hereafter—two of them propel the boat with oars, when the wind fails or is adverse; the third steers with the helm. We take with us a little chest of bread, butter, cheese, corn, cut and dried before it is ripe, beans and a little flour—another chest, also, for carrying bottles, one of which contains wine for religious purposes, six others holy water for the purpose of baptism; a casket with the sacred utensils, and a table as an altar for performing sacrifice; and another casket full of trifles, which we give the Indians to conciliate their affection—such as little

[1] *Relatio Itineris.*

[2] The Susquehannoughs were still in their Fort near Piscataway in 1675, as appears by a letter written in 1705, formerly in the possession of Mr. Jefferson, and now in the Library of Congress. "The beginning, progress and conclusion of Bacon's rebellion in Virginia, in the year 1675 and 1676." The writer of this letter says: "The Susquehannocks were newly driven from their habitations at the head of Chesepiack Bay by the Cinela [*qy.*-Seneca] Indians, down to the head of Potomac, where they sought protection under the Piscataway Indians, who had a fort near the head of that river, and also were our friends."—Campbell's *Maryland Missions.* U. S. Cath. Magazine, 1846.

bells, combs, fishing-hooks, needles, thread and other things of this kind. We have, besides, a little tent when we are obliged to lie out in the open air, which is frequently the case; also a larger one, which is intended to keep out the rain. The servants also bring other things which are necessary for hunting, and preparing for food whatever they have taken in hunting.

"In our excursions we endeavor, as much as we can, to reach by evening some English house, or Indian village, but if not, we land, and to the father falls the care of mooring the boat fast to the shore, then of collecting wood and making a fire, while in the meantime the two others go to hunt—so that whatever they take may be prepared. But if not, having refreshed ourselves with our provisions, we lie down by the fire and take our rest. If fear of rain threatens, we erect our hut and cover it with a larger mat spread over; nor praise be to God, do we enjoy this humble fare and hard couch with a less joyful mind, than more luxurious provisions in Europe."[1]

Our extracts from the missionaries' letters, mention the arrival of two more assistants from England, in 1642, and are then interrupted until the year 1646. We have seen that up to the former date, the gospel had been preached to the Indians with success, not only at the capital of the province, but at Kent Island, along the shores of the Chesapeake bay, at Piscataway and Port Tobacco, on the Maryland side of the Potomac; and at Patowmeck town, on the Virginia side of that river; at Mattapany and Pawtuxent town, on the Patuxent river, besides in many other places, which were visited by the missionaries in their expeditions by water. By the interruption of the annual reports, we are left to the meagre accounts of these missions obtainable from other sources.

One fact of interest connected with the work of the Jesuit missionaries in Maryland deserves to be placed conspicuously on record. The first *printing press* ever worked in any British colony, was set up in Maryland by the Jesuit Fathers. Father White, after he had acquired sufficient knowledge of the Indian tongues, composed a catechism in several dialects, and the press was, no doubt, ordered for the purpose of printing it. Copies of this work are excessively rare; but Mr. McSherry found one in the archives of the Society at Rome. Father White also compiled an Indian grammar and dictionary, but no copies of these are known to exist. The press was probably destroyed when the missionaries were attacked and their property plundered in 1655; but the fact remains that Maryland, first of all the colonies, introduced this great agent for the diffusion of knowledge.

The letters failing us here, we have but fragmentary and imperfect accounts of the acts and sufferings of these missionaries for more than ten years. During Claiborne's rebellion in 1644–5, the venerable Father White was seized by a band of insurgents and sent in irons to England, where he was imprisoned and treated with great harshness. Though worn out by the hardships of ten years of missionary labor in the wilderness, and broken by age and imprisonment, he never relaxed his accustomed austerities, fasting twice a week on bread and water. The keeper of his prison was surprised at

[1] *Relatio Itineris.*

this, and said to him one day, "If you continue in this manner, you will not be strong enough to stand up under the gallows at Tyburn." The meek old man replied, "You must know that my feelings give me strength to bear all sufferings for the love of Jesus Christ." His life was spared; but he was finally banished from England, whither (it is reported) he returned, and died in London, December 27, 1656, O.S., (January 6, 1657, N.S.) in the seventy-eighth year of his age.

Upon the seizure of the missionaries, their Indian flocks were dispersed, as sheep without a shepherd. Again they returned to them, and again were chased away; nor were they ever after allowed to continue their labors without molestation. Although it somewhat anticipates events that will be recited on a future page of this history, we give, as an example of what they had to endure, an extract from the letter of 1656:

"The English who inhabit Virginia had made an attack on the colonists, themselves Englishmen too; and safety being guarantied on certain conditions, received indeed the governor of Maryland, with many others in surrender; but the conditions being treacherously violated, four of the captives, and three of them catholics, were pierced with leaden balls. Rushing into our houses, they demanded for death the impostors, as they called them, intending inevitable slaughter to those who should be caught. But the fathers, by the protection of God, unknown to them, were carried from before their faces: their books, furniture, and whatever was in the house, fell a prey to the robbers. With almost the entire loss of their property, private and domestic, together with great peril of life, they were secretly carried into Virginia; and in the greatest want of necessaries, scarcely, and with difficulty, do they sustain life. They live in a mean hut, low and depressed, not much unlike a cistern, or even a tomb, in which that great defender of the faith, St. Athanasius, lay concealed for many years. To their other miseries this inconvenience was added, that whatever comfort or aid this year, under name of stipend, from pious men in England, was destined for them, had been lost, the ship being intercepted in which it was carried. But nothing affects them more than that there is not a supply of wine which is sufficient to perform the sacred mysteries of the altar. They have no servant, either for domestic use, or for directing their way through unknown and suspected places, or even to row and steer the boat, if at any time there is need. Often, over spacious and vast rivers, one of them, alone and unaccompanied, passes and repasses long distances, with no other pilot directing his course than Divine Providence. By and by the enemy may be gone and they may return to Maryland; the things which they have already suffered from their people, and the disadvantages which still threaten are not much more tolerable." [1]

Such were some of the labors and trials of Father White and his associates in the early days of Maryland. The records, as we have said, are mere fragments, nor can we estimate the extent of their work nor of its success. But one fact is full of meaning to those who study the chronicles of those times, and that is the great and exceptional tranquillity which the colony enjoyed in its early relations with the Indians. There can be no doubt that this happy state of things was due, first to the equity and humanity with which the natives were treated by the settlers, and, secondly, to the devoted labors of the missionaries who spent their lives among them.

[1] *Relatio Itineris.*

How far they were able to bring them to the knowledge of the Christian faith, we cannot now say; but there can be no doubt that these pious men, both by example and precept, introduced them to a more civilized life and higher ideas of morality, and, in part at least, prevented or mitigated the cruel and bloody wars between the tribes, which, in some other colonies where Christianity was professed, were diligently fomented and inflamed.

No stone marks the graves of these devoted men. Of most of them even the names have passed into oblivion, and of the rest we have little more than a few faded yellow lines of antique writing scattered among mouldering and forgotten archives. The tribes among whom they labored have long since passed away. But their work has not perished with them; and if the peaceful, equitable, and generous spirit which characterized the early days of the colony, secured its growth and permanence, and has left its stamp on Maryland institutions, is something to remember with pride, let it not be forgotten how large a part of this is due to the truly Christian example and teachings of the early missionary Fathers. We may or may not share their views in matters of theological doctrine, but bigotry itself must admit the apostolic character of their lives.

CHAPTER IX.

THE wide-spread evils resulting from the civil dissensions in England, affected the remotest provinces, where party spirit ran as high as in the mother country, and Maryland had her full share of the disasters which it bred. While King Charles was a captive in the hands of parliament, Claiborne and Ingle acted under professed authority from the parliamentary commissioners for the regulation of the provinces; but it does not appear that either of them or of their associates undertook to govern in the name of these commissioners. The only attempt to establish a regular and legal government, of which we have any information, was made by a certain Captain Edward Hill, who held a commission from the council, dated July 30th, 1646, under the name of Governor Calvert, though it is probable that the governor never signed such an instrument. As for the Lord Proprietary, he seemed to consider his province lost, and only thought of saving what he could of his private property. On the 15th November, 1646, he sent a warrant of attorney to his brother, Leonard Calvert, the late governor, and Mr. Secretary Lewger, directing them to collect and take charge of so much of his private possessions as might be saved from the general wreck of his fortunes. But Governor Calvert had not retreated into Virginia with the intent of passively resigning his government to the insurgents, and he saw grounds for hope that his brother knew not of. It was true that Virginia had always shown jealousy and hostility to the province; but on the other hand, there was a large body of loyalists there, with stout old Sir William Berkeley, the governor, at their head, who were united by common danger and a common cause with the loyalists of Maryland, and who still managed to hold Virginia in obedience to the king, long after the mother-country had submitted to the parliament. On these Calvert relied for assistance, and not in vain, for he was enabled to gather and organize a force for the reconquest of the province.

The colonists of Maryland in the meantime were growing discontented with their rulers, and daily more disposed to regret the mild and paternal sway of the proprietary. Indeed, within the short space of two years, a disastrous change was apparent in their fortunes: manors and plantations were forsaken, improvements ceased, trade languished, industry was paralyzed, and the province seemed rapidly going to ruin. The steadfast adherents of the Calverts saw the drift of the popular feeling, and, no doubt, kept the governor advised of the state of affairs and the increasing chances of success.

Near the end of 1646, Governor Calvert, at the head of a small force, returned to St. Mary's, where he repossessed himself of the government almost without resistance. Hill surrendered without striking a blow, and retired to Virginia, and the whole western shore returned to its allegiance. Governor Calvert convened the assembly that had been summoned by Hill, and affairs flowed on in their old channels.[1]

The assembly met again on December 29th, 1646, O.S. (January 8th, 1647 N.S.), and in the records of its session we notice for the first time the distinction made between an *upper* and a *lower* house. We find them also copying the form of parliament at the opening of the session: the lower house being sent for to attend the governor in the upper to hear his speech. The journal recites:

"In the upper house present, the Governor, Mr. Lewger, Mr. Greene.—The burgesses being sent for and all appearing, the Governor declares to them that they were called hither as freemen to treat and advise in assembly touching all matters, as freely and boldly, without any awe or fear, and with the same liberty, as at any assembly they might have done heretofore, and that they were now free from all restraint of their persons, and should be free during the assembly, saving only to himself, after the end of the assembly, such charge as he had or hath against any for any crime committed since the last pardon."[2]

Kent Island, the stronghold of the malcontents, still held out against Governor Calvert, who, to reduce it to obedience, on the 16th of January declared martial law, and laid the island under an embargo. In April he proceeded thither with a force and took possession, thus re-establishing his authority over the whole province. On the submission of the inhabitants the governor issued a general pardon, bearing date the 16th of April, 1647, to all the inhabitants therein named, "of and for all crimes of rebellion, or other offences whatsoever committed within the province at any time before."[3]

"He then proceeded to settle the civil as well as military government of the island, and for that purpose issued a commission, on the 18th of April, whereby he appointed Robert Vaughan, gent., to be chief captain and commander under him (the governor) 'of all the militia of the isle of Kent, and with it to command and execute whatsoever shall be by him thought requisite for the defence of the said island against all intestine mutinies or seditions, that shall happen within the said island, and against all invasion of any foreign enemies whatsoever.' He also 'authorised him to constitute and ordain under him all such officers for military service as he should think requisite, and inflict such punishment upon all offenders under his command against martial discipline, as the nature of the offence shall deserve, according to the law martial; provided that where the offence shall deserve the forfeiture of either life or member, that such offender for his trial be referred, and judgment, to the *provincial court* to be held by his lordship's *governor and council* of this province.' He further authorised 'the said captain Robert Vaughan

[1] Burnap, p. 219.

[2] Bozman.

[3] The names of those who were pardoned, and who, therefore, had been engaged in resistance to Lord Baltimore's authority, with others who had fled, are thus stated in the preamble:

"*Whereas* the inhabitants of the Isle of Kent, Thomas Bradnox, Edward Comins, John Metham, Thomas Belt, Robert Short, Francis Lumhard, John Ayres, Zachary Wade, Richard Cotesford, Edward Lannin, and Walter Joanes, have taken the oath of fealty to the Lord Baltimore, and submitted themselves again to his lordship's government," etc.—*Bozman.*

to award all process necessary, according to the law and custom of this province, for or concerning all actions civil and criminal within the said isle of Kent; and he authorised the said captain Robert Vaughan, William Cox, Thomas Bradnox, Edward Comins, Philip Conner, and Francis Brooke, gent., or the major part of them, whereof the said Robert Vaughan to be always one, to hear, try, and judge, according to the laws of this province, all actions and causes civil, which shall happen between party and party within the said . . . . and to award execution upon the same, except where the freehold of any one shall come in question, provided that it shall be lawful for any man, at any time before execution served, to appeal from the said judgment unto the *provincial court* of this province, the appellant first putting in sufficient security to the court, from whence the appeal is made, for treble damages to be satisfied to the adverse party in the cause, in case he be cast in the provincial court in the said cause; and he further authorised the said captain Vaughan and his associates before mentioned, or the major part of them, whereof the said captain Robert Vaughan to be always one, to hear and judge, according to the laws of this province, all crimes and offences committed within the said island, and to cause such sentence, as shall be given by them therein, to be executed, excepting where the life or member of any one person shall come in question.' This arrangement for the administration of justice in the isle of Kent seems to have been similar to what had been before practised in the latter end of the year 1642, when that island appears to have been first considered as a *county* distinct from that of St. Mary's, and not a *hundred* appertaining to it, as it formerly was by the bill entitled, 'an act for the government of the isle of Kent,' passed at the session of 1638–9. The appellate jurisdiction of the provincial court, traced out by this commission, seems also to have been nearly the same as that which continued to be practised from county courts during the existence of the provincial government."[1]

Tranquillity having thus been restored to the province, and the Lord Proprietary happily reinstated in his rights and dominions, Leonard Calvert returned to St. Mary's with the prospect of enjoying the peace he had won by his wisdom, fidelity and courage. But he returned only to die. On the 9th of June he breathed his last, having named Thomas Greene as his successor, who immediately entered upon the discharge of his duties.

Greene's first action was to prevent any attempt to disturb the peace of Maryland on the part of Captain Hill or his adherents who had settled on the opposite shore of the Potomac, where they watched events, hoping for a favorable opportunity to invade the colony, which, in the meantime, they frequently visited, sometimes in secret to confer with those who favored their plans, and sometimes openly and armed. Upon Governor Greene's representations, the assembly passed an act prohibiting their entry into the province under penalties.

Some of the Indian tribes, instigated probably by the white enemies of Maryland, were now giving trouble, as we find by a commission issued on the 4th of July to Captain John Price. The preamble recites that, "the inhabitants of this province have sustained divers great losses in their estates by the Indians of *Nanticoke* and *Wicomick*, enemies of this province, who making incursions here have assailed and set upon divers of the inhabitants of this province, and have committed divers insolencies, rapines, murthers,

[1] Bozman, p. 304.

and other barbarous cruelties, *by the way of trade*, and that divers overtures of peace had been made to them; but notwithstanding, they still persist in their wicked and barbarous intentions toward us." The commission then authorizes him "to take thirty or forty such able men as he shall think fit and make choice of for that purpose, with sufficient arms, provision, and ammunition, and them to embark in such vessel or vessels as he, the said Captain John Price, shall think fit and convenient, and with the said men to go over unto the towns and plantations of the Indians of *Nanticoke* and *Wicomick* aforesaid, lying to the eastward of this province, and then and there to employ his utmost endeavour, skill and force, by what means he may, in destroying the said nations, as well by land as by water, either by killing them, taking them prisoners, burning their houses, destroying their corn, or by any other means as in his best discretion he shall judge convenient." Whether this expedition under this commission took place or not, or if so, what were the incidents of it, we are no where informed. Captain Price appears to have been relied upon, at this time, as a man of some experience in military affairs; and, for his fidelity to the Lord Proprietary during Ingle's rebellion, was subsequently, in 1648, created "muster-master general" of the province; in which commission his "abilities in martial affairs" are highly commended by his lordship.[1] Towards the close of the year the governor summoned an assembly, which met at St. Mary's on January 17th, 1648. At this session a curious incident occurred. Mistress Margaret Brent, the administratrix of Leonard Calvert's estate, applied to the assembly, demanding "to have a vote in the house for herself and another as his lordship's [Lord Baltimore's] attorney." This was refused peremptorily by Governor Greene, and the lady "protested in form against all the proceedings of that assembly, unless she might be present and vote as aforesaid."[2]

At the close of the session, Governor Greene signalized the restoration of good feeling to the province by a proclamation, issued on the 4th of March, granting a general pardon for all offences committed since the 14th of February, 1644, to all persons within or without the province, Richard Ingle only excepted. Thus ended a rebellion conducted with no common skill and audacity, and which—favored as it was by the course of events in England—might have resulted in the permanent overthrow of the proprietary government, had the rule of the Calverts been less mild and wise, or that of the insurgents less oppressive. "Its lingering consequence was longest felt in

[1] Bozman.

[2] Kilty's *L. Asst.*, p. 104.

the threatening aspect of the Indians, who still continued so hostile that the governor found it necessary to adjourn the county court, lest the absence of jurymen, parties and witnesses from the frontier districts should weaken those exposed portions of the settlements and subject them to outrage."[1] For causes not known, the Lord Proprietary removed Governor Greene, and appointed William Stone, who entered upon his duties in the latter part of 1648 or the beginning of 1649. On the 12th of August, Lord Baltimore also sent out "a commission for the great seal," a proceeding rendered necessary from the fact that the great seal of the province had been carried off in Ingle's rebellion, in 1644, and never recovered. In this commission his lordship protests against all acts done under the confirmation of that seal since the 14th of February, 1644, and minutely describes the new seal, which differed slightly from the first.

"On the one side thereof is engraven our figure in complete armour, on horseback, with our sword drawn and our helmet on, and a great plume of feathers affixed to it, the horse-trappings, furniture, and caparison being adorned with the figure of our paternal coat of arms, and underneath the horse a sea-shore engraven, with certain flowers and grass growing upon it, and this inscription about that side of the seal, viz: *Cecilius Absolutus Dominus Terræ Mariæ et Avaloniæ Baro de Baltimore*, and on the other or counter-side of the said seal, is engraven a scutcheon, wherein our paternal coat of arms, to wit: Six pieces impaled, with a bend dexter counterchanged, quartered with another coat of arms belonging to our family, viz: A cross buttoned at each end (and also counterchanged) are engraven; the whole scutcheon being supported with a fisherman on the one side, and a ploughman on the other, standing upon a scroll, wherein is engraven the motto of our paternal coat of arms, viz: *Fatti Maschij Parole Femine.* Next above the scutcheon is engraven a Count Palatine's cap, and over that a helmet with the crest of our paternal coat of arms on the top of it, which crest is a ducal crown with two half bannerets set upright on it. Behind the said scutcheon and supporters is engraven a large mantle, and this inscription is about that side of the seal, viz.: *Scuto Bonæ Voluntatis Tuæ Coronasti Nos.* The figure of the seal is round, and it is of the same bigness that our former great seal was, and cut in silver, as the other was. The impression of all which in wax is hereunto affixed, it being somewhat different (though but little) from our former great seal of the said province. We do hereby declare the said new seal to be from henceforwards our great seal of the said province of Maryland, and that we will have it to be so esteemed and reputed there till we or our heirs shall signify our or their pleasure to the contrary."[2]

[1] McSherry, *History of Maryland*, p. 64.

[2] The blazon here given of the escutcheon coincides with the arms of Lord Baltimore, as represented under his portrait engraved by Blotling in 1657, a copy of which is in the possession of the Maryland Historical Society. The crest and motto, with the first and fourth quarters of the escutcheon, belong to the hereditary arms of the Calvert family. The second and third quarters were derived from the Crosslands of Yorkshire, whose arms are described in Berry's *Encyclopædia Heraldica* (London, 1828) as "quarterly, argent and gules, a cross flory counterchanged." The difference between a *cross bottony* (budded cross) and a *cross flory* (flowered cross) is very slight, consisting in a trifling modification of the terminal ornaments of the arms; and as the former is so identified with our State escutcheon as to be known as "the Maryland Cross," no change should be made in it. The ridiculous and ignorant substitution of an *eagle* for the noble crest, which, in its Palatine's cap, signified the immense privileges conferred by the charter which, distinguishing Maryland above all the other provinces, made her almost independent of the Crown of England, has now, happily, been done away with, and the ancient device restored.

The substitution in the second seal of the ploughman and fisherman as supporters in place of the leopards of his family coat, was a fancy of the proprietary. The engraver of this seal either committed an error, or introduced a

On the 2d of April, 1649, Governor Stone convened the General Assembly at St. Mary's, where, besides the famous "Act concerning Religion," they passed among other laws, a legislative order entitled "An Order of Assembly for the Defence of the Province, as the present times will permit."

"It seems to have been designed as a sort of a militia law, whereby the inhabitants of every hundred in the province were to be assembled at stated times in the year by an officer to be appointed by the Governor, called the Commander of the hundred, for the purpose of making 'such orders and ordinances as they shall judge meet and neccessary for the defence of each particular hundred.' It regulates also the mode of communicating any alarm by what they call 'rounding,' that is, by the discharge of three or more muskets which every master of a family was to answer by the like number of guns, and so communicate the alarm through the hundred and from one hundred to another throughout the province. It further ordered that no inhabitant should go out of the limits of the plantation where he resided, not even to church, without being well armed; and that every master of a family should provide sufficient arms and ammunition, not only for himself, but for his servants and sojourners at his house."[1]

This assembly was dissolved by the governor on the 21st of April, 1649.

We are now approaching one of the most critical periods in the history of the colony. The great wave of revolution that had risen so high in England, and for a time submerged both the church and the throne, found its way across the Atlantic and swept over the little colony of Maryland. Two parties holding opposite views of religion and of government, and widely variant social and moral codes—differing therefore on points the most vital, and to which men cling with the most resolved tenacity—found themselves face to face in Maryland; the one backed by the power and influence of parliament and the dominant party in England, the other supported by the letter of the charter, by the sense of justice and equity, and by the personal affection which bound them to the proprietary and his government. To explain the events we are approaching, we must go a little back in the order of time.

As early as 1639, so unfavorable an opinion of the Puritans prevailed in Virginia, that several laws were made against them, "though there were none yet amongst them," but by way of anticipation, "to prevent the infection from reaching the country;"[2] and so rigorous were these laws in both tenor and execution, that "none but conformists, in the strictest and most absolute sense, were permitted to reside in the colony."[3] Yet it would seem that in

difference by making the bannerets of the crest fly toward the sinister instead of the dexter side, as they are shown in Guillim's *Display of Heraldry*, and other heraldic works. (*Vid.* Clayton Hall, *Address Md. Hist. Soc.*)

This seal was used until the province came under Cromwell's commissioners in 1651, shortly after which it was either lost or stolen. In 1657, after his restoration to his proprietary rights, Lord Baltimore sent out a third seal by his newly appointed lieutenant, Captain Josias Fendall, which was used until the year 1705. In 1713 the Board of Trade made another change, duplicating the original seal of 1633 in all respects except the quarterings of the escutcheon. This we find on the title-page of the acts of the general assembly continuously down to 1765, when a fifth seal, closely resembling the third, was made and used until long after the Revolution.

[1] Bozman, ii., p. 364.

[2] Beverly, *History of Virginia*, p. 51. Burk, *History of Virginia*, ii., p. 75.

[3] Beverly, p. 67.

some parts of the colony the laws were less strictly enforced, or that means were found to elude them; for in 1641, Richard Bennett, (afterwards one of Cromwell's commissioners,) "went to Boston in New England, to desire in the name of some other gentlemen of Virginia that two or three ministers might be sent to them." To this purpose Mr. Bennett carried with him letters from "sundry well-disposed people" of Virginia to the ministers of New England, earnestly soliciting a supply of pastors of their own persuasion. The elders of Massachusetts, after "setting apart a day in which to seek God" touching the matter, despatched to Virginia three of their number "which might most easily be spared."[1] Of the three thus designated as most dispensable, one only could be prevailed on to obey the summons, and this was William Thompson, a native of England, one of the primitive Puritans of Lancashire, and at this time the first minister of Braintree, Massachusetts. In a short time he was joined by Mr. Knolles, of Watertown, and Mr. James, of New Haven. The stay of these gentlemen, however, was but brief, for the legislature in the same year, (1642,) enacted that "for the preservation of purity and unity of doctrine and discipline in the church, and the right administration of the sacraments, no minister be admitted to officiate in this country, but such as shall produce to the governor a testimonial that he hath received his ordination from some bishop in England, and shall then subscribe, to be conformable to the orders and constitutions of the Church of England, and the laws there established; upon which the governor is hereby requested to induct the said minister into any parish that shall make presentation of him; and if any other person, pretending himself a minister, shall, contrary to this act, presume to teach or preach publicly or privately, the governor and council are hereby desired and empowered to suspend and silence the person so offending; and upon his obstinate persistence, to compel him to depart the country with the first convenience."[2] The passage of this act compelled the speedy return of these unwelcome ministers, and prevented them from preaching and propagating their doctrines to "the ungodly Virginians."[3] These Congregationalists or Independents, by secret meetings, notwithstanding the laws against them in Virginia, contrived to keep up a conventicle for some years, which, in 1648, numbered one hundred and eighteen members.[4]

From the first they were objects of suspicion, for the colonists saw plainly that the measures in progress in England, tended to the subversion of the church as well as the throne; so as their increasing numbers drew upon them the attention of the colonial government, a more rigorous execution of the laws was deemed expedient, and the conventicle was broken up and the members expelled from the colony. Mr. Harrison, their pastor, went to Boston, and Mr. Durand, their elder, with Richard Bennett, took refuge in that asylum of the persecuted—Maryland. How they requited the generous

[1] Oliver, Winthrop, Hubbard, Oldmixon, i., 300.
[2] Henning, p. 277.
[3] Chalmers, p. 121.
[4] Hawks, *Virginia*, p. 57.

liberality that gave them a home and the protection of the laws, will be hereafter seen. The Puritans upon the James and Elizabeth rivers, being in like manner expelled, fled to the same sanctuary, and in the years 1649–50, founded several settlements at Greenberry's Point and upon the Severn.[1]

Mr. John Hammond, a contemporary, in his *Leah and Rachel*, published in London in 1656, says of the transactions here related, that—

"Maryland was courted by them [the Puritans] as a refuge, the Lord Proprietor and his Governor solicited to, and several addresses and treaties made for their admittance and entertainment into that province, their conditions were pitied, their propositions were hearkened to and agreed on, which was, that they should have convenient portions of land assigned them, liberty of conscience, and privilege to choose their own officers, and hold courts within themselves. All was granted them; they had a whole county of the richest land in the province assigned them, and such as themselves made choice of; the conditions of plantations, such as were common to all adventurers, were shewed and propounded to them, which they warmly approved of, and nothing was in those conditions exacted from them but appeals to the provincial court, quit-rents, and an oath of fidelity to the Proprietor. An assembly was called throughout the whole country after their coming over (consisting as well of themselves as the rest) and because there were some few papists that first inhabited there themselves, and others being of different judgments, an act passed that all professing in Jesus Christ should have equal justice, privileges and benefits in that province, and that none on penalty (mentioned) should disturb each other in their several professions, nor give the urging terms, either of Roundheads, Sectaries, Independents, Jesuit, Papist, &c.; intending an absolute peace and unison; the oath of fidelity (although none other than every lord of a manor requires from his tenant) was overhauled, and this clause added to it—'provided it infringe not the liberty of the conscience.'

"They sat down joyfully, followed their vocations cheerfully, trade increased in their province, and divers others were by this encouraged and invited over from Virginia."

The Puritans were no sooner seated in their new habitations than they began to raise objections to the oath of fidelity required by the "conditions of plantations" sent by Lord Baltimore to the Governor in 1648, which were agreed to by all immigrants on obtaining patents for their lands. The particular condition referred to, ran thus:

"Every adventurer or planter that shall have any land granted unto him by virtue of these conditions, before any grant be delivered to him, and before it shall enure to his benefit, shall take within the said province the oath of fidelity to his lordship and his heirs, lords and proprietaries of the said province, hereunto specified."

[1] Mr. Davis, after investigating the matter, comes to the following conclusions, which our own examination of the records confirms:

"It is generally believed that the first settlement of the Puritans was at the point where the city of Annapolis stands, and that the foundation of that city was laid almost immediately after their arrival. I can only say there is no recorded evidence within my knowledge of the facts. The earliest settlement which I can discover (the one of 1649) was at Greenberry's Point, a peninsula of the Chesapeake, a little below the mouth of the Severn. My belief is that Annapolis was not founded till many years later. But at Greenberry's Point a town was laid out the very first year of the settlement there; and the tract running down to the point, and now in the possession of Captain Taylor, was originally called Town Neck, as the history of the land-title will clearly show."—*Day Star*, p. 68.

The oath of fidelity was in the following terms:

"I, A. B., do faithfully and truly acknowledge the right honble. Cecilius, lord baron of Baltimore, to be the true and absolute lord and proprietary of this province and country of Maryland, and the islands thereunto belonging; and I do swear that I will bear true faith unto his lordship and to his heirs, as to the true and absolute lords and proprietaries of the said province and islands thereunto belonging, and will not, at any time, by words or actions, in publick or in private, wittingly or willingly, to the best of my understanding, any way derogate from, but will, at all times, as occasion shall require, to the utmost of my power, defend and maintain all such his said lordship's and his heirs' right, title, interest, privilege, royal jurisdiction, prerogative, proprietary and dominion over and in the said province of Maryland. and islands thereunto belonging, and over the people who are and shall be therein for the time being, as are granted, or mentioned to be granted to his said lordship and his heirs by the king of England, in his said lordship's patent of the said province, under the great seal of England. I do also swear that I will with all expedition discover to his said lordship, or to his lieutenant or other chief governor of the said province for the time being, and also use my best endeavors to prevent any plot, conspiracy or combination which I shall know or have cause to suspect is, or shall be intended against the person of his said lordship, or which shall tend any ways to the disinherison or deprivation of his said lordship's, or his said heirs' their right, title, royal jurisdiction and dominion aforesaid, or any part thereof; and I do swear that I will not, either by myself or by any other person, or persons, directly or indirectly, take, accept, receive, purchase or possess any lands, tenements or hereditaments, within the said province of Maryland or the islands thereunto belonging, from any Indian or Indians, to any other use or uses but to the use of his said lordship and his heirs, or knowingly from any other person or persons not deriving a legal title thereunto by, from, or under some grant from his said lordship or his said heirs, legally passed, or to be passed, under his or their great seal of the said province for the time being. So help me God, and by the contents of this book. Given at Bath, under his lordship's hand and greater seal at arms, the 20th day of June, 1648."

This oath "was exceedingly scrupled," says Leonard Strong, a contemporary, "on account, viz.: that they must swear to uphold that government and those officers who were sworn to countenance and uphold anti-Christ, in plain words, expressed in the officers' oath—the Roman Catholic religion."[1] But this objection was conclusively answered by another contemporary, John Langford,[2] who remarks:

"There was nothing promised by my Lord or Captain Stone to them but what was performed. *They were first acquainted, by Captain Stone, before they came there*, with that oath of fidelity which was to be taken by those who would have any land there from his lordship; nor had they any regrett to the oath, till they were as much refreshed with their entertainment there as the snake in the fable was with the countryman's breast; for which some of them are equally thankful. But it is now, it seems, thought by some of these people too much below them to take an oath to the Lord Proprietary of that province, though many Protestants, of much better quality, have taken it, and (which is more than can be hoped for from some of these men) kept it. As to the government there, *they knew it very well before they came thither;* and, if they had not liked it, they might have forborne coming or staying there; for they were never forced to either. The chief officers under my lord there are Protestants. The jurisdiction exercised there by

[1] *Babylon's Fall;* London, 1655.

[2] *Refutation of Babylon's Fall;* London, 1655.

them is no other than what is warranted by his lordship's patent of that province, which gives him the power and privileges of a Count Palatine there, depending on the supreme authority of England with power to make laws with the people's consent; without which powers and privileges, his lordship would not have undertaken that plantation, and have been at so great a charge, and run so many hazards as he hath done for it." "There are none there sworn to uphold anti-Christ, as Mr. Strong falsely suggests; nor doth the oath of fidelity bind any man to maintain any other jurisdiction or dominion of my lord's, than what is granted by his patent. Though some of these people, it seems, thinke it unfit that my lord should have such a jurisdiction and dominion there, yet they, it seems, by their arrogant and insolent proceedings, thinke it fit for them to exercise farre more absolute jurisdiction and dominion there than my Lord Baltimore ever did; nor are they contented with freedome for themselves of conscience, person and estate (all of which are establisht to them by law there and enjoyed by them in as ample manner as ever any people did in any place in the world), *unless they may have the liberty to debarr others from the like freedome*, and that they may domineere and doe what they please."

"But it was not religion," says Mr. John Hammond, another contemporary writer;[1] "it was not punctilios they stood upon, it was that sweete, that rich, that large country they aimed at; and finding themselves in a capacitie not only to capitulate, but to oversway those that had so received and relieved them, began to pick quarrells first with the Papists, next with the oath, and lastly declared their averseness to all conformalitie, wholly ayming (as themselves since confessed) to deprive the Lord Proprietor of all his interest in that country and make it their own." These Puritans who had been "received and protected" by the Governor of Maryland, formed themselves into a community, governed upon their own congregational system, occupying lands without any formal grants, and had no recognized connection with the colony until July, 1650, when their settlement was erected into a county, and a commander and justices of the peace were appointed, as in Kent and St. Mary's.[2]

CHARLES II.

Upon the execution of Charles I., parliament passed a decree declaring it to be treason for any one to acknowledge "Charles Stuart, son of the late Charles, commonly called the Prince of Wales, or any other person, to be king or chief magistrate of England or Ireland, or of any dominions belonging thereunto, by color of inheritance, succession, election or any other claim whatever." In spite of this prohibition, Thomas Greene—the former governor, now acting as governor under a commission from Stone during the temporary absence of the latter in Virginia, with more loyalty than prudence issued a proclamation on Nov. 15, declaring Charles to be "the undoubted rightful heir to all his father's dominions," and signalized the occasion by a general

[1] *Leah and Rachel*; London, 1656.

[2] We find also note of a settlement upon South River about 1650, chiefly of Puritans and Episcopalians from Virginia; and about twenty miles from the mouth of the Patuxent a manor was taken up in the same year by Robert Brooke, with a household of forty persons.

pardon for all offences. Stone soon returned and resumed the government, and this act of folly on Greene's part was not followed by any measures likely to give offence to the parliament, but the audacity was not forgotten. In April, 1650, the assembly met, pursuant to the call of Governor Stone, and passed an order for drawing "An Act for Settling this Present Assembly," as also for rules and orders to be observed in the conduct of its deliberations. On the 6th of April, the following form of government was unanimously agreed to, which, though apparently intended as a temporary arrangement, proved so satisfactory in its working, that it continued almost without interruption, until the dissolution of the provincial government at the American Revolution:

"*An act for settling of this present assembly.*

"Be it enacted by the lord proprietary, with the advice and consent of the council and burgesses of this province now assembled, That the present assembly, during the continuance thereof, be held by way of upper and lower house, to sit in two distinct houses, apart, for the more convenient dispatch of the business therein to be consulted of: And that the governor and secretary, or any one or more of the council for the upper house; and Mr. John Hatch, Mr. Walter Beane, Mr. John Medley, Mr. William Broughe, Mr. Robert Robins, Mr. Francis Poesie, Mr. Philip Land,[1] Mr. Francis Brooke, Mr. Thomas Matthews, Mr. Thomas Sterman, Mr. George Manners, burgesses for St. Mary's county, Mr. George Puddington, and Mr. James Cox, burgesses of that part of the county now called Providence, or any five or more of them, for the lower house, together with the clerk of that house for the time being, who shall from time to time assemble themselves, at the time and place to be by the governor (or whomsoever of the council he shall, by writing under his hand, depute for that purpose) from time to time appointed, during this present assembly, shall have the full power of, and be, two houses of assembly, to all intents and purposes. And all bills which shall be passed by the said two houses, or the major part of both of them, and enacted or ordained by the governor, shall be laws of the province, after publication thereof under the hand of the governor, and the great seal of the provincè, as fully, to all effects in law, as if they were advised and assented unto by all the freemen of the province personally."[2]

The Puritans upon the Severn were now sufficiently reconciled to the government to send two burgesses to the assembly at the summons of the governor, who had visited their colony, which they called "Providence," probably with the view of learning their disposition. This was followed by an act erecting "that part of the province of Maryland, on the west side of the bay of Chesapeake, over against the Isle of Kent, formerly called by the name of Providence," . . . . "into a shire or county by the name of Ann Arundel county."[3]

"This," remarks Bozman, "is the first act of assembly, and indeed almost the only legislative provision for the erecting of any county within the province. It is probable that such regulations for the apportioning of the province into shires or counties were deemed to appertain to the palatine regalia of the Lord Proprietary of the province."[4]

[1] In the list of the members on the journal of the House, the name is *Philip Lane.*

[2] Bacon's *Laws of Maryland.*

[3] From Lady Ann Arundel, daughter of Lord Arundel, of Wardour, and wife of Cæcilius, Lord Baltimore.

[4] Bozman, ii., p. 393.

Claiborne now began to give trouble again, writing arrogant letters to the governor, in which he renewed his claims to Kent Island in a somewhat threatening manner; at which the assembly passed an act forbidding all compliance with him, and prescribing the penalty of death and confiscation to all who should countenance him in any attempt upon the island or any part of the province. An oath of fidelity was also prescribed by the assembly, similar in form to that previously administered; yet differing in one or two points, which can only be attributed to the influence of the burgesses from Providence, whose constituents had begun to show some dissatisfaction with the terms of the oath, because it required them to obey a government that was bound to respect the religious convictions of the Roman Catholics in the province. This they at first submitted to, but, as they gained strength and their friends in England consolidated their power, they more openly manifested their repugnance, and finally refused to take the oath, as it had been prescribed. The objection to the former oath was that the words—"absolute lord and royal jurisdiction" were "thought far too high for a subject to exact, and too much unsuitable to the present liberty which God had given the English subjects, from arbitrary and popish government, as the Lord Baltimore's government plainly appeared to be." These objectionable expressions were now carefully expunged from the oath now prescribed by this act of assembly; and a new clause inserted, somewhat bordering on mental reservation, so as at all convenient times to admit of equivocal meaning, to wit, "that they would defend and maintain all such his lordship's *just and lawful* right, title, interests, privileges, jurisdictions, prerogatives, propriety, and dominion over and in the said province, etc., not any wise understood to infringe or prejudice liberty of conscience in point of religion."

As the proprietary's authority as a lord palatine, unquestionably gave him a *jus regale*, it would seem to be mere squeamishness that carped at the adjective "royal;" but the substitution of such undefined terms as "just and lawful," gave admirable loop-holes for caviling and contention; for raising the favorite "scruples of conscience" against the rightfulness of whatever did not promote their own interests or aims; and for indulging in the practice, not yet obsolete, of professing to obey the letter, while palpably violating the spirit, of the most solemn pledges and compacts.

This clause, however, was but the insertion of the wedge, nor was it pressed further at the time. On the contrary, the next act of the assembly was a strong indorsement of the proprietary's rights, and recognition of his prerogatives, as "absolute lord and proprietary of the province of Maryland," and of "all islands, ports and creeks to the same belonging," by "lawful and undoubted right and title." The preamble is couched in the following memorable words:

"Great and manifold are the benefits wherewith Almighty God hath blessed the colony, first brought and planted within his province of Maryland, at your lordship's charge, and continued by your care and industry in the happy restitution of a blessed peace unto us, being lately wasted with a miserable dissention and unhappy war. But more inestimable are the blessings thereby poured on this province, in planting Christianity among a people that knew not God nor had heard of Christ. All which we recognize and acknowledge to be done and performed next under God, by your lordship's industry and pious intentions towards the advancement and propagation of Christian religion, and the peace and happiness of this colony and province. So we doubt not, but our posterity will remember the same with all fidelity, to the honor of your lordship and your heirs forever. In contemplation whereof we humbly beseech your lordship, that as a memorial to all posterities, among the records of your court and of your great assembly in this province, for ever to endure, of our thankfulness, fidelity and obedience, it may be published and declared by your lordship and assembly, and enacted by the authority of the same. That we being bound thereunto, by the laws both of God and man, do recognise and acknowledge your lordship's just title and right unto this province, by the grant and donation of the late King Charles, of England, etc. And do also recognize and acknowledge your lordship to be true and *absolute lord* and proprietary of this province. And do humbly submit unto all power, jurisdiction, and authority, given, granted and confirmed unto your lordship and your heirs, in and by the said grant and donation : And do hereby submit and oblige us, our heirs and posterities forever, *until the last drop of our blood be spent*, to maintain, uphold and defend your lordship and your heirs, lords and proprietaries of this province, in all the *royal* rights, jurisdictions, authorities and preheminences, given, granted, and confirmed unto your lordship, by the said grant and donation, *so far as they do not in any sort infringe or prejudice* the just and lawful liberties or privileges of the free born subjects of the Kingdom of England."

And now the government of the province appeared firmly established, the rights of the proprietary fully acknowledged, all needful precautions taken to sustain him against attacks upon his charter or the exercise of the powers it conferred, and to secure the peace of the colony; yet a storm was gathering in a quarter where it might have been least expected. The young king, Charles II., though uncrowned, unacknowledged in his own dominions, and an exile in Holland, saw fit to take umbrage with Lord Baltimore for his lenient dealings toward the very party from which he was himself a fugitive. The permission given by the proprietary to the expelled Virginia Puritans to settle in Maryland, aroused indignation in the royal breast, and from his place of refuge, at Breda, he issued an order deposing the proprietary, on the ground that he "did visibly adhere to the rebels in England, and admitted all kind of sectaries and schismatics and ill-affected persons into the plantation." In his stead he appointed Sir William Davenant (known in literature as the author of the indescribably tedious poem "Gondibert") royal governor of Maryland, thus assuming to annul his father's charter at his own pleasure; an act which from a king in the plenitude of his power, would have been arbitrary and tyrannous, but from an exile without an army, without a crown, and without a kingdom, was ridiculous. Its result was quite in keeping: Davenant collected a colony of Frenchmen and set sail from France, but was taken in the English Channel by a parliamentary cruiser and imprisoned in Cowes Castle. His life was only spared at the intercession of two aldermen of York whom he had protected during the civil war, aided by the friendly services of the poet Milton, Cromwell's secretary.

In 1650 parliament found itself free to turn its attention to the disaffected colonies, and on October 3d, made the following declaration:

"Whereas divers acts of rebellion have been committed by many persons inhabiting in Barbados, Antego, Bermudas, and Virginia, who have mutinously, by force, usurped a power of government, and seized the estates of many well affected persons into their hands, and banished others, and have set themselves in opposition to, and distinct from, this Commonwealth, many of the chief actors in, and promoters of, the said rebellion, having been carried over to the said plantations in foreign ships, without the license or consent of the Parliament of England; the Parliament do declare all and every the said persons in the Barbados, Antego, Bermudas, and Virginia, that have abetted or assisted these rebellions, or have willingly joined with them, to be robbers and traitors, and such as, by the law of nations, ought not to be permitted any commerce or traffic with any people whatsoever."

And therefore, enacted, among other things:

"That the council of State shall have power to send ships to any of the plantations aforesaid, and to grant commissions to such persons as they shall think fit, *to enforce all such to obedience as stand in opposition to the Parliament*, and to grant pardons, and settle governors in the said islands, plantations, and places, to preserve them in peace, until the Parliament take further order." [1]

Maryland was not mentioned by name in this ordinance, and having never openly taken sides against the authority of parliament, would probably have been undisturbed, had there not been active enemies watching every opportunity to do her harm. The passage of this act not only gave Lord Baltimore great anxiety in England, but produced unfavorable effects in the colony, as the rumor ran that his charter had been either given up or taken from him. Those of the colonists who favored the cause of parliament began to look with distrust on the existing government and to question its authority. The people of Anne Arundel went so far as to refuse to send burgesses to an assembly called by Governor Stone in March, 1651, their contumacy being evidently due to the belief that the proprietary government would be abolished.

"An account of this conduct of the Puritans on the Severn was in due time transmitted to lord Baltimore in England; who, in return, sent back his letter, or message, addressed to 'William Stone, esqr., his lieutenant of his said province of Maryland, and to his right trusty and well beloved the upper and lower houses of his general assembly there, and to all other his officers and inhabitants of his said province,' bearing date 'the twentieth day of August, one thousand six hundred fifty and one.' In this letter, his lordship, after expressing his 'wonder at a message which he understood was lately sent by one Mr. Lloyd,[2] from some lately seated at Ann Arundel within his said province of Maryland, to his general assembly, held at St. Mary's in March last; and his unwillingness to impute either to the sender or deliverer thereof so malign a sense of ingratitude and other ill-affections as it may seem to bear; conceiving rather, that it proceeded from some apprehensions in them at that time, grounded upon some *reports* in those

[1] Hazard's *Collections*, i., p. 636.

[2] Mr. Edward Lloyd was appointed by the governor in 1650 on his visit to Providence the first commander of Ann Arundel county; and James Homewood, Thomas Meares, Thomas Marsh, George Puddington, Matthew Hawkins, James Merryman, and Henry Catlyn, with him commissioners of said county.

parts of a dissolution or resignation here (in England) of his patent and right to that province;' and, after affirming that 'those rumours and reports were false,' and referring them to Mr. *Harrison*, then in England, their former pastor, for proof of their falsehood, and observing, that 'in consideration of a better complyance from those people with his government there for the future, he should not any further expostulate or make any further reflection on that message, till further occasion given him by them, and if such admonition did not prevail, then that he would make use of his authority, with the assistance of well-affected persons, to compel such factious and turbulent spirits to a better complyance with the lawful government there;' he, accordingly, 'wills and requires his lieutenant to proceed with all such as shall be for the future refractory in that kind; and in case any of the English inhabitants of that province should at any time hereafter refuse or neglect to send burgesses to our general assembly there, being lawfully summoned for that purpose, he wills and requires all the other members of the said assembly, which shall lawfully meet upon such summons, to proceed, as they ought and may lawfully do, in all business belonging to a general assembly there, notwithstanding any such refusal or neglect as aforesaid, and to fine all such refusers or neglectors according to their demerits; and moreover, in case of their persisting in such refusal or neglect, after admonition thereof by the lieutenant, then that they be declared enemies to the public peace of the province, and rebels to the lawful government thereof, and be proceeded against accordingly.'"[1]

Preparations for the reduction of Barbadoes and Virginia, went meanwhile steadily forward in England. By the middle of May, 1651, Sir George Ayscough, with a strong fleet, was ready to sail against the former, but the expedition against the latter was still a subject of discussion in the Council of State. Lord Baltimore now experienced the evil consequences he had apprehended from the ill-timed recognition of Charles II. by Governor Greene, and found it necessary to bring all the influence of which he was master, to bear, to prevent the insertion of the name of his province with that of Virginia, in the instructions about to be issued for the guidance of those appointed to conduct the contemplated expedition. For this purpose he went before the committee, showed that Governor Stone was a Protestant and a parliamentarian, disowned Greene's proclamation, proved by the testimony of the Protestants themselves that they enjoyed their religious liberties undisturbed, appealed to the recently enacted laws for evidence that the principle of toleration was publicly recognized in Maryland, claimed the credit of having given the Independents an asylum when driven from Virginia, and substantiated his assertions by the testimony of several Protestant merchants, who were engaged in trade with the colony, and well acquainted with its condition. His efforts were successful, and he had finally the satisfaction of obtaining a decision from the committee, that Maryland ought not to be disturbed, and of seeing the name of his province erased from the instructions. Baffled in all their attempts in this direction, his enemies, however, managed to have inserted in the commission the disguise under which they afterwards stretched their authority "to reduce all the plantations within the bay of Chesapeake to their due obedience to the parliament of the Commonwealth of England."

[1] Bozman, ii., p. 415.

The following account of these proceedings is given by a contemporary:

"In September, 1651, when the Council of State sent commissioners from hence, to wit: Captains Dennis, Steg and Captain Curtis, to reduce Virginia to the obedience of the parliament, Maryland was at first inserted in their instructions, to be reduced, as well as Virginia; but the Council being aferwards satisfied that that plantation was never in opposition to the Parliament, that Captain Stone, the Lord Baltimore's deputy there, was generally known to have been always zealously affected to the Parliament, and that divers of the Parliament's friends were, by the Lord Baltimore's special direction, received into Maryland, and well treated there when they were fain to leave Virginia for their good affection to the Parliament, then the Council thought it not fit at all to disturb that plantation; and therefore caused Maryland to be struck out of the said instructions; which was twice done, it being by some mistake or other put in a second time."[1]

This was indeed an anxious period for Lord Baltimore. In the north of England, Charles, who had returned from exile, was waging a desperate war with Cromwell, and from his previous conduct the proprietary had every reason to believe that the success of the royal cause would involve his own ruin, or at least the revocation of his charter; while in the action of parliament, and the discussions before the committee, he was made aware that strong religious and political, if not personal, prejudices were working against him. Denunciation of Catholics was the order of the day; the English laws dealt out death, confiscation and banishment to those of that faith, and it was not fitting that they, who were the helots in the kingdom, should be the masters in the province. The clamors of Virginia filled the court of England. Under every change in peace or revolution, before the king, parliament, or protector, Virginia persisted year after year, in her determined hostility to Maryland and her charter. Claiborne the "pestilent enemie to the welfare of the province," perpetually worried, and, in the end, hastened the suspension of the proprietary government. The enmity of the savages was aroused by his intrigues, and the colonists were exposed in their weakness to all the evils of Indian hostility. Amidst these and many other severe trials, the proprietary was firm but prudent. If he suffered injustice in the result, it was only effected by a system of intrigue on the part of his opponents, to which he never condescended to resort. His dominions had been defined with a studious accuracy, unequalled by any other charter. Still he was doomed to interminable contests, and at last saw his province curtailed of her fairest possessions. The peculiar position of Calvert towards the mother-country, rendered efficient opposition impracticable. To the monarchs he was ever the especial object of jealous dislike, as the almost irresponsible lord of a flourishing colony. Nor was he a favorite with the English Parliament, who soon discovered, in the explicit provisions of his charter, an alarming barrier to their commercial usurpation, which could only be surmounted by a bold and open disregard of plighted faith. The great seal of England stared them in the face. It may safely be asserted that Maryland never had the good will of the mother-country, from the moment when first she rose into consequence by the increase of her popu-

[1] *The Lord Baltimore's Case;* London, 1653.

lation and the expansion of her resources. And yet, so well were the people secured by their charter, that, amid all the calamities which harassed the surrounding colonies, Maryland grew apace in the stillness of her forest homes, until the miserable feuds of her own children plunged her into shame and sorrow.

To crown Lord Baltimore's trials at this period, came letters from Governor Stone, apprising him of the reports in circulation in Maryland, the growing disaffection of a portion of the people, and the spirit of aggression manifested by Virginia. To this he replied, August 20th, 1651, mildly rebuking the contumacy of the people of Anne Arundel, and advising the passage of a law for the punishment of persons convicted of spreading false reports, "tending to the disturbance of the minds of the people and of the public peace."

Two days after the signing of this letter, August 22d, Charles, as his ill-fated father had done just nine years before at Nottingham, raised his standard at Worcester, where he had arrived at the head of sixteen thousand men, principally Scotch; and within a fortnight, Cromwell, pressing upon him with a superior force, overwhelmed and scattered his army, extinguished the last hopes of the royalists, and compelled their master, in mean disguises, and with extreme risks, to fly from the kingdom. On the ninth day after the battle, "my lord general," soon to become "my lord protector," attended by an obsequious delegation from parliament, entered London amid the shouts of an admiring multitude. A fortnight after Cromwell's triumphant entry into London (September 26th, 1651), the fleet destined for the reduction of Virginia was ready for departure. The military force consisted of seven hundred and fifty men, embarked on board the ship *John*, and the *Guinea* frigate, the former commanded by Captain Robert Dennis, the latter by Captain Edmund Curtis. There were also on board one hundred and fifty Scotch prisoners, taken in the recent battle of Worcester, and sent over to be sold as servants. The chief command of the expedition was given to Captain Dennis, and with him were named as commissioners, Captain Thomas Stagge, then in England, and Richard Bennett and Captain William Claiborne, residents of Virginia.[1]

The instructions given to the commissioners "for the reducing of Virginia and the inhabitants thereof," were dated Whitehall, 22d September, 1651, and authorized any two or more of them, upon their arrival with the fleet in Virginia, to use their best endeavors "to reduce all the plantations within the Chesapeake bay to their due obedience to the parliament of the commonwealth of England." Ample authorities accompanied this general instruction to render it effectual. They were empowered to offer pardon to all voluntarily submitting, and to use force to reduce the unwilling: and they were even authorized to give freedom to the servants of rebellious masters, upon condition of entering as soldiers into the service of the commonwealth. Upon

[1] Streeter's *Maryland*, p. 59. Hazard's *Collections*, i., p. 556.

the reduction of the colonies, they were directed to administer to the inhabitants an oath of allegiance to the commonwealth, and to cause all process to be issued in the name of the keepers of the liberties of England, by the authority of parliament. They were also to "cause and use the several acts of parliament against kingship and the House of Lords to be received and published; as also the acts *for abolishing the book of common prayers*, and for subscribing the engagement, and *all other acts herewith delivered you*."

"It must be acknowledged by all candid persons," says Mr. Bozman, "that the powers, vested by this clause in the commissioners, carried the authority of an English Parliament over the colonies, to a higher tone than was ever attempted before or since by any English or British Parliament. Supposing that the parliament had power to alter and change the *form of government* adopted and used by any one of the colonies, and to change such government from a monarchy to a democracy (of which some doubts might be entertained), yet assuredly the abolition of the *form of prayer*, in the use of which almost every inhabitant of Virginia had been bred up from his infancy, and to which he was perhaps religiously attached, was such a gross violation of every idea of *religious liberty*, that at this day we cannot but view the authors of such a measure as base hypocrites, renouncing those very principles by which they had artfully worked their way to the tyranny which they now exercised."[1]

On the voyage out, the frigate *John*, in which were Captains Dennis and Stagge, was lost, and with them the original commission; but Captain Curtis had been provided with a copy, and on him devolved the command. Weakened by the loss of the principal ship and her commander, and with sickness prevailing on board, Captain Curtis touched at Barbadoes, where he found Sir George Ayscough held in check by the resolute inhabitants. The reduction of the island had proved a more difficult undertaking than had been anticipated, for, though settled but a few years before Maryland, and under a similar charter, it had vastly outstripped the latter in increase of population and wealth, and had mustered a truly formidable body to repel the invasion. The show of additional force presented by the arrival of the Virginia expedition, enabled Sir George to push his attack and compel the Barbadians to surrender. After a stay of seven days, Captain Curtis sailed for Virginia, and arrived before James city early in March, 1652.

Governor Berkeley had made preparations for resistance, but, finding the means of defence at his command insufficient to withstand even the small force that appeared against him, concluded, with the commissioners, on the 12th March, 1652, an arrangement, by which the most liberal terms were conceded to governor, council, assembly and people.[2]

Virginia being reduced, their attention was now directed to the government of Maryland. Claiborne, who had some time before, in accordance with his usual policy of attaching himself to the strongest party, become an

[1] Bozman, ii., p. 435.

[2] Streeter's *Early Maryland Papers*, p. 60.

avowed Puritan, and who had now, by his ingenuity, the power, wanted no excuse to justify its exercise. They arrived at St. Mary's about the last of March 1652, N.S., and immediately opened negotiations with Governor Stone. Claiborne and the other commissioners assumed the ground that whatever had been the conduct of the colonies, an express submission and recognition by them of the authority of parliament was neccessary to shelter them from the powers of the parliamentary commission; and this was accordingly required of Stone, who was still the governor of Maryland. Stone did not at once accede to their demands; and they, on the 29th of March, 1652, issued a proclamation, divesting him of his government, declaring void all the commissions of the proprietary, and constituting a board of six commissioners composed of Robert Brooke, Colonel Francis Yardley, Job Chandler, Captain Edward Windam, Richard Preston and Lieutenant Richard Banks, for the government of the province, under the authority of parliament. Thus was the province of Maryland completely "reduced," and all authority and power of Lord Baltimore, within the colony which he had planted at so much cost and reared with so much care, were entirely taken out of his hands, with the probable prospect that they would never again be restored.

The commissioners soon after the "reducement," returned to Virginia where we find their proceedings thus recorded:

"James City, April 30th, 1652.—At the *General Assembly*.—After long and serious debate and advice for the settling of the government of Virginia, it was unanimously voted and concluded, *by the commissioners* appointed by the authority of parliament, and by all the burgesses of the several counties and places respectively, *until the further pleasure of the states be known*, that Mr. Richard Bennett, Esq., be governor for the ensuing year, or until the next meeting of the assembly, with all the just powers and authorities that may belong to the place lawfully. And likewise that colonel William Clayborne be secretary of state, with all belonging to that office, and is to be next in place to the governor; next, that of the council of state be as follows:—[naming them in particular,] 'and they shall have power to execute and do equal justice to all the people and inhabitants of this colony *according to such instruction as they have or shall receive from the parliament of England*, and according to the known law of England, and the acts of assembly here established.'"[1]

Mr. Bennett and Mr. Claiborne, having thus provided for themselves honorable, and perhaps profitable stations in Virginia, returned to Maryland about the end of June, to make a more satisfactory settlement of the government of that province also. Accordingly, on the 28th of June, 1652, they issued a proclamation, in which they declared, "that Captain Stone, Esq., be the governor, and Mr. Thomas Hatton, Robert Brooke, Esq., Captain John Price, Mr. Job Chandler, Colonel Francis Yardley, and Mr. Richard Preston be the council of this province, who are to govern, order, and direct the affairs thereof in all matters according to their former power, and the order or proclamation aforesaid."

[1] Burk's *History of Virginia*, ii., p. 83.

Thus it will be seen that Governor Stone and three of his council—Hatton, Brooke and Price—finding all further opposition useless, effected an arrangement with the commissioners, under which they were permitted to retain and exercise their powers, saving to them their oath of fealty to the proprietary until the pleasure of the authorities in England, as to the ultimate disposition of the province should be known. This arrangement answered the purposes of both. By his reservation of the proprietary rights, the governor relieved himself from the responsibility of a voluntary surrender; and the commissioners escaped from the hazard of an unauthorized, or at least, doubtful exercise of power.

Claiborne had hardly become settled in the reduction of Maryland, before we find him bringing up his old claim to Kent Island. In a treaty with the Susquehannough Indians, entered into by Richard Bennett, Edward Lloyd, William Fuller, Thomas Marsh and Leonard Strong "at the river Severn," on the fifth of July, 1652, the first article is in the following words:

> "First, that the English nation shall have, hould, and enjoy, to them their heires and assigns for ever, all the land, lying from Patuxent river unto Palmer's island on the westerne side of the baye of Chesepiake, and from Choptank river to the northeast branch which lyes to the northward of Elke river on the easterne side of the same baye, with all the islands, rivers, creeks, —— fish, fowle, deer, elke, and whatsoever else to the same belonging; excepting the isle of Kent and Palmer's island, which belong to captain Clayborne. But nevertheless, it shall be lawful for the aforesaid English or Indians to build a house or fort for trade or any such like use or occasion at any tyme upon Palmer's island."

By the treaty it will be seen that the Susquehannoughs limited their cession on the eastern shore southward by the Choptank river, thus leaving the territories of the Nanticokes and the Wighcomocoes in the present counties of Dorchester and Somerset unaffected by their grant. No sooner had this powerful tribe thus buried the hatchet, than the Nanticokes and other Eastern Shore Indians showed signs of discontent. And the settlers of the Isle of Kent becoming alarmed, deputed "Mr. Philip Conner, Mr. Thomas Ringgold, Mr. Henry Morgan, and Mr. John Philips, to go to St. Mary's, with a petition to the governor and council, setting forth, 'that whereas formerly there had been by the eastern shore Indians one murthered, and now of late one shot, another killed and stript near to his own house, all of them inhabitants of this island and *subjects of this province*, a dwelling house and much goods burned, as is conceived, by Indians, to say nothing of the continual trade of killing of hogs, they are so emboldened, these murthers being past by, and being so well furnished with gun-powder and shot, that they come about our houses night and day, so that larums and disturbances are occasioned weekly, nay daily, so that some are so dreaded and affrighted, they have left their plantations, and many are resolved to desert the island.' 'We are also informed, that the eastern shore Indians have great store of powder and shot, and many guns, not only in what they formerly bought, and have taken in Captain Gugens his wreck, but they have not long since taken a Dutch sloop with guns, besides very much powder and shot, so that they are very strong, bold, and insolent;—the premises considered, the petitioners humbly crave, that his worship and the council would be pleased to seriously weigh and consider their deplorable condition, and take some speedy course for the suppressing of those heathens, and avenging of guiltless blood, and the preservation of their lives, with their wives and children.'"[1]

In consequence of this petition, Governor Stone convened the council on the 25th day of November, 1652, and ordered every seventh man capable of bearing arms to be mustered into service, at the expense of the remaining six; boats were pressed, and the whole expedition was ordered to rendezvous at Mattapany, under the command of Captain Fuller. The Puritans of Anne Arundel, however, refused to make their levies, selfishly alleging as the reason, the hardships of the season, December and January, and the danger to their health from exposure on the bay and rivers in open boats. Delays thus arose, and, perhaps the note of preparation causing a cessation of outrage, the soldiers already levied were discharged to their homes and the expedition abandoned.

The Lord Proprietary did not rest quietly under the flagrant wrong and injustice which had been done him. He immediately took steps to call the commissioners to account for their illegal proceedings in Maryland, while Colonel Samuel Matthews, their agent in England, presented a petition on their behalf, to the parliament. It was dismissed; and, the parliament having been dissolved by Cromwell, on the 12th December, 1653, and his consequent accession as lord protector, and the Dutch war being then at its height, no further notice was taken of the matter. Lord Baltimore, however, determined to right himself in spite of the Puritans, and directed Governor Stone to require all persons to take the "oath of fidelity" prescribed by the "condition of plantations" in 1650, and to re-establish the proprietary government, which was accordingly done in 1654.

No sooner had Claiborne and Bennett, in Virginia, heard of these proceedings than they "proceeded in their holy work of rooting out the Popish councillors in Maryland." In their declaration dated July 22d, 1654, they state that about the 15th of July, "they applied themselves to Captain William Stone, the governor, and council of Maryland, who, returning only opprobrious and uncivil language, presently mustered his whole power of men and soldiers in arms, intending to surprise the said commissioners, and (as could be imagined) to destroy all those that had refused the said unlawful oath, and only kept themselves in their due obedience to the commonwealth of England, under which they were reduced and settled by the parliament's authority and commission. Then the said commissioners, in a quiet and peaceable manner, with some of the people of Patuxent and

[1] Bozman, ii.

Severn, went over the river of Patuxent, and there at length received a message from the said Captain Stone, that the next day he would meet and treat in the woods; and thereupon being in some fear of a party to come from Virginia, he condescended to lay down his power lately assumed from the Lord Baltimore, and to submit (as he had once before done) to such government as the commissioners should appoint under his highness the lord protector."

They then took possession of the province, and issued, on the 22d of July, 1654, in the name of Oliver Cromwell, whom Governor Stone, on the 6th of May, had already proclaimed lord protector, &c., a commission to Captain William Fuller, Richard Preston, William Durand, Edward Lloyd, Captain John Smith, Leonard Strong, John Lawson, John Hatch, Richard Wells and Richard Ewen, constituting them a board of commissioners to administer the government.

Mr. John Hammond, in his pamphlet of *Hammond vs. Heamans*, published in London in 1655, speaking of Governor Stone's resignation of the government of Maryland into the hands of Cromwell's commissioners, says:

> "At such times as Bennet and Claiborne came into Maryland, and had compacted to take the government out of the hands of Captain Stone, after he had notice of the power they had gathered, he likewise impowered himself for defence, and was in possibility to have cut Bennet and Claiborne and all off, but those few Papists that were in Maryland (for indeed they are but few) importunately perswaded Governour Stone not to fight, lest the cry against the Papists (if any hurt were done) would be so great that many mischiefs would ensue, wholly referring themselves to the will of God, and the Lord Protector's determination; and although the Protestant party, with indignation to be so fooled, submitted to what their Governour was perswaded to do, yet could not but complaine in that particular against the cowardise of the Papists.
>
> "After they had dispossest Governour Stone of his Authority, and had, by promises to dis-bandon their party, perswaded him to do the like, they presented him with a draught for resignation under his hand, which, when he refused, their whole party, upon notice given, on a sudden returned, to the astonishment of himself and affrightment of his wife and children, and required him peremptorily to subscribe to what they had written, which he did, saying, It matters not what it is, I will, being thus enforced; write what ye will have me sign; it cannot be binding nor valid; so here the observance of Bennet and Claiborne's promises; and after this they would have impowered him, as Governour, from them, which, with scorn, he refused; nor did Governour Stone, even in his own esteem, nor in the eyes of those that had been faithfull to his Government, look on himself as lesse or otherwise than Governour, nor even received other title, howbeit he ceased to act until he heard further from England."

The commission issued by Bennett and Cromwell to the ten Maryland commissioners further authorized them to "summon an assembly, to begin on the 20th day of October, (then) next, for which assembly all such should be disabled to give any vote, or to be elected members thereof, as have borne arms in war against the parliament, or *do profess the Roman Catholic religion.*"

As soon as this body, thus constituted, and representing a minority of the people assembled, it proceeded to pass the following law:

"*An Act Concerning Religion.*

"It is hereby enacted and declared, that none who profess and exercise the *Popish* (commonly called the *Roman* Catholic) religion, can be protected in this province, by the laws of *England* formerly established, and yet unrepealed: Nor by the government of the commonwealth of England, &c., but to be restrained from the exercise thereof. That such as profess faith in God by Jesus Christ, though differing in judgment from the doctrine, worship, or discipline, publicly held forth, shall not be restrained from, but protected in, the profession of the faith and exercise of their religion; so as they abuse not this liberty to the injury of others, or disturbance of the peace on their parts. Provided such liberty be not extended to *Popery* or *prelacy*, nor to such, as under the profession of Christ, hold forth and practise licentiousness."

Thus was consummated the first dark stain upon the fair fame of Maryland, and Mr. Bozman truthfully adds that—

"The illiberality and, indeed, ingratitude, of these Puritans, on the present occasion, in respect to the disfranchisement of the Roman Catholics, as above stated, deserves the severest reprehension, and can admit of no palliation. When, through the imprudent liberality of Lord Baltimore, in originally granting indulgence to every sect to settle within his province, and afterwards more particularly, through the special permission of his government at St. Mary's, in allowing these Puritans to form their settlements on the Severn in Maryland, after they had been driven out of Virginia, an asylum had been thus generously granted to them; that they should rise up against their benefactors, seize the reins of the government into their own hands, and then proscribe and interdict these very benefactors from all their political rights, and, as subsequently appears, cruelly *sequester* their property from them as *delinquents*, was such a shameful sacrifice of all *moral* feelings at the shrine of *religious* zeal, as cannot but cover their descendants in the province at this day with confusion and regret."[1]

By the same assembly an act was passed to prevent the taking of the oath of fidelity to the Lord Proprietary, and one recognizing the government of Maryland as settled by Bennett and Claiborne.

On the 3d day of July, 1654, Governor Stone, "for divers reasons, relating to the public good, . . with the advice of the council . . did now erect, make, and appoint both sides of Patuxent river into one county by the name of Calvert county, bounded on the south side with Pynehill river or creek to the head thereof, and from thence through the woods to the head of Patuxent, being the northerly bound of St. Mary's county, and bounded on the north side with the creek upon the western side of Chesapeake bay called the Herring creek, and from thence through the woods to the head of Patuxent river, being the southerly bound of Ann Arundel county; and the governor this day likewise appointed Mr. Richard Collet to be high sheriff of Calvert county aforesaid."

At the session of assembly of this year, under the administration of Cromwell's commissioners, the name was changed to Patuxent county; and it was directed "that the county now called Ann Arundel county should be called

[1] Bozman, ii., p. 505.

and recorded by the name of the county of Providence, this being the first name by which it was known; the bounds thereof to be Herring creek, including all the plantations and lands unto the bounds of Patuxent county, that is, to a creek called Mr. Marshe's creek, otherwise called Oyster creek."

These counties continued to bear the names of Providence and Patuxent until the restoration of the proprietary government in 1658, when the original names of Anne Arundel and Calvert were restored by the general repeal of the acts and orders passed during the defection. The Puritan commissioners, in their excessive zeal, seem to have devoted too exclusive an attention to religious matters; and we find Cromwell presently rebuking them, and commanding them "not to busy themselves about religion, but to settle the civil government." Cromwell had now attained, if not the highest aim of his ambition—the crown—at least dominion and power equal to a king's, and was growing more and more estranged from the Independents, who looked on him with jealousy and suspicion. It was no longer his policy to encourage fanaticism and keep discords alive; but to reconcile factions by liberality, conciliate the nobility, and above all things "settle the civil government;" and this policy he naturally wished to extend to the provinces. On January 12th, 1654, O.S., [1655 N.S.] he addressed the following letter from Whitehall, to Richard Bennett, Governor of Virginia:

OLIVER CROMWELL.

"Sir:—Whereas the differences between the Lord Baltimore and the inhabitants of Virginia, concerning the bounds by them respectively claimed, are depending before our council, and yet undetermined; and whereas we are credibly informed you have, notwithstanding, gone into his plantation in Maryland and countenanced some people there in opposing the Lord Baltimore's officers, whereby and with other forces from Virginia you have much disturbed that colony and people, to the engendering of tumults and much bloodshed there, if not timely prevented:

"We, therefore, at the request of the Lord Baltimore and divers other persons of quality here, who are engaged by great adventures in his interest, do, for preventing of disturbances or tumults there, will and require you, and all others deriving any authority from you, to forbear disturbing the Lord Baltimore, or his officers, or people in Maryland, and to permit all things to remain as they were before any disturbance or alteration made by you, or by any other, upon pretence of authority from you, till the said differences above mentioned be determined by us here, and we give further order herein.

"We rest your loving friend,

"OLIVER P."

Here we may plainly see the conciliatory policy of the protector, and his desire to heal the wounds and assuage the irritations of the civil war, and draw to his support the conservative elements of the commonwealth, without which his new authority was but founded on the sand. In return for Lord Baltimore's submission to his authority, he apparently recognized his proprietary rights in Maryland, yet, at the same time, sustained and protected his commissioners, only curbing the animosities that had arisen between Virginia and that province, on the question of their boundary. This letter seeming not to be properly understood, he wrote again:

"To the Commissioners of Maryland:—

"*Whitehall, 26th September, 1655.*

"SIRS:—It seems to us, by yours of the twenty-ninth of June, and by the relation we received by Colonel Bennett, that some mistake or scruple hath arisen concerning the sense of our letters of the twelfth of January last, as if by our letters we had intimated that we should have a stop put to the proceedings of those of Maryland. Which was not at all intended by us; nor so much as proposed to us by those who made addresses to us to obtain our said letter. But our intention (as our said letter doth plainly import) was only to prevent and forbid any force or violence to be offered by either of the plantations of Virginia or Maryland from one to the other, upon the differences concerning their bounds, the said differences being then under the consideration of ourself and council here. Which, for your more full satisfaction, we have thought fit to signify to you, and rest

"Your loving friend, "OLIVER P."[1]

Lord Baltimore, learning the surrender of Governor Stone, and that the affairs of the province were administered by commissioners appointed by Claiborne and his associates, in the latter part of 1654 despatched a special messenger, William Eltonhead, in the ship *Golden Fortune*, Captain Tilman, to the colony, with a severe rebuke to the governor for so tamely yielding his authority, and an order to him to resume it immediately.

The ship arrived in January, 1655, N.S., and Captain Stone proceeded to issue commissions to officers, and to organize an armed force in the county of St. Mary's. In a short time he found himself at the head of about one hundred and thirty men, when believing himself strong enough to strike, he despatched John Hammond to recover the records of the province which the commissioners had seized and removed to the house of Richard Preston on the Patuxent, and to capture a magazine of arms and ammunition which the Puritans had gathered there. In this expedition he was completely successful. Hammond's own account of this transaction is as follows:—

"Governor Stone sent me to Patuxent to fetch the Records. I went unarmed amongst these sons of Thunder, only three or four to row me, and despite of all their braves of raising the Country, calling in his servants to apprehend me, threatened me with the severity of their new-made law, myselfe alone seized and carried away the Records in defiance."[2]

About the twentieth of March, Stone set out with his little army for Providence. He had pressed into his service eleven or twelve small vessels for the transportation of part of his forces, and part marched by land along the bay shore. Before they reached Herring creek, in Anne Arundel county, they were met by two sets of messengers sent in boats by the people at Providence, with the result thus narrated by Roger Heamans:—

[1] Carlyle's *Cromwell*, ii., p. 182. Campbell's *Virginia*, p. 230.

[2] *Hammond vs. Heamans.*

"A first message having been sent to demand his power, and the ground of such his proceedings;—

"The second message to him being such low terms, that those that sent it were grieved at their hearts that ever it went out of their hands; which was as followeth.

"For Captain William Stone, Esq:—

"Sir:—The people of these parts have met together and considered the present transactions on your part, and have not a little marvelled that no other answer of the last message hath been made, than what tendred rather to make men desperate than conformable; yet being desirous of peace, do once again present to your serious consideration these insuing proposals, as the mind of the people.

"1. If you will govern us so, as we may enjoy the liberty of English subjects.

"2. And that we be, and remain indempnified in respect of our engagement, and all former acts relating to the reducement and government.

"3. That those who are minded to depart the province, may freely do it without any prejudice to themselves or estates; we are content to own yourself as governor, and submit to your government. If not, we are resolved to commit ourselves into the hands of God, and rather die like men than be made slaves.

"WILL. DURAND, Secret.

"But no answer to this was returned, but the same paper in scorn sent back again."[1]

Governor Stone not only returned no answer by the messengers, but detained them in order to take the enemy by surprise. Three of them, however, escaped; and the Puritans, being thus forewarned, began preparations for defence. On the arrival of Stone and his force at Herring creek, they captured one of the commissioners, as we are told by Leonard Strong, a member of Captain Fuller's council, "and forced another man of quality to flie for his life, having threatened to hang him up to his own door; and not finding the man, affrighted his wife, and plundered the house of ammunition and provision, threatening still what they would do to the people at Providence, and that they would force the rebellious factious Roundheads to submit, and then they would shew their power."

Having marched somewhat further, Governor Stone sent Dr. Luke Barber and Mr. Coursey to go on before to Providence, bearing a proclamation addressed to the people of Anne Arundel, in which he declared, "in the presence of Almighty God, that he came not in a hostile way to do them any hurt, but sought all meanes possible to reclaime them by faire meanes; and to my knowledge"—Dr. Barber adds—"at the sending out of parties (as occasion served), he gave strict command that if they met any of the Ann Arundel men, they should not fire the first gun, nor upon paine of death plunder any: these were his actings, to my knowledge, upon the march." The declaration does not seem to have inspired much confidence in Stone's pacific intentions, for, according to Strong, who was probably an eye-witness, the messengers were allowed to read it, "but having no other treaty to offer, they were quietly dismissed to their own company, to whom they might have

[1] *Narrative of a late Bloody Design against the Protestants in Ann Arundel County*; London, July 24, 1655.

gone if they would," but apparently did not. Another messenger was sent by Stone, presumably on a similar errand, who also did not return; and on the evening of the same day, the governor, with his fleet and all his army now on board, made his appearance in the Severn.

Captain Fuller, the commander at Providence, now called his council together, and despatched his secretary, Mr. Durand, and one other, to go on board a merchant ship, the *Golden Lyon*, Roger Heamans, master, then lying in the harbor, and make requisition on the captain for the services of himself, his ship and crew, for the defence of the settlement. Durand went on board, and affixed to the mainmast a proclamation and warrant by which Heamans "was required, in the name of the Lord Protector and Commonwealth of England, and for the maintenance of the just liberties, lives and estates of the free subjects thereof against an unjust power, to be aiding and assisting in this service." Heamans, in his narrative, says that he was at first unwilling to meddle in the matter, "but afterwards seeing the equity of the cause, and the groundless proceedings of the enemy, he offered himself, ship and men, for that service, to be directed by the said councillors." Dr. Barber, in his letter to the Lord Protector, states that "Heamans, commander of the *Golden Lyon*, was *hired* by them," [the Puritans,] "having since received his reward of them; and Mrs. Stone, the governor's wife, in her letter to Lord Baltimore giving an account of this unlucky affair, says, they were 'better provided than my husband did expect; for they hired the captain of the *Golden Lyon*, a great ship of burden. The captain's name is Roger Heamans, a young man, and his brother, who have been great sticklers in the business, as I hear.'"[1]

Hammond declares that there is "not a syllable of truth" in Heaman's pamphlet, and reiterates the charge of "hiring." Heamans was, no doubt, a Puritan, and not unwilling to help his friends, who, we may well suppose, promised that his services should not be unrewarded.

Governor Stone, with his little fleet and army, entered the outer harbor of Providence (Annapolis harbor) late in the evening of March 24. His entrance is thus described by Heamans:—

"Within two hours after at the most, in the very shutting up of the daylight, the ship's company descried off, a company of sloops and boats, making towards the ship, whereupon the Council on board, and the ship's company, would have made shot at them, but this Relator commanded them to forbear, and went himself upon the poop in the stern of the ship, and hailed them several times, and no answer was made, he then charged them not to come nearer the ship, but the enemy kept rowing on their way and were come within shot of the ship; his mates and company having had information of their threatenings, as well against the ship as the poor distressed people, resolved to fire upon them without their commander's consent, rather than hazard all by the enemy's nearer approach, whereupon he ordered them to fire a gun at random to divert their course from the ship, but the enemy kept still course right with the ship, and took no notice of any warning given; he then commanded his gunner to fire at them, but one of his mates, Mr. Robert Morris, who knew the country very well, the malice of the adver-

[1] Langford's *Refutation*.

sary against those people, who were then near worn out with fears and watchings, made a shot at them, which came fairly with them; whereupon they suddenly altered their course from the ship, and rowed into the creek, calling the ship's company, Rogues, Round-headed Rogues, and Dogs, and with many execrations and railing, threatened to fire them on the morning."

"Governor Stone did not think it proper to pay any attention to this signal of war, as it appeared; but, having arrived within the mouth of the creek, which forms the southern boundary of the peninsula on which the city of Annapolis now stands, proceeded to land his men on a peninsula or point of land, which lies on the southern side of both the river Severn and the before mentioned creek, nearly opposite to and in an eastern direction from what is called the *dock* or inner harbor of Annapolis, and on which point or peninsula a small fortress, called fort *Horn*, was afterwards built during the American revolutionary war. While Governor Stone was landing his men on this point of land or peninsula, the commander Heamans, or Mr. Durand, thought it proper to repeat their fire upon the boats of Governor Stone as they were rowing to the shore. The shot thereof lighting somewhere near to them, the governor deemed it most prudent to send a messenger on board the *Golden Lyon* to know the reason of their conduct, with directions to the messenger to inform the captain of the ship, that he (Governor Stone) thought 'the captain of the ship *had been satisfied*.' To which the captain 'answered,' (in a very blustering tone, as it appears), 'satisfied with what?—I never saw any power Captain Stone had, to do as he hath done; but the superscription of a letter. I must, and will appear for these in a good cause.'"[1]

Governor Stone having moved his vessels further up the before mentioned creek, Heamans says:

"The same night came further intelligence from the enemy in the harbor, as they lay there, that they were making fireworks against the ship, whereupon the governor (whose prudence and valor in this business deserves very much honor) commanded a small ship of Captain Cuts, of New England, then in the river, to lye in the mouth of the creek to prevent the enemy's coming forth in the night, to work any mischief against the ship.

"The next morning, by break of day, being the Lord's Day, the 25th of March last, the Relator, himself, and company discerned Captain Stone, with his whole body drawn out and coming towards the water side, marching with drums beating, colours flying, the colours were black and yellow, appointed by the Lord Proprietary. There was not the least token of any subjugation in Stone and his company, or acknowledgement of the Lord Protector of England, but God bless the Lord Proprietary, and their rayling against his ship's company, was Rogues, and Round-headed Rogues, etc."

Stone had no sooner drawn up his force in array upon the shore, than the *Golden Lyon* and Captain Cut's vessel opened fire upon them, killing one man, and compelling him to retire a little up the neck of land. In the meantime, Captain Fuller, at the head of one hundred and seventy men, embarked in boats, and having gone "over the river some six miles distant from the enemy," landed and made a circuit round the head of the creek, proposing to take Stone's force in flank or rear. On their approach, the sentry fired a gun, and an engagement followed, which is thus described by Leonard Strong, one of Fuller's council, in his pamphlet, *Babylon's Fall:*

[1] Bozman.

"Captain Fuller, still expecting that then, at last, possibly they might give a reason of their coming, commanded his men, upon pain of death, not to shoot a gun, or give the first onset: setting up the standard of the commonwealth of England, against which the enemy shot five or six guns, and killed one man in the front before a shot was made by the other. Then the word was given, *in the name of God fall on; God is our strength*—that was the word for *Providence:* the Marylander's word was—*Hey for Saint Maries.* The charge was fierce and sharp for the time; but through the glorious presence of the Lord of hosts manifested in and towards his poor oppressed people, the enemy could not endure, but gave back; and were so effectually charged home, that they were all routed, turned their backs, threw down their arms, and begged mercy. After the first volley of shot, a small company of the enemy, from behind a great tree fallen, galled us, and wounded divers of our men, but were soon beaten off. Of the whole company of the *Marylanders* there escaped only four or five, who run away out of the army to carry news to their confederates. Captain *Stone*, Colonel Price, Captain Gerrard, Captain Lewis, Captain Kendall, Captain Gufther, Major Chandler, and all the rest of the councillors, officers and souldiers of the Lord Baltimore, among whom, both commanders and souldiers, a great number being *Papists*, were taken, and so were all their vessels, arms, ammunition, provision; *about fifty men slain and wounded.* We lost only two in the field; but two died since of their wounds. God did appear wonderful in the field, and in the hearts of the people; all confessing Him to be the only worker of this victory and deliverance."

Strong's pamphlet is, no doubt, strongly colored by partisanship; but whatever the exact details, the Puritans were completely victorious. Their loss, according to Heamans's *Narrative*, was three killed on the field and several wounded, three of whom died soon after.

Heamans says:

"All the arms, bag and baggage, was taken, together with the boats that brought them, wherein was the preparations and fuses for the firing of the ship *Golden Lyon.*

"And amongst the rest of their losses, all their consecrated ware was taken (viz.) their Pictures, Crucifixes, and rows of Beads, with great store of Reliques and trash they trusted in, which, as the Relator is informed, divers was put to the Ancient or Colours" [*i. e.* were attached to the ship's ensign] for their defence; "the variety whereof, as also their great boasting in their own strength, had much confirmed the hearts of the people of God in those parts."[1]

Doctor Barber says that "after the skirmish, the governor, upon quarter given him and all his company in the field, yielded to be taken prisoners; but two or three days after, the victors condemned ten to death, and executed foure, and had executed all, had not the incessant petitioning and begging of some good women saved some, and the souldiers others; the governor himself being condemned by them and since beg'd by the souldiers; some being saved just as they were leading out to execution." The four who were shot, by order of a court-martial, were William Eltonhead, one of the council, Captain William Lewis, John Legatt, and John Pedro. Hammond says that the rest were "saved, but were Amerced, Fined, and Plundered at their pleasure."

[1] *Narrative, etc., ut supra.*

Governor Stone, who was wounded in the engagement, was treated with great severity, being denied the means of communicating with his wife or friends. At last, however, they permitted his wife to visit him and nurse him in his recovery; and shortly before her departure for that purpose, she wrote the following account of the unfortunate affair to Lord Baltimore:

"*For the Right Honourable the Lord Baltemore, these present.*

"Right Honourable:—

"I am sorry at present for to let your honour understand of our sad condition in your province. So it is, that my husband, with the rest of your councell, went about a month agone with a party of men up to *Anne-Arundell* county, to bring those factious people to obedience under your government. My husband sent Dr. *Barber* with one Mr. *Coursey* with a message to them, but they never returned againe before the fight began. Also he sent one Mr. *Packer* the day after, with a message, and he likewise never returned, as I heard: but so it is, that upon Sunday the 25 of March, they did ingage with the people of *Anne-Arundell*, and lost the field, and not above five of our men escaped; which I did conceive ranne away before the fight was ended: the rest all taken, some killed and wounded; my husband hath received a wound in his shoulder, but I heare it is upon the mending. My husband, I am confident, did not thinke that they would have engaged, but it did proove too true to all our great damages; They, as I heare, being better provided than my husband did expect; for they hired the captain of the *Golden Lion*, a great ship of burden. The captain's name is *Roger Hemans*, a young man, and his brother, who have beene great sticklers in the businesse as I hear, captaine *Heman* was one of their councell of war, and by his consent would have had all the prisoners hanged; but after quarter given, they tried all your councellors by a councell of warre, and sentence was passed upon my husband to be shot to death, but was after saved by the enemies owne souldiers, and so the rest of the councellors were saved by the petitions of the women, with some other friends which they found there; onely Master *William Eltonhead* was shot to death, whose death I much lament, being shot in cold blood; and also lieutenant *William Lewis*, with one Mr. *Leggat*, and a Germane, which did live with Mr. *Eltonhead*, which by all relations that ever I did heare of, the like barbarous act was never done amongst Christians. They have sequestred my husband's estate, only they say they will allow a maintenance for me and my children, which I doe beleeve will bee but small. They keep my husband, with the rest of the councell, and all other officers, still prisoners: I am very suddenly, God willing, bound up to see my husband: they will not so much as suffer him to write a letter unto mee, but they will have the perusall of what hee writes. Captain *Tylman* and his mate Master *Cook* are very honest men, and doe stand up much for your honour; they will inform you of more passages than I can remember at the present; And I hope my brother will be downe before captain *Tylman* goes away, and will write to you more at large, for he is bound up this day for to see his brother, if they doe not detain him there as well as the rest; the occasion I conceive of their detainment there is, because they should not goe home, to informe your honour of the truth of the businesse before they make their owne tale in England, which let them doe their worst, which I do not question but you will vindicate my husband's honour which hath ventured life and estate to keep your due heere, which by force hee hath lost. And they give out words, that they have won the country by the sword, and by it they will keepe the same, let my lord protector send in what writing hee pleaseth. The gunner's mate of *Hemans*, since his coming down from *Anne-Arundel* to Patuxent, hath boasted that he shot the first man that was shot of our party. All this I write is very true, which I thought good to informe your lordship, because they will not suffer my husband for to write himselfe: I hope your honor will be pleased for to looke upon my sonne, and for to wish him for to be of good comfort, and not for to take our afflictions to heart. And nothing else at present, I rest your honours most humble servant,

"VIRLINDA STONE.

"*Postscript.*—I hope your honour will favour me so much, that if my sonne wants twenty or thirty pounds you will let him have it, and it shall be payd your honour againe.

"*Hemans* the master of the *Golden Lion* is a very knave, and that will be made plainly for to appeare to your lordship, for he hath abused my husband most grossly."[1]

The following affidavit of three distinguished Protestant gentlemen of the province, gives a more important account of the late transactions, and one that was likely, at the time, to have more weight and influence with the supreme power of the commonwealth:

"The Lord Protector:—

"Henry Coursey, Nicholas Guyther, and Richard Willan, of the Province of Maryland in America, Gent: Maketh oath, That in or about the latter end of May, in the year 1654, His Highness the Lord Protector of the Commonwealth of England, Scotland and Ireland, and the Dominions thereto belonging, was by Captain William Stone, the Lord Baltimore's Governour of the Province, caused to be proclaimed in the head of the people there, they being then summoned in by Capt. Stone for that purpose; and the said Governour took order with Captain Tilman and Mr. Bossworth, two Commanders of ship, then trading in that province, to shoot off severall peeces of ordnance from their respective ships in honour of that solemnity. And they further depose, that in the moneth of July then next following, Mr. Richard Bennet (the then Governour of Virginia) and Colonel William Claiborne, the then Secretary thereof, came from Virginia to Patuxent River, in the said Province of Maryland, and there entertained as Souldiers the Inhabitants of the said River, with those of Ann Arundle, otherwise by them called Providence, as also the Inhabitants of the Isle of Kent, within the said Province, and so forced the said Captain Stone to resign his Government. And the said Deponent, Henry Coursey, further saith, that the said Bennet and Claiborne, afterwards, forced the said Governour to set his hand to a writing, the contents whereof, as this Deponent doth remember, was that he should not meddle with the resuming of the Government again in the Lord Baltimore's behalf. And all the said Deponents further say, that the said Bennet and Claiborne then seized upon the Records of the said Province and put them into the possession of one Captain William Fuller, Mr. Richard Preston and William Durand; and the Deponent, Henry Coursey, saith, that in March last the said Captain Stone sent up to the Inhabitants of Ann Arundle, one Mr. Luke Barber, and the said Deponent, Henry Coursey, with a proclamation, to require the Inhabitants there to yield obedience to the Lord Baltimore's officers, under his Highness the Lord Protector; and that when the said Mr. Barber and this Deponent, Henry Coursey, came thither, they found the people all in arms, and the said Fuller would not suffer this Deponent to read the said Proclamation, and so refusing to give any obedience thereunto, the said Mr. Barber and this Deponent were dismissed, but suddenly after (before conveniently they could get away) were taken prisoners by that party, whereby the said Governour Captain Stone was prevented of any answer, whereupon he proceeded to come up with what force he had into the River, called by some Severn, where these people lived; And all these Deponents say, that when the said Captain Stone came into the said River, there was one Captain

[1] The foregoing letter is taken from a pamphlet, entitled "A refutation of Babylon's Fall," etc., by Mr. John Langford, published in England in 1655.—*Bozman*, ii., p. 687.

Roger Heamans, with a great ship called the *Golden Lion*, whereof he was commander, who presently shot at Captain Stone's boats as they passed by him; and the said Guyther and Willan do further depose, that the said Captain Stone (to avoid the said shot) went into a creek in the said river, where one Mr. Cuts, with another ship (whereof he was master), blocked up the mouth thereof, and upon any discovery fired theire ordnance at the said Captain Stone and his party, untill such time as the said Inhabitants of Ann Arundle had transported themselves over the river, unto the said Captain Stone and his party; where after some dispute, the Governor (finding himself overpowered) yielded upon quarter, whereupon he and most of his party were transported over the river to a Fort at Ann Arundle, where they were all kept prisoners, and about three days after, the said Captain Fuller, William Burgees, Richard Evans, Leo Strong, William Durand, the said Roger Heamans, John Brown, John Cuts, Richard Smith, one Thomas, and one Bestone, Samson Warren, Thomas Meares, and one Crouch, sat us in a Council of War, and there condemned the said Governour Captain Stone, Colonel John Price, Mr. Job Chandler, Mr. William Eltonhead, Mr. Robert Clerk, the said Deponent Nicholas Guyther, Captain William Evans, Captain William Lewis, Mr. John Legat, and John Pedro, to dye; whereof they executed Mr. William Eltonhead, Captain William Lewis, Mr. John Legat, and John Pedro, the rest being preserved at the request of the souldiers and women belonging to the said party of Ann Arundle; after which execution the common soldiers that did belong to the said Captain Stone, were sent away to their severall homes, but the officers and the said messengers were detained longer; and at the discharging of the said Deponents Henry Coursey and Nicholas Guyther, the pretended Councel of War imposed an oath upon them; That they should not write into England to give the Lord Baltimore any information of their proceedings; and not long after they sequestred all the estates of those of the Lord Baltimore's Councel and officers there; and the said Henry Coursey further deposeth, That he was present when Mr. William Eltonhead desired to be allowed an appeale to his Highness the Lord Protector in England, but it was refused him by the said pretended Councel of War at Ann Arundel; and the said Deponents, Henry Coursey and Nicholas Guyther, do further depose that a little before the sending of the proclamation before mentioned to the people of Ann Arundel, they heard the said Capt. Stone declare unto certain the messengers whom these people had sent unto him, That if the said people who he understood were in arms, would repaire unto their severall homes, and submit themselves unto the former established Government under the Lord Baltimore, which did acknowledge his Highnesse the Lord Protector as Sovereign Lord, he would not offer any violence to them, or do them any prejudice, either in their persons or estates, or words to the same very effect; and the Deponent Richard Willan doth also further depose, That about the time when the said Luke Barber and Henry Coursey went with the said Proclamation above mentioned, he heard the said Captain Stone command that none of his party should rob or plunder any upon pain of death.

"HENRY COURSEY,
"NICHOLAS GUYTHER,
"RICHARD WILLAN.

"Sworn all three the second day of July, 1655, before me, NA. HOBART, a Master of the Chancery in Ordinary."[1]

The Puritans being thus undisputed masters of the province, proceeded to confiscate all the property of those who had taken up arms to resist their encroachments and sustain the cause of the proprietary. To this purpose Captain Fuller and his council issued the following order:

[1] John Hammond's pamphlet, entitled *Hammond vs. Heamans*, published in London in 1655.

"It is ordered, that Captain John Smith do take what he may concerning the estates of delinquents, which are sequestered in Patuxent and Patowmack and St. Mary's; to take an inventory thereof, and use such prudential means to save indemnified the said estates, as he shall think fit, until further order come from the governor and council under his highness the lord protector."

The dominion of the proprietary seemed now to be at an end; and in the moment of its downfall, the pretensions of Virginia to his territory were again revived and urged upon the protector, with every circumstance of objection to the charter. On the other hand, the proprietary was as urgent in his request for the restoration of his province; and to counteract his influence, the cause of the Virginia claims was espoused and advocated with great earnestness by Bennett and Matthews, two of the commissioners then administering the affairs of that colony. In opposition to the restitution, several documents[1] were transmitted by them to the protector, embodying every possible objection to the rights of the proprietary. They assail the charter on the old pretext that the territory was not "uncultivated" at the time of the grant; they are eloquent on the subject of Claiborne's wrongs; they seize upon Greene's proclamation of Charles II. and Stone's subsequent conduct, to sustain the allegation that the proprietary was hostile to the protector and an enemy to parliament. Especially do they insist upon the importance of uniting the plantations under one government.

Cromwell, as we have already seen, had, in January 1655, enjoined Bennett to forbear disturbing the people of Maryland until the proprietary's claims had been decided upon. The committee on trade and plantations, to which the matter was referred, reported favorably to Lord Baltimore, on September 16, 1656; and these objections seem to have been meant in opposition to that report, which was kept open for future determination.

The proprietary, however, had not yet lost all hope. A strong party in Maryland were still faithful to him; and no doubt its numbers were increased by the austere rule and oppressive acts of the commissioners. There were even many who openly espoused his cause, and advocated the restitution of his government.

Among these was conspicuous Josias Fendall, who was destined to play an important part in the affairs of the colony. On the 10th of July, 1656, he received a commission from Lord Baltimore as Governor of Maryland, and in the body of the same commission "Captain William Stone, Mr. Thomas Gerard, Col. John Price, Mr. John Chandler and Mr. Luke Barber, and such other person or persons not exceeding three in number, as the said Josias Fendall should nominate," are appointed "to be of his lordship's counsell in the said province." Before Fendall could take any effective steps towards the organization of his government, he was arrested by the Puritans upon "suspicion" and brought before the Provincial Court, composed of Captain William Fuller, Edward Lloyd, Richard Wells, Captain Richard Ewen,

[1] Hazard's *Collection*, i., p. 620 to 630.

Thomas March and Thomas Meares, on the 15th of August, 1656, to answer the charge exhibited against him "of his dangerousness to the public peace." He denied the power of the court to try him, and with his own consent he was remanded to prison, to remain there "until the matters of government in the province of Maryland shall be further settled and fully determined by his highness, the Lord Protector." On the 24th of September following, having grown weary of his confinement, he made his submission by taking the following oath:

"September, 24th, 1656.—Captain Josias Fendall hath this day in open court taken oath, in the presence of God and before the face of the whole court, he will neither directly nor indirectly be any disturber to this present government till there be a full determination ended in England of all matters relating to this government."

The controversy had in the meantime been referred to the Commissioners of Trade in England, and they reported on the 16th of September, 1656, entirely in favor of Lord Baltimore, who now renewed his instructions to Governor Fendall, and directed him to see that the Act of Assembly of 1649, entitled "An Act concerning Religion," "be duly observed in the said province by all the inhabitants thereof, and that the penalties, mentioned in the said act, be duly put in execution upon any offenders against the same or any party thereof; and particularly that part thereof, whereby 'all persons in the said province are to have liberty of conscience and free exercise of their religion.'"

In the third article of these instructions, he directed donations of land to be made to several of those who had been conspicuously faithful to him during the late contests; particularly to Captain Josias Fendall, "his lordship's present lieutenant there," 2000 acres; to Mr. Luke Barber, 1000 acres; to Mr. Thomas Trueman, 1000 acres; to Mr. George Thompson, 1000 acres; to Mr. John Langford, 1500 acres; to Mr. Henry Coursey, 1000 acres.

He moreover instructed his lieutenant and council to take special care of those widows who had lost their husbands by the late troubles—Mrs. Hatton, Mrs. Lewis, and Mrs. Eltonhead; that they should be supplied out of his lordship's rents and profits for their present relief and sustenance in a decent manner, in case they stood in need thereof; and that they let his lordship know, wherein he could do them any good, in recompense of their sufferings, and that they be assured, on his lordship's behalf, that he will continue his utmost endeavours, (by soliciting his highness and council), for procuring of justice to be done them for the lives of their husbands, and satisfaction for their losses from those who have done them so great injuries; which he doubts not but will be at last obtained. He further instructed his governor and council to cherish and comfort, in what they could, all such persons as had approved themselves faithful to his lordship, and done him good service during the late troubles of the province; and that such persons should be preferred before any others to such places and employments of trust and profit as they might be respectively capable of; in particular Mr. Thomas Trueman, Mr. George Thompson, Lieutenant Thomas Tunnell, and Mr. Barton; and that his said lieutenant and council let his lordship understand from time to time, wherein he could, upon any occasion, requite them and others, who have been faithful to his lordship, with any thing in the province for their advantage, according to their respective merits, assuring them that his lordship would be very ready and willing to gratify them in anything, that should be reasonably desired of him and in his power to do.[1]

To aid and give countenance to the new governor, Lord Baltimore appointed on the 7th of November, 1656, his brother, Philip Calvert, secretary of the province, and one of his council.

"The new governor and secretary obtained possession of the capital without difficulty, and soon succeeded in extending their authority over the faithful county of St. Mary's; but beyond this their success did not immediately extend. Maryland was now under a divided rule. The Puritans—Capt. Fuller and his council—governed the north, at Providence, destined hereafter under the name of Annapolis to become the capital of the colony and the state; and Governor Barber, (whom Fendall, being compelled to visit England on the affairs of the province, had appointed by virtue of his commission to act in his absence,) and the friends of the lord Proprietary, held possession of the ancient city of St. Mary's. The Puritans, determined to consider their authority as still undisputed, and probably having possession of the records and public seals, summoned an Assembly, which convened at Patuxent on the 24th of September, 1657, and proceeded to confirm the authority of their party. They also levied a poll-tax to pay the public expenses, and appointed commissioners to collect the fines imposed upon the adherents of the Proprietary. But their domination was near its end.[2]

Through the interference of friends, and to put a stop to the distresses arising from the state of things then existing in the province, the following agreement was entered into and signed in England, on the 30th of November, 1657:

"Articles of agreement between the lord proprietary of this province and Richard Bennett, esqr., which are as followeth, viz.

"Whereas there have bin of late, viz. in the year 1652, and since, some controversies between the right honorable Cecilius Lord Baltimore, lord and proprietary of the province of Maryland and Richard Bennett, esqr., and other people in Maryland, nowe or late in opposition to his lordship's government of the said province upon which have unhappily followed much bloodshed and great distempers there, endangering the utter ruine of that plantation if not timely prevented, and whereas upon complaint made thereof by the said lord Baltimore the matter was by his highness the lord protector referred first to the lord's commissioners, Witlock and Wriddington, whose report thereof was afterwards referred by the councell to the commissioners for trade, who made their report also thereupon to his highness and councell, but they by reason of their great affaires having not as yett leisure to consider of the said report, the same remains yett undetermined, and in the mean time the inhabitants of the said province remaine in a very sad distracted and unsettled condition by reason of the said differences touching the said government there, therefore the said lord Baltimore, upon a treaty with the said Richard Bennett and colonel Samuel Matthews,

[1] Bozman, ii., p. 543.

[2] McSherry, p. 78.

occasioned by the friendly endeavours of Edward Digges, esqr., about the composure of the said differences, and in pursuance of the said report of the said committee for trade, dated 16th of September, 1656, hath for the good of the inhabitants of the said province condescended and is willing to do as followeth, viz., in case the said people in opposition to his lordship's government there as aforesaid, shall forthwith, upon notice hereof, from his lordship's governor or secretary there, for the time being, cease and forbeare for the future, from executing any act or power pertaining to government and administration of justice within the said province, and shall deliver up to his lordship's said governor, or secretary aforesaid, all records of the said province now in their power and also his lordship's former great seale of the said province, if it be found or procured by them, and shall for the future give all due obedience and submission to his lordship's government there, according to his pattent of the said province, that then his lordship doth promise:

"*Imprimis*, that no offences or differences which have arisen in Maryland upon and since the said controversies there, shall be questioned by his lordship's jurisdiction there in the said province, but shall be left to be determined by such ways and means as his highness and councell shall direct.

"2. *Item*, that the said people, in opposition as aforesaid, shall have patents from his lordship for such lands in the said province as they can claime due unto them by his said lordship's conditions of plantation, and in the same manner and with all the same rights as they might have had if the said controversies and differences had not happened, any former order, instructions, proclamations or any other thing proceeding from the said Lord Baltemore, or any deriving any authority from him to the contrary hereof in any wise notwithstanding, provided that they and every of them respectively, who shall desire the same, doe sue out their said patents for the said lands, within nine months after notice hereof, given them by his lordship's said governor or secretary there for the time being, and that before they have theyr pattents they take the oath of fidelity there to his said lordship, with such alteration in it as is mentioned in the said report of the committee for trade, and shall pay or satisfy his said lordship's receiver generall there for his lordship's use, all arrears of rent due to his said lordship from the time they first entered upon the said lands respectively, and due fees to his said lordship's secretary, surveyor, and other officers there, as other inhabitants ought to doe, and according to his said lordship's conditions of plantation for the said province.

"3. *Item*, that such of the said people in opposition as aforesaid, who shall desire to remove themselves or estate from Maryland, shall have free leave and a year's time so to doe.

"4. Lastly, the Lord Baltemore doth promise, that he will never give his assent to the repeal of a law established heretofore in Maryland by his lordship's consent, and mentioned in the said report of the committee for trade, whereby all persons, professing to believe in Jesus Christ, have freedom of conscience there, and do faithfully promise upon his honour to observe and performe as much as in him lies the particulars above mentioned; and his lordship doth hereby authorise and require his lordship's governor and all other his lordship's officers there to give assurance to the people of their due performance hereof. In witness whereof, the said Lord Baltemore hath hereunto sett his hand and seale the 30th day of November, 1657.

"C. BALTEMORE,
"SAMUEL MATTHEWS.

"*Signed, sealed, in the presence of* EDWARD DIGGS, JOHN HARRIS, RICHARD CHANDLER, A. STANFORD, WILLIAM BARRETT.

"This is the paper which was mentioned in my letter to Captain William Fuller, and being of the same date with this.

"R. BENNETT."

On his return from England, in 1658, Governor Fendall brought with him this agreement, also instructions dated November 20th, 1657, relating to grants of lands, ordering, among others, one of ten thousand acres to Edward Eltonhead, who was no doubt a near kinsman of the councillor shot, after quarter given, by Fuller's court martial. Fendall's powers are subjected to certain restrictions by this document, and he is ordered to exercise them subject to the advice and consent of Philip Calvert, the proprietary's brother, and secretary of the province, or, in case of his death, of Thomas Cornwaleys. Barber surrendered his powers back to Governor Fendall, the articles of agreement were publicly read, and the 18th of March following appointed for the meeting of the opposing parties at St. Leonard's creek. Fendall's delegates presented themselves on the appointed day, but the Puritan envoys not having arrived, they adjourned until the 20th, when Captain William Fuller, Richard Preston, Edward Lloyd, Thomas Meares, Philip Thomas and Samuel Withers arrived. The Puritans objected as before to a clause in the oath of fidelity, desired an amnesty for past transactions, and requested that they might not be disarmed on account of danger from the Indians. These demands were conceded, and the oath modified so far as concerned persons already in the province, and the agreement thus amended was adopted two days later. Fendall's commission was read and proclaimed, and a General Assembly summoned to meet at St. Leonard's on the 27th of April, 1658.

Thus, after nearly six years of usurpation, the ascendancy of the Puritans in Maryland was overthrown, and the Lord Proprietary reinstated in his rights and authority.

CHAPTER X.

The principle upon which the European sovereigns of the sixteenth and seventeenth centuries laid claim to all lands discovered by their subjects, and pretended to stretch their sway across a whole continent, because a storm-driven mariner had touched on a spit of sand, or stood for a moment on a point of rock, simple though it seemed, and admirably convenient for rewarding a court-favorite, or satisfying an importunate creditor with immense tracts of land, bestowed all the more lavishly as they were acquired without cost—was not without inconveniences. Of the geography of the western continent nothing was known save of a narrow strip on the Atlantic coast, and a few miles distance up its chief rivers, and even of this the knowledge was very imperfect. Hence, innumerable errors in boundaries, discrepancies in grants, and conflicting claims, out of which were to arise not merely disputes, but bloodshed, war, and manifold calamities. Of these Maryland had her share, and suffered great wrong and loss, being deprived, after a controversy lasting nearly a century, of some of the fairest and most fertile portions of her original domain, upon grounds as unreasonable as they were illegal, as we shall endeavor to show in the present chapter.

On April 4th, 1609, Captain Henry Hudson, an Englishman in the service of the Dutch East India Company, set sail from Amsterdam for the purpose of discovering a northeast passage to India. Baffled by the ice, he changed his plans, and stood across the Atlantic to North America. Passing the banks of Newfoundland he kept southward down the coast, and on August 12th, arrived off the mouth of the Chesapeake bay, which he recognized as "the entrance into the king's river in Virginia, where our Englishmen are." After taking a few soundings, he stood out again to sea, and keeping a north-east course off the coast of Maryland, on the 28th he entered "a great bay with rivers,"—now the Delaware—where he anchored; but finding the navigation difficult, and having no pinnace of light draft to go before and take soundings, he once more stood out to sea, and running northward several days along a low sandy coast with "broken islands" and "high hills," on the 3d of September he reached what is now Sandy Hook, New York.

In the following year, it is stated, Sir Samuel Argall, afterwards governor of Virginia, visited the bay discovered by Hudson, and gave it the name of Delaware, from Lord De la Warr, then Governor. No steps, however, were taken by Europeans looking toward a settlement on its shores until 1614, when Captain Cornelis Jacobson Mey, in the *Fortune*, sailing under a commission from the States General of Holland, with three other vessels, reached the coast of America at the mouth of the Manhattan river. Here, one of the ships, commanded by Captain Block, was accidentally burned; and to supply its place, a small yacht of about 16 tons, called the *Onrest*, or "Restless," was built at a small island, since called Block Island, near the mouth of Long Island Sound, being the first vessel built by European shipwrights in this country. The rest of the fleet then sailed eastward, while Mey steered to the south and entered the Delaware bay, the eastern headland at whose entrance was afterwards named from him Cape May.

Mey's fleet soon returned to Holland, with the exception of the yacht *Onrest*, which was left in command of Captain Hendrickson, with orders to explore the bay and river, and make a careful examination of the coast; and in the same year, 1616, he sailed up the Delaware river as high as the Schuylkill.[1] After this, Hendrickson returned to Holland, where he laid claim to the reward of a discoverer, apparently without success.

The establishment of the Dutch West India Company, in 1621, was followed by preparations for planting a settlement on the Delaware. A vessel called the *New Netherlands* was fitted out by the company and placed under the command of Mey, with whom Adrian Joricz Tienpont was associated as a director of the expedition; a number of colonists, Walloons for the most part, with necessary stores, were put on board, and the expedition set sail from the Texel in the beginning of March, 1623. Reaching the Delaware, which they called the Zuydt, or South, and also Prince Hendrick's river, they ascended for about fifteen leagues, and began to build a fort which they named Fort Nassau, the site of which is supposed to have been on the most northern branch of what is now Timber creek, in New Jersey, about four miles below Philadelphia, and near the present town of Gloucester.

Captain Mey was now formally installed in his office as first director of New Netherland under the Dutch West India Company. During his administration, which lasted but a single year, Fort Nassau was finished and Fort Orange built on the North or Hudson river, on a site now occupied by the business part of Albany.[2] The fur trade was also briskly carried on, and the West India Company were much elated at the prospects of their infant colony. William Verhulst succeeded Mey as director, and during his year of office, appears to have visited the Delaware river, where his name was long commemorated by "Verhulsten Island," near Trenton.

Peter Minuit, of Wesel, was the next director, and took command in 1626. In 1628, by order of the company, the stations on the South or Delaware river, at Verhulsten's Island, and at Fort Nassau, were abandoned, and the colonists removed to Manhattan, the fur trade being kept up by a small vessel that made regular trips to the river.

In 1629, for the purpose of promoting settlements in the territory of New Netherland, the Assembly of Nineteen granted a charter of freedoms and exemptions "to all who should plant colonies there." Under this

[1] Vincent's *History of Delaware*, p. 102.

[2] Barnard's *Address before Albany Inst.*; 1830.

charter, Samuel Godyn, a merchant of Amsterdam, and Samuel Blommaert, on the 19th of June, obtained a grant of land on the west side of Delaware bay, extending northward about thirty-two miles from Cape Henlopen to the mouth of the South river, and running inland for a breadth of about two miles. This they had previously bought from the Indians, having sent two persons "to examine into the situation of those quarters;" and this was the first purchase of land from the Indians within the limits of the present State of Delaware. On October 6, 1630, Godyn and Blommaert formed a partnership with William Van Rensselaer, Jan de Lost, and David Peterszen de Vries, "a bold and skillful seaman, and master of artillery in the service of the United Provinces," and four other directors of the West India Company—Van Cenlen, Hamel, Van Haringhoeck and Van Sittorigh—were soon after admitted as partners. Preparations were immediately made for their two-fold object of making a settlement and engaging in the whale-fishing; and the ship *Walvis*, or "Whale," of eighteen guns, and a yacht, equipped for a whaling voyage, and having on board about thirty colonists with the necessary stores and provisions, sailed on the 12th of December under the command of Peter Heyes, from the Texel, to make the first settlement in what is now the State of Delaware.[1]

The expedition met with a misfortune at the start. Just after sailing, the yacht, through the carelessness of her consort, was taken by a Dunkirk privateer; but the *Walvis* pursued her course, and reached the South river in April, 1631. Running up the west shore of the bay, a few miles within Cape Cornelius, Heyes came to the Horekill, "a fine navigable stream," now Lewes creek in Sussex County. On the banks of this beautiful creek, which offered an admirably safe and convenient roadstead, a brick home, strong enough to serve as a fort as well as a residence, was built and inclosed with a stockade, and Gilliss Hossett, who had acted as Van Rensselaer's agent in purchases of land around Fort Orange the previous summer, was placed in charge. The settlement received the name of "Swaanendael," or "Valley of Swans," from the great number of those birds which frequented the bay; and the Dutch title by discovery, purchase, and occupation was formally asserted by the erection of a pillar bearing a plate of tin engraved with the arms of the United Provinces. The colony thus planted consisted of about thirty souls.[2]

Heyes, after planting his colony, crossed over to the Jersey shore, and, in behalf of Godyn and Blommaert, purchased from the Indians a tract of land extending from Cape May twelve miles northward and along the shore of the bay, and running twelve miles inland; and to the bay itself he gave the name of "Godyn's Bay."

As an offset to Heyes's colonizing success, the other object of the expedition—the whale fishing—proved a failure, which he excused on his return to

[1] De Vries did not go out with this first expedition to the South river, as stated by Vincent in his *History of Delaware*, and other writers. He sailed, for the first time, on May 24th, 1632, and did not arrive until December of that year. De Vries' *Voyages*, pp. 95–101. Albany *Records*, xxvi., pp. 27–30.

[2] Broadhead's *History of New York*, i., p. 206.

Holland, on the ground that he had arrived too late in the season. This ill luck rather dampened for a while the ardor of his partners, but the vision of a profitable whale fishery still haunted Godyn. On the 12th of February, 1632, a new arrangement was made between the "partner patroons" to equip another ship and yacht, with which De Vries himself was to proceed to the South river as "patroon and commander," and test the experiment in person during the next winter. The expedition accordingly left the Texel toward the end of May. But on the 24th, just before it sailed, news brought by Minuit from Manhattan reached Amsterdam, that Swaanendael had been attacked by the savages, thirty-two men killed as they were working in the fields, the fort taken, and the whole colony destroyed.

In sadness and disappointment De Vries proceeded on his way. Misfortune still attended the enterprises of the South river patroons. An unskillful pilot ran the ship on the sands of Dunkirk, and she was forced to put back for repairs. After two months delay, De Vries set sail again on the first of August, arrived at the South river on the 5th of December, 1632, and anchored off Swaanendael, where he found "beautiful land" to cultivate, and promised himself "royal work" with the whales.

"The next day," says Mr. Broadhead, "a well-armed boat was sent into the kill [creek] to open a communication with the savages. Reaching the spot where their little fort had been, they found the house itself destroyed, the palisades almost all burned, and the ground around strewn with the skulls and bones of their murdered countrymen, intermingled with the remains of horses and cattle. The silence of the grave hung over the desolate valley."

After a time De Vries succeeded in opening communications with the savages, when the terrible mystery was explained. One of the Indians had carried off the tin plate bearing the arms of Holland, from the post where Heyes had set it up; upon which Hossett, in command of the post, had made such vehement complaint, that the chief who had committed the petty theft was killed by his men, and a token of the deed brought to Hossett. The latter bitterly regretted this deed which he had been far from intending; but the mischief was done. The friends of the slain chief laid a plan of revenge. Obtaining entrance to the fort under pretence of selling beaver skins, they killed all who were within, of whom Hossett was one, and then despatched those who were at work in the fields, thus cutting off the colony to the last man.

On the 9th of December, the chief and his followers came and ratified a formal peace, receiving presents of "duffels [coarse cloth], bullets, hatchets and Nuremberg toys." After this De Vries remained some time in the neighborhood of the creek; and supposing that no Dutch vessel from New Netherland had yet gone to the Chesapeake, he was ambitious to be the "first Hollander from this quarter that had visited that region."[1] So setting sail

[1] Mey, however, had visited the Chesapeake and ascended the James river as high as Jamestown in his ship, the *Blyde Boodschap*, or "Glad Tidings," as early as 1620.

in his yacht, De Vries reached Jamestown the eleventh of March, and was welcomed by the governor, Sir John Harvey, who came down to the beach attended by a guard of halberdiers and musketeers. "Whence come you?" was the friendly challenge. "From the South Bay of New Netherland." "How far is that from our bay?" demanded the governor. "About ninety miles," answered the Dutch patroon. Harvey then invited De Vries into his house, and after pledging him in "a Venice glass of sack," produced an English chart, on which pointed out the South bay, there named "Lord Delaware's bay," and "it is our king's land, and not New Netherland," insisted the loyal knight. De Vries replied that the South river was a beautiful stream, on which no Englishman had been for ten years, and that several years before, the Dutch had built a fort there, which they called Fort Nassau.

Governor Harvey was surprised to hear that he had such neighbors without knowing it. He had indeed, heard that the Dutch had a fort upon "Hudson's river, as the English called it;" and only in the previous September, he had sent a sloop with seven or eight men to Delaware bay, "to see whether there was a river there." But they had not yet returned; "he did not know whether the sea has swallowed them up or not." De Vries then told Harvey of savages he had seen in the South river, wearing English jackets, and related what he had heard of the tragical fate of the sloop's company.

After a week's sojourn at Jamestown, De Vries took leave of the hospitable Harvey, and returned to Swaanendael with a welcome supply of provisions. In his absence the ship had only taken seven whales, which yielded 32 cartels of oil. Finding that the fishing here was too expensive in proportion to the profit, and the fish poor, he made a final departure from South river, and returned to Fort Amsterdam, and thence to Europe. Once more, Swaanendael was abandoned to its original lords; and, until 1638, European colonization kept aloof from the banks of the Delaware. Such was the extent and condition of the settlements on the Delaware, when Lord Baltimore applied for and received his grant. And it was perfectly justifiable in Baltimore to apply for, as well as lawful for the king to grant all that territory included within the lines of his patent, as the "country was not then cultivated and planted, though, in certain parts thereof, inhabited by certain barbarous people."

We have seen that Cæcilius Calvert, two months after his father's death, on the 20th day of June, 1632, received a charter granting and confirming to him "all that part of the Peninsula, or Chersonese, lying in the parts of America, between the ocean on the east, and the Bay of Chesapeake on the west; divided from the residue thereof by a right line drawn from the promontory, or head-land, called Watkins' Point, situate upon the bay aforesaid, near the river Wighco, on the west, unto the main ocean on the east; and between that boundary on the south, unto that part of the Bay of Delaware on the north, which lieth under the fortieth degree of north latitude from the æquinoctial, where New England is terminated: and all the tract of that land within the metes underwritten, (that is to say,) passing from the said bay, called Delaware bay, in a right line, by the degree aforesaid, unto the true meridian of the first fountain of the river of Pattowmack, thence verging towards the south, unto the farther bank of the said river, and following the same on the west and south, unto a certain place called Cinquack, situate near the mouth of the said river, where it disembogues into the aforesaid Bay of Chesapeake, and thence by the shortest line unto the aforesaid promontory or place, called Watkin's Point."

It will at once be perceived that these boundaries of the province are essentially different from those which, at this day, define the limits of the State. By comparison it will be seen that Maryland has been deprived of the whole State of Delaware, and a strip of territory about twenty miles wide, now forming part of the State of Pennsylvania, including in its limits the present city of Philadelphia, and a great proportion of the counties of Chester, Delaware, Lancaster, York, Adams, Franklin, Fulton, Bedford and Somerset. The whole number of acres of territory lost to Maryland may be summed up thus: To Delaware, one and a quarter millions; to Pennsylvania, two and a half millions; and to Virginia, half a million; making a total of four and a quarter millions of acres, besides about one hundred and fifty thousand acres "left out" between Onancock river and the Scarborough on the eastern shore.

Of the most of this valuable territory Maryland was deprived on the alleged ground that the Swedes and Dutch had established settlements there before Lord Baltimore's chart was obtained; and this plea was not only urged by the Penns, but has been repeated by historians, without any authentic proof of the assertion on which it is founded.

The claim of the English crown to the continent of North America rested upon the discovery and partial exploration of its coast by Sebastian Cabot in the year 1498; and according to the international law of the day, it was a perfectly valid claim. The first discovery made by the Dutch was that of Hudson in the year 1609; and his voyage was one of exploration merely, not for settlement and occupation. As early as 1606, King James's grant to the Virginia Company of the very countries explored by Hudson had been made, and the settlements of the Southern or London Company had already begun. So, whether the Dutch rested their claim on priority of discovery or of occupation, it was valid in neither case.

In 1620, "The Council of Plymouth, for the planting and governing of that country called New England," was invested in a corporate capacity with "the rights of soil and government over all the territory on the continent of North America lying between the fortieth and forty-eighth degrees of north latitude, and the exclusive privilege of fishing and trading therein."[1] This

[1] Hazard's *Collection*, I., pp. 103-118.

was the outstanding grant from the English crown of the territory immediately north of the northern limits of Maryland at the time of the grant to Lord Baltimore. Its southern limit, it will be noticed, lies on the very parallel of latitude which constituted the northern boundary of Maryland. With this common boundary so exactly defined, no room was left for controversy, except as to the territorial location of the parallel. And even this could not be mistaken, as the description of the bounds of the province was manifestly framed by the aid of the admirable and astonishingly accurate map accompanying Smith's *History of Virginia.*

Within the limits of New England, the southern boundary of which, as we have shown, coincided with the northern boundary of Maryland, the settlement of New Plymouth had been planted in 1620, and that of Massachusetts bay, in 1629; but these were so remote that no disputes about boundaries ever arose between them and the authorities of Maryland. The rights of the Plymouth Company had been long extinct, and several distinct colonial governments had been carved out of its territory, before the proprietary of Maryland was involved in contests about the northern limits of his province, all which arose from grants subsequent to his own.

The causes of Virginian dissatisfaction with the grant of Baltimore have already been partially explained. The Maryland grant lay within the limits originally established by the Virginia charter; and though that charter had been afterwards annulled and it had become a royal government, the province continued to retain its ancient boundaries until they were changed by the royal grant to Baltimore. No settlements of any kind had been made upon the territory granted to Baltimore, down to the time of that grant, either under the authority of the crown or of the charter governments, except the trading-post established by Claiborne on Kent Island, and the unauthorized settlement of the Dutch on the Delaware, which, as we have seen, had already been abandoned. True, the Dutch may have regarded their abandonment as but temporary; but from the English point of view they were mere interlopers, who had planted themselves, without permission, on land belonging to the English crown; and Lord Baltimore, in his representations to the king, could not possibly take account of their former residence as in any way obstructing or invalidating his grant. In fact, as early as 1632, Charles I. had notified the New Netherland authorities that some years before, on the complaint of his father, James I., the States General "had interdicted their subjects from trading in those regions." And, in answer to a memorial from the Dutch ambassadors, the British ministry replied the same year (1632), that the roaming savages of America were not "*bona fide* possessors" of the land, and, therefore, they could not alienate it.

The title of the English was asserted to be by "first discovery, occupation and possession," and by charters and patents from their sovereigns, and the ministry boldly denied the Dutch title to any portion of New Netherland, and claimed it as English territory. The strenuous assertion of prior and superior British right was probably the last important American State paper prepared by Sir John Coke, who affirmed that the Hollanders "as interlopers," had fallen "into the middle," between Virginia and New England.[1]

Thus it is seen the British government did not recognize the claims of the Dutch to any part of North America. Up to this period, there is no authentic evidence that the Dutch had effected any permanent settlement on the Delaware; and unless the unfortunate colonists at Swaanendael be an exception, no one had adopted its shores as his home for life, or as an abiding place for his posterity. A report, made to the States General in April, 1638, "on the condition of the colony of New Netherland," furnishes rather conclusive evidence, that no occupation of the Delaware bay was then claimed, as will be seen by the following query and answer extracted from that document:

"Are these limits (limits including the Delaware) in the possession, at the present time, of the West India Company and the inhabitants of this country?"

Answer: "We occupy Mauritius, or the North river; where there are two forts, Orange and Amsterdam; and there is, moreover, one house built by the company, and that is most of the population."[2]

In this connection we also have the testimony of Acrelius, that when the Swedes first arrived, [in 1638], "the Dutch had no establishment on the Delaware." Proud says, that "the commodious situation of New York for the sea trade, induced most of them [the Dutch] who were settled on the Delaware, soon afterwards to quit it, and fix their settlements on both sides of the North river, before any of the Swedes came to America."[3] Campanius says "The Dutch also claimed a right to it [the country,] because they had visited it before the Swedes, and had erected three forts there, which had, however, been utterly destroyed by the Indians, and all who were therein murdered or driven away, so that they had abandoned it entirely when the Swedes came." Gordon says: "At the expiration of twenty-five years from the discovery of the Delaware by Hudson, [1609] not a single European remained upon its shores."[4]

[1] Brodhead, p. 215.

[2] N. Y. *Col. Doc.*, i., p. 106.

[3] Proud's *History of Pennsylvania.*

[4] Gordon's *History of Pennsylvania*, p. 14.

In 1632, Sir Edmund Plowden, the great-grandson of Edmund Plowden, the eminent jurist, whose *Law Commentaries* Lord Coke termed "exquisite and elaborate," made application to Charles I. for a tract of land, to be "exempted from all appeal and subjection to the Governor and Company of Virginia, and with such other additions, privileges and dignities, like as have been heretofore granted to Sir George Calvert K't, late Lord Calvert in New Foundland, together with the usual grants and privileges that other colonies have for governing, and ordering their planters and subordinates, and for supplying of corn, cattle and necessaries from your Majesty's Kingdom of Ireland, with power to take artificers and laborers there."

And in the following month the king, in answer to his petition, wrote: "Our pleasure is, and we do hereby authorise and require you, upon the receipt of these, our letters, forthwith to cause a grant of the said Isle, called the Isle Plowden, or Long Isle, between 39 and 40 degrees north latitude, and of forty leagues square of the adjoining continent . . . to be holden of us, as of our Crown of Ireland, by

It is certain that no permanent settlements were made upon the Delaware until the arrival of the Swedes in 1638. Many authors have assumed that there were Swedish settlements there as early as 1631, even Bozman being led into this error by Proud, whom he quotes; and while the latter is right in asserting that the Dutch built a fort at "Lewistown" in 1630, the former makes the mistake of attributing its erection to the Swedes. The error was first published by Campanius in 1702, and has been repeated by nearly all following writers.

William Usselinx, a distinguished merchant in Stockholm, was the first to propose to the Swedish government a scheme for planting a colony in America. He was a native of Antwerp, and had resided in Spain, Portugal and the Azores, at a time when the spirit of foreign adventure pervaded every class of society. Whether he had ever been in America is uncertain; but he had some connection with the Dutch West India Company soon after its organization, and by this and other means, was able to give ample information to the sagacious sovereign who was then sweeping Germany with his victorious armies, in relation to the country bordering on the Delaware, its soil, climate and production.

In the year 1624, he proposed to Gustavus Adolphus a plan for the organization of a trading company, to extend its operations to Asia, Africa, America and Terra Magellanica. The king recommended it to the States, and a company called the "Swedish West India Company" was formed, and a charter granted by Gustavus, dated June 14th, 1626. But the prosecution of the German war so absorbed the king's attention and the feelings of the people that the enterprise was suffered to die out. Rudman, in his memoirs, says, "ships and all necessaries were provided; an admiral, officers and troops, commissaries, merchants and assistants were appointed. The work was ripe for execution, when the German war, and afterwards the king's death, prevented it, and rendered the fair prospect fruitless." Soon after the organization of the company, the fatal battle of Lutzen, which was fought on the 3d of November, 1632, deprived Sweden of her magnanimous sovereign, and the grand enterprise he had so much at heart was suspended for several years.[1]

the name of New Albion, with such privileges, additions and dignities to Sir Edmund Plowden, his deputies and assigns, as first Governor of the premises," etc.

In accordance with the king's order, a patent was issued to Sir Edmund Plowden in June, 1634, and in a pamphlet published in the year 1648, entitled "A Description of the Province of New Albion in America," its boundaries are thus described: "The bounds are one thousand miles compass of this most temperate, rich province; for our south bound is Maryland's north bound; and beginning at Aquats, or the southernmost or first cape of Delaware Bay, in 38 degrees, 40 minutes, and so runneth by, or through, or including Kent Island, through Chesapeak Bay to Piscataway, including the falls of Patowmack river, to the head or northernmost branch of that river, being three hundred miles due west; and thence northward to the head of Hudson's river, isles, Long-isle or Pamunke, and all isles within ten leagues of the said province."

It is not believed that any settlements were made under this absurd grant, but the preposterous geography of the above statement shows what vague ideas with regard to the western world were current at the time.

[1] Ferris, *Settlements on the Delaware*.

On the death of Gustavus Adolphus, the crown descended to his daughter Christiana, a child six years of age; and the States intrusted the government, during her minority, to a regency, at the head of which was the illustrious chancellor of Sweden, Axel, Count Oxenstierna. Chancellor Oxenstierna viewed the consequences of American colonization as "favorable to all Christendom, to Europe, and to the whole world."

It was more than three years, however, before the scheme was carried into effect, and when it was at length accomplished, it was through the agency of Peter Minuit, who had been commercial agent, and director-general of the Dutch West India Company, and governor of the New Netherlands. After his recall, Minuit went to Stockholm and offered to the regency the benefit of his colonial experience. His counsels won the confidence of the sagacious Oxenstierna, and toward the close of 1637, Minuit, with about fifty emigrants, sailed from Gottenburg with the *Key of Calmar* and a tender called the *Bird Grip*, or "Griffin," under a commission from the infant queen, "signed by eight of the chief lords of Sweden," to plant a new colony on the west side of the Delaware Bay.

In March, 1638, the Swedish expedition put in at Jamestown, where it remained about ten days, "to refresh with wood and water," and then proceeded on its destination to the Delaware, where it arrived in the month of April in the same year.

They sailed up the bay, and about four miles above the present town of New Castle, they entered Minquas creek, (the Christiana,) and proceeding up it for about two and a half miles, cast anchor at the rocks. These rocks form a natural wharf of stone, and are situated at the foot of Sixth street in the city of Wilmington. On this natural wharf the *Key of Calmar* and the *Griffin* landed their passengers and freight.

They at once commenced the erection of a fort and trading-house, which they named in honor of their young queen, "Fort Christiana." They also changed the name of the creek to Christiana creek. A small town, named Christinaham, or Christina Harbor, was also erected behind the fort.[1]

When the Dutch heard of these proceedings of the Swedes, Governor Kieft, who had just before arrived at New Amsterdam, immediately issued a protest, dated May 6th, 1638, against the encroachment, declaring his determination to maintain the rights of the Dutch to the territory invaded. Minuit wisely abstained from taking any notice of the protest, and Kieft, despite his declaration, quietly submitted to this intrusion of the Swedes upon a territory to which they had no claim under any acknowledged principle of international law.

In 1640, the Dutch ship *Fredenburg*, commanded by Captain Jacob Powelson, arrived in the Delaware, laden with men, cattle and everything necessary for the cultivation of the country. This settlement of Hollanders was made under a charter given to Gothardt de Redden, William de Horst

[1] Vincent's *History of Delaware*, p. 149.

and —— Fenland, but was afterwards assigned to Henry Hockhammer and others, they, as the instrument states, "having the intention of establishing a colony in New Sweden."

At this time we also have the first authentic information of the attempt of the English to settle on the Delaware. Turnbull, in his *History of Connecticut*, says: "A large purchase, sufficient for a number of plantations, was made by Captain Turner, agent for New Haven, on both sides of the Delaware bay and river. This purchase was made with a view to trade, and for the settlement of churches in gospel order and purity."[1] Early in the year 1641, a bark was fitted out at New Haven, by Mr. Lamberton, under the command of Robert Cogswell. They stopped at Fort Amsterdam, when Director Kieft, hearing of their intention, entered his protest against their visit, and warned them "not to build or plant on the South river, lying within the limits of New Netherlands, nor on the lands extending along there, as lawfully belonging to us."[2] The English, however, proceeded to South river, and commenced erecting trading-houses at Varkenskill, or Farkenskill, near the present town of Salem, New Jersey, and, it is supposed, also on the Schuylkill. This settlement consisted of sixty persons, comprising twenty families.

The Dutch determined to expel these settlers from the Schuylkill, and on the 22d of April, 1642, issued instructions to their commissary or governor on the South river, Jan Jansen Van Ilpendan, to that effect. John Johnson (as the English call him) appears to have carried out his instructions, for the English, in their complaints afterwards made, say, "that notwithstanding the purchases of the English, on both sides of the river, to which they affirm neither the Dutch or Swedes had any just title, Governor Keith [Kieft], without protest or warning, sent armed men, and by force, in a hostile manner, burnt their trading-house, seized, and for some time, detained the goods in it, not suffering their servants so much as to take an inventory of them." He also seized their boat, and for a while kept their men prisoners, for which treatment they could not, up to 1650, get any satisfaction.

On the 16th of August, 1642, John Printz, a lieutenant colonel in the Swedish army, described by Peterson De Vries as a person "who weighed upwards of four hundred pounds, and drank three drinks at every meal," was appointed Governor of New Sweden. He arrived at Fort Christiana on the 15th of February, 1643, and soon after erected a residence at "Fort Gottenberg," on what is now called Province Island, at the mouth of the Schuylkill river, near the western abutment of Penrose ferry bridge.

Shortly after his arrival, or previous to building this fort, he succeeded in expelling the English who were settled on Varkenskill, under Lamberton. In this outrage he was assisted by the Dutch, who were, with the Swedes, extremely jealous of the pertinacious attempts of the English to settle on the Delaware, and both used their utmost endeavors to prevent them. They

[1] Trumbull, i., p. 116. [2] Vincent, p. 167.

knew that the English claimed the Delaware, and that if they once got a foothold, they could not be expelled. In the year 1646, however, a series of disputes commenced between the Dutch and Swedes, which finally ended, on the 25th of September, 1655, in the overthrow of the Swedish power on the Delaware and their dominion in America. After this, the Dutch extended the boundaries of New Netherlands over the Delaware, and divided the country before called New Sweden into two provinces, Altona and New Amstel. Many of the Swedes emigrated, of whom some came to Maryland, where they were hospitably received, and their descendants still survive among us.

Some years after their conquest of the Swedes, the Dutch grew apprehensive lest their newly acquired territory should be invaded by Englishmen from Maryland, whose claim to the land they very well knew. Among the many fugitives from the severity of Alricks, the Dutch Governor of New Amstel, in 1658, were six soldiers, deserters from the Dutch service, who had taken refuge in Maryland; and at a meeting of the council of New Amstel, on June 20, 1659, it was resolved to request Governor Fendall to return these deserters. But as the council were ignorant of his name and address, the letter was sent to Colonel Nathaniel Utie, "who resides in Bearson Island." Colonel Utie—whose name is still preserved in the island of Spes-Utia, or "Utie's Hope," at the mouth of the Susquehanna—was one of the most adventurous pioneers in the colonization of the country at the head of the Chesapeake, and at this time the first of the twelve magistrates who had jurisdiction there, and a member of the governor's council. Upon receipt of the letter, he promised to forward it to the governor, but, at the same time, informed the messenger that he had himself a commission to go to New Amstel, but that in the meantime Lord Baltimore had arrived, and "had commanded that the lands between the degrees of his grant should be reviewed and surveyed, and when ascertained, be reduced under his jurisdiction, without the intention of abandoning any part of it."[1]

When these tidings reached New Amstel, anxiety and alarm prevailed; business was suspended, and many prepared for flight. In a short time, "fifty persons, including several families, removed to Maryland and Virginia." Scarcely thirty families remained in New Amstel; "and other places, day by day," says Stuyvesant, "are growing worse and worse."

Governor Fendall lost no time in executing the orders of Lord Baltimore, for we find that at a meeting of his council held at Anne Arundel, August 3, 1659, the governor, Secretary Philip Calvert, Colonel Nathaniel Utie, and Mr. Edward Lloyd, being present, it was ordered that Colonel Utie should "repair to the pretended governor of a people seated in Delaware bay, within his lordship's province, without notice given to his lordship's lieutenant here, and to require them to depart the province.

"That in case he find opportunity, he insinuate unto the people there seated, that in case they make their application to his lordship's governor

[1] Albany *Records*, xii., p. 503.

here they shall find good conditions, according to the conditions of plantations, granted to all comers into this province, which shall be made good to them, and that they shall have protection in their lives, liberty, and estates which they shall bring with them."

Governor Fendall at the same time wrote as follows "to the commander of the people in Delaware bay:"

"I received a letter from you directed to me as the Lord Baltimore's governor and lieutenant of the province of Maryland, wherein you suppose yourself to be governor of a people seated in a part of Delaware Bay, which, I am very well informed, lieth to the southward of the degree forty, and therefore can by no means own or acknowledge any for governor there but myself, who am by his lordship appointed lieutenant of his whole province, lying between these degrees, 38 and 40, but do by these require and command you presently to depart forth of his lordship's province, or otherwise desire you to hold me excused, if I use my utmost endeavour to reduce that part of his lordship's province unto its due obedience under him."[1]

Colonel Utie arrived at New Amstel, on the 6th of September, with his brother, his cousin, Major Jacob De Vrintz and a servant, and on the 8th demanded an audience, which was granted. They also brought with them four fugitives, of whom three were apprehended and one escaped. At the meeting, Jacob Alricks, who was governor of New Amstel, and William Beekman, who was vice director and governor of Altona, were present.

On the 12th of September, William Beekman wrote to Director Stuyvesant at New Amsterdam the following account of the Maryland commissioners:

"Colonel Utie first delivered a letter to Alricks; then, at our request, a copy of his instructions; then communicated his orders from the governor of Maryland, and 'declared that we here in the South river have taken possession of Lord Baltimore's jurisdiction, and therefore commanded us to leave it directly, or declare ourselves subject to Lord Baltimore; and if we hesitated to resolve upon it voluntarily, he deemed himself not responsible for the innocent blood which might be shed on that account.' We answered, 'that this communication appeared very strange in every respect, as we had been in possession of this land during so many years, as well as by octroy of the States General and the directors of the West India Company, which we previously obtained.' His honor said 'he knew nothing about it; it was granted to Lord Baltimore, and was confirmed by the king himself, and renewed two years ago, and sanctioned by the parliament, to the extent of forty degrees; when he repeated again he was innocent of the blood which might be shed, as Lord Baltimore was invested to make war or peace, without any man's control.' He said further, 'we ought to take hold of this opportunity, as our men had chiefly deserted us, and they who are yet remaining will be of little or no aid, therefore it is our intention to take hold of this occasion, as we will not let it pass by, convinced as we are of your weakness, and it now suits us best in the whole year, as the tobacco is chiefly harvested; we therefore demand a positive answer, just as you may please;' just as if he would say, 'it is indifferent what you may resolve.' We answered, 'that we could not decide the case, but that it must be left to our lords and principals in England and Holland.' He replied, 'he did not care anything about them.' We answered 'that we would do nothing without them, and were in duty bound to refer the case to the director-general of New Netherland

[1] Albany *Records*, xii., p. 514. Hazard's *Penn. Register*, iv., p. 97.

to whose government we were also subject, and it would require some time to consult them.' He demanded 'what time would be required.' We proposed then 'three weeks,' on which the Colonel said, 'I have no orders to give any respite, nevertheless I will give you the required time.'"

The Dutch officers summoned Colonel Utie to the fort on the 9th of September to receive their written reply, in which, after reciting the facts set forth in Governor Fendall's letter, and Colonel Utie's instructions, they say:

"It is true you declared, in words of more weight, that in case of refusal of immediate departure, to be unaccountable for the much innocent blood that might, by reason thereof, be spilled. Such proceedings and treatment appeared to us unexpected and strange, and so do such proceedings and treatment by Christians and Protestant brethren, and our neighbors, with whom we desired, and of whom we never solicited anything else, nor do it yet, than a sincere cultivation of harmony and friendship, that we yet desire may be uninterrupted, as we, from our side, are confident that we never gave them any reason of discontentment."

They complained of the citizens of the South river being lured away to Maryland by promises of "protection and much liberty," some of whom were bound to their "lords and masters by oaths, and others who were in debt for considerable sums, by which their lords and masters are disappointed, and were frustrated to recover their debts."

They desire that the differences might be settled by the States General and Parliament.

This protest was signed by the Governors Alricks and Beekman, and by the council and Schepens, viz.: Alexander D'Hinoyossa, John Williemsen, John Crato and Hendrick Ripp, and by Secretary G. Van Sweringen.[1]

Immediately on the receipt of Colonel Utie and his instructons, information was sent to Stuyvesant, who expressed his displeasure in a letter dated September 23d, at what he termed "the frivolous, fabricated instructions, without date or place," of Nathaniel Utie, and the "not less frivolous answers and proceedings with him of the governors and council of Altona and New Amstel." He censured them for allowing "Utie to sow his seditious and mutinous seed among the community during four or five days, . . . and with a further written promise signed by the great council, that a further and more satisfactory answer should be given on his frivolous conclusion, and well within three weeks, and all this only on his threatening expressions." This, said Stuyvesant, showed "unquestionable proofs, indeed, of want of prudence and courage" on the part of his governors; and therefore, "to redress the one and correct the misconduct ef others," he appointed his "beloved, discreet and faithful Cornelius Van Ruyven, secretary, and Captain Martain Krygier, burgomaster of this city, [New Amsterdam] to dispose and regulate all the affairs" on South river. He also appointed Krygier commander of all the militia and soldiers on South river, and sent with him a reinforcement of sixty soldiers to assist in protecting the Dutch settlements from invasion from Maryland.

[1] Hazard's *Annals*, p. 265.

Col. Utie did not wait to hear the answer from Stuyvesant, who gave instructions "to arrest him as a spy," but returned to Maryland on the 11th of September. And in consequence of the rumors that he was to return with five hundred men, Governor Stuyvesant, on the 23d of September, determined to send Augustine Heermans (or Herman,) and Resolved Waldron, the underschout of New Amsterdam, on an embassy to the Government of Maryland, to request "in a friendly and neighbourly way, the re-delivery and restitution of such free people and servants as for debt and other ways have been fled, and as to us is given to understand, that for the most part are residing in his honour's government." They were also "especially authorized and commanded seriously to request" Governor Fendall and his council, by virtue of the articles of peace made in 1654 between England and the Netherlands "to give us right and justice against the said Colonel Nathaniel Utie, with reparation of damages already sustained by his frivolous demands and bloody threatening" on South river. Stuyvesant likewise wrote a letter to Governor Fendall, accrediting his representatives, and complaining of Utie's conduct as a breach of the treaty of 1654 between England and Holland.

AUGUSTINE HEERMANS.

On the 30th of September, 1659, Herman and Waldron, the ambassadors appointed by Governor Stuyvesant, accompanied by some guides, mostly Indians, and convoyed by a few soldiers, left New Amstel for Maryland. Mr. Hazard in his *Annals of Pennsylvania*, gives the following abstract of Herman and Waldron's journal, which shows their route, the dangers they encountered, and the manner in which they conducted their negotiations.

"About three miles they came to a small creek which empties into Jagersland Creek; a west-northwest course brought them to another creek; course westward, a march of three miles, they came to another running stream; the savages here refused to proceed, and they encamped for the night. Heard a shot fired towards north, the savages supposed it to be from some Englishmen; the company fired three times, not answered. The next day, October 1st, they pursued a west to south course, crossed two streams, suspected to be branches of South River; they then passed through dry underwood, the land somewhat rising, then a valley, till 9 o'clock, when they arrived at the first current stream, which the savages said emptied into the Bay of Virginia; there they breakfasted, and guessed they were about five miles from New Amstel; the savages called the creek Curriamus, or Horekill, as the whole tract is named after it; from this they passed through woods, south-west and west-south west, without a path, and about a mile further along the creek, where they met with the boat, which the savages informed them had been drawn on land, and thoroughly dried. Dismissing their guides, they proceeded by water, except Sander Boyer, who, with his savages, continued, but soon, the boat being half filled with water, they were obliged to go on shore, caulked it with rags, instead of the tow, which they had left behind, made it tolerably tight with baling, reached Elk River, and at last, at east branch of it, made a fire in the woods, and with the evening tide proceeded on with great trouble, as the boat was very leaky, and had neither rudder nor oars, but only *pagays*, (perhaps paddles.)

"Having rowed nearly all night on Elk River, about 8 o'clock, (October 2,) arrived near Sassafras River, and stopped there at a plantation of one John Turner, where they met Abraham De Fin, a soldier of Altona, who had run away with a Dutch woman; a pardon was offered if they would return to New Amstel or to Manhattan in one month. The woman accepted, she had three months to serve; soldier made many objections, but made two oars for the company; sent Sander Boyer on shore for information; could get none, as *only a few Finns and Swedes* were there, who had run away from Governor Printz. After some rest they continued on, but had scarce left the shore, than Abraham and another, Marcus De Fin, approached in a canoe, and endeavored to obstruct their passage, claiming the boat, although assuring them they should have the boat on their return; they stopped the company by force, drawing a pistol and threatening to fire; they had, besides, two guns with them. At last, with great difficulty, they succeeded in getting rid of them. At the mouth of the river they came to Colonel Utie's; heard strong firing, supposed to proceed from fifty or sixty men, 'neither was the noise of music much less,' which continued through a great part of the night, so that it seemed. they were preparing to visit South River. Looking for information, they came to a beginning plantation, hewing and cutting of timber for a building, but the carpenter, who was known to the company, knew not the object of the firing, unless they were feasting. He invited them to stay with him, as there was no other house nearer Kent, but they pursued their journey two miles further. Wishing to dispatch a savage to New Amstel with the tidings, they could find none.

"Rowed (October 3) with the tide of that day and night, till opposite Pooloo Island; they passed in their leaky boat to the east of it; from here to Kent there is no fresh water. Towards evening arrived at north side of Kent Island, where, meeting a strong flood, and much fatigued, took quarters with Captain Wike, one of the three magistrates of the island. Of him they endeavoured to learn whether the English had laid any regular plan for attacking South River; had understood it belonged to Maryland, and was obliged to sustain Lord Baltimore in his right and title; the company undertook to prove the contrary, and 'he who would have, must get it by force; that we were prepared with more than one hundred soldiers arrived, and double expected, yet we hoped to live on friendly terms.' During the discussion, they heard of a rumour from Mr. Bateman, who had sent for Mr. Wright, an Indian interpreter from above the bay, that the Indians, with regard to the war they were engaged in with the English, had confessed they had been stirred up by the Dutch who lived at Horekill, to murder the English, which took place thus: 'a certain savage met a Dutchman at Horekill, and told him he would kill a Dutchman, because his father had been killed by a Dutchman before, to which the Dutchman replied, that his father had been killed by an Englishman, and therefore ought to take revenge on them, on which a savage went off and killed an Englishman; thus the war was continued, aided by the Dutch, in supplying arms, &c. I denied it at first, then palliated it. Inquired for a boat to take us to the governor, as ours could be no longer used, so he offered his. Inquired what security we could give, to return or pay for it, as he had been frequently deceived; they had none but their word and credentials, or refer to Mr. Brown, who they presumed had arrived with his ketch at Seaforn; they agreed at twenty pounds of tobacco per day for the boat, and twenty pounds for the man. Here we met the soldier's wife, who was willing to go back; he was so lazy as not to earn bread for her, and therefore she ran off.

"Arrived (October 4) at Seaforn; Brown had not; Captain Wickes proposed to procure lodgings for us at Colonel Utie's, who, they understood, was at his plantation; excused themselves, saying they were confident he was on the island, as they heard such a grand firing; took lodging at a savage trader's, who was from home, his wife and child only there; the company blamed her husband for enticing away the people from New Amstel; she excused him by saying they came there, and left scarcely victuals enough for the family.

"Passed (October 5) a draft on Mr. Brown for the boat-owner; not satisfied; must have at Kent or Seaforn 1500 pounds tobacco, or pay at Manhattan in brandy. Declined a visit to Colonel Utie, as they had urgent business with governor. Had a fine run to Billingly plantation, at the cleft, hearing of no preparations against South River.

"Arrived (October 6) at Patuxent, at Colonel Coortsey's, who was 'very courteous, and conversed pleasantly.' Here they learned that Colonel Utie was authorized to communicate to the colony of New Amstel that they had settled on Maryland limits, and ought to submit. The company then presented their claims by possession, &c., for so many years, as before.

"They left at Colonel Coortsey's (October 7) their boat, travelled nine miles by land to Secretary P. Calvert's, Mr. Coortsey with them part of the way; about 3 o'clock arrived at Calvert's; despatched two men to inform him of their arrival; could not forbear to pay him their respects; passed over the creek to Mr. Overfees, where we intended to take up our quarters, previously having communicated to the secretary our commission to the governor of Maryland on important business, and requested him to notify the governor as soon as possible, as he lived several miles off, of our arrival, and recommend an early audience.

"Mr. Overfees invited Calvert to dine with them (October 8), he and his next neighbour also; renewed request to secretary to inform the governor, as expenses were heavy, including the boat, and soldiers all waiting their return, besides more than one hundred soldiers arrived from Manhattans; he promised to do all he could, but it could not be effected before next court. They conversed freely on differences between Virginia and Maryland, wished happiness to Maryland and *Manhattans*. 'This we remarked denoted the whole land, having retained its ancient name from the tribe of savages among whom the Dutch made a beginning of the first settlement, and so gradually we struck on the point of the limits, which he said of Maryland was 38° to 40°, along the sea, by which Delaware Bay was included, and then in a direct course to *Paman's* Island, and thence to origin of Potomac River. We answered 38° to 40° ought to be understood of Chesapeake Bay upward, and then colony of Virginia reached same bay to the sea. He replied, 'not so, and that it ought to meet the limits of New England.' On which we asked, 'where then would remain New Netherlands, if their limits were to join New England?' to which he answered 'he did not know.' Then, we said, 'that we knew it for us both together, that it was a mistake, and that our New Netherlands were in possession of these limits several years before Lord Baltimore obtained his patent, and that they actually settled these spots; alleging further, among other reasons, that Edmund Preyton (Ployden ?) made in former days a claim on Delaware Bay, and that the one pretension had not been better supported than the other;' to which he replied, 'that Preyton had not obtained a commission, and was in England thrown in jail for his debts; he acknowledged that he solicited by the king a patent of Novum Albium, but which had been refused, on which he addressed himself to the viceroy of Ireland, of whom he obtained a patent, but that it was of no value at all.' On this we confounded him entirely with his own words, by saying, that 'it could not be known of my Lord Baltimore's pretension, if he had any on the Delaware Bay, had obtained these by false or foreign representations; neither could it be believed that the king of England, who once took notice of the Dutch plantations in New Netherlands, and who commanded those of Virginia and New England, as we could prove by their own English authors, expressly to remain at a distance of one hundred leagues from one another, determined nothing about it. It was therefore an unquestionable proof that he might reach the borders of New England, that it then was void and of no value whatever.'

"From this time to the 12th, they were waiting the governor's answer; on the 12th they dined at Mr. Overfees, with Secretary Calvert; Minister Doughty accidentally came in; Captain Smith's map of Virginia, and another printed about the date of Lord Baltimore's patent, were introduced, differing with each other, from which they endeavoured to prove Lord Baltimore's claim, 'but we showed that the Bay of Chesapeake, being so much to north-east, would come on our limits; how can that be, as New England was discovered first. On this we answered, the Dutch had been nearly three years, differing perhaps as early in their own quarters as they in theirs; they counted from Walter Raleigh; we then derive our right from Spain. He answered, we were then not a free nation, &c. &c. Waxing warm, they took up other subjects.

"On the 13th, nothing done; on 14th was court day at Patuxent; petitioned for an audience, and a place to be fixed for a reception; on 15th, near sunset, received an answer, and an invitation from Calvert, in name of governor and council, for an audience at house of Mr. Bateman, and sent two horses for them.

"On 16th, they started for Bateman's, at Potusk, about eighteen miles; at about 3 or 4, arrived Governor Fendall, Secretary Calvert, &c., who, after a courteous reception and congratulations, dinner was announced, after which the governor promised an audience, advancing towards the table; Herman was placed on his left, the secretary on the right, then followed Waldron and the members of council, all around the table. During dinner a pleasant conversation ensued.

"When the cloth was removed, their letters and credentials were opened by governor, who seeing they were in Dutch, called Mr. Overfees to interpret them. The commissioners then began their speech in English, delivering at the same time, duplicates of their papers, the secretary comparing as they were read; this being all they had to communicate at this time, copies were exchanged and the originals left. 'We observed an astonishing change. As it appeared council had no corrrect knowledge of what had passed, governor asked if his letter by Utie had not been received by director general and council. We said, no, they received no letter; we were informed on South River that Alricks received a private one in answer to one of his, without date, time, or place, of which he could take no notice.' Governor said he had no intention to meddle with the government at Manhattan, but with that government and people who settled on Deleware Bay lately, within their limits, and that he once did send Colonel Utie to them, and that he should have delivered his instructions, though only given to regulate his conduct, and in behalf of his responsibility, though we were not obliged to deliver to them our instructions; to which we replied, 'that the governor and inhabitants on South River made no separate government, but a subaltern and subject, being only vice-governors and members of New Netherlands,' &c. They answered, 'they knew no better, and had always understood that the general director on South River, in Delaware Bay, did hold his commission from the city of Amsterdam, and had settled there with his people as in a separate government.' We answered, 'No, but that the city of Amsterdam was in possession of that place as a colony and a particular member of New Netherland, in a similar manner as their colonies in Virginia and Maryland were subsisting, and we had many similar colonies in New Netherland, so that any injustice or injury committed against the colony of New Amstel, was perpetrated against the whole state of New Netherland.' Meanwhile, Colonel Nathaniel said, with great vehemence, 'that they might take notice of all what had happened, but that all which was done against people which had dared to settle within the province of my Lord Baltimore, and if governor and council would be pleased to renew his commission, he would do once more what he had done before.' To which we replied, 'If you returned once more, and acted in the same manner as before, you would lose the name of ambassador, and be considered as a perturbator of the public peace, because it is not lawful in an ambassador or delegate to attempt any other thing than to present, in a courteous manner, his message to the magistrates or supreme chief to whom he was sent; but that it was the language of open hostility, a language of war, to summon a place to surrender in such a manner as by fire and sword.' To this he answered, 'that he had not done so, further than his instructions and commission justified.' We again answered, 'that they would only pay regard to the answer which they received in return, and therein he would clearly perceive in what manner he made his.' To this he further said, 'that he too had understood that they had threatened to transport him to Holland, which he wished they had executed.' We replied, 'that if he once more returned there, and acted again in that manner, perhaps nothing better might be his lot.' He answered, 'in what manner then ought he to have conducted himself; he had despatched two of his men before him, to notify his arrival, after which he took up his abode in the city, and if it then was not permitted to take a walk and look at the place, and converse with its inhabitants, who invited him to enter their lodgings.' We answered, 'that it was well permitted to do this, but not to stir up revolt and rebellion against the magistrates, and threaten them, if they would not voluntarily surrender, that they were to be plundered and expelled, so that those altercations caused uneasiness on both sides;' and the colonel particularly glowing with rage, was commanded by the governor to keep himself more reasonable; that nevertheless we remained at full liberty to explain ourselves without interrupting each other; on which we appealed to what we had brought with us in answer from New Netherland, which we had declared and made known, and which we solicited might be taken into serious consideration, so that we might avoid any frivolous discourses. The governor hinted, among other points, that we had arrived there without having demanded or obtained, as ought to have been done, a license, and which they ought to have communicated; to which we answered, 'that we were yet unacquainted with the form of the government, but would conduct ourselves in future in conformity to their customs, as they should deem proper to establish on such a passage.' On this Colonel Utie exclaimed, 'that we ought to have stopped at his island to inquire there, if we should be admitted to land; further, in so many words, that if he had met us, or had known any thing about it, he would in such case have kept us there, and not permitted us to proceed further,' when one of the council interrupting him, said, 'that then we should have been accommodated there with a better vessel, as we declared we arrived in a small leaky boat, as we would not wait to procure a better vessel.' We, however, clearly perceived, that if we had not exerted ourselves to the utmost on the road, to avoid Colonel Utie, he would have left nothing untried to disappoint us, and frustrate our plan. After these discussions, we were requested to retire. After discussing among themselves, we again returned, and were informed that what they had done was under special commission of Lord Baltimore and their oath; to-morrow they would hear Lord's Baltimore's intentions, and we should be despatched on Saturday.

"In the meantime, we had friendly discussions with them individually, on various points. We proposed to submit matters to a committee of both nations, or enter into a friendly correspondence for trade, etc. While they seemed to consent, they were inclined to defend their rights under their patent. Had also a private interview with the governor who showed Lord Baltimore's patent; we asked a copy; permitted to make an extract. Governor and council go to hold a country court. Commissioners found that Lord Baltimore had requested lands not yet settled and cultivated, and only inhabited by savages. Thus we concluded that our South River, named anciently Nassau River, was ours, in virtue of our commission and grant of their High Mightinesses the States-General, and hath long been settled before appropriated and purchased, etc., so that Lord Baltimore's pretensions, as far as related to the Delaware Bay, or part of it, was invalid. At P. M. governor and council returned; after supper delivered our answer in writing; read it to them. We observed a new change in them. Governor observed, that our sayings and acts to the contrary rendered invald said patent, as it was given by his majesty with full instructions that Delaware Bay remains to the English. They required our patent of New Netherland and Delaware Bay; we answered, we did not need expose it at present, as we did not come for the purpose, but only to prepare a day for a future meeting between both parties. Governor then thought he ought not to have shown his. We replied, we intended no other use of it than for Delaware. Governor said Claiborne had before made the same objection regarding island of Kent, of which he had taken possession before the patent, but did not avail, as he had to implore Lord Baltimore to save his life. We replied, this was a different case; we were not subjects of England, but of the Dutch nation, and had as much right to settle parts of America as any others.

"Governor again (on 18th) demanded to see our patent of South River; had it not with us, but would show it at a future meeting. Some members retired to frame an answer, which was read to us. We asked if this was all; said they had nothing else. Some remarks on soldiers' hostilities, that each must pursue his own course. We replied we should prepare ourselves for defence, as before declared and solemnly protested; well knew that they would not attack us in a clandestine manner, etc., etc. They replied, they would use their own pleasure; payment for runaways might be settled by courts, but we could not compel them to return, because they considered Delaware in their jurisdiction; the meeting concluded.

"Governor asked the meaning of 'Dutch Swedes,' which we had used in our declaration; the greatest number being of them; they had been partners and associates, residing for a time under jurisdiction of the company, or rather connived at, but who became more insolent, so as at length, in a traitorous manner, they surprised Fort New Amstel, before called Fort Casimir, by which director-general and council in New Netherland were compelled to cleanse that neighbourhood of such a vile gang.

"October 19, handed an answer to our decision by secretary, neatly written, and bade him farewell, as we could not find that they were inclined to enter into an amicable agreement, without authority from Lord Baltimore, or wait for orders, which he might, perhaps, convey during summer. Had some conversation on trade and commerce between Delaware and Maryland, by land, which might be done without reaching the question of right; desired him to communicate with his brother, Lord Baltimore.

"Inquired with great anxiety about a mountain we had mentioned as a place of meeting, from which the Sassafras River in Virginia, and the kill which empties itself into South River, behind Reedy Island, seem to derive their origin. We had our passage over this mountain, which deserves by us to be examined and surveyed.

"On the 20th they prepare for their departure, and next day despatched Waldron to return by land, with relation of our transactions, and all the papers, while I proceeded to Virginia, to inquire of governor what is his opinion on the subject, to create a division between them both, and purge ourselves of the slander of stirring up the Indians to murder English at Accomac. Signed, "A. HEERMANS."[1]

In the "declaration and manifesto" delivered by the ambassadors to the council of Maryland at Patuxent on the 16th of October, they suggested "by way of advice to prevent further mischief, that three rational persons on each side may be committed out of each province aforesaid, for to meet at a certain day and time, about the middle of between the Bay of Chesapeake and the aforesaid South river or Delaware bay, at a hill lying to the head of Sassafrax river and another river coming from our river almost meet together, with full power and commission to settle there the bounds and limits of between the aforesaid province of the New Netherlands and the province of Maryland for ever, if possible, otherwise to refer the difference they might

[1] Albany *Records*, xviii., pp. 337–364.

find not agreeing, to both Lords Proprietors or sovereigns in Europe." The council, consisting of Captain William Stone, Thomas Gerrard, Luke Barber, Colonel Nathaniel Utie, Baker Brooke and Edward Lloyd, after the commissioners withdrew "resolved, that the business be forthwith taken into debate, and that they would have an answer ready by Saturday, the 18th, at 5 o'clock P. M.," and then adjourned till next day, the 19th, when they met and "after a long debate considering his lordship's instructions and order were only to give the Dutch warning to be gone, that when we are able to beat them out they may not plead ignorance, resolved, that answer be given in writing, by way of letter directed to the general of the Manhattans, in these words, viz.:

"Honourable lords—We have received your letters of credence by the hands of Sirs Augustine Herman and Resolved Waldron, your ambassadors, wherein, as we find many expressions of love and amity, so we account ourselves obliged to return you real thanks in unfolding the causes of that which it seems hath been the reason of your astonishment and wonder, and as the matter shall permit, give you that satisfaction which with reason you can expect, and which we likewise shall exact from you in the rendering to us as substitutes of the right honourable Cecilius, lord baron of Baltimore, lord and proprietary of this province, &c., that part of his lordship's province lying in Delaware Bay, to us entrusted, and by you (as it seems) injuriously seated, in prejudice to his lordship's just right and title. . . . For answer, therefore, unto your demands by your said agents made, we say, that Colonel Nathaniel Utie was by us, in pursuance of a command from the right honourable lord proprietary, ordered to make his repair to a certain people seated upon Delaware Bay, within the 40th degree of northerly latitude from the equinoctial line, to let them know that they were residing within our jurisdiction without our knowledge, much more, without our license, without grant of land from, or oath of fidelity to his lordship taken, both which are expressly, by his conditions of plantation and laws to all comers here to inhabit, conditioned and enjoined; and further, to offer unto them such conditions, in case they intended there to stay, as we ourselves enjoy. But in case of refusal and abode there made, to let them know we should use lawful means to reduce them to that obedience which all people within the degree aforesaid are bound to yield unto us, intrusted within this province by the right honourable the Lord Baltimore, sole and absolute lord and proprietary of the same, by patent under the great seal of England, bearing date 20th of June, in the year of our Lord God 1632, (?) and since by act of parliament confirmed; (a copy whereof we have shown to your said ambassadors;) and since you, by your writing, as well as by your ambassadors, seem to insinuate that the said colony in Delaware Bay is seated there by and under your command, we do protest as well against them and you, as against all other persons, either principals or abettors in the said intrusion upon our bounds and confines. Our damages and costs in due time, and by all lawful means, to recover, which we either have or shall at any time hereafter chance to sustain by the recovery of that place so seated within our bounds and limits, and injuriously by you detained.

"The original rights of the kings of England to these countries and territories, must be our endeavour to maintain, not our discourse to controvert, or in the least our attempt to yield up, as being that which we can neither accept from any other power, nor yield up to any other authority without the consent of our supreme magistracy, their successors in the dominion of England. Though we cannot but mind you that it is no difficult matter to show that your pretended title to that part of this province where those people, (now, if at all, the first time owned by the high and mighty States to be in

Delaware Bay seated by their order and authority,) do live, is utterly none, and your patent (if you have any) from the States-General of the United Provinces void and of no effect.

"And to those instructions by us delivered to the said Colonel Nathaniel Utie, so much insisted on by you, we say, they are such as every person, inhabitant of this province, ought to take notice of, as being subscribed by the secretary of this province, and to no other did we give them, or he make use of them. Neither can we believe the high and mighty States-General, &c., do think or will now own these people at Delaware Bay to be there seated by their authority, since they have heretofore protested to the supreme authority then in England, not to own their intrusion upon their territories and dominions. As to indebted persons, if any be here that are to you engaged, our courts are open, and our justice speedy, and denied to none that shall demand it of us, which we think is as much as can in reason be expected, and the self-same course we take, and the only remedy we afford to our neighbor colony of Virginia, and our fellow-subjects and brethren of England. Thus hoping that you will seriously weigh the consequences of your actions, we rest in expectation of such a compliance as the style you give yourselves imports, having taught us to subscribe ourselves your affectionate friends and neighbours."[1]

Upon receiving this reply, Waldron, on the 20th of October, returned to Manhattan, while Herman went on to Virginia "to inquire of the governor what is his opinion upon the subject: *to create a division between them both,* **and to purge ourselves** of the slander of stirring up the Indians to murder the English at Accomac."

Thus ended the embassy of the Dutch to Maryland, although they were constantly alarmed by rumors of an invasion of their territory by the Marylanders. The directors of the Dutch West India Company, after speaking of the English encroachments on the North and South rivers, wrote to Stuyvesant on the 9th of March, 1660, that "if they won't be persuaded, they must be dislodged. Your honor ought to oppose, in the same manner, those of Maryland, if they undertook to settle on South river, within our district, first warning them, in a civil manner, not to usurp our territory, but if they despise such kind entreaties, then nothing is left but to drive them from there, as our claims and rights on the lands upon South river are indisputable, not so much (which, however, is the case) as first occupants, but by real purchase from the natives, who were the only real progenitors of the soil."

Charles II. had hardly reached Whitehall, before Lord Baltimore, who was in London (July 24, 1660), instructed his agent, Captain James Neal, in Holland, to inquire of the West India Company if they admit his right on the Delaware; if not, to protest against them, and to demand the surrender of the lands, &c., on the Delaware bay. On the 1st of September, Neal had an interview with the representatives of the Council of Nineteen in Amsterdam, who asserted "their right by possession, under the grant of the States General, for many years, without disturbance from Lord Baltimore or any other person." They "resolved to remain in possession and defend their

[1] N. Y. *Hist. Soc. Coll.*, iii., pp. 384-385.

rights;" and "if Lord Baltimore perseveres and resorts to violent measures, they will use all the means God and nature have given to protect the inhabitants." The Council of Nineteen, in November of the same year, addressed a memorial to the States General, praying them to instruct their ambassadors at London to demand of the king that Lord Baltimore should be ordered to desist from his pretensions until a boundary line should be settled.

Doubts had meanwhile arisen in the council of Maryland whether New Amstel was really below the 40th degree of north latitude, and as the West India Company appeared resolved to maintain their possessions by force, and there was no prospect of any aid from the other colonies, in any attempts which they might make to reduce them, all further action had been delayed until the will of the proprietary could be ascertained. Lord Baltimore, however, took care to obtain from the king, on the 21st July, 1661, a confirmation of his patent, and Stuyvesant, receiving the news, wrote to the directors "that Lord Baltimore's brother [Philip Calvert], who is a rigid Papist, being made governor there, has received Lord Baltimore's claim, and protest to your honors in council (wherewith he seems but little satisfied), and has now more hopes of success. We have advices from England that there is an invasion intended against these parts, and the country solicited of the king, the duke, and the parliament, is to be annexed to their dominions." The savages around the South river, showing signs of hostility, D'Hinoyossa and Peter Alricks, with two Indian chiefs, on the 6th of September, 1661, were despatched by Beekman to the Governor of Maryland, to negotiate a general treaty of peace with the neighboring Indians. Governor Calvert, approving of the suggestion, he and his council met the commissioners, together with Mr. Henry Coursey, Mr. Beekman and Mr. Gerrit Smith, at Colonel Utie's residence, at the head of Appoquinimy creek, where a treaty was concluded with the Indian sachem.

News now came that Charles Calvert, the son and heir of Lord Baltimore, was about to visit Altona; and Beekman wrote to Stuyvesant that "here on the river, not a single draught of French wine is obtainable, and requests him to send some, to treat the nobleman with." On the 9th of July, 1663, Charles Calvert came to New Amstel and Altona with a suit of twenty-six or twenty-seven persons. Beekman entertained him at Altona for several days as his guest; and, in conjunction with Van Sweringen, the schout of New Amstel, Governor Calvert, on the 12th of August, renewed the treaty with the Indians; but when it was proposed to define the limits of the two colonies, he replied he would communicate with Lord Baltimore. The young nobleman's intercourse with his Dutch hosts was pleasant and harmonious, and he took his leave with all good feeling. As he proposed to visit Boston the next spring, by way of Manhattan, he desired Beekman to convey his thanks to Stuyvesant for his "offer of convoy and horses."

In the meantime the government of New Netherlands was continually laboring to extend its settlements to the north of Manhattan and across to the Connecticut river, until Charles II., provoked by its continued encroachments, and perhaps animated by that ill-feeling which he is said to have always cherished towards the Dutch, determined to effect the conquest of the whole settlement. To accomplish this, on the 12th of March, 1664, (O.S.,) he granted to his brother James, Duke of York and Albany, all that tract of country extending from the west banks of the Connecticut to the eastern shore of Delaware, (including Long Island). This extensive grant included the whole of New Netherland and a part of the territory of Connecticut.

The Duke of York lost no time in giving effect to his patent. As Lord High Admiral, he directed the fleet. Four ships, the *Guinea*, of thirty-six guns; the *Elias*, of thirty; the *Martin*, of sixteen; and the *William and Nicholas* of ten, were detached for services against New Netherland, and about four hundred and fifty regular soldiers with their officers, were embarked. The command of the expedition was intrusted to Colonel Richard Nicolls, with Sir Robert Carre, Colonel George Cartwright and Samuel Maverick as associates. On the 2d of September, the English ships anchored before Fort Amsterdam, which soon surrendered, and on the 8th, the English flag was hoisted on it, and its name changed to "Fort James." New Amsterdam was named New York in compliment to the Duke. Sir Robert Carre was then sent with the *Guinea*, the *William and Nicholas*, and "all the soldiers which are not in the fort," to reduce the South river settlement. After a long and troublesome passage, prolonged by the ignorance of the pilots and the shallowness of the water, he arrived at Fort New Amstel on the last day of September. The burghers and planters, "after almost three days parley," agreed to Carre's demands, but the governor and soldiery refusing to capitulate, the fort was stormed and plundered, three of the Dutch being killed and ten wounded. With the reduction of Fort New Amstel, fell the Dutch power on the Delaware, and the name of the town of New Amstel was changed to that of New Castle, which name it has ever since borne. Altona again received its old name of Christiana, and the river and the bay into which it flows lost their old names, and received the English name of Delaware.[1]

By the terms of capitulation the Dutch colonists were admitted to all the rights and privileges of English subjects under the new government, and from this period until the grant of Penn from the Duke of York the settlements on the Delaware were dependencies of the government of New York, although clearly within the limits of Maryland.

On the 24th of June, before he had actually received possession of the territory given him, the Duke of York conveyed to Lord Berkeley and Sir George Carteret "all that tract of land adjacent to New England, and lying and being to the west of Long Island, bounded on the east part by the main sea, and part by Hudson's river, and hath on the west Delaware bay or river, and extendeth southward to the main ocean, as far as Cape May, at

[1] Hazard's *Annals of Pennsylvania*, p. 356. Vincent's *History of Delaware*, i., p. 417. McBrodhead's *History of New York*, i., p. 735. Mahon, p. 25.

the mouth of Delaware bay, and to northward as far as the northernmost branch of said bay or river of Delaware, which is in 41° 40′ of latitude, and worketh over thence in a straight line to Hudson's river; which said tract of land is hereafter to be called by the name or names of Nova Cæsarea, or New Jersey."

Lord Berkeley, in March 1674, conveyed his portion of the grant to John Fenwick in trust for Edward Byllinge and his assigns. They were both Quakers. In a short time a dispute arose between them, but instead of having recourse to law, they called in the arbitration of the celebrated William Penn, and his decision was in favor of Byllinge. After an adjustment had been made in accordance with Penn's decision, Byllinge became embarrassed in his fortunes, and made an assignment of all his property to Gawen Laurie, William Penn and Nicholas Lucas, as trustees for the benefit of his creditors.

This is our first introduction to William Penn, whose connection with New Jersey seems to have inspired him with the design of obtaining from Charles II. a grant of the territory westward of the Delaware river. The crown at this time, was indebted to the father of William Penn for services, loans and interest, to the amount of sixteen thousand pounds. The exchequer, under the management of Shaftesbury, would not settle with him, and in lieu thereof he proposed, in June, 1680, to King Charles II., to accept letters-patent for lands in America westward of the Delaware and north of Maryland. His petition was submitted on the 14th of June, by the Earl of Sunderland to the privy council, composed of the Lord President, Duke of Albemarle, the Bishop of London, Mr. Secretary Jenkins, and Sir John Chicheley. Copies were also sent to Sir John Werden, the Duke of York's secretary, and to Lord Baltimore's agents, "to the end that they may report how far the pretensions of Mr. Penn may consist with the boundaries of Maryland, or the duke's propriety of New York, and his possessions in those parts."

Lord Baltimore's agents, Messrs. Barnaby Dunch and Richard Burk, say in their reply, dated June 23:

"It is desired, that if the grant pass unto Mr. Penn, of the lands petitioned for by him, in America, that it may be expressed to be land that shall be north of Susquehanna Fort, also north of all lands in a direct line between the said fort and Delaware River, and also north of all lands upon a direct line westward from said fort, for said fort is the boundary of Maryland northward. It is further desired that there may be contained general words of restriction as to any interest granted to the Lord Baltimore, and saving to him all rights granted. It is also prayed that my lord's council may have a sight of the grant, before it pass.

"On a public account, it is offered, that some due caution be provided, that no arms, powder, shot, or ammunition, be sold, by any that shall settle in this new plantation, to the Indians or natives, for hereby a common mischief may happen unto all his majesty's neighboring plantations."

On the 5th of July Mr. Penn's petition was again read in council, together with a letter from Sir J. Werden, the agent of the Duke of York, and one from the agent of Lord Baltimore. Mr. Penn was then sent for, and "told that it appearing, from Sir John's letter, that part of the territory desired by him is already possessed by the Duke of York, he must apply himself to his royal highness for adjusting their respective pretensions, and Mr. Penn being also acquainted with the matter of the letter from the Lord Baltimore's agents, he does agree that Susquehanna Fort shall be the bounds of the Lord Baltimore's province; and as to the furnishing of arms and ammunition to the Indians, Mr. Penn declares himself ready to submit to any restraints their lordships shall impose."[1]

Mr. Chalmers says both Werden, the Duke of York's secretary, and Lord Baltimore's agents "agreed to the proposals of Penn, provided 'his patent might be so worded as not to affect the rights of others.' To everything that was asked of him he readily agreed, because he knew the importance of concession, while he asked for what might be extremely endangered by opposition. He had the art to procure, not only the consent, but the recommendation, of the Duke of York. And, in November, 1680, the sketch of a patent, which he had chiefly *copied from the charter of Maryland*, was sent to the attorney general 'for his opinion of it:' who, not long after, communicated his observations 'shewing the clauses that are not agreeable to the laws here, though they are in Lord Baltimore's patent.' After a considerable struggle with the Duke's commissioners, who insisted that Penn's southern line should run at least twenty miles northward of New Castle, his boundaries were at length adjusted so as to please both parties."[2]

In January, 1681, the committeé of plantations requested Lord Chief Justice North "to take Penn's patent into consideration," and we find that owing to "the merits of the father, and the good purposes of the son," etc., his majesty, King Charles II., granted to William Penn, as proprietary, on the 4th of March, 1681 (O.S.), that portion of our country which is now called Pennsylvania. In the charter its boundary runs thus:

"I. Know ye, therefore, that we, (favouring the petition and good purpose of the said William Penn, and having regard to the memory and merits of his late father, in divers services, and particularly to his conduct, courage, and discretion, under our dearest brother James, duke of York, in that signal battle and victory fought and obtained against the Dutch fleet commanded by the Heer Van Opdam, in the year 1665: in consideration thereof, of our special grace, certain knowledge, and mere motion,) have given and granted, and by this our present charter, for us, our heirs and successors, do give and grant unto the said William Penn, his heirs and assigns, all that tract or part of land in America, with the islands therein contained, as the same is bounded on the east by Delaware River, from twelve miles distance northward of New Castle town, unto the three and fortieth degree of northern latitude, if the said river doth extend so far northward, but if the said river shall not extend so far northward, then by the said river so far as it doth extend; and from the head of the said river, the eastern bounds are to be determined by a meridian line, to be drawn from the head of the said river, unto the said forty-third degree. The said land to extend westward five degrees in longitude, to be computed from the said eastern bounds, and the said lands to be bounded on the north

[1] Hazard's *Register*, i., p. 270. [2] Chalmers' *Annals*, p. 636.

by the beginning of the three and fortieth degree of northern latitude, and on the south by a circle drawn at twelve miles distance from New Castle, northward and westward, unto the beginning of the fortieth degree of northern latitude, and then by a straight line westward to the limits of longitude above mentioned."

This singular definition of the southern boundary, which left open the question, whether this boundary circle was to be a circle of twelve miles in circumference, or to be drawn around a diameter of twelve miles passing through New Castle, or with a radius of twelve miles beginning in New Castle, was the origin of one of the present boundary lines of this State, and was one of the principal sources of the contention between Baltimore and Penn.

The charter grants the free use of all ports, bays, rivers and waters of the province, and of their produce, and of all mines, and the fee of the soil to William Penn, to be holden in soccage tenure, yielding ten beaver skins annually, and one-fifth of the gold and silver discovered, to the king.

The charter of Pennsylvania, although copied[1] from that of Maryland, differed from it in two cardinal points. One of these reserved to parliament the right to levy taxes and the other required a copy of all colonial laws to be sent to England for the approbation of the privy council. Neither of these restrictions were in the Maryland charter, which was by far the most liberal of any granted to American provinces. Maryland, as a palatinate with the *jura regalia* vested in the proprietary, was almost an independent kingdom, bound to no service to the British crown save the symbolical yearly delivery of two Indian arrows.

Such being the grant, the king on the 12th of April, by a public declaration, announced to all the inhabitants of the province, that William Penn was their absolute proprietary, and invested with all powers neccessary for the government. On the 20th of the same month he commissioned his cousin, William Markham, to be deputy-governor of the province, and in May he was despatched to take possession of it, bearing with him letters from William Penn, and the following letter from Charles II. to Lord Baltimore, apprising him of the grant, and requiring the two proprietaries to adjust the boundaries between their respective provinces according to the limits set forth in their charters:

"Right Trusty & Welbeloved Wee greet you well Whereas by Our Letters Patents bearing date the 4th day of March last past, Wee have been graciously pleased out of Our Royall Bounty & the singular regard Wee have to the merits and services of Sr William Penn deceased to give & grant to Our Trusty & Welbeloved subject William Penn, Esqr son & heir to the said Sr William Penn a certain Tract of Land in America by the name of Pensilvania, as the same is bounded on the East by Delaware River from twelve miles distance Northward of New Castle Town vnto the 43th Degree of Northern Latitude if the said River doth extend so farr Northward, and if the said River shall not extend so farr Northward, then by the said River so farr as it doth extend; And from the Head of the said River the Eastern Bounds to be determined by a Meridian line to be drawn from

[1] Chalmers, p. 659.

the head of the said River vnto the said 43th Degree; the said Province to extend Westward five degrees in longitude to be computed from the said Eastern Bound, & to be bounded on the North by the beginning of the 43 degree of Northern Latitude, And on the South by a Circle drawn at twelve miles distance from New Castle Northward & Westward vnto the beginning of the 40th Degree of Northern Latitude, & then by a straight line Westward to the limit of longitude above mentioned as by Our said Letters Patents doth particularly appear; And to the end that all due encouragement be given to the said Wm Penn in the settlement of a Plantation within the said country Wee do hereby recommend him his Deputies & Officers employed by him, to your friendly aid & assistance, willing and requiring you to doe him all the offices of good neighbourhood and amicable correspondence, which may tend to the mutual benefit of Our Subjects within Our Provinces vnder your respective Proprieties. And more especially wee do think fitt that in order hereunto you do appoint with all convenient speed some person or persons; who may in conjunction with the Agent or Agents of the said William Penn make a true division & separation of the said Provinces of Maryland & Pensilvania, according to the bounds and degree of Northern Latitude expressed in Our said Letters Patents by settling and fixing certain Land Marks where they shall appear to border upon each other for the preventing and avoiding all doubts and controversies that may otherwise happen concerning the same And Wee &c. Whitehall, April 2d, in the 33d year of Our Reign

"By his Maty Command, "CONWAY."[1]

Markham arrived at Upland, now Chester, Delaware, about July, 1681, and soon after, in December, 1682, had an interview with Lord Baltimore at that place when the letter of the king was submitted to Lord Baltimore, and his compliance with it requested. Lord Baltimore received it with respect, but remarked with reference to the mode of adjusting his boundaries prescribed by it: "That his majesty's directions were surely the result of misinformation, as his (Baltimore's) patent granted no specific number of degrees, but merely called for the 40th degree of north latitude as its northern limit, and that such being the right granted by his patent, no royal mandate could deprive him of that right."[2]

This interview, however, much to the astonishment of all parties, resulted in the discovery, from actual observation, that Upland itself was at least twelve miles south of the 40th degree, and that the boundaries of Maryland would extend to the Schuylkill.[3]

This discovery at once ended the conference, and gave fresh incentives to Penn in his efforts to obtain from the Duke of York a grant of the Delaware settlements, inasmuch as without such grant, he had now reason to fear the loss of the whole peninsula.

In this connection, Mr. Chalmers says: "Dissatisfied with the immense region which he had lately acquired, or considering the whole as unprofitable, 'unless he could carry it southward to Chesapeake,' Penn had continually solicited the Duke of York, though in vain, for a grant of *the Delaware*

[1] Public Record Office, Colonial Entry Book, No. 52, pp. 83-4.

[2] McMahon, p. 28.

[3] "The latitude of New Castle, according to an accurate observation taken in 1682 by Lord Baltimore and Markham, was 39 degrees, 40 minutes; that of Chester, 39 degrees, 47 minutes, 5 seconds. So that the 40 degrees intersected the Delaware twenty miles northward of New Castle."—*Chalmers, p. 657.*

colony.[1] Wearied at length, with solicitation, or hoping for benefit from a possession which had hitherto yielded him none, the prince conveyed, in August, 1682, as well the town of New Castle, with a territory of twelve miles around it, as that tract of land extending southward from it, upon the river Delaware, to Cape Henlopen. But no transaction could be more liable to objection; none could reflect more dishonor on both parties, because both knew that the title of what was now sold was extremely exceptionable, since it belonged to another. For the Duke's patents did not include it within his boundaries; and for twenty years his councillors had advised him against procuring an inclusive grant, because they foresaw that the whole must one day devolve on him, with the crown itself. He could transfer, therefore, no other right than mere occupancy, in opposition to the legal claim of Lord Baltimore, whose charter carried up his northern limits '*to that part* of the estuary of the Delaware which lieth under the 40th degree of latitude.' And he conveyed to him only the soil of a territory whose extent it was impossible to describe, because it could not be ascertained, without any of the powers of jurisdiction, which were, however, immediately assumed by Penn, because grave men and philosophers can do, without ceremony, what would cover others with shame. Having thus gratified his followers and his ambition, he departed for Pennsylvania, in order to enlarge the scene of action, because his active mind was never happy except while engaged in intrigue."[2]

Penn being now doubly armed with the grant and release from the Duke of York, the king's brother, and his original charter and a letter from Charles II., directing the proprietary of Maryland to assent to a speedy adjustment of his northern boundary, sailed in September, with many colonists, chiefly from Sussex, and of the Society of Quakers, for Pennsylvania. His arrival at New Castle is recorded as follows:

> "October 28—On the 27th day of October, arrived before the town of New Castle, in Delaware, from England, William Penn, Esq., proprietary of Pennsylvania, who produced two certain deeds of feoffment from the illustrious prince, James, duke of York, Albany, &c., for this town of New Castle, and twelve miles about it, and also for the two lower counties, the Horekills and St. Jones's, which said deeds bore date the 24th August, 1682; and pursuant to the true intent, purpose, and meaning of his Royal Highness in the same deeds, he the said William Penn, received possession of the town of New Castle, the 28th of October, 1682."

He was now eager to adjust his boundaries under these new circumstances, and in conformity to the king's letter, as he was formerly anxious to

[1] "Sir John Werden wrote to Penn in July, 1681: 'that the Duke of York was not yet disposed to grant the lands about New Castle.' He, at the same time, informed him that he thought his claims to the islands in the Delaware ill-founded, because they were not included by the words of his patent, and were never intended to be granted. He immediately warned Dougan, Governor of New York, 'to prevent Penn's encroachments on his province or its dependencies,' giving as a reason, which shews the opinions of men who had done much business with him, 'that he was very intent on his own interest in those parts, as you observe.'"—*Chalmers, p. 660.*

[2] Chalmers' *Annals*, p. 643.

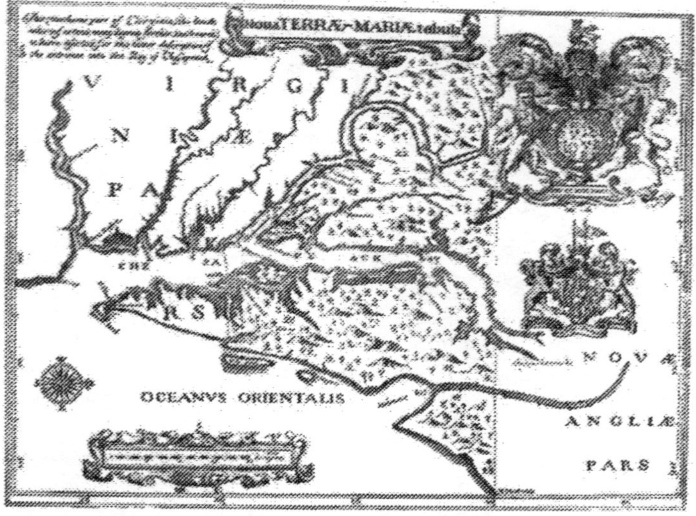

Map of the Relation of Maryland.

evade their adjustment after the discovery at Upland;[1] and immediately on his arrival despatched two commissioners to Lord Baltimore "to ask of his health, offer kind neighborhood, and agree upon a time the better to establish it."

Penn's wishes for an interview with Lord Baltimore were gratified, and it accordingly took place in December, 1682, as will be more fully noticed hereafter.

Having given this slight review of the settlements on the Delaware, to the time of the formation of William Penn's government, we will now briefly consider the disputes which arose as to the situation of Watkins' Point, upon which depends the true location of the boundary line between the Eastern shores of Virginia and Maryland.

As early as 1620, settlements were made on the Eastern shore of Virginia, near Accomack, an Indian town located on Smith's map, near the Cheriton, now Cherrystone river. We have already seen the calamitous consequences to the province of the claims of Claiborne, and under what authority his settlements were made within the territory of Maryland. But no sooner were these claims put to rest, than the adjustment of the boundaries between the two provinces became the next source of contention. These controversies, however, it will be seen, did not originate in the terms of the grant itself, but in claims adverse to the grant, unfortified, indeed, by principle or any sound rule of construction, but in some instances sustained and promoted even by the crown.

In 1634 and in 1635, Lord Baltimore published his "*Relation of Maryland*," a pamphlet with a translation of his charter and a map of his province, showing Watkins' Point to be a neck of land, being the north head-land of the River Wighco, where its waters were discharged into the Chesapeake bay; and it is argued from the limits described in the proclamation dated October 4th, 1638, by the governor and council of Virginia in the name of the king, forbidding Virginians to trade with the Indians within the limits of Lord Baltimore's charter without his license, and defining said limits to be north of the Onancock river on the Eastern shore, and north of Cinquack or Great Wicomico river on the Western shore; that the neck of land must at that time have extended so far south as to have been west of Onancock river, and that an east line from that point to the ocean would have passed along or near that river. It is also stated, from existing facts and tradition, that that headland was subsequently broken into the islands called Fox's and Watts' Islands, and that Watkins' Point was the southernmost end of what afterwards became Watts' Island, at the mouth of the Pocomoke river.

[1] Chalmers says, when Markham discovered the real boundaries of Maryland by "a skillful observation, with an accurate instrument," when Lord Baltimore visited Chester the year previous, Penn "was now as backward as he had been lately solicitous to establish the limits of Pennsylvania. It was to no purpose to renew their conferences at a subsequent day, because the one determined to derive every benefit from the precision of his boundaries, while the other equally resolved to draw advantages from the uncertainty of his."

The next reference to the bounds of Maryland is found in a letter of instructions dated 26th August, 1651, from Lord Baltimore to Governor Stone, in reference to a grant from Governor William Berkeley to Edmond Scarborough, to seat "Palmer's Island within our said province." In another letter of instructions from Lord Baltimore to his governor and council, dated 23d October, 1656, among other items is the following:

"That they do take special care that no encroachments be made by any upon any part of his lordship's said province; for the better prevention whereof, his lordship requires his said Lieutenant and Council *to cause the bounds thereof to be kept in memory, and notoriously known, especially the bounds between Maryland and Virginia, on that part of the country known there by the name of the Eastern Shore, to which* his lordship would have them peruse one of the maps of Maryland, which his lordship formerly sent thither; whereby the said bounds are described, and his lordship hath also for their direction therein, sent herewith, a copy of a proclamation published heretofore by the then Governor and Council of Virginia, for prohibiting any of Virginia to trade with the Indians in Maryland without his lordship's license; which proclamation bore date 4th October, 1638, and therein are described the bounds between Maryland and Virginia; the said copy having been transcribed out of another copy thereof, which his lordship hath, attested by Mr. Richard Kemp, deceased, who was Secretary of Virginia when the said proclamation was made.

"Given under his lordship's seal at arms, 23 October, 1656,

"C. BALTIMORE."[1]

In 1660, an Act of the Virginia Assembly, expelling the Quakers from that colony under severe penalties, compelled them to seek a home and refuge in Maryland. The persecuted Quakers of the Eastern shore of Virginia petitioned Governor Calvert to afford them facilities for settling in Maryland, and in compliance with their petition, in November, 1661, he commissioned Colonel Scarborough, Randall Revell, and John Elzey, then residents of the Eastern shore of Virginia, to grant lands on the Eastern shore of Maryland to those Virginians who wished to come with their families into Maryland.

The offers of the commissioners to the emigrants appear to have been gladly accepted, inasmuch as the report of Revell to the governor and council of Maryland on the 2d of May, 1662, informs us that at that early period settlements had been made at Manokin and Annamessex, which then consisted of fifty tithables, and that the settlers had formed a treaty of amity with the emperor of the Nanticoke Indians. He also desired the "continuance of the commission to himself and the others." On the same day it was ordered, "that the commission for granting warrants for land, dated 6th November last, be renewed to Colonel Edmund Scarborough, Randall Revell and John Elzey, to continue until recalled." This commission seems to have been continued until 4th February, 1663, on which day a commission in similar terms was issued by Governor Charles Calvert to John Elzey, Randall Revell and Stephen Horsey, who had become residents of Maryland.

[1] *Maryland's Statement of the Boundary Line*, 1874, p. 77.

Scarborough was doubtless left out in consequence of a letter he had about that time written to Mr. Revell (who had settled upon Manokin river), claiming that place as belonging to Virginia.

The establishment of these settlements on the very borders of Virginia, and the inducements which they held forth to its inhabitants, naturally excited the jealousy of its government. Hence, about this period, their submission to the authority of Virginia was required by Colonel Scarborough, for and on behalf of that government, and upon the refusal of Elzey, he was arrested, on the 23d of February, 1663, in Accomac, by Scarborough, and released only upon a promise of submission of an equivocal nature.[1]

Scarborough's design was merely to terrify him into submission, and, therefore, after exacting this equivocal promise, he avowed his determination to go up to the settlements for the purpose of exacting the same obedience of all, and declared he would put "*the broad arrow mark*" upon the houses of all such as should refuse. Pursuing these intentions, he entered these infant settlements in October, 1663, in a hostile manner, when, partly by persuasion and partly by force, he succeeded in bending the settlers to a partial compliance with his will, and to a temporary submission.

On Scarborough's invasion of Manokin, the settlers reminded him "of Lord Baltimore's claim to that place, and all other places to Anancock," to which he replied, "that whilst the erroneous proclamation was uncontrolled that declares Anancock to be Maryland's southern bounds, it might be so received, but since occasion made the government of Virginia not only reverse that proclamation, but also by this present Act of Assembly the certain bounds of Lord Baltimore's patent was declared, and if the lieutenant had aught to say, he was referred by the act to persons and place."

In the meanwhile, the governor of Maryland had been apprised by Elzey of all these violent proceedings on the part of Scarborough; and had been importuned by him, to aid the settlers in repelling these hostile incursions, and in repressing the insolence of the surrounding savages; but the former preferring a resort to pacific measures, contented himself with apprising Berkeley, the Governor of Virginia, of all these unwarrantable acts on the part of Scarborough, done avowedly under the authority of the latter.

These acts of unprovoked hostility on the part of Scarborough, were at once disclaimed by Berkeley as wholly unauthorized; and as the best mode of obviating all future difficulties, the Governor of Maryland set on foot a negotiation with Berkeley for the purpose of effecting a final adjustment of the boundary line between the respective possessions of the two governments on the eastern side of the bay. The entreaties and remonstrances of the former were at last crowned with success, and in 1668, Philip Calvert, on the part of Maryland, and Edmond Scarborough, on the part of Virginia, were appointed commissioners to determine the location of Watkins' Point, and to mark the boundary line between the two

[1] Council Chamber *Records*, Lib. H.H., pp. 122-207. McMahon, p. 19.

colonies running thence to the ocean. By them this duty was fully discharged on the 25th of June, 1668, and in confirmation of it, the following articles of agreement were drawn up and signed by each of them, on behalf of their respective governments. It runs thus:

"Whereas his Royal Majesties Commission to the Surveyor Genl. of Virginia, commands setting out the bounds of Virginia, with a reference to his Majesty's Hon'ble Governor and Council of Virginia, from time to time to give advice and order, for directing the said Surveyor General to do his duty appertaining to his office. In order thereunto his Majesty's Hon'ble Governor and Council have by letter moved the Hon'ble the Lord Baltimore's Lieut. Genl. of Maryland to appoint some fitting person to meet upon the place called Watkins' Point with the Surveyor Genl. of Virginia, and thence to run the division line to the Ocean Sea, &c.

"The Hon'ble Philip Calvert, Esq., Chancellor of Maryland, being fully impowered by the Hon'ble Lieut. Genl. of Maryland, and Edmond Scarborough, his Majesty's Surveyor Genl. of Va., after a full and perfect view taken of the point of land made by the north side of Pocomoke Bay and the south side of Annamessex Bay, have and do conclude the same to be Watkins' Pt., from which said point, so called, we have run an east line, agreeable with the extremest part of the westernmost angle of said Watkins' Point over Pocomoke river, to the land near Robt. Holston's, and there have marked certain trees, which are so continued by an east line, running over Swansecute's Creek, into the marsh of the seaside, with apparent marks and boundaries, which by our mutual agreement, according to the qualifications aforesaid, are to be received as the bounds of Virginia and Maryland on the Eastern Shore of Chesapeake Bay.

"In confirmation of which concurrence have set our hands and seals this 25th day of June, 1668.

"PHILIP CALVERT, [SEAL.]
"EDMOND SCARBOROUGH, [SEAL.]"

With the signing of this agreement, all the existing sources of controversy with the government of Virginia about the validity or true location of the charter of Maryland, for the time ceased. But, notwithstanding their precise definition, the bounds here established by authority of the crown and consent of the Lord Proprietary of the province, and which Maryland has held for over two centuries, are not in accordance with the provisions of her charter. It appears from investigation made by Lieutenant Michler, of the United States Coast Survey, in 1858, that either by mistake or design on the part of Colonel Scarborough, then surveyor-general of Virginia, the line of 1668, between Accomac and Somerset (now Worcester) counties, was run 5 degrees and 15 minutes north of east, instead of *east* as the agreement asserts; by which error Virginia obtained possession of 23 square miles, nearly 15,000 acres of Maryland territory.

Despite the Calvert-Scarborough agreement, the controversy about the true boundary between Maryland and Virginia on the Eastern shore, and the sovereignty of the Potomac river, remained unsettled until a century after the American Revolution. Finally, the two States consented to submit their claims to a board of arbitrators to ascertain and determine the true line of boundary. For this purpose, Maryland appointed as her arbitrator the Hon. Jeremiah S. Black, of Pennsylvania; and Virginia selected the Hon. J. B. Beck, of Kentucky. These two distinguished men selected as the third arbitrator, ex-Governor Graham, of North Carolina; but as he died during the progress of their labors, the Hon. Charles J. Jenkins, of Georgia, was appointed in his place. The counsel for Maryland before the arbitrators were Hon. William Pinkney Whyte and Hon. Isaac D. Jones.

After examining a vast amount of evidence, historical, documentary and oral, hearing elaborate arguments of counsel on both sides, and conferring fully on the merits and demerits of this ancient controversy, the arbitrators in January, 1877, came to a final decision, subject, however, to the ratification of the two States and Congress. A majority and a minority report were filed, the former signed by J. S. Black and Charles J. Jenkins, and the latter by Senator Beck. By the decision of the majority Maryland was awarded (in conformity with the claim as presented by ex-Governor Whyte in his argument of the case,) sovereignty over the whole of the Potomac river to its southern bank, except that Virginia was to have dominion over the soil to low-water mark on the south side of the river, and to such use of the river beyond low-water mark as might facilitate the full enjoyment of her riparian ownership without interfering with navigation or with Maryland's proper use thereof. In a long and interesting report upon the boundary line, they sum up their conclusions as follows:

"We run to Sassafras Hammock, and from that to Horse Hammock, because we cannot in any other possible way give Virginia the part of Smith's island to which she shows her right by long possession.

"We go thence to the middle of Tangier Sound, and from thence downward we divide Tangier Sound equally between the two States, because the possession of Virginia to the shore is proof of a title whose proper boundary is the middle of the water. We give Maryland the other half of the sound for the same or exactly a similar reason, she being incontestably the owner of the dry land on the opposite shore.

"The south line dividing the waters stops where it intersects the straight line from Smith's Point to Watkins' Point, because this latter is the charter line, as modified by the compact, and Maryland has no rights south of it.

"From that point of intersection to Watkins' Point we follow the straight line from Smith's Point, there being no possession or agreement which has changed it since 1785.

"At Watkins' Point the charter line has stood unchanged since 1632, and the call for a due east line from thence must be followed until it meets the middle thread of the Pocomoke. At the place last mentioned the boundary turns up the Pocomoke, keeping the middle of the river until it crosses the Calvert and Scarborough line. It divides the river that far because the territory on one side belongs to Maryland and on the other to Virginia.

"From the angle formed by the Scarborough and Calvert line with the line last described through the middle of the Pocomoke, the boundary follows the marked line of Scarborough and Calvert to the seashore.

"It will be readily perceived that we have no faith in any straight-line theory which conflicts with the contracts of the parties, or gives to one what the other has peaceably and continuously occupied for a very long time. The broken line which we have adopted is vindicated by certain principles so simple, so plain, and so just, that we are compelled to adopt them. They are briefly as follows:

"1. So far as the original charter boundary has been uniformly observed and the occupancy of both has conformed thereto, it must be recognized as the boundary still.

"2. Wherever one State has gone over the charter line, taken territory which originally belonged to the other, and kept it, without let or hindrance, for more than twenty years, the boundary must now be so run as to include such territory within the State that has it.

"3. Where any compact or agreement has changed the charter line at a particular place, so as to make a new division of the territory, such agreement is binding if it has been followed by a corresponding occupancy.

"4. But no agreement to transfer territory or change boundaries can count for anything now, if the actual possession was never changed. Continued occupancy of the granting State for centuries is conclusive proof that the agreement was extinguished and the parties remitted to their original rights.

"5. The waters are divided by the charter line where that line has been undisturbed by the subsequent acts of the parties, but where acquisitions have been made by one from the other of territory bounded by bays and rivers, such acquisitions extend constructively to the middle of the water.

"Maryland is by this award confined everywhere within the original limits of her charter. She is allowed *to* go to it nowhere except on the short line running east from Watkins' Point to the middle of the Pocomoke. At that place Virginia never crossed the charter to make a claim. What territory we adjudge to Virginia north of the charter line she has acquired either by compacts fairly made or else by a long and undisturbed possession. Her right to this territory, so acquired, is as good as if the original charter had never cut it off to Lord Baltimore. We have nowhere given to one of these States anything which fairly or legally belongs to the other, but in dividing the land and the waters we have anxiously observed the Roman rule, *suum cuique tribuere*."

As the result of their determination, the majority submitted the following award:

"And now, to wit, January 16, anno Domini 1877, the undersigned, being a majority of the arbitrators to whom the States of Virginia and Maryland, by acts of their respective legislatures, submitted the controversies concerning their territorial limits, with authority to ascertain and determine the true line of boundary between them, having heard the allegations of the said States and examined the proofs on both sides, do find, declare, award, ascertain and determine that the true line of boundary between the said States, so far as they are conterminous with one another, is as follows, to wit:

"Beginning at the point on the Potomac river where the line between Virginia and West Virginia strikes the said river at low-water mark, and thence following the meanderings of said river by low-water mark to Smith's Point at or near the mouth of the Potomac, in latitude 37° 53′ 08″ and longitude 76° 13′ 46″; thence crossing the waters of the Chesapeake bay, by a line running north 65° 30′ east, about nine and a-half nautical miles, to a point on the western shore of Smith's Island, at the north end of Sassafras Hammock, in latitude 37° 57′ 13″, longitude 76° 02′ 52″; thence across Smith's Island south 88° 30′ east five thousand six hundred and twenty yards, to the center of Horse Hammock, on the eastern shore of Smith's Island, in latitude 37° 57′ 08″, longitude 75° 59′ 20″; thence south 79° 30′ east four thousand eight hundred and eighty yards, to a point marked A on the accompanying map, in the middle of Tangier sound, in latitude 37° 56′ 42″, longitude 75° 56′ 23″, said point bearing from Jane's Island light south 54° west, and distant from that light three thousand five hundred and sixty yards; thence south 10° 30′ west four thousand seven hundred and forty yards, by a line dividing the waters of Tangier sound, to a point where it intersects the straight line from Smith's Point to Watkins' Point, said point of intersection being in latitude 37° 54′ 21″, longitude

75° 56′ 55″, bearing from Jane's Island light south 29° west, and from Horse Hammock south 34° 30′ east. This point of intersection is marked B on the accompanying map. Thence north 85° 15′ east six thousand seven hundred and twenty yards along the line above mentioned, which runs from Smith's Point to Watkins' Point until it reaches the latter spot, namely, Watkins' Point, which is in latitude 37° 54′ 38″, longitude 75° 52′ 44″. From Watkins' Point the boundary line runs due east seven thousand eight hundred and eighty yards, to a point where it meets a line running through the middle of Pocomoke sound which is marked C on the accompanying map, and is in latitude 37° 54′ 38″, longitude 75° 47′ 50″; thence, by a line dividing the waters of Pocomoke sound, north 47° 30′ east five thousand two hundred and twenty yards, to a point in said sound marked D on the accompanying map, in latitude 37° 56′ 25″, longitude 75° 45′ 26″ thence following the middle of the Pocomoke river by a line or irregular curves, as laid down on the accompanying map, until it intersects the westward protraction of the boundary line marked by Scarborough and Calvert May 28, 1668, at a point in the middle of the Pocomoke river and in latitude 37° 59′ 37″, longitude 75° 37′ 04″; thence, by the Scarborough and Calvert line, which runs 5° 15′ north of east, to the Atlantic ocean.

"The latitudes, longitudes, courses and distances here given have been measured upon the coast chart No. 33 of the United States Coast Survey; (sheet No. 3, Chesapeake bay,) which is herewith filed as a part of this award and explanatory thereof. The original charter-line is marked upon the said map and shaded in blue. The present line of boundary, as ascertained and determined, is also marked and shaded in red, while the yellow indicates the line referred to in the compact of 1785 between Smith's Point and Watkins' Point.

"In further explanation of this award the arbitrators deem it proper to add that—

"1. The measurements being taken and places fixed according to the Coast Survey, we have come as near to perfect mathematical accuracy as in the nature of things is possible. But in case of any inaccuracy in the described course or length of a line or in the latitude or longitude of a place, the natural objects called for must govern.

"2. The middle thread of Pocomoke river is equidistant as nearly as may be between the two shores without considering arms, inlets, creeks, or affluents as parts of the river, but measuring the shore lines from headland to headland.

"3. The low-water mark on the Potomac, to which Virginia has a right in the soil, is to be measured by the same rule, that is to say, from low-water mark at one headland to low-water mark at another, without following indentations, bays, creeks, inlets, or affluent rivers.

"4. Virginia is entitled not only to full dominion over the soil to low-water mark on the south shore of the Potomac, but has a right to such use of the river beyond the line of low-water mark as may be necessary to the full enjoyment of her riparian ownership, without impeding the navigation or otherwise interfering with the proper use of it by Maryland, agreeably to the compact of 1785.

"In testimony whereof we have hereunto set our hands the day and year above written.

"J. S. BLACK, of Pennsylvania,
"CHAS. J. JENKINS, of Georgia.

"A. W. GRAHAM, Secretary."

Senator Beck, in his minority report, agreed with the majority of the arbitrators in the conclusions reached as to the rights of Maryland on the Potomac river, but differed from them as to the locality of Watkins' Point, called for by Lord Baltimore's charter, and consequently as to the right line of division between the respective States between the mouth of the Potomac river and the Atlantic ocean.[1]

[1] The report of the arbitrators has been confirmed by Maryland, by Virginia, and by Congress, and is now a law.

CHAPTER XI.

Now that the government of Maryland had been restored to the Lord Proprietary, it was believed that a season of peace was about to dawn upon the colony. But there were elements of dissension still active, and conspiracy brooding where it was least to be expected. Governor Fendall, notwithstanding his oath, conceived a plan for enlarging his authority at the expense of the proprietary, and virtually overturning his government by assuming the position of a governor, appointed by the people, through their representatives. To accomplish this, the concurrence of the Lower House was required, which was not difficult to obtain, as they were always ready to extend their own powers, and were already jealous of the position occupied by the Upper House.

At the session, opening February 28th, 1659, the burgesses sent a message to the governor and council, in which they affirm:

> "That this Assembly of Burgesses, judging themselves to be a lawful Assembly, without dependence on any other power in the Province, now in being, is the highest court of judicature. And if any objection can be made to the contrary, we desire to hear it."[1]

This pretension, which denied the right of legislation by the Upper House, it is stated, was a scheme concocted by Fendall, to give color to his designs upon the province. And in pursuance thereof, on the 13th of March, he declared that "the Lord Proprietary, by himself or his deputy, ought to be present, and have a casting voice; and that, as governor, he had not any power to confirm laws made by the burgesses, for any longer time, than until his lordship or his heirs should declare their dissent. But he did believe, the intent of the king, in his lordship's patent, was that the freemen, by writ assembled, either by themselves or their deputies, should make and enact laws, and those laws, so made, were to be published in his lordship's name, and then to be in full force. Provided, they be agreeable to reason, and in no case repugnant to the laws of England." In this view he was sustained by two of his council, Gerrard and Utie.

In the afternoon of the same day, the Lower House, headed by its speaker, came into the chamber of the Upper House and announced that they could not allow the governor and council to sit as an Upper House; but if they pleased they might take seats "in behalf of his lordship and themselves" in the Lower House. The Upper House suggested that in such a case, the speaker of the Lower House must vacate his seat to the governor, who then would be "president of the assembly;" at which the speaker of the Lower House asked

[1] Bacon.

for time to consider. On the 14th, the Lower House demanded a further conference, which, being granted, it was finally agreed that the governor should sit as president of the joint houses, the Lower House reserving the right to adjourn or dissolve itself. The Upper House was now dissolved, and Fendall, with Gerrard and Utie, took their seats in the Lower House, the other members of the Upper House refusing to follow their example. Carrying out his intentions, Fendall now surrendered to the Lower House his commission from Lord Baltimore, accepting from them a new commission for himself as governor. Messrs. Gerrard and Utie, together with the speaker of the Lower House, Mr. Slye, were appointed his council. To give stability to this new government, Fendall gave his assent to several laws, particularly one entitled "an Act for repealing all former acts;" and another entitled, "an Act providing against any disturbance in the present government," whereby it was made felony to disturb the government as established by them; and on the 15th of September following, a proclamation was issued by Fendall, "commanding all persons to own no authority but what came immediately from his majesty or the Grand Assembly of this province." "Thereby," says Mr. Bacon, "colourably sheltering (as the grand jury expressed it) their rebellion under a pretence of his sacred majesty's name, to the great derogation from the just power of his lordship, and the subversion of the government of this province, and contrary to the peace of his said lordship, his rule and dominion."[1]

The rule of this revolutionary government was of short duration. On the 24th of June, 1660, the Lord Proprietary commissioned as governor, his brother, Philip Calvert, and having procured from King Charles II., who was just restored to the throne of England, letters commanding all the officers and inhabitants of the province to aid him in the re-establishment of his government, and a similar command of assistance to the government of Virginia, he ordered Governor Calvert to proceed against the rebels either in the courts or by martial law, but on no account to permit Fendall to escape with his life. Philip Calvert arrived in the province soon after, and on the 11th of December, 1660, was sworn in as governor of the province by the provincial court held at Patuxent. In the meantime, on the 14th September, the Lord Proprietary had published his "declaration" in relation to "that perfidious and perjured fellow, Fendall, whom we lately entrusted to be our lieutenant of Maryland, to cloak his treacherous ambitious designs, and contrary to his oath and trust, to incite the people there to join with him in raising a sedition and faction against our jurisdiction and right of government," and announced a general amnesty to all who were "sorry and repentant," except Fendall and Hatch, for whose apprehension writs were issued. The government of Virginia tendered Governor Calvert all necessary assistance in the execution of his authority, but he had no difficulty in assuming the government, which was abandoned

[1] Bacon's *Laws*; 1659.

by Fendall after a fruitless effort to excite the people to resistance. In a few days, Fendall and Gerrard surrendered themselves at discretion, and being indicted by the grand jury, at the provincial court, on the 22d February, 1660 (O.S.), were tried and found guilty of treason, receiving sentence of banishment and confiscation of their estates. They appealed to the governor and council for the mitigation of their sentence, and, notwithstanding the express injunctions of the Lord Proprietary not to permit Fendall to escape with his life, they received their pardon on the 28th of February, 1660 (O.S.), upon each paying a moderate fine, forfeiting the privilege of voting and holding office, and giving sufficient security for their good behavior towards his lordship and his government. Their accomplices, upon submission and application to the governor and council, without trial or prosecution, received a full and free pardon. Tranquillity was now restored to the province.

A peculiar trait of Fendall's administration, and one which casts light on the spirit underlying the plot against the proprietary, was the severity of the measures taken against the peaceful Friends or Quakers, who now, for the first time, made their appearance in the province. Three missionaries of this sect, Josiah Cole, Thomas Thurston and Thomas Campbell, came from Virginia into Maryland about the end of 1657, and remained until the following August. Whether they made any proselytes or not, we do not certainly know; but by the council records it appears that in July, 1658, Thurston and Cole were arrested for refusing to subscribe the "engagement," or formal act of submission to the authority of Lord Baltimore, and were afterwards set at liberty on condition of their leaving the province. The council also took into consideration "the insolent behavior of some people called Quakers," their offence consisting in their remaining covered in court, and refusing to sign the engagement, "alleging that they were to be governed by God's law, and not by man's law," and ordered that they should either subscribe the engagement or else depart the province by the 25th March following, under pain of being treated as rebels and traitors. From this it would appear that the sect had already gained some footing in the colony.[1]

Thurston returned to Maryland in 1659, and his proceedings soon drew the attention of the council to himself and his sectaries, as will appear from the annexed order in council:

Ordered by the Councill the 23d of July, 1659.

"Whereas It is too well knowne in this Province that there have of late been severall vagabonds & idle persons knowne by the name of Quakers that have presumed to come into this Province as well diswading the people from complying with the Military discipline in this tyme of Danger as also from giving Testimony or being Jurors in Causes depending between party and party or bearing any Office in the province to the no small Disturbance of the Laws and Civill Governm[t] thereof And that the keeping and deteyning them as prisoners hath brought so great a Charge upon this province The Gov[r]

[1] *The Early Friends in Maryland.* By J. Saurin Norris. *Md. Hist. Soc. Papers.*

and Councill taking it into their consid'acon have thought fitt to appoint, And do hereby for the prevention of the like Inconveniency's for the tyme to come require and comand all and every the Justices of the Peace of this province that so soone as they shall have notice that any of the af^d vagabonds or idle persons shall againe presume to come into this province, they forthwith cause them to be apprehended and whipt from constable to constable untill they be sent out of ye Province. "PHILIP CALVERT Sec'ry."[1]

In August, Thurston was brought before the governor and council, and pleaded that the order of July 23d only applied to such as came into the province after its issue, whereas he was in Maryland at the time. This plea was allowed, but he was banished for life under penalty of receiving thirty-eight lashes if contumacious, and any person harboring him was to be fined five hundred pounds of tobacco.

We find no evidence that the penalties provided in the order were enforced in their full severity against any; and, indeed, when so active a missionary as Thurston received no worse sentence than banishment, it would have seemed unreasonable as well as cruel to visit all the rigor of the law upon less conspicuous victims. And with the deposition of Fendall from power the persecuting spirit was for awhile banished. It is true that, in 1661, we find one John Everitt—possibly a Friend—committed for trial, but it is for desertion—"running from his colors when pressed to go to the Susquehanna fort;" in extenuation of which he pleaded conscientious scruples against bearing arms; but this may have been a mere cloak for cowardice. While other colonies were treating these inoffensive, if peculiar people, with extreme cruelty, flogging both men and women, imprisoning, mutilating and hanging; in Maryland they found a secure asylum, and the names of many of these fugitive sufferers appear in our early records.

Some other particulars respecting the Quakers in Maryland may be appropriately introduced here.[2]

George Rofe, a Quaker missionary, visited Maryland about 1661, and wrote to George Fox that there were many "settled meetings" in the province. This shows that even at that early date their numbers had grown, either by "convincement" or immigration, to a considerable body. In April, 1672, George Fox, the founder of the sect, visited Maryland, and attended a general meeting at West river, which he describes as "very large," and "held four days."[3] This was the first general meeting held in the province, and is considered memorable in Quaker history. In October of the same year, Fox attended another "meeting for all Maryland Friends," which was held at Treadhaven, near the site of Easton, Talbot county, and lasted five days. And again in May, 1673, (which he calls "third month," following the old style in reckoning the year,) he was at a "wonderful glorious meeting" at West river, just before he set sail for England. These general or yearly meetings, according to the testimony of Samuel Bownas, an English Quaker,

[1] Bundle, *Maryland*, B. T., iii., D., 33, Public Record Office, London.

[2] From *The Early Friends*, *ut supra*.

[3] Fox's *Journal*.

were not altogether of a devotional character, advantage being taken of the large concourse which attended them, to combine thrift with piety. "Many people," says Bownas, "resort to it and transact a deal of trade one with another, so that it is a kind of market or change where the captains of ships and the planters meet and settle their affairs; and this draws abundance of people of the best rank to it."

In May, 1674, a petition was presented to the assembly asking that they might be exempted from taking judicial oaths, and that their affirmation in the solemn and scriptural form of "yea, yea, and nay, nay," might be accepted as equivalent, subject to the regular penalties for perjury. The petition was not acted on; but from a mention, in the minutes of the yearly meeting of 1677, of "Friends that were chosen assemblymen," it would seem that notwithstanding their peculiar tenets and customs, they were at this early day admitted to public office. In 1688, Lord Baltimore issued a proclamation dispensing with oaths in testamentary cases. In 1695, they set forth, in a petition, the disabilities they are under in regard to oaths, and the evils thence resulting, but without effect.[1] In 1702, however, an act was passed relieving the Quakers from this difficulty.

The Quakers most abounded in the two counties, Anne Arundel and Talbot, where Fox attended the general meetings, and where numbers of their descendants still live. By an order in council of August 10th, 1697, the sheriffs of the various counties were ordered to report on the Quakers and their places of worship; from the returns to which it appears that there was "one timber-work meeting house" at West river, and another at Herring creek, while meetings, monthly, weekly, and quarterly, were held at various private houses, the preachers resident in the county being "Mr. William Richardson and Samuel Galloway's wife." Talbot county had a frame meeting-house at the head of Treadhaven creek (near the present Easton), and three smaller clapboard houses at other points. Kent had one house

[1] "May 17, 1695.—Presented unto his excellency by several persons called Quakers a petition, by way of address, wherein, among several articles there laid down, they do say that they are rendered incapable to serve the king or their country, being under scruple of conscience, and cannot swear, so that if they see a felonious act committed, or hear any seditious words spoken, they cannot, without great danger to themselves, discover the same, because they cannot give such formal testimony as the law requires, and so the parties escape, for want of such testimony, and actions brought against them for slander or defamation, perhaps, for their pains; whereupon his excellency demanded if they did not think they were obliged to discover such matters being made privy to them, who make answer they do hold themselves obliged.

"In another article, they say they have not afforded them the British right of an Englishman; to which his excellency demands, if they did not receive in this province right and privilege equal with their brethren in England; who confess they do, but they expected some other privileges, having been at great charge and expenses in the helping to settle this government." This petition was sent to the House of Burgesses, to which they sent the following answer:

"*By the House of Burgesses, May 17th, 1695*:—As to the first part of this petition, viz., the dispensing with taking the oaths, 'tis the opinion of this House that it is expressly contrary to the known laws of the kingdom of England, and therefore not fit to be dispensed with; and as to the other part of the petition, relating to the 40 pounds of tobacco per poll, this House will not make any distinction, but continue the petitioners under the same circumstances, with all other their majesties' subjects of this province, as to the payment thereof."

on Island creek, and Calvert one near Leonard's creek. In Charles', there were two Quakers but no meeting house, and none in Baltimore, Prince George, St. Mary's, Somerset and Dorchester.

The subject of slavery did not trouble the consciences of Maryland Friends until a hundred years after their settlement in the province, and numerous wills and other records show that they were slaveholders. In 1759 and 1760 the yearly meeting expressed objections to the importation of negroes, but decided that "they were not fully ripe in their judgments" as to buying and selling those already in the province. From this time the question continually arose, until in 1777 the society in Maryland decided against slave-holding, and the members emancipated their slaves, thus proving their conscientiousness by a very heavy pecuniary sacrifice.

The yearly meetings, as we have seen, being largely resorted to for purposes of business as well as religion, gave occasion for very miscellaneous gatherings of people, and were attended with some disorders, so that in 1725 an act was passed to prevent the sale of liquors during their continuance, within one mile of the yearly meeting house in Talbot county, or two miles of that in Anne Arundel.[1]

Thus we have seen that from the first this peaceful people found a home and a refuge in Maryland, while elsewhere they were treated with inhuman severity. The only harsh proceedings against them were those of a revolutionary government under Puritan influences, and ceased with its overthrow. Not merely were they tolerated, but the law itself was modified so as to adapt itself to their innocent scruples, and special legislation was framed for their protection. When we consider their peculiarities of worship and manners, which separated them from all others and made them a people apart; the many points in which their conduct and principles brought them into conflict with the strongest prejudices of others; their non-resistance; their boldness in bearing open testimony against whatever they thought wrong; and the strong animosity which was felt against them in most of the other colonies—when, in addition to all this, we remember that the aggressions of Penn and his colonists gave Maryland more than any other province, grounds for unfriendly feeling toward his peculiar sect—we cannot but admit that the treatment of the Quakers in Maryland forms a bright page in her history.

Having proclaimed Charles II. king, Lord Baltimore made a further display of his loyalty by erecting a new county in 1658, to which he gave the name of that monarch. A county by the name of Charles had been established in 1650, by an order in council, which was repealed in 1654, and the county of Calvert erected in its stead. The bounds of Charles county, as defined by the commission appointing officers for it, were "the river Wicomico, to its head; and from the mouth of that river up the Potomac, as high as the settlements extend, and thence to the head of Wicomico." These vague boundaries stood until 1695, when the territory north of Mattawoman

[1] Bacon, 1725, c. 6.

creek was made Prince George's county, and the limits of Charles county defined by Act of Assembly, its eastern boundary being the line of St. Mary's county; its northern, Mattawoman creek, and "a straight line drawn thence to the head of Swanson's creek, and with that creek to the Patuxent."

About this time Baltimore county was formed out of the territory north of Anne Arundel. The order in council by which it was erected, is lost; but the records show that it did not exist previous to 1659. It is first described in a proclamation of the governor, dated June 6, 1674, declaring that "the southern bound of Baltimore county shall be the south side of Patapsco river, and from the highest plantations on that side of the river due south, two miles with the woods." In 1698, by an Act of Assembly, the boundary line between Baltimore and Anne Arundel was determined by commissioners appointed for that purpose. In 1725 the territory south of the Patapsco, included in Baltimore county by the previous survey, was restored to Anne Arundel, and the head of the Patapsco became the western limit, and so continued until 1748, when Frederick county was erected, and its line determined to run to the Patuxent river, and with that stream to the [western] line of Baltimore county, which it followed to the limits of the province. This left the western line of Baltimore county still uncertain, until it was finally settled by the Act of 1750.[1] Talbot county was established in 1660–1, but, as with Baltimore, the order by which it was created cannot be found. The assembly proceedings, however, show its existence this year. Its bounds were fixed by an Act of Assembly passed in the year 1706, Chapter III., which enacts: "That the bounds of Talbot county shall contain Sharp Island, Choptank Island, and all the land on the north side of the Great Choptank river; and extend itself up the said river to Tuckahoe bridge; and from thence, with a straight line, to the mill, commonly called and known by the name of Swetnam's Mill, and thence down the south side of Wye river to its mouth, and thence down the bay to the place of beginning, including Poplar and Bruff's Island."

Somerset county was erected by the governor's order 22d August, 1666, which assigned to it as its limits, on the south, the southern boundary of the State on the eastern shore; on the west, the bay; on the north the Nanticoke river; and on the east, the ocean.[2]

On the 17th of April, 1661, Governor Calvert convened the assembly "at St. John's, in St. Mary's county," and soon after began to legislate so as to increase the prosperity of the province. Military discipline was promoted, and provision was made for soldiers wounded or disabled in the service of the colony. Though the general court of Massachusetts had, as early as the year 1652, granted to a few French Protestant refugees "liberty to inhabit there," yet the Assembly of Maryland passed, in May, 1666, the first naturalization law of any colonial assembly. And from the many similar laws, which were enacted from time to time till the Revolution, it can be seen that the influx

[1] McMahon, p. 89.

[2] *Ibid.*, p. 90.

of foreigners during this period was large. Among these laws passed in 1661 are: An "Act for the Conveyance of Letters;" another "for the publication of all laws within the province for the future;" one for "prohibiting the importation of all horses, geldings, mares or colts into the province;" and one in 1674, "for erecting a court-house and prison in each county." An act was also passed to prevent horse racing, etc., at Quaker meetings.

On May 1st, 1661, the assembly passed an "Act concerning the setting up of a mint within the Province of Maryland." Before giving the particulars of this measure, it may be well to give a brief account of the early currency of the province, which sheds some light on the state of society.

It is probable that, although the power of coining money was not specified in the charter of Maryland, Cæcilius considered the powers therein conveyed as ample to justify him in such a proceeding, as that power had been granted to Virginia in her patent of April 10th, 1606.[1]

In the earlier times of the colony, trade, to a great extent, was conducted on the primitive principle of barter, and many contracts were drawn on this footing. With the natives traffic was largely carried on, in addition to barter, by the use of the shell-money called *peak* and *roanoke*, which has been explained in a previous chapter, and this, as always available with the Indians, found some currency among the colonists themselves, though never to the same degree that it did in New England. The productions of the soil, such as grain and tobacco, as well as live-stock, were received in early times in payment of taxes, under the name of "country pay." Tobacco, however, as the chief staple of the province, soon became the general medium of exchange, though, perhaps, it never attained the purchasing power it once had in Virginia, where, as Chalmers tells us, in 1621 an invoice of girls, "handsome, and recommended for virtuous demeanor," were purchased as wives by bachelors of the province at 100 lbs. of tobacco apiece, and the demand was so brisk that it soon rose to 150 lbs., and the price of a wife was made recoverable before any other debt.[2]

As the extended cultivation of tobacco reduced the value of that staple, the colonists began to suffer great inconvenience from its depreciation, a trouble which the Virginians had felt, and tried to remedy by legislation in 1640–2–3. Rents of land being payable, in many cases, in tobacco at a fixed rate, the depreciation of the currency was felt severely by the landlords; and as a natural consequence of the presence of an inferior medium, coin was driven out of the colony. Various expedients were resorted to to remedy the evil: in 1650, a levy of half a bushel of corn per poll was made upon Anne Arundel, St. Mary's, and Kent counties, for the support of the governor.

[1] Section 10 of the charter of Virginia runs thus: "And that they shall, or lawfully may, establish and cause to be made a coin, to pass current there between and amongst them and the natives there, of such metal, and in such manner and form, as the said several councils there shall limit and appoint."—Lucas's *Charters of the Old English Colonies*, p. 5. *Sketch of the Early Currency in Maryland and Virginia*, by S. F. Streeter. *Historical Magazine*, ii., p. 42.

[2] Chalmers, p. 46.

Powder, shot and guns were used as currency, and in 1661 the assembly made the port-dues on vessels trading to the province payable in powder or shot, at the rate of one pound of the former, or three of the latter, per ton burthen.

At last, at the suggestion of some of the leading colonists, Lord Baltimore undertook to provide a currency for the colony, and had dies cut in London, and specimen coins struck, which he forwarded to Governor Fendall and council on October 12, 1659. In the letter to the governor which accompanied them, he says:

"Having with great pains and charge procured necessaries for a particular coin to be current in Maryland, a sample whereof, in a piece of a shilling, a sixpence, and a groate, I herewith send you, I recommend it to you to promote, all you can, the dispersing it and by Proclamation, to make current within Maryland, for all payments upon contracts or causes happening or arising after a day to be by you limited in the said Proclamation: And to procure an act of assembly for the punishing of such as shall counterfeit the said coin, or otherwise offend in that behalf according to the form of an act recommended by me last year to my Governor and Secretary; or as near it as you can procure from the assembly, and to give me your advice next year touching what you think best to be further done in that matter touching coin; for, if encouragement be given by the good success of it this year, there will be abundance of adventurers in it the next year."

With this letter was also forwarded the following communication to his brother Philip, then Secretary of State:

"To my most affectionate loving brother, Philip Calvert, Esq., at St. Mary's in Maryland.

"I sent a sample of the Maryland money, with directions for the procuring it to pass, because I understood by letters this year from the Governor and you and others that there was no doubt but the people there would accept of it, when if we find they do, there will be means found to supply you all there with money enough; but though it would be a very great advantage to the Colony that it should pass current there, and an utter discouragement for the future supply of any more, if there be not a certain establishment this year, and assurance of its being vented and current there, yet it must not be imposed upon the people but by a Lawe there made by their consents in a General Assembly, which I pray fail not to signify to the Governor and Council there together from me, by showing them this letter from

"Your Most affectionate Brother,

"C. BALTIMORE.

"LONDON, 12 October, 1659."

Ten days after the receipt of this letter, Fendall's revolutionary act took place, and the confusion that followed rendered it impossible to carry out the proprietary's plan for introducing a specie currency. But at the session of 1661, after the overthrow of Fendall, at the instance of Governor Philip Calvert, an act was passed for the establishment of a mint in the province. After a preamble, setting forth the disadvantages under which the colony labored for want of a sufficient and suitable currency, the burgesses agree to the following enactments:[1]

[1] In the Upper House, Messrs. Brooke and Lloyd dissented from its passage, stating that, notwithstanding the Lord Proprietary, under his charter, had all the rights, etc., of a Bishop of Durham, they did not think that the County Palatine of Durham had liberty to coin.

I. That his lordship be petitioned to set up a mint for the coining of money within the province.

II. That the money coined therein be of as good silver as English sterling money.

III. That every shilling so coined weigh above ninepence in such silver, and other pieces in proportion.

IV. That the offences of clipping, scaling, or counterfeiting, washing, or in any way diminishing such coin, be punishable with death and forfeiture of lands and goods to the Lord Proprietary.

V. That his lordship receive said coin in payment for rents and all amounts due to him.

This act was transmitted to the Lord Proprietary in England, and upon its approval by him, he sent a sufficient quantity of coin into the province to supply its immediate wants. To facilitate its circulation, he invoked the aid of the assembly, and that body, on the 12th of April, 1662, passed an act "to put the coin (struck under the Act of 1661, ch. 4), in circulation." It enacted that "every householder and freeman in the province, should take up ten shillings per poll of the said money for every taxable, at *2d* per pound, to be paid upon tender of the said sums of money, proportionably for every such respective family, &c., for three years, &c."

The passage of this act caused a forced exchange of sixty pounds of tobacco by every tithable for ten shillings of the new coinage; and, as there were at least five thousand tithables then in the province, it is estimated that at least twenty-five hundred pounds sterling of this coin was put in circulation in the province. It is probable that this new currency proved acceptable to the people, as it must have greatly facilitated exchange, yet it by no means superseded tobacco as an article of currency. That still continued largely in use, especially in important transactions; and many of the public dues were still collected in tobacco and not in coin. What was the amount of this new currency in circulation at any time after, we have no means of ascertaining; neither do we know when it began to be disused.[1]

Ogilby, speaking of Maryland, in his work published in London, in 1671, says:

"The general way of traffick and commerce there is chiefly by Barter, or exchange of one commodity for another; yet there wants not besides English and other foreign coins some of his Lordship's own coin, as Groats, Sixpences, and Shillings, which his Lordship, at his own charge, caused to be coined and dispersed throughout that Province. 'Tis equal in fineness of silver to English sterling, being of the same standard, but of somewhat less weight. It hath on the one side his Lordship's coat of arms, stamped with his motto circumscribed '*Crescite et Multiplicamini,*' and on the other side his Lordship's effigies, circumscribed thus '*Cæcilius, Dominus Terræ Mariæ, &c.*'"[2]

[1] Streeter.

[2] *Description of the New World*, p. 188

Oldmixon, whose work was published in 1708, says:

"The Lord Proprietary had a Mint here to coin money, but it never was much used of. . . . Tobacco is their Meat, Drink, Cloathing, and money; not but that they have both Spanish and English money pretty plenty, which serves only for Pocket-Expenses, and not for Trade, Tobacco being the standard of that, as well with the Planters and others as with the Merchants."[1]

From the title of the Act of Assembly of 1661, it might be inferred that a mint was established, and that money was actually coined in the province, but it appears more probable that the coins were struck in England, under the supervision of the Lord Proprietary, and transmitted to the governor, as circumstances made it necessary or convenient. Mr. Streeter says that the operation was a profitable one, "inasmuch as the shilling contained but about seventy-five per cent. of its nominal value in silver, and was exchanged, in the first instance, for tobacco at the ordinary prices."[2]

Specimens of the curious money issued by Lord Baltimore are in the possession of the Maryland Historical Society, and are extremely rare. The shilling has upon the *obverse*: Device—A bust of Lord Baltimore, to left, slightly draped. Legend—CÆCILIVS DNS: TERRÆ-MARIÆ: &C. ✠ Mint mark—A cross patée or formée, ✠ *Reverse*: Device—A lozenged shield surmounted by a crown, and dividing the numerals X II. Legend—CRESCITE: ET: MVLTIPLICAMINI.

The sixpence and groat do not differ from the shilling in any important particulars, the most noticeable variation being in the legends—those upon the sixpence being, CÆCILIVS: DNS: TERRÆ-MARIÆ: &c., ✠ and CRESCITE: ET: MVLTIPLICAMINI.

[1] Vol. i., pp. 204-6.

[2] From the following proceedings before the Council of State in England, it will be seen that the Lord Proprietary's mint was in England:

Tuesday, 4 October, 1659.

Lord Baltimore, to be apprehended:—Upon Information given by Richard Pight, Clerke of the Irons in the Mint, that Cecill Lord Baltamore and diverse others with him, and for him, have made and transported great sums of mony and doe still goe on to make more.

"Ordered, That a warrant be issued forth to the said Richard Pight for the apprehending of the Lord Baltamore and such others as are suspected to be ingaged wth him in the said offence, and for the seizeing of all such moneys, stamps, tooles, & Instrum[ts] to the Councell."

Wednesday, 5 October, 1659.

Lord Baltamore, to attend:—The Councell being informed that a great quantity of Silver is coyned into peeces of diverse rates & values, and sent into Maryland by the Ld Baltamore or his Order.

"Ordered, That the said Ld Baltamore be summoned to attend the Committee of the Councell for Plantacions, who are to inquire into the whole business and to report the State thereof to the Councell."—*State Papers*, Public Record Office, London, cvii., pp. 646-653.

We have been unable to ascertain what action, if any, was taken upon these orders; but as he afterwards coined money, the decision of the Council of State must have been in his favor.

Mr. Sylvester S. Crosby, in his *History of the Early Coins of America*, says:

"Of the groat we find two varieties. The one most frequently met with has the head and shield larger than the other; its legend are CÆCILIVS: DNS: TERRÆ-MARIÆ, &c., ✠ and CRESCITE: ET: MVLTIPLICAMINI. The other variety is extremely rare; its legends are CÆCILIVS: DNS: TERRÆ-MARIÆ, &c., ✠ and CRESCITE ET. MVLTIPLICAMINI. The numerals upon the sixpence are VI, and upon the groat, IV. The punctuation marks upon the reverses of both the sixpence and the groat are so light as to be almost imperceptible upon the plate. The device upon the reverses of the silver coins of this series is the family coat-of-arms of Lord Baltimore. The shield may properly be described as Paly of six, sable and argent, a bend counter-changed. "In the collection of Dr. Clay, of Manchester, England. was an impression in copper, from shilling dies, which differed slightly from any we have seen in silver, the colon after MARIÆ being omitted. There are also in the British Museum impressions in copper, both from shilling and sixpenny dies, but we have no knowledge as to their varieties.

"A coinage of copper seems also to have been intended by Lord Baltimore, although we find no record referring to an issue of copper coin; but, if we may judge from the fact that but a single specimen is known of his coin in that metal, no large amount of it could have been put in circulation. The obverse of the penny is of the same design, and very similar to that of the sixpence; the reverse bears, as a device, a ducal coronet, from which fly two pennants; its legend is DENARIVM: TERRÆ-MARIÆ ✠ The borders of all these coins are milled, and their edges plain; the size of the shilling is 17; the sixpence, 13½; the groat, 11; and the penny, 13. The weight of those in silver is respectively, 66, 34, and 25 grains."[1]

Various acts for regulating the coin current in Maryland were passed and repealed at various times between 1662 and 1694. In the year 1686 an Act was passed for "the advancement of coins," by which the New England shillings and sixpences were rated as sterling, or at an advance of 3*d*. in each shilling; French crowns, pieces of eight, and rix dollars to pass as 6*s*., ducatoons at 7*s*. 6*d*., and all other coins of silver or gold, foreign or not foreign, to be taken at an advance of 3*d*. sterling, in the value of 12*d*. sterling.

[1] Page 123, etc. Ruding describes one of Lord Baltimore's coins as follows: "One shilling has the arms of his wife, a cross botony, quartered on the reverse. This coin, which is supposed to be unique, was in the possession of the late Sir Frederick Morton Eden, bart."

On the accession of William and Mary, in 1688, the government of Maryland was seized by the crown, and the privilege of working a mint was cut off from Lord Baltimore's accustomed rights. Under the royal prerogative, the rates for foreign coins, which had been established under proprietary rule, were continued. An Act of 1692 settled the rates of these coins just as they were established by the Act of 1686, but an Act of 1694 repealed the Act of 1692, and left the people to practise exchanges according to interest or fancy. This state of things continued until about the year 1708, when the legislature of the colony affixed provincial values to a number of foreign coins that had been introduced into the different plantations. Among these coins was the "cross dollar," of Flanders; the "lion dollar," of Holland, called the "Dutch dollar," and the "dog dollar," of which the Act of 1708 says there was "little other money in the province," and "the inhabitants are not so well acquainted with other foreign coins."

About this time there appears to have been much counterfeiting of foreign coins; and the Act of 1708 makes this offence penal, as well as the custom of *clipping* coins, which caused an act to be passed in 1729, providing that gold and silver coins should pass by weight. The mischief of clipping was, therefore, by this act prevented. The practice of clipping was chiefly confined to the Spanish dollar and half dollar cut into four pieces through the centre of the coin to make change, and these pieces were called *sharp-shins, or sharp-change*, on account of the sharp angle made by cutting.

By an Act of Assembly passed in 1763, where payments were made in tobacco, the following species of gold and silver coin, if tendered, were to be accepted at the following rates:

Johannes at	920 ℔. tob. -	Other gold coin (German excepted) by the dwt.	50 ℔. tob.
Half ditto	460 " " -	French silver crowns,	60 " "
Moidore	348 " " -	Spanish milled, Pieces of Eight,	60 " "
English Guinea,	272 " " -	Other good coined Spanish silver per ounce,	68 " "
French ditto,	268 " " -		
Spanish Pistoles, not lighter than 4 dwt, 6 gr.	216 " " -		
French milled Pistoles,	212 " " -		
Arabian Chequins,	108 " " -		

After the revolution, the Act of 1781 declared "what foreign gold and silver coin shall be deemed the current money of the State;" and with the law is published a table of coins in circulation in the province, and whose respective values are fixed. This foreign currency continued to be legalized by successive acts until the year 1812, when an act was passed recognizing the coins struck by the United States, and the values assigned to foreign ones by Congress.

Mr. Crosby says, in 1783, a goldsmith of Annapolis, Maryland, issued silver tokens as a speculative venture of his own. They consisted of shillings, sixpences and threepences, and are all now very rare, the two smaller pieces especially so. The shilling, first to be described, is supposed to be unique.

Obverse:—EQUAL TO ONE SHI., above is a branch, below two hands clasped. Legend:—I. CHALMERS, ANNAPOLIS, 1783. Border:—Finely milled. Reverse: Device,—A chain of twelve rings, linked regularly, another ring interlinked with the three lower rings, the middle one supporting a staff with liberty-cap, above which is an eye; eleven of the rings enclose each a mullet, and at each side of the liberty-cap is a mullet. Border:—Beaded, size, 13.

The centre of the obverse is very indistinct, but faintly shows the inscription, in three lines, "EQUAL TO ONE SHI." The following are descriptions of the more common varieties of these tokens: Obverse:—Device,—Two hands clasped, within a wreath. Legend:—I. CHALMERS, ANNAPOLIS. Reverse:—Device,—Within a beaded and lined circle is a field, divided by a horizontal bar. On the superior portion of the field is a serpent, and on the inferior, two doves holding in their beaks a branch. Legend:—ONE SHILLING, 1783. Borders and edge:—Milled. Size, 14½; weight, 57 grains.

There are two dies of this reverse, not greatly differing; in the more common the bar lies between the N and N, and in the rarer variety, between N and I; the character following "ONE" also differs from that of the other, being here a group of eight points. The Chalmers sixpence has on the Obverse:—Device,—A mullet, within a wreath. Legend:—I. CHALMERS, ANNAPOLIS. Reverse:—Device,—A cross, with hands clasped on the centre, two arms terminating in crescents and two in stars. In each angle of the cross is a leaf. Legend:—I. C. SIX PENCE, 1783. Borders and edge: Milled. Size, 11; weight, 28 grains. We find, also, two dies of this reverse, differing principally in the size of the letters, but only a single die of either of the obverses. The Chalmers Threepence—Obverse:—Device,—Two hands clasped. Legend:—I. CHALMERS, ANNAP[s]. * Reverse:—Device,—A branch encircled by a wreath. Legend:—THREE PENCE, 1783. Borders and edge:—Milled; size, 8; weight, 12 grains. It may be that the edges were not intentionally milled, and that this appearance arises from the manner of cutting the planchets. Dr. John David Schöff, who travelled in this country in 1783 and 1784, gives the following account of the Chalmers coinage:

"In the United States, Annapolis has the honor of having furnished the first silver money for small change. A goldsmith of this place coins on his own account, though with the consent of the government. After the depreciation of the paper money, it became customary and necessary, throughout America, to cut the Spanish dollars in two, four and more pieces for change. This dividing became soon a profitable business in the hands of expert cutters, who knew how to cut five quarters, or nine and ten eighths out of a round dollar, so that shortly every one refused to take this kind of money otherwise than by weight, or at discretion. To get over this embarrassment the said goldsmith assists in getting these angular pieces out of circulation, by taking them in exchange, with a considerable advantage to himself, for pieces of his own coinage."

On the 4th of July, 1790, Mr. Standish Barry, a silversmith, issued in Baltimore, a silver token, known as "The Baltimore Town threepence."

On the obverse side the device is,—A head, facing left, within a plain circle. Legend:—BALTIMORE TOWN. July · 4 · 90 · Reverse:—Inscription, THREE PENCE, within a plain circle. Legend: STANDISH · BARRY · entwined in a beaded network. Border and edge, Milled; size, 9; weight, 13 grains.[1]

The first legal mention made of a paper currency in Maryland, is in 1731. The legislature contemplated the issue of £30,000 in paper, "to ease the inhabitants of the province," provided the act was sanctioned by Lord Baltimore; but doubting the propriety of this new measure, he withheld his approval, and the "bills of credit," as they were called, were not issued. In the following year, however, the Lower House of Assembly, in their message to the Upper House, "being of opinion that a paper currency would contribute to retrieve the trade of the province, and to remove many of the difficulties under which the people labor," agreed that a bill should be brought in for the purpose. Nothing was done, however, until April, 1733, when an act was passed authorizing the issue and making current £90,000 in bills of credit, redeemable in thirty-one years, which was carried into effect; these laws wisely providing a specific mode of redemption for every issue, instances of which will be seen in the following history.

The excessive production of tobacco continued to give trouble. In 1663, the King of England called the attention of Maryland, Virginia and North Carolina to the subject of this staple, which partly from over-production, and partly from deterioration of the standard, had so fallen in price as scarcely to pay for the clothing that the colonists imported. The home government had frequently urged upon the colonies the importance of limiting the growth of tobacco, but without effect. Fears of a famine had as early as 1639, induced the passage of an act compelling every grower of tobacco to plant and cultivate two acres of corn for each member of his

[1] Crosby, p. 328, etc.

household; yet notwithstanding this, and other legislation, scarcity was often apprehended and sometimes felt. It was seen that in this matter the three tobacco-growing colonies must act together, or no good would be effected; and in 1666, the Governor of Maryland appointed Philip Calvert and other commissioners on the part of Maryland to treat with commissioners from Virginia and North Carolina about a plan for checking the production of tobacco. The commissioners met at James city in July, and there entered into an agreement that no tobacco should be planted in either colony for one whole year, and that the respective assemblies should enforce the agreement by suitable legislation. The Legislature of Maryland passed an act for the purpose; but the Lord Proprietary, considering the great inconvenience which would result to the poorer planters, and the serious loss to the revenues of the crown, refused his assent to the act. When this veto was known in Virginia, which was not until October, 1667, they sent a memorial to the king complaining of the conduct of Lord Baltimore, but upon his lordship's explanation of his reasons, the complaint was dismissed.

Philip Calvert, who had conducted the affairs of the province with wisdom and firmness, was superseded in the latter part of 1661 by his nephew, Charles Calvert, son of the proprietary, who held the office of governor until the death of his father in 1675. During his administration he did much to increase the prosperity and well-being of the province, and many salutary measures were passed. Court houses and jails were erected; a state-house and prison provided; coroners were appointed in all the counties; the duties of sheriffs were regulated; the publication of marriage was provided for; inducements held out to farmers to raise English grain; roads and highways were made; ferries established; harbors improved; magazines constructed; rules established for the conveyance of lands, for the protection of orphans' estates, and for regulating the relations between masters and slaves.

As a tribute of gratitude, the assembly ordered a levy of twenty-five pounds of tobacco on every taxable, to be raised annually for Governor Calvert's personal use, which was changed in 1674 to a duty of two shillings per hogshead on all tobacco exported, and given to him for life.

On the 30th of November, 1675, died Cæcilius Calvert, second Lord Baltimore, the founder of Maryland, leaving behind him endearing memories in the affection of his people, and an illustrious name in history as a benefactor of mankind. Throughout all his proprietorship the language and transactions of a body that was far removed from servility, the Assembly of Maryland, abound with attestations of the excellence of his administration. As early as 1640, they declared themselves "thankful to almighty God for the benefits they had received since their colony was first brought here and planted at his lordship's great charge and expense, and continued by his care and industry; and they desire that this may be preserved forever amongst their records as a memorial to all posterity of their thankfulness and fidelity."

And in the "Act for granting one Subsidy," passed in 1642, they set forth in the preamble the motives of that act, by which every inhabitant of the province, female children under twelve excepted, granted to the proprietary fifteen pounds of tobacco per poll, as some compensation for his heavy charges in the settlement of the province. These expenditures, for the two first years alone, and before he received any return, are estimated by Chalmers as not less than £40,000 sterling, for the transportation of colonists and the necessary provisions and stores.

Again in the Act of 1671, Chapter XI., granting the tobacco duty, the two houses of assembly declare that they do it from a sense of "all imaginable gratitude for the great care and favor expressed by his lordship to the people of the province in the unwearied care which his lordship had shewn, and the vast charge and expense he was put to from the time of their first seating unto this instant, to preserve them in the enjoyment of their lives, liberties, and the increase and improvement of their estates and fortunes."

These were no idle words. And certainly if wisdom, justice and clemency; if unselfishness, generosity, and truly paternal care; if a philanthropy which, instead of disturbing others, carried out its benevolent plans at its own cost and risk, and a liberality which exemplified in practice the most generous thoughts of the noblest minds--if these be singular virtues in a ruler, then had the Marylanders of that day reason to feel boundless gratitude and affection to Cæcilius Calvert, and their descendants to cherish his memory.

Charles Calvert, after assuming the titles and estates of his father in the province, meant to return to England; but before doing so, he convened the assembly on May 16, 1676, for the purpose of repealing certain laws, reviving others, and ascertaining what laws were actually in force. The code was revised, the act of toleration confirmed, and after appointing Thomas Notley to act as deputy governor in the name of his infant son, Cecil Calvert, Lord Baltimore returned to England in the same year.

Soon after his arrival, he found a singular complaint preferred against his government. A certain clergyman of the English church, the Rev. Mr. Yeo, had felt the want of an established ministry with its tithes and glebes, its authority and perquisites, to be a grievance; and had written from Patuxent, to the Archbishop of Canterbury, a frightful account of the spiritual condition of the province. "The province of Maryland," he writes, "is in a deplorable condition for want of an established ministry. Here are ten or twelve counties, and in them at least 20,000 souls, and but three Protestant ministers of the Church of England. The priests are provided for, and the Quakers take care of those that are speakers, but no care is taken to build up churches in the Protestant religion. The Lord's day is profaned. Religion is despised, and all notorious vices are committed; so that it is become a Sodom of uncleanness and a pest-house of iniquity. As the Lord Baltimore is lately gone for England, I have made bold to address this to your Grace, to beg that your Grace would be pleased to solicit him for some established support for a Protestant ministry."

The reverend gentleman's zeal doubtless outran his charity in this gloomy picture of affairs spiritual in the province, but he probably thought it important to make a strong impression on the archbishop. The matter of church endowment in Maryland was soon after agitated in the Privy Council, and was resisted by the proprietary on the 19th of July, 1677, who showed the council the Act of 1649, confirmed in 1676, declaring,—

"That for the encouragement of all such persons as were desirous and willing to adventure and transport themselfes and families into the Province of Maryland, a law was there made by the advice and consent of the delegates of the Freemen concerning Religion, wherein a Tolleration is given to all persons beleeving in Jesus Christ freely to exercise theire Religion, and that no person of what judgement soever, beleeving as aforesaid, should at any time be molested, or discountenanced for, or in respect of his Religion, or in the free exercise thereof, and that no one should be compelled to the beliefe or exercise of any other against his consent, upon this act the greatest part of the people and inhabitants now in Mary Land have settled themselfes and families there, and for these many yeares this tolleration and liberty has beene knowne and continued in the government of that Province. That those persons of the Church of England there, who at any time have encouraged any Ministers to come over into that Province have had severall sent unto them, as at this time there are residing there foure that the Lord Baltimore knows of, who have Plantations & settled beings of their owne, and those that have not any such beings are maintained by a voluntary contribution of those of theire owne perswasion, as others of the Presbiterians, Independents, Anabaptists, Quakers & Romish Church are.

"That in every County in the Province of Mary Land there are a sufficient number of Churches and howses called meeting howses for the people there, and these have beene built and are still kept in good repaire by a free and voluntary contribution of all such as frequent the said Churches and meeting howses.

"That the lawes of that Province have beene ever made by the advise and Consent of the Freemen by their delegates assembled as well as by the Proprietor and his Councell, and without the consent of all these no Law there has beene made; The greatest part of the Inhabitants of that Province (three of foure at least) do consist of Presbiterians, Independents, Anabaptists, and Quakers, those of the Church of England as well as those of Romish being the fewest, so that it will be a most difficult task to draw such persons to consent unto a Law which shall compell them to maintaine Ministers of a contrary perswasion to themselfes, they haveing already an assureance by the act for Religion, that they shall have all Freedom in point of Religion and divine worshipp, and no penalties or payments imposed upon them in that particular, That in Carolina, New Jersey & Rhode Island the Inhabitants for the peopleing of those places have had and still have the same Tolleration that those in Mary Land have."[1]

Notwithstanding the satisfactory character of this answer, the council declared that there should be some maintenance for the clergy of the church, "and that he should propose some means for the support of a competent number," to which these exemplary ministers of Charles II. joined an edifying injunction that "the laws against vice should be punctually executed."[2]

[1] Bundle, B. T. Md., I., B. B., p. 3, in Public Record Office, London.

[2] Chalmers.

There is other evidence than that of Lord Baltimore to show that on the part of some of the Protestant laity there was a disposition to make liberal provisions for the support of the clergy. In January, 1675, Mr. Jeremiah Eaton, devised by will his estate of Stokely Manor, containing 550 acres, to the first Protestant minister who should settle in Baltimore county, and to his successors. This liberal bequest induced Mr. Yeo, the archbishop's correspondent, to remove in 1682 from Calvert to Baltimore county, where he was the first resident minister of any denomination of whom we have any notice. In 1676, Robert Cadger conveyed his personal estate to the mayor and municipal government of the city of St. Mary's, in trust "for the maintenance of a Protestant ministry from time to time among the inhabitants of St. George's and Poplar Hill hundred."[1]

Another complaint was laid against Lord Baltimore by the authorities of Virginia, to the effect that his government did not protect its frontiers against the incursions of the Indians. In answer to this charge, he informed the committee of plantations that the peace with the Indians had continued for twenty years and was confirmed annually; and that in all his treaties with them Virginia was especially included. In confirmation of this he produced copies of his commissions and instructions to the governor and council, with other corroborative documents; and the committee reported to the king that "due care had been taken by him to include Virginia; but that in *her* alliances, she had not been equally careful of the interests of Maryland."

Virginia further complained that the proprietary had endeavored to compel vessels navigating the Potomac to enter his ports, that he might collect the anchorage duties; but this proved as frivolous as the former, "for the words and the intention of his charter extended the boundaries of the province, and consequently its jurisdiction, to the southern margin of the river; and such vessels must, therefore, have been necessarily subject to its laws."[2]

Having silenced all complaints for the present, Lord Baltimore returned to Maryland in February, 1680, and resumed the personal management of his government. In order, probably, "to comply with the pious instructions of the "Cabals," an Act was passed "for speedy suppression of crimes, and limiting punishments, when prosecuted in the county courts." A law had already been enacted "for keeping holy the Lord's day." To remove the inconveniences which the province had heretofore suffered from the depreciation of tobacco, laws were enacted for "promoting tillage and raising provisions for exportation." Acts were also passed "restraining the export of leather and hides," for "the support of tanners and shoemakers;" for "encouraging the making of linen and woollen cloth," and "for the advancement of trade." A great number of ports were erected where merchants were to reside, and commerce was to be carried on; and to crown these

[1] Bacon.

[2] Chalmers, p. 36?.

endeavors to promote the interests of the province the assembly, in the year 1682, "to demonstrate its gratitude, duty and affection to the proprietary, prayed his acceptance of 100,000 lb., of tobacco, to be levied this present year," for which the proprietary tendered his thanks, but replied that "considering the great charge of the province, he did not think fit to accept thereof."[1] This was the act of a man familiar with a court where the leading spirits were a Buckingham, an Ashley, a Danby and a Lauderdale, and where the monarch himself was a pensioner of France.

Yet, despite the professed or real attachment of his colonists, events were ripening that threatened Baltimore's ruin and the lasting disgrace of the colony. The spirit that Claiborne, Ingle and Fendall had aroused, was again awaking. The infamous "Popish plot" had provoked the worst passions of bigotry and fanaticism in England, and its effects had crossed the Atlantic and were agitating men's spirits, while the crafty and unscrupulous saw hopes of profit in the coming storm, and inflamed the popular mind with suspicion and hatred of the Catholics. Fendall, who had overthrown the government of Cromwell, and tried to overthrow that of the proprietary, now abused the lenity which had unwisely been shown him, to foment new disturbances. He held out tempting prospects of plunder and aggrandizement to those like-minded with himself, and was assisted in his schemes by one John Coode, "a wretch with no common share of villainy."[2] The plot, however, failed; Fendall was tried in 1681 for seditious practices, and instead of the gallows which he richly deserved, was punished by fine and banishment, while Coode was acquitted.

Of these troubles Lord Baltimore gives an account in the following letter, dated July 19, 1681, to the Earl of Anglesea, president of the privy council:

"My Noble Good Lord,

"I should not presume to offer your Lordshipp the trouble of perusing these lines, did I not hold my selfe obliged to lett your Lordshipp understand in short the present state and condition both of Virginia and Maryland in relation to some Northern Indians, that are lately come downe into both colonies, who have committed outrages and murders in both governments. These Northern Indians pretend no desyne of mischiefe towards the English, but tell us they're resolv'd to destroy all our neighbouring Indians, whome when they're subdued conquered & destroyed, I beleeve their next desyne will be against the Inhabitants of both these colonies, whose stocks of Cattle and hoggs they already make bold with, and especially in Virginia, where these savages kill and destroy hoggs and Cattle afore the faces of the Owners of them, and if the English make any opposition, they're imediately fir'd at by these Indian villians, and upon the like occasion were five men and a woman killed about a month since in Mary Land. Upon these disturbances given us by these heathen Rogues some evill ill disposed spirits have been tampering to stirr up the Inhabitants of Mary Land and those of the North part of Virginia, to meeting, of which I haveing notice, as alsoe being certainly inform'd who were the chiefe contrivers and carriers on of the designe, I immediately sent orders for the apprehending one Josias Fendall and John Coade two rank Baconists; the first of these was some

[1] Chalmers, p. 375.

[2] Hawks, p. 54.

twenty yeares since my Father's Lieut. Governor here, but upon his breach of Trust and beginning a Rebellion here he scaped the gallows very narrowly; since then and in the time of Bacon's Rebellion in Virginia, it was expected every day when he would have fallen in with him, and had there not by the vigilancy care and resolution of my Lieut. Tho: Notley now deceased, been a stop putt to the Rebellion here in Bacon's time, this Fendall had certainly joyned with Bacon, and then Mary Land had been imbroiled and ruined as Virginia was. The encouragement this fellow had now to lay this wicked designe, was the hopes and confidence he had that upon his Majesties meeting his Parliament, there would be such differences, as would occation civill warrs and that then there would be no establisht laws in England and so he and his crew might possess them selves here and in Virginia of what Estates they pleased. This Fendall has a great influence on and interest in most of the rascalls in the North part of Virginia, where he was for some time when he was forced to absent him selfe from Maryland, and at that time I gave notice to Sir Henry Chicheley to sett eyes over him, the same notice I gave to Coll Nicholas Spencer Secretary of Virginia, but I feare the latter either through want of resolution or loyalty did not prevent (what he might) the seditious practises of this Rebell, and I may the more boldly affirm this, since formerly and but few days afore my apprehending this fellow, he had openly entertained and cherist this Rascall in his house, which gives me cause to be confident that he has encouraged Fendall in his designes against Mary Land forgetting or (as I suppose) not considering that a defection in my government may raise an other Bacon in Virginia the people there being as ripe and readdy for an other Rebellion as ever they were, and I know not but one of the two, I've caused to be apprehended might have served their own turne. My Lord if his Majtie please not to send in some Loyall active person to command under Sir Henry Chicheley (who is now super anuated) very speedily, the government of Virginia will be in danger, I pray God Secretary Spencer be owner of so much loyalty, as to deserve the trust and dignity now confered on him, had I the honor to be one houre with your Lordshipp I could give your Lordshipp satisfaction in some things, relating to His Majties service, which I dare not committ to paper in this juncture. I therefore humbly begg your Lordshipp's pardon for breaking in upon you with this fresh trouble, afore I've expiated the rudenesse of my former address as with some evidence of my being, as by infinitt obligations, I am

My Good Lord, Your Lordshipp's most faithfull, obedient & humble servant

"BALTEMORE.

"19th July 1681.

"I humbly beg that the Countesse of Anglesey will permitt the tender of mine and wifes' most humble services to her." [1]

The commander of a ship, who arrived in England from Maryland in October, 1681, upon examination before the Committee of Plantations, stated in relation to the troubles of Maryland, "that there were thirty Protestants to one Papist, between whom there was no quarrel; but that two persons had been apprehended for saying that, were the parliament dissolved, Baltimore should not be quiet in Maryland." [2]

The hydra of revolt derived a sort of immortality from anti-Catholic rancour; and though at first repeatedly struck down, it ever rose with redoubled vigor, and showed its gratitude for the liberality which had been extended to numberless dissenters, by a new and more ruthless onset. Fendall and Coode

[1] Bundle, B. T. Md., I., B. B., p. 22, in Public Record Office, London.

[2] Chalmers, p. 376.

were at this period "the evil geniuses of the colony," others like them, were always ready to foment disaffection, and the banks of the Severn, where the Puritans had been allowed to settle, became the hot-bed of sedition. The "late troubles in Maryland," and his "partiality to papists," formed the prominent subjects of fresh complaints against the proprietary in England. These complaints received from those in authority, countenance to which they were not entitled, as it would seem they were but part of a preconcerted scheme "to root out the abominations of Popery and prelacy," to foster a "thorough godly reformation," and to effect, if possible, the "Protestant revolution." It was in vain the proprietary stated as before, that the governors, from first to last, had sworn to molest no man in the exercise of his religion and to make no distinctions on account of creed, and that the laws of the province gave equal encouragement to men of every sect, without favoring any. He stated that he had endeavored to divide the offices of his government among Protestants and Roman Catholics with as much equality as their different abilities would permit; and that he had given almost the whole command of the militia to the former, who were also entrusted with the care of the arms and military stores.[1] He also appealed to facts, as conclusive evidence of the untruth of the charges brought against him, and in justification of his assertions he submitted, among other evidence, the following "declaration," signed by twenty-five of the leading members of the Church of England in the province of Maryland, in testimony of his impartiality in administering the government of the province to Protestants as well as Roman Catholics:

"LORD BALTEMORE'S DECLARATION.

"*Maryland, 13th May, 1682.*

"To all Christian people to whom these presents shall come greeting, in our Lord God Everlasting: Whereas, through the envy, malice and hatred of some particular turbulent, factious spirits, not only disaffected to this, but also dissatisfied with, uneasie under and averse to, all manner of Rule and government, severall ill reports and foul aspersions have of late been cast upon the government of this Province, under the Right Hon^bl^. Charles, Lord Baltimore, Lord and Proprietor thereof, representing his Lordshipp as violent against the Protestants here inhabiting, concerning and entertaining groundless jealouses against them, and upon all occasions shewing partiality and favour to those of the Popish persuasion, to the great discouragement and oppression of others his majestie's Protestant subjects, who are said (meerely upon the account of their religion) to be kept under and at a distance from all possibility of advancement to any Place of honor or profitt within the Province, and to render the same more odious and contemptible to the world, such reports have not only been scattered abroad amongst severall persons, from one to another, But (as we have seen and heard) through the instigation, means and procurement (as we conceive) of the Authors themselves, have, for the more generall contagion, been exposed to Publick view in Print, thereby to take the deeper impression on the minds of the vulgar, not only to the derogation of his Lordshipp's honor, but also of very ill consequence to the whole Province, in general by terrifying and preventing thereby others his Majestie's loving subjects from resorting hither to cohabit with us as formerly, for our greater strength and fortification against the Indians, and also for the better cultivating and emprovement of this county, to the great damage, detriment and prejudice of

[1] Chalmers, p. 369.

such his majestie's subjects as are here already resident, both as to their lives and estates by that means. We, therefore, the subscribers, professing the gospell of Jesus Christ, according to the Litturgy of the Church of England, and Protestants against the Doctrine and Practice of the Church of Rome, subjects also to his majestie the King of Great Brittaine, etc., and residents as aforesaid, esteeming ourselves (as indeed we are) every one therein particularly and neerly concerned, hold our selves in conscience and duty obliged by this our impartiall, true and sincere remonstrance or declaration to unfold the naked truth, and to undeceive the minds of those before whose eyes the mist may have been against and to purge his Lordshipp and this government whereof we are, from all those false, scandalous and Malitious aspersions which the venimous beasts of such inveterate, Malignant, turbulent spiritts have cast thereon And, therefore, in the first place, we doe hereby unanimously acknowledge and Publish to the world the generall freedome and priviledge which we and all persons whatsoever, Inhabitants of this Province, of what condition soever, doe enjoy in our lives, liberties and estates under this his Lordshipp's government, according to the grand privileges of Magna Charta, as effectually and in as full and ample manner to all Intents and purposes, as any of his Majesties subjects within any Part of his Majesties Dominions whatsoever, with the free and publick exercise and enjoyment of our religion whatsoever it be, whether Protestant or other professing the name of Jesus, according to an Act of Assembly of this Province in that case made and provided, and to which wee and the whole Province in generall, either by ourselves or our representatives in a generall Assembly, have given our assent. We doe also declare and make known that, besides our owne experience, we have observed his Lordshipp's favours impartially distributed, and places of honor, trust and profitt conferred on the most qualified for that purpose and service, without any respect or regard had to the Religion of the participants, of which generally and for the most part it hath so happened that the Protestants have been the greatest number, The halfe of his Lordshipp's Councill neerest to his Person are Protestants, his late governor Thomas Notley, Esq're, and Benjamin Roger, Esq're, of his Councill, also late deceased, both Protestants, The major part of his Lordshipp's commissioners, or justices of the Peace, in each respective County within this Province Protestants, Those likewise that have the charge of the Militia of this Province generally, or for the most Part Protestants, vizt., Coll: Thomas Tailler, Coll: Henry Coursey, Coll: William Steevens, Coll: William Berges, Coll: William Colebourne, Coll: Philœmon Lloyd, Coll: George Wells, Coll: Henry Jowles and Coll: William Chandler, nine Colonells or principal officers of the militia, all Protestants, and but Coll: William Calvert, Coll: Vincent Lowe and Coll: Henry Darnall (when present), onely three of the Romish perswasion, Colonells or principall officers of the militia, within or belonging to the Province, in like manner all other officers and places of honor or profitt within this Province, Civill or Military, impartially and equally (if not for the most part on Protestants) conferred. This not only in vindication of his Lordshipp's honor, and this his government, but also for the Publick Interest of the Province therein concerned, and to discharge a good conscience wee, for ourselves and in the behalfe of severall others whom we know (if not the whole Province in generall), every particular individuall person thereof, who we are confident and doe verily believe would (if requested) readily doe the same, have hereunto subscribed our name, and are and shall be ready further to attest and confirme the same with our Oathes. And for the greater ratification hereof, we have besides our subscriptions, humbly suplicated and obtained his lordship's Command to his Chancellor of this Province to affix hereunto the great seale of this his Lordship's Province, to the end that the greater faith and credit may be given thereunto. Dated at the City of St. Marie's, in Maryland, the thirteenth day of May, Anno Domini, one Thousand six hundred eighty and two.

"Thos. Tailler, Phi. Lloyd, William Hatton, Bar[th]. Ennalls, Will. Stevens, Jo. Rousby, Hen. Smith, Nathaniell Jarrett, W[m]. Digges, Kenelm Cheseldyn, Hen. Trippe, James Dashiell, Tho. Burford, Richard Ladd, John Hynson, Roger Wolford (Attorney Generall), Will. Burges, J. Waterton, John Brooke, Josh. Wickes, John Stone, John Llewellin, Jona. Sibery, James Mills, George Wells.[1]

"*Copia vera.*"

Notwithstanding this complete vindication of his administration against the charges brought, the ministry ordered that all offices in Maryland should be put into Protestant hands.

A short time after this, Lord Baltimore was accused of obstructing the revenue officers in the collection of the duties imposed by parliament. In reply, he did not, as he might have done, deny the lawfulness of these duties, as violating his charter, but used bitter words against the collectors, whom he called "as great knaves to the king, as disturbers of the trade and peace of the province."[2] These charges were investigated, and not being sustained, Lord Baltimore was sharply censured for his erroneous construction of the law, for hindering its execution, and for resisting the restrictions upon the colonial trade. Even the king was irritated, and sent the proprietary the following rebuke on August 16, 1682:

"We are not a little surprised to find that you have obstructed our service, and discouraged our officers in the execution of their duty; and, although by several letters, we have already directed you to be aiding to the collector and officers of our customs in Maryland, and particularly in the due collection of the impositions payable to us by act of parliament, made the 25th of our reign, whereby certain rates were imposed, among which was one penny a pound on tobacco; we are nevertheless informed that instead of your being assisting to our said officers in the due collection thereof, you have hindered and forbidden them to receive the same; and particularly that you have hindered our collector of our customs from receiving the said penny per pound, due for tobacco sent to Ireland, and that you told him that he should not meddle with them, for that he had nothing to do therewith; by means whereof the said ships went away with their cargoes of tobacco, without paying any of the said duties, whereby we are damnified in our customs to the value of £2500 sterling. And although your proceedings above mentioned, in the obstruction of our officers, and contempt for our laws, are of such a nature as that we might justly direct a writ of *quo-warranto* to be issued out, we have, nevertheless, out of our great clemency, thought fit for the present, only to require the commissioners of our customs to charge you with the payment of the said sum, and to cause a demand to be made from you for the same. And we do strictly command you, for the future, to take care that all our laws relating to the trade of our plantations be duly observed and executed; and that all encouragement and assistance be given to the officers of our customs under your government."

[1] Public Record Office, B. T. Md., i., B. C., p. 1.

[2] Between the years 1684 and 1689, two collectors of the customs were slain in the province. Christopher Rousby was killed by Col. Talbot, one of the council, who escaped to Virginia, where he was tried and convicted, but afterwards pardoned by James II. Another by the name of Payne was murdered by the servants of Mr. Sewell, one of the council, during the troubles. The assassins also escaped to Virginia, but were caught, brought back to Maryland, and convicted, and one of them executed. *Chalmers*, p. 377.

Baltimore's answer to the complaints made to the British government on account of these matters, will be found at the end of this chapter.

We have seen that the Susquehannough Indians began hostilities against the whites from the time that the latter undertook to check their incursions against the Yoamacoes and the friendly tribes of Piscataway and Patuxent. In this desultory warfare the Indians got the worst; and in 1652, at the earnest desire of the Susquehannoughs, a treaty of peace was concluded on all sides. By this time this powerful and warlike tribe had been reduced to 700 warriors, but with the assistance of the colonists they still successfully resisted their ancient enemies, the Senecas and Cayugas. But the small-pox broke out among them in 1661, sweeping away more than half their numbers, and they could no longer make head against their foes, and begged the protection of the whites. On the 28th of April, the assembly ordered the governor to raise what force he could for the assistance of the Susquehannoughs "against the Ciniquo [Seneca] or Nayssone Indians that have lately killed some English at Patapsco river."[1]

In 1663, the relations with the Susquehannoughs being unsatisfactory, the governor appointed commissioners to negotiate a treaty with them, which was concluded with "Wastahandow, chief general and councillor of the Susquehannough nation," and in 1666, the following general treaty of peace was concluded with various tribes, which we subjoin in full as a specimen of early colonial diplomacy.

"Articles of Peace and Amity concluded and agreed upon between the Right Honorable Lord and Proprietor of the Province of Maryland and Avalon, Lord Baron of Baltimore, and the Indians of Piscattaway, Anacostanck, Doags, Mikikewomans, Manasguesend, Mattawomans, Chingwanateick, Mangemaick, Port Tobackes, Oacayo, Pangayo, and Choptiko, the 20th day of April, 1666.

"1. The forenamed Indians now ratify and confirm, acknowledge and declare the sole power of constituting and appointing the Emperor of Piscattaway to be and remain in the Right Honorable Cæcilius, Lord and Proprietor of this Province, and his heirs, Lords and Proprietaries of this Province, and do desire the Governor, with what convenient speed he can, to appoint an Emperor in the place of Wahacasso the Second, late deceased.

"2. If an Indian kill an Englishman, he shall die for it.

"3. Forasmuch as the English cannot easily distinguish one Indian from another, that no Indian shall come into any English plantation painted; and that all the Indians shall be bound to call aloud before they come within three hundred paces of any Englishman's clear ground, and lay down their arms, whither gun, bow and arrows, or any other weapon, for any Englishman that shall appear upon his call to take up; and in case that any one appear, he shall there leave his said arms if he come nearer, and that afterwards he shall by calling aloud endeavor to give notice to the English of his nearer approach; and if any Englishman shall kill any Indian that shall come unpainted and give such notice and deliver up his arms as aforesaid, he shall die for it, as well as an Indian that kills an Englishman; and in case the English and Indians meet accidentally in the woods every Indian shall be bound immediately to throw down his arms upon call; and in case any Indian so meeting an Englishman shall refuse to throw down his arms upon call, he shall be deemed as an enemy.

"4. The privilege of hunting, crabbing, fishing, and fowling, shall be preserved to the Indians inviolably.

[1] There was a tribe of Indians at this time, called the Mattawas, inhabiting the lands near Baltimore.

"5. That in case of danger the Governor shall appoint a place to which the Indians of the aforesaid nations shall bring their wives and children to be secured from danger of any foreign Indians; and that in case the men of the aforesaid nations chance to be killed that the women and children shall remain free and not be servants to the English.

"6. That Nicholas Emanson do make the Indians of Mangemaick satisfaction for the damage by him done to their corn, in case George Thompson and John Brown testify that the said Emanson did wilfully throw down the fence about their corn fields.

"7. That the Indians of Mangemaick shall remain upon the place where they now live, and that Mecatahammon son to their last King be King over that people immediately under the protection of the Lord Proprietor of this Province subject to no Indian whatsoever.

"8. That John Roberts and Thomas Morris do pay the Indians of Chingwawateick one hundred and twenty arms-length of Roanoke for the Indian that was slain by them at the head of Port Tobacko Creek in August last.

"9. That every Indian that killeth or stealeth an hog, calf or other beast, or other goods, shall undergo the same punishment that an Englishman doth for the same offence.

"10. That the several nations aforesaid shall continue upon the place where they now live, and that the honorable the Governor be desired to lay out their several bounds as to him in justice shall seem most for the public good, between this and the last of June next ensuing; within which bounds it shall not be lawful for the said Nations to entertain any foreign Indians whatsoever, to live with them without leave from the Lord Proprietary or his Lieutenant Governor here for the time being; and that the said Indians shall not be forced or removed from the said places so to be limited and appointed to them by the Governor as aforesaid, unless the nation or nations, or any particular persons of these nations hereafter to be removed shall signify their willingness to be removed by the consent of their Matchcomicks, to such Commissioners as the Lord Proprietor, or his chief Governor here for the time being, by commission under the great seal of this Province, be authorized to take the same, and license thereupon from his said Lordship or his Governor here, to remove, had and obtained.

"11. That the aforesaid Nations shall, from and after the first of December next ensuing, fence in their cornfields from hogs and cattle of the English; and if any Englishman wilfully throw down any of their fences they shall make the Indians full satisfaction for their damage.

"12. In case any servants or slaves run away from their masters and come to any of the Indian Towns aforesaid that the said Indians shall apprehend them and bring them to the next English plantation to be conveyed to their masters; and if any Indians assist or convey any such fugitive out of the Province that he shall make the respective master or masters of such servant or servants such satisfaction as an Englishman ought to do in the like case.

"13. That all great men here present do immediately sign these articles; and that the great men of these Towns that were here and are returned, or otherwise, did not come but by their proxies, shall come to the Governor when he comes to Piscattaway to make the Emperor, and sign the peace here concluded, or else to be deemed and declared enemies, as well to the English as to the Indians that do join with the Lord Proprietor in this place.

"14. That the said nations shall not make any new peace with our enemies, and shall not make any new war without consent of the Right honorable the Lord Proprietor or by his chief Governor here.

"That from this day forward there be an inviolable peace and amity between the Right honorable the Lord Proprietor of this Province and the Indians aforenamed upon the articles before in this treaty agreed upon, to the world's end to endure."

By 1673, the Susquehannoughs had been reduced by disease and warfare to about three hundred warriors, and in the year following, they were terribly defeated by the Senecas, and driven from their homes at the head of the Chesapeake to the territory formerly occupied by the Piscataways near the Maryland and Virginia boundary, the latter tribe having been removed by the assembly to lands on the Potomac near the head of navigation. Here they established themselves in an old Indian fortification. Hither the Senecas pursued them, and did some damage to the plantations on both sides of the river.

In the summer of 1675, a white man was found lying, covered with wounds, at the door of his house near Stafford, Virginia, and the corpse of a friendly Indian by his side. Before dying, he declared that Indians had been the murderers. Colonel Mason and Captain Brent at once collected a party of militia and followed the trail up the Potomac, and across that river into Maryland. Here the party divided: the detachment under Brent found a wigwam belonging to some of the Doage tribe, surrounded it, and summoned the inmates to come forth. A chief obeyed, and was at once shot dead by Brent. The others within rushed forth, and all, ten in number, were shot down, only a boy being spared. In the meantime Mason's party had also found and surrounded a wigwam, and as the Indians came out to his summons, they were fired on and fourteen killed, the firing only ceasing when a chief running up to Mason called out that they were Susquehannoughs and friends. The survivors denied all knowledge of the murder, which they said had been done by a marauding band of Senecas.

Shortly after this several other murders were committed on both sides of the river, and terror and excitement prevailed. Disbelieving the innocence of the Susquehannoughs, or desirous of ridding themselves of their neighborhood, the Marylanders and Virginians organized a joint attack upon their fortress; the Virginia troops being led by Colonel John Washington (great grandfather of General George Washington), Colonel Mason, and Major Alderton; and the Marylanders by Major Thomas Trueman, one of the Governor's council. The Maryland forces were assisted by Piscataway, Chaptico, Matawoman, Pamunky, and Nansemy Indians. On Sunday morning, September 25th, 1675, the Maryland troops appeared before the fort, summoned the chiefs to a parley, and charged them with the recent murders, which they solemnly denied, laying the blame on the Senecas. These, they said, were now near the head of the Patapsco, and they offered guides for their pursuit. During the conference the Virginians had joined the Marylanders, and their commanders reiterated the charges, which the Indians persisted in denying, insisting that they were friends, and as proof of their assertions showing a silver medal with a black and yellow ribbon—the Baltimore colors—and certain papers which had been given them by Governor Calvert as a safe-conduct and pledge of amity. Trueman, it is said, professed himself satisfied of their innocence, and promised that no harm should befall them.

On the following morning, however, Captain Allen, who had been sent to one of the scenes of recent murder, returned, bringing with him the bodies of the victims, and arrived at the camp while the conference was being held with the chiefs. The passions of the militiamen were roused to fury by the sight of the mangled bodies, and the Virginia officers demanded the instant execution of the chiefs; Colonel Washington, according to the testimony of a witness, being particularly furious, shouting: "What! should we keep them any longer? Let us knock them on the head." Despite the reluctance of Trueman, five of the chiefs were bound, led away and tomahawked, one only being spared. The remainder in the fort bravely defended themselves for six weeks; after which time, their provisions giving out, they made their escape by night.

For his breach of faith, Major Trueman was cited before the bar of the Lower House, and Robert Carville, attorney general, Messrs. Burgess, Cheseldyn, Stephens, and others, brought in articles of impeachment against him, addressed to the proprietary, and supported by affidavits. These charge, First, that he caused the chiefs to be seized and executed, after they had come out under assurance of safety, and had shown the paper and medal as evidence of their being friends to Maryland. Secondly, that he caused the execution without previously obtaining the proprietary's authority. Thirdly, that he failed to procure a signed declaration of the Virginia officers that the execution was by their advice and consent. They, therefore, conclude that Trueman had broken his commission and instructions, and pray his lordship and the Upper House "to take such order with the said Major Thomas Trueman as may be just and reasonable."

These articles and depositions being laid before the Upper House, Trueman was brought to trial on May 27, 1676, before the Lord Proprietary, Colonel Samuel Chew, chancellor and secretary, and Colonels Wharton and Tailler, sitting as a court of impeachment; and it was voted *nemine contradicente* that the accused was guilty of the first article of impeachment; and the Upper House was requested to send a message to the Lower House, desiring them to draw a bill of attainder against him. The bill was at once drawn, and sent to the Upper House, which, on the 1st of June, responded by a message saying that the penalties therein prescribed were far too light for "so horrid a crime" and breach of the public faith. That, if Trueman escaped so lightly, the justice and dignity of the province would be brought into contempt, and the Indians set an example of bad faith likely to have disastrous consequences. That, moreover, the assembly will be looked upon as countenancing, rather than abhorring, the acts of Trueman.

To this the Lower House replied that circumstances were shown at the trial that extenuated the conduct of the accused; for instance, "the eager impetuosity of the whole field, as well Marylanders as Virginians, at the sight of the Christians murdered at Mr. Hinson's," the identification of several of the chiefs as the murderers, and the necessity of the act to prevent a mutiny. They, therefore, refused to recede from their former position.

The Upper House, on the 12th, answered that the bill was an attainder only in name; that they never would consent "to inflict a pecuniary punishment upon a person accused of murder by one house and condemned by the other; and that it was against their privileges for the bill to be pressed on them any further. The Lower House unanimously decided that Trueman, though guilty of the charge, was not deserving of death; and the Upper House remaining firm, he escaped his deserved punishment. He was, however, dismissed from the council.

It has been said that the Indians left in the fort after the massacre of the chiefs, defended themselves until their provisions gave out, and then escaped by night. They went with the fires of rage and revenge burning in their hearts, and marked their southward march by a track of devastation and slaughter. At least sixty settlers paid the penalty of that deed of treachery and cruelty. One of them was a servant of Nathaniel Bacon; and this aroused Bacon, a man of bold and adventurous spirit, to apply for a commission to raise and command a force against the Susquehannoughs, the consequences of which were the utter crushing of the tribe, and the revolt which bears Bacon's name in Virginian history. Col. Henry Coursey, one of the council, was appointed in April, 1677, a commissioner to conclude a peace on behalf of Maryland with the Susquehannoughs and other frontier tribes; and in June, of the same year, the Governor of Maryland invited Governor Berkeley to join with Maryland and New York in making a treaty of peace with the Five Nations, for which purpose a congress was to be held at Albany. Berkeley consented; and until commissioners could attend on the part of Virginia, Colonel Coursey was empowered to represent that province at the congress. The Lords of the Committee on Trade and Plantations, sent out in 1677 a series of queries to the various provinces, respecting their internal government, resources, means of defence, &c. From the answers returned, we learn some interesting particulars as to the size and appearance of the capital of the province in that year.

"The principal place or town is called St. Mary's, where the General Assembly and Provincial Court are kept, and whither all ships trading there do in the first place resort. But it can hardly be called a town, it being in length by the water about five miles, and in breadth upwards, toward the land, not above a mile, in all which space, excepting only my own home and buildings wherein the said courts and public offices are kept, there are not above thirty houses, and those at considerable distance from each other; and the buildings (as in all other parts of the province) very mean and little, and generally after the manner of the meanest farm houses in England. Other places we have none that are called, or can be called towns, the people there not affecting to build near each other, but so as to have their houses near the waters, for convenience of trade, and their land on each side of and behind their houses, by which it happens that in most places there are not 50 houses in the space of 30 miles; and for this reason it is they have been hitherto only able to divide this province into counties, without being able to make any subdivisions into parishes or precincts, which is a work not to be effected until it shall please God to increase the number of the people, and so to alter their trade as to make it necessary to build more close and to lie in towns."[1]

[1] *Report of Virginia Commissioners of the Maryland and Virginia Boundary Line*, p. 217.

The grant to Penn in 1680, brought Lord Baltimore and Maryland into contact with a neighbor who was to give them much trouble, and in the end, heavy loss. The origin of the boundary dispute between the two provinces is explained in another chapter of this history. Had the King or the Duke of York listened to the advice of the Council for Trade and Plantations, and the Privy Council, these troubles would not have arisen; but neither was the man to let considerations of justice or public welfare, or the obligations of a contract stand in the way of a personal interest, or outweigh the importunity of a favorite.

In December, 1682, Penn had an interview with Lord Baltimore at the house of Colonel Thomas Tailler, in Anne Arundel county, and an account of the conference, written by Baltimore, is preserved in the record office, London. The parties present besides the principals, were Philip Calvert, Thomas Tailler, Henry Coursey, Henry Darnall, William Digges and William Stevens. His lordship was at first unfavorably affected by Penn's unctuous manner, which he calls "oily." Penn produced the king's letter: Lord Baltimore exhibited his own patent and a transcript of Penn's, and urged: "I have for my northern bounds the 40° of north latitude; which, by your patent, is your southern bounds, as Watkins' point is mine." This could not be denied, but Penn tried to persuade Baltimore to begin his southern line at 37° 51′. Baltimore insisted that "the certain bounds betwixt us must be the 40° of northern latitude, as I have already shown you by my grant," and "my southern bounds being Watkins' point, was so determined by commissioners from his majesty and others from my father." "Mr. Penn," he said, "you did, I remember, once propose to me in England, that you had offers made you of that part of Delaware from his Royal Highness [the Duke of York], which I lay claim to; but you would not, as you then said, accept thereof, because you knew it was mine. The same, I hear, you have now possessed yourself of. I only desire to know what you claim."

To this Penn replied, as if desirous to evade the question: "If the Lord Baltimore please, I desire we may first conclude our former discourse; and then I shall show myself most willing and ready to give all satisfaction I can on that point." Baltimore replied, "I am willing, and have always been ready to conclude the business of the bounds according as my patent directs me." Penn again urged him to begin his southern boundary at the capes of the Chesapeake, which he said were in 37° 51′ north latitude, as if that narrow strip of sandy peninsula were any equivalent for the vast and fertile territory extending about two hundred and fifty miles westward from the Delaware, on which he had set his heart. Nor did he scruple to tempt Lord Baltimore to steal the territory of Virginia, to which he had not, nor professed to have, the shadow of a claim. Baltimore, being neither fool nor knave, was not to be caught by this bait, but stood firm on the line of his patent, the 40°, to be determined by the height of the sun, and that not taken with a "sea quadrant, but a seven-foot sextant." Penn still pressing the matter of the capes, finally whispered: "If the Lord Baltimore would vouchsafe to discourse with me a word or two in private, I should possibly open myself more fully and freely on this point, and frankly acquaint him what I would request of him; and whether the head of the bay fall within his or my bounds, we should, I doubt not, make all things commodious between us; for which reason I would crave a little private discourse with the Lord Baltimore." Baltimore, having nothing to conceal or plot in private, refused this request, though so obsequiously urged, and whatever disclosures might have followed Penn's opening himself, have been lost to the world. The Lord Proprietary asked Penn, "were it your case, would you not stick to a patent so plain as mine is?" and the other answered: "I do not blame the Lord Baltimore: it may be I should do the same as he does;" by which, if he meant that he would object to barter three and three-quarter millions of acres of territory under the fortieth parallel for the chance of filching a narrow strip of sand from Virginia, we may well believe his sincerity. The conference broke up without coming to an agreement.

Another meeting between the two proprietaries was held at New Castle, on the Delaware, May 29, 1683, but with no result; and in a letter dated from Patuxent, June 11, Baltimore says:

> "The favor that I will now beg of you is this,—that if Mr. Penn should move for any further orders or commands in reference to the bounds of the two provinces, you will please, in my behalf, to request I may have time to be heard, in person, and (God willing) I will, April next, most assuredly embark for England, in order to make my just defence, and also that I may there be heard to make out my just claim to those parts on Delaware Bay and river within the degree of forty, northerly latitude, which the said Penn pretends now to hold by writing from his Royal Highness the Duke of York."[1]

Owing to representations made by Penn and others to the king, Baltimore prepared to depart for England, but first he convened the assembly on April 1, 1684, for the purpose of revising the laws of the province. In his opening speech, after "hoping that he would see no more irregular and unparliamentary proceedings in either house," he continues: "'Tis with some difficulty that I must now acquaint you with my resolution of going speedily for England, where the great exigency of my affairs, not my own inclinations nor love for that place doth now draw me; it is to preserve my interest and settle my child in an undisturbed right before I die, that causeth me to resolve upon this voyage.

"Having given you this assurance, I hope you will believe my stay there will be no longer than the procuring a decision of those matters you all know have been the subject of some differences between Mr. Penn and me. Those once happily ended, I shall soon return to this place, where it is my interest as also my inclination and delight to be."

[1] *Report of Virginia Commissioners of the Virginia and Maryland Boundary Line*, 1873.

The assembly, in reply, presented an address drawn up by Colonel William Stevens and John Darnall of the Upper House, and Messrs. Carville, Benford, and Rousby of the Burgesses, in which, after protesting their high gratitude for the "happiness, peace and tranquillity" they have enjoyed under his lordship's government, and in especial for the revision and codification of the laws, they express their loyal willingness to co-operate with him in all measures for the good of the province.

In the proprietary's closing speech we probably have a corroboration of the statement that Quakers were members of the assembly, as he mildly reproves certain members of the Lower House for "rudely presuming to come before his lordship in the Upper House with their hats on," which breach of good manners, though "for dispatch of business" he had passed it over at the time, he hoped would not be repeated. He also reminds them that there is an act for taking the oath of fidelity, and he expects that "every member of the assembly, and this his lordship's great council," shall take that oath before being admitted to his seat.

Having appointed a council or regency of nine councillors, of whom William Joseph was president, to administer the affairs of the province under the nominal governorship of his infant son, Benedict Leonard, Charles Calvert sailed for England never to return.

In the year 1685 occurred the solitary execution for witchcraft which makes a blot upon the judicial records of Maryland.

The belief in witchcraft and sorcery, that strange survival of barbarous ages, was universal at the time; and the cruelties perpetrated under it form a dark page in the history of Christendom on both sides of the Atlantic. It would be expecting too much even from the liberal people of Maryland, to look for their being entirely free from the prevailing superstition. As early as 1654, a case of witch-hanging appears on the records; but it was not done in Maryland, but on the high seas, and became the subject of judicial investigation. In relation to this matter, Henry Corbyne, merchant of London, being under examination before the governor and council, on June 23d, testified that:

"At sea upon his, deponent's, voyage hither in the ship called the *Charity*, of London, Mr. John Bosworth being master, and about a fortnight or three weeks before the ship's arrival in this Province of Maryland, a rumor amongst the seamen was very frequent that one Mary Lee, then aboard the said ship, was a witch, the said seamen confidently affirming the same upon her own deportment and discourse, and then more earnestly than before, importuned the said master, that a trial might be had of her, which he the said master, Mr. Bosworth refused, but resolved (as he expressed) to put her ashore upon the Barmudas, but cross winds prevented, and the ship grew daily more leaky almost to desperation, and the chief seamen often declared their resolution of leaving her, if an opportunity offered itself, which aforesaid reasons put the master upon a consultation with Mr. Chipsham and this deponent, and it was thought fit considering our said condition, to satisfy the seamen, in a way of trying her according to the *usual custom in that kind, whether she were a witch* or not, and endeavored, by way of delay, to have the commanders of other ships aboard; but stormy weather prevented. In the interim two of the seamen apprehended her without order, and searched her, and found some signal mark of a witch upon her, and then calling the master, Mr. Chipsham, and this deponent with others to see it, afterwards made her fast to the capstan betwixt decks, and in the morning the signal was shrunk into her body for the most part. And an examination was thereupon importuned by the seamen, which this deponent was desired to take. Thereupon she confessed, as by her confession appeareth; and upon that, the seamen importuned the said master to put to death (which as it seemed he was unwilling to do) and went into his cabin, but being more vehemently pressed to it, he told them they might do what they would, and went into the cabin, and sometime before they were about that action, he desired the deponent to acquaint them that they should do no more than what they should justify, which they said they would do by laying all their hands in general to the execution of her.

"HENRY CORBYNE."

The next judicial investigation upon the subject of witchcraft was an action for slander, brought on the 6th of October, 1654, by Richard Manship against Peter Godson and wife, for calling his wife "a witch." This suit, however, was compromised by the defendants making an apology and paying costs.

The judgment of Lord Chief Baron, Sir Matthew Hale, who, in 1664, presided at the trial of two women, Amy Dunny and Rose Cullender, convicted of witchcraft at the Suffolk Assizes, and afterwards executed, is believed to have done much to inspire the witchcraft prosecutions in Maryland, as Hale had the reputation of being one of the first jurists of Europe for wisdom and learning.

In 1674, we find the following entry in the journals of the Upper House:

Upper House, February 17th, 1674.

"Came into this house a petition of the Lower House as followeth, viz:

"To the Honorable Charles Calvert, Esq., Lieut. Genl. and Chief Judge of the Provincial Court of the Right Honorable the Lord Proprietary.

"The humble petition of the Deputies and Delegates of the Lower House of Assembly, Humbly sheweth to your Excellency, 'That, whereas John Cowman being arraigned, convicted and condemned upon the statue of the first of King James of England, &c., for witchcraft, conjuration, sorcery or enchantment used upon the body of Elizabethe Goodall, and now lying under that condemnation, and hath humbly implored and beseeched us, your lordship's petitioners, to mediate and intercede in his behalf with your Excellency for a reprieve and stay of execution.

"Your Excellencie's petitioners do therefore, accordingly, in all humble manner, beseech your Excellency that the rigour and severity of the law to which the said condemned malefactor hath miserably exposed himself, may be remitted and relaxed by the exercise of your excellency's mercy and clemencie upon so wretched and miserable an object.

"And your petitioners, as in duty bound, will ever pray, &c.

"*Upper House, Feb. 17th.*

"The Lieutenant General hath considered of the petition here above, and is willing, upon the request of the Lower House, that the condemned malefactor be reprieved and execution stayed, provided that the sheriff of St. Mary's county carry him to the gallows, and that the rope being about his neck, it be there made known to him how much he is beholding to the Lower House of Assembly for mediating and interceding in his behalf with the Lieutenant General, and that he remain at the city of St. Mary's to be employed in such service as the Governor and Council shall think fit, during the pleasure of the Governor."[1]

[1] *Annals of Annapolis*, p. 59.

But the case in which sentence was carried into execution, happened in 1685; and unfortunately we have but a meagre notice of it. The victim was a woman, designated in our sole authority for the fact, by the initials R. F. She was indicted for witchcraft, and the jury, upon trial, brought "a special verdict, finding the facts, and if," etc. "The court took time to consider their evidence till the next term." "Afterwards, the court having advised themselves of, and upon the premises, it is considered by the court that the said R. F. be hanged by the neck till she be dead," which was carried into execution on the 9th of October following. There were several other cases tried in Maryland, one in 1686, and one as late as 1712, in which the verdicts were "not guilty."[1]

The accession of James II., in 1685, might have seemed a favorable event for Lord Baltimore, as the new sovereign was of his own faith; but James's religion, though narrow to the extreme of bigotry, placed no obstacles in the way of his tyrannous craving for absolute power. The sudden uprising under Monmouth was crushed with a severity and punished with a pitiless vindictiveness that have branded his name and those of the ministers of his cruelty with lasting infamy. He wrote to the proprietary on the 26th of June, telling him of the revolt and its failure, and informing him that "the parliament had cheerfully granted him aid, to be levied on the importation of sugars and tobacco," which he hoped would not be burdensome to the inhabitants of Maryland, as the imposition was not laid on the planter, but on the retailers and consumers.

When Baltimore reached England, he found that he had little to hope from either the sympathy or justice of the king, whose designs against the liberties of the English people were extended to the colonies, where the charters formed a hindrance to his tyranny that he was resolved to sweep away. That of Maryland, as the most liberal, was specially obnoxious; and finally, on April 30, 1687, the king in council, alleging that it was of very great and growing prejudice to his affairs in the plantations and to the customs here, that such independent administrations should be maintained without more immediate dependence on the crown, directed the attorney general, Sir Robert Sawyer, "to proceed in prosecution on the writ of *quo warranto* against the Lord Baltimore's and other proprietary charters."

To avert this issue, Lord Baltimore had pleaded "that the administration of his province had been at all times conducted conformably to his charter and to the laws of England; that he never was informed of the pleasure of his prince, but it was always obeyed; that neither he nor his father had done any act which could incur a forfeiture of a patent which they had dearly purchased in adding a considerable province to the empire."[2] Little would this plea have availed him; but before judgment could be obtained on the writ of *quo warranto*, the king himself had been condemned by a mightier tribunal, and had been deprived of his crown and driven from his kingdom by the revolution of 1688.

[1] Kilty's *English Statutes*, p. 190.

[2] Chalmers, p. 371.

BALTIMORE'S ANSWER TO BLAKISTON'S COMPLAINTS, (REFERRED TO ON PAGE 289).

"The Lord Baltemore's answer to the complaints of Mr. Nehemiah Blakiston mentioned in his Letter to the Commissioners of His Maj[ties] customs dated the 20th of Aprill, 1685.

"It plainly appeareth by a Letter from the Governor of Virginia to the Deputies of Mary Land, that the Escape made by George Talbot out of Prison, was occasioned by the Corruption of the Guard and not procured by any Persons of Mary Land as is falsly suggested in the Letter of the said Blakiston, And that as soon as the governr of Virginia had given notice to the Deputies of Maryland of the said Talbotts Escape, Speciall Care was taken immediately by them for his Apprehension as appears by the Hue & Cry sent out into all parts of the Province, besides what other ways and means could be used for the speedy beginning of the said Talbott, who never was Publiquely seen at his own Plantation though the contrary is affirmed by the said Blackiston but always kept himself out in the Mountaing to the Norward, untill at last he resolved to surrender himself to the Deputies of Maryland where now he is under a strong guard to be disposed off as His Majesty shall think fitt.

"His Lordship is very confident Mr. Blakiston has no just cause to complain of his being discountenanced in the Execution of his Place for that he very well knows his Officers dare not presume to offer any Contempt nor shew the Least disrespect either to his Person or Commission nor would they presume to diswade Masters of Vessells from presenting themselves and their certificats to His Ma[ts] Officers, His Lordship having long since ordered that they should apply themselves to the King's Collector as well as to his own, and such was the Practice whilst Mr. Christopher Rousby was living and the Truth of this may be easily known from severall Masters of ships and others now in Town, After Mr. Christopher Rousby was so unfortunately kill'd by George Talbott, the Deputies of Mary Land did presume to appoint Coll Wm. Diggs and Major Nicholas Sewall (both of them Persons of good repute and Estates) to officiate as collectors for his Majes[ties] dues, until another Person could be appointed by the Commissioners of His Maj[ties] customes. And this they thought their Duty to take Care to doe that His Ma[ties] affairs might receive the less prejudice by that wicked Act of the said Talbott and His Lordship doubts not, but the said Persons so appointed will give a just account of their Proceedings to the Commissioners of His Majesty's Customes. His Lordship cannot believe Mr. Blackiston has bin served (as he alleages in His said Letter) with any warrants or has been threatened in that manner as he has writt and therefore humbly beggs that Enquiry may be made of such Persons as are lately come from those Parts of whom the Truth of all this may be easily known, tho' it may very possibly be, that he has been arrested at the suits of his many creditors, it being known to many that he is much in debt and has bin so for many years. Coll. W[m]. Diggs, one of his Lordship's Collectors is known by the severall Eminent merchants here to be a Person of so much Loyalty as that he would not be guilty of those foul things laid to his charge in the said Letter and 'twere to be wish't that M[r]. Blakiston had at all times express't his loyalty to the King as amply, as the said Diggs has always done both in Virginia and Mary Land. It is not possible for any Person that understands the Trade of Mary Land, to believe His Majes[ty] should be prejudiced several thousand pounds, if His Lordship's officers should be as malicious and as wicked as the said Blakiston doth endeavor by his letter to represent them for whilst M[r]. Chr. Rousby lived who understoood the office well and knew as much as any Person how to make the most of it, there never was much above one hundred pounds in one year received by him, for so he often declared to his Lordship, tis strange therefore to his Lordship as also to all Dealers and traders thither that M[r]. Blackiston should find out that it is possible for his Lordship's Officers by any obstraction which he says is given by them to prejudice His Ma[tie] in so high a measure, were they so undutifull and imprudent as to do it in any matter whatsoever.

But Mr. Blackiston takes care to signify that he doubts he shall receive little Tobacco this year, and gives this as a reason, that his Lordship's Officers threatnen the Masters of Vessels that in case they pay not the penny per pound duty to them, they shall be sued and their Vessels siezed, and yet notwithstanding this complaint, His Lordship is ready to make it appear that the said Blackiston had received several thousand pounds of Tobacco, even afore he had writt that Letter and the same had paid away to his Creditors who never had any hopes of being satisfyed by him until he had obtained His Maties commission. This will be proved if required, so that Mr. Blakiston had no other way this year, to make up his accounts with the Commissioners of his Maties Customes but by pretending great obstructions from his Lordship's Officers.

"What Mr. Blackiston has mentioned concerning Major Sewall is as untrue as the rest of his letter, for when the said Sewall had given him notice of severall Irish Vessels he intended to seize, the said Blackiston neglected to assist him in it, and so the said Sewall was forc'd to proceed without him, and after that those Vessells were seized, the said Blackiston persuades Captain Allen to send boats and men to secure them, who, finding his Lordship's Officers on board, were disappointed, which gave great trouble to them both and is the cause of his writing that he was prevented in the discharge of His office, some of the said Vessells were condemned at a speciall Court and the rest more likely to receive the same condemnation as his Lordship has bin inform'd, and a faithfull account will be given. Suddenly by his Lordship's Officers to the Commissioners of His Maties customes, and His Lordship is assured they will be also ready and able to clear themselves in all Particulars when they shall know and understand what Mr. Blakiston has charg'd them with, for his Lordship doth not doubt but it will in the end appear some prejudice and ill will the said Blakiston has been guilty off in His Office and of which his Lordship has given notice to the Commissioners of his Majestie's Customes.

"Therefore his Lordship humbly beggs that the said Blakiston may be required to prosecute his great charge contained in his said letter, that in case Coll. Diggs and the rest of the officers in Mary Land be found guilty they may suffer, but if innocent, as his Lordship hopes and believes they are, that then they may be clear'd.

"C. BALTIMORE."[1]

[1] Public Record Office, *Colonial Papers*, London.

CHAPTER XII.

No MONARCH ever mounted a throne more unfitted for the time, the circumstances, and the people he had to govern, than was James II. when he ascended that of England. A bigoted Catholic, he undertook to rule a people filled with an intense and unreasoning hatred and dread of the Roman church; an unscrupulous despot, he proposed to destroy the liberties of a nation who had written their rubrics anew in his father's blood. Yet so strong was the conservatism of the English people, that he might have held and transmitted the crown had he possessed either the shrewdness of his grandfather or the easy good-nature of his brother; but he seems to have had all the faults of his race without any of their merits, and with blind infatuation labored at his own overthrow. It was an unfortunate necessity that, during this and the following period of agitation, kept the proprietary away from Maryland. There were not many open signs of discontent with his government; but while the Protestant majority were alarmed at the danger which threatened their religion in England, they could not forget that their own immediate ruler was a "Papist," and that word always suggested mysterious terrors, and roused the irrational spirit of fanaticism. It is but just to Charles Calvert to say that he exercised his power with absolute impartiality, and was at no time disposed to ignore the larger interests of the Protestants. Moreover, his own welfare was so intimately bound up with that of his colony, that it was impossible for him to dissociate them; but calm reason, past experience, and long kindness are as dust in the balance when weighed with strong partisanship and religious hatred. The tyrannical intentions of James, who aimed at reducing all subjects to an immediate dependence upon the pleasure of the crown, and who had already gone far with his scheme for destroying the franchises and independence of the palatinate of Maryland, added to the agitation; and though the handy tool of his tyranny, the writ of *quo warranto*, was struck from his hands by a power stronger than that of his traitorous council and servile courts, men's minds grew familiar with the idea that the proprietary's authority lay at the mercy of the crown; nor was the idea unpleasing, especially when that crown was worn by a Protestant sovereign. It is true, Maryland's only alternative from the proprietary, was the far worse form of a royal government; but so blind is partisanship, that those who would have shuddered at surrendering their franchises into the hands of James, were joyfully ready to place them in the hands of William.

JAMES II.

It was a misfortune, too, that the man to whom the administration of the province was confided, President Joseph, was decidedly unfitted for the emergencies he had to meet. From what we can learn, he seems to have been pedantic, vain, foolish and timid; with an inordinate estimate of his own dignity, a plentiful lack of administrative judgment, and an utter absence of tact and adroitness; talents, which in the crisis he had to meet, were pre-eminently needed.

On November 14, 1688, the president convened the assembly at St. Mary's, and opened the house with a rather labored address, having somewhat the flavor of a sermon. After tracing the descent of the authority under which they were assembled, in a style that would have charmed the royal Stuart on his tottering throne,—from God to the king, from the king to the Lord Proprietary, and from the latter to himself, the speaker, and to them the hearers,—he proceeds to descant on the prevalence of vice, especially swearing, drunkenness and adultery, and to recommend such legislation as may tend to mend the morals of the province in those particulars.[1]

In the winding up of his discourse, he alludes to the growing, though covert, disaffection in the colony, and proceeds to make the direct application of his opening homily on the *jus divinum:*

"I hope that there are not any in the present General Assembly so wicked as, by Machiavellian principles, shall go about to divide the interests of my Lord and of his people, which, indeed, are not two interests, but one; for that whatsoever shall be for the good and welfare of his people is also the undoubted good and welfare of my Lord, whose chief care and study is to increase wealth and ease to the inhabitants of Maryland; wherefore whoever shall endeavor to divide the hearts of the people from my Lord, or my Lord from the people, should, by this Assembly, be declared a traitor to our God, King, Lord and people."

Very fine words; but the president should have known that if there was discontent or a mutinous spirit in the province or the assembly, a pathetic appeal to the *jus divinum* was not the way to allay it. To crown his unwisdom, and show his apprehensions of the Lower House, he next proceeded to an act at once unprecedented, illegal and insulting, which was to demand the Oath of Fidelity from the houses then in session, the members of which had already taken it on being admitted to their respective seats. Anything more adapted to excite suspicion, or provoke animosity, could not well have been devised, and it was destined to bear bitter fruit in brief time.

The Upper House took the oath without demur; after which Major Sewall entered, and having taken the oath, "with the salvo of his allegiance to the king," went to the Lower House with the following message from the Upper:

"This House do desire that the Lower House, before they enter upon business, would take the Oath of Fidelity, according to that part of the President's speech relating thereunto, and according to the province of the Lower House in a message of theirs of the 20th

[1] McMahon's *History of Maryland*, p. 235.

of October, 1686. The members of this House having taken the said oath already, upon notice from the Lower House that they are ready to take the said oath, this House will send a member of the same to administer the said oath as the law directs."

After mature consideration, the Lower House sent, by Mr. George Lingan and Mr. Stephen Luffe, their answer, as follows:

"This House have perused and considered of their message of the 29th of October, 1686, and cannot therein find that this House made any such promise as in the message by the honorable Major Sewall is intimated; this House did then, and still do say, that they always shall manifest their fidelity to his Lordship; and the reason this House then gave for not making any declaration thereof according to the Act of Assembly, was because the same was not proposed in due time; which reasons still remain (this being the same Assembly), and therefore this House conceives the same answer may be satisfactory to the Upper House now as it was then."

To this the Upper House promptly replied:

"This House have considered of the message by Mr. Lingan and Mr. Luffe relating to the Oath of Fidelity, and they do find that the chief reason why the said oath was not taken the last session of Assembly was because the said oath was not proposed to them in due time before they had entered upon the affairs of their House; therefore this House did resolve in this session to send to the Lower House early and before they entered upon other business; but find by the said message of the Lower House, sent by the said Mr. Lingan and Mr. Luffe, that neither is it now proposed in due time for that, this is still the same Assembly. But upon the whole matter for answer this House does say, that although this be the same Assembly, yet, it is not the same session; and the law says it ought to be taken at any time whensoever required by the Chief Governor or Governors or whom they shall appoint; and the Government by this House doth propose the said oath to the Lower House to be taken by the members thereof before any other business be entered upon; and besides it was his Lordship's pleasure to declare at the ending of the session of Assembly in April, 1684 in the presence of both Houses, that every member of Assembly for the future should before they be admitted to sit, take the oath of fidelity to his Lordship; this House therefore do hope that the Lower House will not refuse so legal and reasonable a proposition; and this House neither can nor will deviate from the law and his Lordship's order made therein as aforesaid. This House therefore desire the speedy concurrence of the Lower House in this particular, hoping that those that ought to be conservors of the law will be no breakers thereof."

After several messages had passed between the two Houses, the Upper summoned the Lower to attend in their chamber; which done, the president administered a rather tart reprimand, admonishing them that fidelity was allegiance, and that as the British House of Commons had to swear allegiance to the king, so they were bound, not only as members, but as colonists, by provincial law, under pains and penalties, to swear fidelity to the proprietary; "and further," he added, "I am to tell you that the refusing allegiance implies rebellion; and that you have no privilege to break, contemn, or disobey laws. Wherefore you are desired to return to your House and consider it; for that the government will not permit this House to proceed to any business whatsoever till you satisfy the law and government in this point; for by how much the more you refuse allegiance, by so much the more the government have cause to suspect your loyalty. So God of His mercy direct you."

Neither the crushing logic of the president's speech, nor the pious twang with which he closed it, availed to shake the determination of the burgesses, who, on returning to their own chamber, drew up the following reply and resolutions:

"This House, as is their bounden duty, have attended his Lordship's commands in both Upper and Lower Houses of Assembly, and do declare that it is their duty to express fidelity to his Lordship, and do not know of any one individual member of this House that directly or indirectly refuses so to do, or that hath in any wise either within this House or out of the same used any speech to the contrary; for should this House be made sensible of any such or other misbehaviour by any member thereof, this House, by virtue of the power and authority in them inherent, would proceed against every such person and severely punish the same. But having no knowledge neither of that nor any other unreverent or undutiful deportment in any of their said members whereby to give any offence, cannot but highly resent divers words and expressions contained in a speech made to them by the honorable the President in his Lordship's Upper House of Assembly, and are very sorry that such unusual and such unjust proceedings should be imposed upon them, which this House thinks is prejudicial to the power, authority and validity and privileges of the same, therefore

"1. *Resolved*, that this House to their great grief and trouble have met not only with unexpected, but unreasonable and unjust disturbances; but as by the Journal of this House is in no wise guilty of the same.

"2. *Resolved*, that there is a great difference between the Oath of Fidelity and Allegiance either of which or both we have and are always willing to take according to law.

"3. That what oath is or has been proposed to the House of Commons in Parliament in the Kingdom of England, was never proposed and consequently never refused by the Lower House of Assembly in Maryland.

"4. That we have been and still are as by our former messages willing and ready to take the Oath of Fidelity according to law, not for fear of the penalties intimated in what was spoken by the President, but as it is our duty and the natural direct result of our affection.

"5. That that word rebellion ought not to be in any message from the Upper House to the Lower House, unless accompanied with an impeachment against the person or persons that are guilty.

"6. That this House neither do nor did pretend to have any privilege to break or disobey the law, but do, in the name of the whole Province which we represent, demand the benefit of the laws of England and of this Province as our inherent and just right which we have hitherto been deprived of in not having the last writs of election and Journals returned as desired by this House.[1]

"7. That this house knows not how to satisfy the law and government in the business of the Oath of Fidelity otherwise than they have done already."

Seeing that nothing would prevail with the burgesses, who had evidently the best of the argument, the president summoned them again into his presence and prorogued the assembly to the 19th, thus ending the session, the Lower House having carried its point.

[1] The complaint about writs was that they desired the governor to issue his writs for St. Mary's and Charles counties for the election of two new members, in place of Richard Gardiner and Thomas Burford, which he refused to do until they took the oath. They desired the journals to see if a law, imposing the oath, was ever passed in the province.

In the journal of the Upper House we find here the following

"*Memorandum:* That immediately after the said prorogation, the Honorable the President required Mr. Cheseldyne the Speaker, and the rest of the members to take the Oath of Fidelity to the Right Honorable the Lord Proprietary as the law directs; which, after some debate the said Speaker and the rest of the members did accordingly all take, except Thomas Thurston, a Quaker, who desired to be dispensed with in regard of his opinion, to which the President readily complied."

The law being thus satisfied, the new session carried on its business without further difficulty; but the burgesses had given the Upper House a taste of their temper, from which it might be surmised how they would act if other and more momentous dissensions arose. There is no evidence of any positive apprehension that the Protestant religion was endangered by any recent or anticipated act of the proprietary, but the popular feeling sympathized with the great and growing discontent in England as the magnetic needle quivers and veers when an electric storm gathers in a far-off land. And when, in January, intelligence reached the province of the expected enterprise of the Prince of Orange, certain steps were taken by the authorities which gave a ready pretext for the disaffected to bruit abroad stories of a Popish plot for the destruction of the Protestant religion, planned by the authorities and to be accomplished by the help of the Indians.

Among other things, a treaty with the Indians was renewed, and the authorities began to collect arms and place the province in a state of defence. These things naturally excited attention and gave rise to rumors, which were only exaggerated and the general suspicion and irritability increased by the indiscretion of the authorities, who, by arresting many persons on the charge of "spreading false news," gave these reports importance and heightened the very evil they wished to suppress.

The records of the province from the end of 1688 to the beginning of 1692 are lost; but evidence is still extant in the English State Papers to show that the Protestant revolution in 1689, was the result of a panic produced by the most shameful falsehood and misrepresentation. From these papers we shall quote liberally, as they help to some extent to supply the missing links in the chain of our colonial history.

Immediately upon the success of the revolution in England, the Lord Proprietary gave in his adhesion to William and Mary, and transmitted by a Mr. Broom, to President Joseph, the necessary authority to have the new sovereigns proclaimed in the province, accompanied by the following letter to the president and the rest of the deputy governors:—

"*Gentlemen:* I received the inclosed from the Lords of the Committee for Trade and Plantations, with their order for the proclaiming of their Majesties King William and Queen Mary in Maryland; the which you are to see duly performed with the ceremonies usual on such occasions, according to the directions of the inclosed, to which you are to have due respect, and pay all ready obedience, which is the order of

"Your Friend, "C. BALTIMORE.

"LONDON, Feb. 27th 1688 (1689 N. S.)."

Unfortunately these instructions did not arrive in time, the bearer of them dying at Plymouth; and even after William and Mary had been proclaimed in the adjacent colonies, the authorities of Maryland hesitated to act until they should receive the necessary instructions from the Lord Proprietary. This hesitation gave rise to alarm in the province, and was seized by Virginia as a ground of complaint to be laid before the Board of Trade against the Lord Proprietary. Colonel Spencer, Secretary of Virginia, wrote on the 10th of June, 1689, to Mr. Blathwayt, Secretary of the Committee on Trade and Plantations, a letter containing the following statement:[1]

"The inhabitants of Maryland, most Protestants, are ragingly earnest for the proclaiming their present majesties, and will not believe but orders have come to that government, as well as to this, for proclaiming their Majesties, and that the government have concealed the commands; and are sometimes very positive they will proclaim their Majesties without the order of the government, which, if so, will unhinge the whole constitution of that government and dissolve the whole frame of it."

This letter having been read, Lord Baltimore was ordered to attend the committee on the next day, being the 30th of August, 1689, which he did, and there declared that he "had sent orders to Maryland for proclaiming their Majesties, notwithstanding those orders were not arrived there." Upon this the committee ordered that the proprietary should send them "a duplicate of the orders your lordship has lately sent to those parts for that purpose; their lordships intending forthwith to dispatch a messenger with them to Maryland, the expense of whose voyage the committee think fit that your lordship take care to discharge." A memorandum affixed to this entry in the record, notes that an order of similar term was sent to Mr. Penn, who had been equally dilatory in regard to the proclamation in Pennsylvania. "Whereupon," continues the record, "my Lord Baltimore, attending the committee on the 13th of September, 1689, presents to their lordships the duplicate of the order he had sent for proclaiming their Majesties in Maryland, with copies of their Lordships' letter, the form of the proclamation, and the oaths to be taken instead of the oaths of allegiance and supremacy, which their lordships order to be sent by a special messenger to Maryland, the moiety of whose charges is to be borne by my Lord Baltimore."[2]

This unfortunate delay in the proclamation, helped to bring affairs in Maryland to a crisis. On the 25th of August, Colonel Jowles sent information to the president and council, then in session at St. Mary's, that three thousand Indians were at the head of the Patuxent river, marching toward the interior settlements, and begging that the inhabitants may be furnished with arms and ammunition for their protection. On the receipt of this startling information, the council immediately despatched Colonel Digges with the

[1] This and the following correspondence are from the Public Record Office, London. Colonial Entry Book, iii., pp. 120-5.

[2] The expense was to be shared by Mr. Penn, as the same messenger carried orders to both colonies.

necessary arms. On the next morning, the council desiring further information, sent Colonel Henry Darnall, one of their number, to the house of Colonel Jowles, where he found the people all in arms, who told him they had heard there were three thousand Indians at Mattapany, at the mouth of the Patuxent, and that they had cut off Captain Bowne's family. Darnall assured them that it was a false report; that he had just come himself from Mattapany, and offered to lead them in person against the enemy, if they could show him where they were to be found. Upon this assurance they "seemed very well satisfied," but Darnall suspected that the whole "was only a contrivance of some ill-natured men, who, under this pretence, would raise the country."

After diligent investigations, no hostile movement of the Indians anywhere could be discovered; but "whenever any messenger was sent to the place where it was said the Indians were come there, the inhabitants would tell them they heard they were landed" at some other place. So, after a long search, from place to place, and no sign of Indians appearing, the people became somewhat quieted. Colonel Jowles and others, who had examined into the matter, and were convinced that some sinister influence was at work, prepared and signed the following

"DECLARATION OR REMONSTRANCE.

"Whereas there has been lately many & great disturbances in this province, perticularly in Calvert & Charles County where the people in severall places of the s[d] Counties had gathered themselves in greate parties to defend themselves, as they were perswaded, against a groundlesse and imaginary plott & designe contrived against them as was rumoured & suspected by the Roman Catholicks inviteing the Indians to joyne with them in that detestable & wicked Conspiracy, wee thought fitt for the better satisfaccion of the good people of this province and that the general peace & quiet thereof may be once againe fully & compleately setled, to publish & declare under our hands that wee have made an exact scrutiny & Examination into all circumstances of this pretended designe & have found it to be nothing but a sleevelesse feare & Imagination fomented by the Artifice of some ill minded persons who are studious & ready to take all occasions of raising disturbances for their owne private & malitious interest. And that by all probable conjectures, which shall be also more dilligently searched into, wee doe find the originall of all these mischiefs to arrise from Stafford County in Virginia, who have likewise stirred up some more such like ill minded persons in our Government to continue the same Comocions amongst us, and the rather wee are soe perswaded and have just cause to believe, because that, notwithstanding the many and dayly Rumours of Indians, come downe among us and inforted at the head of Patuxen, and also of another greate body of them landed at Mattapany, Sewall, another party at Cove poynt on the Clifts, another at Choptico & severall more at severall other places of this western side of this province. Wee doe yet find all these reports are notorious false, and that wee can, in noe place trace soe much as the footing of any Indians nor heare any truth or certainty of any designes they have to disturb or molest the good people or peace of this Country. Wherefore wee, whose names are here subscribed, have thought Convenient to Signifie the Premisses to the Magistrates, officers & other the good people of this Country as haveing had the full Examinacion of the whole matter with the hon[ble], the Dep[ty] Govern[r], and from whome also wee have had as much satisfaction as can be desired of their aversnesse to any such unworthy treacherous practices that soe as many others as shall thinke fit may signifie the same Remonstrance for the ample satisfaccion of other parts of this province.

"Given under our hand this 27th Day of March, 1689. Hen: Jowles, Richard Smith, jun^{r}, Will: Garton, Hum: Warren, John Courts, Tho: Brooke, Tho: Tasker, Tho: Greenfeld, Tho: Gant, William Dent, John Bayne, Ninian Beall, Thom: Holliday, John Addison, Wm: Digges, Kenelm Cheseldyn.[1]

For a time these measures quieted the apprehensions of the people, and they began to believe that there was no truth in the rumor which dishonest men had circulated "that a Popish administration, supported by Papists, had leagued with Indians to cut off the whole Protestants in the province."[2]

The nature of things, however, operated against the Catholic Proprietary, and the elements which had been working in the public mind since the usurpations of Cromwell's commissioners, soon swept the old land-marks away. The people, it is true, still felt an attachment for the proprietary, yet, the cry of "No Popery" was abroad, and by the bitterness of the English struggle, which had been infused into the public sentiment of Maryland, his province was soon torn by discord and himself accounted a criminal in his own dominions.

In April, 1689, "An association in arms, for the defence of the Protestant religion, and for asserting the right of King William and Queen Mary to the Province of Maryland and all the English dominions"[3] was formed, at the head of which was placed John Coode, who had already been tried and found guilty of treason and rebellion, and who now found an excellent opportunity of carrying into action those principles which he had before only taught.[4]

[1] Public Record Office, America and West Indies, No. 556.

[2] Chalmers, p. 373.

[3] *Ibid.*

[4] "Coode, although confessedly the leader of the association, appears to have fared worse in the end than the most of the chiefs. *Kenelm Cheseldyn* and *Colonel Jowles* appear to have ranked next. Cheseldyn was the speaker of the Protestant convention, assembled immediately after the close of the Revolution; and also of the assembly of May, 1692, the first which was convened under the royal government. He received a gift of 100,000 lbs. of tobacco for his services, and was soon afterwards appointed *commissary general*, from which office he was dismissed in August, 1697, *for carelessness and negligence in office.*—'*Cl. Proceedings*, H. D., Part II., p. 539.' Jowles also received a gift of 20,000 lbs. of tobacco for his services in raising troops at the beginning of the Revolution. *Coode* was, in a great measure, overlooked, or at least his rewards bore no proportion to his high rank amongst the associators. When we next hear of him, he was in holy orders, and at the same time lieutenant colonel of the militia of St. Mary's county, and receiver of the duties in Potomac river, asserting that religion was a trick, reviling the apostles, denying the divinity of the Christian religion, and alleging that all the morals worth having were contained in Cicero's offices. He had been elected to the assembly about that period, when the doctrine of Horne Tooke's case, '*that once a priest, always a priest*,' was applied to him, and he was declared ineligible; and as he could not lose the character, he does not seem to have been *very apprehensive of soiling it.* His blasphemous expressions were reported to the governor and council; and he was dismissed from all employments under the government, and presented by the grand jury of St. Mary's county for *atheism and blasphemy.* The proofs are recorded at large in *Liber H. D.*, p. 2, 393 to 397. To escape the presentment, he fled to Virginia. Governor Nicholson, whose morals did not particularly qualify him for a castigator of other persons' irregularities, applied to the Governor of Virginia to assist in his apprehension. *There*, although the Governor of Virginia issued proclamations, and made many ostensible efforts for his apprehension, he contrived to remain in security, and even ventured back to St. Mary's, in disguise, to vent the threat amongst some of

From the time of the organization of the "associators," until the middle of July, it seems nothing of importance occurred to disturb the peace of the province, though the rebels must have been engaged in concocting plans for future action. However, on the 16th of July, 1689, the president and his deputies received information that a large force of men was collecting on the Potomac river, under the command of Captain Coode, Colonel Jowles, Major Beale and Mr. Blackiston, under the "pretence that the Papists had invited the Northern Indians to come down and cut off the Protestants; and that their descent was to be about the latter end of August, when roasting eares were in season, and that they, therefore, rose in arms to secure the magazine of arms and ammunition and the Protestants from being cut off by the said Indians and Papists." This was the argument used to those who were apprehensive of the Indians; to others they pretended their design was only to proclaim King William and Queen Mary. Thus organized and under these disguises they marched for the city of St. Mary's.

The president and council had already despatched a person to learn the movements of the enemy, but he was unfortunately captured and held by them as a spy. In course of time, however, they learned of their near approach, and instructed Colonel Digges to organize what force he could to protect the provincial capital. Colonel Digges mustered about one hundred men, and took position in the state-house to await the attack. In a short time Coode and his command marched into the city after being joined by a body of men under Mayor Campbell, and quite a number from Charles county. After a short skirmish and parley, Colonel Digges concluded to surrender, as "his men were not willing to fight," and, moreover, he knew it would be useless to contend against the superior numbers of the rebels who were gaining in strength every hour

Upon the evacuation of the state-house, Coode and his force took possession of it and the records of the province, and immediately issued the following

"DECLARATION.

"Of the reasons and motives for the present appearing in armes of their Majestyes Protestant subjects in the province of Maryland.

"Although the nature and state of affairs relating to the government of this Province is soe well and notoriously known, to all persons any way concerned in the same, as to

his friends, 'that as he had pulled down one government, he would pull down another.' He contrived to keep Nicholson *at bay* throughout the whole of his administration, notwithstanding the unceasing efforts of the latter for his apprehension; and his security in Virginia, notwithstanding the proclamation of its governor, provoked the striking rebuke from Nicholson to that governor: '*Your excellency's proclamation seems to me to be like one of the watch-houses on the Barbary shore, to give notice when the Christians are coming to take them, that they may fly to it for safety.*' Nicholson being removed to the government of Virginia, Coode came in and surrendered himself in May, 1699, and was taken into custody. Being convicted, Governor Blackiston, at the instance of the judges of the provincial court, and in consideration of the services rendered by him at the Revolution, suspended his sentence for six months, in hopes of his reformation. Of this measure the council approved, and advised the governor to pardon him, if he should conduct himself properly during that period. Age, or affliction, or both, seem to have mended his manners and tamed his insurrectionary spirit; for, from this period, he is seen no more in the affairs of the province."—*McMahon*, p. 238.

the people and inhabitants here, who are more immediately interested as might excuse any declaration or apologie for this present inevitable appearance; yet for as much as (by the plottes, contrivances, insinuacions, remonstrances, and subscriptions carryed on, suggested, extorted and detained, by the Lord Baltimore his deputys, representatives and officers here) the injustice and tyranny under which wee groane is palliated, and most if not all the particulars of our grievances shrowded from the eye of observation and the hand of redress, wee thought fitt for generall satisfaction and particularly to undeceive those that may have a sinister account of our proceedings, to publish this declaration of the reasons and motives inducing us thereunto.

"His Lordshipp's right and title to the government is by virtue of a Charter to his father Cecilius from King Charles the first of blessed memory: how his present Lordshipp had managed the powers and authorityes given and granted in the same, wee could mourne and lament onely in silence, would our duty to God, our allegiance to his vicegerent and the care and welfare of our selves and posterity permit us. In the first place in the said Charter is a reservation of the fayth and allegiance due to the Crowne of England (the province and Inhabitants being immediately subject thereunto) but how little that is manifested is too obvious, to all unbyasted persons that ever had any thing to doe here: the very name and owneing of that soveraigne power is some times crime enough to incurr the frownes of our superior and to render our persons obnoxious and suspected to bee ill-affected to the government. The ill-usage of and affronts to the King's officers belonging to the customes here were a sufficient argument of this. We need but instance the busines of Mr. Badcock and Mr. Rousby, of whom the former was forcibly detained by his Lordshipp from goeing home, to make his just complaints in England, upon which he was soone taken sick, and it was more then problably conjectured that the conceit of his confinement was the chiefe cause of his death which soone after happened; the latter was barbarously murthered upon the execution of his office, by one that was an Irish Papist and our chiefe governor.

"Allegiance here, by those persons under whom wee suffer, is little talkt of, other then what they would have due & sworne to, to his Lordshipp the Lord Proprietary, for it was very lately owned by the President himselfe openly enough in the upper house of Assembly that fidelity in his Lordshipp was allegiance, and that the denying of the One was the same thing with the refusall or denyall of the other. In that very Oath of fidelity that was then imposed, under the penalty of banishment, there is not so much as the least word or intimation of any duty, fayth or allegiance to be reserved to our Soveraigne Lord the King of England. How the *jus regale* is improved here and made the prerogative of his Lordshipp, is too sensibly felt by us all in that absolute authority exercised over us, and by the greatest part of the Inhabitants in the service of their persons, forfeiture and loss of their goods, Chattles, freeholds and inheritances. In the next place, Churches and Chappells, which, by the said Charter, should be built and consecrated according to the Ecclesiasticall lawes of the kingdome of England, to our greate regrett and discouragement of our Religion, are erected and converted to the use of popish Idolatry and superstition, Jesuits and seminarie priests are the onely incumbents (for which their is a supply provided by sending our popish youth to be educated at St. Ormes) [St. Omer's]. As alsoe the Chiefe adviser and Councellors in affaires of government, and the richest and most fertile land sett apart for their use and maintenance, while other lands that are piously intended and given for the maintenance of the Protestant ministrye become escheate and are taken as forfeit, the ministers themselves discouraged and noe care taken for their subsistance.

"The power to enact lawes is another branch of his Lordshipp's authority, but how well that has beene executed & circumstanced is too notorious, his present Lordshipp, upon the death of his father, in order thereunto, sent out writtes for four (as was ever the usage) for each County to serve as representatives of the people, but when elected there were two of each respective four pickt out and summoned to that convention, whereby many lawes were made and the greatest leavy yett knowne layd upon the Inhabitants.

"The next session the house was filled up with the remaining two that was left out of the four, in which there were many and the best of our lawes enacted, to the great benefitt and satisfaction of the people; but his Lordshipp soone after dissolved and declared the best of these lawes, such as he thought fit, null and voyd by Proclamation, notwithstanding they were assented to in his Lordshipp's name, by the governor in his absence, and he himselfe, sometime personally acted and governed by the same, soe that the question in our Courts of judicature, in any point that related to many of our lawes, is not soe much the relation it had to the said lawes, but whether the lawes themselves bee agreable to the pleasure and approbation of his Lordshipp, whereby our liberty & property is become uncertain and under the arbitrary disposition of the Judges and commissioners of our Courts of Justice.

"The said Assembly being some time after dissolved by proclamation, another was elected and mett, consisting onely of two members for each County, directly opposite to an Act of Assembly for four, in which severall lawes with his Lordshipp's personall assent were enacted, among the which one for the encouragement of trade and erecting of townes, but the execution of that act was soon after, by Proclamation from his Lordshipp out of England, suspended the last year, and all officers, military and Civill, severely prohibited executing and inflicting the penaltyes of the same, notwithstanding which, suspension being in effect, a dissolution and abrogating of the whole act, the income of threepence p. hogshead to the government by the said act payable for every hogshead of tobacco exported, is carefully exacted and collected.

"How fatall and of what pernicious consequence that unlimitted and arbitrary pretended authority may be to the Inhabitants, is too apparent, but by considering that by the same reasons all the rest of the lawes whereby our libertyes and propertyes subsists, are subject to the same arbitrary disposition, and if timely remedy be not had, must stand or fall according to his Lordshipp's good will and pleasure.

"Nor is the nullifying and suspending power the onely grievance that doth perplex and burthen us in relation to lawes, but these lawes that are of a certaine and unquestioned acceptacion, are executed and countenanced as they are more or less agreeable to the good likeing of our governors: in particular, one very good lawe provides that Orphan children should be disposed of to persons of the same religion with that of their dead parents. In direct opposition to which severall children of protestants have beene committed to the tutelage of papists and brought up in the Romish superstition. Wee could instance in a young woman that had beene lately forced by order of Councill from her husband, committed to the custody of a Papist and brought up in his religion. 'Tis endless to ennumerate the particulars of this matter, while on the contrary, those lawes that enhance the grandeur and income of his said Lordshipp are severely imposed and executed, specially one that against all sence, equity, reason and law, punishes all speeches, practises and attempts relating to his Lordshipp and government that shall be thought mutinous and seditious by the Judge of the Provinciall Court, with either whipping, branding, boreing through the tongue, fine, imprisonment, banishment or death, all or either of the said punishments at the discretion of the said Judges, who have given a very correct and remarkable proof of their authority in each particular punishment aforesaid upon severall the good people of this Province, while the rest are in the same danger to have their words and actions lyable to the construction and punishment of the said Judges and their lives and fortunes to the mercy of their arbitrary fancies, opinions and sentences.

"To these grievances are added excessive Officers' Fees, and that too under execution directly against the law made and provided to redress the same wherein there is noe probability of a loyall remedy, the Officers themselves that are partyes and culpable being Judges.

"The like Fees being imposed upon and extorted from Master and Owner of Vessells trading into this Province without any law to justifie the same, and directly against the plain words of the said Charter that say there shall be noe imposition or assessment without the consent of the freemen in the Assembly to the great destruction of trade and prejudice of the Inhabitants.

"The like excessive Fees imposed upon and extorted from the Owners of Vessells that are built here or doe really belong to the inhabitants contrary to an act of Assembly made and provided for the same, where in moderate and reasonable fees are ascertained for the promoting and encouragement of shipping and navigation amongst ourselves.

"The frequent pressing of men, houses, boates, provision and other necessaries in time of peace and often to gratifie private designes and occasions, to the great burthen and regrett of the Inhabitants contrary to law and severall acts of Assembly in that case made and provided.

"The seizure and apprehending of protestants in their houses with armed forces consisting of Papists and that in time of peace thence hurrying them away to Prisons without warrant or cause of committment there kept and confined with popish guards a long time without tryall.

"Not only private but publick outrages and murthers committed and done by Papists upon protestants without redress but rather conived at and tolerated by the chiefe authority, and indeed it were in vaine to desire or expect any help or other measures from them, being papists and guided by the councills and instigation of the Jesuits, either in these or any other grievances or oppressions and yett those are the men that are our chiefe Judges at the common law in Chancery of the Probat of Wills and the affaires of administration in the upper house of Assembly and chiefe Military Officers and Commanders of our forces being still the same individuall persons, in all those particular qualifications and places.

"These and many more even infinite pressures and calamityes wee have hitherto layne with patience under and submitted to, hoping that the same hand of providence that always sustained us under them, would at length in due time release us.

"And now at length, for as much as it hath pleased Almighty God, by means of the great prudence and conduct of the best of Princes, our most gracious King William, to putt a check to that great inundation of slavery and Popery that had like to overwhelme their Maj: Protestant subjects, in all their Territorys & Dominions (of which none have suffered more, or are in greater danger than ourselves) we hoped and expected in our particular stations and qualifications a proportionable share in soe great a blessing.

"But to our great grief and consternation, upon the first newes of the great overture and happy change in England, wee found our selves surrounded with strong and violent endeavours from our governors here (being the Lord Baltemore's deputye and representatives) to defeat us of the same.

"We still find all the meanes used by these very persons and their agents, Jesuits, priests, and lay papists, that art of malice cann suggest, to divert the obedience and loyalty of the Inhabitants from their most sacred Maj[tyes] to that height of impudence that solemn Masses and prayers are used (as wee have very good information) in their Chappells and Oratoryes for the prosperous success of the popish forces in Ireland and the French designes against England, whereby they would involve us in the same crime of disloyalty with themselves, and render us obnoxious to the insupportable displeasure of their Majestyes.

"Wee every where heare, not only publick protestations against their Majestyes right and possession of the Crowne of England, but their most illustrious persons villified and aspersed, with the worst and most traytrous expressions of obloquie and detraction. Wee are every day threatened with the loss of our lives, libertyes and estates, of which wee have great reason to think our selves in imminent danger, by the practise and machinations that are on foot to betray us to the French, Northern and other Indians, of which some have beene delt with, all and others invited to assist in our destruction, well remembering the incursions and inrode of the said Northern Indians in the year 1681, who were conducted into the heart of the province by French Jesuits, and lay sore upon us, while the representatives of the Country, then in the Assembly, were severely prest upon by our superiors to yield them an unlimited and tyranicall power in the affaires of the Militia as soe great a power of villany cannot be the result but of the worst of principle. Soe we should with the greatest difficulty believe it to be true if undeniable evidence and circumstances did not convince us.

"Together with the premises, wee have with all due thinkeing and deliberation considered the endeavours that are making to disunite us among ourselves to make and inflame differences in our neighbour collony of Virginia, from whose friendshipp, vicinity, great loyalty and sameness of religion, wee may expect assistance in our greatest necessity.

"We have considered that all the other branches of their Majestyes Dominions in this part of the world (as well as wee could be informed) have done their duty in proclaiming and asserting their undoubted right in these and all other their Majestyes territoryes & countrys. But above all with due and mature deliberation, wee have reflected upon that vast gratitude and duty incumbent likewise upon us, to our soveraigne Lord and Lady the King and Queenes most excellent Majestyes in which as it would not be safe for us, soe it will not suffer us to be silent in soe great and generall a jubilee, with all considering and looking upon ourselves discharged, dissolved and free from all manner of duty, obligation or fidelity to the deputye governors or chiefe Magestrates here as such, they haveing departed from their allegiance (upon which alone our said duty and fidelity to them depends) and by their complices and agents aforesaid endeavoured, the destruction of our religion, lives, libertyes and propertyes, all which they are bound to protect.

"These are the reasons, motives and considerations, which wee doe declare have induced us to take up armes to preserve vindicate and assert the soveraigne Dominion and right of King William and Queen Mary to this Province, to defend the protestant religion among us and to protect and shelter the Inhabitants from all manner of violence, oppression and destruction that is plotted and designed against them; then which wee doe solemnely declare and protest we have noe designes or intentions whatsoever.

"For the more effectuall accomplishment of which, wee will take due care that a full and free assembly be called and convened with all possible expedition by whome we may likewise have our conditions, circumstances and our most dutyfull addresses, represented and tendered to their Majestyes from whose great wisdome, justice and speciall care of the protestant religion, we may reasonably and comfortably hope to be delivered from our present calamitye and for the future be secured under a just and loyall administration, from being ever more subjected to the yoke of arbitrary government of tyranny and popery.

"Wee will take care and doe promise, that noe person now in amity with us, or that shall come to assist us, shall comitt any outrage or doe any violence to any person whatsoever that shall be found peaceable and quiet and not oppose us, in our said just and necessary design, and that there shall be a just and due satisfaction made for provisions and other necessaryes had and received from the Inhabitants and the souldiers punctually and duely payd in such wayes and methodes as have beene formerly accustomed or by law ought to be; and wee doe lastly invite and require all manner of persons whatsoever residing or Inhabiting in this Province, as they tender their Allegiance, the Protestant religion, their lives, fortunes and familyes, to ayd and assist us, in this our undertakeing.

"Given under our hands, Maryland this 25th day of July in the first yeare of their Majestyes reign, Anno Domini, 1689.

"JOHN COODE,
"HEN. JOWLES,
"JNO. CAMBELL,
"HUM. WARREN,
"KENELM CHESELDYN,
"JON. TURLING,
"RIC. CLOUDS,
"WM. BLAKISTON."[1]

If invective were argument, or assertion proof, this Declaration might have carried with it some force and plausibility. But they are careful to confine themselves to general charges, or to such specific charges as could not be tested. Had there been any genuine case of such wrongs as alleged, they would have seized upon it with alacrity. But the conclusive evidence of their falsehood is shown by the fact that they had not been brought up in the Lower House, a body, as we know, sufficiently jealous of the rights and franchises of its constituents. Yet the credulous and excited provincials, as in the case of the Indian rumors, were everywhere ready to believe that what had not happened among them, had certainly happened somewhere else.

The falsity of the charges is gross and apparent. The Oath of Fidelity, as we have seen, *was* taken with a salvo of allegiance to the crown. If the proprietary dissented from laws, it was only what his charter allowed him to do, nor are the laws disapproved by him, stated. Mutiny and sedition against the provincial government, was necessarily a penal act in all the colonies.

The pretended seizure of Protestants by "armed forces of Papists" is preposterous, when we remember that the former outnumbered the latter by about thirty to one. As for the other charges, it suffices but to read them to see their falsehood or irrelevance. But whatever its logical or historical defects, if the excellence of a State paper consists in the thorough accomplishment of its purpose, we must admit this Declaration—due probably to the clerical pen of John Coode—to have been an altogether masterly production.

In the meantime, Colonel Darnall and Major Sewall had gone up the Patuxent river to endeavor to organize a force to oppose Coode and his party. In this they found great difficulty, as most of those in the neighborhood were

[1] Public Record Office, America and West Indies, No. 556.

"The declaration of the associators was printed at St. Mary's by the printer of the province. In Virginia, we have seen, no printing press was allowed. In New England and New York there was assuredly none permitted. The other provinces were not more fortunate, because they did not enjoy greater liberty. We may, thence, justly infer that Maryland, under the mild government of the proprietary, and the rational protection of the assembly, of all the colonies enjoyed the most genuine freedom at the era of the Revolution, notwithstanding the ill-founded assertions of those who now overturned the government."—*Chalmers*, p. 384.

possessed with "the belief that Coode rose only to preserve the country from the Indians and Papists, and to proclaim the king and queen," and that he "would do them no harm; and, therefore, they would not stir to run themselves into danger." Most of the officers were willing to join the provincial forces; but they only succeeded in securing one hundred and sixty privates, while Coode's forces now numbered over seven hundred. The council determined to hold Mattapany,[1] and, believing that the people were enticed away "by false reports and shams, in order to quiet them and give them all imaginable assurance that they were clear and innocent of inviting the Indians down, as was laid to their charge, offered to make Colonel Jowles (who was the chief of their party next to Coode) general of all the forces in the province, and sent such an offer to him." Colonel Jowles, however, returned "a very civil answer," and laid the council's communication before his men, who "were extremely satisfied therewith," and gave hopes that he would accept the proposition. He, however, decided not to accept the proffered position, but marched with his entire forces to join Coode at the city of St. Mary's. The president and council also issued their proclamation, granting a free pardon to all who were then in arms, provided they would lay down the same and retire in peaceful order to their respective habitations. Coode prohibited the proclamation to be read in the presence of his army, but read his "Declaration" and "a defiance," purporting to have come from the council, "thereby to enrage and not to pacify them."

While Coode was in possession of St. Mary's city, he forbade any vessel to leave the port, for fear of conveying intelligence of his movements, until his plans were consummated. Having decided to complete the overthrow of the proprietary government, Coode "borrowed some great guns of one Captain Burnham, master of a ship belonging to London," and marched for Patuxent. When he arrived within a short distance of Mattapany house, he sent forward a trumpet and commanded the garrison to surrender; upon which the president and council, who were in the fort, requested "a parley and personal treaty in the hearing of the people," which Coode would not consent to. Colonel Darnall, in a letter to Lord Baltimore, says:

"We knew if we could but obtain that in the hearing the people, we should be able to disabuse them and clear ourselves of what they were made believe against us; but this we could never get at their hands, but to the contrary they used all possible meanes to keep the people ignorant of what we proposed or offered, and made use of such artifices as the following, to exasperate them. They caused a man to come rideing post with a letter, wherein was contained that our neighbour Indians had cut up their corn and were gone

[1] This garrison was located on the south side of Patuxent, about two miles above its mouth. It was originally the Indian town of the Mattapanients, one of the most friendly Maryland tribes; afterwards it served as the store-house of the Jesuit missionaries, and subsequently became the property of the Hon. Henry Sewell, one of his Lordship's councillors. The mansion, during Lord Charles Baltimore's residence, was the government house of the province, and on one occasion the assembly met there. At this period (1689), there was also a fort and a magazine.

from their towns, and that there was an Englishman found with his belly ript open, which in truth was no such thing, as they themselves owned after Matapany House was surrendered."[1]

In the meantime, Michael Taney, the High Sheriff of Calvert county, and an ancestor of the late Chief Justice of the United States, was endeavoring "as an instrument of peace," to negotiate "without shedding blood," an honorable surrender of the fort. Coode becoming impatient at the delay of the provincial forces finally sent the following "Articles of Surrender," which, through the instrumentality of Sheriff Taney, were accepted.

'Gent[lem]:

"Wee have sent you our sumons, and have Received an Answere which desire a parly & personall treaty between us & some of yow; for Answere we doe again demand as in the sumons sent.

"2[ly]. That noe Papist in this province being in any Office Millitary or Civill as by their Maj[ties] Proclamacion & the Laws of England.

"3[dly]. And we doe promise and grant you the gentlemen: and soldiers now in armes in yo[r] Garrison May returne to their Respective homes or Dwellings in order to which we doe assure yow and them safe Conduct protection and security for yow and their persons and attendance.

"4[thly]. These are our absolute Resolutions, Consessions and Demands to w[ch] we desire yo[r] Imediate Complyance being utterly Resolved against any personab!e treaty about the premises Given under our hands this first day of August 1689.

"John Coode, Henry Jowles, Kenelm Chizeldine, John Turling, John Cambell, Ninian Bell, Humphrey Warren."

Their Answere.

"Gent[lm]:

"We doe accept of the Articles Now sent and accordingly are ready to surrender the Garrison. Dated the first August 1689.

"W[m]. Joseph, Henry Darnell, Nicholas Sewell, Edward Pye, Clement Hills.

"Deputy Governo[rs] Then P[r]sent."[2]

Immediately after the surrender of Matapany, Coode retired to St. Mary's, and on the 3d of August drew up the following "Address of the Protestant Inhabitants of Maryland to King William and Queen Mary," which was sent by Captain Johnson, master of a ship bound for London:

"To the high and mighty, the most Illustrious Princes Will[m] & Mary by the grace of God, of England, Scotland, France and Ireland, King & Queene, Defend[rs]: of the Faith, &c.

"The humble Address of your Maj[ties] most Loyall Protestant subjects, Inhabitants of the Province of Maryland.

"Dread Sovereigns:

"As (according to our bounden duty, and the Example of the rest of our fellow Subjects in other parts of your Dominions) wee desire most humbly and heartily to congratulate the happy Success of your Maj[ties] Armes taken up in the defence and restitution not only of the Protestant Religion in generall, but also in particular of the antient Lawes, Liberties and priviledges of our Native Countrey and Kingdom of England to its antient Lustre, purity and Splender, justly intituleing you unto, and placeing on your Royall heads the Imperiall Crowne of the English Territoryes; Soe wee cannot but somewhat

[1] *Narrative of Colonel Henry Darnall*, Public Record Office, America and W. Indies, No. 556.

[2] Public Record Office, America and West Indies, No. 556.

Lament that Wee (who have soe especiall and particular a Share and benefitt in those your soe glorious untertakeings and accomplishm[ts]) have not had the oportunity of appeareing more Early in the testifications of our due Sense and acknowledgm[ts] of your Maj[ties] Royall and Princely care and indefatigable paines therein taken and Sustained, crowned with the blessing of Almighty God upon your pious endeavours, Which the unhappy constitution of this Governm[t] (under which wee have for some time lived and groaned) hath hitherto impeeded, by endeavouring by all the Sinister waies and meanes possible not only to divert your Maj[ties] Loyall Subjects here from the Faith and allegiance w[ch] in Law and gratitude they owe your Maj[ties], but also by threatening and Menaceing with ruin and distruction such as should but dare to acknowledge the same, Stifling and concealing (as we humbly conceive and have just reason to suspect) such orders and Instructions for the proclaiming of your Maj[ties] Lawfull & undoubted right to and possession of the English Monarchy and its Dominions, as the rest of our neighbouring Collonies have received and promulgated; untill at length stirred up by the overruling hand of Divine Providence in opening our Eyes to discern our Duty, Wee have undertaken and hope, in a short time, to compleate throughout this Province the publick and generall acknowledgem[t] of your Maj[ties] undoubted right thereunto as well as other your Dominions and Territoryes; having for that purpose taken up armes in your Maj[ties] names, and without the expence of one drop of blood, blessed be God, rescued the Governm[t] from the hands of your Enemies, and shall reserve the same in such secure manner as wee can for your Maj[ties] Service, untill such time as in your princely wisdom you shall deigne to make Settlem[t] thereof, upon such person and in such manner and form as to your Maj[ties] shall seeme meete and convenient, whereunto wee shall, with all readiness and alacrity imaginable, most heartily and dutifully Submitt and Surrender; (according to the teno[r] of our Declaration, to w[ch] we humbly beg your Maj[ties] relation). Imploring your Maj[ties] serious and speedy consideration and favourable construction of our truly Loyall and dutifull endeavo[rs] herein for your Maj[ties] service and Interest, together with the propagation and Advancement of the Protestant Religion, wherein and for which your Maj[ties] have soe signally appeared and demonstrated to the World your Zeal. The Great God of heaven, who hath hitherto assisted you in your undertakeings, continue still on your Side, and prosper and conduct you throughout the whole Course of your lives, and since in this world you cannot have a Sufficient recompence, lett your reward be an Immortall Crowne of Glory, is, and shall be, the fervent, constant and incessant prayers of

"Your Maj[ties] most humble, Dutifull, Loyall and Obedient Subjects and Servants.

"Dated, in Maryland, the 3rd day of August, Anno 1689." [1]

The piety, loyalty and dutifulness were all for King William's eyes across the Atlantic; but for their fellow-subjects of Maryland, they had harsher language and rougher proceedings, as we presently shall see.

The first act of the associators, when they felt sure that they had the power in their own hands, was to send out precepts in their majesties' names, requiring the sheriffs of each county to notify the people to meet and choose "delegates and representatives," who were to assemble in convention at St. Mary's, on the 26th of August. They also issued a proclamation that "all officers not being papists," or who had not been actually in arms, "or any ways declared against their majesties' service, honor and dignity," should continue in their places; and ordered that the declaration of their motives for taking up arms should be read in all public places.

[1] Public Record Office, America and West Indies, No. 556.

In carrying out these measures, the associators met with considerable opposition. Sheriff Michael Taney, of Calvert county, resisted with tact as well as spirit. In a letter to Mrs. Barbara Smith, dated September 14, he says:

"Col. Jowles, showing me some of those papers, being directed to me, as sheriff of Calvert County, I not being willing to execute their commands, endeavored to excuse myself, saying I look upon myself, by the surrender of the government, to be discharged of my office. Whereupon Col. Jowles took some other course to have it done; but afterwards I, finding most people of our county, and being informed it was so generally through the country, that all people, except such as had been in arms or abetters to their cause, was willing to remain as they were until their Majesties pleasure should be known, and I conceiving that my consenting to choose delegates and representatives to sit in such Assembly, and they countenancing the thing that was done, although they were awed to it, would make me guilty as well as they that did it; therefore, I resolved not to choose, nor consent that any should be chose; however, being modest, forbore railing or speaking grossly of what was done. And when the time appointed was come for the election, Col. Jowles and divers of his soldiers being at the place, and I also and divers of the better sort of the people of our county, discourse arose about choosing representatives, and I and many others, being much the greater number, argued against choosing any. Amongst which discourse, Col. Jowles threatened that if we would not choose representatives freely, he would fetch them down with the long sword, and withall required the deputy clerk to read some papers that he had. Whereupon I asked Col. Jowles whether those papers were their majesties' authority, and if they were I would read them myself, if not, they should not be read. But he still bid the clerk read them. Whereupon I said to him and the rest of the company, 'Gentlemen, if the lord proprietary have any authority here, I command you, speaking to the clerk, in the name of the lord proprietary, to read no papers here.'"[1]

After this, "Colonel Jowles went away in great rage, saying he would choose none, yet afterwards, having got some of his soldiers to drink, he and they did somewhat which they called a free choice."

In consequence of this action, Sheriff Taney and others drew up the following "Declaration of the Inhabitants of Calvert County," giving their reasons for not choosing a representative to the proposed assembly:

"DECLARATION OF CALVERT COUNTY FOR NOT CHOOSING BURGESSES TILL AGAINST OCTOBER.

"*Maryland, 20th Aug. 1689.*

"*Calvert County:*

"Whereas, divers Persons have lately taken up Armes and have taken into their custody the Magazine of Armes and Amunition and also the Records of this Province, and doe pretend their designe is nothing More then the publick good of the Province, and in Order thereto (as they pretend) are now endeavouring to have an Assembly called. But wee whose names are here under written, being very confident and haveing good grounds to believe their Majestys, King William and queen Mary (whom God preserve), will most Certainly take care to protect us their Maj^ties loyall and protestant Subjects, and wee may expect it to be done the more speedily, Considering how great a revenew rises to the Crowne of England from this Province, therefore, believe that in a short time wee shall have some person come from England wth a full and Lawfull Authority and Comission

[1] Public Record Office, B. T. Md., i., B.D., p. 26.

to govern this Province, & most assuredly he will then call an Assembly wch we doubt not will be in Octob^r next, at farthest time enough to perfect and settle the affaires of this province, therefore, are not willing to run ourselves into the Extraordinary Charge of two assemblies, imediately one upon the back of the other, wee likewise are satisfied that noe persons doe nor will disturb those persons that have the possession of the said Magazines, records, and doe expect that they will keepe them safe & deliver them to a Lawfull Authority when it comes from England, therefore wee will choose noe Burgesses or delegates to sitt in Assembly untill a lawfull power from England require the same.

"Wittness our hands this 20th day of August, in the first year of their Maj^ties Reigne, Anno Dom. 1689.

"Mich: Taney, Sheriff of Calvert County; Richard Smith, jun^r, John Griggs, Tho. Clagett, Elisha Hall, Robert Day, Geo. Yougne, Francis Maldin, James Duke, Hezekiah Bussell, John Geyall, John Hume, John Smith, Joh. Holsworth, Jno Chillam, Jno Turner, Tho. Sedwicke, jun^r, Jno Holloway, Jno Manning, Francis Higham, Robt R. (*his* x *Mark*) Spickerwell, Wm Kesoyd, Wm Derumple, Tho. Butterfeild, Andrew (*his* x *Mark*) Bradde, Richd Ladd, Nath. Dare, Geo. Lingan, Richard Shephard, Richd Johns, John ——, Frances Hutchings, W^t Smith, Wm Turner, John Scott, John Grover, Christopher (*his* x *Merke*) Baines, John Renell, John Veitch, Francis Freeman, John (*his* x *Merke*) Kent, Edward Ballson, Jeremiah (*his* x *Merk*) Sherridon, Paule (*his* x *Merke*) Kisby, W^m (*his* x *Merk*) Greenall, Tho. Tasker, Francis Buxton, Edmond Howe, Thomas Hillary, John Willmot, Benjamin Hall, William Wadsworth, John (*his* x *Merk*) Godsgreall, Nath. Manning, Edward (*the* x *Merke of*) Blackborne, Tho. Guenest, Joseph Dawkins, Robt Anderson, James Veitch, William Smith, William Dawkins, W^m (*his* x *Merke*) Whittington, Tho. (*his* x *Merk*) Hinton, Hugh (*his* x *Merk*) Chintons, James (*his* x *Merk*) Baddcock, James Dossey, John Stone.[1]

This declaration, which Sheriff Taney says was signed by "the better sort of people," drew upon him the wrath of Coode and his followers, who ordered his arrest. He thus describes their behavior:

"I was fetched from my house on Sunday the 25th of August, 1689, by James Bigger and six other armed men, by order of the persons assembled at the command of Coad and his accomplices, and kept close prisoner at the house of Philip Lyons, under a guard of armed men, and, upon the 3^d day of September, carried by a company of soldiers before ye said Assembly, where Coad accused me of rebellion against their majesties, King William and Queen Mary, for acting as above written, and withal told me if I would submit to a trial they would assign me counsel. Whereto I answered them that I was a freeborn and loyal subject to their majesties of England, and therefore expected the benfit of all those laws of England that were made for the preservation of the lives and estates of all such persons, and, therefore, should not submit myself to any such unlawful authority as I take yours to be. Whereupon they demanded of me who was their majesties' lawful authority here? I answered, I was, as being an officer under the Lord Balltamore, until their majesties' pleasure should be otherwise lawfully made known. Then they ordered the soldiers to take me away awhile, and soon after ordered my bringing in again before them, with Mr. Smith and Mr. Botler, telling us it was the order of the House that we must find good and sufficient security to be bound for us to answer before their majesties' commissioners and lawful authority what should be objected against us, and in the mean time be of good behavior. To which we answered, their authorities we looked upon not lawful to force us to give any bonds, and that we had estates in this country sufficient to oblige our staying to answer what any lawful authority could object against us. Then we were again ordered away to Mr. Lyons', with a guard

[1] Public Record Office, America and West Indies, No. 556. B. T. Md., I., B. D., p. 8.

to keep us prisoners still, and afterwards, having considered with ourselves, we informed them, by Mr. Johns and several of them themselves speaking with us, that we would give them what bonds they pleased for our answering what should be objected against us by any lawful authority, leaving out the clause of good behavior, for that we knew they would make anything they pleased breach of good behavior, and under presence of that, trouble us again at their pleasure. But that would not do, so at the adjourning of the Assembly we were all ordered by them to be kept in safe custody of Mr. Gilbert Clarke, whom they made Sheriff of Charles County, until we should give bond as above required."[1]

Mrs. Barbara Smith gives the following circumstantial account of these proceedings, drawn up in London, no doubt at Lord Baltimore's request, to be laid before the Council and Board of Trade:

"The narrative of Barbara, wife of Richard Smith, of Puttexent River in Calvert County, in the Province of Maryland:

"Upon the 25th of March last a rumour was spread abroad about the Mouth of Puttexent River that Ten thousand Indians were come downe to the western branch of the said River, whereupon my husband went up to the said Western branch where he found noe Indians but there a strong report that nine thousand were at Matapany and at the Mouth of Puttexent and that they had cutt off Capt. Bownes family and had inforted themselves at Matapany which was all false, upon these rumors the Country rose in Armes but after diligent search and inquiry in all parts of the Province this rumour was found to be only a Sham and noe Indians any where appeared to disturb or molest any the people of our Province All which reports I do verily believe were designedly spread abroad to incite the People to rise in Armes as afterwards by the like than they were induced to doe. For in the latter end of July following one Capt. Code, Coll. Towels, Maj[r] Beal, M[r]. Blakiston with some others appeared in Armes and gave for their pretence that the Papists had invited the Northern Indians to come down cut off the Protestants and that their descent was to be about the latter end of August when roasting hares [ears] were in Season and that they therefore rose in Armes to secure the Magazine of Armes and Ammunition and the Protestants from being cut off by the said Indians and Papists. This was their pretence to those they found very apprehensive of the said Indians to others they said their designe was only to proclaim the King and Queen, but when the aforesaid persons with some others had gathered together a great number of People together they then came and seized upon the government. Who withstood them first at St. Maryes in the State House where the Records are kept, whom the said Code and his party soon overcame and seized upon the Records, from there he proceeded with his party to Matapany House wherein Coll. Darnall with some forces as many protestants as Papists had garisoned themselves, but were soon forced to Capitulate surrender and yield to the said Code & his Aly. They haveing thus possessed themselves of the government, one Johnson Master of a Ship being bound for England they gave him charge he should carry noe Letters but what was sent from themselves and my Husband they arrested and put in Prison for fear he should goe for England with the said Johnson to give an account of their proceedings and as soon as the said Johnson was gone they released him again, the said Code and his complices then sent out letters to all Countyes of the Province to choose an Assembly, what was done in the rest of the Countyes besides Calvert and Ann Arrundell I am not acquainted with, but when the said Letters for the choosing of Burgesses came to our Sheriff to sumon the people for that purpose he refused the same, they then went to M[r]. Elegatt Corroner and he alsoe refused (who are both Protestants) whereupon Coll. Jowles rode about to give the people notice himselfe. When the County were come

[1] London Public Record Office, America and West Indies, No. 556; B. T. Md., i., B. D., p. 8, and Davis' *Day Star*, p. 100, etc.

together most of the Housekeepers agreed not to choose any Burgesses and drew up an abhorence against such proceedings, the which Election was alsoe much opposed by our Sheriff whereupon Coll. Jowles gathered his souldiers and caused the Election to be made by the number he had which was not above twenty and of them not above ten that were capable of Electing, Coll. Jowles himself and Maj^{r}. Beale his next officer were returned for two of the Burgesses Elected and because M^{r}. Taney the Sheriff and my Husband endeavored to oppose the said Election the said Code caused them to be put in Prison. Neither for this Election nor in their Cause did almost any of our County appear that were men of Estates or Men of note, but they to the contrary published an abhorence against such proceedings, and were themselves as are most of our County Protestants. The County of Ann Arrundell which is accounted the most populous and richest of the whole Province, and wherein is but one Papist family unanimously stood out and would not elect any Burgesses. About the 21st of August the Assembly of their calling met before whom was brought M^{r}. Taney our Sheriff and my Husband, and Capt. Code and his complices haveing pretended they had the Kings Proclamation for what they did my husband demanded to see the same, but their answer was, 'Take him away Sheriff.' M^{r}. Taney likewise asking them by what authority he was called before them Code answered, 'What, this is like King Charles, and you are King Taney. Take him away.' Notwithstanding upon the said Codes riseing as before is said, their pretence was chiefly to secure the Country against the Indians, yet all this while nor untill my comeing away which was the 26th of Septem^{r} last there was not the least appearance of any foreign or Home Indians coming to disturb us. What was their further proceedings in their Assembly I am not able to give any account of but M^{r}. Taney and My husband were detained Prisoners at my coming away.

"BARBARA SMITH.

"Dated in LONDON *the 30th of December, 1689.*" [1]

Mr. Peter Sayer, in a letter to Lord Baltimore, dated December 31, 1689, gives a humorous and lively report of such of their proceedings as came under his observation. He says:

"My Lord,

"Since my last to your Lordship (which was in Johnson, the veriest rogue that ever crost saltwater) there has not bin a more tragick comedy of rebellion acted since the Royall bounty of King James and King Charles of blessed memory bestowed upon your Ancestors the Charter of this Province of Maryland. To lay itt downe in all its acts and scenes would be too tedious there being some of the Actors (whom God send safely to arrive) will give your Lordship an orall relation of all. I shall only trouble your Lordship with some few particulars which they (being forc'd to abscond) may not have notice of. As soon as the noise came into our County that one Massinella Coade had gott at the head of five or six hundred men, Griff Jones sends a note to Clayland (then preaching) that he and his auditory must come away presently to the Court house, which they did, where this villanous rascall perswaded the poor silly Mobile that if they did not sign to that paper (a Copy of which your Lordship hath) they should all certainly loose their Estates. Upon this our County (who were before as quiet as lambs) gott to such a head & crying that all their throats should be cutt by the Papists, that if Coade's order for disbanding of every body then in Arms had not come to Will Combes, our temorous Magistrates could never have quitted 'em. With this order came up his declaration, which was read att our Court house the fourth day following which was the 15th of August. All people being warned to come and hear it by the Clearke of our County Nich^{s} Lowe, Coll: Coursey being likewise invited for his advice by M^{r}. Robotham who according came and advised them to lett no papers be read that came from any of the

[1] London Public Record Office, America and West Indies, No. 556; B. D., p. 17.

Rebells, except they would permitt him or that M[r]. Robotham himself would paraphrase, and lett the people know what damn'd falsities were contained in 'em; butt M[r]. Robotham reply'd, that if any body should contradict any thing, in that humour the people were in, they should have all their braines knockt out: Sayes Coll. Coursey, 'What did you send for me for, if you won't take my advise; would you have me hear a company of lyes tould against my Lord Baltemore, to whom I have sworn fidelity, and so have you. If your conscience will, mine won't permitt me to doe itt.' After a great many arguments the Court was call'd butt no Coll: would appear with 'em: In short my Lord, the declaration was read, with Coad's other orders by Nick Lowe, after which Mr. Robothom (without mentioning the goodness or badness of the things read) asks them how they should dispose of the County Arms, and who should be their officers, never mentioning the duty or faithfulness they owed to your Lordship and your substitutes (which I believe was forgettfulness) but hoped that none of them (by what they heard read) would act any thing against your Lordship, or your Country, and to be quiett and peaceable and in a small time all would be well. Two or three dayes after came up Coade's circular letters commanding every County to choose four delegates who were to be ready att St Maries on the 26th of August. The 24th they sent for my Arms and Amunition, and Mad[m] Lloyd's, betwixt thirty and forty men headed by Sweatman, who had a warrant (in their Maj[ties] names) from Edward Man, Will[m] Combes and J[no] Edmondson to take what arms and amunition they could find for the Country's use, for that our Indians (haveing fled from the Towne and cutt up their corne) had reported, that they onely staid 'till the two great men came from the North, meaning Coll Darnall and Major Sewall who the day before parted from my house. I was resolved to find out who was the inventor of those falsities, and rid downe to Oxford to our Burgesses, who were just then takeing boat, where I met a great company of people, who askt me whether I knew not of Coll Darnall and Major Sewall's being at our Indian Towne. 'No,' said I, 'butt I know they were last night at Coll: Lowes, and are now gone home.' Upon this I desired the burgesses to send some people to the Indians, to know the cause why they deserted the Towne, and betook themselves to the Swamp; they said, itt was a folly to go, for the Indians would not come out except Coll: Coursey came, I tould 'em a Tackahick from him would doe, and I would frame one, and send Mr. John Hawkins with itt: Att last they pickt out four or five men (who knew best where the Indians were) and signed Instructions for 'em to enquire as above. They went, and brought the answer which your Lordship has a copy of. This was the Tuesday, and because Will Combes was to muster by Coade's order on Thursday, I stay'd with him to see how my old souldiers would look upon me being cashier'd. On Thursday night I came home. The Wednesday following came a Justice of peace and three or four more, who had a kindness for me and ask'd me where I was last Saterday? 'Where?' sayes I, 'Here.' 'Lord Jesus!' said they, 'what lyes goes abroad?' 'Why, what's the matter?' said I; 'Begod,' said the Justice, 'Dick Sweatman had much adoe to keep Capt. Halfield and his Company from comeing to take you.' 'Take me,' said I; 'for what?' 'Why,' sayes he, 'there's two men att old Watt's will swear that last Saturday they see you over against the Indian Towne, where you shot off two pistols, and three or four cannows full of Indians came over to you, to whom you tould that within ten dayes you would be with 'em at the head of a thousand other Indians.' I asked the fellows names; and they tould me, and that they lived by the Indian Towne, and desir'd me withall to make hast to Maj[r] Combes, for that Sweatman was gone to tell him the story. The next day I went to Combes's where meeting his wife at the doore, she imediately cryed out, 'O Lord! Coll: I was allweys glad to see you, butt now am ten times gladder than ever I was.' 'Why?' says I; 'why,' sayes she, 'there's a parcell of lying devills would perswade the people that you were att the Indian Towne last Saturday; butt that I tould 'em you were a Thursday att our house, they would all come to your house. My husband's gone to the Indian Towne to know the certainty well.' Saies I, 'I'll stay till he comes back and he shan't be hang'd for your sake.' 'Nay Gad,' sayes she, 'if I knew this would have excused him, I had not spoke a word.' I stay'd till they came back and tould me that the fellows said they were tould so by an Indian, and the Indian being questioned, said, he heard itt from two of the Nanticoke Indians, and so it was put off from one to t'other 'till itt was lost, and they all say now (being deceived so many times by these sham reports) that if I should really deal with the Indians against the protestants (which God forbid I should be so wicked) they would never believe itt; yett those damn'd malicious stories was in a fair way to pull my house downe about my Ears, and which has really turn'd your Lordships Government out of the Province, for they doe not pretend to meddle with your Lordships title to itt. Coll Darnall & Major Sewall won't come so well off about their treaties with the Northern Indians, altho' there is as much truth in one as t'other."[1]

As for the reports of the hostile disposition of the Indians, they were the merest falsity, but quite of a piece with all the other proceedings of Coode and his followers, who, working on the credulity of the people, obtained the countenance of many who would have shrunk from them with abhorrence had they known their true character.

On August 23d, a committee who had been sent to confer with the Indians, and see how they were disposed, made the following report:

"These may acquaint you that we, whose names are under written, have, according to request, bin and treated with the Indians, and doe find 'em to be very civill and kind, and desire nothing butt peace and quietness, butt that in part thorough the instigation of bad people, and chiefly doe instance Andrew Gray, that the English in one moone would cut them all off; likewise concerning an Indian woman, wch they say was killed by Cornelius Mubraine's wife, wch they have expected some satisfactory answer concerning, which as yett they have not received. Also that the said Cornelius, since their departure, offered great abuse in robbing them of their cannous, corn matts, bowles, and basketts, and they say their chests have been broke open, and since they have bin gone out, the said Gray hath bin with 'em and threatened them if they would not come home he would gett a party of men and fetch 'em pér force. Likewise they say they have ten Indians wch went between Oxford towne and Coll. Lowe's, and that their time of return is elapsed, and are not satisfyed what is become of 'em. Whereof all these things being computed together, hath seized them with feare; butt that they were very joyfull att our comeing, and were takeing up their goods to return to their habitations.

"John Stanley, John Hawkins, Clement Sales, Wm. Dickinson, Wm. Stevens, Wm. Bealey."[2]

By the same ship which carried out the associators' address, his lordship's council endeavored to send an account of the revolution to him in London. Captain Johnson, "the veriest rogue that ever crossed salt water," received the letters and promised to deliver them with others as directed, but immediately upon their receipt betrayed his trust by turning them over to Coode. When the council found out their mistake they requested Johnson to allow Colonel Darnall and Major Sewall to take passage in his vessel for London, so as to enable them to convey in person the information they desired to impart to his lordship. This he also refused, and the gentlemen were compelled to

[1] London Public Record Office, America and West Indies, No. 556; B. D., p. 24.

[2] London Public Record Office, B. T. Md., 1, B. D., p. 25$\frac{1}{4}$.

go to Pennsylvania to procure, if possible, a passage from that province. Upon their arrival there, they found that they had just missed a passage, and hearing that Coode was endeavoring to impress upon the minds of the people that they had gone to bring in the Northern Indians, they returned to Ann Arundel, county ("which never had joined with Coode and his party"). Here they remained until the 26th of September, when Major Sewall being sick, Colonel Darnall took passage in the ship *Everard*, and arrived safely in England, where he gave Lord Baltimore a full account in writing of these proceedings.[1]

Mr. Sayer in his letter to Lord Baltimore, previously cited, gives the following quaint account of the meeting of the Associators' "convention." He says:

"The first thing they did, after they voted themselves a full house, tho' there were ten of the forty-two absent, viz. Ann Arundle, Somersett, and two of Cecil; but Somersett came over the last day and excused their delay, saying, they heard all things were done in your Lordship's name, but indeed they intended to own no other power but their Majesties', which excuse was readily accepted of *nemine contradicente*: Little Jenkins was chief, whom your Lordship may remember, and I hope will. They fixed upon the State House door a prohibition that no Papist should come into the city during the Assembly. The rest of the transactions your Lordship will see in the papers which Jack Lewellin has promised to give to my man, who is going down with him, only I must tell your Lordship, that the Committee of Secrecy appointed for the discovery of Col. Darnall's and Major Sewall's dealing with the Northern Indians, is kept on foot still. It is composed of Blackstone, Jowels, Gibt. Clark, and one or two more I forgott. Upon their report to the house (which was presently voted to be entered), a vote passed that letters should be sent to each neighboring governments as far as New England, that the house had found by several substantial evidences that your Lordship's Deputies have been tampering with the Northern Indians to come in and cutt off the protestants and therefore desires all of 'em to hold a strict correspondency with this goverment and to take up all persons of this Colony that shall seem any way suspicious; This is the purport, but I'me promis'd a copy of the letter itt self. The grand ordinance is not yett come up, which must give the measure to all their Actions both civill and Millitary. Your Lordship will see in itt all the officers, and by that know that those that have gott Estates under your Lordship are as ready to serve Jack Coade as your Lordship butt there are some entered that I'me sure will never comply with itt. People in debt think itt the bravest time that ever was. No Courts open, nor no law proceedings, which they pray may continue as long as they live. I ask'd why Coade and his Councill divested themselves of that supream power which they usurped att first, and t'was tould me that Coade proposed to the house to have a standing Committee to receive all appeals and be as the grand Councill of the Country, butt the house would be all alike in power, that the officers civill and Millitary of each respective County should give definitive sentences in all matters whatsoever, till further orders out of England, so that Coade and his adherents now have no more power out of their County than we cashiered officers. They have drawne many Impeachments against severall, which are not sent home, and which they keep untill the king sends or orders Commissioners. It's a pleasant thing to see the Rascalls in their cupps. Coade calls himself Massinella, butt vaunts he has outraigned him, and little Taylard is his Wiggins, Jowels will be Count Scamburgh and

[1] The narrative of Col. Henry Darnall and Mr. Hill, to Lord Baltimore and the letter of Mr. Johns to Mr. Groome, on account of these matters, will be found at the end of this chapter.

Ninian Beal, Argyle, Furlin glories in the name of Ferguson and Cheseldyn is Speaker Williams, butt the Dog will never have so much witt, and I believe that if those persons of honor whose names they usurp did butt know what villians they were, instead of a recompence (which they expect from his Maj[tie]) would gett an order that they mat, be try'd & hang'd. And now I think I have given your Lordship trouble enough to spoile your next meale yett my Lord, this comfort remains still that the best men and best protestants such as Coll: Coursey, Coll: Codd, Coll: Wells and a great many others (men of the best Estates and real professors of the protestant Religion) stand stiffly up for your Lordship's interest. This onely more I have to say in my own behalf, being att present much afflicted with the gout, as I have been this pretty while, which will be enough (I hope) to gain your Lordship's pardon for all faults committed in this Relation. Committing your Lordship and family to the protection of Almighty God, presenting my humble duty to your Lordship and Lady, and my humble service to little Master and the young Ladies, I am, My Lord, your Lordship's most humble servant,

"PETER SAYER."[1]

On the 28th of August, 1689, after the "Convention" met, "The Committee of Secrecy," referred to in Mr. Sayer's letter to Lord Baltimore, made the following report:

"The Committee of Secrecy appointed by this present Assembly, the Representative Body of this Province, doe make their Report as followeth, viz.:

"Wee have diligently, faithfully, and with all due circumspection, made inquisition into the severall affaires and concernes committed to our care, for discovering of the truth thereof, and we find, First, that the late Popish Governors have contrived, conspired and designed by severall villanous practices and machinations, to betray their Maj[ties] Protestant subjects of this Province to the French, Northern, and other Indians; and that there hath been, and still is, eminent danger of our lives, libertyes and estates, by the malitious endeavors and combinations of the said Governors with the Indians and Papists to assist in our destruction and the subversion of our Religion. And wee also find, by the informations, examinations, evidences and depositions by us taken, that the late Governors did prorogue and obstruct the last Assembly from meeting, least the truth of their unjust contrivances and wicked designes should be made manifest.

"And wee, the Committee aforesaid, doe also discover and apparently find the trayterous undertakings of the said Governours in their Renunciation, disowning and denying the right, title and Soveraignty of King William and Queen Mary to the Crowne of England and its Dominions.

"The verity of the above particulars is to be further proved by other numerous circumstances and evidences that are now in the custody of the said Committee, for their Maj[ties] service.

"Read, approved of, and ordered to be entered in the Journall of the House of Assembly."[2]

On the same day the "convention" addressed a letter to the governors and presidents of Virginia, Pennsylvania, New York and New England, informing them of the "conspiracies and combinations against the Protestant inhabitants of Maryland," which had "caused the present commotion," and

[1] S. P. O., B. T. Md., i., B. D., p. 24.

[2] On the back of this report is the following endorsement: "Memorandum, notwithstanding the Country have often desired a proofe of the accusations this Committee charged upon some of y[e] Lord Proprietaryes Dep[tys], yet the same could never be obtained, or was any wayes made appear."—S. P. O., B. T. Md., i., B. D. S.

asking the "hearty affections, love and good will" of their neighbors. On the 4th of September they drew up and adopted the following address to the king:

"THE ADDRESS OF THE REPRESENTATIVES OF THEIR MAJ[TIES] PROTESTANT SUBJECTS IN THE PROVINCE OF MARYLAND ASSEMBLED.

"To the King's most excellent Maj[tie]:

"Whereas, Wee are, with all humility, fully assured that the benefitt of your Maj[ties] glorious undertakeings and blessed Success for the Protestant Religion and civill rights and libertyes of your Subjects was graciously intended to be extensive, as well to this remote part, as to all others of your Maj[ties] Teritorys and Countreys, being thereby influenced to express our utmost zeale and endeavours for your Maj[ties] Service and the Protestant Religion, here of late notoriously opposed, and your Maj[ties] Soveraign Dominion and Right to this your Maj[ties] Province of Maryland, invaded and undermined by our late Popish Governo[rs], their Agents and Complices:

"Wee, your Maj[ties] most dutifull, Loyall Subjects of the said Province, being assembled as the representative body of the same, doe humbly pray your Maj[ties] gracious consideration of the great grievances and expressions wee have long layne under, lately represented to your Maj[tie] and directed to your Maj[ties] principall Secretarys' of State, in a certain Declaration from the Commanders, Officers and Gentlemen in Armes for your Maj[ties] Service, and Defence of the Protestant Religion.

"And that your Maj[tie] would be graciously pleased, in such waies and methods as to yo[r] Princely wisedome shall seeme meete, to appoint such a Deliverance to your Suffering People whereby, for the future, our Religion, Rights and Libertyes may be secured under a Protestant Governm[t] by your gracious direction especially to be appointed.

"Wee will waite with all becoming Duty and Loyalty your Maj[ties] pleasure herein, and will, in the meane time (to the hazard of our lives and fortunes), persevere and continue to vindicate and Defend your Majestie's Right and Soveraign Dominion over this Province, the Protestant Religion, and the civill Rights and Libertyes of your Maj[ties] Subjects here against all manner of attempts and Oppositions whatsoever, Hereby unanimously declareing that as wee have a full sense of the blessings of heaven upon your Maj[ties] Generous undertakeings, Soe wee will endeavour to express our due gratitude for the same, as becomes professors of the best of Religions, and Subjects to the best of Princes.

"Maryland: Dated in the Assembly sitting at the State house, in the City of St. Maries, the 4th day of September, 1689, in the first year of their Maj[ties] Reign."[1]

The address to William was ingeniously contrived. That monarch had just seized the crown of England by violent measures, and even though those measures had the approval of the majority of the English people, they were none the less revolutionary; consequently he could not with consistency severely blame an act which seemed a consequence and a reflection of his own. He mounted the throne as the champion and protector of the Protestant religion, and the Associators professed to be merely carrying out in the colony the same measures of defence against "Popish" tyranny that had been successfully accomplished in England. A foreign prince, he was likely not to understand very clearly, or feel very stringently if he understood, the solemn obligations of a charter granted by the father of the monarch whom he had

[1] London Public Record Office, America and West Indies, No. 556; B. T. Md, 1., B. D., p. 13.

dethroned; and wise and good though he may have been, he was not the king to refuse to take the franchises of a people who seemed servilely eager to lay them in his hands.

The freemen of the counties—or at least such of them as favored the movement—hastened to send addresses to their majesties, of which the following are specimens:

"ADDRESS OF THE JUSTICES OF THE COUNTY OF KENT TO THE KING.

"To The High and Mighty Prince William, by the Grace of God, of England, Scotland, France & Ireland, King, Defendor of the Faith, &c.

"The Humble Address of yo[r] Majestys most Loyall protestant Subjects, the Justices and Grand Jury of the County of Kent, within yo[r] Majesty's province of Maryland, in America, in Court now Sitting:

"Wee, yo[r] Majesty's most Loyall & Dutifull Subjects, doe, in all Humility, Render our most hearty and Dutyfull thankes unto yo[r] most Sacred Majestys for yo[r] great and unwearied Care and the hazzard of yo[r] Royall persons you have been pleased (with the Assistance of Almighty God) to take over uss, in rescueing uss out of the hands of popery and Tyranny, which, like a cloud, had over spread this yo[r] Majestys province; And, in persuance of yo[r] Majestys most gratious declaracion, Dated at yo[r] Majestys Court of White Hall, the nineteenth of February, in the first year of yo[r] Majestys Reign, wee, with the Consent of all the rest of yo[r] Majestys most Loyall Subjects within yo[r] Majesty's province of Maryland, and in a parliamentary way Assembled, have displaced all Roman Catholicks whatsoever from beareing any office, Civill or Military, within this yo[r] Majesty's province. And forasmuch as yo[r] Most Sacred Majesty hath been gratiously pleased (with the Assistance of Almighty God) Even to the Hazzard of your Royall person, to rescue uss from those Evills and Eminent Dangers, which, like violent flouds, weere breaking in upon uss, Wee doe, therefore, most Humbly Implore the Continuance of yo[r] Majesty's most Royall favours towards uss, & wee doe, and shall, soe long as life is in uss, pray to Allmighty God to bless yo[r] Majesty and yo[r] Royall Consort with long and happy Reign over uss, and with Joy and bliss in the World to Come, which is and shall bee the Constant prayers of yo[r] Majesty's most Loyall and Dutyfull Subjects.

"Dated at Kent County this Twenty Eight day of November, in the first yeare of yo[r] Majesty's Reign, Anno Domini 1689.

"Signed by order of the said Justices and Grand Jury.

"MILLER, *Clericus Comita: Kent.*"[1]

"ADDRESS OF THE INHABITANTS OF THE COUNTY OF SOMERSETT, TO THEIR MA[TYS].

"*Novem'r the 28th, 1689.*

"To the King and Queen's most Excellent Majestys:

"Wee yo[r] Majesty's Subjects in the County of Somersett and Province of Maryland, being refreshed and Encouraged by yo[r] Majesty's great and prosperous Undertakeings, and by yo[r] late gracious letter to those of this Province, doe Cast our Selves at yo[r] Majestys Feete, humbly desireing and hopefully Expecting the Continuance of your Majesty's care of us, as our Case and Circumstances doe or may require, in the Confidence whereof Wee resolve to continue (By the grace of God,) in the Profession of the Protestant Religion, and yo[r] Majesty's title and intrest against the French and other Papists That Oppose and trouble us in soe just and good a Cause, not doubting, but yo[r] Majesty's wisdome and Clemency will afford unto us all Needfull suitable Aid and Protection for secureing our Religion, Lives and libertys under Protestant Governors and Government, and for

[1] London Public Record Office, America and West Indies No. 556; B. D, p. 35.

Inableing us to defend ourselves Against all Invaders: thus Praying for yo[r] Majesty's long and happy Reigne Over us, Wee Avow ourselves to bee with due Reverence and sincerity,

"Yo[r] Majesty's Loyall, Obedient And Humble Subjects,

"John Huett, W[m] Coulbourne, Jun[r], Thomas Wilson, Henry Phillips, John Parsons, Thomas Shiles, Thomas Stivenson, James Knox, John Browne, W[m] Alexander, Randolph Revell, Peter Elzey, James Smith, Ephraem Wilson, Thomas Smith, Archibald Smith, John Knox, Thomas Walter, John Knox, Thomas Walter, Alexander Knox, Alexander Proctor, John Renshaw, James Conner, John Goldsmith, John Browne, W[m] Owen, Malcom Knox, William Knox, William Hacaland, Richard Jarrett, Nathaniell Clark, George Bozman, John Nelson, William Waller, George Phebus, John Rawley, John Jones, George Park, W[m] Polk, W[m] Wilson, Edward Surnam, William Wilmot, Micajah Sadler, John Chanceleer, John Smocke, Nicholas Cornwell, Robert Cade, John Miller, Adam Spence, Tho. Midgley, John Baron, John Deale, Martin Curtis, Clement Giles, Robert Johnson, William Bowen, Devoraux Diegas, Robert Simson, Edw[d] Evans, Hugh Tingle, John Colston, Richard Warren, Mathew Jones, Richard Hill, Thomas Edwards, Alexand[r] Mackcullah, George Beniam, Andrew Miller, Patrick Reed, Henry Reed, John Steel, William Browne, Thomas Bromley, William Wouldhane, Richard Wildgoose, John Lucas, John Johnson, Richard Cole, William Oswell, John Snow, George Latcham, William Law, William Alexander, Jun[r]., John Gray, Robert Polk, Thomas Pollett, Charls Mullen, Arnold Elzey, Charls Ractlife, (*sic*,) William Melvell, William Smith, Richard Mackclure, John White, William White, John Rowell, John Killam, John More, Sam[ll] Hopkins, Jun[r]., Benjamine Kezar, Ralph Milbourne, Henry Hall, Francis Heap, John Pope, Thomas Oxford, William Hearne, Richard Pepper, John Saunders, Nathaniell Abbott, William Coard, William Hall, William Davis, Joshua Light, John Rust, Nathaniell Vesey, Richard Woodcraft, Tobias Pepper, Walter Read, John Peterfranck, Stephen Page, John Tarr, Alexander White, William Nelson, Michaell Hannah, William Lawrence, John Swaine, Ambroce Archer, William Stevenson, James Barber, Sam[ll] Showell, William Turvill, John M[ck]nitt, W[m] Coulbourne, James Marrah, John Roach, Owen M[ck]graw, William Round, Richard Farwell, Alexander Kyll, Thomas Poynter, John Strawbridge, Adam Hitch, William Burch, Thomas Gordan, Nicholas Carpenter, John Henderson, Francis Joyce, Richard Hill, Edm[d] Beachamp, Allen Ross, Geo. Nobell, Richard Britten, Peter Whaples, William Layton, William Bozman, Geo. Lane, John Crawley, Sam[ll] Worthington, Robert Perry, Moses Fenton, John Porter, Ninian Dulan, James Henderson, James Duncan, John Barber, John Hicks, William Mead, Robert Nearne, Henry Mills, Richard Dennis, Thomas Morgan, Humphrey Read, William Shankland, David Dredan, John Watt, John Ellis, Thomas Ellis, John Starret, William Fossit, Thomas Dalahide, Arthur Hauley, Robert Boyer, Nicholas Todvin, Geo. Layfield Comp[r], Michaell Clugstone, Lawrence Cranford, W[m]. Traile, Thomas Wilson, Sam[ll] Davis, Peter Dent, John West, John Bozman, James Sangster, John Tayler, Edward Jones, Thomas Poole, Roger Burkham, John Emmit, John King, William Planer, William Planer, Jun[r], Richard Tull, Thomas Tull, Robert Hall, John Braughton, William Nobell, John Colhoune, John Williams, Richard Chambers, John Trupshaw, Mathew Dorman, James Langreene, Nath[ll] Horsey, Alexander Thomas, John Mackbride, John Christopher, Phillip Askew, Roger Phillips, Robert Crouch, George Baley, Lazurus Maddux, John Davis, Henry Hamon, Miles Harrison, Tho. Dixon, Alexander Maddux, John Frankland, W[m]. Coulbourne, David Brown, Francis Jenkins, W[m]. Brerton, John Winder, Rob[t]. King, James Dashell, Stephen Luff, Thomas Newbold, James Round, Sam[ll] Hopkins, Edm[d]. Howard, Thomas Jones, Henry Smith.

"This is a true Coppy taken from the Originalls, Examined and signed by the Ord[r] of the respective p'sons above named.

"Peter Dent, dpty Collect[r] of his Majesty's Customes in the County of Somersett."[1]

[1] London Public Record Office, America and West Indies, No. 556; B. D., p. 38.

"ADDRESS OF TALBOT COUNTY TO THE KING, REC[D] FROM MY L[D] SHREWSBURY THE 7 FEB: 1689–90.

"*Maryland, 1689.*

"To the most sacred Maj[ties] of Great Brittain &c.:

"The Humble Address of your Maj[ties] most Loyall Protestant Subjects, Inhabitant of Talbot County in the Province of Maryland.

"Dread Sovereigns,

"The congratulations of your Maj[ties] happy Access to the Throne and Imperiall Crowne of our Native Countrey of England together with the Recognition of your Maj[ties] undoubted Right and Soveraignty thereunto and also to this your Maj[ties] Province and other your Dominions and Territoryes (which hath been already represented to your Maj[ties] in a Generall Address from this Province). Wee have not deemed sufficient to Demonstrate our Zeale and Affection for your Maj[ties] Royall persons and Interest. And therefore humbly acknowledging and rendering thankes to Almighty God for your pious and Princely care and endeavours for the restitution of our Antient Lawes Religion and properties to their primitive purity Lustre and Splendor Soe happily accomplished and Effected, Wee presume now particularly to Address your Maj[ties] humbly prostrating our Selves at your Royall Feete, and Imploreing your Gracious Answer to our Humble Supplications therein sett forth; That your Maj[ties] would favourably receive and accept us into your Royall protection, and vouchsafe to Settle the Governm[t] of this Province in the true Protestant Religion, in such manner and forme as to your Maj[ties] in your Royal and Princely wisdom shall seeme most meete and convenient, That Wee may participate the happy Influences of your Maj[ties] Glorious Atchievements and Accomplishments with the rest of our fellow Subjects in our Native Countrey of England, and others your Dominions and Territoryes: and be the better Enabled to serve your Maj[ties] with all imaginable Alacrity, joineing with them in the hearty and Sincerely well wishing your Maj[ties] Long Life and happy Reign in this world, and a Crowne of glory in the next And that there may never want of your Royall Offspring to succeed you in the Throne, As is and for Ever shall be the constant fervent and incessant prayers of

"May it please your Maj[ties] your Maj[ties] most humble Dutifull Loyall and Obedient Subjects and Servants,

"Edward Man, William Combes, George Robotham, Thomas Smithson, Mich[ll] Turbutt, James Smith, W[m] Finney, James Sedgwick, Sam Withers, John Edmondson, W[m] Sharp, Rob. Smeth, Anthony Rumball, Tho. Bruff, James Ross, John Dally, William Ridgaway, James Edmondson, Walter Quinton, Abraham Morgan, John Barker, William Troth, John Whittington, Richard Sweatnam, James Downes, James Benson, Michell Hacket, Robert Norest, Charles Holkinworth, Andrew Hamillton, Jn[o] Swaine, John Lambe, Joseph Lambert, John Stanley, T. Delahay."[1]

"ADDRESS OF THE INHABITANTS OF ST. MARY'S COUNTY, RECEIVED FROM MY L[D] SHREWSBURY, 7 FEB: 1689.

"*Maryland, 1689.*

"To their most Sacred Majestys:

"The humble address of your most dutyfull and Loyall Protestant Subjects, the Inhabitants of S[t]. Mary's County, in y[r] Maj[tys] Province of Maryland, etc., etc., etc.

"Kenelm Cheseldyn, Jn[o] Coode, W[m] Blackiston, John Turlinge, Ric. Cloude, John Dent, Joh. Davies, John Llewellin, Edw[d] Greenhalgh, Jo. Watson, George Plater, Sam[el] Cooksey, Tho. Lord, John Hilton, Edward Henly, Thomas Sikes, Ralph Foster, Danell Crew, W[m] Hodgson, Edward Fair, Edward Tedman, Upgate Reeves, Robert Frazer, Clement Hely, Henry Lawrence, John Rosse, James Simmons, Peter Johnson, John Green, Absolon Tennison, Abraham Price, Robert Fletcher, Tho. Jordan, John Greaves,

[1] London Public Record Office, America and West Indies, No. 556; B. D., p. 39.

Daniel Hanley, James Swann, Joshua Houlldsworth, Henry Portter, John Cheverill, Rich^d (*his* x *Merk*) Scot, John Hastins, Wm Blankenstein, John Shanks, Walter Watkins, Michel Coutis, Robt Foster, Wm Taylor, Edward Crevin, Sam (*his* x *Merke*) Abell, Tho. (*his* x *Mark*) Reynolds, Tho. Waughon, John Marttyndall, William Aisquith, Thomas Hebb, John (*his* x *Mark*) Redman, Peter (*his* x *Mark*) Watts, Edwd (*his* x *Mark*) Killsha, Daniel (*his* x *Mark*) Smith, William (*his* x *Mark*) Wherrett, Henry (*his* x *Mark*) Lewis, Edward Sissons, John Millner, Robt Fargason, John Little, Robt Crane, Tho. Hixon, Henry Morgan, David Holt, John Reerely, William Rylands, Tho. Price, jun^r, William Stinson, Edwd Probe, Jo^n Skipper, John Loe, Tho. Carvill, Jo^n Blomfield, John Tan, Tho Marrum, W. Taylard, Tho. Attaway, Robt Carss, John Cambell, Charles Gough, Thomas Green, William Hardy.[1]

"ADDRESS OF THE INHABITANTS OF CHARLES COUNTY TO THEIR MAJ^TIES REC^d FROM MY LORD SHREWSBURY, 7 FEB. 1689.

"*Maryland, 1689.*

"To their most Excellent Majesties, King William and Queen Mary:

"The Humble Address of the Gentlemen, Merchants, Planters, Freeholders and Freemen, their Majesties Protestant Subjects in Charles County, in the Province of Maryland, etc., etc., etc.

"Hum. Warren, James Smallwood, William Hawtan, Hen. Hardy, Cha. Shepherd, John Wilder, Cleborne Lomax, John Wincott, Joseph Manning, Philip Lynes, Robert Thompson, Stephen Mankin, W^m. Stone, Joseph Bullox, George Pleter, Will. Hutchison, Edward Middleton, Michaell Mynock, Jno Marten, W^m. Newman, Phill. Frost, Henry Hawkins, Abell Wakefeild, Fra. Adams, Ralphe Shawe, Tho. Parker, Thos. Wakefeild, Edwd Eaton, James Kingsbury, Richard Land, Thos. Whichaley, John Courts, Jno. Allward, Jno. Goazly, Wm Barton, Senr., John Cuncey, John Callock, Rich. Dodd, James Thomson, Jno Cage, Arthur Eathey, John Knolewater, Henry Franklin, Henry Belcher, Valentine Hill, Edw. Philpott, Bennjamen Posey, Mathew Dyke, Edward Rookewood, George Breett, W^m. Taylor, W^m. Spikeman, Jo^n. Cornish, Rich. Wade, John Ratcliff, Robert Powel, John Payn, George Newman, James Turner, Edward Turner, Peter Oat, Robert Powell, Randolph Hinson, John Addison, Richard Newton, John Gibbs, Alexander Mckarter, Hugh Bawden, Law. Rochford, P. Deyzer, Gilb^t. Clarke, Vicecom. Comitat."[2]

"ADDRESS OF CALVERT COUNTY, REC^D FROM MY L^D SHREWSBURY, THE 7 FEB: 1689.

"*Maryland, 1689.*

"To the King and Queens most Excellent Maj^ties. The humble Recognition and Addresses of Calvert County in the Province of Mary Land, etc., etc., etc.

"Henry Jowles, Saml Bourne, Francis Collier, Tho. Gantt, John Griggs, Th^o. Tasker, *Justices of Peaces*; Andrew Abington, *Sheriffe*; Henry Trueman, E. Batson, Hen. Ferneley, John Payne, Charles Tracey, Joseph How, John Lirigatt, I. Woodroffe, Samuell Warner, William Haines, Tho. Collier, Thomas Parslow."[3]

Notwithstanding the signers to these addresses favored the rebellion against Lord Baltimore, there were not wanting generous and honorable spirits who remembered with gratitude the paternal government of the Calverts, and were not disposed to renounce and vilify it in the day of its adversity. As Protestants they knew how false were the allegations that Protestants were treated with injustice or oppression, or their religion imperilled under the rule of the

[1] London Public Record Office, America and West Indies, No. 556; B. D., p. 37.

[2] *Ibid.*, p. 36.

[3] *Ibid.*, p. 40.

proprietary; and they viewed with honest indignation the treachery and falsehood of Coode and his associates. They saw clearly that "their rights and freedoms were interwoven with his lordship's prerogative," and that in his hands, whose equity they had experienced, and whose interests were one with theirs, those rights and freedoms were far safer than if they depended on a king that was a stranger to them, and a parliament that contemned them.[1] In this spirit ran most of the addresses, of which the following are specimens:

"To the King's Most Excellent Majestie:

"Wee, your Majestie's most Loyall and dutifull Subjects, the antient Protestant inhabitants of Talbott County in your Majestie's province of Maryland, who have here enjoyed many halcyon daies under the imediate government of Charles Lord Baron of Baltemore, & his honorable father, Absolute Lords proprietaries of the said province by Charter of your royall Progenitors, wherein our rights and freedomes are soe interwoven with his Lordship's Prerogative, that wee have allwaies had the same liberties & priviledges secured to us, as other your Majestie's Subjects in the Kingdom of England; and wee again, by vertue of the said Charter (as it enjoin'd us) have alwaies paid our obedience to the said Lord Baltemore and his honorable father, by whom equally and indifferently were justice, favor, authority & preferment, administred, bestowed, conferred, and given to, & upon your Majestie's Subjects of all persuasions; doe in prostrate & humble manner testify to your Majestie, that wee abhorre and detest the falsehood, and unfaithfulnesse of John Coade & others, his Assotiates and agents who first by dispersinge untrue reports of prodigious armies of Indians, and French papists invadinge us did stirre up unjust jealousies and dismall apprehensions in the lesse cautious sort of people of this Province, and then havinge thereby created in them unnecessary feares & dispos'd the people to mutiny and tumult, made further insurrection, and extorted the lawfull government from the Lord Proprietary, who was alwaies as ready to redresse our aggreivances as wee to complain. And now the said John Coade and his accomplices havinge assum'd the Government upon themselves and procured a Convention to be tumultuously assembled, did tirannically imprison, restrain & turn out of civill & military comission severall of your Majestie's good subjects, of unquestionable loyalty & affection to the Church of England, who approved not his actions, and who might justly, by your Majestie's proclamation, have continued in authority & done your Majesty good service. And those Delegates in that manner convened (beinge part of or most of them factious persons of noe commendable life and conversation) have arbitrarily decreed and ordained many things to the inconvenience of your Majestie's People, placed the Militia of severall Counties in the hands of unworthy and infamous persons, and the better to make their decrees be observed, many of the said Delegates have procured themselves to be putt in judiciall places, to the terror of your Majestie's more peaceable Subjects. From the dangers and oppressions whereof wee your Majestie's most loyall, Dutifull & Protestant Subjects in these, our Addresses, humbly crave by your princely care and prudence to be freed and enlarged, and that the government, together with your Majestie's favour, and a lastinge settlement may be again restored to the right honorable Lord Baltemore, which will make him and us happy, and give us new occasion to blesse God & pray for your Majestie's life and happy reign.

"James Murphey, Hugh Sherwood, John Newman, Ralph Dawson, Wm. Hambleton, John Power, Richard Pedderman, Henry Frith, Henry Adcocke, Charles

[1] It is worthy of notice that a considerable proportion of the signers of the addresses against the proprietary, sign by their *marks*, while in the counter-addresses all the names are fairly written.

Cartwright, Robart Harrison, Isaace Corson, Thomas Evans, Michael Turbutt, Charles Robinson, Ralph Dawson, ju., Zerubable Wells, Joseph Greene, Samuel Taylor, Thomas Wetherby, Francis Shapard, Tho. Smithson, Ro. Gouldsbrough, William Crump, John Hawkins, Will. Coursey, Richd. Macklin, Rich. Jones, Daniel Glaer, Robert Macklin, Robert Kent, William Tonge, Richard Tilghman, John Chaiers, John Johnson, Nathanell Tucker, John Nabb, Henry Price, Richard Parnes, George Powell, James Smith, William Hackit, John Whittington, John Hambleton, Tho. Hopkins, and divers more." [1]

ADDRESS OF PROTESTANTS OF KENT COUNTY.

"*November*, 1689.

"To the King's Most Excellent Majestie:

"Wee, your Majestie's most loyall and dutyfull subjects, the ancient Protestant Inhabitants of Kent County, in your Majestie's Province of Maryland, who have here enjoyed many halcyon dayes under the imediate Government of Charles, Lord Baron of Baltemore, and his honorable Father, absolute Lords Proprietaries of the said Province, by charter of your Royall Progenitors, wherein our Rights and Freedoms are so interwoven with his Lordship's prerogative, that wee have allwaies had the same liberties and priviledges secured to us as other your Majestie's subjects in the Kingdome of England. And wee againe by vertue of the said Charter (as it enjoyned us) have alwayes paid our obedience to the said Lord Baltemore and his honorable Father, by whom equally and indifferently were justice, favour, authority & preferment administered, bestowed, conferred and given to and upon your Majestie's subjects of all perswasions: Doe in prostrate and humble manner testifie to your Majesty that we abhorr & detest the falsehood and unfaithfullness of John Coade and others his Associates and Agents, who first by dispersing untrue reports of prodigious armies of Indians and French Papists invadeing us, did stirr up unjust jealousies and dismall apprehensions in the less cautious sort of people of this Province, and then haveing thereby created unnecessary feares & disposed the people to mutiny and tumult, made further insurrection, and extorted the lawfull government from the Lord Proprietary, who was alwayes as ready to redress our aggrievances as wee to complaine. And now the said John Coade and his accomplices haveing assumed the Government upon themselves, and procured a Convention to be tumultuously assembled, did tyrannically imprison, restrain and turn out of civill and military Comission severall of your Majestie's good subjects of unquestionable loyalty and affection to the Church of England, who approved nott of his actions, and who might justly by your Majestie's proclamation have continued in authority, and done your Majestie's good service. And those Delegates in that manner convened, (being part or most of them factious persons of no comendable life and conversation) have arbitrarily decreed and ordained many things to the inconvenience of your Majestie's people, placed the Militia of severall Counties in the hands of unworthy and infamous persons; and the better to make their decrees to be observed, many of the said Delegates have procured themselves to be putt in judiciall places, to the terror of your Majestie's more peaceable subjects. From the dangers and apprehensions whereof, Wee your Majestie's most loyall, dutyfull, and Protestant subjects, in these our Addresses humbly crave by your Princely care and prudence to be freed and enlarged, and that the Government together with your Majestie's favour and a lasting settlement may be again restored to the Rt. Honorable Lord Baltemore, which will make him and us happy, and give us new occasion to bless God, and pray for your Majestie's life and happy reign.

"(Signed) Wm. Frisby, Griffith Jones, Robert Burman, Philemon Hemsley, Simon Wilmer, William Peckett, Josias Lanham, Thomas Ringgold, Tho. Smyth, Henry Coursey, Josh. Wickes, Jno. Hynson, George Sturton, Lambart Wilmer, Gerrardus Wessels, Richard Jones, Philip Conner. [2]

[1] London Public Record Office, B. T. Md., I., B. D., p. 41.

[2] *Ibid.*

"BALTEMORE COUNTY IN THE PROVINCE OF MARYLAND. ADDRESS TO HIS MAJESTIE.

"Whereas by King Charles the first of ever blessed memory, a Charter for the Province of Maryland was granted unto Cæcilius, late Lord Baltemore, &c., &c., &c.

"George Wells, Edward Bedell, John Wallston, James Salmon, Matthew Goldsmith, Thomas Hedges, Richard (*his* x *Mark*) Adams, Mark Richardson, Anto: Crew, Miles Gibson, James Phillips, Wm. Hollis, Will: Wilkeson, Richard Hills, Roger Matthews, George Goldsmith, John Bevanes, Thomas Jones, Daniell Peverill, Samuel Browne, Thomas Hodges, John A. Arding, John Gold, John Haies, Moses Groom, Joseph Peake, Charles Gorsuch, Lodwick Martin, Thomas Preston, Wm. Digges, Edward Dorsey, with divers more."[1]

"AN ADDRESS FROM THE PROTESTANTS OF CALVERT COUNTY TO HIS MAJESTIE.[2]

"Geo: Lingan, Thomas Johnson, Richard Smith, junior, Walt: Smith, Enoch Comet, Will: Brookes, Henry Orton, Robert Day, Robert (*the* x *Marke of*) Johnson, Jno. Smith, John Smith, Wm. (*his* x *Marke*) Whittington, W. Akeroyd, Joseph Hall, Nathan Veitch, John Towman, Jno. Veitch, Elisha Hall, Hugh Chinton, Richd. Rake, John Faney, Francis (*the* x *Marke of*) Hutchins, Jno. Leach, jun., Samuel Holdeworth, Jno. Holdeworth, Wm. Daukins, Jos. Edwards, Mich: Taney, Rich: Keene, Hugh Hopewell, John Nutthall, Symon (*the* x *Marke of*) Garling, Wm. Chaplaine, Daniel Rawlings, James Wainless, Morris Davis, John (*the* x *Marke of*) Gyatt, Wm. (*his* x *Marke*) Needham, Jno. (*his* x *Marke*) Austin, Edwd. (*his* x *Marke*) Wood, senior, Edward Wood, junior, Marttin (*the* x *Marke of*) Beale, Henry Cox, James Downall, Benjamin Hall, Henry Deakes, Richard (*his* x *Marke*) Evins, Francis Buxton, Jno. (*the* x *Marke of*) Magdowell, Wm. (*the* x *Marke of*) Wooderd, Richard Looke, Roger Skrine, Edward Dickinson, Tho: Clagett, Robt: Claike, Joseph Wright, Robert Shepheard, William Hutchings, William Fiiming, James Veatch, Edward (*the* x *Marke of*) Blackburne, James Duke, Wm. Turner, Wm. (*the* x *Marke of*) Kidd, Sam: (*the* x *Marke of*) Fouller, John Bullocke, Josiah Willson, Joseph Wilson, Tho: (*the* x *Marke of*) Cole, Thomas Hills, Daniell Brown, Tho: Blake, Francis Maldin, John Manning, Ja. Crawfford, George (*the* x *Marke of*) Sealing, Wm. Wilkeson, Natthannell Mannyng, Henry Lowe, Tho: Collin, John Reade, Tho: Beevin, Humphrey Swift, Thomas Simmons, junior, John Turnor, Paul Kisbe, Alexander Llewis, George Young, Thomas Kingcart, Ambrose Leach, John Leech, senior, John (*the* x *Marke of*) PeeCock, Jonathan (*the* x *Marke of*) Smith, Wm Wadsworth, Benjamin (*the* x *Marke of*) Evins, John Sollers, John Sunderland, Jno. Scot, Fran: Freman, John (*the* x *Marke of*) Kent, George Busser, Peter (*the* x *Marke of*) Fouler, Christopher B. (*the* x *Merke of*) Beanes, William (*the* x *Merke*) Cheathe."[3]

CECIL COUNTY IN THE PROVINCE OF MARYLAND, ADDRESSED TO HIS MAJESTIE.[4]

"The humble petition of the Inhabitants of Cecill County in the Province of Maryland, &c., &c., &c.

"George Stevens, Geo. Oldfeild, Wm. Chamberlain, Henry Eldest, Robert Crook, St Leger Codd, Casper Agust: Herman,[5] Gideon Gundry, G. Wroth, Isaac Caulk, York Yorkson, George Beestone, Thomas Killton, Daniell Smith, John Durby, Wm. Nowell, George Warner, Thomas Deakston, Robert Randell.

[1] London Public Record Office, America and West Indies, No. 556.

[2] *Ibid.*

[3] There are six small seals on this Document to fasten the three sheets together of which it consists—the seal being a sword with death's-head at the point and a wreath (of laurel) surrounding it and the motto: "*Gratia et Patientia*."

[4] London Public Record Office, America and West Indies, No. 556.

[5] Herman, a son of the map-maker of Bohemia manor.

In the Public Record Office, London, are also preserved many letters from leading men of the province to the proprietary on the state of affairs, of which the following from Charles Carroll will be read with interest:[1]

"*St. Marye, September the 25th, 1689.*

"My most hon'd Lord:

"I believe your Lordship has ere now had some intelligence either by Captain Burneham or Johnson, of the strange rebellion your ungratefull people of this your Lordship's Province have involved themselves in, moved by the wicked instigations of Code, Jowles, Blackston, Chiseldon, Parson Thurling, and several others to that degree, that they have quite unhinged your Lordship's Government: and (as if there were noe Justice to be had but such as they please to distribute, or as if the whole body of the lawes were to be annulled by their wild fancyes,) have taken upon themselves to declare your Lordships charter forfeited, as your Lordship may see by their malitious declaracion, (which the bearer will shew your Lordship,) they have further taken upon themselves to give commissions to Sheriffs and Justices of their own stamp, and constitute other officers, both civill and military, utterly excluding not onely all Roman Catholiques from bearing any office whatsoever contrary to any express act of assembly, but allsoe all protestants that refuse to joyne with them in their irregularities, imprisoning such of them as declare against their illegall proceedings, and arbitrarily threatening to hang any man that takes upon him to justifie your Lordship's right; they have assumed the power of calling an assembly, the Election of which was in most Countyes awed by their souldiers, one Countye disowned their power, and would chuse noe members, but in fine they have packed up an assembly after the most irregular manner that ever was knowne wherein they have layd downe the methods of their future conduct, but is as yet kept private, but am informed that your Lordship shall speedily have sent you a Copy of their journall.

"But soe it is that neither Catholique nor honest protestant can well call his life or Estate his owne, and if your Lordship, according to your wonted care and tenderness of your people, by a speedy application and true representation to his Majesty of these most inhuman actions doe not procure some orders whereby to allay their fury a little, all your friends here will be reduced to a miserable condition, for dayly their Cattle are killed, their horses prest, and all the Injury imaginable done to them, and to noe other. Certainly your Lordship's Charter is not such a trifle as to be annulled by the bare allegations of such profligate wretches and men of scandalous lives, as Code, Thurling, Jowles & such fooles, as they have poysoned by the most absurd lyes that ever were invented. If the King thinks that your Lordship or your Deputy Governors have done any thing that may render your Charter forfeited, his Majesty and his Councill know the way of trying it is by a quo warranto, which way of proceeding (as I understand) is not much favour'd by the King or parliament, much less I believe will they approve of such unheard of actions as were committed against your Lordship and Government by these evill speritts without commission or order from any superior power, whereby they have not onely rebell'd against your Lordship, but allsoe committed high treason in takeing up armes as they have done without warrant from his Majesty or your Lordship. I fear I have been too tedious upon this ungratefull Subject, yet could enlarge much now; and would but that the bearer can informe your Lordship to the full much better than I can, he haveing been noe small Sharer in the general calamity, whereof likewise I had my parte mingled with a hard seasoning of which I am now thank god allmost recovered.

[1] This name, afterwards so distinguished in Maryland history, here appears for the first time on our pages. Mr. Carroll had come to Maryland shortly before the revolution of 1688. He was a warm friend of the proprietary, whose full confidence he enjoyed, and who afterwards appointed him his agent and receiver-general in the province.

"I believe an act of indemnity, with a few exceptions of the most notorious transgressors, would prove a great means to reduce the people to their obedience, tho' the heads of them are soe arrogant as to declare that in case the King should send orders not to their likeing, they would not obey them, and a deal of such stuff; the Coll: will informe your Lordship at large; therefore will at present conclude with my hearty prayers that your Lordship may meet with noe great difficultye in composeing these matters, as allsoe with a full assurance that I allwayes shall strive in the station I am in to deserve in some measure the name of, My Lord,

"Your Lordship's most humble and most faithfull Servant,

"CHARLES CARROLL.

"Addressed:—For the Right Honorable the Lord Baltimore, at his home in Bloomsbery Square in London."[1]

The Associators assembled again in convention in September, 1690, but at neither of their sessions do they seem to have made any attempt at a permanent organization of the government, but apparently awaited the pleasure of the king, whom they had besought to assume the executive power. On February 1st, 1689, O. S. (1690 N. S.), William recognized them in a letter in which he approves the motives which induced them to take up arms, and empowers them to continue in the administration of the government, but at the same time commands that they shall preserve the peace. The complaints made against Lord Baltimore were investigated before the Privy Council, by which an order was passed on the 21st of August, 1690, directing the Attorney General to proceed by *scire facias* in the matter of the charter, and present proof of the alleged abuse of power under it, that it might be lawfully vacated. While the case was still pending, in 1692, the Maryland Council, now in league with the Associators, passed the following address, which was submitted by Mr. Wynn, and after receiving the signatures of all the members, was forwarded to the king:

KING WILLIAM III.

"To their most excellent Majesty's, William and Mary, by the Grace of God, King and Queen of England, Scotland, France and Ireland, defenders of the faith, &c.

"We, your Majesty's Council, and the Freemen, Inhabitants of this, your Majesty's Province of Maryland, by their representatives in a General Assembly now convened and met together, having seriously and maturely perused, considered and debated, and enquired into the several acts of impeachment or charge exhibited by your agents against the Lord Baltimore and his deputies, do upon strict search thereunto and the several depositions, examinations, papers and records thereof, find the same to be punctually and exactly true according to the several parts thereof, now by us abridged and hereunto annexed, the which we are able, ready and willing to prove, defend and maintain by such further testimony, proofs and evidences as may be reasonably required of us whensoever your Majesty shall please to call us thereunto by your Royal Commission of enquiry unto the premises; and not only so, but several insolencys, misdemeanors and outrages done

[1] London Public Record Office, America and West Indies, No. 556; B. D., p. 19.

and perpetrated since by his Factors and agents here to the disturbance of your Majesty's good and liege subjects, inhabitants hereof, aiming at and designing nothing less than total subversion of this, your government and your Majesties royal authority over us which they have (as much as in them lie) endeavored to obliterate and erase out of the minds of your Majestie's loyal subjects.

"The moiety of 2s per hhd. by Act of Assembly vested in his Lordship for the support of government and the contingent charges thereof, we likewise find to be misapplied, and that his lordship, the Lord Baltimore in arrears indebted to the country six or seven and thirty thousand pounds sterling at the least, whereof his Lordship's agent here hath obstructively, [and] peremptorily refused to give any account or produce his book of entry whereby he is to make out the same, which we humbly pray (by your Majesty's Royal commission) may be inquired into and an account thereof duly rendered, and satisfaction for the balance duly made by his Lordship, by which means we, your Majesties most loyal subjects, may the better be enabled to express our gratitude to your Majesties for answering our petitions in giving us a Protestant Governor, by rendering him able and sufficient to support and maintain the honor your Majesties designed him and the satisfaction we retain in placing him among us."

It cannot be wondered at that William was quite ready to take the authority thus thrust upon him in the name of the people of Maryland. His own title to the crown was disputed at home by the Jacobites, then an active and powerful party, assured of the sympathy of France, whose intrigues against his crown were always formidable, and under better leaders would probably have succeeded. Every accession of strength, and every open acknowledgment of his title was therefore most welcome to him, nor was he disposed to weigh too scrupulously the manner in which it was obtained. The proceedings against the charter under the writ moved slowly, and the king determined to anticipate the expected decision. The proprietary, represented by able counsel, pleaded in vain. The privileges of his charter had long been viewed with a jealous eye by the crown as an encroachment on its sovereignty, and the vineyard of Naboth has often proved a temptation to better monarchs than Ahab. The shrewd Puritans, seventy years before, had shown their knowledge of royal nature, when they said that "if there should be a purpose or desire to wrong them, though they had a seal as broad as the house floor, it would not serve the turn, for there would be means enough found to recall it or reverse it." And there was no difficulty here in obtaining a legal "opinion" to sanction the king's wishes, even from so eminent a jurist as Lord Holt. He did not yield without some qualms of conscience however, as may be gathered from his own declaration:

"I think it had been better if an inquisition had been taken, and the forfeiture committed by the Lord Baltimore had been therein found, before any grant be made to a new governor; yet since *there is none*, and it being *a case of necessity*, I think the king may, by his commission, constitute a governor, whose authority will be legal although he must be responsible to Lord Baltimore for the profits. . . . An inquisition may at any time be taken, *if the forfeiture be not pardoned, of which there is some doubt.*"[1] The

[1] Chalmers' *Opinions*, p. 29.

charges alleged had not been proved, had not even been inquired into; the party impleaded had had no hearing; it was not certain even that the forfeiture, if incurred, had not been pardoned; yet "it being a case of necessity" (according to the report of the Associators and the wishes of the king), Maryland might be legally seized by the crown.

We must not judge too harshly of the Protestant inhabitants of Maryland for lending what countenance they did to the schemes of a party of adventurers, whose leaders for the most part were aliens to the soil. These were quick, daring, and reckless in action; the cry of a "Popish plot" was enough to spread a panic; they were doubtful of the expediency of any regular opposition, and it was believed that the crown would sustain the revolutionary movement. The Proprietary was away, his representatives timid and inefficient, and so the blow was struck at Maryland's liberties.

"THE NARRATIVE OF COLL. HENRY DARNALL, LATE ONE OF THE COUNCILL OF THE RIGHT HON^BLE THE LORD PROPRIETARY OF THE PROVINCE OF MARYLAND.

"On the 25th of March last, Coll. Jowles sent word to the councill (then at St. Maryes), that three thousand Indians were comeing down on the Inhabitants, and were at the head of Pattuxent River, and required Armes and Amunition for the people to goe against the said Indians, all which was with all expedition sent him by Coll. Digges. The next morning I went up myself to Coll. Jowles', where I found them all in Armes and they told me they heard there was three thousand Indians at Matapany (from whence I then came). I assured the people it was a false report, and offered myself to goe in person if they could advise me where any Enemyes were, Indians or others, whereat they seem'd very well satisfied. I began to suspect this was only a contrivance of some ill minded men, who under this pretence would raise the Country; as by what happened afterwards we had reason to beleeve. Upon the most diligent search and enquiry into this whole matter, noe Indian anywhere appeared, and when ever any Messenger was sent to the place where it was said the Indians were come, there the Inhabitants would tell them they heard they were landed at such a place, but after long search from place to place and noe sign of any Indians, the people were pretty well pacified, and Coll. Jowles himself wrote a remonstrance (the copy whereof is here inclosed) which he signed, as did severall others who had the Examination of this matter, the which was published in order to quiet the People, who in a few days seemed to be freed from their apprehension. From this time untill the 16th of July following, the Country was all quiet and noe appearance of any Enemy to disturb them, Indians or else. On the said 16th of July, a Messenger came to me at Matapany in the night time to acquaint me that John Cood was raising men up Potowmeck, whereupon I informed the Councill thereof, who imediately dispatched a person to know the truth, but the said person was taken by Cood as a spy and by him kept, soe the Councill had no notice untill two dayes of any thing, when they were assured that Cood had raised men up Potowmeck, and that some were come to him out of Charles County, who were all marching down toward St. Maryes and in their way were joyned with Maj^r. Campbell and his men. Coll. Digges having notice whereof got together about an hundred men and went into the State House at St. Maryes which Cood and his party came to attack, and which Coll Digges, (his men not being willing to fight) was forced to surrender; wherein were the records of the whole Province which Cood and his party seized. In this while Majr Sewall and myself went up Patuxent River to raise men to oppose said Cood and his party, where wee found most of the officers ready to come in to us, but their men were possessed with a beleef that Cood rose onely to preserve the Country from the Indians and Papists, and to proclaim the King and Queen, and would doe them noe harm, and therefore, would not stir to run themselves into danger, soe that all the men wee could get amounted not to one hundred and sixty, and by this time Cood's party was encreased to seaven hundred. The Councill seeing how the people were led away by false reports and shams, in order to quiet them and give them all imaginable assurance they were clear and innocent of inviting the Indians down as was laid to their charge, offered to make Coll. Jowles (who was the chief of their party next to Cood) general of all the forces in the Province, and sent such an offer to him, who returned a very civill answere, that haveing communicated what we wrote to his own men he had with him, they were extreamly satisfied therewith, and gave us hopes he would come down to us, but to the contrary, he went and joyned Cood at St. Mary's, to whom and to all, then in Armes there, the Councill sent a Proclamation of pardon, upon condition they would lay down their Armes and repair to their respective Habitations, the which Cood (as we were credibly informed), instead of reading to the people what was therein contained, read a defyance from us, thereby to enrage, and not to pacify them. Cood and his party haveing thus made themselves Masters of the State House and the Records at St. Mary's, borrowed some great gunns of one Capt Burnham, Master of a ship belonging to London, and came to attack Mattapany House, the which when he came before, he sent a Trumpeter and demanded a surrender. We desired a parlay and personall treaty in the hearing of the people, which Cood would never consent to. We know if we could but obtain that in the hearing of the people, we should be able to disabuse them and clear our selves of what they were made beleeve against us, but this we could never get at their hands, but to the contrary, they used all possible meanes to keep the People ignorant of what we proposed or offered, and made use of such artifices as the following, to exasperate them: they caused a man to come rideing post with a letter, wherein was contained that our Neighbor Indians had cut up their Corn and were gone from their Towne, and that there was an Englishman found with his belly ript open, which, in truth, was noe such thing, as they themselves owned, after Matapany House was surrendered. We being in this condition and noe hopes left of quieting or repelling the People thus enraged, to prevent Effusion of blood, capitulated and surrendered. After the surrender of the said House His Lordship's Councill endeavored to send an account of these transactions, by one Johnson, Master of a Ship bound for London, to his Lordship, the which the said Johnson delivered to Cood. When we found we could send noe Letters, Majr Sewall and myself desired of Johnson we might have a passage in him for England, to give his Lordship account of matters by word of mouth, which the said Johnson refused, upon pretended orders to the contrary from Cood, whereupon Majr Sewall and my self went to Pensylvania, to endeavor to get a passage there, upon which Cood and his party took occasion to give out we were gone to bring in the Northern Indians, but we missing of a passage there, came back and stay'd in Ann Arundell County (who never had joyned with Cood and his party) untill the 26th of September, when (Majr Sewall then being sick) I myself got a passage hither in the *Everard*. As to their proceedings in their Assembly I can give no account, only that they have taken severall prisoners.

"HENRY DARNALL.[1]

"*London, December 31st, 1689.*"

[1] London Public Record Office, America and West Indies, No. 556; B. D., p. 16.

"FROM Mr HILL TO Ld BALTEMORE, RECd THE 29TH SEPT., 1689.

"*Maryland, Sept: 20th 1689.*

"My Lord:

"My education and imploymt hath left mee unfurnish'd wth Language sutable to adress my selfe to yr Lordship for that I humbly begg yr pardon for offering this trouble; but as I have been long happy under yr Lordship's just governmt, soe cannot but bee sencible of the late fatall mischeifs befallen us here by which my Selfe and thousands more are deprived of such Happiness; and as my Selfe and all others living under yr Lordship's protection for these many years past haveing allwayes Enjoyed our free Libertie in the Exercise of our Religion, together wth the benefit of the Lawes of our Native Countrey, England, & all other Rights and properties that a free Englishman could desire or wish to enjoy; for my Lord wee Cannot but Lament and Condole our Late Losse of all those privilledges of which wee are now utterly deprived, and that by the mallice, pride & ambition of Some Restless Spirits here; as by a late Confederacie have endeavoured by whome wee are brought under the aprehention of nothing Lesse then the Inevitable Ruine & destruction, not only of us and ours, but alsoe of yr Lordship's peaceable governmt, and as much as in them lyes of yr Lordship's Just prerogative and Interest here haveing by force of Armes depos'd yr Lordship's Deputies and governours; and divested them of the Legall power and authoritie they Exercised under yr Lordship, making voyd all yr Lordship's Comissions, both sivill and millitarie, by which they have broken, disolved & Extinguished all Lawes, disjointed and unsettled the whole frame & order of this, yr Lordship's governmt, under Such pretences as plainly apears they have neither power nor authority to maintain (otherwise plawsible) but soe Contrary are their practices & proceedings, that they are not only Contrary, but in defiance of all Lawes, both Humane and divine, some few people here out of each County only, Sideing and taking part wth them soe that they might, wth ease, have been subdued; but that for a handfull of people to take armes one against another, & other Reasons wch Induced us Rather to suffer that wth patience which Could not bee prevented but by making the Case worse; for as hither to noe blood hath been Spilt altho wee are in great fear & terror that it will not end wth out; exept Some Speedy means from yr Lordship to prevent the same; yr Lordship's presence here would doe the worke for which wee dayly pray; My Lord, I am heartily Sorry that such distractions should befall us here, which is all exept the obligations of my duty & fidellity to yr Lordship, whose I am in all dutifull Respects to my power,

"RICHd HILL."[1]

"Mr JOHNS' LETTER TO Mr GROOME, RECd FROM MY Ld BALTEMORE, 31 DEC: 1689.

"Mr Richd Johns' Letter to Mr Samuel Groome. Mr Johns, the person the Assembly directed a Letter to, & call him a person of good credit & repute.

"*Maryland 27th. m 7. 1689.*

"My friend Samll Groom:

"I should have sent to thee at Some former opertunity to give thee Some account of the Great Distraction amongst the Inhabitants of this (once peaceable governed) Province but to that passe wee are now brought that its difficult to send or receive any lettor for feare of its being opened: wee live in dayly hopes of the forward ships but more Especially some order from the Crowne of England to settle & Compose our present distractions. Here is a small Ketch or Packett boat that have brought lettors for this govermt, & private lettors alsoe, but all is kept husht, & some private lettors I have seen yt have been opened before they Came to the owners hands. If thee or Jno Tayler did send any by the said Ketch, they are kept up. I'le say but little more only tell thee the

[1] London Public Record Office, America and West Indies, No. 556; B. D., p. 18.

long Soard in the Rables hands is our master. Coll. Darnell & alsoe Richd Smith's wife comes in this Ship. I referr thee to them for a full Information of matters here. I'le add that I am Confident the least scrip of order or Comand from King William would be, gladly Received & Readily acknowledged wth a Generall submission from the Freeholders of this province; God grant it may Come Quickly. I hope when the Ships comes thou will send the goods I sent for, or at least those y^t are most necessary for my family. Else I Cannot keep house. I leave all my Consernes to thy Care. My Selfe, wife & family are in health.

"I am thy true friend,

"RICH'D JOHNS.

"Pore Edward Talbot is Dead."[1]

[1] London Public Record Office, America and West Indies, No. 556; B. D., p. 23.

CHAPTER XIII.

King William, as may be supposed, was by no means reluctant to accept the fruits of a successful revolution which seemed but a corollary of that which had placed him on the throne; and the convention which had usurped control of affairs in Maryland seemed eager to show, not merely their loyalty, but their servility. Though the charter still continued in force, he determined to send over a governor to administer affairs as the representative of the crown. Lord Baltimore, as a last resort, offered to place the government in Protestant hands, though he firmly refused to surrender a charter, no condition of which he had broken, and no privilege of which he had abused. This proposition was not accepted; and on August 26, 1691, Sir Lionel Copley, who had earned the king's gratitude by securing for him the port of Hull on his first landing in England, received his commission as the first Royal Governor of Maryland. But the commissioners of the Privy Seal were doubtful of the legality of the warrant, and refused to confirm the commission until they were peremptorily ordered by the privy council to do so. Indeed, before the commission was issued, the ministers thought it prudent to obtain the explicit approbation of the chief justice, and the countersign of the attorney general. Nor were they yet entirely satisfied of the legality of their proceedings; so they ordered a writ of *quo warranto* to be issued, that they might have their act confirmed by the verdict of a jury. The facts alleged were found to be impossible of proof; and Treby, the attorney general, refused to proceed without a written order from the privy council; and so no judgment was obtained against the proprietary, though he was deprived of his rights and of the protection of the laws.

Governor Copley arrived in Maryland early in 1692, and received the government from the hands of the "Committee of Safety." He convened an assembly at St. Mary's on May 10th, and the Upper House was organized with Sir Thomas Lawrence as secretary, and Colonel Henry Jowles, Colonel Nehemiah Blackiston, Colonel George Robotham, Colonel Nicholas Greenbury, Colonel David Browne, Thomas Tench, Captain John Addison, Colonel Charles Hutchins, Captain John Courts, and Thomas Brooke, as councillors. Colonel Blackiston was chosen president of the Upper House, and Kenelm Cheseldyne, speaker of the Lower House. Both Houses being assembled in the chamber of the Upper, the new governor made them an address, the chief burden of which was to exhort them to make liberal provision of money for the support of the government, and of himself in particular. "I conceive," he says, "it will be an advantage to the country, as well as satisfaction to myself, to know what you intend for me, to support the honor of the post the king hath placed me in."

The members having taken the prescribed oaths, except Thomas Everdine, of Somerset, and John Edmundson, of Talbot, who, as Quakers, were permitted to make the usual "declaration," they signed the following "humble address," to their sacred majesties, William and Mary:

"Gracious and Dread Sovereigns:

"The due sense and acknowledgements of those great blessings it hath pleased God to bestow on us, in redeeming us from the arbitrary will and pleasure of a tyrannical Popish government, under which we have so long groaned, leads us to pay and render to your Majesties (as the only instruments and authors, under God, thereof) the just tribute of our humble and hearty thanks for the same, more especially for that your Majesties have graciously vouchsafed to incline your sacred ears to the hearing and granting our humble petitions and former addresses to your Majesties, by taking and receiving us into your immediate care and protection, and to that end sending amongst us a Protestant governor, of whose loyal candor and integrity, as your Majesties have had good experience, so that small time he has been amongst us gives us that assurance as most humbly and sincerely to bless and praise Almighty God, and give your Majesties our cordial thanks therefor, rendering us thereby true Englishmen and good subjects, immediately to the crown of England, and you, our lawful and liege sovereigns, the rightful and undoubted possessors thereof."

And the address winds up with an elaborate prayer for their Majesties' welfare and prosperity.

It seems not to have occurred to these martyrs of a "tyrannical Popish government" that four years before, the last Proprietary Assembly, of which a number of them were members, had signed an address to Lord Baltimore, thanking him, "with all imaginable gratitude," for the "happiness, peace and tranquillity" they enjoyed under his "care, vigilance, and august government," and for "the many signal favors and benefits and immunities" they had "in general received from his lordship's bounty and clemency." And they, therefore, returned their most humble and hearty thanks for his lordship's "kindness, love and affection to, and studious care for the good and welfare of the good people of this, your lordship's province." But, then, this address had been framed before the revolution of 1688 had broken out. Since then the times had changed, and the kindness and studious care for their good had been discovered to be Popish tyranny.

The first act passed by the Assembly was one recognizing the title of William and Mary; a formal recognition in which Maryland was joined by but one other province—New York. The next was an act making the Church of England the established church of the province, and thus putting an end to that equality in religion which had hitherto been Maryland's honor. It provided for the division of the ten counties into thirty-one parishes, and imposed a tax of forty pounds of tobacco upon each taxable person, as a fund for the building of churches and the support of the clergy.

As the province was now governed, all Acts of Assembly required the assent of the king and council to give them validity, and before this was obtained, they had to be examined and reported on by the attorney general.

This act—which contained the clause that "the Great Charter of England should be observed in all points," was rejected by the privy council, the solicitor general, Trevor, objecting "that he knew not how far the enacting thereof will be agreeable to the constitution of the colony, or consistent with the royal prerogative."[1]

Besides passing an act repealing all laws hitherto made in the province, they endeavored by legislation to appropriate a great part of the revenues of the proprietary arising out of certain duties; but Lord Baltimore's claim to these was sustained, and from this period to his restoration he does not appear to have been interrupted in the collection and enjoyment of his revenues.

In this year treaties of peace were concluded with the Mattawoman, Choptico, and Piscataway Indians.

The administration of Governor Copley was ended by his death, on or about September 12, 1693, and Sir Thomas Lawrence, his former secretary, assumed the government *ad interim* as president until a new governor should arrive.[2] The right of succession was with Francis Nicholson, who was then in England. Nicholson had been Deputy Governor of New York until the revolution of 1688, when he was made Lieutenant Governor of Virginia, and administered the affairs of that province until Sir Edmund Andros arrived as governor in 1692, and superseded him. In 1691, he was commissioned Lieutenant Governor of Maryland, and was entitled to assume the government immediately upon Copley's death. He being absent, however, Sir Edmund Andros claimed the government by virtue of a commission, which, upon examination, was found only to take effect in the event of Nicholson's death. Andros, however, was used to arbitrary proceedings, and seized the government, despite the decision of the assembly, which, after examination of the commissions, declared Nicholson alone entitled to the office. He held his position for about ten days only, when he returned to Virginia, and Colonel Nicholas Greenbury of the Upper House assumed the government as president. On May 7th, 1694, Sir Thomas Lawrence—the order annulling his suspension from office, having reached the province—was duly installed as president, which place he held until the arrival of Nicholson, about the end of July.

SIR EDMUND ANDROS.

Soon after his arrival, Governor Nicholson convened the assembly to meet on the 21st of September, not in St. Mary's, but at Anne Arundel town, afterwards called Annapolis. This choice foreshadowed the doom of the former city, the cradle of the province; and at this session the removal of the seat

[1] Chalmers' *Revolt*, etc., i., p. 250.

[2] Lawrence was appointed secretary and chancellor of the province when Copley was made governor; but soon after his arrival, he was, for some cause, suspended by Copley, and imprisoned without bail. Lawrence appealed to the king in council, who decided, on September 28, 1693, that the arrest was illegal and arbitrary.

of government was decided upon. The reasons alleged for the change were not without weight; but it is probable that the true motives were to be found in the fact that St. Mary's was especially a Catholic settlement, was, beyond other towns, devoted to the proprietary government, and was closely connected with all those ties and associations which it was the policy of the new government to break up. Great was the consternation at St. Mary's at a change which brought her certain ruin, and a pathetic appeal was made to the assembly to reconsider their action. We subjoin the petition and the reply of the Lower House, as they serve to illustrate the feelings and spirit of the time:

"To His Excellency, Francis Nicholson, Esq., Captain General and Governor in Chief in and over this their majesty's Province and territory of Maryland.

"The humble address of the Mayor, Recorder, Aldermen, Common Councilmen and Freemen of the City of Saint Mary's, in the said Province, and principally from the bottom of their hearts they congratulate your Excellency's happy accession to this your Government, and sincerely pray for your peaceable and quiet enjoyment thereof, and long and prosperous continuance therein for the glory of God, their majesty's service, the good and benefit of their subjects, and your own particular comfort and satisfaction.

"From whence they proceed humbly to supplicate your Excellencies grace and favor, and granting and continuing to them their ancient franchises, rights and privileges granted them by their charter, with such other benefits and advantages as hath been accustomed and usually allowed, and from time to time confirmed to them by your predecessors, rulers and Governors of this Province, humbly offering and proposing to your Excellency these following reasons as motives inducing thereunto, viz.:

"*Imprimis*—As that it was the prime and original settlement of this province, and from the first seating thereof for above sixty years hath been the ancient and chief seat of Government.

"II. In consideration whereof the Lord Baltimore by his letters patents did incorporate and constitute the same a city with several immunities, rights, benefits and privileges thereunto belonging, above and beyond all other parts and places in the province.

"III. The situation in itself is most pleasant and healthful, and naturally commodious in all respects, for the purpose being plentifully and well watered with good and wholesome springs, almost encompassed round with harbor for shipping, where five hundred sail of ships at least may securely ride at anchor before the city, having also most suitable and convenient points of land and proper places for the erecting and building of Forts, Block houses and other fortifications and edifices for the security and defence of such shipping, the keeping and preserving the public magazine and records of the Province.

"IV. And as such and for divers other reasons then appearing in the year 1662, a convenient part or portion of the said land, was, by the representative body of the province, bought and purchased for the building of a State House and prison, and twelve years after to wit A.D. 1674, his Lordship by and with the advice and consent of the representative body of this province, passed an act for the building of a State House and prison in the said place which cost the country at that time three hundred and thirty thousand pounds of tobacco.

"V. That the inhabitants of the said City themselves for their further security in having the Courts of Judicature and other public officers and meetings continued among them, humbly moved his Lordship with their free offering of one hundred thousand pounds of tobacco towards the erecting and building for his Lordship a dwelling house at West Saint Mary's, convenient and adjacent to the said city, which sum of tobacco they duly and punctually paid and complied with.

"VI. His Lordship, notwithstanding to gratify the request of some persons, and studying the ease and conveniency of the people according to some motives to him then made, did, in the year 1683, remove the records together with the officers and courts of Judicatures as also the assembly then convened to the ridge in Ann Arundel County, whereby the inhabitants in those parts finding themselves grievously burdened and altogether incapable to make provision, for so great a concourse of people became suitors to his Lordship to remove to some other place which accordingly he soon after did to Battle Creek, in Patuxent river, where the provincial Court after it continued for the space ot three days only were for want of necessary accommodations obliged to break up abruptly great part of their business unfinished.

"VII. After all his Lordship's having made trial of the most probably convenient places for the holding of his Courts of Judicature and other public meetings as aforesaid found the same altogether incommodious and most inconvenient, and at last by the advice of his Council found himself obliged to return to the first and ancient place of Saint Mary's.

"VIII. And for the encouragement of the inhabitants of the same and the better to enable them to make provision for the accommodation of such persons as should have occasion to apply themselves there in times of assembly, provincial courts or otherwise, his Lordship was pleased to signify to the corporation under his hand his promise and full assurance of continuing the same and not to be removed thence during his life.

"IX. Upon which encouragement given, several of the inhabitants of the said city have launched out and disbursed considerable estates to their great impoverishment and almost utter ruin if they should be defeated of such their promised encouragement, and not only so but divers others the inhabitants, for several miles about contiguous and adjacent to the said county, upon the same encouragement of his Lordship, have seated themselves upon mean indifferent lands and laid out their estates, and made improvements thereon barely for the raising of stocks, wherewith to supply the said city for the end and purpose aforesaid, which is now become their whole and only dependance for the future support and maintenance.

"X. The city of St. Mary's, situated as aforesaid, is undeniably the most convenient port or place for all masters of ships, or other persons whatsoever, at their arrival into or going out of the province to make their application to his Excellency, and also for the receipt and dispatch of all public letters and expresses relating to their majestys' service and the good of the whole province, from and to any parts of the same, as lying in a manner equally distant from Patuxent and Potomac rivers and the main Bay, and is most commodious and contiguous to its neighboring colony of Virginia, with whom a mutual intercourse and correspondence is most undeniably necessary and material.

"XI. For which reasons amongst others best known to their Majesties, your supplicants humbly conceive that (as they have been informed,) their Majesties' late Governor Copley was by his instructions commanded to apply primarily and principally to Saint Mary's, and there enter upon his government as the known and generally accepted ancient and chief seat of government in this province.

"XII. It hath hardly been known, and indeed scarce any precedent can be produced of so sudden a change as the removal of the ancient and chief seat of government upon the care, suggestion and allegations of some particular person for their own private interest and advantage, neither is it in the power we humbly conceive, of the subject, but the prerogative royal invested in your Excellency as their majesties' Lieutenant, at whose feet we humbly cast ourselves for relief and support against the calamities and ruin wherewith we are threatened, and wholly relying upon your Excellencie's grace and favor therein, with whom we also conceive should be good manners in all persons, first to treat and intercede before they presume to make any peremptory result in case of so high a nature as this may be.

"XIII. We cannot omit to represent to your Excellency that the very last assembly held in the time of the late deceased Governor, A. D. 1692, it was put to the vote of the full house whether the holding of Courts and an Assembly's at Saint Mary's were a grievance or not, and carried in the negative.

"XIV. At which time we humbly conceive that house did well consider all difficulties as well as the vast charge and expence they already had been at (to no purpose if the courts, &c., should be removed,) as also what must necessarily follow, (and it may be to as little purpose) in building of new courts and offices in other places, and making provisions for the holding and keeping the same, besides the hazards and casualities of removing and transporting the records from one place to another, of which already some experience hath been had.

"XV. To remove some scruple and objection, and, as we humbly conceive the main one that hath been made against the conveniency of the place, that the gentlemen, the members of the house, have been forced to their great trouble oftentimes to travel on foot from Patuxent to Saint Mary's, and so back again.

"It is humbly proposed, and we do offer to obligate ourselves forthwith, and so soon as possibly workmen and materials can be provided for the great ease and convenience of all persons at such times as also at all other times to provide and procure a coach, or caravan, or both, to go in all times of public meetings of assemblies and provincial courts, &c., every day daily between Saint Mary's and Patuxent river, and at all other times once a week, and also to keep constantly half a dozen horses at least with suitable furniture for any person or persons having occasion to ride post or otherwise, with or without a guide, to any part of the province on the Western Shore.

"XVI. That the situation of the place being not in the centre of the province, and consequently not so convenient for some persons to apply to we hope the proposal above may somewhat mitigate that objection, besides we humbly represent even the place of our nativity, the Kingdom of England and the Imperial court, there held in the City of London as far from the centre of England as Saint Mary's, in this province, Boston in New England, Port Royal in Jamaica, James Town in Virginia, and almost all other their Majesties' American plantations, where are still kept and continued in their first ancient stations and places, the chief seat of government and Courts of Judicature.

"Philip Lynes, *Mayor;* Kenelm Cheseldyn, *Recorder;* Henry Duton, John Lewellen, Jo. Watson, Thomas Beal, Philip Clark, Edward Greenhalgh, *Aldermen;* Thomas Waughop, William Aisquith, Thomas Price, Richard Benton, Robert Mason, W. Taylard, Samuel Watkins, *Common Councilmen;* Wm. Digges, J. Bouye, *Clerk;* G. Vansweringen, Josh Brodbert, Ro. Carvile, Chas. Cand, Robt. King, George Layfield, John Coode, Henry Wriothesley, W. Bladen, James Cullen, Thomas Hebl, James B. Baker, Stephen Blatchford, Daniel Bell, Jonathan Clarke, Edward Kelsey, Abraham Rhodes, Joseph Edto, Roger Tolle, Henry H. T. Taylor, James Reckets, John Wincoll, Edward Fisher, John F. Noble, Thomas Huchins, Richard Sowler, Thomas (*his* x *Mark*) Guyther, Robert Drury, Claudius Dutitre, Samuel Wheeler, *Constable;* John I. M. Mackye, Peter Dent, Wm. Guyther, John (*his* x *Mark*) Janner, John (*his* x *Mark*) Little, Thomas H. Hickson, William Nuthead, Richard Griffin, Isaac Paine, Peter Watts, Robert Carss, John Evans, Wm. Lowry, Anderson, Eben Cooke, Lacharias Vansnearingen, Leon D. Hukenett, William Harpanus, Michael Chevers, Elias Beech, Thomas Guinurn, John Freeman and Joseph Doyne—*Freemen.*"[1]

[1] In another address to the governor and council, the mayor and municipal authorities urge another plea They say that, hearing the assembly are preparing a bill to remove the courts and principal seat of government, and settle them at Severn, in Anne Arundel county,

Their pathos and humility were but thrown away on the Lower House, the coarse and almost brutal scorn of whose reply shows the acrimony of the dominant party. It was addressed to the governor, and ran as follows:

"BY THE ASSEMBLY, OCTOBER THE 11TH, 1694.

"This House have read and considered of the petitions and reasons of the Mayor, Aldermen and others, calling themselves Common Council and freemen of the City of Saint Mary's, against removing the courts and Assemblies from this corner and poorest place of the province, to the centre and best abilitated place thereof, although we conceive the motives there laid down are hardly deserving any answer at all, many of them being against the plain matter, some against reason, and all against the general good and welfare of the province. Yet, because your Excellency has been pleased to lay them before us, we humbly return this our sense of the same, that 1, 2, 3, 4, 5, 6, 7 and 8 reasons relating to what his Lordship has thought fit to do to the City of St. Mary's, it is no rule nor guide to their Majesties, Your Excellencies nor this House. It seems, in some part, to reflect on his Lordship more than this House believes is true or deserved by his Lordship.

"II. As to the 9th, this House say that it is against the plain matter of fact, for we can discerne no estate either laid out or to lay out, in or about this famous city, comparable with other parts of this province, but they say and make appear that there has been more money spent here by three degrees, or more than this city and all the inhabitants for ten miles round is worth, and say that having had sixty-odd years experience of this place, and at most, a quarter part of the province devoured by it, and still, like Pharaoh's kine, remain as at first, they are discouraged to add any more of their substance to such ill improvers.

"As to the 10th and 11th, we conceive the being of Saint Mary's so near Virginia is not so great an advantage to the province as the placing the courts in the centre and richest part of the same, which is no great distance from thence, or Virginia either, and nearer New York and other governments which we have as much to do with as Virginia, if not more, and the place as well watered and as commodious in all respects as Saint Mary's, which has only served hitherto to cast a blemish upon all the rest of the province, in the judgment of all discerning strangers, who, perceiving the meanness of the head, must rationally judge proportionally of the body thereby.

"To the 12th, 13th and 14th they say that they do not hold themselves accountable to the Mayor and his brethren for what they do for their country's service, nor by what measures they do the same, nor what time they shall do it in, nor for what reasons, and are and will be as careful of the records and properties of the people as the petitioners.

"To the 15th the House say, the petitioners offer fair as they have done formerly, but never yet performed any; and this house believes that the general welfare of the province ought to take place of that sugar plum, and of all the Mayor's coaches, who, as yet, never had one.

"To the 16th this House conceive that the city of Saint Mary's is very unequally ranked with London, Boston, Port Royal, etc.

"All which we humbly offer to your Excellency's judicious consideration."

they represent "that the appointing a place for the Supreme court of judicature and seat of government in any kingdom, colony, province or territory, belonging to the Crown of England, is a peculiar prerogative of the crown; and that the upholding and maintaining the king's prerogative is as essential and undoubted a part of the laws of England as the liberty and property of the subjects; and that when either the former is intrenched upon by the subjects, or the latter invaded by the princes, the State is in a convulsion." . . . . .

"Wherefore your petitioners do most humbly pray that, lest this province may be so blemished as to have it said that it was the first of the American plantations that offered violence to the prerogative of so worthy a prince, by passing the said bill into a law, your excellency and your honorable council will be pleased to reject the said bill until such time as leave be first obtained from their majesties (as the method ought to be in such a case), for preparing and bringing in the same."

Remonstrance and appeal were all in vain. The ancient city was stripped of her privileges, of everything that gave her life, and she was left to waste and perish from the earth. Her population departed, her houses fell to ruins, and nothing is now left of her but a name and a memory. Yet it may be at some future day, when Marylanders care more than they now do for the history of their State—possibly when they have learned to prize liberty by its loss—some fitting monument may be erected to the honor of Cæcilius Calvert on the memorable spot where religious liberty first became a reality.

The first session of the assembly after its removal, was held in Anne Arundel town, at the house of Major Dorsey, on February 28, 1694, O.S., (1695 N.S.) The only remarkable incident recorded of its proceedings is their adjournment one day in a body, to an ale-house—whether for their greater convenience, or for the assuagement of thirst, is not stated; but the act gave high offence to the governor. In the next session, they gave the town the name of Annapolis, and made provision for the erection of public buildings and a parish church. Good brick-clay having been found in the neighborhood, contracts were made with Casper August Herman, a burgess from Cecil county[1] for the erection of the parish church, school-house, and State house.[2] From the first no effort was spared by the government of the province to enlarge its population and increase its prosperity. A writer, who visited Annapolis at a very early date, is quoted by Oldmixon in his *British Empire in America*, as saying:

"There are indeed several places alloted for towns; but hitherto they are only titular ones, except Annapolis, where the Governor resides. Col. Nicholson has done his endeavor to make a town of that place. There are about forty dwelling houses in it; seven or eight of which can afford a good lodging and accommodations for strangers. There are also a State House and a Free School, built of brick, which make a great show among a parcel of wooden houses; and the foundation of a church is laid, the only brick church in Maryland. They have two market days in a week; and had Governor Nicholson continued there a few months longer, he had brought it to perfection."[3]

This year, 1694, is memorable for the first provision made for a free school in the province. The earlier colonists had so much work on their hands with clearing, planting, building, and in all ways providing for their immediate necessities, that but little time and means were left them for education, though it was not wholly neglected. The earliest effort to establish a public educational institution in Maryland was made in the year 1671, only thirty-seven years after the first settlement at St. Mary's. In the assembly of April 13th, of that year, an act was read for founding and erecting a school or college within the province of Maryland for the education of youth in learning and virtue. It passed the Upper House, and was then sent to the Lower House, who returned it with a message proposing the following amendments:

[1] He was third son of Augustine Herman, of Bohemia manor.

[2] The State-house, or "Stadt-house," as it was at first called (probably as a delicate compliment to "Dutch William"), was finished about 1697. In 1704 it was destroyed by fire, and the assembly held its sessions in a house rented at £20 a year from Col. Edward Dorsey, until it was rebuilt.

[3] Volume i., p. 333.

1. That the place where the college shall be erected be appointed by the assembly most convenient for the country.

2. That the tutors or school masters of the said school or college may be qualified according to the Reformed Church of England; or that there be two school-masters, one for the Catholic and the other for the Protestant children, and that Protestants may have leave to choose their school-masters.

3. That a time be appointed when the work shall be set on foot.

4. That the Lord Proprietor be pleased to set out his declaration of what privileges and immunities shall be enjoyed by the scholars that shall be brought up or taught at such school.

The amendments were rejected by the Upper House. Up to this time and for twenty years after, this was the first and only legislative movement in the matter of public education. True, the population was small, not being over 25,000, so late as 1692, and this was scattered widely along the bay and river shores, though to great distance inland. But private education was not wholly neglected. Fathers and mothers and the Parish ministers were the teachers of the children of the early colonists, and occasionally an emigrant from the mother country took the place of schoolmaster.

"On the 24th of September, 1694, Governor Nicholson sent a message to the assembly in which he proposed, that 'a plan be framed for the building of a free school for the Province and the maintenance for a school-master, and usher, and a writing master, that can cast accounts, the which, if it can be agreed upon, His Excellency proposed to give £50 towards the building of the said school, and £25 sterling a year towards the maintenance of the master during his Excellency's continuance in the government. The Honorable Sir Thomas Lawrence, the Secretary of the Province, would likewise give 5,000 lbs. of tobacco towards the building of the free school, and 2000 lbs. yearly during his being Secretary, towards the maintenance of the masters. Cols. Robotham, Jowles, Greenbery and Mr. Brooke, would give 2,000 lbs. of tobacco each; Cols. Hutchins and Courts, 1200 lbs.; Cols. Tench, Brown and Frisby, 1000 lbs. each; Mr. Thos. Brooke, £5 3s yearly towards the maintenance of the Masters, and Auditor General, Randolph, £10 sterling.'"

In reply to this message, the Lower House sent by Mr. Hawkins and Major Smallwood, the following:

"Having received your Excellency's instructions of the 24th of September and considered your Excellency's proposals and large contribution towards the establishing a free school, we have endeavored as far as able to follow your Excellency's example and in order thereunto have contributed towards the building such a free school as your Excellency hath proposed the sum of 45,400 pounds of tobacco and some absent members as yet have not subscribed; and doubt not that every well-minded person within this province will contribute towards the same; and upon consideration thereof have had some debate concerning the building of one Free School on the Western and another on the Eastern Shore, and have nominated Severn and Oxford for the two places, which debate we leave to your Excellency's consideration and appointment. And to that end and purpose humbly desire a conference with your Excellency and Council to consider of the best ways and methods to establish the same."

The following were the subscriptions of the several burgesses of the House towards the building of the free school, and are deserving of being remembered. The subscriptions are in pounds of tobacco:

"Mr. Robert Smith (Speaker), 2,000; Mr. John Watson, 800; Captain Thos. Waughop, 800; Kenelm Cheseldyn, 4,000; Edward Boothby, 1,200; Francis Watkins, 800; Capt. Jas. Maxwell, 800; John Ferry, 800; Robert Mason, 1,000; Philip Clark, 2,000; Capt. John Bayne, 2,000; Hans Hanson, 1,000; John Hinson, 800; Col. Henry Coursey, 3,000; Thos. Smithson, 800; Capt. Wm. Whittington, 1,000; Mat Scarborough, 1,000; Thomas Dickson, 400; John Bozman, 400; Henry Hooper, 800; Thomas Tasker, 1,500; William Frisby, 1,000; Thomas Smith, 1,000; Capt. John Hammond, 2,000; James Sanders, 800; Maj. Edward Dorsey, 2,000; Capt. Richard Hill, 1,000; Thomas Greenfield, 1,200; Francis Hutchins, 800; George Lingan, 800; Henry Hawkins, 1,000; James Smallwood, 800; Capt. Wm. Dent, 2,000; Wm. Hutchinson, 1,000; Thomas Hicks, 800; John Pollard, 800; Thos. Ennals, 1,200; Col. St. Leger Codd, 800; Col. Wm. Peirce, 400; Captain John Thompson, 800; Col. Casparus Herman, 2,000; Nicholas Low, 1,200; Capt. George Thompson gave a guinea piece in gold."

In October, 1694, an act was passed for the maintenance of free schools, by laying an imposition on furs, beef, bacon and exports out of the province, and on the 16th of October, the assembly ordered an address to be sent to their majesties William and Mary about this free school, another to the Bishop of London, and a third to the Archbishop of Canterbury, asking him to accept the patronage of the school. The letter to the Bishop of London is as follows:

"*Maryland, Oct. 18th, 1694.*

"To the Right Rev. Father in God, Thomas, Lord Bishop of London:

"May it please your Lordship, Under so glorious a reign, wherein by God's providence, his true religion has been so miraculously preserved, should we not endeaver to promote it, we should hardly deserve the name of good Protestants or good subjects; especially considering how noble an example is set before us by their majesties' royal foundation now vigorously carried on in Virginia, in William & Mary College chartered in 1693. We have therefore in Assembly attempted to make learning a hand-maid to devotion, and founded free schools in Maryland, to attend on their college in that colony. We only beg their Majesties' confirmation of an act which we have proposed for their establishment and of your Lordship a share of that assistance and care which you have taken in promoting so good and so great a design as that of the college in Virginia, so charitable a founder of a school in opposition to that shop of poisoning principles set open in Savoy.

"We are confident that you will favor our like pious designs in this Province wherein instructing our youth in the orthodox religion, preserving them from the infection of heterodox tenets and fitting them for the service of the church and state in this uncultivated part of the world, are our chiefest end and aim." * * * * * *

In the letter to the Archbishop of Canterbury they say:

"We did in the last Assembly by the truly worthy Sir Thomas Lawrence, their Majesties' Secretary of this Province, desire your Grace's assistance in behalf of a Free School which we design to found, and now we presume to entreat your Grace to take upon you the patronage of the same.

"This is to be presented to your Grace by the said Sir Thomas Lawrence and Mr. William Frisby, a very worthy member of our House of Burgesses.

"We shall not be further troublesome to your Grace than to beg your Grace's blessing and to pray God that your Grace may long preside in the chair to his honor and glory and the glory and good of the Church of England."

The archbishop's answer accepting the place of patron was received and laid before the General Assembly, October 13th, 1695; and on the 15th, the governor and council sent a message to the burgesses that they write again to his grace and thank him for his patronage of their schools.

At the session of Assembly of 1695, an act was passed "for the encouragement of learning," which provided that no person residing in the province should export any furs or skins mentioned in the act, except by paying the duties therein mentioned, for the maintenance of free schools in the province. As the fur trade was a large and profitable trade at this period, the revenue derived from it was the "school fund" for nearly thirty years. By this act every bear skin was charged 9*d* sterling; beaver, 4*d*; otter, 3*d*; wild cats', foxes', minks', fishers', wolves' skins, 1½*d*; muskrat, 4*d* per dozen; raccoons, 3 farthings per skin; elk skins, 12*d* per skin; deer skins, 4*d* per skin; young bear skins, 2*d* per skin, and all non-residents were to pay double.

In the year 1696 the assembly, in order to encourage "good learning" and "for the propagation of the gospel and the education of the youth of the province in good letters and manners," passed a "Petitionary Act," for the establishment of "a Free School or Schools, or place of study of Latin, Greek, writing and the like, consisting of one master, one usher and one writing-master or scribe, to a school, and one hundred scholars more or less, according to the ability of the said free school." By this law the Archbishop of Canterbury was nominated Chancellor of the said school, which, in honor of the king, was to be called "King William's School," and to be built at Anne Arundel town. Other schools were to be erected "at such other place or places, as by the General Assembly of this province, shall be thought convenient, and fitting to be supported and maintained in all time coming."[1]

The visitors and trustees (who were the largest contributors to the original establishment) were Governor Francis Nicholson, Honorable Sir Thomas Lawrence, secretary of the province; Rev. Peregrine Coney, of William and Mary Parish, St. Mary's County; Rev. John Hewett, of Somerset Parish, Somerset County; Colonel George Robotham, Colonel Charles Hutchins and Colonel John Addison, of the council; Robert Smith, Edward Dorsey, Francis Jenkins, Edward Boothby, Kenelm Cheseldyn, Thomas Ennals, William Dent, John Thompson, Henry Coursey, Thomas Tasker, Thomas Smith and John Begger, gentlemen.

By the law these trustees and visitors had all the necessary corporate powers and privileges to establish a free school or college in Annapolis, and with the further power, whenever adequate funds could be obtained, to establish a similar free school at Oxford, in Talbot; and "as fast as they shall be enabled, as aforesaid, proceed to the erection of other and more free schools in this province, that is to say, in every county of this province at present one free school."

[1] Bacon.

Besides the money given to the building and the annual amount promised by him to the master, Governor Nicholson gave a lot in Annapolis, upon which the trustees immediately commmenced the erection of a brick school house.[1]

The Law of 1696 gave to "King William School" in Annapolis its existence; but the rector, governors and visitors, for the want of funds, did not establish schools in any other parts of the province. The colony, however, was not deterred from further attempts to carry into effect the original plan; and in 1723 was passed "an Act for the Encouragement of Learning and Erecting schools within the several counties in this Province." At that period there were twelve counties, and in each of them seven visitors were appointed.[2]

They were authorized to purchase one hundred acres of land in order to erect "one school in each county within this province, at the most convenient place, as near the centre of the county as may be, and as may be most convenient for the boarding of children." "For the encouraging of good school-

[1] It was a plain building, containing school-rooms and apartments for the teacher and his family, and stood on the south side of the State-house, between it and the present iron railing. It was not completed until the year 1701. In the meantime, however, the Bishop of London sent over, in 1696, Mr. Andrew Geddess to take charge of the school, but not finding it finished, he was sent to All Saints' parish, in Calvert county, to officiate there as reader, at a salary of 10,000 lbs. of tobacco per annum, until it was completed. He was to receive, as master of the school, £120 per annum. In 1697, a rector was presented to the charge of All Saints' parish, and a reader not being needed, he was sent to William and Mary College, Virginia, and, perhaps, never returned to the province, for we find in the ministerial records of St. Ann's parish, Annapolis, the following entry: "Died November 9th, 1713, Rev. Edward Butler, rector of St. Ann's, and master of the free school, Annapolis." At what time he became master we are unable to find out, but previous to the time of his becoming rector of the parish, which was April 14th, 1711, he had been a resident of the city, and was then probably master of the school.

[2] They were as follows: St. Mary's County—Rev. Leigh Massey, rector of William and Mary parish; James Bowles, Nicholas Lowe, Samuel Wilkinson, Col. Thomas T. Greenfield, Thomas Waughop, Captain Justinian Jordan. Kent County—Rev. Richard Sewell, rector of Shrewsbury parish; Rev. Alexander Williamson, rector of St. Paul's parish; James Harris, Colonel Edward Scott, Simon Wilmer, Gideon Pearce, Lambert Wilmer. Anne Arundel County—Rev. M. Joseph Colbatch, rector of All Hallows' parish; Col. Samuel Young, William Lock, Captain Daniel Moriartee, Charles Hammond, Richard Warfield, John Beale. Calvert County—Rev. Jonathan Cay, rector of Christ Church parish; John Rousby, Col. John Mackall, Col. John Smith, James Heigh; Walter Smith, of Leonard creek; Benjamin Mackall. Baltimore County—Rev. William Tibbs, rector of St. Paul's parish; Col. John Dorsey, John Israel, William Hamilton, Thomas Tolley, John Stokes and Thomas Sheredine. Charles County—Rev. William Maconchie, rector of Portobacco parish; Gustavus Brown, George Dent, Captain Joseph Harrison, Robert Hanson, Samuel Hanson and Randal Morris. Talbot County—Rev. Henry Nicolls, rector of St. Michael's parish; Colonel Matthew Tilghman Ward, Robert Ungle, Robert Goldsborough, William Clayton, John Oldham and Thomas Bozman. Somerset County—Rev. Alexander Adams, rector of Stepney parish; Rev. James Robertson, rector of Coventry parish; Joseph Gray, Robert Martin, William Stoughton, Robert King and Levin Gale. Dorchester County—Rev. Thomas Howell, rector of Great Choptank parish; Colonel Roger Woolford, Major Henry Ennalls, Captain John Rider, Captain Henry Hooper, Captain John Hudson, Govert Lockerman. Cecil County—Colonel John Ward, Colonel Benjamin Pearce, Major John Dowdall, Stephen Knight, Edward Jackson, Richard Thompson and Thomas Johnson, Jr. Prince George's County — Rev. Jacob Henderson, rector of Queen Anne parish; Governor Charles Calvert, Robert Tyler, Colonel Joseph Belt, Thomas Gantt, George Noble and Colonel John Bradford. Queen Anne County—Rev. Christopher Wilkinson, rector of St. Paul's parish; Philemon Lloyd, Richard Tilghman, James Earle, Sr., William Turbutt, Augustine Thompson and Edward Wright.

masters, that shall be members of the Church of England, and of pious and exemplary lives and conversations, and capable of teaching well the grammar, good writing, and the mathematics, if such can conveniently be got; and that they allow every such master for his encouragement for the present (besides the benefit and use of his plantation) the sum of twenty pounds per annum." It was also enacted that the money already raised for the use of county schools, and that in the public treasury should be "divided into twelve equal parts, answering to the number of county schools now to be erected;" and thus was secured to each county an equal part of the money then in the hands of the treasurer; and the same distribution was made of the money which might afterwards come into his hands for the same purpose. The laws of 1704, chapter XXVII; 1717, chapter X; 1723, chapter XI; 1763, chapter XXVIII; provided funds for those free schools by duties upon certain exports from and imports into the province.

Certain fines and forfeitures also constituted a fund for the support of these schools, and in 1719, the estates of persons who died intestate in the province, and without known legal representatives, were given to the free school of the county wherein the deceased died. The revenues arising from these sources, together with the tuition money, which the masters were allowed of others than the children of the poor (who were to be taught without charge) was quite sufficient to enable the trustees to employ competent masters, and to build up respectable schools.

Having given a brief sketch of the early education in Maryland, we will now retrace our steps to that eventful period when France was pursuing with vigor her scheme for securing dominion in America. The designs of this power had been regarded with jealousy from the first settlement of the colonies; and when the Five Nations desired peace with the English in 1684, Governor Dongan, of New York, invited a conference of the colonial governors at Albany to meet the chiefs of these tribes. It was held in July, 1684, the colonies being represented by "The Right Honorable Francis Lord Howard, Baron of Effingham, Governor General of Virginia," also acting for Maryland; Colonel Thomas Dongan, Governor of New York, and the magistrates of Albany; Stephanus Van Cortlandt, as the agent of Massachusetts, and several sachems. In this conference the North and South met for the first time, and formed a treaty with the Indians which embraced territory extending from the St. Croix river to the Albemarle.

After the accession of William and Mary, hostilities were declared between England and France, which extended to America, and thus began the first inter-colonial war. The French planned an invasion of Massachusetts and New York, and soon the country was startled by the intelligence that a war-party of French and Indians had massacred the inhabitants of the town of Schenectady and burned their houses. As the colonies were left to their own exertions, a joint effort was proposed by holding a congress with a view to some organization. The call for a meeting is dated the 19th of March, 1690, and recites "that their majesties' subjects had been invaded by the French and Indians; that many of the colonists had been barbarously murdered, and were in danger of greater mischiefs; and it proposed as a measure of prevention, that the neighboring colonies, and Virginia, Maryland and the parts adjacent, should be invited to meet at New York and conclude on suitable methods for assisting each other for the safety of the whole."[1]

Such was the first call for a general congress in America. John Coode, who was then acting Governor of Maryland, in a letter dated May 19th, 1690, wrote to the Hon. Jacob Leisler, Governor of New York, that it was the design of the Convention of Maryland to send arms and men to aid the general defence; though the great distance between that province and New York, the unsettled state of their "constitution" and the uncertainty respecting his Majesty's intentions toward the province, so discouraged their councils that they could come to no definite conclusion on this point; they had, however, sent Mr. William Blankersteine and Mr. Amos Nicholls to the conference to act in their name, and report to the convention the proceedings of the meeting.[2]

The commissioners of the four colonies met at New York, and on the 1st of May an agreement was signed in behalf of the five colonies, to raise a force of eight hundred and fifty men to strengthen Albany, and resist the French and Indian enemies. Of this number, Maryland promised to raise one hundred soldiers.[3]

The congress resolved to attempt the reduction of Canada by two lines of attack, one to conquer Acadia, and thence to move on Quebec, and the other by the route of Lake Champlain to assail Montreal. Acadia and Port Royal were taken, but beyond this the expedition proved a complete failure.

The French now waged a savage war on the remoter settlements. The settlers felt equal to their defence against the French colonists, but as these were reinforced by troops from France, they petitioned the home government to help them with forces from England. The request was not granted, and for seventy years the colonists had to rely on their own resources for their defence. This was a period of hard trial, of frequent alarm and constant anxiety, of heavy taxation, and of all the horrors that accompany warfare in its most barbarous forms; but it served to loosen the ties which bound the colonies to England, to teach them self-reliance, and to prepare their minds for the thought of independence. It is true that war was not waged incessantly during this time; but the persistence of France in her schemes of extension was a continued menace.

[1] Frothingham's *Rise of the Republic*, p. 89.

[2] New York *Doc. Hist.*, ii., p. 249.

[3] Among those who served we have the names of the following: Captain Gabriel Towson, Lieutenant Rodgar Barton, Ensign Ebennazar Wakeman, Sergeant Joseph Rumsey, Sergeant Thomas Sturgis, Thomas Hunt, Samuel Wall, Matha Randall, Abraim Brown, Joseph Boils, Samuel Couch, Daniel Gori, John Ogdin, John Cable, Josiah Hunt, Samuel Shered, Philip Trauis, Loeling Philips, Thomas Brodgat, Robert Graims, George Scot, James Camioll, John Owen, Nathaniel Furbush, Sergeant Jonathan Horton, John Fergeson, Richard Feloo, William Danford, John Knap, Richard Cozens, Thomas Poor, Philip Galpin, Philip Prise, Joseph Cable, John Green, Isaac Rumsey, Thomas Mathias. *Ibid.*, p. 215.

On the 16th of October, 1694, Governor Nicholson laid before the assembly a letter from the king, requesting the province to raise supplies of men and money for the assistance of New York and Albany; also letters and papers from Governor Fletcher, of New York, proposing a new plan with the co-operation of the Five Nations. The Lower House, after due consideration, replied that "the great, unavoidable, and continual charges occasioned here by the late revolution, and the vast sums of money expended by our several agents in England out of the public revenue, together with the vast sums of money and tobacco in arrears, which are now come to be paid, besides the continual charge of several troops constantly kept out for the security of our frontier plantations; these, with other like circumstances, do incapacitate us to yielding supply or assistance to the said government of New York and Albany, at this juncture. As to the several articles contained in the said treaties relating to the covenant chain[1] renewed, in which we find ourselves together with the several colonies included, for which we return our hearty thanks, and shall ever esteem it both our duty and interest upon all occasions to use our utmost endeavor for the preservation, safety, and welfare of all their majesties' subjects within their majesties' territories of America and more especially for those whom we acknowledge ourselves so signally and highly obliged." The Upper House concurred in these "sensible representations."

On the 22d of August, 1694, the king again wrote to the governor fixing a quota of men and supplies; and the assembly resolved "according to their utmost abilities," they would "at all times be ready to assist that government [New York] with such number of men and arms when need shall require and his excellency the governor shall intimate, the same as the strength and ability of this province will afford." In consequence of this resolution they forwarded a considerable sum of money by Colonel Tasker, and in July, 1695, sent the quota of men. Thus the system of crown requisitions on the colonies was begun; and for her share of the burden, Maryland had only herself to thank.

In the year 1699, an Indian war threatened the frontiers of Maryland, Virginia and Pennsylvania, and as the Piscataway and Clecocick Indians had wandered off their reserved lands on the upper part of the Potomac, Lieutenant Colonel James Smallwood and Mr. William Hutchinson were appointed commissioners, on the 5th of July, by the governor and council, to make a treaty and induce them to return for fear they might join the enemy. On the 8th of May, 1700, the council resolved "that the friendship of the Susquehannock and Shawanese Indians be secured by making a treaty with them, they seeming to be of considerable moment and not to be slighted," and advised the "reissuing of the order for running out the Choptank and Piscataway Indian lands, and all acts of justice done them."

[1] A figure of speech continually used in negotiations with the Indians. The chain was said to be "rusted" or "tarnished" when any misunderstanding had arisen; "brightened" when good feeling was restored; "broken" when conditions were violated, and "renewed" or "joined" when another treaty was made.

The treaty of Ryswick, in 1697, by which Louis XIV acknowledged William as King of England (Queen Mary having died in 1694), brought about a general peace, but it was not of long duration. The great increase of power which France was likely to obtain by the succession of Louis' grandson to the throne of Spain, in 1700, aroused the apprehensions of William; and when, in September, 1701, on the death of James II., Louis, in defiance of the treaty, recognized his son, "the Pretender," as king of Great Britain, general indignation was excited, and parliament requested the king to make no peace with France until reparation had been made for this insult.

In March, 1702, the Governor of Maryland submitted to the assembly a royal letter, making a requisition of men and troops for the assistance of New York. To this the Lower House replied on March 24th:

"His Majesty's letter of the 19th January, 1700, and your Excellency's speech on that subject touching a supply of money to New York, has been seriously debated and considered, and our loyalty and duty to his Majesty having carried us on throughout the difficultys and obstructions, we have resolved on a supply of money to the utmost degree of what we have or can by any means attain to, which with trouble of mind we are forced to acknowledge will not amount to above £300, which, although it be not the whole sum mentioned, yet it is all we have or can get, and by which we are constrained to leave some just debts of the public unpaid and ourselves in a weak state of defence against our common enemy, the Indians, who are daily annoying our frontiers.

"And because we have great reason to believe that our neighbors of New York have not used us fairly in representing our condition to his most Sacred Majesty, otherwise that what really is and are well assured that it will be much more for his Majesty's service to apply the said money, and also strength we are able to exert to the defence of his Majesty's Province of Maryland in as great or greater danger than New York, and not to them who are much abler to defend themselves than we, and from whose fortifications or other strength we can have no manner of safety or security, we beseech your excellency plainly and sincerely to represent the truth of our condition to his Majesty, imploring his Majesty's grace and favor to make good these assertions, which are plain matter of fact and undoubted truths:

"I. That the Indians of New York have as easy and open access to us as to them, who being a light, flying, wild, barbarous kind of enemy, are not obliged by carrying of any baggage or artillery, to keep the improved roads or pass by our forts, but can easily and suddenly descend upon us over the unbeaten and unoccupied mountains, as we have found by experience.

"II. We have several nations of Indians on our frontier, some between us and New York and some to the westward of us and wide of New York, and some among us who are frequently committing rapines and murders on our frontier inhabitants, to secure whom, as well as the Province in general, this Province has, within this 3 years, been at the charge of many hundred thousand pounds of tobacco; and though we have for this last 3 or 4 months been quiet, by the winter season we are in great fears of new incursions in the spring, having no assurance of their faithfulness to us.

"III. We have no means of raising money but by imposition of goods exported and imported, of which commodities, as exportation of tobacco, is twenty times more than all the rest, and in laying any thing upon that we are constrained to be very tender, by occasion of the duty payable on the same in England, and the commission that is thereby advanced to the merchant, to whom the same is consigned for sale.

"IV. To raise money by tax on the inhabitants is utterly impracticable here, for there is several hundred families pay the greatest part of the whole Province, have not 5 shillings by them, nor any means to raise it, because there is very little amongst us, and that a base coin that is not current with our neighbors, nor have we any liberty yet from his Majesty to advance coin so as to introduce it among us, by means whereof the best in the Province are oftentimes put to a straight to procure money for their traveling pocket expences.

"V. This Province has several times heretofore been reduced to very great extremity and danger by those very nations on our back, to the impoverishing and almost destruction of the men and substance of this Province, which we always sustained without any assistance from New York or any other neighboring government, except Virginia, who was equally concerned in the same.

"VI. The great charge we have lately been at in raising money to build a State House, free school, church, and prison, on a new seat of government at Annapolis, hath put on us another great burthen which is not yet discharged.

"VII. That it may be considered how far the money will compass the designed end, and when all our neighbors (under better circumstances than we) have not answered their proportion, and how discouraging it will be to us to remit our treasure and strength to New York, and lay our nakedness and defenceless condition open to our aforesaid enemy, whilst our neighbors retain their strength for their own defence, and which we believe is the best service to his Majesty.

"VIII. Let it be considered that 2,000 pounds of tobacco per year is one with another what every laborer makes in this Province, and that none but laborers, or the best of this Province, can be sent to make up the quota of men demanded, and it will easily be found, considering the inability to us of raising money and the duty tobacco pays at home, that the maintaining the quota of men mentioned will ruin this Province in one year, and lessen his Majesty's revenue more than double the sum that we pay, besides the danger of this Province of being overrun and destroyed by the savages in the meantime.

"And that his Majesty, on consideration thereof, and his gracious regard of our safety, will be pleased to exempt from that or any other contribution to New York, and direct that the said money, or what other strength we can raise, may be applied to the defence of this Province of Maryland against the incursions of his Majesty's and our enemies, that so we may with comfort and quiet apply ourselves to our manufacture of tobacco for our own support and increase of his Majesty's Revenue."

In the meantime the French privateers were ravaging the colonial shipping and often entered the Chesapeake bay, sometimes landing their crews on the Eastern shore and plundering the plantations. These incursions, together with the pirates who were then infesting the seas, naturally created considerable alarm in the province, and almost completely paralyzed commerce. They sometimes came up within sight of Annapolis, and the inhabitants, for their protection, erected the first fort in the town.

The superintendence of colonial affairs continued until the year 1696, in the hands of the privy council; but in that year, at the instance of Lord Somers, a board was established in England, entitled "The Lords of Trade and Plantations," who ever evinced a desire to interfere in the internal affairs of the colonies, and it became the lion's mouth into which the royal agents dropped their accusations and complaints against the colonies.

It was strongly urged at this period, in consequence of the common danger of the colonies, that there should be a union to provide for the general defence. "Without a general constitution for warlike operations" it was said, "we can neither plan nor execute. We have a common interest and must have a common council—one head and one purse."[1] The mode that suggested itself to remedy these evils and to obtain a "free constitution" was through the representative principle and by a congress, or by forming a union. Among those who submitted the earliest plans were William Penn, Charles Davenant, Daniel Coxe, "a Virginian," and Robert Livingston, of New York. The "Virginian," in his *Essay upon the Government of the English Plantations on the Continent*, proposed that the deputies to the proposed general assembly should be as follows: Virginia, four; Maryland, three; Pennsylvania, one; the two Carolinas, one; and each of the two Jerseys, one. And Robert Livingston, in a letter dated May 13th, 1701, to the Lords of Trade, recommended that "one form of government be established in all the neighboring colonies on this continent. That they be divided into three distinct governments, to wit: That Virginia and Maryland be annexed to South and North Carolina. That some part of Connecticut, New York, East and West New Jersey, Pennsylvania and New Castle, be added together. And that to the Massachusetts be added New Hampshire and Rhode Island, and the rest of Connecticut."[2]

Besides the citations showing the germs of the union that finally grew into favor, the governor and council of New York in a petition as early as August 6th, 1691, to the king says: "There can be nothing in America more conducive to your Majesty's dignity and advantage, and for the safety of your Majesty's subjects upon this continent than that Connecticut, East and West New Jersey, Pennsylvania, and the three lower counties [Delaware] be re-annexed to your Majesty's province [New York] which will then be a government of sufficient extent."

Thus, New York was eager to aggrandise herself by devouring the smaller colonies, regardless of their interests or their wishes. Maryland could no longer protect herself behind the shield of her charter, as she had renounced its protection and placed her rights and liberties in the hands of the king. She had abdicated her high position as an almost independent palatinate, such as none of her sister colonies enjoyed, and now the crown could make and unmake her laws, could tax her to build northern forts and take her children to defend them, and might even merge her very existence in that of her neighbors. The arguments of New York chimed in so well with the views of the Lords of Trade, that a remodelling and consolidation of the colonies became a principle of their policy. As early as 1697, petitions had been presented to the board for such a consolidation under a general governor, and in their report, after presenting the various arguments, they pronounced the plan not practicable at that time, but recommended the appointment of a military commander-in-chief.[3]

[1] *Essay on Government*, p. 53. By a Virginian. London; 1701.

[2] New York *Col. Doc.*, iv., p. 874.

[3] Frothingham, p. 115.

Governor Nicholson, after his removal from Maryland to Virginia in 1698, urged upon the crown the importance of bringing all the colonies under one head and one viceroy, and keeping up a standing army; and painted in dark colors the growing spirit of independence, which should be stifled in the birth. A bill was brought into parliament in 1701, proposing the destruction of all the colonial charters and the establishment of royal governments, but it was finally defeated. The Lords of Trade applied to the government of Maryland in the same year for "information in regard to the ill-conduct of the proprietary governments," and the assembly, who had so long "groaned under" Lord Baltimore's "tyranny," can only allege that there was no oath of allegiance to the crown, that the laws were not submitted to the king for approval, nor was there any appeal to the English courts, and that the tonnage duty of fourteen pence per ton properly belonged to the province.[1]

The fact is, they were beginning to see their mistake, and were growing alarmed at the designs of the crown and the ambition of their neighbors. In 1704, Governor Seymour laid before them an extract from a London letter, giving notice of—

—"a design New York hath of making all the colonies tributary to them, in order to support or rather enrich them, and they seem to push the thing for the half as to have a member to be chosen out of the Northern and Southern governments to represent these colonies, and meet at New York instead of their own Assembly, and to have one Vice-Royal and General of all the forces of the Continent, and that of Virginia and Maryland &c., to be dependents under them; a project to this effect is lodged with the Lords."

At a conference held by the governor, council and the Lower House, to consider of and advise and lay before her majesty such reasons as may induce her majesty to put a stop to all proceedings levelled against the constitutions of this province by the Governor of New York, it was resolved:

"I. It is conceived by this conference that if the seat of government be at New York, it will not only be a means to allure and entice many tradesmen, artificers and others now among us who follow the trade of planting tobacco here, to desert this Province and fly to that of New York, where they may follow their several trades and callings and gain to themselves more ease and advantage, thereby lessening the revenue of the Crown of England, and also by these means we shall in a short time be enabled to supply us with such manufactures and other necessarys which we now have imported from England, and inevitably destroy our commerce with the same.

"II. We do conceive that New York having power and authority, will upon all occasions command from us such forces as they shall think fit for the safety and strengthening themselves, as will in a great measure weaken this Province (now but thinly seated), and thereby leave the remaining part of the inhabitants here, open to the incursions of the common enemy, the Indians, by whom we are environed and many of them as near to us as those of New York who are often committing murders on the inhabitants here, and have lately destroyed several persons and having opportunity of joining with the several nations of Indians now among us to effect their designs, leaving us in a deplorable condition, the lives of the inhabitants greatly hazarded thereby, and the Province in general in danger of being totally laid waste.

[1] McMahon, i., p. 270.

"III. That it will be very disadvantageous to the inhabitants of this Province, upon all occasions, as Councils, Assemblys, General Courts, and upon appeals and differences betwixt party and party, to travel thither, it being near four hundred miles distant from us, and the ways impassable in the winter season by reason of the desert roads, violent frosts, deep snows and the difficulty in passing the rivers and bays, so that the poorest sort of people will not be able to undergo such great charge and fatigue, and the richer, to avoid it, will remove themselves and their estates to England or other parts, and so tend to the ruin of the tobacco trade, and, consequently, lessen the revenue of the crown.

"IV. That the constitution of this Province to theirs is so disagreeable and of so different a nature, both in traffic and other things, that the laws there composed cannot be agreeable to the trade and affairs of the country nor the constitution of the inhabitants thereof."

The Upper House then sent to the Lower House the following message:

"It is humbly offered to the consideration of the' Honorable House of Delegates whether it may be of service to the country, that a certain sum of money be raised and lodged in the hands of some able merchant or merchants in London, ready to be called out upon any occasion, for the better encouraging the persons negotiating this affair; and whether or no it may not be thought of service to the country that some person be appointed by the House and sent home with such packets for their more safe and speedy conveyance."

And the assembly, in compliance with the governor's wishes, adopted the following resolution of the council:

"We have moved his Excellency that, whereas, in the year 1702, the then Assembly did vote £300 for the assistance of New York, which since was directed to be paid out of the public treasure of this province to the order of that government, when sent for; for as much as the government of New York has not yet thought fit to send for that sum of money, we are induced to suspect they have greater designs against us, and, therefore, desired his Excellency would admit the same sum to be remitted to Mr. John Hyde, in England, ready for that service, in case the Lord Corpebury shall require the same; otherwise, that our agent might make use of all or any part thereof to obviate any machinations of the said government of New York against our constitution, if any such be prosecuted; to which his Excellency has been pleased to assent."[1]

Before the year 1661, letters were sent in Maryland by private hand, and dispatches from the government by special messengers. But in this year (1661), an act was passed by the General Assembly "for conveyance of letters concerning the State and public affairs." This act continued in force with slight changes until the year 1695, when a regular post was established from the Potomac river to Philadelphia. John Perry was appointed post-rider at a salary of £50 a year, and was required to traverse his route and carry all public messages, and to deliver all letters and packages for the inhabitants eight times a year. His route extended from Newton's Point on the Potomac river, thence to Allen's Mill, Benedict, Leonardtown, George Lingan's, Mr. Lawkin's, South river, Annapolis, Kent, Williamstadt, Daniel Toass, Adam Peterson's, New Castle, and thence to Philadelphia. The thinly

[1] Ex-Governor Blackiston, upon his retirement from office, was appointed the agent of the province in England, to represent her interests in all matters. He was to serve the first year without pay, and afterwards to receive £120 per annum.

settled condition of the country, and the distance which separated the scattered towns along the coast, prevented the speedy growth of the post-office. The first regular post-office established in all the colonies by parliament was in 1710. By its provisions a general post-office was established in North America and the West Indies. And in 1717 a settled post was established from Virginia to Maryland, which went through all the northern colonies, bringing and forwarding letters from Boston to Williamsburg in Virginia, in four weeks. In 1727, the mail to Annapolis was opened, to go once a fortnight in summer, and once a month in winter, by way of New Castle, etc., to the Eastern shore; managed by William Bradford, in Philadelphia, and William Parks, in Annapolis.

We have seen that at the time of the first settlement at St. Mary's, a printing-press, the first in the colonies, was set up. This, however, was doubtless destroyed or carried off in Claiborne's rebellion. The next mention we have of a press is in 1666, when an act was passed for the publication of the laws within the province. Up to 1696 the province had no public printer; but in October of that year, William Bladen, clerk of the Upper House, petitioned the assembly to establish the office, offering to procure the necessary press and material, if he should receive the appointment. The petition was approved; Bladen brought out a press and all needful apparatus, and in 1700 the governor and council recommended to the Lower House that all blanks for writs and other legal documents be printed by Bladen, "writs, citations, and summons at one penny or one pound tobacco per piece, and letters testamentary or administrative, bail-bonds, etc., at two pence or two pounds tobacco."

Bladen printed the laws then in force; and in 1718 the laws were again printed, as they then stood, by William Bradford, of Philadelphia. The next "printer of the province" was William Parks, of Annapolis, who published in 1727 the laws then in existence, known as "the old body of laws." From that period to the present time the laws of each session have been separately published. Mr. Parks having removed to Williamsburg, Virginia, the laws and journals were printed by his partner, Edmund Hall, until 1740, when Jonas Green, of Annapolis, was given the office. In 1765, the Rev. Thomas Bacon, rector of All Saints' parish, in Frederick county, a man of great learning, excellence and intelligence, published his *Laws of Maryland*, giving the course of legislation in the province from its beginning down to 1764; a work well known, and indispensable to all students of Maryland history.

We have traced the beginning of the English Church in the province down to the time when it was made the Established Church. That of the next most important Protestant denomination, the Presbyterians, is involved in much obscurity, but the fact is certain that the first regular Presbyterian church was established in Maryland. The first adherents of this church came over in small companies, and nowhere, not even among the Independents or Congregationalists of New England, did they find the liberty of worship that was afforded them in Maryland under the Calverts. The earliest settlements of Presbyterians were made in Somerset county; but in 1690 a considerable number, through the influence of Colonel Ninian Beale, settled in the neighborhood of the present cities of Washington and Georgetown.

In the famous Act of 1649, we find the name Presbyterian included among the terms of reproach which were forbidden to be used, from which it would seem that persons of that faith were already in the colony. In the letter of Lord Baltimore before mentioned, giving an account of the state of religion in the province, he speaks of dissenting ministers being "maintained by a voluntary contribution of those of their own persuasion, as others of the Presbyterians, Independents, Anabaptists, Quakers, and Romish church are." And in speaking of the proportions of the different sects, he says: "The greatest part of the inhabitants [of Maryland], three of four, at least, do consist of Presbyterians, Independents, Anabaptists, and Quakers, those of the Church of England, as well as those of the Romish, being the lowest." This great numerical proportion, and the fact that they were able to support their churches and ministers, shows that they must have existed in the province from very early times.

The first regularly constituted Presbyterian church in the United States, so far as we can discover, was erected at Rehoboth, then in Somerset, but now in Wicomico county.

In 1697, we have a report of Governor Nicholson, from information furnished him on his requisition by the sheriffs of the counties, made to the Bishop of London, in which he says Somerset county had no "Popish Priest, lay brothers, or any of their chapels, and no Quakers." But it had three Presbyterian places of worship. In 1710, the minutes of the presbytery mention at least five congregations in Maryland. These were Rehoboth, Snow Hill, Upper Marlborough, Manokin, and Wicomico.[1] Upper Marlborough was formed by a company of Scotch emigrants under the pastorate of Rev. Nathaniel Taylor, about the year 1690. The other four churches were in Somerset county, and were the fruits of Rev. Francis Mackenzie's labors, who is believed to have been the first regularly ordained Presbyterian minister in America. The congregations of Manokin and Wicomico were organized under the pastoral care of the Revs. Mr. McNish and Hampton, before the year 1705. Mr. Hodge says: "It can hardly be presumed that these five Presbyterian congregations with distinct church edifices, some of them within fifteen miles of each other, could, at so early a period, and in so thinly settled a part of the country, have been formed in a few years." And Mr. Spence calls Somerset county "the fatherland of American Presbyterianism."[2]

In the years 1694–5 an epidemic disease broke out among the cattle and hogs and destroyed immense numbers; and two years later a terrible pesti-

[1] Hodge, *History of the Presbyterian Church*, i., p. 77. Irving Spence, *Letters on the Early History of the Presbyterian Church*, p. 82.

[2] Philadelphia writers maintain that the first regularly constituted Presbyterian church in America was organized in that city in 1698.

lence made its appearance among the people of the lower counties. Whatever faults may have been alleged against the Catholic clergy, they have never been charged with shrinking from their duties in times of peril; and while the disease was raging they went from house to house, helping the sick, and administering the consolations and last offices of their faith to the dying. This conduct was not unnoticed by the Lower House, who made it the subject of the following message to the governor:

"Upon reading a certain letter from a reverend minister of the Church of England, which your Excellency was pleased to communicate to us, complaining to your Excellency that the Popish priests in Charles county do, of their own accord, in this raging and violent mortality in that county, make it their business to go up and down the county, to persons' houses when dying and frantic, and endeavor to seduce and make proselytes of them, and in such condition boldly presume to administer the sacrament to them; we have put it to the vote in the House if a law should be made to restrain such their presumption, or not; and have concluded to make no such law at present, but humbly intreat your Excellency that you would be pleased to issue your proclamation to restrain and prohibit such their extravagance and presumptuous behavior."

A short time later, the Upper House think it necessary to bring a specific offender to the governor's notice, in these terms:

"It being represented to this board that Wm. Hunter, a Popish priest, in Charles county, committed divers enormities in disswading several persons, especially poor, ignorant people of the Church of England, from their faith, and endeavoring to draw them to the Popish faith, consulted and debated whether it may not be advisable that the said Hunter be wholly silenced and not suffered to preach or say mass in any part of this province, and thereupon it is thought advisable that the same be wholly left to his Excellency's judgment to silence him or not, as his demerits require."

On the 4th of October, 1698, Governor Francis Nicholson was transferred by the king to Virginia, and Colonel Nathaniel Blackiston was appointed in his stead. He qualified on the 2d of January, 1698 O.S. (1699 N.S.) Before Nicholson's departure, however, the assembly appropriated £100 to purchase of Mr. John Dent, Cool Springs, now called Whitemarsh, in St. Mary's county, and fifty acres adjoining, and for the erection of "small tenements for the good and benefit of such poor, impotent and lame persons as shall resort thither." Governor Blackiston alludes to this as a subject of special thankfulness, in an address to the assembly, wherein, after enumerating many blessings for which the people should be thankful to the Almighty, adds: "and for restoring health to us, and blessing us with several beneficial and healing springs of water, called the Cool Springs, which, by His blessing, have wrought many wonderful and signal cures amongst several distempered and impotent persons."

By this we learn that the epidemic had subsided. Notwithstanding their serious misfortunes, the colony seems at this time to have been in a thriving state, as the governor declares:

"As for public workhouses, we adjudge them altogether needless. None need stand still for want of employment. The province wants workmen; workmen want not work. Here are no beggars; and such as are superanuated are reasonably well provided for by the counties."

Upon the council records we find the following entry of an event which happened on the day of the delivery of this address:

"*Friday, July 13th, 1699.*

"It pleasing Almighty God that a great clap of thunder and lightning fell upon the State House, the House of Delegates sitting therein, which splintered the flag staff, shook down the vane, burnt the flag, and set the roof of the house in a flame of fire, and striking through the upper rooms shattering the door posts and window frames, stroke down and greviously wounded several of the delegates and more particularly Col. Hans Hanson, Lieut. Col. Thomas Hicks and Mr. George Ashman, and passing through the room where the committee of laws were sitting, struck dead Mr. James Crawford one of the delegates of Calvert County and one of the said Committee, to the great astonishment of all persons. But it so pleased God, by the active care and personal presence of his Excellency the Governor, the said fire was quickly quenched, a shower of rain happening immediately thereupon, and the records preserved, as also the house with little or no considerable damage, and this occasioned the adjournment of this board till 8 of the clock to-morrow morning."

By way of precaution against the recurrence of a similar danger, the council recommended to the House "that four or five small water engines and twenty leather buckets may be sent for by the present shipping, which may be hung up in the Court House and ready upon any such unhappy occasion."

We have seen that the first law for the establishment of the Church of England in the province was made in 1692, but whether this was confirmed by the king we are unable at this time to tell. In 1694, an additional act was made on the subject, and in 1695, another was passed by which both the former were repealed and a new law substituted, the strong opposition of the Quakers and Roman Catholics caused the various changes in these laws. In 1696, another new law was made, and that of 1695 repealed. This law contained a clause "that the Church of England within this province, shall enjoy all and singular her rights, privileges and freedoms as it is now, or shall be at any time hereafter, established by law in the kingdom of England, and that his Majesty's subjects of this province shall enjoy all their rights and liberties according to the laws and statutes of the Kingdom of England, in all matters and causes where the laws of this province are silent." This law again roused the Quakers and Catholics in the colony, and as its terms were open to attack, they opposed it in the King's Council, and in the autumn of 1699 it was annulled on the ground that it contained "a clause declaring all the laws of England to be in force in Maryland; which clause is of another nature than that which is set forth by the title in the said law."[1] In 1700 a new act was passed by the assembly, which again furnished strong ground of remonstrance to the dissenters, and it also failed to receive the assent of the crown.

By this law it was enacted "that the book of Common Prayer and Administration of the Sacraments, with the rites and ceremonies of the church

[1] Bacon.

according to the use of the Church of England, the Psalter and Psalms of David, and morning and evening prayer therein contained, be solemnly read, and by all and every minister, or reader in every church, *or other place of public worship*, within this province." This law, which required the use of the book of Common Prayer "in every church, *or other place of public worship*" in the province, practically destroyed all toleration of dissenters, and they naturally took strong ground against its adoption.[1]

In the meantime, however, the Rev. Dr. Bray, the founder of "The Society for Promoting Christian Knowledge," and "The Society for Propagating the Gospel in foreign parts," who had been appointed by the Bishop of London, commissary of Maryland, and who had arrived here in March, 1700, summoned all the clergy of the province to a general visitation at Annapolis, on the 23d of May, 1700. This "ecclesiastical legislature," the first held in America, is memorable as having originated "the first missionary effort made by any part of the church on this continent. The field selected was Pennsylvania, among the Quakers.[2]

The law passed by the Assembly of 1700, which had been referred by the Lords Commissioners of Trade and Plantations to the attorney general for his opinion upon the objections raised by the dissenters upon the words we have already alluded to, that officer gave it as his opinion "that those words '*or other place of public worship*,' were so general that they might be construed to extend to the places of worship of dissenters; and, though this construction was probably not intended by the framers of the law, yet it might endanger liberty of conscience in the province; and therefore it was submitted whether this clause should not be so far explained as to remove the objection stated."[3] Dr. Bray, who had been sent to England to look after the bill, induced the Lords of Trade to grant him permission to have another bill drawn, with the objectionable features stricken out, and in accordance with the views of the board, and then to be returned to Maryland to be passed without amendments into a law. Upon doing this, it was promised that his majesty would confirm it; and in the interval the law already before the board was not to be considered as being "totally disannulled." Dr. Bray availed himself of the permission granted,

[1] In May, 1701, John Field, Edward Haistwell and Joseph Wyeth, in behalf of the Quakers of Maryland, presented a memorial to the Board, in which they stated their objections against the Act.

[2] The following clergymen were present at this visitation: John Tilliston, rector of St. Paul's, in Talbot county; Benjamin Nobbes, of William and Mary's, in St. Mary's county; Christopher Platts, of King and Queen parish, in St. Mary's county; Robert Owen, of St. Paul's, in Prince George's county; George Tubman, of Port Tobacco, in Charles county; Hugh Jones, of Christ Church, in Calvert county; Thomas Cockshute, of All Saints', in Calvert county; Henry Hall, of St. James', Herring creek, in Anne Arundel county; Joseph Colbach, of All Hallows', in Anne Arundel county; Edward Topp, of Annapolis, in Anne Arundel county; George Trotter, of Somerset, in Somerset county; Thomas Howell, of Great Choptank and Dorchester, in Dorchester county; Richard Marsden, reader of St. Michael's, in Talbot county; Stephen Beardley, rector of St. Paul's, in Kent county; Richard Sewell, of North and South Sassafras, in Cecil county; and Jonathan White and Alexander Strahan.

[3] Hawks', p. 108.

caused the bill to be prepared under the advice of counsel, and after it had received the approval of the board, it was sent to Maryland. The assembly adopted it on the 25th of March, 1702, when it was returned to England to receive the royal assent. The Quakers now redoubled their efforts in resisting its approval. They filed their objections with the board, who submitted the same to the king for his examination, and he appointed the 5th of June, 1701, to hear them urged. Upon this occasion the objectors were represented by Joseph Wyeth and Theodore Eccleston, of Maryland; but, notwithstanding their efforts, the council confirmed the law the 18th of January, 1702, O.S. (1703, N.S.)

"By this law," Dr. Hawks says, "every congregation and place of worship, according to the usage of the Church of England, for the maintenance of whose minister a certain revenue or income was directed by law to be raised, was to be deemed as part of the established Church. Every minister presented, inducted, or appointed by the governor, was to receive forty pounds of tobacco per poll, out of which he was required to pay, yearly, a thousand pounds of tobacco to a parish clerk. The sheriffs were directed to collect the minister's tobacco. Each parish was directed to have a select vestry, consisting of six at the least; the incumbent being in all cases placed at the head of the vestry, as principal thereof. On the death or resignation of a vestryman, the freeholders of the parish supplied the vacancy; and on every Easter Monday two of the vestry of the previous year were to retire from office, and two new ones were to be appointed. A parish register was directed to be kept; the vestries were required to meet once a month, under a penalty; and to them it belonged to keep the churches, chapels, and churchyards in repair. For this purpose they were empowered to receive and apply all fines or forfeitures which might arise under this act; and should they prove insufficient, the justices of the county courts, upon application from the vestries, were to lay a tax, not exceeding ten pounds of tobacco per poll in any one year, which the sheriffs were to collect and pay over to the vestry. No minister was allowed to hold more than two livings at one time, and the consent of both the parishes concerned was made necessary even to hold two. In case a parish was destitute of a minister, the vestry were authorized to select a lay reader, and present him to the ordinary, who might (if he approved of him,) grant him a licence, and sequester so much of the forty pounds per poll as he deemed proper to pay such reader for his services. Nothing, however, was permitted to be read but what the ordinary appointed. The English acts of toleration were extended to Protestant dissenters and Quakers, and they were permitted to have meeting-hours, provided the same were certified to, and registered by the county courts."[1]

Such were the provisions of the law for the establishment of the Church of England in the province, by which "the Catholic inhabitant was the only victim of intolerance." But this unjust and ungenerous policy did not end here: disfranchisement was followed by a system of persecution so tyrannous as to cast an indelible blot on the ancient glory of Maryland.

Early in 1701, Governor Blackiston solicited the queen to allow him to return to England on account of his impaired health. In June he received the permission, and soon after embarked, leaving the administration provisionally in the hands of Thomas Tench, one of the council. On the 12th of February, 1702, O. S. (1703, N. S.), John Seymour was appointed governor,

[1] Hawks, C. C. *History of Maryland*, p. 113; Bacon's *Laws*, 1702, ch. 1.

and soon after entered on the duties of his office. Some time after his installation he received complaints from a number of the Protestant inhabitants against Robert Brooke and William Hunter, two Catholic priests of St. Mary's county. He immediately summoned them to answer the charges before the council. They signified their obedience, but requested that they might be accompanied by Charles Carroll, their counsel, which request the board unanimously refused. Upon the appointed day, September 11, 1704, they appeared before the governor and council, and in the council proceedings we find the following minute of the affair:

"The said Mr. William Hunter and Mr. Robert Brooke appeared and are told on what occasion they were called before his Excellency, Mr. William Hunter gives his Excellency many thanks for the opportunity of appearing before his Excellency, and says he is very sorry for any annoyance in his conduct. As to his consecrating the chapel, he did not consecrate it, for that is an Episcopal function, and that nobody was present but himself in his common priest's vestments, and that neither under his Excellency's eye nor in his presence, but if any such thing was done, it was above fourteen months ago and long before his Excellency's arrival. Mr. Brooke says he did say mass in the Court time at the chapel of St. Mary's, but found that others had formerly done so.

"Advised that this being the first complaint the said Mr. Hunter and Mr. Brooke be severely repremanded, and told that they must not expect any favor, but the utmost severity of the law upon any misdemeanor by them committed; and being called in, his Excellency was pleased to give them the following repremand:

"'It is the unhappy temper of you and all your tribe to grow insolent upon civility and never know how to use it, and yet of all people you have the least reason for considering that if the necessary laws that are made were let loose, they are sufficient to crush you, and which (if your arrogant principles have not blinded you), you must need to dread.

"'You might, methinks, be content to live quietly as you may, and let the exercise of your superstitious vanities be confined to yourselves, without proclaiming them at public times and in public places, unless you expect, by your gaudy shows and serpentine policy, to amuse the multitude and beguile the unthinking, weakest part of them, an act of deceit well known to be amongst you.

"'But, gentlemen, be not deceived, for though the clemency of her Majesty's government and of her gracious inclinations leads her to make all her subjects easy, that know how to be so, yet her Majesty is not without means to curb insolence, but more especially in your fraternity, who are more eminently than others abounding with it; and I assure you the next occasion you give me you shall find the truth of what I say, which you should now do, but that I am willing, upon the earnest solicitations of some gentlemen to make one trial (and it shall be but this one) of your temper.

"'In plain and few words, gentlemen, if you intend to live here, let me hear no more of these things; for if I do, and they are made good against you, be assured I'll chastise you; and least you should flatter yourselves that the severities of the laws will be a means to move the pity of your Judges, I assure you I do not intend to deal with you so. I'll remove the evil by sending you where you may be dealt with as you deserve.

"'Therefore, as I told you, I'll make but this one trial, and advise you to be civil and modest, for there is no other way for you to live quietly here.

"'You are the first that have given any disturbance to my government, and if it were not for the hopes of your better demeanour you should now be the first that should feel the effects of so doing. Pray take notice that I am an English Protestant gentleman, and can never equivocate.'

"After which they were discharged. The members of this board taking, under their consideration, that such use of the Popish chapel of the City of Saint Mary's, in Saint Mary's County, where there is a Protestant Church, and the said County Court is kept, is both scandalous and offensive to the government, do advise and desire his Excellency the Governor, to give immediate orders for the shutting up the said Popish Chapel, and that no person presume to make use thereof under any pretence whatsoever.

"Whereupon it was ordered by his Excellency, the Governor, that present the Sheriff of Saint Mary's County lock up the said chapel and keep the key thereof."

The House of Delegates, on the 19th of September, 1704, took into consideration the remarks of the governor to the two priests, and sent him the following address:

"By a paper read in the House, we perceive what your Excellency was pleased to say to two Popish Priests, on the occasion there mentioned, and, as all your actions, so this in particular, gives us great satisfaction, to find you generously bent to protect her Majesty's Protestant subjects here against insolence and growth of Popery, and we feel cheerfully thankful to you for it."

The dread of Popery must have been excessive at this period, if we may judge from the penalties of an act made at the September session of Assembly of 1704, "to prevent the growth of Popery within this province." By this act it was enacted, that "whatsoever popish bishop, priest or jesuit, should baptize any child or children, other than such who have popish parents, or shall say mass, or exercise the function of a popish bishop or priest within this Province, or should endeavor to persuade any of his majesty's liege people of this province to embrace and be reconciled to the Church of Rome," should upon conviction, pay the sum of £50 and suffer an imprisonment of six months. And, if after such conviction, any popish bishop, priest or jesuit should say mass or exercise any function of a priest within the province, or if any persons professing to be of the Church of Rome should keep school or take upon themselves the education, government, or boarding of youth, at any place in the province, upon conviction, such offenders should be transported to England to undergo the penalties provided there by statutes 11 and 12, William III., "for the further preventing the growth of Popery."[1] "And that Protestant children of Popish parents might not, for want of a suitable maintenance, be compelled to embrace the Popish

[1] "This act, contrasted with the law of 1649, reveals the difference between the charity of the Protestants of the latter period and the Catholics of Cæcilius Calvert's day. By its provisions, Section 1 provides a reward of £100 to anyone who shall 'apprehend and take' a Popish bishop, priest, or Jesuit, and prosecute him 'until convicted of saying Mass, or of exercising any other part of the office or function of a Popish bishop or priest.' Section 3 inflicts perpetual imprisonment on any Popish bishop, priest, or Jesuit, that shall say Mass, or exercise any function proper to such bishop, priest, or Jesuit; or on any person professing the Catholic religion, who shall keep school, or educate, or govern, or board any youth. Section 4: That if any Popish youth shall not, within six months after he attains his majority, take certain oaths prescribed (oaths inconsistent with the faith of Catholics), he shall be incapable of taking lands by descent, and his next of kin, being a Protestant, shall succeed to them; that any person professing the Catholic faith shall be incompetent to purchase lands. Section 6: Any person sending his child abroad, to be educated in the Catholic faith, should forfeit £100."—*Letter of William M. Addison upon Religious Toleration in America*, p. 9.

religion contrary to their inclinations, it was enacted, that if any such parent refused a proper support to his Protestant child, then the governor or keeper of the great seal had power to make such order therein as suited the intent of the act; in other words, was at liberty to deprive a father of the earnings of his labor, for the sake of promoting the orthodoxy of his child." "Little comment," adds Dr. Hawks, "is here necessary. The enactment enforced a gross violation of the best feelings of human nature; it forbade a parent to fulfill the first duty which he owed to his offspring, that of instruction; and dissolving the filial obligations, offered to a wayward child a premium for youthful hypocrisy. He who can speak of such a law in any terms but those of indignant reprobation, deserves himself to endure all its penalties."[1] A subsequent provision of another law passed this year (1704) with more generosity, permitted a priest to officiate in a private family of the Roman Catholic communion, but in no other. Out of this privilege grew a custom of providing chapels, under the same roof, and connected with the dwelling of some Roman Catholic family.[2]

In 1715, with tyranny still more atrocious, it was enacted, that the children of a Protestant father might be taken from a Papist mother, and placed where they might be securely educated in the Protestant religion. In 1718, Catholics were rendered incapable of giving a vote in any election of delegates without having renounced their faith by taking the test oath. The fourth chapter of the same year repeals all former legislation against the growth of Popery, but adopts the full measure of English severity in the statute of 11th and 12th, William III.[3]

After such acts, whose recital may well make the Marylander of the present day blush with indignant shame at the deeds of his predecessors, one turns with almost a feeling of amusement to the policy pursued by our earlier legislators with respect to the Irish Catholics. In 1704, an import of twenty shillings per poll was laid on all negroes and Irish Papists imported into the province, while Irish Protestants were admitted duty free. A later

[1] *Rise and Progress of the Protestant Episcopal Church in Maryland*, p. 126.

[2] As in the old residence of Charles Carroll, of Carrollton, at Annapolis, and Doughoregan manor, Howard county.

[3] By an act of the Assembly passed in 1723, it was provided: That a person convicted "of wittingly, maliciously and advisedly, by writing or speaking, blaspheming or cursing God, or of denying our Saviour Jesus Christ to be the Son of God, or denying the Holy Trinity, or the Godhead of any of the Three Persons, or the unity of the Godhead, or of uttering any profane words concerning the Godhead," should for the first offence be bored through the tongue and fined £20, or if unable to pay the fine, be imprisoned six months; for the second offence, should be branded in the forehead with the letter B and fined £40, or if too poor to pay it, be imprisoned twelve months; and for the third offence should "suffer death without benefit of clergy." This law was not repealed until 1820.

The number of Catholics in the province in 1708 was 2,974, as appears by the subjoined list, sent out by Governor Seymour:

"A list of the number of Papists inhabiting in the several counties of this province, as taken by the respective sheriffs, Anno Domini 1708, viz: In Anne Arundel county, 161; in Baltimore county, 53; in Calvert county, 48; in Prince George's county, 248; in Charles county, 709; in St. Mary's county, 1,238; in Cecil county, 49; in Kent county, 40; in Queen Anne's county, 179; in Talbot county, 89; in Dorchester county, 79; in Somerset county, 81. In all, 2,974." (London Public Record Office, Maryland, B. T., Red, No. 4, H., p. 79.) The whole population of the province at this time was over 40,000.

act repealed this, and imposed a penalty of £5 in each case for the concealment of their importation; and not long after, it was enacted that certain test oaths should be tendered by the naval officers to Irish servants on board of any ships arriving. In the year 1717, the tax upon Irish servants was doubled. No less than twelve acts, in the space of sixteen years, were levelled against their entering Maryland. But like the wheat-fly, they showed themselves in spite of precaution; and the legislatures, in despair, at last prevented owners of vessels from shipping them. But while the Irish Catholic was forbidden our coast, the branded convict was, to a certain extent, welcomed to the shores of Maryland, and permitted to mingle with the native population.

The practice of transporting the king's "seven year passengers for the better peopling of the American plantations," began under the reign of James I., who adopted the policy of sending "dissolute persons" to Virginia. This plan was afterwards extended to the other colonies, and finally legalized and regulated by acts of parliament. By these acts, persons convicted of burglary, robbery, perjury, forgery and theft, and by the laws of England subject to death, might be transported to the American colonies for seven or fourteen years. By the statute of 4th, George I., those guilty of minor offences and entitled. to the benefit of clergy, as well as others convicted of crimes, might by order of the courts be transported in the same manner. One of the reasons assigned for this act was, that "in many of his majesty's colonies and plantations, there was a great want of servants, who, by their labor and industry, might be the means of improving and making the said colonies and plantations more useful to his majesty." Thus it was that those whose crimes had made them unfit for society in England, were let loose upon society in America, and deemed fit servants for the colonist.

These "seven year passengers," or "king's passengers," as they were generally termed by the journals of the day, were transported by private shippers, under a contract with the government, and were afterwards sold for the advantage of the shipper.

It must not be supposed, however, that all these convicts were criminals of the deepest dye. Insurgent peasants, who resisted the enclosure of common lands, minor offenders, and at some periods, as we shall see hereafter, political offenders, were those usually sentenced for life, "to his majesty's tobacco plantations in America." We must not forget how small an offense was a felony under the barbarous English penal code of the seventeenth century; a code which punished over four hundred different offences with death; a code which, under Cromwell's commonwealth, executed three thousand unfortunate wretches for witchcraft; a code which in the days of the Stuarts, and even till our own day, made the unlicensed shooting of a partridge a felony.

The number of convicts imported into Maryland before the revolution of 1776 must have amounted to at least twenty thousand. From the year 1750 to 1770 not less than from four to five hundred were annually brought into the province. The evils of the system excited the indignation of the colonists, and Maryland, as early as 1676, had passed "an Act against the importation of convicted persons into this province." This drew upon her the reprobation of the crown lawyers, who contended that every law of the colonial legislature, passed to restrain a measure that was allowed and encouraged by acts of parliament, was void *ab initio.* This law was continued at different times, till the year 1692, when a new law was passed. The Lower House of Assembly, during the French and Indian war, passed a law imposing a tax upon imported convicts, which the governor and council resisted upon the ground that it was in conflict with the acts of parliament authorising the importation. During the controversy that arose between the two houses the subject was submitted to Mr. Murray, the attorney general—afterwards Lord Mansfield--who pronounced the opinion that "no colony had power to make such laws, because they were in direct opposition to the authority of parliament; and if they were proper, the colonial legislatures might, with equal propriety, lay duties upon, or even prohibit the importation of English goods." The argument was an unfortunate one, as it happened, for under the charter of Maryland (which the attorney general admitted *he had not examined*) the assembly had power to impose duties on imported British merchandise. It seems a flagrant outrage that a high public officer, in considering so important a question as this, involving the fundamental rights of a whole province, should give less attention to the evidence than he would have done in a case between John Doe and Richard Roe, involving the ownership of an acre of meadow; but we must remember the general obsequiousness of crown lawyers toward the crown, and the special disposition of this particular jurist, as memorably shown some years later.[1]

A large portion of the early emigrants to Maryland belonged to the class called in colonial phrase "redemptioners" or "indented servants." These were persons who, being unable to pay their own passage over, bound themselves by contract to serve a certain period in the colonies, to redeem their passage. The importation of these white indented persons was extensively carried on. In Maryland, the term of indented service, where no express contract had been entered into, was limited by the Act of 1715. A servant being above the age of twenty-five was obliged to serve five years; if between eighteen and twenty-two, six years; if between fifteen and eighteen, seven years; and if under fifteen, they were to serve until they reached the age of twenty-two.[2] On the expiration of their terms of servitude they became free

[1] This convict business gave occasion for frequent interchanges of sarcasm among the colonies. In 1752, the Virginia *Gazette*, noting the arrival of a ship in the James river with "150 convicts bound for Maryland," remarks: "We *congratulate* the Marylanders on the safe arrival of these recruits!" To which the Maryland *Gazette* retorted: "Thanks for this Virginia compliment! But the author, it is probable, did not think of the old trite proverb—'The pot should not call the kettle black.' It is said that Captain Gracey, who brought these recruits into Patowmack, sold the chief part of them on the *south* side of that river."

[2] Bacon.

citizens and were absorbed into the general mass of freemen. In Alsop's time,[1] the conditions of servitude were very mild: "Five days and a half in the summer weeks is the allotted time that they work in; and for two months, when the sun predominates in the highest pitch of his heat, they claim an ancient and customary privilege, to repose themselves three hours a day within the house; and this is undeniably granted to them that work in the field." When the four years of servitude are over, and the servant became a freeman, "there's a law in the province that enjoins his master whom he hath served, to give him fifty acres of land, corn to serve him a whole year, three suits of apparel with things necessary to them, and tools to work withal."

The female immigrants, according to the same authority, were eagerly sought in marriage. Their former condition of servitude entailed no disabilities nor disgrace upon the redemptioners of either sex, when their time of service had expired; and many of them became distinguished citizens. Indeed, some of the most honored names in our history were redemptioners, such as Charles Thomson, secretary of congress during the revolution; Matthew Thornton, a signer of the Declaration of Independence; and the parents of Major-General and Governor Sullivan.

About the years 1752–3–4, there was a considerable influx into Maryland of what were called "the German Palatines." These were originally the inhabitants (or their descendants) of that beautiful country lying on the Rhine and the Neckar, which, during the Thirty Years' War, and afterwards during the wars of Louis XIV. was again and again ravaged and desolated with horrible cruelty. Numbers of the inhabitants fled to Holland, and for years there was a drain of emigration from the ruined and devastated country. We can not doubt that, in the flat and chilly land of sluggish canals and continual fogs, they yearned for the bright waters, the glowing sunshine, and the vine-clad hills of their native home, and this may have prompted them to seek a more congenial clime beyond the stormy Atlantic, where they found so satisfactory a home, that they invited over great numbers of German and Swiss Protestants, who were all known in the colonies as "Palatines." About the period mentioned, at least three thousand of them came into Maryland, chiefly from Rotterdam, and settled mostly in the western part of the province. We shall hear of them again in the border difficulties with Pennsylvania.

QUEEN ANNE.

On the death of William III., the crown, in accordance with the Act of Settlement, descended to his wife's sister, Anne, who ascended the throne March 8, 1702. Her accession was proclaimed in all the colonies, but Mary-

[1] *A Character of the Province of Maryland.* By George Alsop. London, 1666 [Gowans's Reprint]. Alsop was himself a redemptioner; so spoke from personal knowledge.

land alone passed an "Act of Recognition" of her title, which, though regarded as an instance of loyalty, was rejected by her majesty, because she was advised that while it seemed to respect the law which had placed her on the throne, it really *impugned Parliamentary jurisdiction.*[1] During her reign, Maryland enjoyed almost undisturbed peace and prosperity, with but one slight breeze, which shall presently be mentioned, to ruffle the calm. The year 1704 was signalized by a proclamation of the governor against immorality, profaneness, and breaking the Lord's day, which only lacks the word "Sabbath" to have quite a Puritan flavor; and an act for marking roads, which is worthy of some notice. As early as 1666, the Assembly of Maryland passed "an Act for marking highways and making the head of rivers, creeks, branches and swamps passable for horse and foot." This law, with a few amendments, was continued down to 1704, when a new act was passed. About the time of the passage of the first act, Augustine Herman of Bohemia manor, commenced the construction of a cart road between Bohemia river in Cecil county, Maryland, and the Appoquinimink creek in New Castle county, Delaware. The making of this road, the first in Delaware, was the foundation of the present thriving town of Odessa, in that State, and the ancient town of "Cecilton," on Bohemia river, in Maryland. Writing to Beekman about this period, Herman says: "I am now engaged in encouraging settlers to unite together in a village, of which, I understand a beginning will be made before next winter. From there we may arrive by land in one day at San Hoeck [New Castle]. . . . . The Maquas [Christina] kill, and the Bohemia river are only one mile distance from each other, by which it is an easy correspondence by water, which would be greatly encouraging to the inhabitants of New Netherlands." The contemplated village is now called Port Herman.[2]

The General Assembly of 1704, however, "thought convenient, and very much for the benefit of the inhabitants of the province, that roads and paths be marked, and the head of rivers, creeks and branches be made passable." It was enacted, therefore, that all public and main roads, be hereafter cleared and grubbed, fit for travelling, twenty feet wide. "And that all the roads that lead to any ferries, court houses of any county, or to any church, or leading through any county to the Port of Annapolis, shall be marked on both sides of the road with two notches; if the road lead to Annapolis, the road that leads there, at the leaving the other road, shall be marked on the face of the tree, in a smooth place cut for the purpose, with the letters AA set on with a pair of marking irons and colored; and so with two notches all along the road: and where, at any place it leaves any other road, shall be again distinguished with the mark aforesaid, on the face of the tree, with a pair of marking irons, and colored as aforesaid. And any road on the Eastern shore, in Talbot county, that leads to the Port of William Stadt [Oxford], at the entering into the same, and upon parting with or dividing from any other road, shall be marked on the face of a tree, in a

[1] Chalmers' *Revolt of the Colonies*, i., p. 314. [2] Vincent, *History of Delaware*, p. 374.

smooth place cut for that purpose, with the letter W and so with two notches all along the road. And the roads that lead to any county court house, shall have two notches on the trees on both sides of the road as aforesaid, and another notch a distance above the other two. And any road that leads to a church, shall be marked at the entrance into the same, and at the leaving any other road, with a slip cut down the face of the tree near the ground. And any road leading to a ferry, and dividing from other public roads, shall be marked with three notches of equal distance at the entrance into the same." This curious "road law," certainly shows how much of the country then settled, was a wild wood, and at the same time, the primitive guide marks along the public roads and paths leading to ferries, towns, court houses, and also to the places of public worship.

The exception to the general quietude of this time happened in 1705, when the repose of Maryland was somewhat disturbed by a conspiracy of discontented debtors and others who attempted, with the aid of the negroes and Indians, to seize the government, in order to discharge their incumbrances by assuming the administration. The provincial court house was burnt, together with a number of other buildings. A timely discovery frustrated the plans of the conspirators, and Richard Clarke, the principal ringleader, and a number of others were arrested, others outlawed and attainted by the assembly. In 1707, however, this same Clarke was charged with the "design of burning Annapolis, destroying the public records, sacking, and blowing up the public magazine within the limits of the town; with making and passing base coin of dollars and pieces of eight; and with the intention of pirating, after he had succeeded in carrying into execution his diabolical and villainous designs."[1] He was "convicted and attainted of high treason," and sentenced to suffer death, but whether this was carried into effect our records do not furnish us with the evidence.

The unsettled state of the boundary between Maryland and Pennsylvania now began to be a source of trouble to the colony, as settlements were made in the lands in dispute, giving rise to lawsuits and other difficulties. So, on April 15th, 1707, the governor and council petitioned the queen to take steps to settle the question, which, however, was not done.

As early as 1588, a company of English merchants trading to Africa, associated themselves under the name of the African Company, which received a charter in 1618. Other companies bearing the name were successively formed in 1662, 1672, and 1695, which latter continued in existence till 1821. A large, perhaps the chief part of its profits arose from the importation of negro slaves into the colonies, and this traffic was greatly encouraged by the crown. In 1708 the Board of Trade wrote to Governor Seymour, inquiring what negroes had been imported into the province, and we subjoin his answer in full, as referring to important facts in Maryland history.

[1] *Annals of Annapolis*, p. 108.

"May it please your Lordships:

"I have your Commands of the 15th of Aprill, which came to hand by a Chance Sloope from Barbados; but not untill the 13th of October, by which your Lordships may perceive how tedious and uncertain that Conveyance is; And, therefore, have not the least apprehensions your Lordships' Justice will impute any neglect to me; since, in Obedience thereto, I imediately made the best Inquiry I could, what numbers of Negros have been supplyd to this her Ma'ys Province by the Royall Affrican Company, or by the separate Traders, who pay the tenn ℔ ct., Since the 24th of June, 1698. And by the List here inclosed, which is as exact as the speedy dispatch of this Answer, would admitt. Your Lordships will find the Royall Affrican Company have not supplyd one Negro to this province during that tyme; Nor can I, on Enquiry of above twenty years last past heare of any ship belonging to the Company that has come hither, but Wee have been wholy supplyd by the seperate Traders, as your Lordships may perceive, tho by the Death and Removeall of severall Officers of the Customes here, I cannot learne the Owners or Importers, further than the Names of severall shipps and Commanders; yet am satisfied they were exclusive of the Royall Affrican Company.

"And these Negros have been sold for Bills of Excha payable in London, generally men at £30 sterling, ℔ head, and Women at five & six and twenty pounds.

"I have, pursuant to your Lordships' directions, discourst many of the principall planters here, by whom I am informd that before the year 1698, this province has been supplyd by some small Quantitys of Negros from Barbados & other her Ma'ys Islands and Plantations, as Jaimaica & New England Seaven, eight, nine or ten in a Sloope, & sometymes larger Quantitys, & sometymes, though very seldom, whole ship Loads of slaves have been brought here directly from Affrica by Interlopers, or such as have had Lycenses, or otherwise traded there. At present the Trade seems to run high, there having been between six and seaven hundred Negros imported hither this yeare (1708), and the Planters owne themselves obliged to the seperate Traders for these supplys, having never had any from the Company, and now the price of Negroes begins to abate, as Wee suppose by reason of the plentifull Importation by the seperate Traders, so that 'tis the Opinion of most here, should the seperate Traders be totally excluded, the Company would take no better care to supply them with slaves, than they have formerly done, which would not only be a great Detriment to the planters, but also to her Ma'ys Revenue of so valuable Customes on tobacco.

"As to shipping belonging to this Country & imployd to the Coast of Affrica at present, I cannot learne of any, nor above two or three persons concernd therein with the Merch'ts in London.

"I humbly begg your Lordships pardon that the Account of what number of Negros the province has been yearly supplyd with, and at what Rates has not been transmitted, which, being interwoven with the Encouragem't and Protection, I am enjoyned to give the Royall Affrican Company, made me mistake to be intended of those to be supplyd by them only. And to convince your Lordships of my future exact Complyance with Commands I esteeme so sacred, have sent you a list of those imported this present year (1708), and shall, in all other matters, punctually observe & obey your Commands on all Occasions transmitted to, my Lords,

"Yor Lordships' most obedient & humble serv't,

"JO: SEYMOUR.

"*Maryland, November 18th, 1708.*"[1]

[1] London Public Record Office, Maryland, B. T., Red, No. 4, H., p. 91.

"*An Exact Account of Negroes Imported into Her Majesties Province of Maryland from Midsummer, 1698, to Xtmas, 1707.*[1]

Time of Importation.	By Whome.	In What Vessells.	Of What Place.	The Owners' or Traders' Names.	No.
May 2, 1699...	George Laurence.....	Hopewell Jacob..	London...	....	86
July 20, 1699.	Richard Bradshaw....	African Galley...	London...	....	76
Aug. 9, "	Saml. Thornborrough.	Fairfax...........	London...	....	190
July 20, 1700.	Henry Munday........	John Hopewell. .	London...	Mrs. Smith & Petit & Co.	320
Oct. 7, 1701...	Edward Briscow......	Betty Galley......	London...	....	64
July 4, 1702..	Stephen Jerome.......	Endeavour	London...	....	49
" " " ..	Roger Carnaby........	Hunter Galley....	London...	....	152
Sept. " " ..	John Gunnell..........	Providence	London...	....	136
July 13, 1703.	John Lewis............	Pinck Mary.......	Barbados.	....	55
June 11, 1704.	Roger Carnaby........	Dolphin	London...	....	200
July 2, 1705...	John Hays............	Brigt'n Adventer.	London...	Mrs. Bascow...........	131
July 9, " ...	John Woodward......	Olive Tree........	London...	Mrs. Perry Browne & Co	150
Aug. 11, 1705.	Richard Hinton.......	Brigt'n Adventer.	London...	....	90
Same time.....	John Hunt............	Sloop Swallow....	Barbados.	....	71
July —, 1706..	John Woodward......	Olive Tree........	London...	Mrs. Perry Browne & Co	163
Aug. 4, 1707 .	James Frisby.........	Young Margarett.	London...	Mrs. Perry Browne & Co	265
Aug. 11, 1707.	Daniel Lewis..........	Brigt'n Adventer.	London...	....	92
Total.........					2290

In 1712, the census was taken of the inhabitants of the province, by counties, showing an aggregate of 46,073 souls, as shown by the annexed report:

"*A Complete List of the Number of Christian Men, Women and Children, and also of Negro Slaves.*

Counties' Names.	Masters and Taxable Men.	White Women.	Children.	Negroes.
Ann Arundell county..............	985	881	1,574	1,559
Calvert county.....................	644	597	1,080	1,179
Charles county.....................	993	783	1,507	724
Prince Georges county.	790	600	1,198	1,202
Baltemore county.........	785	572	1,114	452
St. Marys county..................	998	812	1,768	512
Cecil county...........	504	435	873	285
Kent county.........................	830	575	996	485
Queen Anns county......	1,011	843	1,446	550
Talbott county................ ..	1,114	864	1,708	492
Dorchester county................	759	747	1,582	387
Somorsett county..................	1,616	1,368	2,787	581
Total	11,025	9,077	17,641	8,330

"*Memd.*—The 11,025 masters of families and taxable men are generally reputed fitt to beare arms, being persons from sixteen years and upwards, of which there are not many old and decrepit."[2]

On July 30, 1709, Governor Seymour died, and the government of the province devolved upon the President of the Council, Major General Edward Lloyd, by whom it was administered until the arrival of Governor Hart, in 1714.

In February, 1710, O. S. (1711, N. S.), Charles Calvert, the third Lord Baltimore, petitioned the crown that the government of his province might be restored to him, but this was denied him, on account of his religious belief; nor was his application granted to have Col. John Corbet appointed governor. On the 20th of February, 1714, (1715, N. S.), he died at Epsom, in the county of Surrey, England, at the advanced age of eighty-five. During King William's reign (in 1690), he had been outlawed for high treason in Ireland, a country he had never visited; but the king, upon proper representation, in 1691, ordered the act to be annulled.

[1] London Public Record Office, Maryland, B. T., Red, No. 4, H., p. 92.

[2] London Public Record Office, Maryland, B. T., Red, No. 5, I., p. 64.

CHAPTER XIV.

UPON the death of Queen Anne, in August, 1714, official notification of the accession of George I. was sent to the colonies, but the vessel bearing the despatches being shipwrecked, they never came to hand. Of all the plantations thus left without formal notice of the change of dynasty in the mother country, Maryland alone thought herself bound "by the laws of God and man," to declare by Act of Assembly that, "on the dissolution of Anne, of pious memory, George was, and of right ought to be, by the laws of the realm of Great Britain, our sovereign liege lord."

Scarcely was the new monarch seated on the throne, when the second attack upon the charters of the colonies was made in parliament. In the same month of August, Sir Edward Northey declared that "the mischiefs in proprietary governments cannot be remedied but by an act of parliament, since they have power to make laws by their charters, which cannot be regulated but by an act of the supreme legislature." The Board of Trade, being informed that eight of the twelve colonies enjoyed real independence under chartered forms, advised "that, since neither Carolina nor Maryland, Connecticut nor Rhode Island, were obliged to submit their laws to royal revision, an act of parliament was necessary to compel them to do that, without which it was impossible to enforce their submission;" and to carry out this purpose, a bill was brought in the House early in the next year for regulating charter governments. A petition was immediately presented, in the name of the youthful Lord Baltimore, stating that he and his brothers and sisters were Protestants, and that upon their revenues from Maryland they depended for their support, and praying that his province might be spared. The other colonies also made a vigorous opposition to a measure so threatening to their interests and their independence.

GEORGE I.

This change of faith in the Calvert family had probably been the result rather of policy than conviction. On the death of Charles, the third Lord Baltimore, his son, Benedict Leonard Calvert, succeeded to the title and his possessions in Maryland. From 1692, down to this time, the powers of the proprietary government had been withheld from the Calverts because of their adhesion to the Catholic faith; and as the inhabitants of the colony were for the most part Protestants, they willingly concurred in the policy of the crown, which, while it protected the proprietary in the enjoyment of his private rights and revenues, denied him the government of his province.

The new proprietary perfectly understood his position. The unwise attempts of the adherents of the pretender, James III., which kept England in agitation and apprehension about this time, only served to inflame Protestant zeal, and strengthen the crown in the policy it had adopted; and Lord Baltimore clearly saw that if he remained true to the faith of his family, he must resign all hope of recovering his proprietary rights and authority. He was not of the stuff of which martyrs are made; and he renounced the faith which his illustrious ancestor had embraced for that of the Church of England.

In a memorial to the king dated February 2nd, 1714, O. S., (1715, N. S.,) he thus announces his change of religion:

"*To the King's most Excellent Majesty:*

"The humble petition of Benedict Leonard Calvert, son of Charles Lord Baltemore, sheweth—

"That he having for some years expressed to severall his Inclinations to become a member of the Church of England, determined in November, 1713, to declare himself so, and accordingly soon after publicly renounced the Romish Errors, and received from the hands of the Bishop of Hereford the blessed Sacrament of the Lord's Supper, in the Church of St. Anne Westminster.

"That the Lord Baltemore, his Father (whom he had some time before acquainted with his Resolutions), resented this so much, that he withdrew Four hundred & Fifty Pounds per Annum of what he had for several years allowed him, which he (a little before yor Petitioner's changing his Religion), assured him (by a letter under his own hand) he intended to continue.

"That by this unkindness of his Father, yor petitioner was reduced to live upon his marriage settlement, which is but Six hundred Pounds per Annum, & out of which he allows his Wife two, for her separate Maintenance.

"That yor Petr hath Six Children, four Sons & two Daughters, all which his Father Educated, & at his own charge maintain'd in Popish Seminaries abroad, without any deduction, either from the monys arising from his marriage settlement or the Four Hundred & Fifty Pounds per Annum above mentioned.

"That yor Petr immediately after his changing his Religion, sent for his children, and placed them all in and about London at Protestant schools, where they now are.

"That her late Majesty was Graciously pleased out of her Royall Bounty, in Consideration of yor Petrs hard usage from his Father, & his slender fortune, during his Father's life, to grant him a Pension of Three hundred Pounds per Annum, for the maintenance of his Children during the life of his said Father, who is Eighty Five Years old, & longer than his Father's life yor Petr neither did, nor doth desire any Pension.

"That (at yor Petrs request, & that he might have some farther relief in his present Circumstances), her Majesty was also pleased to appoint Captain John Hart, Nephew to the prsent Archbishop of Tuam, who had served several Years both in Spain & Portugall, Governr of Maryland, who out of the Proffits thereof has obliged himself to render yor Petr the sume of £500 per Annum.

"That the Government of Maryland is a proprietory Governmt, & will be in yor Petr upon the decease of his Father.

"That yor Petr having severall times taken all the Oaths to the Governmt as well as the Sacrament in the Church of England, & having always demeaned himself with the utmost Duty & affection towards yor Majesty & Government,

"Therefore humbly prays, that yor Majty will be graciously pleased to continue his Pension, for the support of his children, during his Fathers life, & farther prays that

Captⁿ Hart's commission may be renewed: But if there are any objections that may avail against Captⁿ Hart's being continued, yoʳ Petʳ humbly craves, he may himself be sent Governor of the said province, during his Fathers life, with a saving to all the Rights of the Patent, which is his inheritance.

"And yoʳ Petʳ shall (as in Duty bound) ever Pray &c.

"BEN: LEO: CALVERT."[1]

The king received the petition of Benedict Leonard with great satisfaction, and, in accordance with his suggestion, appointed Captain John Hart Governor of the province, who set sail at once for Maryland, and on his arrival, May 29, 1714, assumed the administration of the government. He convened the assembly at Annapolis on June 22, which, after passing a few laws, was prorogued until October 5, and again prorogued until April 26, 1715. This was the last session held under the royal government, and "is as conspicuous," says McMahon, "in our statute-book, even at this day, as the 'blessed Parliament,' in that of England. A body of permanent laws was then adopted, which, for their comprehensiveness and arrangement, are almost entitled to the name of 'a Code.' They formed the *substratum* of the statute law of the province, even down to the revolution; and the subsequent legislation of the colony effected no very material alterations in the system of general law then established. Several of the important statutes of that session are in force at this day. . . . . The internal administration of the government, from this period, was in general, but the regular and ordinary operation of established forms; and presents nothing worthy of record in the history of that government, but the increasing and unwearied vigilance of the assemblies and the people, in preserving the spirit of these forms, and in restraining the power of their rulers within their proper orbits. At every period of this era, the eye rests upon memorials of the constitutional history of Maryland."[2]

Benedict Leonard survived his father scarcely long enough to be formally recognized as proprietary;[3] and by his death, on the 5th of April, 1715, his title and rights devolved upon his infant son, Charles Calvert, who was now being brought up as a Protestant. The pretext for the suspension of the proprietary government having now ceased to exist, Francis, Lord Guilford, the guardian of Charles, petitioned for its restoration; and the king, "to give encouragement to the educating of the numerous issue of so noble a

[1] London Public Record Office, Maryland, B. T., Red, No. 5, I., p. 81.

[2] *History of Maryland*, p. 282.

[3] Cæcilius Calvert, second Lord Baltimore, married Ann, daughter of Thomas, Lord Arundel of Wardour. She died in 1639. Charles Calvert, third Lord Baltimore, married the daughter of Hon. Henry Sewall, of Matipany, on the Patuxent. Benedict Leonard Calvert, fourth Lord Baltimore, married Charlotte, daughter of Edward Henry Lee, Earl of Litchfield, May 2, 1698. She died July 20, 1731, and was buried at Woodford, England. His children were: Charles, successor to the title; Benedict Leonard, Governor of Maryland in 1726; Edward Henry, in 1728 commissary general and president of the Council of Maryland; Cecil died in 1765; Charlotte married Thomas Brerewood; Jaule; Barbara, born October 3, 1704, but died young.—*Irish Compendium*, p. 488; J. G. Morris, Lords Baltimore *Maryland Historical Society*, Fund Publication No. 8; Charles Browning's *Appeal to the Citizens of Maryland*, p. 35. Same, *An Abstract of the Condition of Granting of Lands in Maryland*, p. 27.

CHARLES CALVERT, FIFTH LORD BALTIMORE.

family in the Protestant religion," restored the government of the province to the infant proprietary, the Fifth Lord Baltimore. The administration was immediately assumed in his name, by his guardian, and a new commission, dated May 30, 1715, issued in both their names, continuing Captain Hart as governor. So soon as the latter received his commission and instructions from the king, he summoned the assembly, and, at its opening session, thus announced the restoration of the proprietary government:

"His most Sacred Majesty, King George (whom God long preserve), has been most graciously pleased, out of his abundant wisdom and justice, to restore the Right Honorable the Lord Proprietary of this province to the government thereof, and also has the clemency and bounty to approve of me in the station I now have the honor to be employed in, as appears by his Majesty's royal instructions, under the sign-manual and privy seal given at St. James's, the first of July, 1715.

"His Majesty (who is the true Defender of the Faith) was readily induced to reinstate the noble family of Baltimore in their ancient right of governing this province, from the pious consideration of their having embraced the Protestant religion, which has not only removed that umbrage which has been wisely conceived against their administration of the government thereof, for reasons of state, but I have strong hopes this better change of principles will prove a continued happiness to you.

"It is with great pleasure that I am ordered to assure you, from my Lord Guilford, the noble guardian of the young Lord Proprietary, that his Lordship will make it his constant care to promote the welfare of this province; and I can assure you, from the personal knowledge I have of the gentle and sweet disposition of the Lord Proprietary, that there is a promising aspect his Lordship will prove a growing blessing to Maryland."

Notwithstanding the comfortable assurances of Governor Hart, the restoration of the proprietary government was the signal for alarm in the province, which was increased by the foolish conduct of a few over-zealous Catholics in Annapolis, who, after drinking the health of the pretender and the new Lord Proprietary, "took the government guns down to the fort and fired a salute." These things caused serious uneasiness among the Protestants, who dreaded the establishment of the pretender's power in the colony; and at the first session of assembly, held under the restored government at Annapolis, on the 17th of July, 1716, an act was passed, which introduced the qualifying test oaths of England in all their rigor, and effectually excluded the Catholics from all participation in the government. In the preamble to the act they say "that nothing can be more effectual to secure to his lordship the quiet and peaceable enjoyment of his government, than the easing of the minds of the people, by having their religion, liberty and property secured, which has of late been daringly threatened by persons disaffected to the Protestant succession, who have openly, in treasonable manner, taken upon them to give the pretended Prince of Wales the title of King of Great Britain, and drunk his health as such." All persons, "that already have, or hereafter shall be admitted to have or enjoy any office or place of trust within the province," were required to take certain oaths, called the oaths of allegiance, abhorrency, and abjuration. The oath of allegiance was that they would "be faithful and bear true allegiance to his majesty, King George." The oath of abhorrency ran thus: "I, ——, do swear from my heart that I abhor, detest and abjure, as impious and heretical, that Damnable Doctrine and Position, That Princes may be excommunicated or deprived by the Pope, or any Authority of the See of Rome; and do declare, That no foreign Prince, Person, Prelate, State, or Potentate, hath or ought to have any Jurisdiction, Power, Superiority, Pre-eminence, or Authority, Ecclesiastical or Spiritual, within the Kingdom of Great Britain, or any the Dominions thereto belonging. So help me God." The oath of abjuration consisted in abjuring the claims of the pretender, and declaring "King George" to be the "lawful and rightful King of the Realm of Great Britain, and all other Dominions and Countries thereunto belonging." They were also required to declare "That I do believe that there is not any transubstantiation in the Sacrament of the Lord's Supper, or in the Elements of Bread and Wine, at or after the Consecration thereof, by any person whatsoever." None were capable of holding offices or places of trust who refused to take these tests; and in case of such refusal, if the person refusing attempted to hold or exercise any such office, his commission or appointment was declared void, and he himself subjected to a fine of two hundred and fifty pounds sterling. It was also enacted, "That in case any person who holds any office or trust within this Province, and has taken the oaths appointed by this law, shall afterward be present at any Popish assembly, conventicle or meeting, and join with them in their services at Mass, or receive the Sacrament in that Communion, he shall not only forfeit his office, and incur the penalty in this act limited, but also be incapable of taking, holding, or executing any commission or place of trust within this Province, until he shall be fully reconciled to the Church of England, and receive the Communion therein."[1]

The government of Maryland thus became and continued until the revolution, exclusively Protestant; and the Catholics were taxed to sustain a religion which they believed heretical, and a government in which they had no share. This system of disqualification did not end here, but was extended by the act of 1718, chapter I, which enacted, "That all professed Papists whatsoever, be, and are hereby declared incapable of giving their vote in any election of a delegate or delegates within this province, either for counties, cities, or boroughs, unless they first qualify themselves for so doing by taking the several oaths appointed to be taken, ... and subscribe the oath of abjuration and declaration." These were but a few of the oppressions practised upon the Catholics of Maryland during many years. Catholic priests were prohibited from the administration of public worship; the council granted orders to take children from the pernicious contact of Catholic parents; Catholic laymen were deprived of the right of suffrage, and the lands of Catholics were assessed double when the exigencies of the province required additional supplies. Besides the oppression of legislative enactments, personal animosity was carried to such an extent that the Catholics were considered as beyond the pale of fellowship, not suffered to walk with their fellow-subjects in front of the Stadt House, at Annapolis, and finally obliged to wear swords for their personal protection.[2]

During the period immediately preceding, none of the provinces had enjoyed higher prosperity than Maryland. In 1715 it was found to contain forty thousand seven hundred adult white males, and nine thousand five hundred negroes; the numbers of both having doubled during the last fifteen years.[3]

The people were described by Governor Hart, at a time when he no longer expected anything from their favor, as "a well-natured and most hospitable

[1] Bacon, *Act of 1716*, ch. v.

[2] Sanderson's *Biographies of the Signers*, vii., p. 240; McMahon, p. 280.

[3] The following table shows the population of each of the eleven colonies in the year 1715:

	White Men.	*Negroes.*	*Total.*
New Hampshire..	9,500	150	9,650
Massachusetts....	94,000	2,000	96,000
Rhode Island.....	8,500	500	9,000
Connecticut......	46,000	1,500	47,500
New York.........	27,000	4,000	31,000
New Jersey.......	21,000	1,500	22,500
Pennsylvania.....	43,300	2,500	45,800
Maryland.........	40,700	9,500	50,200
Virginia..........	72,000	23,000	95,000
North Carolina...	7,500	3,700	11,200
South Carolina....	6,250	10,500	16,750
	375,750	58,850	434,000

—Chalmers' *American Colonies*, ii., p. 7.

In 1749, the population of Maryland was 85,000, but she had fallen from the third to the sixth place in point of numbers, being surpassed by Pennsylvania, Massachusetts, Connecticut, New York and Virginia.

people, who, for the much greater part, were zealously affected to the present government and Protestant interest." The general industry of these two provinces, Maryland and Virginia, supplied Great Britain with 25,317,981 pounds of tobacco, of which were afterwards exported 17,142,755 pounds, leaving 8,175,226 pounds for domestic consumption. Without considering the revenue which the British government acquired from duties, etc., these figures show that these two colonies alone were of greater commercial importance to the mother country than the other nine provinces combined.

The transportation of Maryland's staple of thirty thousand hogsheads of tobacco yearly, employed one hundred ships and sixteen hundred seamen. And so great was the demand at one time for sailors that the assembly took into serious consideration the establishment of a "seamen's training-school." In this they were encouraged by Governor Hart, who, in his opening speech to the assembly on April 26, 1715, said:

"The want of seamen to navigate your vessels is a mighty obstacle to the trade of this province; and since the humour of the generality of the people is such that they will not send their children to sea, if some method were found of disposing annually of a certain number of the youth maintained by the several counties, it would in a few years be of considerable use and advantage to this province in particular, and promote navigation in general.

"It is with compassion I observe so many young men of admirable natural parts grow up without the least improvement of art to form their minds and make them more useful to their country. It is more than time to repair this great neglect that is shewn to learning here. It lies at your door to accomplish the good work of laying a foundation for sufficient schools. The consequence of such education will be to see your sons increase in knowledge and virtue, as well as in wealth and honour. You will likewise have the blessings of the poor in this life, and posterity will praise you as benefactors of your country."

During this year the assembly endeavored, by imposing taxes, to obstruct the importation of negroes, and also of Irish servants, on account of their religion; and enacted that each man servant should have, at the expiration of his servitude, "one new hat, coat and breeches, either of kersey or broadcloth, one new shift of white linen, one new pair of French fall shoes and stockings, two hoes and one axe, and one gun of twenty shillings price, not above four feet by the barrel nor less than three and a half." All women servants, at the expiration of their servitude, were allowed "a waistcoat and petticoat of new half-thick, or pennistone, a new shift of white linen, shoes and stockings, a blue apron, two caps of white linen, and three barrels of Indian corn."[1]

The legislature also attempted to resist a tyrannous and very unwise policy on the part of parliament, which was injuring and degrading the colonies into penal settlements by making them the places of deportation for convicts. It is true, these convicts came out as prisoners, and their services were sold to the planters; but at the expiration of their terms of punish-

[1] Bacon, *Act 1715*, ch. xli., sec. 9.

ment they became freemen, and thus introduced a very undesirable, and possibly dangerous element into the community. The provincial legislature took alarm, and began to consider the best mode of preventing this. It is possible that their apprehensions were no less aroused by the influx of political culprits—the transported Jacobites, two ship-loads of whom were sent over after the defeat of Mar and Derwentwater's rising in 1715–16, and sold as servants. They came over in the spring and summer of 1717, in the ships *Friendship* and *Good Speed.*

The following proceedings relative to the political prisoners are of considerable interest:

"A Copy of the proclamation about the 80 Rebbells Transported in the Ship Friendship. In Governor Hart's office, April 28th, 1717. Att a Councill held at his Excellency's house, in the City of Annapolis, the 28th day of August, in the third year of his Majesties Reign, &c., And the first of his Lordship's Dominion. Anno Domini, 1716. Present: His Excellency John Hart, Esquire, Captain General & Governor in Chief, &c. The Honorable Thomas Brooke, Esquire, Coll: Wm. Holland, Coll: Wm. Coursey, Lt: Coll: Saml. Young, Coll: Tho. Addison, Phil. Lloyd, Esquire, Lt: Coll: Richd. Tilghman, Coll: Thomas Smyth, of his Lordship's Council.[1]

"*Resolved & Ordered*, That the following proclamation Issue, viz.: By his Excellency John Hart, Esquire, Captain Generall, &c.

"A Proclamation.

"Whereas, his most Sacred Majesty, out of his abundant Clemency, has caused eighty of the Rebbells (most of them Scotsmen) lately taken at Preston, in Lancashire, to be transported from Great Brittain into this province, in the Ship Friendship, of Belfast, Michael Mankin, Commander, and Signified to me his Royall pleasure by one of his principall Secretaries of State, that the said Rebbells, to the number aforesaid, should be sold to the Assignes of the Merchants, who should purchase them for the full Term of Seven Years and not for any lesser time. And that I should cause the said Rebbells to enter into Indentures to performe such service, or otherwise grant the respective purchasers proper Certificates of their being so sold them by his Majesties royall Command, and cause the said Certificates to be recorded, the better to enable them to detain them, least they should at any time attempt to make their escape not being bound. It appearing to be his Majesty's pleasure the aforesaid Rebells should continue in this province for & dureing the whole term and Space of Seven Years aforesaid. And, whereas, the said Rebells, Notwithstanding his Majesty's Clemency & Pleasure, signified as aforesaid, have Obstinately refused to enter into such Indentures, And that the greatest part of them already have been sold, And the rest will, in all probability, be disposed of with such proper Certificates, by me granted to the respective purchasers, as by his Majesty directed, In order to enable them to retake any such of them who may at any time hereafter attempt to make their Escape. I have thought fitt, by and with the advice of his Lordship's Councill to Issue this my proclamation, Notifying the same and Straitly requiring, charging, & enjoyning all and Singular the Sherriffs, Constables, Magistrates & their Officers, within this province, Military and Civill. And also all and every the Inhabitants thereof to be very vigilant in putting in due execution the Act of Assembly of this province relating to runaway Servants, and to use their utmost endeavors upon any suspicion notice or discovery of any of the said persons transported, attempting or endeavouring to get out of this province before the Expiration of the full time of seven years from their arrivall here, viz: the 20th of August instant, to stop and prevent them

[1] London Public Record Office, America and West Indies, No. 27.

from so doing, and to apprehend and cause such fugitive Rebbells to be returned to their respective masters and Owners, who have so bought and purchased them as aforesaid, after such manner as is used in this province for the apprehending, secureing & returning runaway Servants to their respective Masters, Dames or Owners, and foreasmuch as it may probably happen that some of the persons so transported as aforesaid by themselves or friends, may purchase or otherwise obtain their freedomes from their respective Masters or Owners, and attempt to go out of this province to some other plantation or province, where they may not be known, and consequently have the greater opportunity to returne to Great Brittain in order to pursue their wicked and rebellious practices and designs against his Majesty and the Protestant succession, I do hereby, with the advice of his Lordship's Councill aforesaid, direct, require, and comand the aforesaid Sheriffs, Magistrates, Constables, and all other Officers, Civill and Military, within this province, to use their utmost endeavours to prevent the same by useing all possible diligence to apprehend all or any of them who shall so attempt to escape out of this province contrary to his Majesty's Intention and to take Care that they be brought before myself or the Governour for the time being, in order to oblige them to give good security not to go out of the province until the Expiration of the aforesaid time of seven years; and that all persons within this province may have due and sufficient notice hereof, and use their faithfull endeavours for the apprehending and discovering the said Rebells, who shall, or may endeavor or attempt to escape from their Masters' Service or otherwise go out of this province, I do hereby Strictly Charge & comand the severall Sherriffs of the respective Counties within this province, to cause this my proclamation to be published at all Court houses, Churches & Chappells and others the most publick and frequented places in their respective Counties, and by affixing attested Copies thereof at all such places, whereof they are not to fail at their perills. Given at the City of Annapolis, under the great Seale, this 28th day of August, in the third year of the Reign of our Sov[r] Lord George of Great Brittain, France and Ireland, King, defender of the faith, and the first year of his Lordship's Dominion &c., Anno Domini, 1716.

"JNO. HART,
"JNO. BEARD, *Cl. Council.*

"*Vera Copia.*"

"A List of Rebbells Transported in the Shipp the *Friendship* of Belfast, Michael Mankin, Comander, the 20th of August, 1716:

Rebbells' Names.	*Purchasers' Names.*	*Rebbells' Names.*	*Purchasers' Names.*
John Pitter,		James Webster,	Steph. Warman.
James Nithery,	Wm. Holland, Esq.	Wm. Cumins,	
Dugall Macqueen,		Allin Maclien,	Thos. Macnemara.
Alex. Smith,	Samuel Chew, Jr.	John Robertson,	
Abraham Lowe,	Thomas Larkin.	Farq. Macgilvary,	Saml. Young, Esq.
Henry Wilson,	John Gresham.	David Mills,	Evan Jones.
Alexander Gorden,		Patrick Cooper,	Albertus Greening.
John Hay,	William Homes.	Jeremiah Dunbarr,	Hugh Kenneday.
William Simm,	Wm. Nicholson.	John Degedy,	
Alex'der Spalding,		William McBean,	Phile. Lloyd, Esq.
Leonard Robinson,	Thomas Doccora.	Thomas Lawry,	
John Blondell,	Benjamin Wharfield.	John Glancy,	Hugh Spedden.
John Sinclear,	Joseph Hill.	Wm. Macgilvary,	Robt. Ungle, Esq.
William Grant,	Thomas Davis.	Alexandre Nave,	Thomas Broadhurst.
Thomas Spark,	Philip Dowell.	James Hindry,	John Oldham.

Rebbells' Names.	*Purchasers' Names.*	*Rebbells' Names.*	*Purchasers' Names.*
William Mobbery,	Henry Tripp.	John Mac Intire,	DanielS herwood.
James Small,	Samuel Peele.	William Onan,	
James White,		Alex. Macqueen,	
John Macbayn,	John Ford.	Alex. Macdugall,	
Rot. Henderson,	Edward Penn.	David Macqueen,	Robert Grundy.
Thomas Potts,	Wm. Bladen, Esq.	John Macdonald,	
George Thompson,		John Poss,	Edgar Webb.
John Ramsey,		Robert Stobbs,	John Valliant.
Alexandre Reind		Finley Cameron,	Wm. Elbert.
Thomas Forbus,		John Mertison,	Peter Anderson.
William Davidson,	Mordecai Moor.	Alex. Swinger,	Phil Sherwood,
James Mitchell,	Benjamin Tasker.	Wm. Macgilvary,	Thomas Mackell.
James Lowe,		Patrick Hunter,	James Calston.
James Denholme,	John Clark.	Henry Farchaser,	Darley Dullany.
James Allein,	Eliz. Brown.	Alex. Mortimore,	Henry Ernallse.
James White,	Benjamin Dufour.	Jas. Robertson,	Joseph Hopkins.
Thomas Donolson,	John Cheney.	Thomas Butter,	Francis Bullock.
James Hill,	Humphrey Godman.	Andrew Davidson,	
David Steward,	Jacob Henderson.	Thos. Smith,	Joseph Bullock.
Henry Lumsdale,		Thos. Mac Nabb,	Wm. Thomas.
Arch. Macdonall,	W. Fitz Redmond.	James Shaw,	Thos. Robbins.
alias Kenneday,		Donald Robertson,	
Charles Donalson,	Aaron Rawlings.	Andrew Daw,	Roger Woolforde.
William Mare,		John Coucham,	Philip Kersey.
Hector Macqueen,		Henry Murry,	Wm. Holland, Esq.
John Maclean,	Edward Parish.	In all 80 Rebells.	

"Att a Councill held at the City of Annapolis, in the Province of Maryland, on the Eleventh day of January, in the third year of the Reign of our Sovereign Lord, King George, and in the second of his Lordship's Dominion, &c. Annapolis, Anno Domini 1716. Present: His Excellency, John Hart, Esq., Governour in Chief, &c; The Honorable Col. Wm. Coursey, Lt. Col. Sam'l Young, John Hall, Esq'r, Phile. Lloyd, Esq'r, Col. Rich. Tilghman, & Col. Tho. Smyth.

"*Resolved & Ordered*, That a proclamation issue, declaring whosoever setts free any of the Rebbells transported into this Province, in the Ship *Good Speed*, shall give security for their abideing in this province, and be of good behaviour for the term of Seven Years, as follows: By his Excellency, the Capt. Generall, &c.

"A PROCLAMATION.

"Whereas, There has been transported into this province by his Majesty's Royall Command, fifty-five persons, most of them Scotts, men taken in the late Rebellion at Preston, and Imported in the Ship the *Good Speed*, of Liverpoole, whereof Arthur Smith is Comander, concerning whom his Majesty has been graciously pleased to Signify to me by Letter from the Right Honourable James Stanhope, Esq., One of his Principall Secretarys of State, dated at Whitehall the fourth day of May last, that it was his royall pleasure that the Rebbells so taken & Imported as aforesaid should either enter into Indentures to serve such persons as would Purchase them for the term of Seven Years, or otherwise, that on the Sale of such who should refuse so to do, I should grant to the respective purchasers or Masters under my hand and Seale a proper Certificate that it was his Majesty's pleasure the said Rebbells so transported into this province should be sold by the factor of Messrs. Richard Guildard & Company to serve the term aforesaid, And foreasmuch as fifty of them have been sold to the severall purchasers as by the list hereunder written is expressed, and that John Shaftoe is dead, And Humphrey Sword and Alexander Macgiffin have exempted themselves To the end, that his Majesty's pleasure may be duly complyed with in this province, and that the said runaway Rebbells be retaken and Subjected to his Majesty's commands by proper certificates by me to be granted therefore; And that the traiterous & wicked attempts and designations of the said Rebbells may be entirely Obviated, and their persons secured within this province during the term aforesaid. I have thought fitt by and with the advice of his Lordship's the Lord Proprietary's honourable Councill to issue this my proclamation notifying the same, and Comanding and requireing all Officers, Military & Civill, and Especially all Sherriffs, Magistrates & Constables, to use their utmost endeavours upon notice or knowledge of any the said Rebbells absenting themselves from their said Masters or purchasers to apprehend and secure their persons, and oblige them to remain in their bounden Service according to his Majesty's royall directions, and particularly to apprehend the aforesaid Humphrey Sword and Alexander Macgiffin, and bring them before me to be dealt with according to Justice and their Demerritts, and further, I do hereby will and require all Officers, Magistrates, Sherriffs & Constables, and other his Majesty's good Subjects within this province in case of any the said Rebbells being sett free by their respective Masters or purchasers, immediately to Apprehend and bring them before the next Magistrate, who is hereby required to oblige them to give good security not to depart, but remain in this province dureing the term of Seven years from their Arrivall in this province, and also to be of good abearance towards his Majesty and his Lordship's Government in this province, or otherwise comitt them to the County Gaole, there to remain till such further proceedings may be had against them as their Demerritts shall require, And to the end that all persons may have due notice hereof, and none pretend Ignorance, I do hereby in his Lordship's the Lord Proprietary's name command and require the respective Sheriffs of the severall Counties in this province to publish this my proclamation at all Churches & Chappells of Ease, and others the most frequented places in their said Counties, whereof they are not to fail at their perills. Given at the City of Annapolis under the broad Seal of the province the eleventh day of January, in the 2nd year of his Lordship's Dominion, &c., Anno Domini, 1716.

"God save the king.

"JNO. HART.
"JNO. BEARD, *Cl: Councill.*

"*Vera Copia.*"

"A List of the Rebell prisoners transported into this province in the Ship the *Good Speed*, on the 18th Day of October, Anno Domini 1716, with the names of the persons who purchased them:

Prisoners' Names.	*Purchasers.*	*Prisoners' Names.*	*Purchasers.*
Wm. Macferson,		James Crampson,	Francis Clavo.
Tho. Shaw,	Michael Martin.	John Stewart,	John Middleton.
Miles Beggs,		Patt Smith,	Gustavus Brown.
John Macgregier,	Rich'd Eglin.	Geo. Hodgson,	John Nelly.
Daniel Steward,		Malcolm Maccolm,	John Wilder.
Duncan Ferguson,	John Fendall.	James Mac Intosh,	Henry H. Hawkins.
John Mackewan,		John Cameron,	Wm. Penn.
David Graham,		David Lander,	Francis Goodrich.
Wm. Johnson,		Francis Macbean,	Charles Born.
Jas. Mallone,	Charles Digges.	Wm. Simpson,	John Rogers.
Geo. Nuelson,		John Kennery,	Marmaduke Simms.
John Chambers,		James Bowe,	John Philpott.
James Sinclare,	Henry Wharton.	Laughlin McIntosh,	Henry Miles.
Alexr. Orrach,		Alexr. McIntosh,	Daniel Steward.

Prisoners' Names.	*Purchasers.*	*Prisoners' Names.*	*Purchasers.*
Wm. Ferguson,	John Bruce.	Hugh Mac Intire,	John Vincent.
James Dixon,		Finloe Mac Intire,	John Penn.
Richd. Withington,	Randall Garland.	Richd. Birch,	Benj. Tasker.
Tho. Berry,		James Shaw,	Jno. Donalson.
Jas. Maclearn,		Danl. Grant,	Wm. Macchonchia.
Rowl'd Robertson,	Thomas Jameson,	Hugh White,	Danl. Bryant.
Ninian Brown,		James Rutherford,	Arthur Smith.
Daniel Kennedy,	John Courts.	Tho. Hume,	Judith Bruce.
Patrick Mackoy,		James Renton,	Unsold.
Angus Macdormott.		Alexr. Macgiffin,	Runaway.
James Mac Intosh,	Robt. Hanson.	Humphrey Sword,	—— ——
Hugh Macdugall,		James Sumervill,	—— ——
John Maccollum,	John Hawkins.	John Shaftoe,	Dead.
Wm. Shaw,			

"*Maryland, 28th April, 1717.*

"Sire:

"I am honored with the Favour of yours of the 16th of August post, Signifying His Royall Highness, his Pleasure, to return exact Lists of the Rebel Prisoners that have been landed in this Province.

"In obedience to His Royall Highness, to whose Commands I shall ever pay a most dutifull Submission, I have inclosed you exact Lists of all the Rebel Prisoners that are come into this Province, Indorsed on the Proclamations I published by the advice of the Councill here which were formed from the Letters I had the honour to receive from the Right Honorable Mr. Secretary Stanhope on that occasion, And exprest in such a manner as might be consonant to his Majesty's mercifull Intentions of sparing the Rebels' lives, and securing their Persons for the space of seven years in the plantations, and also to give due encouragement to the Inhabitants of this Province to Purchase them for servants.

"I was comanded by Mr. Secretary Stanhope's Letters (which I have answered,) to oblige the Rebel Prisoners to enter into Indentures to serve for seven years, and upon their Refusing to Indent, I published the Inclosed Proclamation, which had the Effect propos'd, of their being immediately purchased by the Respective Persons whose names are likewise sent to you for your further sattisfaction, that his Majesty's Pleasure has been punctually obey'd.

"Some of the Rebel Prisoners have run away from their Service, but on Complaint of their Masters I have given strict orders for the Apprehending of them whereever they shall be found in this Province.

"I hope that what I have transacted in relation to the Rebel Prisoners will be considered by you as agreable to that Duty I owe to his Sacred Majesty's Commands for whose Service I have a most Inviolable Zeal, and shall embrace all occasions to demonstrate it, and that I am with very great respect, Sir,

"Your most obedient and most faithfull humble Servant,

"JN. HART."

Notwithstanding the oppressive laws enforced against them, the Roman Catholics of Maryland steadily increased in numbers and influence, and about this time began to entertain hopes, as Governor Hart's address of April 23d, 1718, informed the assembly, of regaining at least a share in the administration of the government. But there were many to whom such a result seemed doubtful and distant at the best, and who naturally chafed at finding themselves treated as aliens and inferiors in a colony which had been founded by their ancestors and fellow-believers, who, out of Christian charity, had opened an asylum for the very party that was now denying them the rights of freemen. Among these were Charles and James Carroll, who, with a small band of Catholic gentlemen[1] had conceived the plan of emigrating to the territory belonging to France. Charles Carroll, during a visit to his son in France, applied to the French government for a grant of land on the Arkansas river; but the extent of the tract demanded startled the minister as Mr. Carroll pointed it out on the map. He considered it too vast to be given to a subject; and Mr. Carroll was obliged to return without having gained the concession. Soon after his return, the rigour of the objectionable laws was relaxed, and the project of emigration was abandoned. Mr. Carroll, who had been for twenty-five years the proprietary's agent in the province, was re-appointed by Lord Baltimore with increased authority; and this act gave great offence to Governor Hart, who represented to his Lordship that Mr. Carroll was "a professed Papist, and the first fomenter of our late disturbances, and had acquired a vast estate in this province by the office he formerly occupied, and his practice in the law." At the opening session of the Assembly in 1720, Governor Hart thus recites his grievances:

"I shall not entertain you with an historical relation of obtaining the first grant of this province, nor yet mention the administration of the government under the late Lord Proprietary, believing it will suffice that I acknowledge the Papists had more than an equal share with the Protestants in holding judicial and ministerial offices here from the date of the Charter in 1632, to the year of our Lord 1691, when their late Majesties, King William and Queen Mary, were pleased to send you a Governor of their appointment. After this Maryland continued happily governed for 24 years, the respective governors in that space receiving their commissions and instructions immediately from the crown, of which I had the last honor. But so soon as his present sacred Majesty condescended to restore the now Lord Proprietary (on his professing himself a Protestant) to his hereditary government, the Papists instantly laid in their claim to be also restored to their former pretended privileges, which, when offered to me for my approbation by their principal agent [Charles Carroll], was dismissed with the answer I would oppose it to the utmost of my power. Hence our troubles took their rise.

"Upon the first insurrection of the Rebels in Great Britain against his Majesty's person and government, those of the same evil disposition here were so elated with the hopes of their imaginary success, and so open and daring on that presumption, that I was early obliged to check and restrain their follies by a proclamation published the 14th of February, 1715, to which I refer you for my reasons of so doing.

"On the 19th of June following, the supposed birth-day of the pretender, the great guns of this city were fired off late in the night. These offenders were soon discovered by a reward published in a proclamation, and afterwards punished according to their demerits.[2] Soon after this transaction, Mr. Charles Carroll, a professed Papist, arrived

[1] Among these we find the names of Henry Darnall, Henry Darnall, Jr., William Diggs, John Diggs, Benjamin Hall, Clement Hall, William Fitz Redmond, Henry Wharton, Charles Diggs, Peter Attwood (priest), Major Nicholas Sewell, and Richard Bennett.

[2] Charles Carroll's nephew was among the number arrested for firing the guns.

On the 5th of May, 1684, Charles Calvert, the third Lord Baltimore, commissioned Col. Henry Darnall, Col. William Digges, Major Nicholas Sewall, and John Darnall, his "especial and

from London with a commission of so strange a nature, that, under pretence of being his Lordship's agent, it included, with his instructions, many essential parts of government; this he produced to me, wherein he had power given him to receive all the money raised for the support of government, and even that for purchasing arms for the defence of the country."

In May, 1720, Francis, Lord Guilford, the guardian of Lord Baltimore, deemed it expedient to remove Governor Hart, and he applied to the king and council for permission to appoint Captain Charles Calvert, of the First Regiment of Foot Guards, and uncle of Lord Baltimore, to succeed him. Permission was given, and the new governor at once sailed for Maryland, and presided at the session of assembly held in Annapolis in October.

About this time, the Bishop of London, Dr. Gibson, propounded certain queries to the clergy of the province, respecting the condition of the Established Church in Maryland. From the replies to these queries, Dr. Hawks has gathered the materials for the following sketch:

"The province contained thirty-eight parishes in its twelve counties; of these, fifteen were on the eastern, and twenty-three on the western side of the Chesapeake. There was a commissary on each shore, who visited the several churches once in three years. The clergy were assembled, however, annually; and on such occasions their consultations were on the discharge of their ministerial functions alone. Most of the clergy had been settled in the province for many years. There was a minority of such as had held their cures less than ten years; the greater part had lived in Maryland from ten to twenty years, and about one-fifth had been occupying their fields of labor from twenty to thirty years. Of these the majority consisted of natives of England; they were, however, nearly equalled in number by the Scottish clergy, while a few others were Irishmen. The parishes were all too large in extent of territory; but the population was so sparse, that had they been smaller, the annual levy of tobacco would not have sustained the clergymen. None were less than nine miles in length, and some were as much as seventy. There were between ten and eleven thousand families of Episcopalians in the province, and about three thousand communicants. The Sacrament was generally administered not less frequently than once in two months, and in many of the parishes much oftener. The children were duly catechised for a part of the year at least, in every parish, and the livings of the clergy averaged about £50, which was paid in tobacco."[1]

At this session of the assembly the Lower House adopted a series of resolutions vindicatory of their liberties, and exposing the grounds on which they

select council." Col. Henry Darnall was also his lordship's agent and receiver general, to receive and collect all his dues and revenues in the province. About the year 1692 he was succeeded in this duty by Charles Carroll, who became Lord Baltimore's chief agent, in conjunction with —— Somerset, who had married Maria, his lordship's sister. When Lord Baltimore was deprived of his government, on account of his religion, all who held prominent positions under the proprietary were, at the same time, displaced. The first step Charles, the fifth Lord Baltimore, took on assuming control of the government of the province, was to reinstate those, or their descendants, who had been deprived of their offices on account of their religion. Among the first of those who were reappointed was Charles Carroll, whose appointment much displeased Governor Hart, who thought that Mr. Carroll had too much power—that he would infringe on the rights of the governor, and that his authority was more than an agent ought to have. In 1720, however, John Hart was displaced and Charles, Lord Baltimore, appointed his uncle, Charles Calvert, in his place, which ended, for a time, all religious feuds.

[1] *History of the Protestant Episcopal Church in Maryland*, p. 170.

claimed the benefit of the English statutes. They declared that "the province was not to be regarded as a conquered country, but as a colony planted by English subjects, who had not by their removal forfeited any part of their English liberties; that the inhabitants of the province had always enjoyed the common law, and such general statutes of England as are not restrained by words of local limitation, and such Acts of Assembly as were made in the province to suit its particular constitution as the rule and standard of its government and judicature; such statutes and acts being subject to the like rules of common law, or equitable construction, as are used by the judges in construing statutes in England; and that all who advised the proprietary to govern by any other rules of government, were evil counsellors, ill-wishers to the proprietary and to their present happy constitution, and intended thereby to infringe the English liberties of the province, and to frustrate in a great measure the intent of the crown in granting it to the proprietary." To prevent any misconstruction of the temper or drift of these resolutions, they declared "that they were not occasioned by any apprehension that the proprietary had ever infringed, or intended to infringe, the liberties or the privileges of the people, or to govern otherwise than according to the usage and custom of the country since its first settlement; but were intended merely to assert their rights and liberties, and to transmit their sense thereof, and of the nature of their constitution, to posterity."

These resolutions, so characteristic of the firm and manly spirit which in early times inspired the people of Maryland, became the Magna Charta of the province. Though they sprang from the principles involved in the contest then pending, they were not limited to the occasion which gave them rise, but extended far beyond the immediate subject. The discussion ranged over all their chartered rights and privileges, and shed over these all the light which the ablest writers and debaters of the province could impart. It familiarized the colonists with the character and extent of these rights, and instilled into their minds just notions of government. The colonists nourished in their breasts a spirit of stern and sturdy adherence to their rights, which was perceived and felt down to the period of the revolution.[1]

In 1715, the Quakers had been disturbed in their religious worship, by the irregular and turbulent conduct of some of the inhabitants in the immediate vicinity of their meeting houses, and in May they presented the following address to the governor and council:

"The address of the people called Quakers inhabiting in the said Province is in humble manner presented. Shewing that about forty years past the said people have yearly kept a religious meeting for the worship of Almighty God at West river in Ann Arundel, and at the head of Tred Haven, in Talbot county, in the said Province. Which said meetings have been yearly kept by the said people in peaceable manner until of late years they have been greatly disturbed by means of several persons that at those meeting times bring drink or sell and dispose of it near or within some distance of the said meeting places whereby great evils and immoralities have been committed by drunkenness,

[1] McMahon.

fighting, whooping, hallowing, swearing, cursing, wrestling, horse racing and abundance of wickedness and immoralities, and notwithstanding, that upon application made to former Governors of the province or council, several orders for suppressing the said evils have been published, yet in contempt of government have the same been continued, and rather grows worse. Wherefore the humble request of the said people that some effectual measure may for the future be taken for suppressing the said evils as in your wisdom you shall see meet."

Upon receipt of which the governor and council passed the following order:

"It being thought reasonable the said people in their request should be gratified and enjoy his majesty's royal protection, it was considered what may be the most effectual means to protect the said people in their said peaceable yearly meetings. And resolved and ordered that no booth be set up or any liquors sold within two miles of either of the said meeting houses, except at a licensed ordinary, and that no person whatsoever presume to make any disturbance by wrestling or horse racing, or using any other sports or exercise by which any annoyance may be given the said people, called Quakers."

This order of council it seems did not cure the evils complained of, and upon the renewal of complaints in 1725, the legislature interposed, and sought by legal penalties to protect them in the quiet enjoyment of their religious observances. Indeed, considering the strong opposition made by the Quakers to the Established Church, there was more forbearance towards them than the temper of that age would lead us to expect. Their scruples on the subject of oaths were so far respected that, by a law of this year (1725), their affirmation of allegiance was accepted as the equivalent of an oath; and we have found no instance of any serious grievance or infringement on their peculiar tenets, unless their contribution of forty pounds of tobacco per poll in common with every one else, to the support of the Established Church, be so considered.

At this session of the legislature, all that portion of the south side of Patapsco river, which was in 1698 added to Baltimore county, was now restored to Anne Arundel county.

Governor Charles Calvert died, and in November, 1726, Lord Baltimore appointed his brother Benedict Leonard Calvert in his place. He was a member of Parliament for Harwich, but presided at the first session of the assembly on the 10th of October, 1727. In 1728, Lord Baltimore appointed another brother, Edward Henry Calvert, commissary general and president of the council.

The year 1727 deserves especial remembrance in the history of Maryland, from the fact that in it was printed the first newspaper published in the province.[1] It was called the *Maryland Gazette*, and was published at Annapolis.

[1] It was the *sixth* in the provinces. The others were the Boston *News-Letter*, weekly, from 1704 to 1776; the *Gazette* in Boston, and the *Mercury* in Philadelphia, in 1719; the *New England Courier*, started by James Franklin, in Boston, in 1721, and the *Gazette*, in New York, in 1725.

Mr. Charles Browning, in his *Abstract of the Condition of Granting of Lands in Maryland*, says: "The proprietaryship was taken from Lord Baltimore on account of his religion, by King William and Queen Mary. It was remarked, at this time, that there was a printing press in this colony for many years, and that none of the others had one."

It was well printed on rough foolscap, and the first number appeared about August. The printer and publisher was William Parks, "by whom," as his advertisement runs, "subscriptions are taken for the paper at fifteen shillings a year; and advertisements to be inserted in it at three shillings for the first week, and two shillings for every week after." Extracts from foreign journals, usually about three months old, formed the substance of the paper. The editor's duties seem to have been limited to selection and compilation; his own pen was seldom employed, and but little information concerning affairs in the province can be culled from the columns of the *Gazette*, except so far as they appear in the advertisements, which are to us now the most interesting features of the paper. From the few copies in the possession of the Maryland Historical Society, we select a few notices, illustrative of customs and incidents of the times. In No. 89, which contains three advertisements, notice is given "that there is a ship arrived in South river with about two hundred choice slaves, which are to be sold, by Daniel Dulany, Richard Snowden and Peter Hume." "Annapolis, June 16, [1729.] On Tuesday last, George Plater, Esq., was married to Mrs. Rebecca Bowles, the relict of James Bowles, Esq., a gentlewoman of considerable fortune.

"On Friday last, died James Carroll, at the house of Charles Carroll, Esq., in this city." "Annapolis, June 24. On Friday last, the Honorable Patrick Gordon, Esq., Governor of Philadelphia, attended by several gentlemen of that Province, arrived here, to visit our Governor. His Excellency received them very kindly, and they were saluted with the discharge of our great guns, colors flying, &c., and their entertainment has been made as agreeable as this place could afford. This morning his Honor, the governor of Pennsylvania, departed this city under discharge of our guns, &c." "Annapolis, March 4th, Saturday last being the birth day of our most gracious Queen Caroline, was celebrated here in the manner following: His excellency, Benedict Leonard Calvert, our Governor, invited the gentlemen of this city to a very handsome entertainment at dinner, and in the evening there was a ball at the Stadt House."[1]

Benedict Leonard Calvert, the governor, was compelled by ill-health to return to England in 1731. In answer to his farewell address, the assembly

[1] During the publication of the *Maryland Gazette*, which continued but a short time, William Parks published the votes and proceedings of the Lower House of Assembly, and sold this official journal at three pence *per diem*. In December he published "A complete Collection of the Laws of Maryland, with an Index and marginal Notes directing to the several Laws and the chief matters contained in them. Collected and printed by authority. Annapolis. Printed by William Parks, MDCCXXVII." He also printed various other small works, including a catechism, "The Rights of the Inhabitants of Maryland to the Benefit of the English Laws," a primer, several prayer-books, explanations of the fasts and feasts, almanacs, etc. In 1727 he was made "public printer of the province," a position he held until 1742, when he was succeeded by Jonas Green, who held the office until his death in 1768. In 1736, Parks, being then resident in Williamsburg, Virginia, began the publication of the *Virginia Gazette*. He printed Stith's *History of Virginia*, the *Laws of Virginia*, and other works now of great rarity. On the 27th of January, 1745, Jonas Green issued the first number of his *Gazette*, which he continued to edit for twenty-one years. After his death, it was continued by his widow, assisted by his son William, and was published by their successors down to the latter part of the year 1830. A complete file of this paper was presented to the State by its last editor, and is now in the State Library at Annapolis. The first newspaper published in Baltimore was the *Maryland Journal and Daily Advertiser*. The first number was issued August 20, 1773.

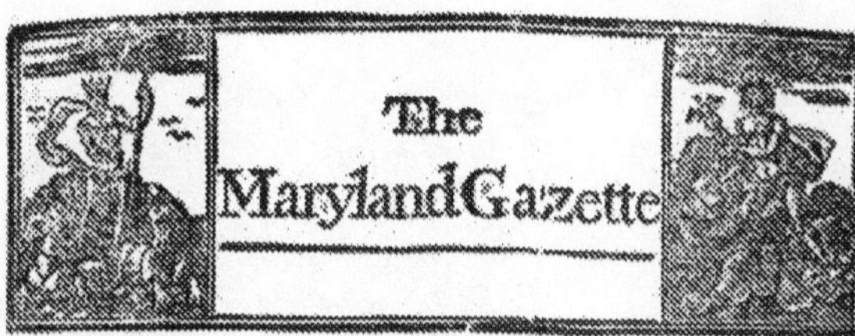

From Tuesday December 10, to Tuesday December 17, 1728. (Numb. LXVI.

Cujusvis est hominis errare: Nullius nisi insipentis, perseverare in errore. CICER. Philip.

SIR,

HAVING treated of *Philosophical Doubting*, in my Third Lecture, I shall this Day recommend it again to my Readers, and attempt to shew the Reasonableness and the Necessity of it, in other (and perhaps more familiar) Lights; that the Plainest Capacity may be capable to apprehend the great Advantages of this Disposition of Mind; without which we can never be thoroughly convinced of any Truths, that are not *Self-Evident*.

I desire the Lovers of Truth and Sincerity, to consider that no Man, of common Reflection, can be Unblamable in his Opinions, who [illegible] them upon Trust, and never once doubts of their Validity. In order to be fully persuaded of the Truth of an Opinion, (without which Perswasion it can never be justifiable to embrace it,) Common Sense requires we should not neglect the Proper and Ordinary Methods of Information: Now all Information comes by Enquiry; and all Enquiry comes by Doubting. He that is positive cannot Doubt; and consequently cuts himself off from the Possibility of being Informed: Neither ought he, that never Doubted, to be Positive.

OF Truths which are *Self-Evident*, the Number is but small; whereas the Variety of Truths, that require Examination and Reasoning, before they can be rightly apprehended, is Infinite. Besides, through Prejudice or Negligence, many Notions are taken for *Self-Evident Truths*, which upon an impartial Examination, would prove manifest Falshoods: And this Deception is the main Source of the most Popular Errors. Therefore an honest Man cannot be too much upon his Guard, by accustoming himself to a Habit of Doubting. Let him remember, that he lives in a degenerate Age, and that he is besieged on every Side with Errors: That he should therefore Garrison his Mind, and keep a constant Watch within Himself, so as to give no Admittance to new Opinions, before he takes a strict Account of them; neither to harbour old Ones, which, upon being question'd, cannot give sufficient Assurance of their Truth.

I am sensible that this Lesson about Doubting, cannot be learnt without great Difficulty by Persons, who are grown Old in Obstinacy and Prejudice, who have perhaps Borrowed all their Opinions upon Credit; and who if they were to be judged by Right Reason, and call'd upon to give an Account of the Methods, by which they came by their Stock of Notions, perhaps would not be found to be rightly possessed of any One of their Favourite Tenents. But I hope the more Ingenuous, who generally speaking are the more Youthful Readers, who have not yet laid in their Provision of Opinions for Life, may be perswaded to be Cautious in their Choice; not to Lumber up their Understandings with old-fashioned Trumpery, on one Hand; nor to be fond of every New-fangled Toy on the Other: But to select such a Set of Furniture as shall be at once Useful and Ornamental, and never grow out of Fashion amongst wise Men.

THERE are Persons, who have as great a Facility in Doubting, as Others have in Believing: The One affect Singularity; the Other Popularity. Whereas the Man who THINKS FREELY, whose Heart is set upon Truth, Doubts only in order to be Certain; removes his Doubts by Doubting; and Believes or Disbelieves a Proposition, in Proportion to the Evidences, that appear to him for it or against it. The Extreams of Credulity and Incredulity, do often proceed from an equal Positiveness of Temper. And the only Cure for these Two Imperfections in the Understandings is a Rational Doubting; such as will make Us wary in Receiving New Opinions, and not unwilling to part with old Ones.

THERE is as great a Libertinism of Mind in Believing without a reasonable Conviction, as in Disbelieving upon precarious Suppositions and unwarrantable Surmizes. An Over-Forwardness to Assent to Opinions, is a Prostitution of our Understanding: And an Over-Backwardness to Doubt, implies a Distrust of the Truth of our Perswasion, or at least a Consciousness of our Inability to defend it. A Truth is no Truth to Him, who believes it Implicitly, and never enquires into the Reasons, upon which it is founded. And an Error is not chargeable as an Error to the Man, who (after due Pains to be rightly inform'd,) takes it for a Truth.

THERE are Opinions, which have prevailed in the World through many Ages, and are received almost Universally; and yet may be far from being True. There may likewise be Opinions which may be very New and very Singular; and yet may be as far from being False. So that neither the Antiquity nor Universality of the One, nor the

Novelty

(July 14th, 1731,) express great satisfaction with his official conduct, and avow their unfaltering attachment to the proprietary and his family. Governor Calvert died on his voyage out, and was succeeded by Samuel Ogle in September, who continued in office for eleven years.

Lord Baltimore, finding his presence necessary to settle the boundary dispute with Pennsylvania, arrived in the province in 1732, and assumed the government in his own person.[1]

From the year 1685, when the decree relative to the boundary controversy between Maryland and Pennsylvania was passed by the king in council, the good understanding between the two provinces had been kept up by mere temporary expedients, which were every now and then frustrated by some act of border aggression. Immediately upon the death of William Penn, in 1718, his sons, John, Richard, and Thomas, who became joint proprietaries by the will of their father, revived the old dispute, and succeeded in obtaining from Charles, the Fifth Lord Baltimore, in 1732 a written agreement conceding to the Penns all their claims. The boundary adjustment provided for a line drawn due west from Cape Henlopen[2] across the Peninsula, from the centre of which another line should be drawn tangent to a circle twelve miles from New Castle, while a meridian from the tangent point should be continued to within fifteen miles south of Philadelphia, whence should be traced the parallel westward that was to divide the provinces. Should the meridian cut a segment from the circle, the segment was to be a part of New Castle county. This parallel is the famous Mason and Dixon's line.[3]

The agreement provided that within two months, seven commissioners should be appointed by each of the contracting parties, any three of whom should be a quorum, to run and mark the said boundaries; that the commissioners should begin operations in October, and finish in December of the same year, with all fairness and despatch; that the line should be well marked by trees and other natural objects, and further designated by stone pillars, sculptured with the arms of the contracting parties, facing their respective possessions; and that in case of a quorum of the commissioners of

[1] He was born September 29th, 1699, and on July 20, 1730, married Mary, daughter of Sir Theodore Janssen, Baronet of Wimbledon Surry, by whom he had several children. On June 27, 1731, he was Gentleman of the Red Chamber, to Frederick, Prince of Wales, father of King George III., and on December 10 following he was elected a Fellow of the Royal Society. On his return to England, in 1734, he was chosen a member of parliament for St. German's, in Cornwall, and in 1741 and 1747, for the county of Surry. On March 9, 1741, he was appointed Junior Lord in the Admiralty, which place he resigned in 1745. In April, 1747, he was made Cofferer to the Prince of Wales and Surveyor General of the Dutchy Lands in Cornwall. He died April 24, 1751.—John G. Morris, *Lords Baltimore*, p. 44.

In 1732, Thomas Bladen, a son of one of the early settlers of Maryland, went to England, where he married Barbara, daughter of Sir Thomas Janssen, and eldest sister of the wife of Lord Baltimore. He returned to Maryland in 1742, and was appointed governor. William Janssen, Lord Baltimore's brother-in-law, accompanied him to Maryland in 1732, and was made a member of the council and also Lord Baltimore's secretary.

[2] The Cape Henlopen here referred to is not the point now known as such, opposite to Cape May . . . but the point where the States of Maryland and Delaware now abut together upon the ocean, marked Fenwick's Island on the latest map of Maryland, and about fifteen miles to the southward of the present Cape Henlopen.—*History of Mason and Dixon's Line*, p. 22. By J. H. B. Latrobe.

[3] *Ibid.*

either party failing to attend, the defaulting party should forfeit to the other the sum of five thousand pounds.

In pursuance of this agreement, commissioners were appointed, who were to meet at New Castle to commence operations. Lord Baltimore, who had now arrived in Maryland in 1732, to settle the dispute in accordance with the agreement, in a letter to Governor Patrick Gordon, of Pennsylvania, dated February 15th, 1733, gives the following account of the treatment of his commissioners by the Pennsylvanians:

"My arrival in this Province afforded me an opportunity of taking more than ordinary care that my commissioners of Pennsylvania, at Newcastle, the first of this instant; pursuant to the adjournment jointly made by the commissioners on both sides, the third of last November; for this purpose I thought fit to nominate a new commissioner, to supply the place of an infirm one, and for the same reason my commissioners, notwithstanding the unusual extremity of the present season, and the distance of place, were so assiduous in their journeys as for some of them to arrive at Newcastle many days, and all of them before the day appointed. This behaviour on our part, might justly challenge the same strict observance from the Commissioners of Pennsylvania. And I should still have depended on their unwillingness of being guilty of any infraction, if on the sudden return of my Commissioners I had not been informed, that the Commissioners of Pennsylvania so little observed the adjournment made by the Commissioners on both sides, of their meeting at ten o'clock on Saturday, the third instant, in the morning, pursuant to their accustomed way of proceeding, as that not only one of them left the place of meeting abruptly at the very instant my commissioners desired to proceed on business, of whereby there was not a sufficient number present, but also that the others (tho' sent for and repeated declarations made by my commissioners of breaking up the meeting for their non-attendance) seemed willfully and obstinately to neglect attending that morning, which ended the appointment made by the joint commissioners on Friday the second instant in the afternoon. I forbear to mention many other circumstances reported to me by my commissioners, and which too plainly shewed a design in the Commissioners of Pennsylvania, to violate the measures entered into in that particular. Was I inclinable to make the strict use of this failure, nay, voluntary one, on the side of the Pennsylvania Commissioners, I might not only disregard all further notice, but entitle myself immediately to the forfeiture incurred by the failure of the Commissioners of Pennsylvania. But I think myself not a little fortunate by my being in my Province at this juncture, that I may have an opportunity of doing in this affair, what my Commissioners perhaps could not reconcile to themselves the liberty of, which is to recede in some measure of the advantage I may claim from the proceeding of the Commissioners of Pennsylvania. Upon this account I am willing, and now offer, and have accordingly given directions to my Commissioners that they should meet the Commissioners of Pennsylvania, on the first Monday in May next, at the town of Joppa in Baltimore County, in the Province of Maryland, but with this salvo of all the right, benefit, and advantage, I may claim from the non-attendance or failure of the Pennsylvania Commissioners, on the third instant, in the morning, according to the last adjournment.

"I think myself obliged to name the place at Joppa, not only because my Commissioners have attended twice at Newcastle, but also by reason of a behaviour of your Commissioners to some of mine in Newcastle, which possibly without having the command over the inhabitants, would never have been attempted, and to prevent any apprehension of the like conduct from my Commissioners, I do assure you I shall give a strict charge to the contrary."[1]

[1] Pennsylvania *Colonial Records*, III., p. 486.

Governor Gordon in his answer to Lord Baltimore, dated Philadelphia, March 28th, 1732, denies the allegations set forth in the letter of Lord Baltimore, and ridicules the idea of selecting Joppa as the place of meeting. It is stated, however, that at the first meeting of the commissioners at Newcastle, disputes arose as to the application of the terms of the agreement, and the manner of carrying it into execution. And as Lord Baltimore no doubt soon found out that the Penns had taken advantage of his ignorance of his rights, and did not really desire a fair adjudication of the controversy, he withdrew from this attempt at a fair settlement.

Lord Baltimore was now uneasy at learning what unfair advantages the Penns had obtained, and sought to relieve himself from all further controversy, by obtaining from King George II. a confirmation of his charter, *non obstante* the language of description contained in it, which represented it "as uncultivated and inhabited by strangers." "These unfortunate words," says Mr. McMahon, "which the sagacity of Penn had turned to good purpose, in his objections to the charter as obtained by misrepresentation, at least as to the peninsular territory, had been the source of his most serious difficulties, and they now suggested an expedient which it would have been well for the Proprietary of Maryland to have adopted in the very origin of the controversy. To adopt this expedient, was indeed to admit the force of the objection, and hence the tardy resort to it; yet it is probable, that if instead of relying with entire confidence upon the efficacy of the charter, the proprietary had, upon the first appearance of this objection, petitioned for this confirmation, it would have been at once accorded by the justice of the crown, and thus in all future contests, his claims would have rested upon an unquestionable chartered right. Fortified by this right, whatever might have been the result during the reign of James, the principles of political liberty and the respect for chartered rights, which rose in triumph when he fell, must ultimately have restored Baltimore to the full enjoyment of his original grant. As it was, the Proprietaries of Maryland had suffered difficulty to accumulate upon difficulty, and objection to spring upon objection, until it was too late to retrace their steps. Had the confirmation been sought and obtained in the first instance, it would have been a preventive; but now it was applied for as a remedy, and only when all else had failed. The application thus made was strenuously opposed by the proprietaries of Pennsylvania, who interposed Baltimore's voluntary agreement and surrender of territory as a bar to his application."[1]

GEORGE II.

The result was that John, Richard and Thomas Penn filed in 1735 a Bill in Chancery against Lord Baltimore, praying for a decree of specific perform-

[1] *History of Maryland*, p. 39.

ance of the articles, which, from the death of John Penn, and the necessity of adding other parties, and the delay incident to proceedings in that court, was not fully decided until the year 1750, when Chancellor Hardwicke decreed the specific execution of the agreement.

In the meantime the quiet of the provinces continued to be interrupted by riots and disturbances, occurring from the violent conduct of Pennsylvanians, on the borders of Lancaster and Baltimore counties. One of these is referred to in the following letter from Lord Baltimore to Governor Patrick Gordon of Pennsylvania:

"*Annapolis, December 15th, 1732.*

"Sir:

"By the enclosed precept, founded upon information given upon oath to a magistrate here, you will see that a most outrageous riot hath lately been committed in my Province by a great number of people, calling themselves Pennsylvanians.

"It appears, by the same information, that some of your magistrates, instead of preventing or discouraging these violences, countenance and abet the authors of them; whether with or without the approbation of your government, you best know.

"For my own part, I think myself in honor and justice obliged, and I am determined, to protect such of his Majesty's subjects who are my own tenants, in all their rights; and therefore, to the end the persons complained of may be punished, if upon a fair trial they shall be found guilty, I desire that they, or such of them as can be found in your Province, may be sent without loss of time into this, as the only and proper place, where the fact with which they are charged is cognizable, and where my officers will be ready to receive them, particularly the sheriffs and justices of my counties of Baltimore and Cecil.

"I also desire that such of your magistrates as shall appear to have encouraged the commission of these or any other violences in my province, by the people of Pennsylvania, may be punished for their abuse of authority and that you'l favor me with a categorical answer to these my just demands, by this bearer. Your humble servant,

"BALTIMORE."

In the "Precept" referred to in the foregoing letter, is the following:

"Whereas Charles Jones, James Patison, Alxr. McKey, John Capper, John Hart, John Pattan, James Pattan, James Patison, Jr., John Trotter and William Macmanac being, or pretending themselves to be inhabitants of Pennsylvania, together with several other persons unknown, are charged upon the oath of John Lowe of Baltimore County, planter, taken before me Robert Gordon, Esq., one of his Lordship's Justices of the Provincial Court of Maryland, who having assembled themselves armed with weapons, offensive and defensive, in a riotous manner, and on the plantation of him the said John Lowe, in the said County, in the night of the 26th of November last, and riotously assaulting and beating the said John Lowe, his wife and family, and imprisoning the said John Lowe and his two sons, to the great terror and damage of the said John Lowe and his family, against his Lordship's peace, good rule and government."

Governor Gordon and his council "fully considered the said letters and affidavits, making some observations on the style and manner of the Lord Baltimore's letters, which they conceived too peremptory."[1] About the same time an unhappy fray took place on the borders of Dorchester county. In May, 1734, John Hendricks and Joshua Minshall, from their settlements on

[1] Pennsylvania *Records*.

the Susquehannah, and two others from the borders of New Castle county, were carried off by the Maryland authorities and confined in the Annapolis jail.

The most prominent event of these border feuds was the attack upon the house of Thomas Cresap, a citizen of Maryland, which was made by a body of armed men from Pennsylvania, who set fire to the house in which himself and family and several of his neighbors were, and attempted to murder them as they made their escape from the flames. On the other hand the Pennsylvanians allege that "Many Palatines had settled west of the Susquehannah (now York county,) under Pennsylvania titles, but in order to avoid the payment of taxes imposed by the province, they accepted titles from Maryland and attorned to Lord Baltimore; but, becoming satisfied that adhesion to him might ultimately prejudice their interests, they formally renounced their allegiance, and sought protection from Pennsylvania." This tergiversation irritated the Maryland authorities, and the sheriff of Baltimore county, with three hundred men, marched to eject the Palatines from their possessions. The sheriff of Lancaster county (Samuel Smith,) drew out his *posse* for their protection, and without violence, succeeded in inducing the Maryland party to return without attempting their purpose, on a pledge of the Germans that they would consult together, and give an answer to Lord Baltimore's requisition to acknowledge his authority. But, an association was soon after formed, with the knowledge of Governor Ogle, consisting of at least fifty persons, headed by a captain, Thomas Cresap, expressly for driving out the Germans, and dividing their lands among the associators, two hundred acres being promised to each. In the prosecution of their design they killed one Knowles Dant, who had resisted them. Cresap was in his turn assailed by the sheriff of Lancaster, and after a sharp contest, in which one man was killed and Cresap himself wounded, was made prisoner and conveyed to Philadelphia jail.[1]

"Governor Ogle, on receipt of intelligence of this, despatched Edmund Jennings and Daniel Dulany to Philadelphia to demand reparation, and the release of Cresap. Both were refused by the President and Council, who earnestly remonstrated against the encroachments of the people of Maryland, encouraged and protected as they were by their Governor.

"Governor Ogle immediately ordered reprisals. Four German settlers were seized and carried to Baltimore, and a band of the associators, under one Higginbotham, proceeded forcibly to expel the Germans. Again the Council ordered out the Sheriff of Lancaster, and the power of his county, with directions to dispose detachments in proper positions to protect the people; and they despatched Messrs. Lawrence and Ashton, members of the Board, to support him in the execution of their orders. When the Sheriff entered the field the invaders retired, but returned as soon as his force was withdrawn.

[1] Colonel Brantz Mayer, in his *Tag-Gah-Jute*, or *Logan and Cresap*, page 25, says: "Cresap lived at this time at Wright's Ferry, opposite the town of Columbia, where he obtained a Maryland title to 500 acres of land, 'and was borne off in triumph' to Philadelphia, where the streets, doors and windows were thronged with spectators to see the *Maryland monster*, who taunted the crowd by exclaiming, half in earnest, half in derision—'Why, this is the finest city in the Province of Maryland!'"

Captures were made on both sides; the German settlers were harassed perpetually; in many instances driven from their farms, and in others deterred from every attempt to plant or improve.

"In May, 1737, the Council sent Samuel Preston and John Kinsey on an embassy to Governor Ogle, to treat on some measure which might preserve the quiet of the border, until the pleasure of the King should be known, to whom both parties had appealed. But Governor Ogle requiring some concessions incompatible with the rights of the Proprietaries of Pennsylvania, the deputies returned without having made any agreement. In the succeeding October, a party of Marylanders, to the number of sixteen, under the direction of one Richard Lowder, broke into the jail at Lancaster, and released the rioters who had been apprehended by the Sheriff, among whom was a brother of their leader."[1]

In the report of the Governor of Pennsylvania to his council, we find the following account of the arrest of Thomas Cresap for the killing of Knowles Dant:

"The Sheriff of Lancaster, having called to his assistance twenty-four persons, went over Susquehannah on Tuesday night, the twenty-third November [1736], in order to be at Cresap's early next morning, and to have taken him by surprise, but they being discovered, Cresap secured himself in his house, and having six men with him, he stood on his defence; that the Sheriff read the warrant to Cresap and required him to surrender, but he and those with him swore they would defend themselves to death; that the Sheriff finding all persuasive means ineffectual, sent for more assistance, but Cresap had so fortified his house, and fired so furiously on the Sheriff and his company, that they could not storm the house without the utmost hazard, there being near a hundred fire-arms in it; that they had endeavored to persuade some of those who were with Cresap to desert him, but they had taken an oath to stand by one another, with a resolution to kill any that offered to capitulate; one however found means to desert him by getting out at the chimney; that the Sheriff and his assistants having waited till near sunset, and finding they must either return without executing their warrant or destroy the house to come at him, they set fire to it, but offered to quench it if he would surrender; he nevertheless obstinately persisted in his refusal, neither would he suffer his wife or children to leave the house, but fired at those who proposed it; that when the fire prevailed and the floor was ready to fall in, those with him rushed forth loaded with arms, which, as they fired at the Sheriff and his assistants they threw away, and in this confusion one of Cresap's men, Michael Reisner, shot down by mistake another of the gang, name Lauchlan Malone, on whose body the Coroner was taking an inquisition; that Cresap was at length apprehended."[2]

These border outrages were now of so alarming a character that the Governor, and Upper and Lower Houses of Assembly of Maryland, found it necessary to make the following full representation of the facts, to the proprietary and to the king in council:

"The humble Address of the Governor and the Upper and Lower Houses of Assembly of the Province of Maryland.

"May it please your Majesty:

"We Your Majesty's most dutiful and Loyal Subjects, the Governor and the members of the Upper and Lower Houses of Assembly of the Province of Maryland, most humbly presuming on your Majesty's constant Goodness and gracious condescension to receive the petitions and Complaints of all your Subjects, do hope for your Majesty's Royal

[1] Gordon's *History of Pennsylvania*, p. 219. [2] Pennsylvania *Colonial Records*, iv., p. 110.

permission to represent the impious treatment which this Province in General, and more particularly your Majesty's Subjects, residing on the Northern Borders thereof, have of Late Suffered from the Government and Inhabitants of the Province of Pennsylvania.

"His late Majesty, King Charles the first, by his Royal Grant of Letters Patent, under the Great Seal and bearing date the 20th day of June, in the eighth year of his Reign, did grant unto Cecilius, late Lord Baltimore, his heirs and assigns, a tract of Land described by and included within the particular Limits, Metes and Bounds, expressed in the said Grant, and which was by the said Grant erected into a Province, and Stiled by the name of Maryland; by Virtue of which Royal Grant the said Lord Baltimore immediately took possession thereof, and which the present Lord Baltimore, now our Lord Proprietary, claims, and we must beg leave further to lay before your Majesty that the late William Penn, Esq., Claiming some Lands to the Northward of and near to the said Province of Maryland, now called Pennsylvania, under a Royal Grant from his late Majesty, King Charles the second, and taking Advantage of the Bounds of Maryland not being Sufficiently known and fixed by Proper Land Marks, both he and his Heirs have intruded and encroached on considerable Quantities of Land, far within the Descriptions, Bounds, and Limits, of the Province of Maryland, as comprised in the Royal Charter or Grant.

"This Truth, may it please your Majesty, is so notorious that the Government of Pennsylvania, ever despairing to justify their frequent Incroachments by a Denial thereof, have endeavored from time to time to insinuate that some Limit was set by a Lord Baltimore to himself many years ago, whereas they must be sensible there is little Reason or Justice to rely on that assertion or the strength of that pretended Limit, for even after the supposed time of fixing thereof an Order was made by the late King James the second in Council on the particular application, and greatly in favor of Mr. Penn, without any regard to that limit, or Mr. Penn's mentioning the same or so much as pretending there ever was one; but extended Lord Baltimore's right as far to the Northward as was comprised within the Charter, and which Order we most humbly presume Mr. Penn would not have so earnestly contended for, and his Heirs would not have since so much and only replied thereon if that pretended Limit to the Southward of the Bounds expressed in the Charter, could have been sufficiently supported.

"But your Majesty's Subjects, the Inhabitants on the Northern Borders of this Province, have on too many Occasions lamentably experienced the little Knowledge or Opinion the Inhabitants or persons pretending to act under the Authority of Pennsylvania, have of any Limit or Bound to their violent and Intruding dispositions, which always hurry them to extend the Authority of the Government of Pennsylvania by Encroachments to the Southward of every Limit they at any time before thought proper to set to themselves under these circumstances, the Lord Baltimore, our Proprietary, was prevailed in the year 1732, to hearken to Overtures made by the Proprietaries of Pennsylvania for the fixing and ascertaining some certain Limits and Bounds, between the Provinces of Maryland and Pennsylvania, and accordingly Articles of Agreement were entered into and Commissioners were appointed by the Lord Baltimore and the Proprietors of Pennsylvania for that purpose, in which Articles a time was Limited for Carrying them into Execution, and a Provision made that if they were not executed in the time so limited, they should be void, which Articles, partly from the Difficulty of the execution and partly from the unreasonableness, objections and demands of the Commissioners of Pennsylvania and the different constructions put upon the Articles themselves, were not executed yet, those concerned in the Government of Pennsylvania, who have ever been careful to slip no Opportunity or omit any Pretence to incroach into Maryland, pretended that though the Articles were never carried into Execution and that the time for so doing was actually elapsed, yet, that they were equally Binding as if really Executed, and even went so far as to Cause Lines to be run and Boundaries to be marked by Persons

Appointed by themselves without the knowledge of the Lord Baltimore or any Body concerned in the management of his Affairs, and gave out that they would maintain the Limits made and Boundaries so marked, at all events. This Conduct, may it please your Majesty, Occasioned new Incroachments, which were supported by Force and Violence, such as the Imprisonment and ruin of some of your Majesty's Subjects, who had the Misfortune of setling on the northern parts of Maryland, bordering on Pennsylvania, to the great Terror of such others who had the good Fortune to escape such severities, to prevent which Violences and to secure the peace and Property of your Majesty's Subjects until the Bounds of the two Provinces could be settled, so as to end all disputes Concerning them, this Government offered to join with the Government of Pennsylvania in an humble address to your Majesty for the fixing Our Limits and determining our Differences, and to prohibit any Person from settling and encroaching in the meantime further to the northward or southward of the then respective Settlements in each province, but the Government of Pennsylvania was not pleased to concur in such measures, which must have Greatly added to the happiness of all, and saved the Lives of some of your Majesty's Subjects.

"Then, may it please your Majesty, the Lord Proprietary of this Province became apprehensive of the Consequences of such Unwillingness in the Government of Pennsylvania, to that Peace and Good will which your Majesty so Gloriously defends and preserves to your Subjects, and most justly respects and Commands should be observed amongst them, and in Compliance with his Duty to your Majesty in the safety and Preservation of us, your Majesty's Subjects, under his Government, as well as in maintenance of his own right and Property, his Lordship our Lord Proprietary did, by his most humble petition to your Majesty, set forth his Title to this Province under the said Charter, and for the Reasons in the said Petition mentioned, his Lordship most humbly prayed your Majesty's further Charter or Letters Patent to Confirm the whole of the Tract of Land called a Peninsula in the said Charter to his Lordship, which petition your Majesty was most Graciously pleased to refer to the Consideration of your Majesty's Lords Commissioners for Trade and Plantations, upon which their Lordships having made their Report to your Majesty, your Majesty was most Graciously pleased to refer the same to the right Honorable the Lords of Committee of Council for Plantation affairs, and their Lordship's were pleased to report to your Majesty that your Majesty having been pleased to refer unto that Committee a Report made by the Lord's Commissioners for trade and Plantations upon the Petition of Charles, Lord Baltimore, praying for a Grant of Confirmation of such part of a Peninsula in America as is contained within the Limits of the Charter granted to his Ancestors in the Reign of King Charles the first, notwithstanding the words *Hactenus inculta*, which are inserted in the Recital of the said Charter, and that your Majesty, having been pleased likewise to Refer unto that Committee two petitions, the one in the name of Richard Penn, Esq., the youngest surviving Son of William Penn, Esq., deceased, in Behalf of himself and his two Elder Brothers, John and Thomas Penn, Esqs., then in Pennsylvania, setting forth their right to the three Lower Counties of New Castle, Kent and Sussex, lying within and Contiguous to the said Peninsula, and therefore praying to be heard against confirming the said Peninsula to the Lord Baltimore, and the other in the name of the People called Quakers, inhabitants of the said three Lower Counties, praying also to be heard against Confirming the said Lands to the Lord Baltimore; that their Lordships took the said Report and Petitions into their Consideration, and were attended by Council, as well for the Lord Baltimore as the other petitioners; and that, it appearing that on the 10th of May, 1732, Articles of Agreement had been entered into between the Lord Baltimore and the said John Thomas and Richard Penn, for adjusting the boundaries of the Land Granted to them by their respective Charters, which Articles had not been carried into Execution within the time thereby Limited, but notwithstanding such Lapse of time, the Validity of the said articles being insisted on by and Behalf of the said John Thomas and Richard Penn, the Lords of the Committee did agree humbly to report to your Majesty as their Opinion, that the Consideration of the said Report and petitions should be adjourned until the end of Michaelmas term, then next in order to give an opportunity to the said John Thomas and Richard Penn to proceed in a Court of Equity to obtain the said Articles of Agreement so insisted upon by them, as they should be advised, and that after the Expiration of the said time, either party should be at Liberty to apply to the Committee of Council for Plantation affairs, as the nature of the case might require; which Report your Majesty was pleased to approve and order agreeable thereto, and to Direct that all Persons whom it might concern were to take notice and govern themselves accordingly.

"This, your Majesty's Royal Notice and Interposition, gave immediate Ease and quiet to every poor Inhabitant on our Borders, nor would our awful duty to your Majesty suffer us to entertain the least Apprehension or distrust that any of your Majesty's Subjects would be so presumptuous and daring to break in and disturb that Tranquility which your Majesty had so Graciously taken under your own so immediate Royal Cognizance.

"But we most humbly represent to your Majesty, that although your Majesty was pleased, on the Petition of the Proprietary of Pennsylvania, to adjourn the Consideration of the Report of the Lords for Trade and Plantations, till the end of Michaelmas term, then next in order to give them an opportunity to proceed in a Court of Equity to Obtain Relief upon the said Articles of Agreement, so insisted upon by them, as they should be advised, yet the Government of Pennsylvania very soon after seemed to imagine they had a right to determine by violence what your Majesty had so lately given your Royal Directions About, and which then was, and still is, depending in your Majesty's high Court of Chancery, by your Majesty's Royal Indulgence to the Proprietaries of Pennsylvania.

"That several Germans and Palatines being arrived some time ago in these parts of your Majesty's Dominions in America, made their Applications and requests to this Government for the Liberty of Seating and settling with their Families on Lands within this Province, which desires this Government not only thought reasonable, but the People so deserving Encouragement that several Considerable Quantities of Land lying on the Borders of this Province, adjoining to the Province of Pennsylvania, were allotted and assigned them for their Residence and Support under the Authority of this Government, and accordingly not less than fifty or sixty families of that nation immediately took Possession of these Lands, and paid their Proportion of the Taxes and demeaned themselves in every other Respect as peaceable subjects to your Majesty, and unquestionable Inhabitants and Tenants of this Province until very Lately, when through unwariness and too much Credulity they suffered themselves to be prevailed on by the Emissaries of Pennsylvania, under Pretence of more than ordinary advantages, to renounce openly their Submission to this Government, and to declare their Resolution to transfer their obedience to the Government of Pennsylvania; and in order to account for this their extraordinary proceeding, they declared their unwillingness to Contribute towards the Maintenance of the ministers of the Church of England by the Law established in this Province, or to Conform themselves to such Laws and Rules for the regulating the Militia as this Province in their Legislature has thought expedient and necessary for their Safety and Defence against any Foreign Enemy, which the said Emissaries among other things, promised they should be entirely free from in consideration of their withdrawing their Obedience from this Government.

"So Surprising a Behavior, endeavoured to be Justified by such Pretences, so Greatly alarmed this Government with the Dangerous Consequences which might ensue, not only to this Province, but to every other part of your Majesty's Dominions in America, that they thought their indispensable Duty required their utmost Care to disabuse these deluded people, to make them sensible how much they had misbehaved themselves as

Subjects to your Majesty; for this purpose the proper Sheriff of the County has orders as well to demand and levy on those inhabitants their Just Proportion of the Legal Taxes due to this Province, as to apprehend and secure so many of them as he could find, in order that they might be forthcoming to answer in a due course of Law for their Misdemeanor in attempting to disturb the Peace of this Province by their avowed Disobedience to the Laws thereof, and as this Government was not ignorant that these unfortunate people had been privately encouraged by some persons daring enough to protect them against any Prosecution, therefore the said Sheriff had directions to take to his Assistance in the Execution of his said Office, some of the Militia of his County, in pursuance of which Commands the said Sheriff, attended by several of the Militia, Repaired to that Part of his County where those Inhabitants resided, there he found them shut up in an House which an armed number of men, Inhabitants of Pennsylvania, had taken possession of, and after his demand of their being delivered to him was obstinately refused, the said Sheriff with the said Militia, departed in a peaceable manner and Distrained some few of their Goods for their Proportion of Taxes.

"This Conduct of the Government of Maryland, we humbly hope, will Appear in your Majesty's Great wisdom proper and reasonable, but we presume to Acquaint your Majesty that the Government of Pennsylvania thought fit not only to consider it in another Light but to make use of it for purposes destructive of the Lives and Properties of your Majesty's Subjects; for that Government, under pretence that those parts of the Country lay to the northward of a Line mentioned in the Agreement now under the Cognizance of your Majesty's high Court of Chancery, to Determine whether it should bind the Lord Proprietary of this Province, was pleased to issue a Proclamation under a specious Colour of preserving Peace, but really to inflame and incite the Inhabitants of their Borders, which that Government then acknowledged was filled with people of more than ordinary Spirit to the Commission of horrid and Cruel Violences.

"It is with the most sensible Concern, may it please your Majesty, that we found those designs of the Government of Pennsylvania had too soon their desired effect, for divers of your Majesty's Subjects who had nothing to support themselves with but their Labor and Industry, were violently Dragged from their Habitations, and thrown into Loathsome Gaols to the ruin of their poor families; and not Content with these Violences, an armed multitude, pretending to be Inhabitants of the Province of Pennsylvania, headed by a Sheriff and a Magistrate of that Province, beset the house of one Thomas Cresap, who had always held the Land he then Lived on under a Title from the Lord Proprietary of Maryland, acknowledged himself Tenant of that Province, and Constantly paid his Taxes and Dues to the same, and acted for some time past as a Magistrate thereof and in further Execution of their pernicious intentions, these outrageous people set fire to the house (in which there was then the Owner, his Wife and Children, and Six other men), and burnt the same down to the Ground, with all the Effects of the said Owner to a very Considerable Value; nor was the Spirit of these Incendiaries allayed by the bold Violation of your Majesty's Laws, but when the unhappy Wretches, then in the house, endeavored to save and Defend themselves from the Flames and those merciless men, a Continual firing of Guns followed, which Occasioned the Death of one and Wounding others of your Majesty's Subjects who had been in the House; then the Owner, with four of his Companions, were Seized and Hurried into the Gaols of the Province of Pennsylvania, where one of them actually perished for want of Sustenance; and the rest now Lye.

"This Proceeding by Fire and Sword to establish the Bounds which are now in Dispute in your Majesty's high Court of Chancery, filled your Petitioners as well as others, your Majesty's Subjects of these two Provinces, with such terrible apprehensions, that an immediate Application was made from this Government to the Government of Pennsylvania for their Assistance in Discountenancing such Violences, and Bringing the offenders to Condign Punishment; and Lest they should escape a Just Return for their wickedness by any Doubt which the Government of Pennsylvania might pretend to entertain of the place where they ought to be tried, this Government Requested that Government to cause the offenders to be immediately Apprehended, in order that they might be amenable to Justice in such Place as your Majesty should be pleased to direct; but, contrary to all reasonable Expectations, the Government of Pennsylvania was pleased to decline any Compliance with that demand by deferring their apprehension till your Majesty's Pleasure should be signified therein; nor could any Remonstrance from this Government of the Probability of the offenders' escape, and Eluding by that means your Majesty's Justice, prevail with that Government to alter their Resolution.

"We further humbly presume to lay before your Majesty Our Unhappiness, that this Government is not able to procure from the Government of Pennsylvania the release of those unfortunate Sufferers who are still Confined in Pennsylvania Gaols; this desire was refused, on pretence that Thomas Cresap, the owner of the house, had been guilty of a former murder, and that the others were present at the aforementioned Confusion, when one of your Majesty's Subjects was killed. That accusation of a former murder against the said Cresap will, we humbly hope, appear very extraordinary, when we presume to say that the man was killed by him in defence of his Own House, when the very Same House was in the night time attacked and broke into some years ago by another number of Pennsylvanians, and the Owner then threatened with the Loss of his Life, which he had no Means or Possibility of preserving but by defending himself the best way he could, and therefore in defence of his house fired a Gun and Shot the deceased in the Leg or thigh, of which wound he died; for this Fact the Owner of the House was brought to his Trial in this Province, and the late Governor of Pennsylvania was so sensible of this being the Truth of the case that he often declared the Owner of the House ought not to be accountable for that man's death, and those Concerned in the Government of Pennsylvania are so well satisfied of the said Cresap's and his fellow Prisoners' innocence, that during eight months' imprisonment there has been no prosecution against them, nor any Legal Opportunity Given them to shew their Innocence, and only groundless Slanders raised Against the poor, unhappy man and his fellow Sufferers to furnish a Pretence to Deprive them of their Liberty and to Violate the Laws securitative of the Rights of British Subjects.

"This being the melancholy Situation of many of your Majesty's Subjects who have been ruined and Deprived of their Liberty, and of others who are in danger of the like Rigorous Treatment from a Neighboring Government and people, who, under the specious Pretence of peaceable principles of Religion, have used the most subtle Arts to incroach into the Limits of this Province, and have not Scrupled to Excite Bold and desperate men to commit the most Deliberate Cruelties upon several of your Majesty's Subjects, and to Countenance, Protect and reward these their instruments, at the same time that they have pretended they would not encourage the Violences committed, or the Authors of them, and your Majesty's Subjects, who have the honor of having any Share in the administration of the Government of Maryland, conceiving it to be their undoubted Duty to use all possible endeavors to preserve the Lives and secure the Peace of all your Majesty's Subjects, and even to avoid repelling force with force, but in the most humble manner to have recourse to your most Sacred Majesty, and to implore your Protection and Defence, we most humbly beseech your Majesty to take the Sufferings of your Majesty's Subjects, who are and long have been deprived of their Liberty in the manner already mentioned, and such others of the Inhabitants of this Province as are in danger of the like rigorous usage, into your Royal Consideration, and to vouchsafe to grant them Such Relief as to your Majesty in your Royal Wisdom shall seem meet.

"Your Majesty's most Gracious Condescension in hearkening to these Our complaints must the more (if possible) inforce Our inviolable duty in praying for the Blessings of Length and Happiness to your Majesty's Reign, and an ever Continuance of the Crown in a succession of the illustrious House of Hanover, whose chief Good is placed only on that of Mankind, and more Especially of its Subjects, amongst the most Dutiful and Obedient of whom we humbly presume to Declare Ourselves.

"SAM. OGLE.

"Signed by Order of the Upper House.

"RD. TILGHMAN, *President.*

"Signed by order of the Lower House.

"JAMES HARRIS, *Speaker.*"

This address drew from the king an order in council, dated August 18th, 1737, in which it is commanded:

"That the Governors of the respective provinces of Maryland and Pennsylvania, for the time being, do not, upon pain of incurring his Majesty's highest displeasure, permit or suffer any tumults, riots or other outrageous disorders to be committed on the borders of their respective provinces; but that they do immediately put a stop thereto, and use their utmost endeavors to preserve peace and good order amongst all his Majesty's Subjects under their government inhabiting the said borders, his Majesty doth hereby enjoin the said Governors that they do not make grants of any part of the lands in contest between the Proprietors respectively, nor any part of the three lower counties, commonly called New Castle, Kent and Sussex, nor permit any person to settle there, or even to attempt to make a settlement thereon, till his Majesty's pleasure shall be further signified."

The dangerous situation of affairs in the two provinces at this time, and the desire to conciliate the crown, induced a ready compliance with this order in council; to carry which into effect, the governors of both provinces issued their proclamations, setting forth the terms of the order, and afterwards, in May, 1738, entered into an agreement providing for the running of a provisional line between the provinces, which line was not to interfere with the actual possessions of the settlers, but merely to suspend all grants of the disputed territory as defined by that line, until the final adjustment of the boundaries. When this agreement was reported to the council, his majesty was pleased to order "that the proprietaries of the respective provinces of Maryland and Pennsylvania do cause the said agreement to be carried into execution." The order was accordingly promulgated by proclamation in the provinces, and commissioners were, in 1639, appointed to run the "temporary line:" Colonel Levin Gale and Samuel Chamberlaine on the part of Maryland, and Richard Peters and Lawrence Growden on that of Pennsylvania. These commissioners commenced their operations in the spring of 1739; and, after proceeding as far as the eastern bank of the Susquehannah, were interrupted by the departure of Colonel Gale, on account of death and sickness in his family, and the declaration of Mr. Chamberlaine that he had no authority to continue operations without the attendance of his colleague. The Pennsylvania commissioners received orders from Governor Thomas to proceed alone and accordingly ran the line westward of the Susquehannah "to the most western of the Kittochtinny hills."

In conformity with this provisional line between the provinces, which was not to interfere with the actual possession of the settlers, all grants of the disputed territory, as defined by this temporary line, were suspended until the final establishment of the respective rights of the Lord Proprietary by the British Court of Chancery. Accordingly, a decree was pronounced by Chancellor Hardwicke, in May, 1750,[1] and, in pursuance thereof, commissioners were appointed by each of the parties to carry it into effect. The death of Charles, Lord Baltimore, in April, 1751, suspended the progress of the work, and upon the succession of Frederick, the last Lord Baltimore, fresh sources of controversy were at once opened. The question remained unsettled until the 4th of July, 1760, when an agreement was entered into between Lord Baltimore and Thomas and Richard Penn, the surviving proprietaries of Pennsylvania, when the controversy was finally determined.

This agreement adopted that of 1732, and the decree of 1750, in their full extent, as to the definition of the boundaries; and to carry it into effect, Governor Sharpe, Benjamin Tasker, Jr., Edward Lloyd, Robert Jenkins Henry, Daniel Dulany, Stephen Bordley and the Reverend Alexander Malcolm were appointed commissioners on the part of Maryland, and Honorable James Hamilton, William Allen, Richard Peters, Benjamin Chew, Lynford Lardner, Ryves Holt and George Stephenson, on behalf of Pennsylvania.[2]

They assembled at Newcastle on the 19th of November, 1760, and immediately began their operations. They were engaged from time to time in the prosecution of their labors, until the 9th of November, 1768, when they finished their work and made a final report to the proprietaries. After referring to the authority under which they had performed their duty, they reported as follows:

"1st. We have completely run out, settled, fixed and determined a straight line, beginning at the exact middle of the due east and west line mentioned in the articles of the fourth day of July, one thousand seven hundred and sixty, to have been run by other commissioners, formerly appointed by the said Charles, Lord Baltimore, and the said Thomas Penn and Richard Penn, across the peninsula, from Cape Henlopen to Chesapeake Bay, the exact middle of which said east and west line is at the distance of thirty-four miles and three hundred and nine perches from the verge of the main ocean, the eastern end or beginning of the said due east and west line; and that we have extended the said straight line eighty-one miles seventy-eight chains and thirty links up the peninsula, until it touched and made a tangent to the western part of the periphery of a circle drawn at the horizontal distance of twelve English statute miles from the centre of the town of New Castle, and have marked, described and perpetuated the said straight or tangent line, by setting up and erecting one remarkable stone at the place of beginning thereof, in the exact middle of the aforesaid due east and west line, according to the angle made by the said due west line, and by the said tangent line; which stone, on

[1] *1st Vesey Sen'rs Reports*, pp. 444-456.

[2] In the progress of this tedious and protracted work, the Rev. John Barclay, George Stuart, Daniel of St Thomas Jenifer, and John Beale Bordley, were appointed on the part of Maryland, to fill the vacancies occasioned by the declension of several of its original commissioners; and the Rev. John Ewing, William Coleman, Edward Shippen and Thomas Willing, Esqs., were appointed to fill vacancies similarly occurring in the Pennsylvania Board.

the inward sides of the same, facing towards the east and towards the north, hath the arms of the said Thomas Penn and Richard Penn graved thereon, and on the outward sides of the same facing towards the west and towards the south, hath the arms of the said Frederick Lord Baltimore graved thereon; and have also erected and set up in the said straight or tangent line, from the said place of beginning to the tangent point, remarkable stones at the end of every mile, each stone at the distance or end of every five miles, being particularly distinguished by having the arms of the said Frederick Lord Baltimore graved on the side thereof turning towards the west, and the arms of the said Thomas Penn and Richard Penn graved on the side thereof turning towards the east, and all the other intermediate stones are marked with the letter P on the sides facing towards the east, and with the letter M on the sides facing towards the west, and have fixed in the tangent point a stone with the arms of the said Frederick Lord Baltimore graved on the side facing towards the west, and with the arms of the said Thomas Penn and Richard Penn graved on the side facing towards the east.

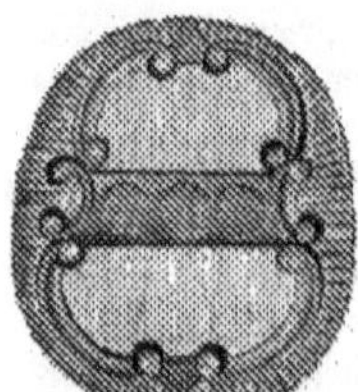

ARMS, WILLIAM PENN.

"2d. That from the end of the said straight line or tangent point, we have run out, settled, fixed and determined, a due north line of the length of five miles one chain and fifty links, to a parallel of latitude fifteen miles due south of the most southern part of the city of Philadelphia, which said due north line intersected the said circle drawn at the distance of twelve English statute miles from the centre of the town of New Castle, one mile thirty-six chains and five links from the said tangent point, and that in order to mark and perpetuate the said due north line, we have erected and set up one unmarked stone at the point where the said line intersects the said circle, three other stones at a mile distance from each other graved with the letter P on the sides facing the east, and the letter M on the sides facing the west, between the said place of intersection of the said circle and the said parallel of latitude, and a third stone at the point of intersection of the said north line and parallel of latitude, which last stone on the sides facing towards the north and east, hath the arms of the said Thomas Penn and Richard Penn graved thereon, and on the sides facing towards the south and west hath the arms of the said Frederick Lord Baltimore graved thereon.

ARMS, LORD BALTIMORE.

"3d. That we have run out, settled, fixed and determined such part of the said circle as lies westward of the said due north line, and have marked and perpetuated the same, by setting up and erecting four stones in the periphery thereof, one of which, at the meridian distance of one mile from the tangent point, is marked with the letter P on the east and the letter M on the west sides thereof.

"4th. That we have run out, settled, fixed and determined a due east and west line, beginning at the northern point or end of the said due north line, being the place of intersection of the said north line, with the parallel of latitude, at the distance of fifteen English statute miles due south of the most southern part of the city of Philadelphia, and have extended the said line, two hundred and eighty miles, eighteen chains and twenty-one links due west from the place of beginning; and two hundred and forty-four miles, thirty-eight chains and thirty-six links due west from the river Delaware; and should have continued the same to the end of five degrees of longitude, the western bounds of the Province of Pennsylvania, but the Indians would not permit us. And that we have marked, described, and perpetuated the said west line, by setting up and erecting therein stones at the end of every mile, from the place of beginning to the distance of one hundred and thirty-two miles, near the foot of a hill, called and known by the name of Sideling hill; every five mile stone having on the side facing the north, the arms of the said Thomas Penn and Richard Penn graved thereon, and on the side facing the south, the arms of Frederick Lord Baltimore graved thereon, and the other intermediate stones are graved with the letter P on the north side, and the letter M on the south side; and that the country to the westward of Sideling hill, being so very mountainous as to render it in most places extremely difficult and expensive, and in some impracticable, to convey stones or boundaries which had been prepared and marked as aforesaid, to their proper stations, we have marked and described the said line from Sideling hill to the top of the Alleghany Ridge, which divides the waters running into the rivers Potowmack and Ohio, by raising and erecting thereon, on the tops of ridges and mountains over which the said line passed, heaps or piles of stones or earth, from about three and a half to four yards in diameter, at bottom, and from six to seven feet in height, and that from the top of the said Alleghany Ridge westward, as far as we have continued the said line, we have set up posts at the end of every mile, and raised round each post, heaps or piles of stones, or earth of about the diameter and height before mentioned."

Thus was finally settled what are now the eastern and northern boundaries of Maryland, which separate it from Delaware and Pennsylvania. The east and west line between Pennsylvania and Maryland is known as Mason and Dixon's line. It is so called from the following facts: On the 4th of August, 1763, Lord Baltimore and Thomas and Richard Penn, being in London, employed Charles Mason and Jeremiah Dixon, "two mathematicians or surveyors, to mark, run out, settle, fix and determine all such parts of the circle, marks, lines and boundaries, as were mentioned in the several articles or commissions, and were not yet completed." They left England at once, and arrived at Philadelphia on the 15th of November, 1763. Having settled upon their "tangent point, they proceeded to measure on its meridian fifteen miles from the parallel of the most southern part of Philadelphia, the north wall of a house on Cedar street occupied by Thomas Plumstead and Joseph Huddle."[1] They thus ascertained the northeastern corner of Maryland, the beginning of the parallel of latitude that had been agreed upon as the boundary between the provinces. On the 17th of June, 1765, they had carried the parallel of latitude to the Susquehannah, and thereupon received instructions to continue it "as far as the provinces of Maryland and Pennsylvania were settled and inhabited." Having run their lines two hundred and forty-four miles from the river Delaware, and within thirty-six miles of the whole distance to be run, they were ordered to stop by the Indians, and retracing their steps they returned to Philadelphia, where they were honorably discharged on the 26th of December, 1767. Subsequently the line was completed by other surveyors to its termination.

Having adjusted her eastern and northern boundaries, Maryland next turned her attention to the settlement of her southern and western boundaries. This related to, and grew out of the description of "the first fountain of the Potomac," as the terminus of the western and southern boundaries of Maryland. This was predicated upon a grant made by Charles II. in the first

[1] Latrobe's *History of Mason and Dixon's Line.*

year of his reign, to Lord Hopton, Lord Jermyn, Lord Culpeper, Sir John Berkeley, Sir William Morton, Sir Dudley Wyatt, and Sir Thomas Culpeper, of "all that tract of land, lying and being in America, and bounded within the heads of the rivers Rapahannock and Quiriough, or Potomac (the courses of the said rivers as they are commonly called and known by the inhabitants) and the Chesapeake bay." After the restoration of Charles, the validity of the grant was drawn in question, when it was surrendered, and a new one given in May, 1669, to the Earl of St. Albans, Lord Berkeley, Sir Wm. Morton, and John H. Trethaway, Subsequently the title of this grant vested in Thomas, Lord Culpeper, to whom a new patent was granted of the northern neck of Virginia by King James II. in the fourth year of his reign, and from him it descended to his daughter and only child, who was married to Lord Fairfax, and thus passed into the Fairfax family. This grant of the northern neck called for the lands lying on the south side of the Potomac to its *head*, while the charter of Lord Baltimore called for all the land to the *fountain* or *source* of the Potomac, which was of course its *head*. At first there were no disputes about the true location of the common call, but as soon as the settlements began to extend towards the head of the Potomac, jealousies and difficulties broke out between the two proprietaries. Lord Baltimore, who claimed from the head of the south branch of the Potomac its first fountain, remonstrated at a very early period with the Virginians, who had undertaken to define his limits by granting lands to the north branch. Notwithstanding these protests, since the year 1753, Fairfax continued to adhere to the line as adjusted by him, and the Proprietary of Maryland continued to assert his claim to the first fountain as provided by his charter. In 1771, Colonel Thomas Cresap made the first actual examination and survey of the two branches of the Potomac, and he decided that the south branch was the most western source, and therefore *the first fountain*. Various attempts have been made from time to time by Maryland to settle the controversy, but Virginia has rejected all propositions up to this day (1878), except that of unqualified submission to her demands. The extent of territory between the two branches is estimated at half a million of acres, including some of the most fertile lands of Virginia.[1]

As Maryland increased in population and importance, as a natural result, villages sprung up here and there, and some of these assumed later, others at the very outset, the style and consequence of towns. The erection of towns by legislation was quite a hobby of the early law-makers and land-speculators of the province; some being fixed at points where a village, or small aggregation of houses had already appeared, and others, again, laid out on open ground, because the people needed a market, or a port, or the site seemed promising. There were, as may well be thought, none of these sudden and amazing growths with which the magic powers of the railway have made us familiar in recent times; and those towns of Maryland which succeeded

[1] See an extended review upon this subject in McMahon, p. 49.

in attaining any share of prosperity, grew, for the most part, slowly and regularly, in conformity with the needs of the growing population. The situation was always on some one of the navigable streams or estuaries, in which both shores of the bay abound, furnishing cheap and convenient means for the exchange of commodities with their neighbors or with the outside world; while the actual location was determined by the depth of water, commodious harborage, or sometimes by trivial circumstances, such as the site of an Indian village, or the crossing of highways. As each county required a place for the administration of justice, and one for the incarceration of offenders, a court-house and a jail, with its apparatus of pillory, stocks and whipping-post, often formed the nucleus around which crystallized the county town. Some of these towns grew and flourished, in their simple fashion for a while, then, as if stricken by a blight, they perished away—in some cases so utterly that their very existence is only revealed to us by ancient records; others have retained a quiet respectability and modest prosperity down to our own times; one or two are still growing and thriving; but all have been outstripped, and many checked in their growth, by the preponderating development of Baltimore.

The mode of erecting a town was nearly always the same. Commissioners were appointed to agree with the owner of the land for a tract of fifty, a hundred, or more acres, which was then staked off and divided into lots of an acre each, intersected by proper streets, lanes and alleys. The lots being numbered and prices attached to them, the owner of the land was allowed to select one lot, and the rest, or so many as there were applications for, were divided among the "takers-up," who received the freehold in consideration of a yearly quit-rent, usually of one penny, to the Lord Proprietary.[1] In case the experiment failed, as it often did, another act declared the former towns to "be annulled and untowned," and the land reverted to its former owner.

That uncertainty exists as to the sites of some of these ancient vanished towns, is less surprising when we consider the imperfection of the topographical knowledge of the province, and the way in which they were described, which was usually "on such a river," or "creek," "on Mr. A's land," or "near Mr. B's plantation." Since then the land has passed to other owners, the stream has changed its name, perhaps its course, or has disappeared altogether; the harbor has been choked up, and we cannot even conjecture the spot on which once such hopes were built. Even the counties were

[1] The following list comprises most of the towns thus erected previous to the Revolution: Benedict-Leonard town, Charles county, 1683; Milford, Kent county; York, Talbot county; Snow Hill, Worcester county; Islington and Bristol, Dorchester county, 1686; Wicomico, St. Mary's county; Gloucester, Kent county; St. Joseph's, Calvert county; Dorchester, Dorchester county; Talbot, Talbot county, 1688; Oxford, Talbot county, 1694; Chestertown, Kent county; Upper Marlborough, Prince George's county, 1706; Leonardtown, St. Mary's county, at a place formerly called Seymour town, 1708; Charlestown, Charles county, 1726; Ceciltown, Cecil county, 1730; Salisbury, Somerset county; Kingstown, Queen Anne county; Ogle, Queen Anne county; Bridgetown, Queen Anne county, 1732; Princess Anne, Somerset county; Jansentown (Elkridge Landing), Anne Arundel county, 1733; Fredericktown, Cecil county; Georgetown, Kent county, 1736; Bladensburg, Prince George county, 1742; Newport, Worcester county, 1744; Frederick town, Frederick county, 1745; Georgetown, Frederick county, 1751.

defined in a very vague and loose way, which has since given rise to much inconvenience and confusion. The mode of erecting a county varied: the most of them were created and defined by orders in council; others by Act of the Legislature.

Anne Arundel county was erected by legislative act in 1650; Prince George's, in 1695; Queen Anne's, in 1706; Worcester, 1742; and Frederick, in 1748. Charles county was erected in the same year as Anne Arundel, 1650, by an order in council issued in compliance with an order of the proprietary in the previous year, appointing Robert Brooke to be "commander of one whole county," to be "set forth round about and next adjoining the place he shall settle in," "by such a quantity and number of miles, and such extent and circumference of ground as other counties in our said province, or as counties in Virginia are usually allotted and extended."[1] This order was rescinded in 1654, and the present Charles county erected four years later. We need not, therefore, be surprised to find, as early as 1695, an act passed to determine the boundaries of St. Mary's and Charles counties; and in 1698, another to ascertain the limits of Anne Arundel and Baltimore counties, in which the lines are fixed by marked trees, roads and private paths; while again and again acts have to be passed for "laying out towns anew," owing to the uncertainty of boundaries.

The first recorded commission for organizing the government of the province, bearing date April 15th, 1637, authorizes Governor Leonard Calvert "to appoint fit places for public ports for lading, shipping, unlading and discharging all goods and merchandises," and also "to erect and establish convenient places for the holding and keeping of fairs and markets."[2] It seems that succeeding governors exercised similar powers; for it is not till 1683 that we find any action of the legislature in the erection of towns; though, in 1671, the commissioners of county courts are empowered by act of assembly to levy taxes on tobacco to defray the expenses of the county; and in 1674 an act is passed for providing each county with a court-house and prison.[3] Doubtless, justice had a local habitation in the counties long before this, for, in 1663, acts were passed for furnishing each county in the province with a pillory, stocks, ducking-stools, and irons for branding malefactors.

Long before the mineral wealth of the region at the head of Chesapeake bay was known, the fine estuaries and harbors of that country attracted the attention of settlers. Colonel Utie's settlement on the island named by him Spesutia, ["Utie's Hope"] at the mouth of the Susquehannah, has already been mentioned, and in 1659 patents were issued to him conferring lands described as being within the limits of Baltimore county, which is the nearest approach we can make to the date of its erection. Its bounds we find first laid down in a procla-

[1] Bozman, p. 377. The counties erected previous to the Revolution were: St. Mary's, 1634; Anne Arundel, 1650; Kent, 1650; Calvert, 1654; Charles, 1658; Baltimore, 1659; Talbot, 1660; Somerset, 1666; Dorchester, 1669; Cecil, 1674; Prince George's, 1695; Queen Anne's, 1706; Worcester, 1742; Frederick, 1748; Harford and Caroline, 1773; Washington and Montgomery, Sept. 6th, 1776; Allegany, 1789; Carroll, 1836; Howard, 1851; Wicomico, 1867; and Garrett, 1872.

[2] Bozman, p. 572.

[3] Bacon's *Laws of Maryland*.

mation of 1674. In July, 1661, a county court was held at the house of Captain Thomas Howell, from which we may infer that no court-house for the county then existed; nor was there one built, in all probability, until the passage of the act of 1674, before referred to. Singularly enough, neither record nor tradition preserves the date of construction of the first Baltimore county court-house, nor even the place on which it stood. But in the act of 1683—the first relating to the establishment of towns—a town is authorized to be laid off on Bush river, "on the town land near the court-house," by which we learn that the court-house was then in existence, and that there was some sort of settlement there aspiring to the name of a town. The early maps show[1] the location of this town to have been on the east side of the river near its mouth; and all give it the name of "Baltimore." Tradition still attaches the name of "Old Baltimore" to a spot about a mile south of the eastern terminus of the present railway bridge over Bush river; though its annals have perished, and no stone now marks the site of this elder sister and namesake of the present metropolis of the State. We can only surmise that, after a placid existence of about half a century, this ancient Baltimore dwindled and faded before the rising glories of Joppa.

Another Baltimore, in another county, died in infancy, and may almost be said to have been strangled in the birth. In 1744, fifty acres of land were ordered to be laid out on Indian river, in Worcester county, and erected into a town called Baltimore. But the county surveyor, for some unexplained reason, refused to stake out the lots; and by an act in the next year, it is ordered that the said Baltimore shall be laid out on a more commodious and navigable part of the river, and the surveyor and commissioners are commanded to have the work done before the following May. Whether the surveyor again proved contumacious or not, we cannot say, nor whether the town ever had any existence more substantial than this order for its erection; no further trace of it appears in the record.

The venerable town of Joppa, on the Gunpowder river, which succeeded to the Baltimore on Bush river, as the county seat, was once a place of no small consequence, as the various "Joppa roads," once highways of active traffic, still remain to testify. Yet Joppa had a rather serious struggle in coming into existence, and seemed in her infancy the sport of misadventure. In 1706, the assembly conceiving that the State needed more ports, towns and loading-places, to encourage the trade which it was hoped would grow up, erected a batch of forty-two by a single act, three of which were in Baltimore county: "at Whetstone Neck, on Patapsco river; upon the land called

[1] Map of Augustine Herrman, 1670. (This Herrman was a Bohemian by birth, who emigrated to the Dutch settlement at Manhattan. After his visit to Maryland, as one of the Dutch commissioners, he removed to the latter province, where he was naturalized in 1666. He took up land on Elk river, Cecil county, where "Bohemia manor" and "Port Herrman" still preserve his memory.) Vaugondy's map, 1755. Eman Bowen's map of North America, 1763. Bowen's map of Virginia and Maryland. Fry and Jefferson's map, 1775. In a map prepared to accompany Jefferson's *Notes on Virginia*, Baltimore appears on the northwest branch of the Patapsco, and the town on Bush river has dwindled to "Bush town."

Chilberry, in Bush river; and a town on Forster's Neck, on Gunpowder river."[1] Whether any beginning of the town was made or not, does not appear; but in the next year the assembly ordered the site at Forster's Neck "to be deserted, and in lieu thereof fifty acres to be erected into a town on a tract of land on the same river, belonging to Anne Felks, and called "Taylor's Choice," and the court-house to be built there."[2] Now the act had no validity—the province being then under royal government—until the queen's assent was obtained; but this would take a year, and probably no one imagined that Queen Anne, with her mind full of Marlborough and the French war, would have any objection to Forster's Neck as the location of the county court. So the commissioners went actively to work, laid off the town and had the court-house partly built, when the surprising news came that the queen had refused her assent to the bill. So matters stood; nor do we know where the court was held until 1712, when (the Tories being then in power, and Marlborough disgraced) a new act was passed, setting the county court at the house built on Taylor's Choice, "in the town of Joppa"—for here the name first appears.[3]

But Joppa had not yet reached the end of her troubles, and, indeed, seems to have been born under a disastrous planet. The court-house had been first built without legal authority, and now that this difficulty was got over, it was found that the commissioners had built it on the land of a minor, who could convey no valid title. This stumbling-block hindered Joppa's progress for twelve years more. The court-house and prison were built, but not a dwelling-house. Again the assembly came to the rescue, and legalized the conveyance by special act, but reduced the area of the town to twenty-one acres.[4]

After so many false starts, Joppa was now fairly on her way.[5] Like all these towns of the legislature's making, she was laid off into lots, intersected by streets, lanes and alleys; but, as if the assembly wished to punish the town for its own rashness and negligence, the lots were ordered to be of half

[1] Bacon's *Laws of Maryland.*

[2] *Ibid.*

[3] *Ibid.*

[4] *Ibid.*

[5] The "Act for erecting a town at Joppa, in Baltimore county, and for securing the land whereon the court-house and prisons are built," was passed by the General Assembly at the October session, in 1724. By this act, Thomas Tolley, Captain John Taylor, Daniel Scott, Lancelot Todd and John Stokes were appointed town commissioners. On the 20th of April, 1725, Messrs. Tolley, Taylor and Scott met at Joppa, and proceeded to lay off twenty-one acres of land—one acre for the use of St. John's parish Church—for the use of the town. The town was laid out into forty lots, exclusive of the church lot, and divided by Court street and Church street running east and west, and Low street and High street running nearly north and south. The lots were offered for entry at one pound, seven shillings each, to be paid to Colonel James Maxwell, whose land had been taken by the commissioners for the use of the town. Among those who took up lots were Colonel James Maxwell, Asaell Maxwell, son of James Maxwell, Colonel John Dorsey, for the use of his son Greenbury Dorsey, John Crockett, John Stokes, David Hughes, Thomas White, clerk of the town, Roger Matthews, Captain Thomas Sheredine, Aquila Paca, sheriff of the county, John Hall, Jr., John Roberts, Joseph Ward, inn-holder, Richard Hewitt, Nicholas Day, Thomas Tolley, Aquila Hall, William Hammond, Benjamin Jones, William Lowe, Joseph Calvert, late merchant of Kent county, James Isham, Catharine Hollingworth, widow, Samuel Ward, carpenter, Benjamin Johns, Abraham Johns, Stephen Higgins, Samuel Maccubbin, Hannah Ward, John Higginson, inn-holder, and Benjamin Rumsey.

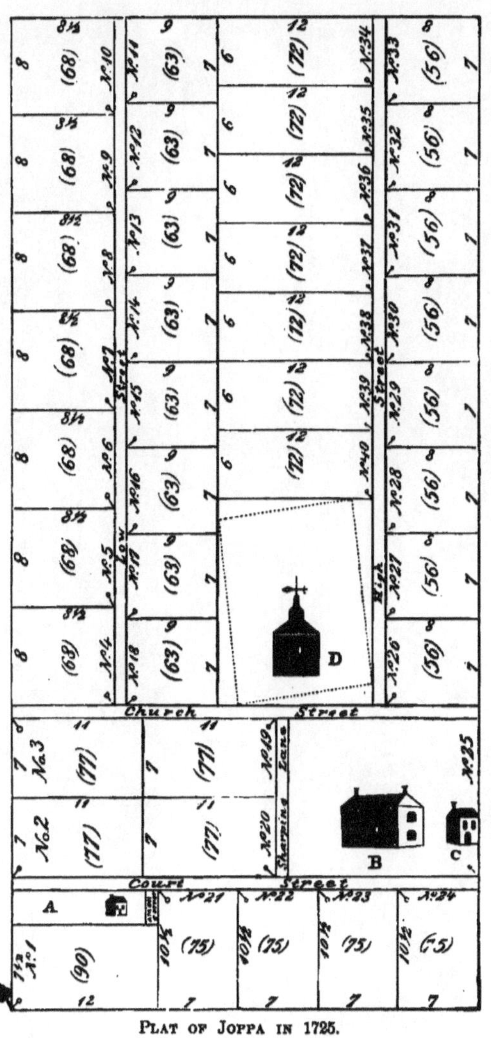

PLAT OF JOPPA IN 1725.

A—New Prison.
B—Court House.
C—Old Prison.
D—St. John's Parish Church.

the usual size, or half an acre each. Takers-up of lots were bound to build each a dwelling-house, covering not less than four hundred square feet, with a good brick or stone chimney. And so the new town flourished and became a great tobacco market, to which hogsheads were brought from all the upper parts of the country by a simple but practical contrivance then generally in use, which made each hogshead its own vehicle. A gudgeon, or pin, was fastened in each end, on which hoop-pole shafts were attached, and fastened to the horses' collar, who thus trundled the cask behind him; and the roads used for this transportation were called "rolling roads," by which name many of them are still known. To build up still further her commerce, all debtors paying their debts in tobacco at Joppa, were allowed a reduction of ten per cent. She became a port of entry, and had a respectable trade with Europe and the West Indies. Tradition says that so late as the American revolution a vessel of war was built there.

But the grandeur of Joppa was not destined to endure. As old Baltimore on Bush river had faded before her, so she wás to fade before Baltimore on the Patapsco. Her trade was drawn off, her population dwindled, her store-houses fell to ruin, her wharves rotted, and her harbor filled up with mud. Yet the ancient town has not, like old Baltimore, utterly vanished. A solitary house, once a stately mansion, built of bricks imported from England, and a few mouldering grave-stones, overgrown by weed and grass, still mark the site of the once flourishing town of Joppa.

Great expectations were built upon Charles town, in Cecil county, which was laid off in 1742, and which, it was hoped would gather in all the trade of the important region lying at the head of the bay. The unusual space of two hundred acres was laid out, and three hundred acres of adjacent woodland reserved for a common. Squares were laid off for a court-house, market-house, and other public buildings; a public wharf and stores were built, and a ship-yard constructed. The quit-rent to the proprietary was two pence per lot, or twice the usual rate. Two annual fairs were established, with privilege of exemption from arrest (except for felony or assault), for all persons attending them. A flour inspector was appointed, and an overseer of town matters in general. Forestalling, or buying provisions on their way to market, was forbidden under penalties. Finally, residents were relieved of the yearly poll tax of 40 lbs. tobacco for the support of the clergy, and from all other parochial dues. Such extraordinary immunities and privileges were granted to residents and traders, that Philadelphia grew alarmed, expecting her trade to be drawn off to this new centre of commerce; yet, thirty years later, a correspondent of the Pennsylvania *Chronicle*, asks, "What, I beseech you, is Charles town?—a deserted village, with a few miserable huts thinly scattered among the bushes, and daily crumbling into ruin." Though she did not fulfill the sanguine expectations of her founders, Charles town is still a thriving borough.

We have spoken of towns that have disappointed the hopes of their founders, but Baltimore—the Baltimore on the Patapsco—was destined far to surpass them. The Baltimore of to-day is, in fact, a congeries of three towns: "Baltimore town," a small settlement on the west side of Jones' Falls; "Jones' town," which was an earlier settlement on the east of the same stream; and "Fell's Point," which grew up to the southeast, on the outer basin. The first land taken up was on Whetstone Point, where Charles Gorsuch, a member of the Society of Friends, patented fifty acres in 1662. The next year, Alexander Mountenay took up two hundred acres on the other side of the northwest branch, in the bottom lands on both banks of Harford Run, and

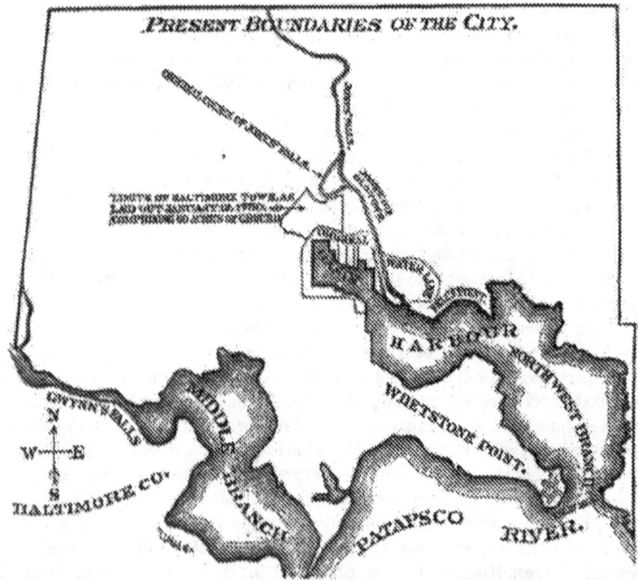

PLAT OF BALTIMORE.

gave his place the name of "Mountenay's Neck." In 1668, "Timber Neck," lying between the middle and north branches of the Patapsco, was taken up by John Howard, and in the same year the tract north of it—the site of the original Baltimore town—was granted to Thomas Cole. This tract, which was called "Coale's Harbor," contained five hundred and fifty acres, and extended from Mountenay's Neck, westward, along the north shore of the river for a mile, and northward about half a mile, having a rhomboidal form, and was divided into nearly equal parts by the stream afterwards known as Jones' Falls. Other patents were granted for lands on the east—Long Island Point, Kemp's Addition, Parker's Haven, and Copus's

Harbor (afterwards known as Fell's Point)—on the west, for Lunn's Lot, and Chatsworth; and for Darby Hall, Salisbury Plains, and Gallow Barry, on the north. All these lands, at a later date, were included within the limits of Baltimore.

In the course of time the mouth of the Patapsco began to be looked to as a favorable place for a town; but the flat lands along the southern branch, instead of the hilly slopes of the northwestern, seemed to offer the most desirable location, and Moale's Point, on Spring Garden, was pitched upon as the site. But the owner, John Moale, a merchant from Devonshire, had discovered an iron mine on his land by which he set prodigious store; and no sooner did he find that it was proposed to build a town on his territory, than he hurried off to Annapolis, and being a member of the legislature, succeeded in defeating the scheme. The projectors then turned their attention to the hilly country, bordered with marshes, on the northwestern branch, and here the town was to be.

It was on the 8th of August, 1729, that the "Act for Erecting a Town on the north side of Patapsco, in Baltimore county, and for laying out into lots sixty acres of land in and about the place whereon John Flemming now lives," was passed, at the application of "the leading men of Baltimore county." John Flemming was a tenant of Mr. Carroll, and his house stood on the bank of Uhler's run, about the present intersection of Charles and Lombard streets. The act made Baltimore a privileged place for landing, loading and selling goods; and Major Thomas Tolley, William Hamilton, William Buckner, Dr. George Walker, Richard Gist, Dr. George Buchanan, and Col. William Hammond, were appointed commissioners to lay off the new town, which was to be called "Baltimore Town."

On the 1st of December, 1729, these commissioners bought from Daniel and Charles Carroll the tract of sixty acres, paying therefor the price of forty shillings per acre, in money or tobacco, or one hundred and twenty pounds for the whole; and on the 12th of January, with the assistance of Philip Jones, the county surveyor, they laid off the town. The boundary began at a point near the northwest corner of the present Pratt and Light streets, and ran thence northwesterly along or near Uhler's alley towards what was then called a "great eastern road," and "a great gully" or ravine at or near Sharp street; thence across the present Baltimore street, keeping to the east of the gully, and in a northeast direction, to the precipice overhanging the Falls about the present southwest corner of St. Paul and Saratoga streets; then along the bank of Jones' Falls (which at that time made a sudden bend in its course, bringing it to the last-named corner) southwardly and eastwardly various courses, to the low grounds lying ten perches west of Gay street; then due south along the margin of those low grounds to the bank on the north side of the river, which then came up nearly to the site of the present custom-house; and thence by that bank various courses nearly as Lombard street runs, westwardly and southwardly to the place of beginning.

27

The town was next divided by Long street, now Baltimore street, four perches wide, and running 132¾ perches east and west, intersected at right angles by Calvert street (not then named,) also four perches wide, running 56¾ perches from the hill near the falls north, to the river-side south, and by Forrest street (now Charles,) three perches wide, and 89¼ long, in the same course. There were also nine lanes of the width of one perch each, eight of which, afterwards widened, became German, Hanover, St. Paul, Light, South, North (formerly Belvidere,) Second and East streets, while Lovely lane retains its original dimensions. The land intersected by these streets was then divided into rectangular lots, averaging about an acre each, and num-

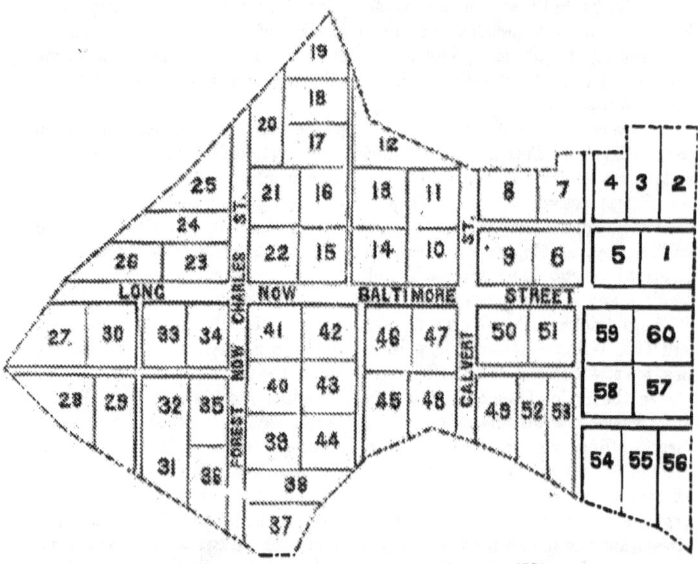

ORIGINAL PLAN OF BALTIMORE AS LAID OUT IN 1730.

bered from one to sixty, beginning on the north side of Long street and running westward, then returning eastward on the south side. Two days later, the 14th, an office was opened for purchasers of lots, and the proprietor of the soil, Mr. Carroll, selected No. 49, on the east side of Calvert street, running down to the river, Mr. Gist taking the corresponding lot on the other side of the street. Other lots were taken up by residents of the vicinity, and some, remaining untaken for seven years, reverted to the original proprietor.

Thus began the original town of Baltimore, which formed the nucleus of the present city, and still remains its centre It was comprised, as we have seen, within the western basin of the Patapsco, which then reached up about as high as Lombard street, on the south, the clay hills of Charles and Saratoga streets on the north, the deep drain and gully which ran down nearly in the course of Liberty street and McClellan's alley on the west, and on the east by the great marsh which bordered Jones' Falls, and ran up by its west bank to somewhere about the junction of Frederick and Gay streets. The Falls, its absolute easternmost limit, swept round in a deep horseshoe curve, convex toward the southwest, a short distance above the present Gay street bridge, the toe of the horseshoe reaching as far as the corner of Calvert and Lexington streets. The course of the stream was afterwards straightened, and the piece of meadow-land in the curve brought into Baltimore proper.

It would seem from the small dimensions of the original plan, and its narrow natural limits of hills, waters and marshes, that no great extension of its boundaries was anticipated. While this diversity of surface gives great beauty and variety to the present city, it has placed obstacles in the way of its extension which few other American cities have had to contend with. Marshes have been drained, hollows filled up, hills levelled, streams bridged, walled in and tunnelled; and still as the city grows, difficulties present themselves, requiring all our engineering skill to master; while the eccentricities of Jones' Falls, a pacific brook for the most part, but subject at long intervals to freshets which convert it into a swollen and boiling torrent, laying the lower part of the city under water, still perplex the city authorities. Despite these disadvantages, however, the site presented so many desirable features that the town was enabled to hold its own. The hills to the north and west, with their rapid streams, afforded abundant water-power for milling; the soil was more fertile than in the sandy regions to the south and east; the harbor was admirably safe, and deep enough for the light-draft vessels that carried on our first commerce; the climate was less rigorous in winter than that of the regions nearer the mouth of the Susquehannah, and more healthy than that of the coast settlements lower down the bay. Forests of fine timber surrounded it: oak, chestnut and other deciduous trees to the north and west, and yellow or pitch pine and other conifers to the south and east; building stone of fine quality, and mines of rich iron ore, were within easy hauling distance. In fact, Baltimore lies at the junction of two botanical and two geological systems, and enjoys the advantages of both.

Of these advantages, however, not all were known at the time of the first settlement; and the original settlers seem to have been most impressed with those of the harbor, as we find that within the first three days all the lots toward the river were taken up, and but one of those on Long street. Yet but a single street—Calvert street—actually reached navigable water; for the alluvion carried down by the Falls made the northern side of the basin a mere mud shoal, with islands overflowed at high tide; while between the eastern limits of the city and the Falls was a large marsh, reaching down to the

owner of the land refused to build, any person building a substantial warehouse, not less than twenty feet square, thereon, acquired the fee simple of a lot forty feet square, including the ground on which his warehouse stood. Four rolling-roads are laid out. To encourage trade, merchants, or the officers of ships that made two voyages to the port, were to have the privileges of freemen of the town during their sojourn. By a Petitionary Act, a school, or academy, is founded, bearing the name of King William School, with a board of trustees, at whose head was Governor Nicholson, who were constituted rectors, governors, and visitors of the free schools of Maryland, and were empowered to found schools throughout the province, and to make laws and receive donations for them. Of this school, one of Maryland's most distinguished citizens, William Pinkney, was, in after years, a student.

In 1697, the new state-house[1] is completed; and minute directions are given in an Act of Assembly for locating the various offices of government in it. King William is petitioned "that some part of the revenue given towards furnishing arms and ammunition for the use of the province, be laid out for the purchase to be added to the books which had been presented by the king, to form a library in the port of Annapolis, and that a portion of the public revenue be applied to the enlargement thereof."[2] Many of the books given by the king are now preserved in the library of St. John's College.

In 1699, Annapolis is made the chief place and seat of justice in the province; all assemblies and provincial courts are to be held here, and here all writs are made returnable. In 1704, the state-house was burnt, and another immediately begun, which was finished in 1706. The next year the good town was thrown into commotion by the nefarious conduct of one Richard Clarke, who, if the charges alleged against him were true, must have been a miscreant of no common magnitude. He is charged with counterfeiting, and with plotting to destroy the public records, blow up the magazine, burn the town, and then take to the high seas as a pirate. It would seem that he proposed to perpetrate these enormities single-handed, as we find no action taken against any confederates. An act for his attainder was passed, and as he refused to surrender himself, he was attainted of high treason and condemned to death. But the worthy Annapolitans, like the Nuremburgers of old, "never hung a man until they had caught him"; and it is probable that Richard Clarke took good care to keep out of their clutches.

[1] This building is frequently called the "Stadt-house," the Dutch word *Stadt*, with many others of that tongue, having grown familiar to English ears since the accession of "Dutch William." A short time before, the assembly conferred upon Oxford the name of "Williamstadt."

[2] It is possible that this petition may have been suggested by King William's celebrated gift of books to the (Whig) University of Cambridge, at the same time that he sent a troop of horse to (Tory) Oxford. This distribution of the royal favors gave rise to the following epigram by a Tory wit:

"The king, observing with judicious eyes
The state of both his universities.
To one he sent a troop of horse—for why?—
That learned body wanted loyalty.
To the other he sent books, as well discerning
How much that loyal body wanted learning."

To which it was not less happily replied:

"The king to Oxford sent a troop of horse,
For Tories own no argument but force;
With equal care to Cambridge books he sent,
For Whigs allow no force but argument."

In 1708, Annapolis was erected into a city under a charter from Governor Seymour, and obtained the privilege of sending two delegates to the assembly; while the venerable town of St. Mary's, which had been declining from the time she ceased to be the capital of the province, was deprived of her representation, which seems to have been the last blow to her falling fortunes. Annapolis, on the contrary, grew and prospered exceedingly, and became famous for the wealth, luxury and elegance of her inhabitants.

Frederick city, the next in wealth and population to Baltimore, was laid out in the year 1745, and its name given in honor of Frederick, the son of the proprietary. The first house within the present limits of the city was built in 1748.[1]

In the same year Frederick county was erected, embracing the territory now included in Frederick, Montgomery, Washington, Alleghany, Garrett, and part of Carroll counties, being about three-fourths of the land-area of the province. Most of its early settlers were of German birth or descent, though a few were of Scotch and Irish lineage. They were an industrious, frugal, temperate people, tilling their farms, accustomed to conflict with savage and other enemies on the border, and distinguished for their bold and independent spirit. Their history forms a conspicuous part of the annals of Maryland during the French and Revolutionary wars.

We have seen how pacific and just a policy was pursued by the Maryland colonists in acquiring lands from the Indians by purchase rather than conquest, and the happy results that followed this course in the general friendliness and mutual confidence that for a long time prevailed between the white settlers and the natives. In those cases where the local attachments of the Indian tribes outweighed their cupidity, they were not only permitted to retain their lands, but protected in their possessions. Thus in 1698 an act was passed, and renewed in 1704 and 1723, to assure to Panquash and Annotoughquan, two chiefs of the Nanticokes, the possession of their lands in Dorchester county. In the preamble to this equitable law, the assembly say, "It being most just that the Indians, the ancient inhabitants of this province, should have a convenient dwelling-place in their native country, free from the encroachments and oppressions of the English, more especially the Nanticoke Indians in Dorchester county, who, for these many years have lived in peace and concord with the English, and in all matters in obedience to the government of this province."[2] As an acknowledgment of the authority of the proprietary, they were only required to pay him annually the nominal tribute of one beaver skin.

In the next year (1705,) some hostile symptoms being apparent among the Indians, Colonel Thomas Ennalls was commissioned by Governor Seymour to negotiate a treaty with the Nanticokes; and on May 19th articles of peace

[1] The commissioners, in laying out the streets, intended that they should run toward the cardinal points; but their surveyor, having but very rude instruments and a defective compass, accomplished this object but imperfectly.

[2] Bacon, ch. lviii; 1704.

were concluded with the two chiefs above mentioned, they having been duly appointed to act on behalf of "Asquash, 'Emperor' of the Nanticokes, Winnoughquargno, 'King' of the Babcoes and Ahatchwoops, and with Robin Hood, chief of the Indian River Indians, on behalf of his queen Wyraufconmickonono, queen of the said Indians." The treaty is similar to that made with the Piscataways in 1666, with the exception of a stipulation that Asquash should pay yearly to Colonel Ennalls, for the use of the Queen of England, four arrows and two bows, to be delivered to the Governor, "as a tribute or acknowledgement to her majesty, and as a token of the continuance of this peace." The chiefs complained to Colonel Ennalls that the English brought spirituous liquors into their territory and sold them to their people; and in consequence of this complaint the governor issued a proclamation the same year, empowering "the great men of the Indian towns, upon such liquors being brought thither, to break and stave the bottles, casks, and barrels, or overset and spill such other vessels wherein such liquors shall be, without being troubled to answer any complaint on that score." This proclamation, it seems, did not put an end to the traffic, and probably the "great men" were indisposed to exercise the powers conferred upon them, for in 1715 we find an act passed forbidding all persons from carrying liquor to any Indian town or within three miles thereof, and selling the same to any Indian, under penalty of 5000 lbs. tobacco; or selling above one gallon of spirits or fermented liquor to any Indian in one day; or exchanging liquor for their guns or "match-coats."[1]

In this year (1705,) the chief, Robin Hood, represented to the governor that his tribe had at first occupied "a town called Buckingham," and that by the continual encroachments of the whites they had been compelled to remove, first to Assawamen, and then to Indian river, where they now were; and he made petition that they should be confirmed in their present habitations, and a thousand acres of land granted them; which was asssented to. By an Act of Assembly in 1711, Lieutenant Colonel George Gale, Samuel Worthington, Captain Charles Ballard, and Benjamin West, were appointed commissioners to lay out three thousand acres of land on Broad creek, in Nanticoke river, Somerset county, on which the Nanticokes were settled, "to remain to the use of the said Indians so long as they shall occupy the same."[2]

In 1742, the Six Nations advanced a claim to a considerable portion of Maryland territory lying along the Susquehannah and Potomac rivers, and including the Eastern shore of the Chesapeake bay. A war between England and France then being imminent, this claim created great uneasiness in Maryland, Virginia and Pennsylvania, as the alienation of the Indian tribes at such a time was much to be dreaded. Other causes of uneasiness arose, in which the province was more particularly concerned. John Armstrong, an Indian trader, and his two servants, were murdered by Delaware Indians on the

[1] Bacon; 1715.

[2] Bacon, ch. 1; 1711.

border. Governor Thomas of Pennsylvania, was requested by the Six Nations "to write in their behalf, to the governor or owner of the land in Maryland and to the Governor of Virginia, to let them know that they expected some consideration for the same, and were willing to leave it with their brethren in Philadelphia." If their request was refused, they proposed to appeal to the "Great King over the great sea." Governor Thomas sent a messenger to Governor Bladen, and despatched Conrad Weiser, the provincial interpreter, to the Indians to renew assurances of friendship and to offer mediation.

As it was of great moment that the province should not be involved in hostilities with this powerful confederacy, which it seemed but too plain was seeking a pretext for quarrel, Governor Bladen recommended that a peaceful settlement be attempted by purchasing the lands claimed. The assembly concurred in this view; but a contest arose on the question whether they or the governor had the right of appointing the commissioners for the negotiation. The governor made his appointments, but the assembly asserted their right by adding to them Dr. Robert King and Charles Carroll, and drew up instructions for their government.

This gave great offence to the governor, who regarded the act as a usurpation of his powers, and refused to confirm their proceedings. The house remained firm and the negotiations were suspended.

In the meantime at a conference held with the Six Nations at Philadelphia on the 7th of July, 1742, Conassateego, chief of the Onondagoes, gave the alarm when he said "that the lands on the west side of the Susquehannah were paid for by the proprietary, [of Pennsylvania] but that those taken up by the people in the south of the province was not." He also said that they (the Six Nations,) had written to the Governor of Maryland and had as yet heard nothing, and he now said to Governor Thomas:

> "If you have not done anything, we now renew our request, and desire you will inform the person whose people are seated on our lands, that that country belongs to us in right of conquest, we having bought with our blood, and taken it from our enemies in fair war; and we expect as owners of that land to receive such a consideration for it as the land is worth. We desire you will press him to send us a positive answer. Let him say yes or no. If he says yes, we will treat with him. If no, we are able to do ourselves justice, and we will do it, by going to take payment ourselves."

The governor replied that he would write to the Governor of Maryland, and he had no doubt they would receive justice.[1]

The threats thrown out by this Indian chief did not have the desired effect on the assembly, for they adhered with unshaken firmness to the position they had taken, as incident to their control over the public interests and the public revenue.

The Shawnee Indians, however, became dissatisfied at the failure of the claim which the Six Nations had made to the lands west of the Susquehannah in Maryland, and endeavored to induce the Eastern shore Indians to enter

[1] Ridgely's MS. of the *Archives of Maryland*, in the Land Office.

into a conspiracy with them to rise and massacre the settlers. The plot was discovered by a few friendly Indians and communicated to the authorities, who promply placed the frontiers in a state of defence.

The following account of the visit of the Shawnee emissaries to the Nanticokes and Choptanks, is taken from the affidavits on record at Annapolis:

"The examination of Jemmy Smallhommoney, one of the Atchawamp Indians of Great Choptank, taken before me, Henry Hooper, one of his Lordship's Justices of the Provincial Court, taken this 25th day of June, 1742. This examinant saith that about the middle of May last, there was an agreement made between some Indians that came from Shawan (being 23 in number) and the several nations of our own Indians, to rise and cut off the English, and that two of our Indians went up with them in order to know the time, which was agreed on to be this moon; and to be assisted with 500 of the Shawan and Northern Indians, and about the same time the French, with the assistance of other Indians were to attack the back inhabitants of Maryland and Pennsylvania. This examinant further saith that the several nations of our Indians have built a lodge house about 20 feet long and 15 feet wide in Pocomoke Swamp for a repository to secure their arms and ammunition, and that they now in the said house have several guns with a good deal of ammunition, and a large quantity of poisoned arrows pointed with brass, and that they intended to begin the attack in Somerset and Dorsett, and several places in one and the same night, and when they had cut off the English in those two counties, to extend their conquest upwards till they had joined the other Indians and the French.

"This Deponent further saith the said Indians intended to destroy man, woman and child, as far as they extended their conquest, &c.

his
"JEMMY x SMALLHOMMONY.
mark."

"Taken the day and year above written by me,
"HENRY HOOPER."

Having failed to bring the Lower House of Assembly to subjection, Governor Bladen was at length, in 1744, driven to the necessity of appointing the commissioners upon his own responsibility, and of accomplishing the objects of the mission by the ordinary revenue of the government. The commissioners sent by him were Edmund Jennings, Philip Thomas, Robert King, and Thomas Colville, by whom, in conjunction with the representatives of Virginia and Pennsylvania, a treaty was concluded with the chiefs of the Six Nations, at the town of Lancaster, Pennsylvania, on the 30th of June, 1744, under which their claims to the territory of Maryland were satisfactorily settled. The Indians engaged to prevent the French, and the Indians in their alliance, from marching through their country to attack the English settlements; and that they would give the earliest information they received of the enemy's designs; and in consideration of four hundred pounds, they recognized the title of the king to the colonies of Virginia and Maryland as they were then, or should be, afterwards, bounded. The favor of the Indians was obtained by Pennsylvania presenting them with three hundred pounds currency; Maryland one hundred pounds; and Virginia two hundred pounds, with the addition of a promise to recommend the Six Nations to the consideration of his majesty. The following is the tenor of that part of the treaty, which extinguished the Indian claims to the Maryland settlements:

"Now know ye, that for and in consideration of the sum of three hundred pounds current money of Pennsylvania, paid and delivered to the above named sachems or chiefs, partly in goods and partly in gold money, by the said commissioners, they, the said sachems or chiefs, on behalf of the said nations, do hereby renounce and disclaim to the right honorable the Lord Baltimore, lord proprietary of the said province of Maryland, his heirs and assigns, all pretence of right or claim whatsoever, of the said Six Nations, of, in, or to any lands that lie on Potomac, alias Cohongaroutan, or Susquehanna rivers, or in any other place between the great bay of Chesapeake and a line beginning at about two miles above the uppermost fork of Cohongaroutan or Potomac, on the north branch of the said fork; near which fork Captain Thomas Cresap has a hunting or trading cabin, and from thence, by a north course, to the boundaries of the province of Pennsylvania, and so with the bounds of the said province of Pennsylvania to Susquehanna river; but in case such limits shall not include the present inhabitants or settlers, then so many line or lines, course or courses, from the said two miles above the fork, to the outermost inhabitant or settlement, as shall include every settlement and inhabitant of Maryland, and from thence by a north line to the bounds of the province of Pennsylvania, shall be deemed and construed the limits intended by these presents; anything herein before contained to the contrary, notwithstanding. And the said sachems or chiefs do hereby, on behalf of the said Six United Nations, declare their consent and agreement to be, that every person or persons whatsoever, who now is, or shall be hereafter settled or seated in any part of the said province, so as to be out of the limits aforesaid, shall, nevertheless, continue in their peaceable possessions free and undisturbed, and be esteemed as brethren by the Six Nations. In witness whereof, the said sachems or chiefs, for themselves, and on behalf of the people of the Six Nations aforesaid, have hereunto set their hands and seals, the thirtieth day of June, in the year of our Lord, one thousand seven hundred and forty-four."

The Nanticokes, who had yielded to the mild influence of the colony, and became peaceful dwellers under its protection, now began to remove from the province. The causes that induced their tribe to leave the colony, were, that the game, on which they mainly depended for subsistence, had either been destroyed or driven away; their numbers were rapidly diminishing; and crowded as they were on all sides, by a population whose vices their young people were more prone to adopt, than to imitate their virtues, they saw that their choice lay between extermination or removal to a country better adapted to their habits. They, therefore, after the treaty at Lancaster, made application to the governor and council for permission to remove from the province. In the council proceedings for the year 1744, we find the following entry, relating to this subject:

"Simon Alsechqueck and three other Nanticoke Indians appeared at this board, and on behalf of themselves and the rest of the said Nanticoke Indians now residing in this province, desire that they, the said Nanticoke Indians, may be permitted to leave Maryland, and to live amongst the Six Nations of Indians, and that this board would be pleased to direct a pass might be given them. Which being granted, they had a pass in the following words, viz: 'Maryland, SS: Whereas, in the late treaty with the Six Nations of Indians, the commissioners for this province promised the chiefs of the said Six Nations that the Nanticoke Indians should be permitted, if they should desire it, to leave Maryland, and live amongst the Six Nations, or where they (the Six Nations) should appoint, and whereas, the said Nanticoke Indians have applied to the governor and council for leave to depart this province and to remove to the Six Nations, or to such place as they shall appoint them to live in out of this province. In compliance, therefore, with the said promise made to the Six Nations, the said Nanticoke Indians are hereby permitted to depart this province, and all his Majesty's subjects inhabiting the same are strictly charged and required to suffer the said Indians to pass, without any molestation or disturbance, they behaving quietly and peaceably. Given under my hand and seal this 13th day of September, Anno Domini 1744."

By degrees they began to remove, and in 1748 the great body of them departed from the Eastern shore to different places, and became scattered abroad. Some went to the head waters of the Susquehannah: some to the northern parts of New York, and some into Canada. Rev. Christian Pyrlaeus, a Moravian missionary, at the settlement on the Forks of the Delaware, says that "On the 21st of May, 1748, a number of the Nanticokes from Maryland passed by Shamokin in ten canoes, on their way to Wyoming."[1]

These Indians, among others, had the singular custom of removing the bones of their deceased friends and ancestors to the country to which they emigrated. "In earlier times they were known to go from Wyoming and Chemenk to fetch the bones of their dead from the Eastern shore of Maryland, even when the bodies were in a putrid state, so that they had to take off the flesh and scrape the bones clean, before they could carry them along." "I well remember," adds Mr. Heckewelder, "having seen them between the years 1750 and 1760 loaded with such bones, which, being fresh, caused a disagreeable stench, as they passed through the town of Bethlehem." Not all the Nanticokes, however, left the province, for we find there were still a sufficient number remaining who desired to be governed by an "Emperor," as was shown by the petition of the Nanticokes of Dorchester in 1757 to Governor Sharpe, to appoint Peter Monk to that dignity; and in July of the same year a large number of them assembled at Nanticoke, their town, and selected as their chief George Pocatous, "a descendant of the family of old Panquash, one of those Indians to whom his lordship gave the grant for the Nanticoke town lands" in 1704. The several remnants of this once numerous tribe, numbering nearly one hundred persons, were, in 1853, settled on lands upon the upper waters of the Grand river, north of Lake Erie. The Choptank Indians never left the State, but remained upon their lands and drew yearly their annuities. They intermarried with the negroes until the race became entirely extinct. It is said the last survivor of their tribe died a few years before the late war between the States.

We note about this time the appearance of the Baptist denomination as an important element of the colony. The first prominent Baptist of whom we have notice was Henry Sator, an immigrant from England, who settled near

[1] Heckewelder. p. 75.

Chestnut Ridge. He organized a congregation at his house, of which George Eglesfield, of Pennsylvania, was pastor. He was succeeded by Paul Palmer, and Henry Loveall; and in 1742 a church was formed with fifty-seven members, who subscribed a declaration of faith laid before the governor. In four years the church numbered one hundred and eighty-one members, and its membership extended into Virginia. A church of Particular Baptists was organized in Harford county about 1772, which extended to Baltimore, where a church was erected on the southeast corner of Fayette and Front streets; Messrs. David Shields, George Presstman, Richard Lemmon, Alexander McKim and others, furnishing the means, and opened in 1785.

On June 29th, 1740, the king made a requisition on Maryland to raise and equip five hundred volunteers for service against Spain, with which country war had broken out the previous year. The assembly voted £2,560, afterwards increasing the sum to £5,000. The volunteers thus raised were sent to Carthagena to join the forces of Wentworth and Vernon, and, it is said, that nine-tenths of the colonial levies perished in the terrible mortality that raged in the British forces, and carried off, as we are told, twenty thousand men. During this war the Spanish privateers did considerable damage to colonial commerce; and several entering the Chesapeake, plundered plantations on the Eastern shore.

NOTE ON AUGUSTINE HERMANN AND THE LABADISTS OF BOHEMIA MANOR.

This Hermann was a man of some importance in the early days of the colony. He was a native of Prague, Bohemia, whence he emigrated to the Dutch settlements at Manhattan. We have already given some account of his mission from Stuyvesant to the Maryland authorities, after which he visited Virginia. About this time, 1660, he proposed to Lord Baltimore to make an exact map of the country, if his Lordship would be pleased to grant "him a certain tract of land as an inheritance to his posterity, and the privileges of a manor."

"By letter, September 18, his Lordship, in acceptance thereof, recommended the granting to the Honorable Philip Calvert, Esquire, then governor—and was then supposed, the one tract to contain about 4,000 acres, the other 1,000 acres, good plantable land—danger of Indians not then permitting a certain inspection nor survey of that far remote, then unknown wilderness.

"Whereupon, January 14, a Patent of free Denization issueth forth out of the office; and Augustine Hermann bought all the land there (by permission of the Governor and Council) of the Susquehanoh Indians, then met with the great men out of the Susquehanoh Fort at Spes-Uty Isle, upon a treaty of Soldiers, as the old record will testify, and thereupon took possession; and transported his people from Manhattan, now New York, 1661 (with great cost and charge), to inhabit."[1]

This land was patented to him on October 12, 1663, under the name of Bohemia, or Bohemia Manor. By subsequent additions it was increased to nearly twenty thousand acres, lying in both Maryland and Delaware, and just west of Elk river. From the conditions attached to the grant of a manor, as well as from the expressions about the transportation of "his people" above quoted, it will be seen that Hermann was a man of considerable substance. In 1664, he and his family were naturalized as citizens of Maryland by an Act of Assembly—the first act of the kind passed in the colonies.

[1] Herman's *Journal*.

In 1670, his map was published, copies of which are still extant. It is adorned with his portrait, representing a gentleman of about fifty years of age, of rather saturnine, but not unpleasing features, set off by the full-bottomed periwig of Charles the Second's time, the whole surrounded by the legend, "*Augustine Hermann, Bohemensis.*"

Mr. Lednum says of him: "It is said that the Dutch had him a prisoner of war at one time, under sentence of death, in New York. A short time before he was to be executed, he feigned himself to be deranged in mind, and requested that his horse should be brought to him in the prison. The horse was brought, finely caparisoned, Hermann mounted him, and seemed to be performing military exercises, when, on the first opportunity, he bolted through one of the large windows that was some fifteen feet above ground, leaped down, swam the North river, run his horse through Jersey, and alighted on the bank of the Delaware, opposite New Castle, and thus made his escape from death and the Dutch. This daring feat, tradition says, he had transferred to canvas—himself represented as standing by the side of his charger, from whose nostrils the blood was flowing. It is said a copy of this painting still exists. He never suffered this horse to be used afterwards, and when he died had him buried, and honored his grave with a tombstone. . . . . . Hermann was the great man of the region; he had his deer park—the walls of it are still (1859) standing; he rode in his coach, driven by liveried servants; his mansion commanded a fine view of the Bohemia River to the Chesapeake Bay."[1]

On the 11th of August, 1684, Augustine Hermann conveyed by deed to Peter Sluyter, *alias* Vorsman, Jasper Dauckaets, *alias* Schilders, of Friesland, Petrus Bayard, of New York, and John Moll and Arnoldus de la Grange, of Delaware, in company, 3,750 acres of land, bounded on the west by Long Creek, north by the great cart-road leading to Reedy Island, in the Delaware, east by the Appoquinimink path leading from the great cart-road to the head of Bohemia river, and south by Bohemia river, known afterwards as the Labadie tract.

"The whole of this tract, with the exception of a few acres, lies within the State of Maryland in Cecil county, the line between Delaware and Maryland crossing its eastern extremity just before reaching the Bohemia River.

"The grantees in the deed from Herman, were members of a religious community at the small village of Wiewerd, in Friesland. They professed a kind of mysticism, regulating their lives by the divine light of the inner man, and seeking to bring together all the elect of God, separate from the world, into one visible church, which, as they said, like a city set upon a hill, could not be hid. In doctrine they held the tenets of the Dutch Reformed church; but they also maintained other opinions and adopted practices not recognized by the authority of that church."[2]

Its founder, Jean de Labadie, an enthusiast who had been dismissed from the order of Jesuits, founded this new "Evangelical church" in Amsterdam about the year 1669. Owing to the burgomasters forbidding any one from attending the services of de Labadie, he and his adherents removed to Erfurt, where, owing to their peculiar customs, the Imperial Diet compelled them to remove in 1672 to Altona where de Labadie died. In a short time disputes arose between them and the authorities, and after various migrations they settled at the village of Wiewerd, in Friesland. To secure a safe retreat for the society and extend the boundaries of the church, the community, shortly after their removal to Wiewerd, resolved upon colonization in America. As a measure of precaution, however, they sent Jasper Dankers and Peter Sluyter, two of the ablest members of the community, on a tour of observation through New York and the adjoining colonies. The two travellers, after visiting the settlements in the colonies of New York and New Jersey, along the Delaware, and as far as the Chesapeake, were most pleased with a portion of Bohemia Manor. They returned to Friesland and made a favorable report, and the consequence was that a company of men and women came from Wiewerd, inclu-

[1] *Methodism in America*, p. 277. [2] H. C. Murphy, *Memoirs Long Island Historical Society*, I., p. 12.

ding several families; a few persons from New York also removed thither. "Thus really was formed not only a new colony in America, but the daughter church, *dochter gemeente*, as they themselves were pleased to style it, of the Labadists of Walta House, of which Peter Sluyter declared himself the bishop, under Yvon, archbishop at Wiewerd."

Sluyter became the sole proprietor of the land and sole director of the church, and exercised the severest discipline over the members. He, at the same time, carried on a brisk trade in planting tobacco and selling negroes. Mr. Samuel Brownas, a Quaker preacher, who visited Bohemia Manor, in 1702, thus briefly describes his visit:

"After we had dined we took our leave, and a friend, my guide, went with me, and brought me to a people called Labadies, where we were civilly entertained in their way. When supper came in, it was placed upon a long table in a large room, where, when all things were ready, came in at a call, twenty men or upwards, but no women. We all sat down, they placing me and my companion near the head of the table, and, having passed a short space, one pulled off a hat, but not the rest, till a short space after, and then, one after another, they pulled all their hats off, and in that uncovered posture sat silent, uttering no words that we could hear, near half a quarter of an hour; and as they did not uncover at once, so neither did they cover themselves again at once; but as they put on their hats, fell to eating, not regarding those who were still uncovered, so that it might be ten minutes' time or more, between the first and last putting on of their hats. I afterwards queried with my companion, concerning the reason of their conduct, and he gave for answer that they held it unlawful to pray until they felt some inward motion for the same; and that secret prayer was more acceptable than to utter words; and that it was most proper for every one to pray as moved thereto by the spirit in their own minds.

"I likewise queried if they had no women amongst them? He told me they had, but the women eat by themselves, and the men by themselves, having all things in common, respecting their household affairs, so that none could claim any more right than another to any part of their stock, whether in trade or in husbandry; and if any had a mind to join with them, whether rich or poor, they must put what they had in the common stock, and afterwards, if they had a mind to leave the society, they must likewise leave what they brought, and go out empty-handed.

"They frequently expounded the scriptures among themselves, and being a very large family, in all upwards of a hundred men, women and children, carried on something of the manufactory of linen, and had a large plantation of corn, tobacco, flax and hemp, together with cattle of several kinds."

Mr. Murphy says: "They slept in the same or adjoining buildings, but in different rooms, which were not accessible to each other, but were ever open to the father, or such as he appointed for the purpose of instruction or examination. Their meals were eaten in silence, and it is related that persons often eat together, at the same table, for months, at Wiewerd, without knowing each others' names. They worked at different employments in the house, or on the land, or at trades, and were distributed for that purpose by the head of the establishment. Their dress was plain and simple, eschewing all fashions of the world. Gold and silver ornaments, jewelry, pictures, hangings, carpets, lace, and other fancy work were prohibited, and if any of the members had previously worked at such trades, they had to abandon them. They worked for the Lord and not for themselves. . . All the desires or aversions of the flesh . . were to be mortified or conquered. These mortifications were to be undergone willingly. A former minister might be seen standing at the wash-tub, or a young man of good extraction might be drawing stone or attending cattle. If any one had a repugnance to a particular food, he must eat it nevertheless. They must make confession of their sinful thoughts in open meeting. Those who were disobedient, were punished by a reduction of clothing, or being placed lower down the table, or final exclusion from the society."

In the year 1722, Peter Sluyter, the founder of the colony at Bohemia Manor, died, and the "mother church and daughter church" expired about the same time.

CHAPTER XV.

DIFFICULTIES between England and France had arisen at intervals since the peace of Utrecht (1713), though not assuming the character of war. In 1741, however, the wretched war of the Austrian Succession (arising from the pragmatic sanction of the Emperor Charles VI., by which he settled his Austrian dominions upon his daughter, Maria Theresa) broke out, and Great Britain, to her extreme disgust, became embroiled in it through her Hanoverian connexion. War was declared between her and France in March, 1744; and this involved the American colonies of both nations in what was known as "King George's War," a phrase which indicates the way in which it was regarded by Englishmen in both hemispheres. Before the declaration had reached the provinces, an armament was fitted out at Louisburg under Duvivier, which surprised the English garrison at Canseau, May 13th, took eighty prisoners, and broke up the fishery. Other places being threatened, Governor Shirley, of Massachusetts, conceived the design of attacking the French settlements at Cape Breton, and, if possible, taking Louisburg, its capital, which afforded a safe harbor for the largest French vessels, and a place of rendezvous for their numerous privateers now infesting the western shores of the Atlantic. As the design originated with the people of New England and had not been sanctioned by the crown, Commodore Warren, the English commander on the American station, declined to co-operate in the attack. The plan, however, was soon communicated to the British government, and was warmly approved. Arrangements were made for carrying it out promptly, and circulars were addressed to the other colonies as far south as Pennsylvania, asking their help; but with the exception of a grant of provisions from Pennsylvania and New Jersey, and a train of artillery from New York, no general assistance was furnished, and the charge of the expedition devolved upon New England. After two month's siege, during which the provincial forces displayed courage, activity, and fortitude that would have distinguished veteran troops, the town, on June 17, surrendered.

The capture of Louisburg "filled Europe with astonishment and America with joy." In London the cannon of the Tower and Park were fired, and at night there were great rejoicings, with bonfires and illuminations, and a general elation was felt throughout the kingdom. When the news reached Annapolis, by an express from Governor Shirley to Governor Bladen, on the 15th of July, unbounded enthusiasm prevailed. Bells were rung, cannon fired, bonfires blazed, and everywhere there were "drinking of healths and other demonstrations of joy." No event had ever filled the province with such excitement. In some of the counties subscriptions were made for the benefit of the soldiers and their families, and the Lower House of the Assembly voted £2,000—afterwards raised to £3,000—"to be laid out in provisions; with half a ton of gunpowder, and two tons and a half of lead and leaden bullets, to be taken out of our magazine; to be forthwith sent to his majesty's garrison at Louisburg, Cape Breton."[1] This being the most brilliant, and only decisive advantage gained during the war, the British officers attempted to arrogate to themselves the chief credit of the exploit by magnifying the services of the fleet; but the conspicuous merit of the provincial forces extorted at length the recognition it deserved. Colonel Pepperel, an officer of little experience, but great spirit and activity, was rewarded with the title of baronet, and a regiment was given him in the English e blishment in America. A like honor was conferred upon Governor S .rley, and parliament voted the reimbursement of the expenses incurred in the expedition.

While these things were happening in the North and East, the Shawanese Indians on the Ohio, who had long shown symptoms of disaffection to the English, and a leaning toward the French cause, openly assumed the hostile character. The French had long been endeavoring to seduce all the Indian tribes from the English interest, but their efforts were but partially successful, for the powerful confederacy of the Six Nations, the most warlike of all, showed no disposition to be drawn into the contest. Governor Bladen prudently prepared to repel any inroads of the Shawanese; and in January 1745 (O.S.) issued a proclamation "to acquaint the back inhabitants of this province with the mischievous designs of our enemies." Their plan, it was understood, was to penetrate to the south and attack the Catawbas, a tribe friendly to the English, who lived on the Catawba river in South Carolina. The proclamation ran as follows:

"*Whereas*, I have received information that the French Indians intend to pass through the back parts of this province in order to attack the Catawbee Indians (who are in Amity with his Majesty's subjects,) and will, as it is said, attempt to plunder and annoy as many of the said subjects as they can, I have, therefore, with the advice of his Lordship's Council of State, issued this my Proclamation to acquaint the back inhabitants of this Province of the mischievous designs of our enemies to warn them to be upon their guard, and strictly to charge and require all his Lordship's officers to use their utmost endeavors to oppose, distress and destroy the said Indians, and to that end to arm and assemble together the inhabitants when and as often as there shall be occasion, and from time to time to give me the earliest and most speedy intelligence of the motions and proceedings of the enemy. And I do hereby strictly charge and require the sheriff of Prince George's county to make this my Proclamation public in the said county, in the usual manner, as he will answer the contrary at his peril.

"Given at the City of Annapolis, this 21st day of January, in the 31st year of his Lordship's Dominion, A.D. 1745.

"THOMAS BLADEN, *Governor*."

During this war our shores were much annoyed by French privateers, some of which ascended the Chesapeake bay almost as high as Baltimore, and made frequent landings on both shores, plundering the defenceless inhabitants.

[1] Maryland *Gazette*.

Although Maryland at this time had no ships of war, occasions arose in which the commanders and crews of the merchant shipping showed that they lacked neither courage nor conduct, and gave earnest of the time when Maryland valor was to be as famous on the sea as on the land. On January 7th, 1744, O.S. (1745, N.S.,) the merchantman *Cunliffe*, Captain John Pritchard, bound from Maryland to Liverpool with a large and valuable cargo, when almost in sight of Ireland, being about ten leagues northwest of Cape Clear, had her attention attracted by the suspicious manœuvres of a strange sail, which presently displayed French colors. Although the *Cunliffe* was bound on a peaceful errand, she was not altogether unprepared for defence, all merchant vessels at that time carrying some small armament; and Captain Pritchard determined to fight rather than surrender. After some manœuvering, the vessels came to close quarters, when the Frenchman, who proved to be a privateer carrying twenty broadside guns, besides swivels, and upwards of two hundred men, as if to finish the contest at a blow, poured in her whole broadside, and then attempted to grapple the *Cunliffe* and carry her by boarding; but in this she was foiled. Although the merchantman had but thirty-eight men and boys, was deeply laden, and for her whole armament carried but one long gun and a few carronades, she was handled with such skill and resolution that the fight was prolonged for ten hours, her "Long Tom" raking the enemy's deck with terrible effect, and her carronades doing good service at short range. All the Frenchman's attempts to grapple and board were baffled; and to his repeated summons to surrender, the *Cunliffe's* crew replied with shouts of defiance and derision, at last hoisting the black flag, to show that they would neither give nor ask quarter. At nightfall the privateer was driven off with heavy loss, and disappeared under the cover of darkness, while the victorious *Cunliffe* came triumphantly into port. Her victory was dearly bought, however, by the death of her heroic captain and a number of his gallant crew.

The easy acquisition of Louisburg revived the often-disappointed hope of the conquest of Canada; and Governor Shirley submitted to the Duke of Newcastle a plan for a colonial army to carry on the enterprise. But the Duke of Bedford, then at the head of the British marine, took alarm at the idea of "the independence it might create in these provinces when they shall see within themselves so great an army, possessed of so great a country by right of conquest."[1] The old plan was therefore preferred of sending a fleet and army from England to capture Quebec, to be joined at Louisburg by the New England levies, while the forces of the other colonies operated against Montreal in the rear.

This plan was cordially approved by the colonies, who furnished their quotas with alacrity. On June 26, 1746, the Assembly of Maryland voted a supply of forty-five hundred pounds to raise a body of men for the expedition. The call was met with promptness; and on September 15, three

[1] Hildreth's *United States*, ii., p. 398.

companies raised in the province by Captains Campbell, Crofts, and Jordan, sailed from Annapolis "with cheerful hearts, in high spirits, and all well-clothed and accoutred, to join the main body of the forces" at Albany, New York. In November a further appropriation of eleven hundred pounds was made to pay the additional expenses of this volunteer force.[1] Though the attempt on Canada was abandoned, the troops were retained nearly eighteen months at Albany.

In 1745, occurred that unhappy rising in England of the partisans of Prince Charles Edward, "the Young Pretender," the disastrous result of which crushed forever the hopes of the house of Stuart. When the news of this rebellion was received in Maryland, the assembly unanimously pledged their support to the house of Hanover, and drew up an address to the king, signed by all the members of both houses. The news of the decisive battle of Culloden, fought on April 16, 1746, was joyfully received in the province, and celebrated in Annapolis and Baltimore by bonfires, processions, illuminations, and general festivities.

After the suppression of this rebellion, the participators in it were punished with vindictive severity. Great numbers were put to death, and multitudes transported. The Scottish prisoners were taken to England for trial, lest their own countrymen should be disposed to deal with them too leniently; and at one time there were no less than three hundred and eighty-five crowded in Carlisle jail. Of these the rank and file were permitted to cast lots, one man out of every twenty to be tried and hanged, and the rest to be transported. One ship-load of the latter were sent to Maryland. They came by the ship *Johnson*, of Liverpool, William Pemberton, master, and arrived at the port of Oxford, on July 20, 1747.[2]

The Lord Proprietary, in 1747, appointed Samuel Ogle Governor of the Province; and on the 12th of March the new governor and his lady arrived

[1] Maryland *Gazette*.

[2] Their names, taken from a worm-eaten, certified list among the records at Annapolis, are as follows: John Grant, John ——nald, John Newton, John Cameron, —— Stutton, Patrick Ferguson, Thomas Ross, William Cowan, —— Nacooon, Patrick Macintergall, Mary Shaw, Alice Pimmarrage, James Allen, William Beverley, John Brandy, John Bowe, Alexander Buchanan, John Burnett, Robert Boy, Robert Craigin, Alexander ——agie, William Connell, Duncan Cameron, John Cameron, Donald ——, James Chapman, Thomas Claperton, Sanders Campbell, William ——, Charles Davidson, John Dunham, John Duff, Robert ——, James Erwyn, Dunkin Farguson, Dunham Farguson, Allen Grant, Peter Gardiner, John Gray, John Hector, —— Hamilton, James King, Dunham Macgregor, Alexander ——, Patrick Murray, Archi MacAnnis, William Melvil, William Murdock, John Mean, John Magregor, Roderick Macquerrist, Roderick Macferrist, John Macdaniel, John Macquerrist, John Macnabb, Dan'l MacDaniel, Hugh Macclean, Peter Maccloughton, James Macduff, Patrick Morgan, Peter Maccoy, James Mill, John Macgregor, John Nesmith, Adam Norvil, Peter Ruddoch, David Russell, Naile Robertson, Alexander Smith, William Stewart, James Simson, Michael Steele, John Suter, John Taylor, Andrew Fillery, Saunders Taylor, Minnian Wise, John Warair, George Walson, John Watt, Sanders Walker, William Yeats, Alexander ——, Adam Sutherland, Augus Maccleod, Archi Macintire, —— Macdaniel, Augus Grant, Alexander Macoelod, Daniel Magellis, —— Macintosh, Donald Macintosh, Gilbert Maccullum, —— Gwyn, John Cameron, John Arbuthnot.

in the ship *Neptune*, at Annapolis, from Liverpool.[1] On the 9th of June ex-Governor Bladen sailed for London. In December, at the request of the king, Governor Ogle called the assembly together for the purpose of providing means for the support of the Maryland troops in Canada. In his opening speech to the assembly, he said his Majesty desired money "to be raised as a present supply to our own levies, until such time as the whole expense of the American troops can be laid before the Parliament of Great Britain, that provision may be made for the payment thereof."

The assembly took into consideration the request of the king, and in a few days returned the following message to the governor:

"We, his Majesty's most dutiful and loyal subjects, the Delegates of the freemen of Maryland, in Assembly convened, taking under consideration the extract of the Duke of Newcastle's letter laid before us, recommending the advancing money for the payment of the levies raised by this province, on the late intended expedition against Canada, as well as all the ways and means in our power for complying with his majesty's hopes and expectations therein, beg leave, under the greatest concern, to represent to your Excellency, that the vast charge and expense the people of this province have already been at, in levying, maintaining here, transporting to Albany in the province of New York, the place of general rendezvous, and further supplying those levies with provisions there; together with the heavy taxes and other difficulties, under which the people we represent labor; have rendered it altogether impracticable for us to raise or advance any sum for payment of the said forces. And as no further business lies before this house, we pray your Excellency will please to put an end to this meeting."

To which the governor returned the following message:

"I wish with all my heart you could have thought of any way of answering his Majesty's expectations at this time, in relation to our own levies, agreeable to the zeal you have hitherto shewn upon the like occassions; but as you represent it impracticable for us to raise or advance any further sum for the payment of the said force, nothing remains for me to do, but to put an end to this assembly."

In answer to certain queries, proposed by the Board of Trade in England to Governor Ogle, the governor and council in December, 1748, made the following interesting report of the state of the province:

"Concerning that part of the Peninsula which lies to the Eastward, a dispute is now depending between the Lord Baltimore and Messrs. Penns in the high court of Chancery; nor are the boundaries on the northward as yet fixed between Maryland and Pennsylvania, but a temporary line hath been run by order of his Majesty, from the East side of the river Susquehannah, down so far South as fifteen miles, and a quarter of a mile south of the latitude of the most southern part of the City of Philadelphia, and on the West side of the said river Susquehannah down so far South as fourteen miles, and three quarters of a mile south of the latitude of the most southern part of the City of Philadelphia, for the present quieting the disturbance on the borders of each province. The Constitution is founded

[1] Mr. Browning says: "Lord Baltimore, about this time [1747], sent out an illegitimate son of his, named Benedict Swingate, who, at the instigation of Governor Ogle with his lordship, was afterwards called Calvert, for whom Lord Baltimore bought the Mount Airey estate of his brother-in-law, —— Hyde, Esq., merchant, London, and gave it to Leonard Calvert, Esq., who was for several years one of the council, and one of the judges of the Land Office."—Page 28, *ut supra*.

on the aforementioned Royal Charter. The legislative power is in the Governor and the Upper House (which is composed of twelve councillors), and the Lower House of Assembly, which consists of the delegates of the people.

"The trade of the Province consists chiefly in the exportation of tobacco to Great Britain, in vessels yearly sent thither from thence to the number of about two hundred, of the burthen of about 12000 tons, navigated with about 4000 men. The vessels owned by the inhabitants of the Province are not above 50, navigated with about 400 men, and of the burthen of about 400 tons, and are decreased within these few years, occasioned by the captures since the war.

"The inhabitants take annually from Great Britain all sorts of fine and coarse woolens and linens, great quantities of wrought leather and wrought iron, and all kinds of British manufactures; but the quantities of each cannot be ascertained from the great variety of persons to whom the same are consigned or shipped.

"This province has very little trade with any foreign plantations, except to some of the Portuguese islands for salt by a few small vessels which carry lumber and provisions, and a vessel or two in a year to Maderas loaded with wheat, Indian corn, bread, flour and staves, which brings back Madera wine, nor has the Province any trade to any part of Europe besides Great Britain, except an inconsiderable quantity of wheat and lumber sent to Lisbon, and that but seldom, and sometimes a vessel to Ireland which carries wheat and lumber thither.

"The methods used to prevent illegal trade, are by the appointment of the collectors and surveyors of his Majesty's customs by the commissioners of the customs in London, and naval officers appointed by the Governor in all the districts in the Province; and considering the number of rivers and creeks in the said Province, this method is as effectual to prevent illicit trade as can well be.

"The exportation of the commodities and manufactures from hence, exclusive of tobacco, is wheat, lumber, Indian corn, bread flour, pig and some bar iron, skins, furs to the value of about sixteen thousand pounds sterling annually, of which the pig iron and furs are exported only to Great Britain.

"There are a great many iron mines and several of them very good in the Province, and there are eight furnaces for making pig iron and nine forges for making bar iron, and great shews of copper in many places, but of the several attempts that have been made to discover veins of that metal, none has been yet made that quitted cost.

"The number of inhabitants is, as near as can be computed, about ninety-four thousand, and of blacks, about thirty-six thousand, and are increased of late years by the many Germans and others brought into this Province.

"The number of militia is about twelve thousand five hundred.

"The Six Nations of Indians, though not neighboring on our borders, are in friendship and alliance with this government, and are about seventeen hundred, but as those Indians are nearer the government of New York, that Province can give a more exact account of them.

"The friends and allies of the Six Nations upon the river Ohio, are about seven or eight hundred more.

"The French settlements being at Quebeck and on the river of St. Laurence or Canada and the Mississippi, can have very little immediate effect on this Province.

"The revenue arises and is appropriated by the several following Act of Assembly.

"1661, Port duty of fourteen pence per ton on all ships and vessels trading into the Province, due to and received by the Right Honorable the Lord Proprietary thereof and his ancestors, from the payment whereof ships and vessels wholly belonging to the inhabitants are exempt.

"1694, Francis Nicholson, Esq., being then Governor, an act was made, giving three-pence per ton on tonnage of all trading vessels (except such as belonged to the inhabitants) to the Governor, which was made perpetual in the year 1704. Col. Seymour being Governor, 1704, a perpetual law was made (the government of the Province being then immediately in the crown) to raise twelve pence per hhd. upon tobacco for the support of government, which is the only one now in being.

"1704, By an act made in that year, impositions of three pence per gallon on rum, wine, brandy and spirits imported (except from England) twenty shillings per poll on negroes, and twenty shillings per poll on Irish servants, were laid, which duties have hitherto been continued by subsequent acts, excepting on Irish servants being Protestants, and also vessels wholly owned by the inhabitants of this Province, which duty is applied to the maintaining a free school.

"1715, An act was then passed for laying an additional duty of twenty shillings per poll on Irish servants being Papists, to prevent the importation of too great a number of them into this Province, and an additional duty of two shillings currency per poll on negroes imported, for raising a fund to support public schools within this Province, which act is still in force.

"1723, An act was passed for laying a duty of twelve pence per barrel on pork, for every hundred weight, sixpence, for every barrel of pitch, twelve pence, &c., for every barrel of tar, sixpence, the said commodities being imported by any other than the inhabitants of this Province.

"1732, An act was then passed, laying a duty of fifteen pence sterling for every hogshead of tobacco which shall be exported for and during the space of thirty-one years next ensuing, the twenty-ninth day of September, in the year aforesaid, for the better supporting the credit of ninety thousand pounds emitted and made current in bills of credit.

"The ordinary expenses are: Support of the Governor, an allowance to the council and Upper & Lower Houses of Assembly during their attendance, and the payment of the superior courts of law, and officers in several inferior stations. As the extraordinary expenses are only made on particular occasions, they rarely happen so as to amount to a considerable sum, except lately for raising, supplying and transporting several forces by his Majesty's command for the West India and Canada expeditions, and a treaty of peace with the Indians, and for which provisions were made by the Assembly.

"The establishments, as well civil as military, depend on the power granted by the Royal charter to the Lord Baltimore, under whom all the officers (except the collectors and surveyors of his Majesty's customs,) hold their places."

In another account published this year in London, we have the following additional particulars of the trade, etc., of the province:

"Two-thirds of the inhabitants at least are of the Church of England; about a fourteenth part are Roman Catholics, and the rest Presbyterians, Quakers and other sectaries.

"The chief branch of the trade of this province is the importation of goods from Great Britain; and the annual exportation of about 28,000 hhds. tobacco thither in vessels annually sent hither from thence to the number of about 120 of the burthen of about 18,000 tons. The vessels owned by the inhabitants are about forty, most of them sloops and schooners, about 13,000 tons burthen; these are generally employed in the West India trade, and in carrying corn, bread, and flour to the northern colonies. The exact value of the goods imported annually from Great Britain cannot be ascertained; but must cost at least £180,000; large remittances being made by the way of Lisbon, the West Indies, and by bills of exchange and specie to pay for it over and above the proceeds of the tobacco, which might be rated at about £150,000 (the freight and merchants' commissions for selling it being about the same sum.) Near two-thirds of the tobacco is carried to the London market, and the rest to Glasgow, except about 2,000 hhds. to Bristol, Liverpool, Biddeford and Whitehaven. The commodities exported hence, besides tobacco, are pig and bar iron (to the amount of at least 2,000 tons,) wheat, corn, bread, flour, skins, furs, flaxseed, to the value of about £90,000. Most of the wheat, perhaps 150,000 bushels, is sent to Lisbon or up the Mediterranean, for which remittances are made to Great Britain. The importation of rum, molasses, sugar, from the British islands is very considerable, but not equal to the exports thither. The balance of every other branch of trade, except that to Great Britain, is in our favor.

"There are about twenty navigable rivers in the province, but large ships load in only twelve of them."[1]

The peace of Aix-la-Chapelle, concluded in October, 1748, produced a temporary suspension of hostilities between England and France.[2] By the terms of this peace, the island of Cape Breton, with Louisburg, so dearly purchased by provincial blood and treasure, was restored to the French. English policy, however, at this time, took small account of colonial prosperity; and the people of America on this as on other occasions, were made sensible that they were looked on as mere dependencies of the crown, and that their interests were to be sacrificed at the caprice of the dominant powers. "Of such consequence to the French was the possession of that important key to their American settlements, that its restitution was, in reality, the purchase of the last general peace in Europe."[3]

No one versed in the political secrets of the day could by any possibility have believed that this peace was to be a lasting one. It was deficient in every element of coherence. Nothing was settled by the treaty; conquests all over the world were to be eventually restored; some trifling shiftings of territorial proprietorship on the part of the Italian and other minor princes engaged in the war were agreed upon; a few other articles relative to European affairs, of little or no consequence in proportion to the cost at which they were effected, were inserted, and the treaty of Utrecht, as well as all former treaties, confirmed in existence. In short, matters were essentially placed *in statu quo ante bellum*, at a cost to England of £110,000,000.[4]

In the war just past, Maryland was not immediately concerned, nor directly threatened; and her participation in it consisted in furnishing occasional supplies of men and money to the northern colonies. But a new contest was at hand, in which she was to have deep and perilous interest, and which was to bring the horrors of Indian invasion over her borders. The treaty of 1748 left the controversy between England and France with respect to the boundaries of their American possessions still unsettled. Neither party admitted the right of the other to the valley of the Penobscot, nor to that of the Ohio. The French, on the ground of discovery, laid claim, not

[1] MS. Maryland Historical Society.

[2] The Maryland *Gazette* announced the event on the 5th of May, 1749, though it was not formally proclaimed in the province until September 19.

[3] Massachusetts *Hist. Coll.*, vii. Minot, i., p. 81.

[4] Sargent, *Hist. Braddock's Expedition*, p. 16.

only to the great lakes, but to the Mississippi, with its affluents and the vast valley they drained, as well as to the Ohio and its tributaries, which extended their claim within the territories of Virginia and Pennsylvania. They had begun to establish a chain of military and trading posts from Canada down to New Orleans, and as a symbol of their jurisdiction, had carved the lilies of France on the trees, or on plates of metal sunk in the ground. On the other hand, the English grants of territory, starting from the Atlantic coast, extended westward (when not otherwise limited) as far as the Pacific ocean. So long as the English colonists confined themselves to the seaboard, these claims of the mother country attracted comparatively but little attention from their rivals; but as they began to push their settlements beyond the Alleghanies, and to encroach upon what the French regarded as their rightful domains, it became evident that a collision could not be much longer deferred.

In the north and east, France was now sparing no effort to extend her power and crush that of England. This vexatious contest was continued with feeble efforts and various success, almost down to the period of the war of 1756. It came at last to be distinctly understood, or fully believed, that a preponderating ascendency in America must decide the long and arduous contest between those rival powers. It was certainly a singular phenomenon, that a great question of national aggrandizement, between the courts of London and Paris, should be decided in the interior of America. Such, however, was the fact; and the banks of the St. Lawrence and the shores of the American lakes, and the borders of Maryland and Virginia were destined to be the theatre on which the great prize was to be contended for. The vigor of the contest was proportionate to the magnitude of the stake. The efforts of England were cheerfully and promptly seconded by those of her colonies, through four successive years, until, at length, the Plains of Abraham witnessed the triumph of their united valor, and the gallant and lamented Wolfe planted the cross of St. George upon the ramparts of Quebec. The peace of Fontainebleau, which soon followed, secured the conquest which valor and perseverance had won. France relinquished her pretensions, and left Great Britain without a rival on this extensive field of glory and of enterprise. The first signal of alarm to the French was a grant of five hundred thousand acres of territory, on the south side of the Ohio, between the Monongahela and Kanawha rivers, and west of the Alleghanies, made by the English government in the year 1749, to a small number of Marylanders and Virginians of wealth and influence, styling themselves "The Ohio Company." To accomplish its commercial purposes, trading posts were soon established, which the French followed by prompt and decisive measures of reprisal. Some of the English traders, amongst the Indians, were seized and imprisoned; and several of the trading posts of the comany were reduced and pillaged. Indignant at these outrages, Governor Dinwiddie introduced upon the theatre of affairs, a youth—George Washington—to perform an important and hazardous

FREDERICK, SIXTH LORD BALTIMORE.

mission for his native colony, and to prepare himself to serve his whole country. Colonel Washington was dispatched to the French commandant to protest against his proceedings and to demand an evacuation of the territory. On the 30th of October, 1753, Washington set off from Williamsburg on his dangerous mission, through a hostile Indian country, with that courage, zeal and perseverance which afterwards, in a higher station, made him the saviour of his country. He reached Wills' creek on the 14th November, where he engaged Colonel Nathaniel Gist, the intrepid pioneer, to accompany him in the expedition.

The demands of Virginia were rejected, and nothing was left but a recourse to hostilities. In the war which ensued, Maryland became involved simply in self-defence and for the assistance of the sister colonies—while Virginia and Pennsylvania were contending for the acquisition of a large and fertile territory.

Charles, the Fifth Lord Baltimore, died on the 24th of April, 1751, aged 52 years, and was succeeded by his only son, Frederick, the sixth and last of the Barons of Baltimore. Before the death of Charles he made and published his will, which was afterwards proved in the prerogative court of the Archbishop of Canterbury, England, bearing date 17th of November, 1750, whereby he devised to trustees therein mentioned, the Province of Maryland, and all his estates, "of what nature or kind soever the same were (except the manor of Anne Arundel, in the county of Anne Arundel, in the said province) to the use of his only son Frederick Calvert, afterwards Lord Baltimore, in strict settlement, with the reversion in fee to his, the testator's, eldest daughter, Louisa Calvert."[1]

Governor Ogle, who had been re-commissioned in 1746–47, died on the 3d of May, 1762, in the 58th year of his age. Upon his death, the government of the province devolved upon Benjamin Tasker, then President of the Council, until the arrival of Horatio Sharpe, the new governor, on the 10th of August, 1753.

The intentions and movements of the French being now understood, the Governor of Virginia prepared for immediate war. He summoned the House of Burgesses to meet at an early day, and also wrote letters to the governor's of the other provinces, calling on them for aid, drawing a vivid picture of the common danger, and making moving appeals to their patriotism and sense of duty to their sovereign. The English government recognized the dangerous

[1] Charles Browning's memorial to the Legislature of Maryland, dated September 29, 1820, for compensation for the losses sustained by the Baltimore family in the confiscation of their property during the Revolutionary war, of which he and his mother were then the sole legal representatives. Mr. Daniel Dulany estimated the loss of the Baltimore family by the results of the Revolutionary war, as follows: "The revenue for the support of government, fines, forfeitures, appointments to offices, presentations to livings, caution money for vacant lands, quit-rents, fines of a year's rent upon every alienation, escheat manors (as they are called), reserved lands, as well as the tonnage, constitute the subject intended to be devised to Mr. Browning, a subject which, I think, if purchased at the price of £400,000, would be purchased at a very moderate rate, and it would seem to carry a fiction of a recompence beyond the supposition, there being no possibility of a repetition, as there is no instance of a similar estate or subject."

Mr. Browning, in his memorial, says: "Frederick Calvert, afterwards Lord Baltimore, [married Diana, daughter of the Duke of Bridgewater], departed this life on the 4th day of September, in the year 1771, without issue. That, on the 13th day of May, 1762, the above named Louisa Calvert intermarried with John Browning, late of [Horton Lodge] Epsom, Surrey aforesaid Esquire, deceased, your memorialist's late father. That the said John Browning departed this life on the 13th day of May, 1792, leaving issue of his marriage with the said Louisa Calvert only one son, your memorialist, who was born on the 29th day of July, 1765. That the said Charles Browning, on the 7th of April, 1795, married Elizabeth Anne More, daughter of Sir William More, Baronet, [Stamford], by whom he has issue living, three sons and two daughters. [Charles, born and died an infant, buried at Hamilton. Charles Calvert, born at Epsom 27th of May, 1798; Louisa, born Londonderry, Ireland, September 2, 1799; Frederick, born at Epsom, January 23, 1801; Cecil, born at Epsom 26th May, 1802; and Elizabeth, born at Epsom, June 25, 1804. All of these children, except the first, were christened at Epsom, by the Rev. Jonathan Boucher, formerly of Maryland.] . . . That, on the 9th day of February, in the year 1779, your memorialist's said mother, Louisa Browning, being unable, through mental derangement, to govern herself or her affairs, and which took place very shortly after the birth of her said son, Charles Browning (considerably above fifty years since), a commission was issued under the Great Seal of Great Britain, to enquire of the lunacy of the said Louisa Browning, and she was, by inquisition taken thereon, found to be a lunatic, and the custody of her person was granted to your memorialist's late father, and afterwards, on his decease, to your memorialist; as also the committeeship of his said mother, Louisa Browning's estates, soon after the decease of Sir Cecil Wray, Bar't, who acted in that capacity for several years under a similar order."

GOVERNOR HORATIO SHARPE.

consequences likely to result to her possessions from these encroachments, unless they were instantly repelled, and responded fully to the spirit of Virginia. Upon representations made by Governor Dinwiddie, to the Earl of Holderness (then secretary of state), circulars were addressed to the English colonies to repel by force all attempts by the French to intrude upon the settlements within the colonies. That addressed to the colony of Maryland, was submitted to its assembly, at October session, 1753; but its requisitions, although sustained and urged by its executive, were without effect. The Lower House assured the governor, "that they were resolutely determined to repel any hostile invasion of the province by any foreign power; and that they would cheerfully contribute to the defence of the neighboring colonies, when their circumstances required it; but they did not deem this a pressing occasion."[1]

While the colony thus withheld herself for the present from active co-operation in the enterprises not called for by any direct attack upon her settlements, or those of the sister colonies, but merely intended to anticipate

[1] McMahon, p. 294.

their occurrence; yet she was determined to resist any and every foreign invasion, and to contribute her assistance to the neighboring colonies when their necessity required it. At the next session of the assembly, held in February, 1754, in pursuance of letters received from Governor Dinwiddie, who was apprehensive of an invasion of his province, and called for aid; the Upper House in reply to the address of Governor Sharpe, say: "The encroachments of the French, and their depredations on his majesty's lands and the sufferings of our fellow subjects, give us the greatest alarm, and we should think ourselves wanting in our duty to his majesty and our country, should we not give all the assistance in our power to repel the common enemy; and as one step towards it will be to secure the affections of the Indians, at this critical juncture, we shall concur to do what is necessary towards the attaining so desirable an end."

To secure the fidelity and aid of the Six Nations who had before placed themselves under the protection of the British crown, the Board of Trade, in September, 1753, sent instructions to the colonial governors to make a treaty with them, to hear their complaints and redress their grievances, and to gratify their wishes in relation to their lands. The requisitions of the English government in this respect were cheerfully complied with, and the assembly in May, 1754, appropriated £500 for the purchase of presents; and Benjamin Tasker, Jr., and Major Abraham Barnes were appointed by the governor to represent Maryland in that convention. After some delay, delegates from all the colonies north of the Potomac met in June, 1754. The members, both for abilities and fortune, were among the most prominent in America. There were De Lancey, Murray, Johnson, Chambers and Smith, from New York; Welles, Chandler, Hutchinson, Patridge and Worthington, from Massachusetts; Atkinson, Wibird, Weare and Sherburne, from New Hampshire; Pitkins, Wolcott and Williams, from Connecticut; Hopkins and Howard, from Rhode Island; Penn, Peters, Norris and Franklin, from Pennsylvania, and Tasker and Barnes, from Maryland. After the organization of the congress, the negotiations with the Indians were conducted at intervals, and the "chain of friendship" was thoroughly brightened. But the matter of most importance was the consideration of a plan for a union of all the colonies for common action and mutual defence. On Monday, June 28th, a committee was appointed of one from each province, to "prepare and receive plans or schemes for the union of the colonies, and to digest them into one general plan for the inspection of this board." On the 28th "hints of a scheme" of union were presented, which were debated for several days, but no decision was reached until the 10th of July, when "Mr. Franklin reported the draught in a new form" which was "read paragraph by paragraph and debated, and the further consideration of it deferred to the afternoon," when it was adopted.

"By its terms, the general government was to be administered by a president, appointed and supported by the crown, and a council, chosen by the representatives of the several colonies. This council was to consist of forty-eight members, of which Massachusetts and Virginia were each to choose seven, New Hampshire and Rhode Island two each, Connecticut five, New York, Maryland, North Carolina and South Carolina four each, New Jersey three, and Pennsylvania six. A new election of members was to be made triennially; and on the death or resignation of any member, his place was to be supplied at the next sitting of the colony he represented. After the first three years the quota of each province was to be determined by the proportion it paid into the general treasury; though no province was to be entitled to more than seven, or less than two, councillors. This council was empowered to choose its own speaker, but could neither be dissolved nor prorogued, nor could it continue in session longer than six weeks at one time without the consent of its members or the special command of the crown. The assent of the president was required to all acts of the council to give to them validity; and it was his duty to cause such acts to be executed. With the advice of the council he could likewise hold treaties with the Indians, regulate trade, make peace or declare war, purchase their lands for the crown, if not within the limits of particular provinces, settle such purchases and make laws for their government until the crown should form them into distinct governments. The council was further authorized to raise and pay soldiers, build forts for public defence, equip vessels to guard the coast and protect the trade on the ocean and lakes, and levy such duties as were necessary to defray the expenses accruing; but no men were to be impressed in any colony without the consent of its legislature. A quorum of the council was to consist of twenty-five members, among whom there was to be one or more from a majority of the colonies; and the laws made by that body were not to be repugnant, but 'as near as may be agreeable,' to the laws of England, and were to be transmitted to the king for approval as soon as practicable. If not disapproved within three years, they were to be considered in force. All military officers were to be nominated by the president, and approved by the council before receiving their commissions; and all civil officers were to be nominated by the council, and approved by the president. The first meeting of the government was to be held at Philadelphia, and was to be called by the president as soon as convenient after his appointment."[1]

Such was the confederacy of 1754, framed in July, just twenty-two years before the Declaration of Independence, and assented to by two persons, at least, whose names are affixed to that memorable instrument; and such was the first official suggestion of what grew afterwards to be our present Federal Constitution. It is worthy of remark that this plan met with no favor from either the colonial assemblies or the Board of Trade. "The assemblies," says Franklin, speaking of it some thirty years after, "all thought there was too much *prerogative* in it; and in England it was thought to have too much of the democratic in it." Maryland, ever jealous of her colonial independence, proud of her charter, and fearful of the invasion of her rights of internal sovereignty, had constantly resisted every attempt to effect a union of the colonies under one government; and now the proposed scheme, when submitted to the assembly, (as required by the convention) encountered the most decided opposition. The Lower House of Assembly disapproved it, as appears from their address to the governor:'

"We do not conceive" says the address, "that the commissioners were intended, or empowered, to agree upon any plan of a proposed union of the colonies, to be laid before the parliament of Great Britain, with a view to an act, by which one general government

[1] Barry's *History of Massachusetts*, ii., p. 179. *Doc. History of New York*, ii., p. 545, etc.

may be formed in America; and therefore do not deem it necessary to enter into any particular notice of the minutes of their proceedings relative to it. But as it appears to us, we cannot, in consistence with our duty to our constituents, refrain from remarking, that the carrying of that plan into execution, would ultimately subvert that happy form of government to which we are entitled under our charter, (the freedom of which was, doubtless, the great inducement to our ancestors, to leave their friends and native country, and venture their lives and fortunes among a fierce and savage people, in a rough uncultivated world); and destroy the rights, liberties, and property, of his majesty's loyal subjects of this province."

In the meantime the French had not been idle. In the spring of 1753, they had built, at Presqu' Isle, on Lake Erie, a strong fort, and leaving a large garrison there, they marched to the Rivière aux Boeufs, where they erected another fort, cutting a wagon road twenty-one feet in width between the two. Here garrisons were maintained during the winter of 1753–4, and here a strong force gathered in the spring of 1754, fully prepared to march to and occupy the head of the Ohio.

On the 17th of April, 1754, M. de Contrecoeur, the French commander, at the head of from five hundred to a thousand men, with eighteen pieces of artillery, captured the defenceless works afterwards known as Fort Du Quesne, which occupied the spot where now stands the city of Pittsburg. Washington was at Wills' creek (now known as Cumberland, Maryland,) when the tidings reached him of the surrender of the fort; he resolved to proceed to the mouth of Redstone creek,[1] and there to erect a fort and await the advancing foe. He arrived at the Great Meadows on the 28th of May, and encountered a detachment of thirty-five men under M. de Jumonville, sent out from Fort Du Quesne as ambassadors, as was alleged by M. de Contrecoeur, to warn him to withdraw. Washington, however, mistook their character, and a sharp skirmish ensued, in which M. de Jumonville and several of his men were killed, and the rest surrendered, and were sent, under guard, to the governor of Virginia. Having heard of large reinforcements at Fort Du Quesne, and expecting an attack, Washington retreated to the Great Meadows, where he commenced the erection of a fort, to which was given the suggestive title of Fort Necessity. While thus engaged, they were surprised by the approach of a superior French force, and after a conflict of some hours, obliged to surrender on honorable terms. On the 4th of July, 1754, the little garrison evacuated its feeble fort and retreated to Wills' creek; and the unprotected frontiers of Pennsylvania, Maryland and Virginia were exposed to the plundering bands of French and Indians. Leaving his force at Wills' creek under the command of Colonel Innes, Washington hastened to Williamsburg, to communicate in person to Governor Dinwiddie the result of his expedition; while messengers were dispatched with letters to the governors of Maryland and Pennsylvania, explaining his weak and exposed situation, and soliciting aid. Governor Sharpe, however, aware of the situation of affairs, had already convened the assembly, who met in Annapolis on the 17th of July. In his opening speech he urged in the most earnest and forcible terms

[1] Brownsville, Pa.

the propriety of making instant provision for the defence of the frontier, and the protection of their Indian allies. The occasion was one of that very character, previously indicated in the history of the colony, as entitled to her exertions; and the assembly, true to its obligations and professions, was now as prompt as as it had before been remiss. The news of the defeat of Colonel Washington reached Annapolis on the day after the assembly met, and created great surprise and alarm; and it had the effect of hastening the action of the legislature, who, on the 25th of July, appropriated £6000 "to his excellency Horatio Sharpe, Esq., for his majesty's use, towards the defence of the colony of Virginia, attacked by the French and Indians; and for the relief and support of the wives and children of the Indian allies that put themselves under the protection of this government."[1]

Immediately upon the passage of this act, Governor Sharpe notified Governor Dinwiddie, who received the announcement with great satisfaction, and recommended that a company of one hundred soldiers should be raised in the province to act in conjunction with the forces that were then gathering at Wills' creek, to serve under the command of Colonel Innes. Governor Sharpe issued a commission to Captain Thomas Cresap, who "had behaved himself on all occasions as a good servant to the government," to raise a company of riflemen to serve beyond the Alleghany mountains. In August the governor gave orders that two additional companies should be raised to join Colonel Innes; and on the 15th The *Gazette* announced that we "are now raising recruits to go against the French on the Ohio." The privates were to receive eightpence a day, and clothes, arms, and accoutrements. On the 23d of September, a part of a company left Annapolis under the command of Lieutenant John Forty, on their way to Frederick; and on the 30th, another detachment marched for the same place under the command of Lieutenant John Bacon. John Ross also enlisted a company. All were to serve under the command of Captain Dagworthy.[2]

Colonel Innes, who commanded a few companies of the North Carolina troops, was ordered after the battle of the Great Meadows, to march to Will's creek and construct a fort, which should serve as a rallying point and a defence to the frontiers. It was built by Rutherford's and Clarke's independent companies of foot from New York, Demerie's independent company from South Carolina, and the three independent companies under the command of Colonel Innes, from North Carolina, assisted by a company which arrived there in November from Maryland. When finished it received the name of Fort Cumberland, in honor of the Duke of Cumberland, captain-general of the British army.[3]

[1] Bacon, *Act of 1754*, ch. ix. McMahon, p. 297.

[2] In a letter to Charles Calvert, dated September 2, 1754, Governor Sharpe speaks of him as follows: "I have given the command thereof to one Captain Dagworthy, a gentleman born in the Jerseys, who commanded a company raised in that province for the Canada expedition, since the miscarriage of which he has resided in this province upon an estate which he purchased in Worcester county."

[3] Sargent, p. 144. Sparks, i., p. 63.

"The greater portion of Fort Cumberland

In October, the Virginia House of Burgesses made an appropriation of twenty thousand pounds for the public service; and with the grant of ten thousand pounds and supply of arms made by the home government, Colonel Washington contemplated an extensive expedition against Fort Du Quesne.

At the same time, "for settling the rank of the officers of his majesty's forces when serving with the provincials in North America," the king directed:

"That all officers commissioned by the king or his general, should take rank of all officers commissioned by the governors of the respective provinces; and further, that the

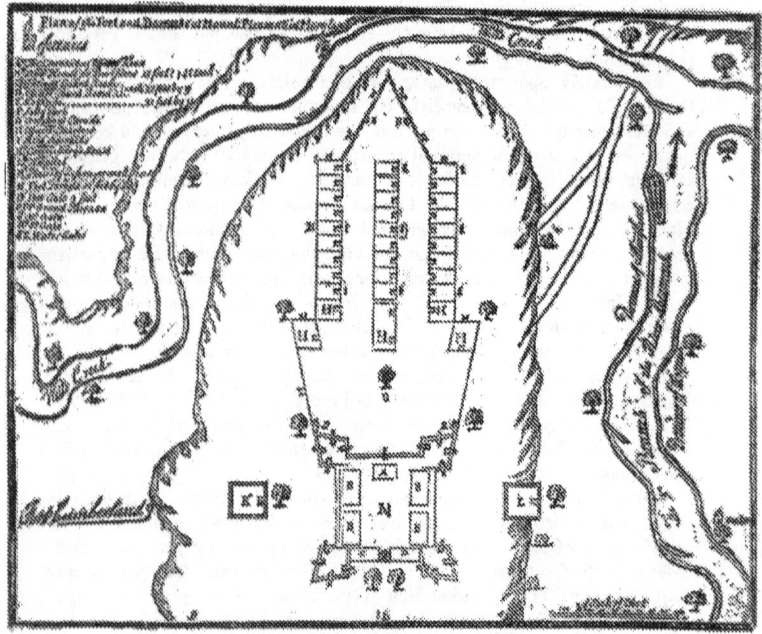

PLAN OF FORT CUMBERLAND IN 1755.

was a pallisade work—all of it, in fact, except the small bastioned work on the western end. The pallisades were logs cut to a length of eighteen feet, and planted in the earth to a depth of six feet, forming a close, wooden wall twelve feet in height. These logs were spiked together with strips and pins on the inner side, and the wall was pierced with openings for musketry along its entire face. Two water-gates are shown in the plat [among the king's manuscripts, in the library of the British Museum in London], and from each of these a trench was excavated leading to the creek, so that the men might secure therefrom a supply of water, without being exposed to the fire of the enemy. In 1756, after Braddock's defeat, the Indians became so numerous and so bold as to approach near enough to shoot those who ventured to the water's edge; and in consequence thereof, a well was sunk inside of the pallisade, near the main gate on the south side. . . . Inside the stockade were built

general and field officers of the provincial troops should have no rank when serving with the general and other commissioned officers commissioned by the crown; but that all captains and other inferior officers of the royal troops should take rank over provincial officers of the same grade, having senior commissions."

The effect of these instructions was to reduce Washington from the rank of colonel to that of captain. This humiliation he was not content to submit to, but resigned his commission and retired to private life. The Duke of Newcastle upon learning of the resignation of Colonel Washington, issued a commission to Governor Horatio Sharpe, appointing him commander of the provincial forces at Fort Cumberland. Immediately on the receipt of information that the vessel bearing it had arrived, Governor Sharpe proceeded to Williamsburg and "received his majesty's commission appointing him commander in chief of all the forces that are, or may be raised to defend the frontiers of Virginia and the neighboring colonies, and to repel the unjustifiable invasion and encroachments of the French, on the river Ohio."[1]

After an interview with Governors Dinwiddie, and Dobbs of North Carolina, who brought out the commission, he returned to Annapolis November 3d. It was concluded to raise immediately 700 men, with whom and the Independent companies, the French fort should be attacked and reduced before reinforcements could be brought thither from Canada or Louisiana. This effected, that post and another which he thought it would be necessary to erect on a small island in the river, were to be held for the king. To garrison these and Fort Cumberland would require all his forces; and he concluded it would be useless for them to attempt anything further against the enemy on La Rivière aux Boeufs and Lake Erie, "without they be supported by such a body of troops from home as he dared not presume to hope for the direction of."[2]

barracks sufficient to furnish quarters for two hundred men and the company officers. Besides, there was a parade or drill ground for the companies. At the west end of the stockade was built a fort with bastions, parapets and ditches, where sixteen guns were mounted, which commanded all the ground north, west and south, as well as the north and south lines of the stockade. These guns were of different calibre, four of them being 12-pounders, and twelve 4-pounders. Besides these, there were several swivels. A part of this armament was ships' guns, brought from Admiral Keppel's fleet. On the west face was a sally-port, and inside the fort were the houses used as quarters for the commanding officer, for storing provisions, and for the guard details while on duty. The entire work was 400 feet in length and 160 in width, extending from the point indicated, below Emanuel Church, to within a short distance of Prospect street, the northern line extending along nearly the centre of Washington street. . . . The ground to the northwest was somewhat higher, but a small earthwork of a temporary character was constructed on the crest. . . . The ground on the south side of the river, opposite the fort, was high enough to overlook the work, and somewhat interfered with its efficiency. The company parade and drill ground was inside the pallisades, but the dress parades were held on the ground now occupied by the court-house and academy. Quite a number of log houses for barracks were built near the crest, and as far back as Smallwood street, but these were made use of only when there were present a greater force than could be accommodated in the fort and the barracks immediately adjoining." — Will H. Lowdermilk, *History of Cumberland*.

[1] Maryland *Gazette*.

[2] Sargent, p. 108.

Governor Sharpe, who was now commander-in-chief of all the forces engaged against the French, with instructions to make his headquarters in Virginia, attended by some officers of the Virginia regiment and a few personal friends, set out from Annapolis on the 12th of November, to take command of the army. During the occasions of his absence in visiting the military posts, and in attending to his official duties as governor, Colonel Fitzhugh, of Virginia, was to have command of the forces. Knowing the value of Colonel Washington's experience and reputation, Sharpe at once took steps to induce him to re-enter the army; and before he left Annapolis he requested Colonel Fitzhugh to endeavor to influence him to change his resolution. Washington, however, who was deeply wounded at what he considered an act of gross injustice, was not to be persuaded.[1]

An officer writing from Fort Cumberland, on November 21st, thus speaks of the arrival of Governor Sharpe at that place:

"We have now got a fort completed, with barracks for our men at the back of it, well-built, comfortable for the winter. We had the pleasure of being joined three days ago by his Excellency, Col. Sharpe, with one company from Maryland. Mr. Sharpe appears to be a stirring, active gentleman, and by his method of proceeding, I believe a very good soldier; cheerful and free, of good conduct, and one who won't be trifled with. In the spring, if we have a good body of men, I make no doubt but we shall be able to do something to purpose. By the present situation of the French, they are not to be drove out of their forts without our numbers are greatly increased."[2]

Governor Sharpe now carried on with vigor the preparations for the spring campaign. Military stores, ordnance, etc., were collected in Frederick and Alexandria, and the militia were properly organized and disciplined. Indeed, an unwonted energy seems at this time to have inspired the people of the province. Finding the militia law defective, the governor convened the assembly on December 24, when they passed an act to levy troops for the following campaign. As an inducement to enlistments they enacted "that if any citizen of the province should be so maimed in the service as to be incapable of maintaining himself, he should be supported at the public expense."[3] In the ensuing session of February, 1755, they regulated the rates of transportation of military stores, and the mode of quartering soldiers in the province, and prohibited by severe penalties any inhabitant from supplying the French or their Indian allies with stores, ammunition or provisions.[4] Governor Sharpe, however, did not find it a difficult matter to procure volunteer soldiers, for he had more applications than he could provide for; as an instance the Maryland *Gazette* of February 6th, 1755, says: "We are assured that at Chestertown, in Kent county, several men enlisted immediately on the arrival of the officer in that town, before the drum was beat, and that the officer, who wanted but 30 men, got his complement and marched with them." The *Gazette* adds "such is the commendable spirit of that place! They are gone

[1] Sparks, II, p. 64.

[2] Maryland *Gazette*.

[3] Bacon, ch. xxi.; 1754.

[4] *Ibid.* McSherry, p. 131.

for Wills creek, and some young Maryland gentlemen (true patriots,) are gone from thence as volunteers; the mother of one of them, at parting, took leave of him with saying, 'My dear Son, I shall with much greater pleasure hear of your death, than your cowardice or ill conduct.'" And Governor Sharpe, in a letter to Lord Baltimore, dated January 12th, 1755, also says:

> "As to levying any number of men, I conceive we shall not find it difficult, . . . but the difficulty will be to get money from the Assemblies to support them after they are raised; indeed this I look upon as impracticable, or not to be expected without the legislature of Great Britain shall make a law to be binding on all these several colonies, and oblige them to raise such a fund as may be thought expedient for the support of their own troops."[1]

The appointment of Governor Sharpe to the chief command, was but a measure of temporary expediency. His friends would have persuaded the king to retain him in this position, urging in his behalf his exceeding honesty, while compelled to admit that he was not possessed of remarkable ability. "A little less honesty," replied the king, "and a little more ability, might, upon the present occasion, better serve our turn." The government, though still attempting to amuse the French with professions of peace, had decided to maintain vigorously all its pretentions on this continent; and with this view to send out at the head of an adequate force, one of the bravest and most accomplished soldiers of the empire. Such, in the opinion of the Duke of Cumberland, captain-general of the army, was Major-General Edward Braddock; whom Horace Walpole describes as "desperate in his fortune, brutal in his behavior, and obstinate in his sentiments," but admits that he was still "intrepid and capable."[2] General Braddock was ordered to proceed to Virginia as commander-in-chief of all the British troops in North America, on the 24th of September, 1754, but did not sail until the 21st of December. He set sail in the *Norwich*, convoyed by the *Centurion*, flag-ship of Commodore Keppel, and arrived in Hampton Roads on the 20th of February. He was soon followed by the rest of the fleet, with two regiments, each of five hundred men, one under Colonel Sir Peter Halket, and the other under Colonel Thomas Dunbar. Two more regiments, each of one thousand men, were to be raised in the colonies, at the king's cost, and commanded by Sir William Pepperell, and Governor Shirley, of Massachusetts. These, with the independent companies, the levies expected of the several colonies, and such Indians as enlisted, it was thought would make up an effective force of not less than twelve thousand men.

GENERAL BRADDOCK.

[1] MS. *Letter-Book* of Governor Sharpe, in the Land Office, Annapolis.

[2] Lossing, *Washington and the American Republic*, i., p. 135.

When Governor Sharpe received information of the appointment of General Braddock, he proceeded, on the 13th of January, 1755, on a tour of inspection to the scenes of anticipated operations, in the neighborhood of Wills' creek. In one week after his arrival, he was joined by Sir John St. Clair, lieutenant-colonel of O'Farrell's 22d regiment of foot, and quartermaster general of all the British forces in America. Colonel St. Clair had just arrived in America, and was then actively engaged in visiting military posts, making contracts for supplies and acquainting himself generally with the nature and the scene of his future operations. Having procured, from every source, all the maps and information that were obtainable, respecting the country through which the expedition was to pass, he and Governor Sharpe descended the Potomac river two hundred and fifty miles in a canoe, and reached Annapolis on the 2d of February, whence they went to Williamsburg, Virginia, to await General Braddock's arrival. Governor Sharpe, in a letter to Lord Baltimore, dated March 12th, 1755, gives the following account of his trip:

"I departed for the camp at Wills' Creek, to put in execution what I then mentioned. After I had been there a week, I had the pleasure to see Sir John St. Clair arrive also; after which we tarried there only one day, and in order to examine the channel of that river, we came down the Potomac by water, for the distance of about 250 miles. The many falls and shoals in that river will, we find, render the conveyance of artillery and other stores to the camp by water, impracticable. The 5th day from our leaving the camp we reached Alexandria, or Belhaven, a town on the south branch of the Potomac, just below the great falls of that river, having purchased and secured all the provisions and forage that was to be gotten on each side the water as we came down. Staying a day at Belhaven, we proceeded to Dumfries and Fredericksburg, Virginia, providing and engaging quarters for the troops in each of those places; and from thence we journeyed to Williamsburg, where we hoped to find General Braddock by that time arrived. We have agreed to quarter five of the companies from Europe for a month or so, to refresh themselves after their voyage, if the general approves thereof, in your Lordship's pro vince; one company at Marlborough, one at Bladensburg, a third at Rock Creek, three towns in Prince George's county, and two at Frederick Town, which stands on Monocacy river, in Frederick county. Beside the Maryland Company, which I have before mentioned to your Lordship, I had raised 80 more recruits in this Province, but have reason to fear they will be so much approved of that 150 from the company and them will be drafted into the English regiments. In that case I shall form two companies, each consisting of 56 men, in your Lordship's government, for the honor of the Province, even though the Assembly should determine to grant no further supplies."

Braddock's arrival was hailed with great joy by the people of Maryland, Virginia and Pennsylvania, as they looked forward with confidence to the defeat of the French and the early termination of the war; and possibly thought that the cost of the undertaking would mainly fall where it justly belonged—upon the mother country.

On the 10th of March, General Braddock forwarded letters to the governors of the different colonies, desiring them to meet him at Annapolis on the first of April, for consultation and to settle a plan of operations. On the twenty-sixth, accompanied by Governor Dinwiddie and Commodore Keppel, he arrived at Alexandria where the troops were encamped, and issued his first general order the next day. Here Governor Sharpe paid him a visit on the 28th. On the third of April the general, with a numerous suite, arrived at Annapolis, but owing to the absence of Governors Shirley, De Lancey and Morris, the council was postponed to the 14th, the place of meeting being changed to Alexandria. On the 11th and 12th, Governors Shirley of Massachusetts, De Lancey of New York, and Morris of Pennsylvania arrived at Annapolis, and, in company with Governor Sharpe, proceeded to the general's head-quarters at Alexandria, where on the 14th he laid before them his instructions, and his plans for the summer's operations. He proposed to proceed in person against Fort Du Quesne, while Shirley commanded an expedition against Niagara, and Sir William Johnston one against Crown Point. The plan having been agreed upon, and the details arranged, the council broke up, and Governors Shirley, De Lancey and Morris returned to Annapolis on the 17th with Governor Sharpe, whose hospitality they enjoyed for several days. In a letter to Lord Baltimore dated April 19th, the Governor gives the following account of his proceedings:

"The letter that I did myself the honor to write the 12th of March, informed your Lordship that General Braddock was then arrived, together with the train of artillery. I can now acquaint your Lordship that the regiments too, mustering about 500 men each, were the 28th of that month all disembarked in good health and spirits at Alexandria, where they received the general's orders to encamp till enough drafts from the Maryland and Virginia companies, and recruits could join and compleat them to near 700 each. Since his arrival the general has received instructions to have those regiments increased to 1,000 each; for which purpose officers and parties of men have been ordered into each part of this Province, as well as Pennsylvania and Virginia, to recruit. The second day after proroguing the Assembly I waited and paid my respects to general Braddock at Alexandria, and the Tuesday following, the General, Commodore Kepple, Gov. Dinwiddie, and the general's aid-de-camp and secretary, came hither in expectation of meeting the Governors Shirley, Delancey and Morris at this place; but they not arriving according to appointment, the general and company returned to Alexandria the Monday following and gave orders for the troops to march. Col. Dunbar's on this side and Col. Halkett's on the other side of the Potomac towards Will's Creek; and I expect that ere this the regiments are encamped at Frederick Town on Monaccy, and at Winchester in Virginia; and the train of artillery is also on the road through Virginia to Will's Creek. Of the 180 men that I had raised only 60 are left (the rest being drafted into the regiments) which compose one company from this Province; and the Virginia troops are formed into companies of the same number to be distributed of and employed as General Braddock shall think proper. At present two Virginia and the Maryland company are engaged in opening a road to Will's Creek, and thence towards Juniata River, in Pennsylvania, which flows into Susquehanna. Two of the independent companies will, I believe, remain at Will's Creek during the campaign; and the third will march to the westward with the other forces. The three Governors above mentioned from the Northward came hither the 11th and 12th instant; and this day, same night, I proceeded with them to Alexandria, which place we left again Tuesday morning, and they are now on their way returning to their respective governments. General Braddock departs from Alexandria to-day, and I have promised to be with him next Tuesday evening at Frederick Town where I shall tarry till the 1st of May when all the troops will be in motion, and he will proceed to Will's Creek, and thence without any stop or delay for the Ohio. The general and Mr. Shirley seem to expect and insist on the assemblies of your Lordship's province, Pennsylvania, Virginia, and the two Carolinas, being once more summoned on the same business that has been lately so earnestly recommended to them. Governor Dinwiddie intends to shew his ready compliance by meeting the Virginia Assembly the 1st of May, Governor Morris his the 10th; Governor Dobbs and Glen will also follow the example, and I promise to take the advice of your Lordship's Council thereon next Monday morning. The plan of operations proposed to be pursued, I take the liberty to inclose to your Lordship, and also a copy of some minutes taken at a Council which was held at Alexandria. Some sections thereof will shew your Lordship the opinions of the gentlemen present thereat, to whom the General proposed several questions and desired their particular sentiments thereon and answers thereto. I apprehend the general (somewhat dissatisfied that no such fund is already established) will solicit the ministry to obtain an act of Parliament whereby these several colonies may be compelled to contribute towards a general fund or stock, their several quotas. In case such an act should be moved for, it might perhaps provide and order that the quota imposed on each province be proportionable to the number of their inhabitants respectively; but that it be left to the Assemblies' option in what manner to raise that quota; and to prevent useless disputes and controversies, it might perhaps also direct that if the several branches of each legislature do not concur about ways and means within a certain time, the Governor and Council to proceed to levy the money in some particular way, or after any manner that may be deemed most ready and convenient. What the Generals or the other Governors may determine to do or wish as to the matter, I know not; but I thought it my duty to hint to your Lordship what possibly may happen."[1]

At the council held in Alexandria, this subject of revenue for the support of the army was the first presented. General Braddock stated that his instructions commanded him to insist that a joint fund be established for the benefit of the colonies, collectively, and he exhibited displeasure that such a thing had not already been done. The governors present mentioned their controversies with their assemblies, and Governor Sharpe, in particular, stated that nothing of this nature could be accomplished here, but by the direct interposition of parliament; this he had maintained from the first in all his letters to Lord Baltimore, and his friends in England.

"Having found it impracticable to obtain in their respective governments the properties expected by his Majesty toward defraying the expense of his service in North America, they were unanimously of opinion that it should be proposed to his Majesty's ministers to find out some method of compelling them to give it, and of assessing the several governments, in proportion to their respective abilities, their shares of the whole money already furnished, and which it shall be thought proper for them further to furnish, towards the general expense of his service."[2]

The requisitions of the crown for the supply of money, although backed by the entreaties and remonstrancces of the governors, were, in almost every instance, disregarded by the Assembly of Maryland. For the colonial statesmen scouted the pretence that England was graciously expending her treasure here exclusively for our benefit; and held "that these colonies were an object

[1] Sharpe's MS. *Letter-Book.*

[2] *Minutes of Council* at Alexandria. Pennsylvania *Colonial Records*, vi., p. 366.

of the highest importance to the mother country, and already the chief basis of its trade and independence;" and "that it was more for the interest of the nation to carry on a war with the French, in America, than in any other part of the world, since all the money circulated in the colonies returned, in the end, to Great Britain."[1] The British government now discovered that Maryland, at least, far from being a mere humble dependency of the crown, was inhabited by a high-spirited and resolute people, sincerely attached to the mother county, but by no means disposed tamely to surrender the inestimable rights of regulating their own affairs and imposing their own taxes, which were guaranteed to them by their charter. To be thwarted by this insignificant province was more than the haughty ministry could brook; and even Mr. Pitt, afterwards the champion of American liberty, was so highly incensed at the course of Maryland, that he avowed his intention of bringing the colonies, when peace should be restored, into such subjection as would enable the English government to compel obedience to its requisitions.[2] General Braddock wrote to Lord Halifax: "I cannot sufficiently express my indignation against the provinces of Pennsylvania and Maryland, whose interests being alike concerned in this expedition, and much more so than any others on this continent, refuse to contribute anything towards the project." But if these provinces, who certainly did not spare what was far more precious than treasure—the lives of their own citizens—in this cause, were really censurable, the blame should not fall on the people alone, or their representatives. Again and again, during the war, the Lower House of Assembly brought in money bills, which were rejected by the Upper House and the governor, under the color that the proposed mode of levying taxes was an encroachment upon the prerogative of the lord propriеary. This apparition of the prerogative was, at this time, certain to arise whenever any measure of benefit to the people was presented for the approval of the governor. The Lower House was never unwilling to render assistance when the necessities of the people required it. The proprietary owned vast tracts of land in the province; and the Lower House justly insisted that these lands, and the revenues which he derived from the people, being equally benefited by the defence, ought to bear an equitable proportion of the cost incurred in maintaining it; and they reported money bills on this basis; but the governor and his council, the Upper House, refused to concur, and the bills fell to the ground.

WILLIAM PITT.

Nor were matters any better in Pennsylvania. "The proprietaries, our hereditary governors," says Franklin, "when any expense was to be incurred for the defence of the province, with incredible meanness, instructed their

[1] Bradford's *Magazine* for November, 1757. [2] McMahon, p. 271.

deputies to pass no act for levying the necessary taxes unless their vast estates were, in the same act, expressly exonerated; and they had even taken bonds of their deputies to observe such instructions."

In addition to the £6000 currency voted by both houses on July 25th, 1755, the Lower House, at the October session, appropriated an additional sum of £20,000 for "the encouragement of the service;" but because the grant was not in "a more acceptable manner," Governor Sharpe states, "the bill was stopped in the Upper House; and as it was evident to us that nothing could be expected from them, and that they would make no concessions, I thought myself under the necessity" of proroguing the session until he was "honored with his lordship's further instructions, and to receive more particular instructions."[1] These quarrels continued for years between the governor and Lower House, and left but little leisure for other business. The course of the Assembly of Maryland was remembered long afterwards; for we find that in the examination of Dr. Franklin, in 1766, when the repeal of the Stamp Act was under consideration, the conduct of Maryland, during this war, was brought up as one of the objections to its repeal. The query propounded to him during that examination, relating to the course of Maryland, and his answer thereto, are as follows:

> "*Query*: Did you never hear that Maryland, during the last war, had refused to furnish a quota towards the common defence?"
>
> "*Answer*: Maryland has been much misrepresented in that matter. Maryland, to my knowledge, never refused to contribute or grant aids to the crown. The Assemblies, every year during the war, voted considerable sums, and formed bills to raise them. The bills were, according to the constitution of that province, sent up to the council or upper house for concurrence. Unhappy disputes between the two houses, arising from the defects of that constitution principally, rendered all the bills but one or two abortive. It is true, Maryland did not then contribute its proportion, *but it was, in my opinion, the fault of the government, and not of the people*."[2]

General Braddock had written to the Duke of Newcastle from Williamsburg on the first of March, that he should be beyond the Alleghanies by the end of April; and in compliance with this promise, he now hurried his arrangements for a forward movement. By Colonel St. Clair's advice, it was decided to march from Alexandria in two divisions; one regiment and a portion of the stores were to be sent to Winchester, Virginia, whence a new road was nearly completed to Fort Cumberland, and the other regiment, with the remaining forces, were to move by way of Frederick, Maryland. Accordingly, on the 8th and 9th of April, the provincials and six companies of the 44th regiment, Sir Peter Halket, set out for Winchester; Lieutenant Colonel Gage and four companies remaining to escort the artillery. On the 18th of April, the 48th regiment, under Colonel Dunbar, marched for Frederick, detaching a company to the mouth of the Conecocheague creek (a large stream which flows into the Potomac in Washington county) to hasten the

[1] Sharpe's MS. *Letter-Book*.

[2] Franklin's *Works*, iv., p. 172.

forwarding of the stores gathered there. Arriving at Frederick, Colonel Dunbar found there was no road through Maryland to Fort Cumberland; and he accordingly, on the first of May, crossed the Potomac at the mouth of the Conecocheague and took the Winchester route. For the purpose of expediting the necessary preparations for transporting the supplies, Governor Sharpe, on the 22d of April, went to Frederick, where a portion of the army was then quartered. At this point he met General Braddock, Colonel Washington and Benjamin Franklin, the two latter having met for the first time. Washington had been invited by the General to serve as one of his aides-de-camp in the campaign. Franklin, then the British postmaster-general for the colonies, had met Braddock here to concert a plan for forwarding despatches; and, learning the scarcity of wagons, undertook to furnish them from Pennsylvania. By adroit means he succeeded in obtaining from the counties of Lancaster, York and Cumberland, one hundred and fifty wagons with four horses to each, and fifteen hundred saddle or pack horses needed for the expedition. Besides this assistance Governor Sharpe tells us, General Braddock did "not scruple in enlisting and taking away a good many servants from the inhabitants of Frederick, Prince George's and Baltimore counties, as well as impressing their wagons, horses, teamsters, carriages and carriage horses." To such an extent were the seizures made, that the contractors for the new court house which was then being erected in Frederick, found it impossible to obtain horses to haul the materials to the site of the building. "He was extremely warm and angry" at this time "and stormed like a lion rampant."

Braddock, while at Frederick, purchased of Governor Sharpe an English chariot with six horses, in which he rode; and on the 1st of May accompanied by his guard of light horse, he left Frederick and by various routes reached Fort Cumberland on the 10th.

The erection of Fort Cumberland (sometimes called "Fort Mount Pleasant"),[1] and its strength, have already been described. It stood upon the bank of Will's creek, near its junction with the Potomac, "opposite to the New Store,"[2] on the site of the present city of Cumberland, in Alleghany county, Maryland. In ancient days the site of this fortification had been a Shawanee village, and its Indian name, "Cucucbetuc," is still preserved. Here, after a series of disappointments and delays, Braddock at length assembled his forces, which amounted to more than two thousand effective men. The regiments of Halket and Dunbar, originally one thousand strong, were now increased to fourteen hundred by volunteers and conscriptions principally procured in Maryland; and besides these there were the two independent companies from New York; five companies of rangers, and two of carpenters and pioneers principally from Virginia; one company of rangers from Maryland; one company of rangers from North Carolina; and thirty

[1] Pennsylvania *Colonial Records*, vi., p. 180. [2] *Ibid.*

seamen, under a lieutenant of the navy furnished by Admiral Keppel, having four pieces of cannon, which they were to assist in dragging over the mountains.

Among the officers present who afterwards distinguished themselves in the Revolution, we find Thomas Cresap, Hugh Mercer, George Washington, Daniel Morgan, Thomas Gage and Horatio Gates.

Being at last ready to undertake the long and tedious journey that was before him, General Braddock gave orders for the army to advance. On the 30th of May, Sir John St. Clair, with Major Chapman and 600 men of the 44th regiment, were sent forward to clear a road to the Little Meadows, on

FORT CUMBERLAND.[1]

the Youghiogeny, thirty miles distant, where they were to erect a fortified camp. The army followed in three divisions, the first under Col. Halket, on the 7th of June; the next under Lt. Col. Gage, on the 8th, and the third under Col. Dunbar on the 10th. Braddock delayed his departure until the 10th, when he set off with his aides-de-camp and others of his staff, and his body guard of light horse. Fort Cumberland, with the hospital filled with invalids, was left under the care of Col. Innes. The advance through the forests and over the steep mountains with wagons loaded with unnecessary luggage and camp equipage, as well as with munitions and supplies, was, as Washington had foretold, a "tremendous undertaking." Roads were to be cut, streams to be bridged, and morasses made passable. Passing the great

[1] From Lowdermilk's *History of Cumberland*.

Savage Mountain, and the gloomy pine forest known as the "Shades of Death," they reached the Little Meadows, but twenty-four miles from Fort Cumberland, at the end of ten days.

While these events were occurring in the western part of Maryland, the governor and the Lower House of Assembly were quarrelling over the requisitions made by General Braddock for supplies for his army. In consequence of an appeal for assistance from General Braddock, Governor Sharpe, on the 23d of June, convened the assembly and laid before them the letter he had lately received. In reply to the governor's message the Lower House said:

"We shall take the subject matter therein recommended under our immediate and most attentive consideration, and flatter ourselves our speedy resolutions thereupon will fully demonstrate our readiness to embrace the opportunity that now presents itself of manifesting an unshaken Loyalty to the best of Kings, a just sense of his royal and paternal care of all his subjects, however remote from the happy influence of his more immediate protection; and at the same time a steady adherence, and immoveable attachment to the true interests, rights and privileges, of those from whom our power of forming resolutions is delegated.

"We still continue (as we always have been) in the strongest inclination to do every thing reasonably within our power, which may contribute to this laudable end, and entertain the most sanguine hopes that we shall not now, in the course of our proceedings, meet with any rock upon which we shall split, or which may in the least obstruct the granting supplies, with the dispatch necessary to render effectual our sincere intentions for his Majesty's service, and the common safety of ourselves and fellow-subjects."

On June 28th, the Governor sent to the Lower House the following message:

"Gentlemen of the Lower House of Assembly:

"I have just received letters from Colonel Innes at Fort Cumberland, and from the back inhabitants of Frederick County, advising me that a party of French Indians, last Monday morning (June 23) fell on the inhabitants of this Province, and killed two men and one woman (who have been since found dead); eight other persons they have taken prisoners and carried off. The names of the persons who were murdered and left, are John Williams, his wife and grandson; and with their bodies was also found that of a French Indian. The persons carried off, are Richard Williams (a son of John who was murdered) with two children, one Dawson's wife, and four children. Richard William's wife, and two brothers of the young man that is killed, have made their escape. This accident, I find, has so terrified the distant inhabitants, that many of them are retiring and forsaking their plantations. Another letter from Winchester in Virginia informs me that a party of Indians have also attacked the back inhabitants of that Province, of whom they have killed eleven, and carried away many captives. Apprehending the French would proceed in this manner as soon as General Braddock and the troops under his command should have passed the mountains, and being confirmed in my opinion by an intimation in the General's letter, I issued a proclamation near a month since, cautioning the distant and other inhabitants of this Province to be on their guard, and unite for their common defence and safety. At the same time I sent peremptory orders and instructions to the officers of the militia of Frederick County, frequently to muster and discipline their several troops and companies, once a fortnight at least; and in case of an alarm that the enemy was approaching or had fallen on the inhabitants, to march out and act either offensively or defensively, and use all means to protect and defend the inhabitants from the devastations of the French or their Indians. However, I find neither the proclamation or instructions will be effectual unless the militia can be assured that they shall receive satisfaction and pay for the time that they shall be out on duty. I should consider it highly proper for us to have about a hundred, or at least a company of sixty men, posted or constantly ranging for some time on the frontiers, for our protection. In this I desire your advice, and that you will enable me to support such a number.

"Gentlemen:

"At the General's request, and that I might receive early intelligence at this time from the camp and the back inhabitants, I have engaged several persons, between this place and Will's Creek, to receive and speedily convey any letters that shall come to them directed for the General or myself. I doubt not you will be convinced of the necessity of such a measure, and provide for the expence thereof.

"HORO. SHARPE."

The House, on the same day, took into consideration the governor's message, and immediately passed the following resolutions:

"RESOLVED, That this House will make suitable provision for the maintaining eighty men, including officers, for four months (if occasion) for ranging on the frontiers of this Province, to protect the same against the incursions and depredations that may be attempted or made by the French or their Indian allies.

"RESOLVED further, That this House will defray the reasonable expense of conveying intelligence from Wills' Creek to Annapolis and back thither, for four months."

With some slight amendments, the Upper House agreed to the resolution, and £2,000 was appropriated for the purposes therein mentioned.

On the 5th of July, the governor sent another message to the Lower House, informing them that bands of hostile Indians were entering the province, and that fifteen of the people of Frederick county, on their way to Fort Cumberland for protection, had been killed or captured by savages. The result of these communications to the assembly is given in the following extract from a letter of Sharpe's to Charles Calvert, dated July 9, 1755:

"The Lower House still perseveres in their obstinacy, and I believe will never recede from what they have been contending for, though half the province should be depopulated. They have not yet addressed me to be prorogued; but I expect they will to-morrow morning, and 'twill be absolutely to no purpose ever to meet them again. I have not since heard from the General; but I am not without apprehensions that he will be obliged to desert the fort when he has taken it, for want of provisions which he cannot now expect from the colonies. In that case I fear the French will again take possession of that country, and then let the General's success be ever so great, we shall be in as bad, if not a worse situation than we were last winter."

In his letter of July 9, the governor touches another subject which was disquieting the Lower House:

"I prorogued our Assembly yesterday evening, after they had twice requested me to be dismissed. In the course of the session they presented me with a furious address against Roman Catholics, which you see inclosed. As I thought it contained some indecent reflections, I thought it improper to let it pass unanswered, as you will see by the papers herewith transmitted. The occasion of it was the late preferment of the Attorney-General, who unhappily is no favorite with the people, to the Naval Office of Patuxent

I believe, too, their warmth was increased by some letters written thither some time since, intimating that if Mr. Hanbury had not prevented it, you would have got Mr. Darnal appointed to a seat in the Council. For my part I have not heard but the Papists behave themselves peaceably and as good subjects. They are, I imagine, about one-twelfth of the people; and many of them are men of pretty considerable fortunes. I conceive their numbers do not increase, though I have reason to think the greater part of the Germans which are imported profess that religion. As the Lower House first resolved that all the Penal laws mentioned in the Toleration Act are in force within this Province, though some of them have been entirely, and others in part, repealed by later acts of Parliament, I declined granting the request in the conclusion of their address, lest the courts should govern themselves in some sort by the resolve of the Lower House of Assembly, and a fiery persecution should ensue. This part of my conduct will not, I hope, be disapproved of by his Lordship or yourself; and I hope you will think that nothing has been left undone to bring the Assembly to reason and temper, though our endeavours have failed of success.

"A bill for an agent was sent to the Upper House, but immediately rejected. Governor Morris informs me that all his endeavors have proved equally unsuccessful, and that he cannot think of meeting the Assembly of that province again, unless some reformation be first made in their Constitution."

On the 9th of July, the day of Braddock's defeat, Governor Sharpe writes to Charles Calvert, from Annapolis:

"From our receiving no letters from the general since those dated the 22d of June, we apprehend that those Indian parties have cut off the communication between him and Fort Cumberland and taken the carriers. I am about to depart for Fredericktown (where I have given orders for all the military officers of that county to meet), to try what can be done with the militia for the defence and protection of our distant inhabitants. I propose to draft a company of 60 or 80 from the militia, by lot, and oblige them to keep ranging on the frontiers for a few months, without any pay. Provisions they must impress, and take it where it can be found; and if money be ever granted, the people from whom it is taken must be satisfied for the same. Unless some such step be taken, the people will not be persuaded to stay on their plantations, being already struck with an universal panic. The representatives for Frederick and some of the other counties on this side of the Bay would have gladly done anything to obtain assistance and protection, but as the gentlemen whose counties are not so immediately exposed, did not so sensibly feel for the sufferings of the poor people as they would were they less retired from danger. All propositions for an accommodation were vain and fruitless."

And on the same day he writes to Lord Baltimore:

"When the gentlemen of the Lower House came to the resolution that your Lordship was before advised of, I was not without hopes that they would fall on some unexceptionable means to raise a small sum of money for the protection of your Lordship's tenants who are exposed to the encroachments and devastations of the French and the Savages, by whom twenty-six of the distant inhabitants have already perished. However, I with sorrow find that they will set nothing in competition with the points for which they have been contending; and that the lives and safeties of the people must submit to their caprice and humour. . . . . . . Governor Morris advises me that the Assembly of that province have behaved and concluded their session just in the same manner; and are determined to abide by their former resolutions, unless they be compelled to recede by some superior authority."

The fact is, the Lower House, while by no means indifferent to the perils of the border, expected that these would soon be put an end to by Braddock's triumph, and were jealous of making concessions which might throw an unreasonable share of the expenses of the war upon Maryland. Moreover, the relations between the province and the proprietary had altogether changed from what they had been under the paternal rule of the earlier Calverts. Frederick, the last Lord Baltimore, was a degenerate scion of a noble stock. Dissolute in life, selfish in character, he looked upon his province merely as a source of revenue, from which as much was to be drawn, and to which as little was to be conceded, as possible; the people, in return, resolved to grant as little and to extort as much as possible; and the present occasion, when his lordship might, perhaps, be apprehensive of losing his province altogether, seemed to the Lower House a favorable moment for urging their demands. Two points they had especially at heart. The first of these was the abolition of a port duty of fourteen pence a ton on all vessels trading to the port and owned by non-residents, (which yielded £800 or £900 yearly, for his lordship's use), and an excise of one shilling a hogshead on all tobacco exported, yielding about £1400, the greater part of which went to the governor, as his salary. These duties the people looked on as illegal exactions and grievous burthens; and as the proprietary refused to abolish them, the Lower House more than once attempted to have an agent appointed to lay the matter before the king in council; a step which the proprietary had always opposed and prevented, thereby confirming the people that these duties were illegal, and would not bear investigation. This was an old grievance of many years standing; a more recent one was the refusal of the proprietary to allow his vast landed estates to bear their proportion of the tax laid for the common defence.

To these demands Frederick turned a deaf ear; while the delegates were resolved to insist upon them to the uttermost. The position of the governor, on the one hand bound by his oath and duty to guard the proprietary's interests, as his representative, and to see that none of his rights suffered impairment; and on the other, conscious of the equity of part at least of the popular demands; looked upon by the people with some mistrust as the upholder of selfish tyranny, and by the proprietary with dislike as the mouthpiece of popular discontent; with plenty of enemies assailing his credit with his lordship, and plenty more undermining his authority in the province; conscious, moreover, that a great crisis was at hand in which nearly everything would depend on his judgment, tact, and firmness, and he would assuredly be held responsible for any misadventure—the position of Horatio Sharpe at this juncture was far from enviable.

On the fifteenth of July—so long was the bad news in reaching the interior—Sharpe writes to Charles Calvert:

"I have myself received no letter from the General or the camp since that dated the 22d of June; but a person belonging to the train in a letter to a gentleman of this place, dated the first of this month, at their camp near the Great Meadows, expresses himself in the following manner: 'On the 9th of last month the whole army (except 600 men with Genl. St. Clair who marched 2 days before) went from Will's Creek, and with infinite difficulty, through the worst roads in the world, arrived 10 days afterwards at the Little Meadows, where an abbatis was made by St. John and two engineers, encircling the whole camp. Here the whole halted 3 days; then the Bart. with his party moved forwards, and the second day after, the General, with four howitzers, four 12 pounders, 13 artillery waggons, besides ammunition carts, followed him, and have kept marching on ever since; and this evening he expects his Excellency will be within 25 miles of the fort. Col. Dunbar, with the remainder of the army, 4 artillery officers, 84 carriages with ordnance stores, and all the provision waggons from the rear, amongst whom I have the honor to be, though contrary to my inclination, as all the sport will be over long before we can reach the General. The night before last we were alarmed four different times by the skulking Indians, on whom our out-guards and sentries fired. We have had 3 people scalped, but it happened through their own imprudence in loitering behind too far. 'Tis said this morning the General has had advice that 500 regulars are in full march to the Fort; which is the reason he is determined to be there before them. As we have had but very little fresh provisions since we left the fort at Will's Creek, the officers as well as the private men, have been and still are extremely ill with the flux, and many have died. To-morrow morning we march again, and are to emerge on the western side of the Great Meadows; thence we are to proceed after the General, but I am fearful it will not be before we have built some fortification there and left a strong party of men with a great deal of provisions and artillery stores; our horses being so weak for want of food and rest that it is impossible for the whole rear to join the front in 25 days."

During all this time the possibility of Braddock's defeat had been as little dreamed of by the colonists as by that confident commander himself. The immense superiority of English over French troops had become, since Marlborough's time, an article of the British creed; and to the regulars at least, their Indian allies who knew nothing of drill and discipline, who never met a foe in the open field, and carried into warfare the tactics and strategy of the forest hunter, seemed beneath contempt, and only formidable to sentinels, stragglers, and "raw militia-men." The colonists, however, knew them better; and the general had been warned of the possibility of a surprise, and had received the caution with the scorn which he freely bestowed on the militia and all their doings. But even of the provincials, only a few who were with the army thought any serious disaster possible; elsewhere victory was regarded as certain. Preparations were made in Philadelphia and Annapolis for celebrating the assured triumph; and money was freely subscribed for illuminations and general festivities so soon as the couriers should bring the joyful news.

On the 9th of July the advance of Braddock's army, under Col. Gage, had approached within about seven miles of Fort Du Quesne. It was followed by the working-party under St. Clair, whose duty had been to make the road as they advanced; and behind this came the main body, guarded by flanking parties on each side. The march had hitherto been unmolested; the crossing of the Monongahela had been effected without the sight of an enemy, and the goal of the expedition seemed already within their grasp. To produce a striking impression on the enemy, the men were dressed in their brightest uniforms, and as they marched to the stirring sounds of martial music the forest-glades were illuminated with glowing color and flashing light as the rays of the July sun fell upon their coats of scarlet, or glanced from burnished gold and polished steel. Suddenly a small party of Indians were seen, who immediately vanished. The next instant, from unsuspected ravines on either side the line of march, an unseen foe opened a murderous fire on both flanks, throwing the advance into confusion. St. Clair's party advanced to support Gage, and Braddock ordered up the main body, all was in vain. In the narrow road, but twelve feet wide, the men were huddled into a confused mass, firing at random into the trees, while the enemy, whom they could not see, but whose numbers seemed multiplied ten-fold by their hideous yells and whoopings, mowed them down by a well-directed fire. Frantic with rage and excitement, Braddock endeavored to restore order and extricate his force from this slaughter-pen; and four horses were shot under him, as, reckless of his own life, he flew from point to point. His officers dismounted and formed into platoons, to set their men an example, and thus made themselves fair marks for the Indian rifles; but their self-devotion was fruitless. The provincials, skilled in forest-fighting, had at once sheltered themselves behind trees; and the regulars would have followed their example had Braddock allowed it, but he refused to give the order; and such was the force of discipline, or the bewildering effects of panic, that the men were mowed down as they stood, neither flying nor taking cover. Many were slain by the fire of their own comrades, who had lost the power of distinguishing friend from foe.

Thus for hours the slaughter went on. The ammunition was giving out, the officers were nearly all killed or wounded, not a single aide but Washington being left; more than half the army had fallen, and the rest could do nothing where they were but die. Braddock gave the order for retreat, and almost at the same moment a ball pierced his right arm and entered his lungs, inflicting a mortal wound. The retreat became a headlong flight, which the dying general in vain attempted to check. A few men gathered around him, bore him from the field, and obeyed his orders; and despite his agonies he employed every remaining moment of his life in endeavoring to provide for the safety of the survivors, repair in what slight measure he could, the disaster his rashness had caused, and bring back the shattered remnant of his army to Great Meadows, where he died.

On July 11, Colonel Innes, who had been appointed by Braddock Governor of Fort Cumberland, received the first uncertain news of a great reverse to the army, and hurried away expresses to the neighboring provinces. On the 16th, the tidings reached Annapolis; and on the next day Governor Sharpe set out for Fort Cumberland, accompanied by his secretary, Mr. Ridout, Lieutenant Gold, Ensign Russell, of his majesty's forces, and a band of volunteers who had taken up arms to aid in the defence of the frontier. On the 23d, while still on the way, the governor received a more full account, which he hastened to communicate to Lord Baltimore in the following letter:

"I am sorry to have such an occasion to write, but as we have a ship just about to sail, I embrace the opportunity to acquaint you that I have this instant received a letter from Captain Orme (who is at Fort Cumberland ill of his wounds) in which he gives me a brief account of the unfortunate engagement between the troops commanded by General Braddock and the French from Fort Du Quesne on the 9th inst. In the morning of that day the General crossed the Monongahela twice, the last time about 7 miles from the French Fort. A party of 300 men having passed the river advanced toward the Fort, and was immediately followed by another of 200. The General with the column of artillery, baggage and the main body of the army got over about one o'clock, when they heard a very heavy and quick fire in the front; the General and the main body immediately advanced in order to sustain them, but the two advanced detachments giving way and falling back on the main body caused great confusion, and the men were struck with such a panic, that afterwards no military expedient which could be used, had any effect. They were deaf to the exhortations of the general and the officers, who advancing sometimes in bodies and sometimes separately, were sacrificed by the soldiers declining to follow them. The general had 5 horses shot under him before he received a wound through his right arm into his lungs, of which he died the fourth day after. Sir Peter Halkett and the general's secretary were killed on the spot. Sir John St. Clair is wounded, but there is room to hope he will recover. The inclosed is a particular account of the officers that fell and of those that survived the action. The number of private soldiers killed and wounded is about 600. My last letter dated the 15th, will inform you that at the Little Meadows, the general, finding it impracticable for all the troops to advance farther together, selected 1200 of the best, and proceeded with as much of the artillery, ammunition and provisions as he thought necessary, leaving the main body of the convoy under the command of Col. Dunbar, who had orders to join him as soon as possible. The four howitzers, 4 twelve-pounders and 14 cohorns that the general had with him, with the ammunition, baggage and provisions are fallen into the hands of the enemy. When Col. Dunbar (who I have reason to apprehend, was about 40 miles behind the general), was apprized of this fatal accident, finding the troops extremely reduced and weakened by this action and sickness, he judged it impossible to attempt anything with them at that time with probability of success, and is returning to Fort Cumberland with every thing that he is able to bring with him, but as his horses were reduced and much enfeebled and many carriages wanted for the wounded men to prevent their falling into the hands of the enemy, he has destroyed most of the ammunition and the superfluous provisions that was left to his care. Captain Orme does not describe to me the situation of the place where the battle happened, how great were the number of the enemy, and whether they consisted principally of regular troops or Indians.

"When I received this account, I was on my way to Fort Cumberland with a number of gentlemen and volunteers, who had entered into an association to bear arms and protect the frontiers. I shall now halt at Frederick Town; and if I find the troops are not well supplied, shall expend part of a sum of money which the council and gentlemen of the country had subscribed upon the Assembly's refusal at their last meeting to grant any supplies, in purchasing a quantity of fresh provisions and such things as I think necessary for the troops, and escort them, with such men as I can persuade to join me, to Fort Cumberland, where I expect, in case I go thither, to find Col. Dunbar by that time arrived."

When the Governor reached the fort, all was alarm and confusion. Numbers of the terrified inhabitants had hurried to its walls for safety from the now defenceless frontier; and to complete their misery, Colonel Dunbar had announced his intention of abandoning everything and retreating to

Philadelphia, there to put his troops into winter quarters in the month of July; and all Sharpe's remonstrances and pleadings were unavailing to turn him from this disgraceful purpose. Indeed he succeeded in convincing the governor that under the circumstances there was nothing else to be done, as we may see from the close of his (Sharpe's) letter of August 12th, to Charles Calvert:

"The 23d of July I addressed a letter to his Lordship and another to yourself, acquainting you with the fatal engagement that had happened near the banks of the Monongahela. I was then proceeding westward with an intention to send up a supply of fresh provisions and wine to Fort Cumberland, which I imagined the troops must have been in need of. On my arrival at Conogsgee [Conecocheague], which is thirty miles beyond Frederick Town, I was informed that they had plenty of everything at the camp and that Col. Dunbar had determined, and was about to leave Fort Cumberland and to march with the remains of the two regiments and the three independent companies to Philadelphia. This news, so soon after the depredations of the Indians and the General's defeat, had much alarmed and thrown our distant inhabitants into great consternation. They concluded that when the troops should retire from the frontiers, the enemy would repeat and renew their devastations; and that it was better for them to fly naked and leave their habitations than remain an easy prey to an enraged and cruel enemy, who may now have free and uninterrupted access to these two infatuated and defenceless colonies. Some that were retiring to their friends in the more populous parts of this and the neighboring Provinces, I persuaded to return back, with assurances that a sufficient body of troops would be left at Fort Cumberland for the security of that place; and that I would take proper measures to prevent the inroads and incursions of any French or Indian parties; which I hope will be effectually done by the small forts that I have ordered to be built, one on Tonallaway Creek, and three under the North Mountain, in each of which I shall place a small garrison with orders to them to patrol from one to the other and to Fort Cumberland, and in case of alarm to receive the neighboring families into their protection. The subscription that had been made in this county and some other parts of the Province has enabled me to take this step for the security of our frontiers, and to continue on foot the Maryland company, which the late resolves of the Lower House had made me desire the General to distribute between the two regiments.

"It was as surprising a defeat, I think, as has been heard of; for 'tis supposed that the Indians that day opposed to General Braddock were not less than 1,500 or 2,000, and yet none of the English that were engaged will say they saw a hundred, and many of the officers who were in the heat of the action the whole time, will not assert that they saw one enemy. It seems they had most advantageously posted themselves behind the large trees that grew on the eminences or hills that were on the right flank and in the front of our troops, thence they fired irregularly on the English beneath them, who being in a compact body became a fair mark to their enemies, against whom they fired in platoons almost as fast as they could load, without doing, as I conceive, any great execution. The men had not been used to, nor had any idea of this kind of fighting, which dispirited them and soon threw them into confusion. They refused to obey the voice of their officers, and having wasted all their ammunition, retired in great disorder, leaving the enemy masters of the field, and of all the artillery, ammunition, baggage and everything that had passed the river. It is supposed that 800 or 900 stand of arms have fallen into the enemy's hands, and that what Col. Dunbar by the General's orders destroyed, was worth at that place £100,000. This loss of all the artillery except four six-pounders which Col. Dunbar has taken with him, together with the loss of so many officers and the disability of many that survive to enter again on action, as also the present condition of the troops who have been harassed almost to death by the laborious campaign they have made, has determined Col. Dunbar to retire from Fort Cumberland: which step I think the present temper and disposition of the troops must incline any one who saw and conversed with them, to approve."

Such was the battle of the Monongahela, fought on the 9th of July, 1755; a scene of panic and carnage, in proportion to the relative numbers engaged, which is, perhaps, unexampled in the annals of modern warfare. Of the fourteen hundred and sixty officers and privates who went into the engagement, four hundred and fifty-six were slain outright, and four hundred and twenty were wounded; making a total of eight hundred and seventy-seven men, or *sixty per cent.* Of eighty-nine commissioned officers, sixty-three were killed or wounded, not one of the field-officers escaping unhurt. Everything was abandoned to the victors: artillery, small arms, ammunition; all the wagons, provisions, baggage and stores; the military chest containing £25,000 in specie, and even the general's cabinet, with his instructions and private papers. But few of the wounded fell into the enemy's hands, all who were able to escape having done so; and those who were left on the field the Indians speedily put to death. A score of regulars, however, and one Virginian, being cut off from flight, surrendered. Half of these were tomahawked before they reached the Ohio; the others were taken to Fort Du Quesne, and there tortured to death at the stake, in the sight of the French garrison, who crowded to witness the atrocious spectacle.[1]

The body of Braddock was buried privately, on the morning of July 14, in a spot selected in the middle of the road, in order to efface any marks by which the enemy might recognize it, and disinter and insult his remains.[2]

Braddock was at least fortunate in his death, which spared him the humiliation of knowing his reputation blasted, and hearing his name everywhere mentioned with opprobrium, as of one who had disgraced his country and the service. The unreasoning popular anger charged him, not only with rashness, arrogance, and obstinacy, but with cowardice, though he was ignorant of fear, and in his vain efforts to redeem his fatal negligence, his conduct on the field had been heroic. In the colonies, the *prestige* of British invincibility was at an end. This battle, for the first time in our history, tested on the same field, the disciplined regular of Europe, and the rifleman and bushfighter of America, and taught the latter that on his own ground, amid forests, thickets, rocks, and mountains, the other was no match for him. It was the beginning of a contest in which the colonies became schools of arms; and a martial spirit was fostered and trained among the people, who gained

[1] Sargent, *Braddock's Expedition*, p. 258.

[2] Until the opening of the National road, Braddock's road was the thoroughfare between Baltimore and the Ohio. About 1823, some laborers at work on it exposed the general's remains, still recognizable by the insignia of his rank. A few of the bones were taken by the discoverers, and the rest re-interred under "a tree on the hill near the National road." Mr. Stewart, of Uniontown (father of the Hon. Andrew Stewart), afterwards collected the scattered bones from those who had taken them, and sent them, it is believed, to Peale's museum in Philadelphia.—Day's *Pennsylvania*, p. 334.

confidence in themselves and learned their own strength: a lesson which stood them in good stead twenty years later. It is more than possible that had Braddock obtained the easy victory he anticipated, the course of American history would have been changed.

Shortly after the defeat, Washington wrote to Governor Dinwiddie:

"The dastardly behavior of the regular troops (so called) exposed those who were inclined to do their duty to almost certain death; and at length, in spite of every effort to the contrary, they broke and ran as sheep before hounds; leaving the artillery, ammunition, provisions, baggage, and in short, everything, a prey to the enemy; and when we endeavored to rally them, in hopes of regaining the ground and what we had left upon it, it was with as little success as if we attempted to stop the wild bears of the mountains, or the rivulets with our feet.

"It is supposed that we had three hundred or more killed, and about that number were brought off wounded. It is conjectured (I believe with much truth) that two-thirds of both received their shot from their own cowardly regulars, who gathered themselves into a body, contrary to orders, ten or twelve deep—would then level, fire, and shoot down the men before them."

No allowance was made for the peculiar training of the British troops, drilled to obey orders with the precision and unintelligence of machines, never relying upon their own judgment, but blindly following the word of command; who here found themselves in a situation where no routine tactics were available, and where each man had to act for himself. Falling under the bullets of an invisible foe, they could only huddle into squads and fire at random, until terror overcame them, and they broke into headlong flight. Their conduct was attributed to stupidity and abject cowardice; and from this time "king's troops" were held to be a dear bargain in the colonies.

So soon as Braddock was buried, the retreat was resumed, under the command of Colonel Dunbar, who arrived at Fort Cumberland on the afternoon of Tuesday, July 22d, with three hundred wounded in his ranks. On the 2d of August he again set out with 1200 men. and on the 29th reached Philadelphia unmolested, and encamped on Society Hill. This pusillanimous retreat excited the greatest indignation and alarm throughout the colonies, for it left the whole frontier uncovered, and the inhabitants, unarmed and undisciplined, had to make a hasty choice between a desperate and unorganized defence or precipitate flight. The enemy now, astonished at his own success, harried at his pleasure all the western borders of Maryland, Virginia and Pennsylvania, plundering and murdering everywhere. To add to the alarm, the Shawanese and Delaware Indians, who had hitherto continued faithful, but had repeatedly solicited employment against the enemy, with threats of defection in case of refusal, now went over to the French side, allured by hopes of recovering the lands they had sold, and tempted by the booty that was so abundant, and began to ravage and slay the unhappy colonists. The outposts were everywhere driven in, some of the smaller forts taken, and universal panic prevailed, the remoter inhabitants crowding for safety to the interior, and by their terror and the exaggerated rumors they disseminated, increasing the general fright.

Meanwhile, the people of Maryland were not idle. Fort Cumberland was still held by the provincials, under Captain Dagworthy; but this isolated post could afford no protection against the roving bands of savages who plundered the country round; and the garrison were themselves subject to frequent annoyance. There are two high knobs of the mountain, one on the southern, or Virginia side of the Cohongoruton, and the other on the Maryland side, within a short distance of the fort. The Indians frequently took possession of these heights, from which they could fire into the fort. On one occasion a rather large party of savages were posted on the knob on the Maryland side, and had given considerable annoyance, when a captain and seventy men volunteered to dislodge them. On a very dark night they sallied out from the fort, surrounded the knob, and cautiously ascending until they were within musket-shot of the foe, waited for daybreak. As soon as it was light they opened a brisk fire from all sides upon the Indians, which threw them into utter confusion. Not knowing which way to escape, they were killed almost to a man; and the knob, to this day, bears the name of "Bloody Hill."

Shortly after this "Kill-buck," a distinguished chief, attempted to take the fort by stratagem. He approached it at the head of a large force of warriors, and pretending that they came as friends and allies, asked to be admitted. The commander appeared to be deceived by the stratagem, and opened the gates; but no sooner had the chief and his principal warriors entered, than the gates were closed, and the wily savage caught in a trap. The commander charged him with his treachery, and as a punishment dressed his prisoners in women's clothes, and drove them from the fort; a humiliation which, to the haughty savage, was more bitter than a torturing death.[1]

The alarm which the disaster on the Monongahela, the flight of the British troops, and the advance of the enemy occasioned, spread over the whole province. Many of the inhabitants of the western settlements fled to Baltimore, and preparations were even made by the people of that town to place the women and children on board the vessels in the harbor and send them to Virginia; while some of the Virginians were so alarmed as to think there was no safety short of England itself.[2] But there were others of firmer temper, who prepared to meet the coming danger. In September, Lieutenant Stoddert, assisted by fifteen pioneers from the surrounding settlements, erected a stockade fort, which served as a rallying point for the settlers of the country round. All those who lived beyond Tonalloway creek abandoned their habitations; and the country, as far to the eastward as thirty miles east of Colonel Thomas Cresap's, who lived about five miles west of the mouth of the south branch of the Potomac, was deserted. Colonel Cresap himself removed down the river to the plantation of his son, Michael Cresap, who lived near the Conecocheague. The two Cresaps were distinguished among the hardy frontiersmen for courage, intelligence and skill in Indian warfare; they were always on the alert,

[1] Kercheval, *History of the Valley of Virginia*, p. 107.

[2] McSherry.

and their timely warnings saved many of their neighbors from massacre. Their block-house, which was strong enough to resist the savages, served as a place of refuge in case of expected invasion, and as a rendezvous for the settlers in more peaceful times, where they met to hear and tell the news, to try their skill as marksmen, or engage in friendly trials of strength or dexterity, and at night, seated around a huge log fire, they would tell adventures of war or of the chase; and if by good luck any of the company possessed a fiddle or jewsharp, and had the cunning to awaken its harmony, the evening wound up hilariously with a dance.[1]

So now the frontiersmen gathered at Cresap's and strengthened his block-house for defence; others sought protection at Fort Cumberland and

CRESAP'S HOUSE IN 1770.

Frederick. Governor Sharpe, as we have already seen, had raised a number of volunteers at this town, when on his way to the fort; and to defray their expense, subscriptions were raised throughout the province, Annapolis and the surrounding country alone furnishing in a very few days one thousand pounds. The people of Baltimore raised a large sum with which they purchased arms and ammunition, and established a public armory in the town. The news from the frontiers, telling of Indian raids and massacres, kept up the alarm. In the Maryland *Gazette* of October 9th we have the following account of affairs in the west:

[1] About 1770, Michael Cresap removed further west, beyond the Alleghany, where he built himself a house of hewed logs, with a shingle roof nailed on, which is believed to have been the first shingled house west of the Alleghany mountains. He retained the title to this land for years, and at last disposed of it to Thomas and Basil Brown, two brothers from Maryland. From them the town of Brownsville, Kentucky, takes its name.—*American Pioneer*, ii., p. 61.

"By a person who arrived in Town last Monday (Oct. 6th,) from Col. Cresap's, we are told that last Wednesday (Oct. 1st) morning, the Indians had taken a man prisoner who was going to Fort Cumberland from Frazier's, and had also carried off a woman from Frazier's plantation, which is four miles on this side Fort Cumberland. The same morning they fell in with a man and his wife who had left their plantations, and were retiring into the more populous parts of the country; they shot the horse on which the man rid, but as it did not fall immediately, he made his escape; the woman it is supposed, fell into their hands, as neither she nor the horse on which she was riding have been since seen or heard of. The same party of Indians have also killed or carried off Benjamin Rogers, his wife and seven children, and Edmund Marle, of Frederick County. On Patterson's Creek many families have within this month been murdered, carried away, or burnt in their houses, by a party of these barbarians, who have entirely broke up that settlement.

"Another person, who left Stoddert's Fort last Sunday, acquaints us that the inhabitants of that part of the country were in the greatest consternation; that near 80 persons were fled to the said fort for protection, and many more gone off in the greatest confusion to Pennsylvania. This, it seems, has been occasioned by an express that was sent to Lieutenant Stoddert and the neighborhood by Col. Cresap, advising them that a party of 17 Indians had passed by his house, and had cut off some people, who dwelt on the Town Creek, which is a few miles on this side Col. Cresap's. One Daniel Ashloff, who lived near that creek, is come down towards Conococheague, and gives the same account. He says also, that as himself and father with several others were retiring from their plantations last Saturday they were attacked by the same Indians, as he supposes, and all but himself were killed or taken prisoners. It is said that Mr. Stoddert, who has a command of 15 men, invited a few of the neighborhood to join him, and to go in quest of the enemy, but they would not be persuaded, whereupon he applied himself to Major Prather for a detachment of the militia, either to go with a party of his men in pursuit of the savages, or garrison his fort, while he made an excursion. We hope there will be no backwardness in the militia to comply with such a reasonable request, especially as any party or person that shall take an enemy prisoner, will be rewarded with six pounds currency, and the person who will kill an enemy, with four pounds, provided he can produce witnesses, or the enemy's scalp, in testimony of such action."

In consequence of these outrages Governor Sharpe, on the 18th of October, called out the militia of the province. At the same time Captain Alexander Beall and Lieutenant Samuel Wade Magruder with thirty volunteers from the lower part of Frederick county, and Colonel Henry Ridgely with thirty more from Anne Arundel county, hastened to the invaded district. A few days afterwards sixty more volunteers, fully armed and equipped, went from Prince George's county to the west at their own expense. They arrived too late to punish the marauders, who had already made off with their booty and prisoners, but they remained to protect those who were left from further outrage.

Meanwhile the alarm increased, and the wildest rumors were afloat. It was reported early in November, that a large body of French and Indians were advancing upon the interior settlements; and this rumor reaching Frederick town on Sunday, November 2d, the inhabitants, expecting an immediate attack, rang the bells as an alarm, and despatched messengers to Baltimore and Annapolis for help. Several companies of volunteers at once mustered in Baltimore and the neighborhood, and marched without delay.

Even distant Annapolis caught the infection of terror, and on the 6th of November the citizens began to fortify the town. A correspondent in the *Gazette* of that date, reflects the general apprehension. He says:

"The Indians, as we are now informed by certain intelligence, are within a hundred miles of this city, the metropolis of our Province, and that in a considerable and formidable body. . . . . I know of no fitter place than Annapolis at present to answer their purpose: the places to the northward are in a proper posture of defence. The metropolis of Virginia, Williamsburg, is not a seaport town, and would not answer their purpose; the ports in the Carolinas are too far from the scene of action; Philadelphia is very populous, and might by her numbers make a stand; in fine Annapolis is the place they will probably pitch on, as being a place at present utterly defenceless, and is so well situated to fortify. If this advice of fortifying the town is not followed, I have one piece of counsel to give those who have any value for the lives of themselves and children, to pack up and be gone with all speed, and seek out some safer habitation than this desolate and infatuated place; for there is no time to lose, and they cannot now go to bed of a night in safety, it being probable that the enemy will burn their houses and cut their throats while they are sunk in sleep."

On the same day a report reached Baltimore that the French and Indians were within thirty miles of the town; and in a short time about two thousand volunteers had assembled for defence. This was a false alarm; but reports, which were unfortunately true, poured in, announcing slaughter and devastation in the western part of the province.

In November, Governor Sharpe, who had been active in measures for the defence of the frontier regions of the province, set out for New York to attend a council of governors summoned by Governor Shirley, commander-in-chief of the forces since Braddock's death, to arrange plans for the coming campaign. It was determined to prosecute the war with vigor, and on a large scale: an army of six thousand men was to make its way to Niagara; Crown Point was to be invested by ten thousand, and another attempt on Fort Du Quesne was to be made by a force of three thousand. Sharpe returned to Annapolis at the close of December, and convened the assembly to meet on the 23d of February to adopt the necessary measures for carrying out these plans.

In January, 1756, reports came to Maryland that Lancaster, Pennsylvania, had been burned by the French and Indians who were advancing into the interior. There was then a considerable body of friendly Indians living near Snow Hill, in Worcester county; and as a matter of precaution, Colonels Robert and John Henry proposed that they should be mustered in the town, and asked "if they were still friendly to the English, and whether they were inclined to leave Maryland and join the Indians at the North." They also proposed that they should be deprived of their arms. This proposition was not agreed to by the citizens; but the great men of the Indian town were summoned to Snow Hill, where, on being interrogated, they reported the numbers of their people as forty-three men, thirty-eight women, twenty-one boys and eighteen girls, making a total of one hundred and twenty souls.

Efforts were made to induce them to migrate to the north and "join their brethren, the Six Nations," and supplies were offered them for the journey, "but they answered with one voice they never would, as they were here born, and they would live and die in this place."[1]

Andnow while Fort Cumberland was the only considerable rallying point in the invaded region, its effectiveness was weakened by the old bickerings and jealousies between royal and provincial officers. Colonel Innes, who had been appointed by Braddock, "governor" of the fort, was called away to North Carolina soon after the disaster of the Monongahela. Captain Dagworthy, who commanded the Maryland troops, asserted his right of precedence over the other colonial officers at the post, upon the grounds that he had been an officer in the previous war, and still held a royal commission, in addition to his provincial commission from Governor Sharpe. In this position he was sustained by Sharpe, who claimed the fort as a Maryland post, and therefore properly under the command of a Maryland officer. Governor Dinwiddie took the ground that it was a king's fort, built in obedience to an order sent him by the king, and chiefly for the king's troops; so in no sense subject to the authority of Maryland. As for Dagworthy's alleged royal commission, this was held to have been annulled by his having commuted his half-pay for a sum of money. Colonel Washington, who claimed the command as chief of the Virginia forces, endeavored to move Dinwiddie to decisive action in the matter; but not succeeding in this—which indeed would probably have brought about a serious misunderstanding between the authorities of the two provinces, at a time when harmonious action was more than ever needed—to settle the dispute, by the request of his officers, and with the approval of Governor Dinwiddie, he set out for Boston to lay the matter before Governor Shirley. It was now mid-winter; but attended by his aide-de-camp, Captain George Mercer, and Captain Walter Stewart, of the Virginia light horse, he safely accomplished the journey of five hundred miles on horseback.

Shirley confirmed Washington's position, and on March 5th issued an order, declaring Dagworthy simply a provincial captain, acting under a commission from the Governor of Maryland, who could only rank as such, under the command of all provincial field-officers, where there were no regular troops, and giving Washington the command of Fort Cumberland.[2]

After ten days spent in Boston, Washington started on his return to Virginia, arriving in Annapolis on the 22d; and after informing Governor Sharpe of the result of his mission, left the next day for Williamsburg.

The year 1755 connects Maryland with another melancholy page in American history—that of the unfortunate Acadians, whose wrongs have been since so widely celebrated in prose and verse.

By the treaty of Utrecht (1713) this harmless people had been brought under the dominion of the English, but it had been expressly stipulated that on conditions of their not assisting their French countrymen to regain the

[1] *Council Proceedings.* [2] Sparks, ii., p. 133.

territory, nor bearing arms against the English, they should retain their lands unmolested. Here they lived peaceful and patriarchal lives, in primitive simplicity, probably the most inoffensive people then dwelling on the earth They were treated, however, with great harshness by their new masters, (on the ground that at the capture of Fort Beaujeu, a number of Acadians had been found in the garrison, who asserted that they were kept there against their will) and their property seized and their services demanded with brutal severity. Finally, Governor Shirley, of Massachusetts, procured an order from England that they should be expelled from their homes, not as exiles, but as prisoners, who must find other places of settlement among the English. Lawrence, the lieutenant-governor of the province, and his council, entered upon the task with alacrity, and the execution of the sentence was entrusted to the New England troops. At a general assembly of the Acadians at Grand Pré on August 30th, they were notified to quit the province at once, retaining only their money and household effects; not only their lands, whose fertility had long excited provincial cupidity, but even their live-stock, being declared forfeit to the crown.

Vessels were provided for their transport to the main land, and into these the unhappy Acadians were driven rather than led. During all the fall and winter the deportation continued; fathers being separated from children, husbands from wives, the aged and infirm from their natural protectors; and as the different vessels had different destinations, the separation in many cases was eternal. Whether this was in the orders, or was merely a gratuitous cruelty on the part of the New Englanders, we are not informed. A few escaped and hid in the woods; and to insure their perishing, the crops were destroyed, and the barns and houses burnt.

The number of these exiles scattered along the coast from New Hampshire to Georgia, was about seven thousand, of these about nine hundred came to Maryland.

It was certainly an unpropitious time for French Catholics to appeal to provincial sympathies. French and Indians had been so often and so recently associated in deeds of blood and cruelty upon their friends and kindred, and the alarm at anticipated invasion was so great, that as much abhorrence was felt for a subject of his Most Christian Majesty as for the painted savage of the forest. In addition, the war had aroused the anti-Catholic feeling, and the colonial governors did what they could to inflame it, in their frequent appeals to the reluctant assemblies for money, who, even in their paroxysms of terror, were slow to loosen their purse-strings. The ministers from the pulpit had harped on the same theme; and the universal alarm gave additional fierceness to bigotry. The general state of feeling may be seen from the reports and records of the day. In November, 1754, the citizens of Prince George's instructed their delegates to urge a law "to dispossess the Jesuits of those landed estates which under them became formidable to his majesty's good Protestant subjects of this province; to exclude Papists from places of trust and profit; and to prevent them from sending their children to foreign Popish seminaries for education, whereby the minds of youth are corrupted and alienated from his majesty's person and government."[1] The Lower House of Assembly, on the 1st of July, 1755, urged the governor to "issue his proclamation commanding all magistrates and other officers duly to execute the penal statutes against Roman Catholics within this province." The church-wardens of various parishes adopted an order commanding "all persons not having lawful excuse, to resort to their parish church or chapel on every Sunday and other days, and then and there to abide in decent manner during the time of Common Prayer, Preaching, or other Service of God."[2]

It was to this excited atmosphere of public feeling that these unfortunate exiles came. On the first of Decmber, 1755, five vessels arrived at Annapolis with the Acadians on board. The people of the town were at first uneasy at the thought of having domiciled among them a number of "French Papists," quite capable, they thought, in their quality of French, of betraying them to the invading enemy, and in their quality of Papists, of plotting to overthrow the Protestant religion. But they did not altogether do violence to Maryland traditions, nor stain the glory of the "Land of the Sanctuary." The hapless exiles were soon found to be rather the objects of pity than apprehension; and blankets, provisions, and clothing, which they sorely needed, were promptly supplied them. Governor Sharpe being then absent, attending the council of provincial governors in New York, the president of the council sent one vessel to the Patuxent river, one to Oxford, on the Chesapeake, one to Wicomico, and one to Baltimore, retaining one at Annapolis, so as to distribute the exiles throughout the province. Those sent to Oxford were fortunate in being placed under the superintendence of Mr. Henry Callister, a merchant of that port, who had from the first interested himself in their behalf.

Shortly after their arrival, Mr. Callister prepared an address from them to the king, asking for relief and redress; and forwarded it to Mr. Anthony Bacon, of London, for presentation to his majesty. In the letter which accompanied it, dated December 25th, Mr. Callister says to Mr. Bacon:

"This serves to cover the inclosed address to his Majesty, which your innate sentiments of humanity will prompt you to put into proper hands. These poor wretches have been here at Oxford ever since the 8th current, and nothing yet has been done for them by the public—the Governor being gone to the northward, and not yet returned. Nobody knows what to do; and few have charity for them. I see no one interested for them but myself. They are pleased to mention me, but I assure you it is not my vanity which approves of it, though they insist on it; and I think it shows their gratitude—in which, you may say, I indulge myself and them. I think it a happy [qy. "unhappy"?] event that has put them into our hands at this time, when Papist principles are dangerous, even in sworn subjects. But our aversion to their principles must not be allowed to destroy the seeds of humanity. The case of these French is grossly misrepresented among us to their disadvantage, which, added to the aversion we have to their principles as Papists, seems to have destroyed the seeds of charity in us, and eradicated the principle of

[1] Maryland *Gazette*, November 28, 1754. [2] Maryland *Gazette*.

humanity. Some of the fraternity, who are dispersed in other parts of Maryland, and the other colonies, we daily hear the most shocking accounts of. Particularly, Mr. Lowes sent up this way to inquire what was done in behalf of those sent hither, and made a dismal representation of the condition they were in in Somerset, where they were obliged to betake themselves for shelter to the swamps, now and a long time full of snow, where they sicken and die. I have had the good fortune since I interested myself for them, yet not without potent opposition and much difficulty, to dispose of their sloop-load; almost every family being now placed in good houses for the winter. There's a number of them now about me in tears, craving relief for their sick, &c."[1]

On January 17th, Mr. Callister addressed the following letter to Governor Sharpe:

"Your Excellency's sensibility of the sufferings of these wretched exiles among us, emboldens your petitioner, on behalf of them and myself, to make a direct application to the fountain-head, having met with great obstacles in forming a regular approach, though I have not spared pains to touch the souls of those whose immediate care it ought to be (especially in your Excellency's absence,) at least to have assisted me, from the same motives I assisted them; which I am confident were not simply just and humane, but also political. The trouble I had is as extraordinary as the expense. I have been shocked in a particular manner by the opposition of the Honorable Col. Lloyd; and because I could not quit the principle I acted on, it required an uncommon resolution to support me. I shall stop here (lest I should say anything that might be disagreeable to you, or seem injurious to him,) and lay my cause at your feet. Inclosed is an account of the charge these people have put me to since they landed. You will easily imagine to yourself there are a thousand articles I could not with decency make a charge of. When the distressed see a man's breast open for their relief, they come in at that door; and it is sufficient to give a hint of the trouble and expense of it. I did imagine that the King's allowance would be due till the day the transport sloop was regularly discharged; and as the captain gave out no provisions from the day they began to land, which was the 8th of December, there would be due to these people more than sufficient to pay me, and moreover, something to mend their clothing. This I shall not say further upon, humbly submitting it. The simple French at Annapolis, I am told, called themselves prisoners of war. They did so here likewise at first; but they were soon made sensible of their mistake. Indeed they might easily be forgiven, when one considers. See the inclosed address to his Majesty, where they declare themselves accordingly. This is yet a dilemma to them, and may well puzzle wiser heads, especially as they say in their address, that they were treated as prisoners of war by Governor Lawrence. They might have thought themselves not only in duty bound to declare themselves prisoners, but also in that character to be entitled to better treatment than they have met with as faithful subjects. For the justice of this remark I appeal to the consistency of Governor Lawrence's letter to Sir T. Robinson, with the capitulation of Beau Séjour. They may be both seen in "The Uni-

[1] Among those who materially assisted Mr. Callister, we find the Rev. Thomas Bacon—rector of All Saints' parish in Frederick county, domestic chaplain to Lord Baltimore, and the well-known compiler of the early laws of Maryland—the most prominent. A collection was taken up in his parish church (White Marsh), on the 14th of December, "for the relief of the poor, distressed French exiles of Acadia;" and we find that he contributed, personally, three times as much as the entire congregation. Among those who gave them quarters, we find H. Callister, P. C. Blake, Rev. Thomas Bacon, Thomas Browning, Jacques Tilghman, Michael Hacket, Jean Caile, Matthew Tilghman, Charles Brown, Guill Goldsborough, Mrs. Sarah Blake, Pollard Edmondson, Philemon Hambleton, David Robinson, Colonel Ennalls, Edward Niel, David Jones, Simon Jones, Samuel Chamberlaine, Mrs. Marguerite Lowe, Thomas Willson, Colonel Joseph Ennalls, Corneille Daly, Robert Howe, Edward Tilghman, Thomas Browning, Colonel Edward Lloyd.

versal Magazine" of July last, from "The Whitehall Gazette" of that month. If I would be thought a patriot, I should have as much regard for the honor as the interest of my country. For my part I am not sorry that we shall play the political artillery upon the French, and beat them at their own weapons. The laws of reprisal will perhaps bear us out here. But methinks there should be a *cœteris paribus* in the case. These people here do not seem to be the subjects to justify the experiment on. A good point gained it certainly is, that they are removed and dispersed; and it would certainly be bad to restore them. However, I am sorry the above mentioned letter was not new modeled before it was published. We are very liberal to the French of the epithet of *perfidious*, and with justice; but those who sow thorns should not go barefoot. There is a parallel case to that of these people to be seen in Harris's *Voyages*, vol. 2, p. 369, in relation to the settlement of the Island of Tobago, by the Lampsins. The passage is short and curious, and will be worthy of your Excellency's perusal, and to see the author's judgment upon the affair, who was a zealous patriot. You'll pardon me for daring to claim so much of your attention. I shall only add, to prevent any imputation of arrogance or vanity to me, on account of suffering my name to be inserted in the enclosed address, that as they thereby give a small token of their reconnoissance, it may be no disadvantage to them; and as to me, I have no reason, I hope, to be ashamed of the part I have acted. The people are well, so far as I can hear. There's only an old woman dead in Dorset, aged 87. There are five families here not yet lodged. One of them I ordered back from the house of a Papist.[1] If the magistrates will do anything about them it will be well; but I perceive I must support them yet a while. But I have no assurance from any, even the best people, who approve of my conduct. If your Excellency but approve of what I have done, I shall not despair of an indemnification in due time. If their effects had been sent out with them, it would be but justice to the colonies who take them in. The families sent to Wye are all lodged; but I have not yet received an account at what houses. Those who are in Papist houses may be distributed very easily in Queen Anne's County, and we can make up the complement for Dorset county out of those on hand here. With an humble reliance on your Excellency's bounty and candor to take my case into your generous consideration, and to forgive this direct application, I resign myself with the profoundest respect and submission. * * * * * * * * *

"H. CALLISTER."[2]

As a token of the gratitude which the Acadians felt towards Mr. Callister for the many acts of kindness which they had received from him, they signed the following testimonial, which was enclosed in the foregoing letter to Governor Sharpe:

"We the undersigned, residents of Acadia, declare with truth that we have not received any provisions from the King since the 7th of December; and since our arrival here Mr. Callister has provided us with provisions, or by his means, until the present time. Our captain has declared to us that he had no more provisions to give us. We were reduced to die of hunger, saving the assistance of Mr. Callister. We can say with truth that he has saved our lives."[3]

This humane gentleman incurred at his own risk, relying upon the justice of the public, a very considerable expense in the support of these exiles, to such an extent, indeed, as to embarass him seriously in his business; nor does

[1] The council passed an order to the justices, to prohibit the Roman Catholic inhabitants of the province to lodge them.

[2] Goldsborough's MS.

[3] *Ibid.*

it appear that he was ever reimbursed, though the assembly, on the 22d of May, 1756, passed "an act to impower the justices of the several county courts to make provision for the late inhabitants of Nova Scotia, and for regulating their conduct," which was continued in force until the 10th of May, 1758, when it expired.

In February, 1757, the electors and freeholders of Talbot county presented an address to John Goldsborough, Matthew Tilghman, Pollard Edmondson, and———Edge, their representatives in the assembly, in which they represent:

"That the wretched Acadians, in a manner quartered upon us, are become a grievance, inasmuch as we are not at present in a situation, and in circumstances, capable of seconding their own fruitless endeavors to support their numerous families, as a people plundered of their effects. For though our magistrates have taxed us, perhaps sufficient to feed such of them as cannot feed themselves, they cannot find houses, clothing, and other comforts, in their condition needful, without going from house to house begging, whereby they are become a nuisance to a country hardly able to afford necessary comfort to their own poor. And as it is no easy task for a Christian to withstand the unfortunate cravings of their distressed fellow-citizens, those among us especially who possess the greatest degree of humanity, must of course be the greatest sufferers. But this is not all. Their religious principles, in a Protestant country, being dangerous, particularly at this juncture, and their attachment to their mother-country, added to their natural resentment of the treatment they have met with, render it unsafe to harbor them in case of any success of the enemy, which visibly affords them matter of exultation on the slightest news in favor of the French and Indians. We therefore pray that you will use your endeavors in the assembly to have this pest removed from among us, after the example of the people of Virginia or Carolina, at their own expense, as they request, or otherwise, as the Assembly shall, in their wisdom, think fit. We humbly conceive that any apprehensions of their adding to the strength of the enemy, if transported into their colonies, would argue a degree of timidity not to be approved of. That, on the contrary, they would rather be burthensome to their country in their present circumstances encumbered with their wives and children, whose immediate wants will, for a long time, employ the utmost industry of the few able-bodied fathers amongst them. Besides, they need not be discharged without first binding them as strongly as people of their principles can be bound, by an oath of neutrality for so long time as may be judged needful. It will have perhaps this further effect, that since they so earnestly desire to quit his Majesty's protection, in a manner renouncing it, they enfeeble their claim to the restitution and restoration they contend for; a point it would be greatly the interest of the colonies to gain with a good grace."[1]

We would fain trust that the language of this address, and especially the base suggestion of the last paragraph, did not fairly represent the sentiments of the people of Maryland, nor even those of the freeholders of Talbot county. It is evident that there was no legitimate ground of complaint against these hapless exiles, who were neither turbulent nor idle, but only French and Papists, wretchedly poor, and miserably unhappy. But we must own, with shame, that if not treated with positive inhumanity, they were almost everywhere viewed with suspicion and dislike, and even the charity which their meek wretchedness extorted, was grudgingly bestowed.

[1] Maryland *Gazette*, February 10, 1757.

Not all the Acadians, however, were so unfortunate. Those who were sent to Baltimore were received with a ready and generous hospitality. They were at first lodged in private houses, and a number were sheltered in the unfinished dwelling of Mr. Edward Fottrell, "the first brick house in Baltimore with free-stone corners, and the first which was two stories high, without a hip-roof," which stood on or near what is now the northwest corner of Fayette and Calvert streets. The owner of this house, an Irishman, had returned to Ireland, where he died, and the house remained unfinished; so the Acadians were quartered in it, occupying such rooms as were habitable. Here they established, without molestation, their little chapel, the first Catholic church in Baltimore. There being no Catholic priest in the town, they were visited once a month by the Reverend Mr. Ashton, resident priest at

DOUGHOREGAN MANOR.

Doughoregan (Carroll's) Manor, who celebrated mass, bringing with him the vestments and vessels used in the service. A temporary altar of the rudest description was erected for each occasion; and the congregation consisted sometimes of not more than twenty, and rarely more than fifty persons, principally of the "Neutral French," with whom were joined a few Irish Catholics. In a short time these peaceable, frugal, and industrious exiles were able to construct some small but comfortable houses upon south Charles street, near Lombard, giving to that quarter the designation of "French town," which it long retained. The names of Guiteau, Blanc, Gould, Dashield and Berbine are still preserved, and their descendants are to-day numbered among our best and most honored citizens.

In anticipation of the summer's campaign, recruiting was actively begun in all parts of the province. It seems that Maryland had been the recruiting ground for most of the royal and provincial regiments, owing, no doubt, to the fact, that she had no regular organization in the pay of the province. Thus the services they rendered were credited to other organizations. In this respect, the zeal and energy of the Maryland volunteers surpassed the expectation of the English officers, for their regiments were mainly kept full by recruits obtained from this province. As an evidence of this, Governor Sharpe, in a letter dated April 10th, 1755, speaking of General Braddock's regiments, says: "With the general's approbation all the men that had been raised in this Province are taken into the English regiments except a company of fifty-three, which is still kept up for the honor of his Lordship's Province."[1] Not content with receiving the volunteers and levies, the provincial and royal regiments enlisted a large number of indented servants, which gave great offence to the merchants and farmers. Governor Sharpe, alluding to this, said: "I shall not be much surprised if some of them [the assembly] express a dissatisfaction of the behavior of the troops before they left this province, and mutter at their enlisting and taking away a good many servants from the inhabitants of Frederick, Prince George's and Baltimore counties, as well as in pressing their carriage horses."[2] In February, 1756, several of the recruiting officers of "General Shirley's regiment," enlisted a large number of indented servants on the Eastern shore. The planters of Kent county became very indignant and attacked the recruiting officers, upon which a conflict ensued "in which some blood was spilt," and the former were successful.

The assembly, being convened on the 23d of February, were urged by the governor to further exertions for the defence of the frontier. The Lower House immediately took into consideration the state of the province, revived an embargo-law, prohibiting trade with the enemy, and prepared a bill in contemplation of the summer campaign in conjunction with the other colonies. While this bill was pending, owing to the dissensions between the two houses of assembly, the western counties of Maryland were kept in continual alarm by the inroads of the savages, and the sufferings of the settlers throughout that range of border territory, were distressing in the extreme.

Some of the scalping-parties approached within thirty miles of Baltimore; and though many of them were killed, terror spread from the very fact of their approach. But in the west the peril was real and constant; scarce any out-door labor was carried on except under the protection of the troops, or of armed bodies of settlers. It was at the risk of life that any one ventured a few rods from his door; women visiting their sick neighbors were shot down or carried off; children bringing in the cattle from the field were

[1] Sharpe's MS. [2] *Ibid.*

tomahawked and scalped by the ambushed murderers. The plantations were being deserted, and homes and property abandoned to plunder or the torch; and all the remoter settlements were fast becoming a wilderness.

Washington, harassed by want of sufficient support, and deeply pained by the scenes which he witnessed, wrote to Governor Dinwiddie April 16, 1756:

"I have done everything in my power to quiet the minds of the inhabitants, by detaching all the men that I have any command over, to the places more exposed. There have also been large detachments from Fort Cumberland in pursuit of the enemy these ten days past; yet nothing, I fear, will prevent the people from abandoning their dwellings, and flying with the utmost precipitation."[1]

Six days later he writes:

"The supplicating tears of the women, and moving petitions of the men, melt me into such deadly sorrow, that I solemnly declare, if I know my own mind, I could offer myself a willing sacrifice to the butchering enemy, provided that would contribute to the people's ease."

On the 24th he writes:

"The deplorable situation of this people is no more to be described than my anxiety and uneasiness for their relief. You may expect, by the time this comes to hand, that without a considerable reinforcement, Frederick county will not be mistress of fifteen families. They are now retiring to the securest parts in droves of fifties.[2]

In consequence of this state of things, Governor Sharpe authorized Major Prather to organize all the forces on the frontiers, except those at Fort Cumberland, and operate between the Potomac and the Pennsylvania line. By the 11th of March, Prather had under his command one hundred and fifty efficient and hardy backwoodsmen skilled in Indian fighting. Captain Alexander Beall, who commanded a company of volunteers, was also authorized to raise a force of one hundred men, and join Major Prather.

Extracts from the papers of the times will show the state of affairs, and the public excitement. The Maryland *Gazette* of the 4th of March, says:

"Our accounts from the westward are truly alarming. All the slaughters, scalpings, burnings, and every other barbarity and mischief that the mongrel French, Indians, or their chieftain, the *Devil*, can invent, are often perpetrated there, and approach us nigher and nigher.

"By a person come to Town this day from Frederick County, we are told that last Sunday two boys, near Lawrence Wilson's, in that County, were killed and scalped, and a son of one Mr. Lynn was found dead and scalped, himself and three more of his family missing. At the Little Cove all the houses were burnt last week. The house of Ralph Matson, about half a mile from Stoddert's Fort, was burnt on Tuesday last week. Some sheep which were in a pen near the house, the Indians flung in the fire alive, others they killed, and some they scalped."

And on March 11 the *Gazette* published this extract from a letter dated Conecocheague, February 29:

[1] Sparks, ii., p, 138.

[2] *Ibid.*, p. 149.

"My last was of the 26th instant. On our march to Toonaloways, about 5 miles this side Stoddert's Fort, we found John Myer's house in flames, and 9 or 10 head of large cattle killed, besides calves, and several horse-kind and sheep. About 3 miles and a-half further up the road, we found a man (one Hynes) killed and scalped, with one arm cut off and several arrows sticking in him; we could not bury him, having no tools with us for that purpose. Half a mile further (within a mile of Stoddert's Fort), we found Ralph Matson's house burnt down, and several sheep and hogs killed. When we came to Stoddert's Fort, we found them all under arms, expecting every minute to be attacked. From thence we went to Combes's Fort, where we found a young man about 22 years of age, killed and scalped; there were only four men in this Fort, two of which were unable to bear arms, but upwards of forty women and children, who were in a very poor situation, being afraid to go out of the Fort, even for a drink of water. The house caught fire during the time the Indians were surrounding the Fort, and would have been burnt down, but luckily there was some soap suds in the house, by which they extinguished it. The young man mentioned above, was one Lynn's son, and was sitting on the fence of the stock yard with Combes' son, when they discovered the Indians, upon which they ran to get into the Fort, and before they reached it, Lynn's son was shot down, and an Indian pursued the other man with a tomahawk within thirty yards of the Fort, but he luckily got into the Fort and shot the Indian. We searched the woods to see if we could discover where the Indian was buried (as they supposed him to be mortally wounded); we found in two places a great quantity of blood, but could not find the body. We saw several creatures shot, some dead, and others going about with arrows sticking in them. About half a mile on this side Mr. Kenny's (in little Toonaloways), we found a load of oats and a load of turnips in the road, which two boys were bringing to Combes's, and it's imagined the boys are carried off by the Indians. When we came to Mr. Kenny's we saw several sheep and cattle killed. From thence we went to one Lowther's, about two miles further, where we found his grain and two calves burnt, two cows and nine or ten hogs killed, and about 150 yards from the house found Lowther dead and scalped, and otherwise terribly mangled; his brains were beat out, as it is supposed with his own gun-barrel, which we found sticking in his skull, and his gun broken; there was an axe, two scythes and several arrows sticking in him. From here we returned to Combes's and buried the young man, and left ten of our men here to assist them to secure their grain, which, as soon as they have done, they purpose to leave that Fort and go to Stoddert's. From hence we went to Stoddert's Fort, where we laid on Friday night, and yesterday, on our way down here, we buried the man we left on the road.

"ISAAC BAKER."

At this time an effort was made by the enemies of Washington to remove him and place Colonel Innes in the chief command of the Maryland and Virginia troops. In consequence of this, Washington again threatened to resign; but men who knew his worth, and the injustice of his calumniators, urged him to entertain no such thoughts while the peril and distress were so extreme. Governor Sharpe, in a letter to Governor Shirley, dated April 10th, 1756, says:

"The inclosed letter I am desired to forward to your Excellency from Col. Washington, and to request you to commissionate and appoint him second in command, in case these colonies shall raise a sufficient number of troops for carrying on an expedition or making a diversion to the westward this summer. As Mr. Washington is much esteemed in Virginia, and really seems a gentleman of merit, I should be exceedingly glad to learn that your Excellency is not averse to favoring his application and request.

"The Assembly of this province is still sitting, but no supply bill is yet passed; and I hear that the Virginians have not yet come to any resolution to grant such supplies as you have recommended to them and required."

In another letter, to the same, four days afterwards, he says:

"The measures taken by the Assembly of this Province, and the delay of those of the two neighboring Colonies to grant any supplies, obliges me to acquaint your Excellency that I have now very little hopes of seeing such a number of men raised by them this summer as would be able to carry your Excellency's scheme for the reduction of Fort Du Quesne into execution."

Again in a letter to Governor Morris, of Pennsylvania, dated April 24th, 1756, he informs him:

"Our Assembly is still sitting, but as the Lower House seem to be absolutely determined to grant no supplies, unless they can at the same time carry certain points which manifestly tend to subvert, in a great measure, the constitution, and render it more similar to that of Pennsylvania, which I believe you do not think the most perfect, I expect to find myself under a necessity of proroguing them in three or four days."[1]

In the meantime the people of Frederick, Prince George's, and Baltimore counties, assailed the Lower House of Assembly with petitions. A memorial from the inhabitants of Frederick town urged them to decline unnecessary disputes, and demanded that means should be adopted to defend their lives and the protection of their property; as the destructive inroads of the enemy were now compelling them to desert their homes. Of these, on the 25th of April, 1756, forty-one persons—six men, five women, and thirty children, with a small portion of their cattle, to avoid the fury of the enemy, deserted their cabins and clearings near Conecocheague, and came to Baltimore. Their houses were destroyed and cattle killed. And on the 23d of April, Thomas Cresap, Jr., and Daniel Cresap, sons of Colonel Thomas Cresap, with sixty riflemen, "dressed and painted like Indians," with "red caps," started on an expedition "to kill the women and children in the Indian towns, and scalp them, while the warriors are committing the like destruction on our frontiers." The result of this expedition is given in the Maryland *Gazette*, as follows:

"On the 23d of April, as Thomas Cresap, jr., and his party lay in ambush near the Little Meadows, they saw a party of Indians coming by them; but one of the party firing too soon, alarmed them, and they fled as fast as possible into thickets, leaving their horses and baggage, which our people took and brought off with them; among their baggage one scalp was found. One of the Indians taking a different course from the rest, Mr. Cresap and two others ran after him near a mile, when the Indian finding that Mr. Cresap gained on him and would overtake him, he dodged behind a large tree, and Mr. Cresap stopped behind one smaller, and they fired at one another so near together, that it could not be distinguished which fired first. Cresap was shot with large shot in the breast, and the others of his party coming up, he told them not to mind him, he was a dead man, but to pursue the enemy; and then dropped down dead. The Indian was shot

[1] Sharpe's MS. *Letter-Book.*

through the right breast, but was not dead when they came up to him, and so they despatched him with a tomahawk and scalped him. Mr. Cresap's body they buried as privately as they could. He was a young widower, and left two little children, and his death was lamented by all who knew him."[1]

Thus, "*Dum Romæ disputabatur Saguntum peribat.*" But the complaints and earnest solicitations of the people were now changed to something more determined. The interminable disputes between the governor and the assembly at length wore out the patience of the western settlers, and they threatened to adopt the emphatic measures of their friends in Pennsylvania.[2] The resolute men of Frederick county, under the leadership of Thomas Cresap the elder, assembled in Frederick town, threatening to march with guns and tomahawks to Annapolis and compel the assembly to cease their unseasonable wranglings and come to their relief. A bill was, however, passed, and Governor Sharpe, in a letter of May 2d, to his brother, William Sharpe, then in London, gives the following account of its progress, and also of certain grievances both public and private:

"I am sorry to find the scheme for raising so many regiments here under Swiss officers is approved of because no step could have been taken that would have been more disagreeable to his Majesty's American subjects, and because I look upon it as absolutely impracticable. Have the four established regiments, notwithstanding they entertained servants, been unable to compleat themselves because the recruiting officers were not natives of this country; have the Virginians sunk so many thousand pounds without being able to raise and keep 500 men, because Governor Dinwiddie could not help shewing whence he came by his nomination of the officers, and can it be supposed that 4000 of our inhabitants will hasten to enlist and serve under foreigners? for I shall be much deceived if these Swiss are not esteemed as such by the Germans who have for any considerable time resided among us, as well as by the English. Whence comes it that such numbers have been speedily collected in the Northern provinces? must it not be attributed to the officers' commissions being given to popular gentlemen who raise their men in their respective neighborhoods, and in a month or two a regiment is completed. It is not for want of men in these parts that I must go to New England for such an instance. I am glad you pressed Mr. Calvert to persuade my Lord to make his tenants a present of some arms, and if he would recover their affections let him do so; but I dare not speak lest it should be thought that I am courting the people's favor at another's expence. I am concerned to find the instructions lately sent concerning ordinary licences was given with so much regret, or that it is thought a great favor, I assure you the concession does not appear to many here in that light, and I heartily wish for his Lordship's sake more than my own that I had been ordered to waive the dispute about them before. [It was through your interest I was honored with a Lieutenant Colonel's commission.] Our assembly is now

[1] This account was not quite correct. Cresap was shot with a bullet and seven buckshot, the ball going through his breast; and he was not shot behind a tree, but in an open space, while pursuing his foe.

[2] Governor Sharpe, in a letter to Lord Baltimore dated New York, November 27, 1755, says that the Assembly of Pennsylvania would have continued obstinate in their refusal to pass a supply bill of £55,000, "if a body of near four thousand people had not come in from the back country and insisted on their sending up such a bill as the governor was impowered to pass. The bodies of three people that had been scalped were brought down to Philadelphia by the distant inhabitants, and exposed in the streets, which, it is probable, would have excited unusual commotions among the people, if the supply bill had not been before passed, and the governor and assembly been out of the city."—Sharpe's MS. *Letter-Book.*

sitting, and have framed a bill for granting £40,000 for his Majesty's service, but as it does not exempt his Lordship's manors and some lands which he has ordered to be reserved in the populous parts of the Province from the Land tax which is imposed as one of the funds for sinking the money, I ought in obedience to a letter which I have lately received from Mr. Calvert to reject the bill and be guilty of such reasoning as Gov. Morris has been in defending his superiors instructions; but by what I can find, his Lordship's council and best friends will advise me very differently, and insist on my disobeying for once Mr. Calvert's order, unless those arms should happily arrive before the bill can be offered me. Whether I shall be approved or condemned for this step I cannot predict, but am in hopes that the arguments which may be used to convince his Lordship that the preservation of his province depends on a supply, bills being passed at this juncture, and that his lordship's annual proportion of the intended tax will be less than the interest of the money which, according to his agent's account, he lost last year, will excuse me for not insisting so strenuously on what his lordship and Mr. Calvert distinguished by the name of prerogative. I would not imply by anything that has been said that I at all approve of the Assembly's conduct; on the contrary, I think them absolutely inexcusable for the part they have acted on this occasion, and if an act of generosity in his lordship had afforded me the least room, I would not have despaired of making them ashamed of their behavior and of rendering them odious to their own constituents. My journey to Fort Cumberland last summer, and in the winter to New York, where I was obliged to wait for and attend General Shirley near two months, put me to about £150 expense, for which I shall never receive more than thanks at most; to this let there be added what the frequency and length of our sessions of assembly, and the number of military officers who call on me lay me under a necessity of expending, together with part of my house rent, and also the £220 which I am annually to pay Mr. Calvert for his correspondence, and deduct the whole out of my yearly salary and perquisites, which amount to about £1400., The remainder is for the support of the honor and dignity of his lordship's governor, and for him to lay by against a future day. I think I have already hinted to you that I am not permitted to dispose of any of the most honorable or lucrative offices, because another person loves to have all applications made to himself. This, perhaps, is of itself sufficient to lessen the weight and influence that a governor would otherwise have, but as it has been thought proper of late to saddle those officers with about £550 per annum, and I am charged with the care of making the most advantageous bargains. I submit to your own judgment whether it is possible for a person in my situation to continue always popular. Any body that can get introduced to Mr. Calvert is sure to bring me an open letter, desiring I will appoint him to this, or that, or the first vacant office, and should I have an objection to the person introduced and recommended to me, or for any other reason, neglect to comply with the terms of such letter, that man thinks himself hardly dealt by, and immediately commences my enemy. It has been the policy of my predecessors always to have three or four gentlemen of abilities in his lordship's council, and the rule was a good one, such three or four gave the whole board weight, and made the Lower House more cautious how they attacked a superior branch of the legislature. Since my arrival I have had the misfortune to lose Jennings and two other gentlemen of very good abilities from that board, whereby it is exceedingly reduced, though these accidents have made no more than three seats vacant. To fill the first I recommended the son of one of those deceased, a gentleman in my opinion, of the best natural and acquired abilities of any in the province, and therefore a more desirable friend and a more formidable enemy. His services while in the Lower House supported my recommendation, but my repeated applications in his favor, for what cause I know not, have hitherto proved ineffectual, and instead of him am I ordered to put into the council a person whose merit and qualifications are to me all invisible, unless I am to reckon as such an easy disposition and his having lately contracted marriage with a niece of his lordship, who was lately in England, and whom possibly you might have seen at the council office. On these matters I have often writ in the most pressing manner, but have the mortification to see that I have done so to very little purpose. There are several matters about which disputes have subsisted many years, between the Lord Proprietary and the people, which, would his lordship suffer them to be brought to a hearing at home, and a final determination, would, I am well convinced, be decided without the least hesitation, in his lordship's favor, however some of the violent patriots, as they are called, think, and persuade the people to think otherwise. A cause is not to be brought before his Majesty in council without money and an agent; the people have repeatedly desired to be allowed an agent for a short time, but granting this request, his lordship says, would plunge him into a sea of trouble, and therefore enjoins me to take every measure to prevent anything of that sort, unless the people will put their confidence in Mr. Calvert and nominate him their agent, this I am to recommend to them as warmly as possible, but as it can be easily foreseen, with what indignation they would hear the proposal, I shall never act so unpolitically as to give them a hint of it."

In another letter to the Hon. Henry Fox, secretary of state, dated May 3d, 1756, he says:

"I have recommended the building a strong fort on an eminence at the conflux of the North and South branches of Potomac, for the expediency of which I took the liberty in February last, to communicate my sentiments to the Rt. Hon'ble, the Lords of Trade, which, with a small fort between that place and that where our people intend to build one, would always keep open the communication between the inhabitants and Fort Cumberland, and would be very convenient, or rather absolutely necessary as a place of arms in any future expeditions to the westward; a body of 500 or 600 men, which, had I wherewith to support them, I could easily raise from among our inhabitants, posted in those forts with orders to be constantly patrolling or ranging on the frontiers, would effectually prevent any incursions of Indians, and be always ready to act in conjunction with any troops that should be raised in the neighboring colonies, or able of themselves to send detachments to annoy the Indians in their own country; but as our Assembly imagine such measures would involve them in greater expences than they think their constituents can well bear, and oblige them to keep up a body of troops much longer than they propose by the bill that is now under their consideration, I am afraid it will be impossible for me, as I have already hinted, to prevail with them to do what the safety of the back inhabitants requires, and without which they may expend considerable sums of money to very little purpose. I have been advised that a Captain of the Virginia Regiment, which consists of about 500 men with a detachment of sixty, fell in lately with a party of Indians, by whom they were entirely defeated. The Captain, Lieutenant and 15 men being killed, the rest retired to a little sort of a fort that was near the place where the action happened. Another party of Indians have been attacked in Virginia with better success, and a French ensign that led them being killed, there were found in a little bag tied about his neck, instructions from Dumas the commandant at Fort Du Quesne, ordering him to make an incursion with a party of 50 savages, to Conegochiegh (a place about seventy miles on this side Fort Cumberland), and destroy the magazine of stores and provisions that has been left there ever since last summer. This inclines me to think that the French do not expect any expedition will be carried on by us to the westward this season, and that they are so anxious to prevent a possibility of it destroying the ammunition and stores, that they may detach as many of their garrisons as they can possibly spare to the Northward, where they cannot be ignorant that large preparations are making against them. Some of the back inhabitants who have escaped from the Ohio, whither they had been carried by the savages, report that the artillery which fell into the enemy's hands last summer, have been carried up that river, and that the French purchase the men which the Indians have taken from the frontiers of these Colonies, and keep them constantly employed in building barracks for the reception and convenience of the Indian tribes that have lately come into their alliance, and are to be employed this summer in harrassing and depopulating these provinces. The Cherokees or Carolina Indians have, I hear, made great professions of friendship to the commissioners that were sent from Virginia to make a treaty and enter into a League with them, but they will not declare openly in our favor, or commence hostilities against the French or their allies, till we have an army able to act offensively, and till we have constructed a strong fort in their country for the security of their wives and children, while their young men act in conjunction with our troops. In this, the commissioners promised to gratify them, and Governor Dinwiddie has ordered a detachment from the Virginia regiment in that service."

In another to Calvert dated May 5th, 1756, he says:

"I might refer you to my letters dated the 18th of March and 17th of April for an account of our present situation. The Assembly is still sitting on the bill that was prepared; some of the gentlemen of both houses are holding a conference, but what will be the event of it I cannot predict, as there are many obstacles to be removed before they take that part which imposes a tax on lands into consideration. I am apt to think the conference will break up, and perhaps the assembly be prorogued without his Lordship's manor lands coming into dispute. A few days I think will determine the fate of this bill and bring matters to a conclusion; but if we do nothing for the protection of the frontiers, God knows what will be the consequence. Conegochiegh is already our most western settlement, and if the inhabitants of that part of the country do not stand their ground, and I think there is little probability of their doing so, I believe one might foretell without the spirit of prophecy that all that part of Frederick County that lies beyond Frederick Town will be abandoned before this time twelve months at farthest. The inhabitants of all that part of Virginia which lies westward of the Shennandoah river have, I am told, left their plantations; and notwithstanding a great part of the £60,000 granted by the Pennsylvanians has been expended in building forts and keeping troops in the frontiers of the Province, the settlers have for many score miles deserted their houses and retired to the more populous parts of that colony. Several of the small forts that were built in Virginia and Pennsylvania have been attacked by large parties of Indians, and some reduced. Capt. Mercier, of the Virginia regiment, with a detachment of 60 men from Fort Cumberland was fallen upon and defeated about a fortnight ago many miles on this side Fort Cumberland. The captain, his lieutenant, and 15 men were killed and left to the enemy, the rest of the detachment retired to a little stockade fort near Cacapehon which runs into Potomac. Two of Captain Dagworthy's company that were with the above mentioned detachment were found tied to trees and their bodies most horribly mangled, it is supposed that they were tied while living and put to the most cruel death. Ensign Bacon, of Capt. Dagworthy's company, was scalped as he was returning from Col. Cresap's to the fort; and one of Col. Cresap's sons, who put himself at the head of a party of volunteers and went in pursuit of the Indians, is also killed. At present the garrison at Fort Cumberland consists of no more than 150 men, 80 of the Carolina company and the rest of the Virginia regiment which consists of about 450. I cannot learn that the Pennsylvania Assembly have as yet come to any resolution."

The bill which passed, notwithstanding the prognostications of the governor, appropriated £40,000 for purposes of defence. Of this sum £11,000 were to be applied to the erection of a fort and block-houses on the frontier, and for raising, arming, and maintaining a body of two hundred men to garrison them; £3,000 were appropriated for engaging the services of the Southern Indians, for which purpose two commissioners, Colonel Benjamin Tasker and Charles Carroll, the younger, were appointed to take charge of the fund and conduct the negotiations. One thousand pounds were allotted as bounties for Indian scalps or prisoners, at the rate of £10 for each; and £25,000 were set apart for the proposed joint expedition against Fort Du Quesne. William Murdock, James Dick, and Daniel Wolstenholme, were appointed agents to pay out these sums, with a commission of 2½ per cent.

Of the whole amount, £34,000 were raised by the emission of bills of credit; and to redeem these a sinking fund was provided, by laying additional taxes and increasing the duties on imports. Carrying their great point, for which they had contended so pertinaciously, they imposed a share of the common burden on the proprietary's estates; but, less justifiably, they gratified the prejudices of the time by a double tax on the lands of Catholics. Evidently regarding an active compliance with the motto of the colony, "Increase and Multiply," a main means for repairing the depopulations of war, and a public duty which no good citizen should shirk, they laid a tax on "all bachelors of twenty-five years and upwards," on those worth £100, and less than £300, five shillings per annum, and on those worth over £300, twenty shillings. As the general treatment of the Acadians shows that it was only the Protestant population whose increase was thought desirable, equity would seem to have demanded that Catholic bachelors should have been exempted from this tax; but this does not seem to have occurred to the legislators, who evidently regarded celibacy as a luxury, and in their schedule of taxable articles, placed it between "wines and spirits," and "billiard tables."[1]

On May 27, Governor Sharpe gave the following account of the passage of this bill, in a letter to his brother, John Sharpe:

"As to the quantum, they seemed to comply with my requisition, by voting £40,000 for the services I had desired them to provide for, but as some of the leading men in the house were averse to giving more than a small sum for the immediate protection of our own frontiers, though they could not directly oppose the vote and sentiments of a great majority, yet as it is a new and difficult matter to raise large sums in this Province, it was easy for them to get such funds proposed and insisted on for raising the money as would damn the bill; and they hoped that by such a clamor would be raised against the government, or that the sum voted might afterwards be reduced and made as small as themselves wished and desired. Accordingly, when a Committee of Ways and Means was appointed, and orders given for framing a bill, among other exceptionable matters a land-tax was proposed by these gentlemen, and that all his lordship's manors and reserved lands should be subjected to the payment of it, as his Tenants', the inhabitants' lands are, was carried by a great majority. You may be assured, the flaming patriots, or rather inflaming demagogues, on this occasion made great use of the arguments that have by the Pennsylvanians been urged to Mr. Morris; in short, at the end of seven weeks, the bill made its appearance, and was sent to the Upper House in such a form as was expected, and was

[1] Bacon, ch. v.; 1756.

by them returned again after some days, with a negative and their objections in writing to many parts of it. A conference was afterwards agreed on by both houses, and after a warm engagement between the conferees, that lasted above a week, the principal obstacles were removed and the bill assented to.

"The Burgesses had at first, as I before hinted, insisted that all his Lordship's manors and reserved lands should be made liable to the tax, and none exempted but such as remain still vacant; but to give you a clear idea of what is meant by manors, reserved and vacant lands, it will, perhaps, be necessary to inform you that at times the Lords Proprietaries or their Governors have, on an appearance of copper or other ores, or on account of the extraordinary fertility of the soil, or their contiguity to Towns or his Lordship's manors, ordered a reserve to be entered on certain tracts of lands; or in other words, forbade those officers who are impowered, to sell, grant, or make away, such tracts on any consideration whatever. These differ from the manor lands in this, that the latter are regularly and properly surveyed, and the description and bounds of them entered in the public records; but the reserved lands have never been surveyed or laid out, are not distinguished or known by proper names as the manors are, but are in the records described only in the general terms or words as 'all the land that lies between such and such hills and rivers,' or 'between two roads for its breadth, and so many miles for its length,' &c.; however, parts or parcels of these reserves are leased, and his Lordship's agent receives rent for the same as he does for those parts of the manors that are let to tenants.. Lands that are unoccupied or have never been taken up, but are by His Lordship's Officers to be sold to any that will purchase them at the common rates, are called vacant lands; from such his Lordship receives no immediate revenue and profit, neither did our Assembly offer to burthen them, though the Pennsylvanians had endeavored to make their Proprietaries' vacant lands liable to the tax that was proposed to be laid in that Province. Upon the conference that I have already mentioned, the Lower House receded from what they had at first insisted on, so far that instead of taxing all his Lordship's reserved lands, they agreed that only those parts of them that are actually leased out and pay rent to his Lordship, shall be made liable, and that the rest shall be deemed vacant and exempted accordingly; but the whole manors according to the true contents of each, whether tenanted or occupied, are subjected to the payment of the tax in the same manner and form that the inhabitants' lands are. I think the annual rents that his Lordship receives from such parts of his manors and reserved lands as are leased, amount to about £600—and it is supposed that his Lordship's proportion of the tax imposed, will, in the five years for which the act is to endure be about £400 currency.

"Was his Lordship's case my own, I am sure I should never have hesitated a moment to contribute my share with the people to defend the province and annoy the enemy, and I am well convinced that if his Lordship had been on the spot, he would have suffered his estate to be more burthened than I have done; but as his Lordship might possibly in England think very differently from what he would in America, I am not without some apprehensions that this step, which, at the importunity of his friends, I have taken, will be censured as a culpable concession and subversive of his Lordship's rights and prerogatives. In a letter that I have lately received from him (Mr. Calvert) says: 'His Lordship does not doubt of your following and guarding against any invasion on his rights, similar, in your defence on his behalf, as Governor Morris has done for the Proprietors of Pennsylvania.' By this I understand that his Lordship is absolutely against my suffering his estate or property to be subjected to any burthen or tax on any account or consideration whatever.

"From Messrs. Penns having made the Province or people of Pennsylvania a present of £5,000, there was room to suspect that Governor Morris had pushed matters further than was desired by his superiors, or perhaps than was agreeable to the ministry or

During this time the audacity of the Indians had increased with their success, and they had begun harrying the settlers in the neighborhood of Emmittsburg. Many were killed and wounded, and the affrighted people deserted their homes and began flying to the interior. Colonel Washington being unprovided with the necessary men and means for defence, appealed to Lord Fairfax for aid from the militia "to save the most valuable and flourishing part of the country from immediate desertion." "The whole settlement of Conecocheague, in Maryland, is fled," he adds, "and there now remain only two families from thence to Frederick town. That the Maryland settlements are all abandoned is certainly a fact, as I have had the accounts transmitted to me by several hands, and confirmed yesterday by Henry Brinker, who left Monocacy the day before, and who also affirms that three hundred and fifty wagons had passed that place, to avoid the enemy, within the space of three days."[1]

Governor Sharpe, in a letter to Lord Baltimore, dated September 13, thus alludes to the enemy, who had captured Fort Granville, on the Juniata, and was devastating the country west of the Susquehanna:

> "The flight of the Pennsylvanians from the western parts of that province, has left our northern frontier, beyond the Monocacy, much exposed. The enemy has now free access to us through Pennsylvania; and if some measures are not speedily taken for the defence of that colony, neither Fort Frederick nor its garrison can be of much service; for our people will follow the Pennsylvanians' example: a passion very different from true patriotism and courage seeming to have entire possession of their souls. Besides the garrison at Fort Frederick, we have at present two hundred men from the militia of Baltimore and Prince George's counties, distributed on this side that fort, and about Conegochegh; yet that settlement is, I am advised, almost broken up, and several hundred persons have lately retreated thence and retired to the more populous parts of the county."[2]

In consequence of these outrages the people below Conecocheague raised a subscription sufficient to arm and equip a patrol of twenty men, under Lieutenant William Teagard, of Captain Rench's company of militia, for their protection. Their services were soon demanded, for on August 18th, the enemy plundered the settlers near Baker's Ridge, and on the 20th attacked a funeral train, killing two persons, when they were in turn attacked by a detachment of the patrol, under the command of Luke Thompson, and driven back towards the Pennsylvania line.

The British Parliament was not inattentive to the state of affairs on this side the Atlantic; and though it was its policy to cast the burden of the war in America as much as possible on the colonies themselves, it granted in August the sum of £115,000 as a reward for the services of the colonial troops for the past year. Of this sum Massachusetts received £54,000; Connecticut, £26,000; New York, £15,000; leaving £20,000 to be apportioned among the other colonies. As it was intimated in England that the services of Governor Shirley had been greatly overestimated, that he was deficient in military

[1] Sparks, ii., 183.

[2] Sharpe's MSS.

capacity, and lacked the urbanity of manners essential to his position, he was displaced at the suggestion of the Duke of Cumberland and Secretary Fox, and the Earl of Loudoun, the friend of Halifax, was appointed Governor of Virginia and commander-in-chief of the forces in America, with powers superior to, and independent of, the other provincial governors.

In addition to these measures, during the session of 1756, the authority of parliament over colonial affairs was notably extended. It was enacted that "foreign Protestants might be employed as engineers and officers to enlist a regiment of aliens; that indented servants might be accepted as soldiers, and their masters compensated by the several assemblies; volunteers were exempted from the process of law for petty debts; the naval code of England was extended to all persons employed in the king's service upon the lakes or rivers in North America;[1] and each northern province was forbidden to negotiate with the Indians, the management of Indian affairs being intrusted exclusively to Sir William Johnson, with no subordination but to Loudoun."[2]

Lord Loudoun was prevented from an immediate assumption of his authority, and sent over in his stead his second in command, General Abercrombie, who arrived in April. It was not until the middle of May that his lordship left England, and the season was then so far advanced without anything having been done, that Governor Sharpe, not unreasonably, remarked, "We shall have good reason to sing *Te Deum* at the conclusion of this campaign, if matters are not then in a worse situation than they are at present."[3]

Matters were in a worse situation, for the disasters and reverses of the campaign of 1756, were greater even than those of the preceding year. North Carolina, Virginia and Pennsylvania having failed to co-operate with Maryland in the proposed expedition, for which the assembly at its last session had voted twenty-five thousand pounds, Governor Sharpe, at the instance of Lord Loudoun, convened the assembly on September the 14th. In his opening address, besides asking for supplies to support the provincial forces, in pursuance of royal instructions he proposed to lay an embargo on all vessels laden with provisions.

Five thousand pounds were appropriated to raising and maintaining three hundred men for the Royal American regiment, and for the purchase of wheat and its shipment to New York for the use of the forces; three thousand pounds for bounties, for Indian scalps, or prisoners at fifty pounds each; and thirty-four hundred pounds for raising, equipping and maintaining one hundred men, to be incorporated with two hundred already raised, one third of this whole force to be employed for the protection of the frontiers.

[1] In accordance with this law, a number of gentlemen at Chestertown, in Kent county, in September, 1756, fitted out "a fine, new ship called the *Sharpe*, commanded by Captain Edward Scott, carrying twenty-six carriage guns and twenty swivels; and manned by two hundred men, to cruise against his majesty's enemies.—Maryland *Gazette*, September 12.

[2] Barry's *History of Massachusetts*, ii., p. 213.

[3] Bancroft, iv., p. 235.

Twenty-four hundred pounds were to be employed in finishing and garrisoning Fort Frederick; thirty-one hundred for the purchase of arms and munitions of war; and six hundred and twenty pounds were to reimburse the governor for sums expended by him in raising and supporting the rangers in the previous spring.[1]

The position and conduct of the assembly at this juncture, form one of the most interesting portions of Maryland history. On one side was the proprietary, selfish and rapacious, caring little or nothing for his province except as a source of revenue, and quite indifferent, so a golden stream flowed into his coffers, how much parliament might encroach upon the franchises of his charter. On another side were parliament and the crown, anxious to make it appear that the war in America was one waged by England for the sake of the colonists, the brunt of which should rightfully be borne by the latter; and not unwilling, moreover, to curtail the too great independence of the proprietary governments. On the third side were the people of the province, terrified by the growing storm of invasion advancing upon them from the northwest with carnage, rapine, and flame in its train, and exasperated at what they thought the obstinacy and indifference of their legislators. But though menaced on all sides, the delegates stood firm, determined to maintain so far as in them lay, the rights of the people, and the franchises of the charter. It was a memorable and momentous contest; for in it, as we shall see, lay hidden the germs of American independence.

Between the clamors of the people, the exactions of Lord Baltimore, the demands of Loudoun, and the resistance of the Lower House, Sharpe had by this time completely lost his temper. In a letter to his brother John, dated October 9th, the day of the adjournment, he says:

"The bill received my assent yesterday, and I have rid myself of a parcel of wretches whose company I begin sincerely to detest. The Virginia Assembly met a few days after ours, and having granted £8,000 for raising five hundred men for the Royal American regiment, and a pretty large sum for the support and encouragement of a body of Cherokees that they expect will join them, broke up within a week; while we have, to our reproach, sat five times as long, doing less business * * * * * * * *

"I am now to communicate to you something that more particularly relates to myself, and to desire your good offices in case a set of people whom I have some reason to suspect, should think proper to become my enemies. You may remember that I told you in a former letter that the Roman Catholics were much dissatisfied at my having assented to the act for granting a supply of £40,000 for his Majesty's service, because it imposes a double tax on the lands of all persons of that persuasion. They are, I find, determined to apply to his Lordship or the King in Council for relief; and to remonstrate against my conduct in assenting to the bill.

"The penal statutes, by an Act of Assembly made long since, are declared to extend to this province. Their priests have large tracts of land among us, and their children are frequently sent to St. Omer's for education. These are, in my opinion, great indulgences, and such as are allowed in none of the colonies but Maryland and Pennsylvania. I believe about one-twelfth part of our inhabitants are of that persuasion; and many of them are persons of considerable fortune.[2]

[1] Bacon.

[2] Sharpe's MSS.

To Secretary Calvert, Lord Baltimore's kinsman, he writes, November 3d:

"I have long been persuaded that nothing to effect will be ever done by these colonies unless an Act of Parliament is made for obliging them to contribute their respective quotas and to exert their united force in defence of themselves and his Majesty's dominions. The Assemblies of Pennsylvania and this Province more particularly, have, I think, sufficiently shewn that they have nothing so much at heart, and desire nothing more than to increase their own power and render the other branches of the Legislature odious or contemptible. They perceive that nothing can be now done without their concurrence, and thence conceive a great opinion of their own importance. The oftener they are convened the less tractable they grow, and become more extravagant in their demands on the government. I hear Lord Loudoun has written in a more peremptory manner than usual to Governor Denny, demanding a large sum of money from that province towards establishing a general fund for his Majesty's service, and requiring them to build barracks at Philadelphia for the reception and accommodation of a battalion of the American regiment."[1]

Fort Cumberland, which had long been a subject of contention between the governors of Virginia and Maryland, now threatened to become the source of further trouble. In August, Washington wrote to Dinwiddie that it was so distant as to be of no service; the Indians ravaging with impunity on the hither side of it, and the garrison "seldom hearing of these things within a month after they were done; that it took more forces to garrison it than could be spared; that it contained valuable stores that might easily be lost, as it was an outpost accessible to the enemy, and not capable of an hour's defence if they were to bring a single half-pounder against it," and, in short, "I wish we were clear of it." He recommended that a fort should be erected at the joint expense of the three contiguous provinces, near the Little Meadows; and if it was deemed absolutely necessary to retain Fort Cumberland, that it should be garrisoned by Maryland troops alone.[2]

Now Fort Cumberland was to Governor Dinwiddie as the apple of his eye; and these comments and propositions of Washington irritated him exceedingly. He wrote to Loudoun, giving his views of the matter, to which the commander-in-chief replied:

"I can not agree with Colonel Washington in not drawing in the posts from the stockade forts in order to defend that advanced one; and I should imagine much more of the frontier will be exposed by retiring your advanced posts near Winchester, where I understand he is retired; for from your letter I take it for granted he has before this executed his plan without waiting for my advice. If he leaves any of the great quantity of stores behind, it will be very unfortunate; and he ought to consider that it must lie at his own door."

Fortified by this approval of his views from so high a quarter, Dinwiddie ordered the garrisons withdrawn from the smaller frontier forts, and sent, with most of the troops from Winchester, to Fort Cumberland, which was made the headquarters of the army. To conciliate Washington, however, the

[1] Sharpe's MSS.

[2] Sparks, ii., p. 169.

governor proposed to refer the whole matter to a council of officers, to be held at the fort itself. This council met, and after reviewing the reasons on both sides, declined to decide positively whether the fort should be abandoned or retained. They agreed that "the fort itself was defenceless, imperfectly constructed, and commanded by several hills within gunshot; but they thought it important that a post should be maintained in that quarter, since the only road to the west for wheel-carriages passed in that direction."[1]

As Loudoun had summoned the Southern governors to a military council to be held in Philadelphia, in March, 1757, to concert measures for the coming campaign, Washington obtained permission from Dinwiddie to attend it, and lay his views in person before the commander-in-chief. At this council, at which Sharpe, Dinwiddie, Governor Dobbs, of North Carolina, and a number of prominent gentlemen from the several provinces were present, the question of Fort Cumberland was discussed at length; and it was decided that the Virginia troops, provisions, and stores should be removed to Fort Loudoun, a fortress built the preceding year, and that Fort Cumberland should for the future be garrisoned by Maryland troops only. Dinwiddie thereupon ordered its immediate evacuation; but a council of war decided that this step should not be taken until the Maryland garrison, under Captain Dagworthy, had arrived.

The day after Sharpe's return from Philadelphia, he called together the assembly; but as the small-pox was raging in Annapolis, he prorogued them and re-convened them at Baltimore, when they met on April 8. Here he laid before them the plan of operations agreed upon in Philadelphia, and exhorted them to do their part with despatch, as the season was now well advanced. The Lower House replied with protestations of loyalty to the sovereign, and promises to act in the matter with alacrity and unanimity. There being still £7,469 remaining out of the £25,000 originally appropriated, and the £3,000 intended to secure the services of the Cherokees being yet unapplied, this whole sum was devoted to the raising, equipping, and paying five hundred men, including Dagworthy's command. To promote the recruiting service, those who enlisted were exempted for three years from all levies, highway labor, and ferriages, and if maimed in the service, should receive a yearly pension.[2] After passing a number of laws, the assembly adjourned on the 9th of May.

The diversion of the Cherokee fund seems to have been a little premature, as on May 9, Sharpe writes to Dinwiddie, that he had just received a message from a body of Cherokees who had come to Fort Frederick to offer their services, and that he had sent them £100, which was all the assembly had appropriated for that purpose. The message of the Cherokees was as follows:

[1] Sparks, ii., p. 200.

[2] Bacon.

"*Fort Frederick, April 29, 1757.*

"To the Governor of Maryland:—

"*Brother of Maryland:* This day I came into your Province, with a company of our nation, on our way to war against the French, Shawaness, and all their Indians, hearing they had killed some of our brothers, not knowing when we set off from Winchester but the murder was committed in Virginia; but coming to this fort, found we were in another Province; and on being informed by Capt. Beall, that our brother, the Governor of this Province, had a real love for our nation, and that he had provided clothes for our nation, though unacquainted with us, I have just now held a council with my young warriors, and have concluded to write to you, to acquaint you, our brother, our design of coming into this country, was, hearing from our good brother, the Governor of Virginia, that it was the desire of our father, King George, that we would join the English in war against the French and their Indians. On hearing this news we immediately took up the hatchet against the French and their Indians, and hold it fast till we make use of it, which I expect will be in a few days. We intend to set out immediately from this fort, and immediately on our return expect to meet you, our brother, here, to make ourselves acquainted with you. If you cannot come yourself, you will send one of your beloved men with your talk, which we will look upon as from your own mouth. I hope you will let the Province of Pennsylvania know that I am come this length to war, and if they are in need of our assistance, I have men plenty at home, and will not think it troublesome to come and fight for our brothers. I set off from home with 150 men, part of which are gone to Fort Cumberland; forty more by this are come to Winchester. Our people will be so frequent among you, that I wish you may not think us troublesome. Our hearts ache to see our brothers' bones scattered about the country, but you will hear in a short time we have got satisfaction for our brothers, and in confirmation of what I have spoke, I have sent you these few white beads to confirm my regard to this Province. Likewise I have sent you these black beads, to convince you that I have taken up the hatchet against all the English enemies. We intend to stay as long amongst our brothers as there is use for us. I hope our good brother will not be backward in providing necessaries for us. I have sent you a list of what is useful for us, and have got our good friend Mr. Ross to carry this letter to you, whom we shall always acknowledge as a particular friend to us. As we expect to see you soon, we will add no more at present; but remain your loving brother,

His
"WAHACHY x OF KEEWAY."
Mark.

The governor's secretary, John Ridout, and Daniel Wolstenholme were sent as commissioners to Fort Frederick, to treat with these Indians, carrying with them a wagon-load of presents and £200 in goods for the scalps of four hostile Indians, whom the Cherokees had killed while waiting for an answer; and with this earnest of the province's bounty they professed themselves well satisfied.

The enemy, however, still kept up their forays, almost under the walls of the forts, and the settlements west of the Blue Ridge were well-nigh deserted. In the summer there was a general flight from the upper waters of the Potomac; and on the 18th of June the report came that a large force of French and Indians, with artillery, were advancing on Fort Cumberland. Sharpe immediately called out the militia, and gathering a body of volunteers, started to relieve the threatened post, but on reaching Frederick found that it was a false alarm.

Shortly after his return, on the 6th of July, the governor wrote a letter to his brother William, then secretary to the privy council, in which he gives an account of his grievances, and some interesting particulars concerning his position toward the Catholics, the Lower House, and the proprietary:

"I am glad to find by your letters, as well as by one that I have received from Mr. Calvert, that the Roman Catholics of this province have not so much interest at home as they would have me believe. His Lordship has confirmed the act against which they petitioned, and for passing which they regard me as a professed enemy. One Mr. Charles Carroll, who is at the head of that sect, and is possessed of a fortune of £30,000 or £40,000 among us, has taken a passage to England in a vessel that lately sailed hence, and will probably be in London before this can be received. What his views or intentions are in taking such a voyage at this time, I know not. It has been said that he has thoughts of leaving Maryland and carrying his fortune to Europe. He has a son about twenty-two years of age, now at Paris; and if he should determine to spend the remainder of his life in Europe, it is not improbable that he will take up his residence in some part of France, as he seems, by sending his son to that kingdom while he was very young, and by supporting him there since he has finished his studies, to prefer that country. He is a sensible man, has read much, and is well acquanited with the constitution and strength of the American colonies. If he is inclined to give the enemy any intelligence about our American affairs, none is more capable; but, indeed, I do not conceive that he has any such inclination. He was heretofore a bitter enemy to the Lord Proprietary; but having behaved with moderation since I came hither, we were on good terms till I incurred his displeasure by assenting to an act which I thought equitable, and which you say appears to you in the same light. Since that time all correspondence between us has been broken off. I presume he will be much among the merchants while he stays in London, and in particular with his friend, Mr. Philpot. Should he endeavor to do me any prejudice with his Lordship or any one else, during his residence there, I hope you will be able to render his attempts abortive. * * * * * * * * * * * * *

"I am exceedingly obliged to you for your kind offer to use your interest in my favor with Lord Halifax, and to endeavor to procure me the government of New York, in case I should think that government a desirable one. In this you continue to act the generous part that you have always done; and I shall think myself wanting in gratitude if I failed to make you my grateful acknowledgements; but as you say that you have been assured, by those that know best, that it is not worth more than £1600 a year, I am at a loss whether to accept or decline the offer. It has been usually estimated in America at a much higher value; but I suppose that as the lands are almost all sold, the profits must have been considerably lessened. With regard to the people that a governor has to deal with there, they are much the same, I believe, as in the other colonies. They have, I know, shewn more generosity and spirit since these disturbances began than the people of Maryland, for they have agreed to support the men that were required of them, and they have defrayed the governor's expense, or made him a considerable present as often as he has gone to Albany, or taken any journey for his Majesty's or his colony's service; while I have been obliged to spend upwards of £500 on such journeys, and have not been reimbursed a shilling. Indeed, our Assembly is, in this respect, a hundred times worse than the Pennsylvanians, for they have never declined paying any expenses that their Governors or Commissioners have been at in holding treaties with Indians or journeying to the frontiers; though such expenses have, within these three years, amounted to many thousand pounds. Was it a time of peace, or would our Assembly make a reasonable allowance for my extraordinary expenses on these occasions, I would not complain, though I am obliged to pay so much to Mr. Calvert out of my salary, which no governor, before 1751, ever did; but really, what with the burthen of these expenses and other incidental charges which the late Lord Baltimore used to make an allowance for, out of the fines and forfeitures, but which I defray out of my own purse, I really believe I am as ill off as any Governor on the continent, except those that are elective, in some of the New England republican governments. As his Lordship has lately writ to me, desiring I will, by some means or other, get £100 a year remitted to one Mr. Wogan, a friend of his, I am determined, by the next opportunity, to acquaint his Lordship with the difficulties that I already labor under, as do also all the principal officers in his Lordship's government- We already pay to Mr. Calvert as much as the places can bear; and really, if his Lordship will increase the burthen, some or other will be obstinate and endeavor by violence to throw it entirely off. The gentleman who used to act as his Lordship's predecessors' secretaries in England, were rewarded with £100 per annum; and that sum was never increased till the late Lordship's decease. At this time we pay £750, and yet his Lordship tells me that he thinks it hard that when he has so many places in Maryland in his gift he cannot procure an annual present of £100 for a friend in England whom he has a great desire to serve."[1]

To enable him to support the garrisons he had placed in Forts Cumberland and Frederick, the governor determined to call the assembly together on September 28th, though not without many misgivings that they would insist on the conditions that the proprietary's estates should be taxed, as he confides to his brother in a letter of the 18th, in which he reverts to what had now become a fixed idea with him, the desirableness of an Act of Parliament compelling this contumacious body to furnish the necessary supplies. As the proprietary had peremptorily forbidden his assenting to any taxation of his estates, and as there seemed no likelihood that any money was to be had without it, this Act of Parliament seemed to the sorely-tried governor the only means to cut the knot.

The assembly met on the day appointed, and justified Sharpe's prophetic instinct that they would give trouble, by at once taking the position that if the troops were stationed beyond the frontiers, it was a violation of the terms of the act under which they were raised; and the responsibility of supplying them rested upon those who had placed them there. They went further, and denied the authority of Lord Loudoun to control the forces raised and paid by the province; upon which that astonished commander protested to the governor against this doctrine as without precedent, and peculiar to Maryland alone; and reported their contumacy to the home government as "a most violent attack on his majesty's prerogative." Sharpe in reply reverts to his fixed idea, and assures his lordship that "the superior class of people in every part of the province are already much dissatisfied at the assembly's proceedings, and declare publicly that they should be well pleased if the Legislature of Great Britain would ease the assembly of the trouble of framing supply bills by compelling us by an Act of Parliament to raise £20,000 annually by a poll-tax as the quota of this province toward carrying on the war." And thinking the opportunity a favorable one, he forwards a sketch of such an act.

[1] Sharpe's MSS.

While Sharpe was thus urging his favorite measure, and, aided by Secretary Calvert, endeavoring to gain the assent of the Board of Trade to an act which would have been a flagrant violation of the charter, Pitt, the secretary of state, though solicited to interfere, regarded the whole contention with calm impartiality, and looked on both proprietary and assembly as to blame for the disputes which kept Maryland from contributing her quota to the expenses of the war. In October, the governor wrote to Pitt, reciting the difficulties of his position, and adds that he has recently received a letter from Admiral Holburne, "wherein he required me to furnish him with a number of seamen for the fleet that his majesty had been graciously pleased to order to America under his command. As soon as the assembly met, I submitted the admiral's letter as well as yours to their consideration, and pressed them to enable me to comply with the admiral's demand. In answer to my message they were pleased to assure me that they were sorry it was not in their power to comply with my request; but that the trade of the province must be entirely ruined if any more of our seamen should be taken away; and indeed so many of those that have been usually employed in our trade have left us to serve on board his majesty's ships or privateers, that it is not without the greatest difficulty the masters of our vessels homeward bound can engage a few seamen to navigate them."

To Secretary Calvert he writes on November 9th, still pressing his pet scheme of a poll-tax imposed by parliament, which he has good hopes of seeing adopted, now that Lord Loudoun has represented the state of affairs to government. And by way of putting arguments in the secretary's mouth, he adds:

"You will be pleased to remember that no considerable sum of money (except what has arisen from the duty on tobacco), has ever been raised in this province otherwise than by a poll-tax; that as the people have been always accustomed to that mode of taxation, they all prefer it to any other, except some few leading men of the Assembly who desire nothing more than to throw things into confusion, and thereby to exempt themselves and their constituents from all taxes whatever, and that in fact it is the most equitable way of raising money in this colony that can be proposed, because as our estates consist for the most part in servants and negroes, those who have most property pay the greatest share of the tax; that the Assembly-men's wages (which amounts annually to a considerable sum), and other public charges, are always paid and defrayed by a poll-tax; that by a perpetual law of this province it is enacted and provided that whenever the governor shall find it necessary to order the militia to march for the defence of the province, a poll-tax shall be laid for the payment of such militia, and that they shall not be paid after any other manner whatever.

"These hints you will make use of as you shall see occasion. I can truly say that nothing would have given me so much pleasure as the Assembly's making the interposition of Parliament unnecessary; but really if an Act of Parliament is not made for us very shortly, instead of reducing the power of the French in America—which, if these colonies exerted themselves properly, might be easily done—we shall be ready to fall a prey to their first attempts."

As we are now approaching a period when the political agitations in Maryland led to results far more important than the exasperation of a governor, or the astonished indignation of a pompous commander-in-chief, it will be well to pause for a moment here and see in what direction political affairs in Maryland had already drifted, and how they were still drifting.

The Charter of Maryland, as we have seen, made that province not so much an outlying dependency of Great Britain, as a miniature England. The charter represented the English constitution. In place of the king was the Lord Proprietary, a petty monarch by virtue of his royal rights (*jura regalia*) as Palatine, alone empowered to make war or peace, to regulate ecclesiastical matters, to levy taxes, to appoint officers, and to give or withhold his assent to laws, which without it had no force. When present in the colony, he exercised his authority—*reigned*, as we may call it— in person; but when absent, as was usually the case, he was represented by a viceroy, or lieutenant governor, of his appointing.

The English House of Commons was represented by an assembly first composed of all the freemen of the province, and then by their elected delegates, who, acting jointly with the proprietary or his representative, proposed and voted on laws. At first the governor was president of this assembly, and therefore held a double capacity: as speaker of the House he presided over its deliberations; as representative of the proprietary, he convened or prorogued the assembly, protected the rights of his principal, and in his name gave or refused his assent to laws, and appointed or removed officers.

Here we see the king and the commons both represented; but one essential feature of the English Constitution is wanting: the peers. Now the proprietary or the governor, like the King of England, was assisted by a council of his own appointing, with whom he deliberated on all executive acts, and who, in the earlier days of the colony, took upon themselves no inconsiderable part of the functions of legislation, as numerous Orders in Council show. In 1650, as we have seen, this council was constituted an Upper House, with the governor as president, and sat separately from the Lower House, who chose a speaker of their own. Bills originating in the delegates passed to the Upper House, and were voted on by that body, but though approved by both houses, they had no validity until subscribed by the governor, as representing the proprietary. Here, it would seem to a hasty observer, was a House of Lords; but in reality, it was a quite different body. Its members were neither the holders of great feudal offices, nor were they the great land-holders; they did not, like the British peers, represent great interests. Their office was not hereditary, nor was it for life; appointed at the pleasure of the proprietary or the governor, and removable at their pleasure, they remained under the new name simply a council, with enlarged functions, the constitutional advisers of the executive.

Thus the second estate, or aristocratic element, was as entirely wanting in the political system of Maryland as the first estate, or clergy. A feudal aristocracy, which the proprietary might have tried to found under the provision of his charter which allowed him to confer rank and title, was never attempted, and would probably have failed, as did the experiment in the Carolinas. A landed political aristocracy never grew up.

A certain division of sentiment, and partially of interest, did, however, exist between two classes of the population, which by some has been supposed to indicate the existence of an aristocratic and a democratic class. The great land-holding interest, originally Catholic and liberal, as it became Episcopalian became haughty and exacting, and so lost its early influence. The non-land-holding class, to which we may join the small farmers, originally Puritan, aggressive and obstructive, became liberal and dissenting as it grew by accessions of traders, sailors, craftsmen and pioneers. To this class Sharpe was especially antagonistic, but they had the majority in the assembly. With this class the Catholic land-holders were most in sympathy, after they had become the victims of oppressive legislation, because to them they looked for redress and rehabilitation.[1]

Thus the two parties in the province were the sovereign (the proprietary) represented by his viceroy or lieutenant, the governor, supported by his council (called an Upper House,) and a minority among the delegates; and the people, represented by the great majority in the Lower House. As the power of the popular branch continually grew, they were ever disposed to encroach upon the privilege of the sovereign, who, having no peerage and no body of nobility as his natural allies, turned for support to his overlord, the king, and to the parliament of the mother country, and was willing even to divest himself of his most important chartered privileges, such as the independence of his province from British rule or parliamentary taxation, for the sake of their support. The people, however, were by no means disposed to concur in this abnegation by which the proprietary gave away their rights as well as his own; and hence the Lower House found themselves drawn to an attitude of opposition to parliament; and the idea of resisting by all lawful means all encroachments by that body upon their chartered privileges or their birthright of English freemen, grew stubbornly fixed in their minds. The restraining influences—personal affection for the proprietary, and the conviction that his welfare was identical with their own—were wanting; for in Baron Frederick they saw nothing but selfishness, rapacity, and indifference to their interests. Their belief in the invincibility of "disciplined British valor," had been considerably shaken by the foolhardiness of Braddock, the imbecility of Loudoun, and the helplessness of the regulars; and a dim consciousness of their own powers of resistance, even in the last resort, was assuming form in their minds.

Thus we see how the spirit of democracy grew and strengthened, though as yet blind and inarticulate, unconscious of its identity as a babe in the

[1] This division of feeling subsisted in modified form down to our own times, when the great bondholders of the State were mostly Whigs, but the Catholic landholders mostly Democrats.

womb; but hardening its bones and knitting its sinews in preparation for its mighty birth in the fulness of time. But to Sharpe, who could not see this, their action was mere factious opposition, and a desire to affront and despoil the proprietary; to the western settlers, who saw nothing but reeking scalping-knives and blazing homes, it was infamous neglect and inhumanity; to Loudoun, who despised the provincials, it was arrogance inconceivable; while even to the Virginians and Pennsylvanians, it was temerity hardly to be approved.

At this particular period the standing controversy had taken the feature of objections made by the Lower House to the claims made by the Upper to the appointment of officers, and the supervision of the acts of the former, which in this case had resulted in the rejection of two supply-bills, on account of the usual objectionable conditions. The delegates rightly saw that the so-called Upper House was no estate, but merely the council of the proprietary and creatures of his creation. Lord Baltimore obtained an opinion on the point from Mr. Pratt, Attorney General of England, afterwards Lord Camden; but the views of that eminent jurist were much impaired in value by the fact that he had never seen the Charter of Maryland, and was consequently ignorant of the very essence of the dispute. Guided however by his *á priori* views of what colonies ought to be, he sustained the position of the Upper House, decided that certain taxes imposed by the assembly were improper, and concluded his remarks with the following edifying admonition:

> "The Upper House should take care how they admit encroachments of this kind, when they are supported by arguments drawn from the exercise of the like rights in the Commons here. The constitutions of the two Assemblies differ fundamentally in many respects. Our House of Commons stands upon its own laws; whereas Assemblies in the colonies are regulated by their respective charters, usages, and the common law of England, and will never be allowed to assume those which the House of Commons are justly entitled to here, upon principles that neither can nor must be applied to the colonies."

Here we see that singular feeling of contempt for the colonists which seemed to them so strange, and especially to the Marylanders, who could not conceive why free Englishmen who had removed to a distant part of English territory, and by developing its resources were adding to the wealth of the empire—why these, or their descendants should be considered as having forfeited a part of their common birthright, and in some inexplicable way become inferior before the law to their kinsmen who remained in the island. If the Maryland assembly was regulated by the charter, usages, and the common law of England, so the House of Commons was regulated by the constitution, that is, precedents, usages, and the common law. If the charter were infringed by any of their actions, it could not be difficult to point out the infraction; and certainly if the extraordinary position was assumed, that the principles of English legislation neither could nor ought to prevail in that colony, they were, at least, entitled to know the reason why.

"We observe," say the Delegates in reply to the message of the governor accompanying the opinion, "your Excellency's particular and pathetic admonition to us, to avoid the rock on which we have heretofore split; and as you have thought proper to give us the opinion of his majesty's attorney general, (though given, we presume, only as private counsellor to the lord proprietary,) relative to the two supply bills, being desirous to pay to it all due regard, we cannot but wish that opinion had been accompanied with the state of the facts on which it was founded, especially as we are not at present convinced that the Upper House could not have assented to those bills, without a breach of their duty and a violation of the constitution."

On the 2d of December, 1757, the Lower House, in an address to the governor, declared that they "knew nothing about the rights and privileges of those gentlemen that are said to constitute another branch of the legislature, as it is a branch undevised in our charter, and unknown in its original."

The legal objection, founded on the charter, to the usurpations of the council, was probably an after-thought—the formula invented by the lawyers to express the popular discontent. The assembly refused supplies because, as Sharpe contended, these were to be raised by a poll-tax, which had become hateful to all classes except the Episcopalian land-holders, because it had been so rigidly enforced for the benefit of the Established Church. Yet in some respects Sharpe was right. This tax was not oppressive when paid by the landlords *per capita* of their servants, since then it was in effect a land-tax, no man being able to till more land than the number of his servants permitted; but it grew obnoxious and oppressive when these servants and their descendants became freemen with small holdings; while there was no poll-tax paid for negroes.

Governor Sharpe, in a letter to his brother William, dated January 1, 1758, gives his views of this address as follows:

"Our Lower House of Assembly has, of late years, claimed a right of calling before them any person they thought proper, and their commands have been generally obeyed, though as generally inveighed against as oppressive. Magistrates have been brought before them to answer for offences they were never guilty of, and to gratify the private pique and resentment of any particular member, gentlemen have at times been put to a great deal of trouble and expence. They assumed all the powers in such a manner as tended to render all the inferior courts of judicature contemptible or subservient to their purposes. Before this time, however, they had not presumed to meddle with any one of a Governor's family; nor did they pretend any authority over the gentlemen of the Council, so far as to call them before the House, till the present session, on occasion of the controverted election. Whether the extraordinary declaration they made in their address to me concerning the Upper House, must be attributed to their absolute ignorance of our constitution, or to a worse motive, I cannot tell; but they have, I find, taken abundance of pains to convince the people of the inutility, or rather impropriety, of an Upper House of Assembly in this Province; and I have great reason to believe that if they had not at this time given me an opportunity of stopping them in their career, they would in a year or two have offered their bills directly to myself instead of first sending them to the gentlemen of the Upper House for their concurrence; and their constituents would no doubt have been told that it was agreeable to the usage for them to do so."

In his reply to the address of the delegates, the governor proceeded to enlighten their ignorance with a long historical account of the origin of the Upper House, and its growth from a council to a nominally distinct branch of the legislature. How far they profited by this, does not immediately appear; but on the 4th of December he has new grievances to pour into the sympathetic ear of Governor Dinwiddie, now about to sail for England.

"About ten days ago a bill was indeed sent to the Upper House for reducing the men in the pay of this province to three hundred, and for restraining the service of those to the distance or space of about fifteen miles on our frontiers, viz: between Fort Frederick, Conogocheague and the temporary line [between Maryland and Pennsylvania]. None of them were to be marched beyond the North mountain, on any account whatever, nor to obey any orders that should be sent them by the Earl of Loudoun, or any other officer whatever. This bill has, for these and about a hundred other reasons, been returned to them with a negative. What scheme they will now go upon, I cannot tell; nor do I believe that they themselves yet know. In the meantime, to relax their minds after the toil and fatigue that they have undergone while this bill was framing, they have thought proper to ask what necessity I can have for a secretary; and to insist that if I employ any gentleman under that or any other title, to write for me, they will compel him to appear at the bar of their house and to answer all such questions as they shall, out of curiosity, or in their great discretion, be pleased to put to him.

"On my advising the Earl of Loudoun of their resolution to have our troops withdrawn from Fort Cumberland, he has given me hopes of seeing him here in a very few days. What good effect his Lordship's presence among us will have, I know not; but to provide against all accidents I have given orders for four companies of our militia to march upon the first notice."

The views of the House in reference to Fort Cumberland, are set forth in full in their annexed address:

"ADDRESS OF THE HOUSE OF DELEGATES, DECEMBER 15TH, 1757.

"Fort Cumberland, we are informed, was first begun by some gentlemen of the Ohio Company, as a storehouse of their goods designed for the Ohio Indian trade, and never was garrisoned by troops stationed there by the direction of any law of this province, but commonly by Virginia forces. That fort, we have too much reason to believe, from an extract of a letter from your Excellency to the Secretary of State, laid before the lower house in September session, seventeen hundred and fifty-six, in which are the following words:—'There are no works in this province that deserve the name of fortifications; just behind and among our westernmost settlements are some small stoccado or palisadoed forts, built by the inhabitants for the protection of their wives and children; and besides these, there is one larger, though in my opinion not much more capable of defence, on Potowmack, about 56 miles beyond our settlements. It has been distinguished by the appellation of Fort Cumberland, and is at present garrisoned by three hundred men from Virginia. It is made with stoccadoes only, and commanded almost on every side by circumjacent hills; a considerable quantity of military stores that was left by General Braddock, still remain there, and ten of the carriage guns that his majesty was pleased to order to Virginia, two years ago, are mounted therein;—'is not tenable against even a trifling force, should they come with any cannon; and therefore humbly submit it, whether it might not be a prudent measure to remove his majesty's artilley and stores, (though indeed the provisions, we are told, are chiefly spoiled) from thence to a place of greater security.

"Though Fort Cumberland may be constructed, for anything we know, near a place proper for the stationing a garrison at, for his majesty's service in general, yet being, as we have been informed, between eighty and ninety miles from the settlements of the westernmost inhabitants of this province, and in the truth of that information, are confirmed by your Excellency's message of the 11th of this instant, wherein you say, 'the distance from Fort Frederick to Fort Cumberland, by the wagon road, is 75 miles,' and consequently the carriage of provisions thither very expensive; we humbly conceive it cannot be reasonably desired, that the people of this province should be burthened with the great expense of garrisoning that fort, which, if it contributes immediately to the security of any of his majesty's frontier subjects, it must be those of Virginia or Pennsylvania, who do not at present contribute any thing towards the support of it, that we know of.

"We understand, the most common track of the Indians, in making their incursions into Virginia, (which have been lately very frequent) is through the wild desert country lying between Fort Cumberland and Fort Frederick, and yet, we cannot learn that the forces at Fort Cumberland (though the most of these that are in our pay the summer past, have been stationed there, contrary, we humbly conceive, to the law that raised them) have very rarely, if ever, molested those savages in those their incursions; from whence we would willingly presume their passage is below the ranges which troops stationed at Fort Cumberland, can with safety to that fort, extend themselves to; and consequently, that any security arising from those troops, even to the Virginians who are most in the way of being protected by them, must be very remote, and to us much more so.

"When, from the incursions and horrid depredations of the savage enemy in the neighboring colonies, an opinion prevailed that a fort was necessary for the defence and security of the western frontier of this province, it was thought most likely to be conducive to those ends, to have it placed somewhere near the place Fort Frederick is now constructed; because from thence, the troops that might be judged proper to be kept on foot for the security of the frontier inhabitants, might have it in their power to range constantly in such a manner as to protect them against small parties; and in case any considerable body of the enemy should appear, or the fort should be attacked, the troops might, at a very short warning, be assisted by the inhabitants.

"Near the sum of £6,000 has been expended in purchasing the ground belonging to and constructing Fort Frederick, and though we have not any exact information what sum may be still wanting to complete it, (if ever it should be thought proper to be done) yet we are afraid the sum requisite for that purpose must be considerable; and we are apprehensive that fort is so large, that in case of attack it cannot be defended without a number of men, larger than the province can support, purely to maintain a fortification."

To punish the assembly for their contumacy, Loudoun in December quartered five companies of the Royal Americans upon the citizens of Annapolis, and notwithstanding all remonstrances, kept them there until March 22d. Even Sharpe expostulated at the severity and inefficiency of this measure, which oppressed and annoyed the citizens, who had given no offence, and left untouched the burgesses who were the real offenders. As Annapolis contained at that time considerably less than a hundred families, of whom many were barely able to provide for themselves, the whole burden of supporting these soldiers fell upon those who were in better circumstances, of whom many were office-holders of the governor's appointing, and consequently his partisans.

This act of the imbecile Loudoun, "whom a child might outwit, or terrify with a pop-gun," fitly terminated the inglorious campaign of 1757, which might have been a brilliant and victorious one, but by procrastination in England and bad management in America, left matters in a very much worse state than it found them. Nothing of any importance had been done; and what few laurels were gained fell to the lot of the provincials.

William Pitt, appointed secretary of state the previous June, resolved that the campaign of 1758 should be conducted after a different fashion; and by way of beginning, recalled Lord Loudoun, and superseded Abercrombie by an abler general. It was proposed that the campaign should consist of three expeditions; the first against Louisburg and the East, the second against Ticonderoga and Crown Point, and the third against Fort Du Quesne. He addressed a circular to the Southern governors requesting their hearty co-operation in aid of General Forbes, who was to command the last expedition. The crown would provide arms, ammunition, tents and provisions for the colonial levies; the colonies had only to raise, pay and clothe them; and for these expenses he promised that they should be reimbursed by parliament. Sharpe, in reply, promised to do his best, but held out but feeble hopes that anything would be obtained from an assembly that had left the garrisons in forts Cumberland and Frederick without pay for more than five months. To Sir John St. Clair he writes in a similar strain, remarking sarcastically, "It is well Captain Dagworthy and the rest of our officers taught their men to live without victuals last summer, otherwise they might not have found it so easy a matter to keep them together six months without pay in the winter." * * * * *

"I wish you had told the General [Forbes,] when he was writing to me to get a quantity of forage laid at the mouth of Conegochegh, that it will be impossible to get anything in those parts without ready money, there being more than £2,000 still due to the people of Frederick county on account of General Braddock's expedition. I will, however, write to a trusty man, a colonel of militia, who lives in that neighborhood, and desire him to engage as much as he can get at a reasonable price; but you must not expect that a ration will be delivered till the people are well assured that the cash is at the mouth of the creek."

The assembly met on March 28th, and the governor urged them to provide means for bringing a larger force into service for the coming campaign, and the usual issue followed; the Lower House passing a bill, including a tax upon the proprietary's estates, and the governor and Upper House rejecting it.

In this month about ninety Cherokee Indians, under their chief "Round O" came to Fort Frederick and tendered their services. The chief and several of the warriors with an interpreter visited Annapolis, and while there the assembly voted them an appropriation of £300.

In June the forces of Maryland, Pennsylvania and Virginia received orders from General Forbes to begin their march upon Fort Du Quesne. The troops destined for this expedition numbered between six and seven thousand, of whom Maryland furnished a contingent of about five hundred under

Lieutenant Colonel Dagworthy. Early in July the Maryland and Virginia troops were assembled at Fort Cumberland, and the Pennsylvanians at Raystown (now Bedford) in their own province, about thirty miles from the fort.

As soon as the advance was ordered, Sharpe hastened to the front, and to garrison the forts left vacant by the departure of Dagworthy's command, he called out the militia in the western section of the province. So soon as Col. Washington with his Virginia regiment had evacuated Fort Cumberland and joined the main army now assembling at Raystown, the governor took possession. Washington, who at this time showed a good deal of jealousy in regard to the command of others, wrote on August 21 to Colonel Bouquet:

> "Governor Sharpe may be expected here in a day or two.
>
> "I am at a loss to know how he ranks, and whether he is entitled to the command. In the British army his rank is that of lieutenant-colonel only; but what it may be as Governor, in his own Province, I really do not know; nor whether he has any out of the troops in his province. I should, therefore, be glad of your advice, being unwilling to dispute the point with him wrongfully, or to give up the command if I have a right to it."

To this Colonel Bouquet replied:

> "The Governors in America have no command of the troops, even in their own provinces, when they are joined with any other of his Majesty's forces, unless they have a commission from the commander-in-chief for that purpose. Governor Sharpe will not expect to have the command as governor; and as lieutenant-colonel he cannot, nor do I suppose he would choose to serve in that rank."

During the spring companies of militia were ordered by the governor from Kent, Calvert, Baltimore, Charles, and Prince George's counties, to patrol the western frontier. This order the Lower House resisted as an encroachment on the governor's part; but Sharpe paid no attention to their resolutions, and with his usual spirit and energy he placed himself at the head of two hundred men in August, and marched from Fort Cumberland to relieve the Virginia troops under Washington still in garrison there. Before marching, he addressed a letter to Secretary Calvert, informing him of the state of affairs in the province, and advising that the parliament be induced to pass an act compelling Maryland to raise £30,000; and he again forwarded a sketch of such an act as he wished to see passed. The governor was absent from Annapolis five months, returning on the 16th of October.

An army of seven thousand men had now assembled under the command of General Forbes, who, disregarding the advice of Washington to advance by the road already opened by Braddock, ordered a new road cut from Raystown. The working party, under the command of Colonel Bouquet, to whom this task was assigned, had early in September arrived at Loyal Hanna, ten miles beyond Laurel Hill; and on the 21st of September, Major Grant, of Montgomery's battalion, with eight hundred Highlanders, a part of Washington's regiment, eighty-one Marylanders, and a number of Pennsylvanians, were detailed from this advanced post to reconnoitre the enemy's position at Fort Du Quesne.

The French commander of that fort, observing the want of precaution with which Grant executed his orders, took speedy measures to punish him. Having posted Indians in ambuscade on his enemy's flanks, he made a sudden sally from the fort, and soon spread dismay and confusion among the ranks of the British soldiers. With gleaming knives and brandished tomahawks, the Indians rushed yelling from the thickets and fell upon the astonished Highlanders with terrible effect. Hand to hand they fought, until overpowered, the whole detachment fled in dismay, pursued by the furious savages. The Highlanders, for a time, stood their ground well, but the Marylanders and Virginians bore the brunt of the battle; the Pennsylvanians breaking at the first fire. The Marylanders behaved with the greatest gallantry, and gave evidence of the thorough manner in which they had been trained for border warfare. Out of eighty-one men their loss was twenty-seven privates and one officer—Lieutenant Duncan McRae—killed, and nearly one-half of their whole force missing. "The Marylanders," says the Maryland *Gazette*, "concealing themselves behind trees and the brush, made a good defence, . . . but were overpowered by numbers, and not being supported were obliged to follow the rest."[1] The total loss was two hundred and seventy killed and forty-two wounded.

The fugitives were rallied by Captain Bullitt, who checked the enemy until the whole force could retreat out of danger. Captain Ware, Lieutenant Riley and Ensign Harrison brought off in safety the remaining Marylanders. On the 12th of October the enemy, who had watched the movements of the army, thinking it a favorable time to make another blow and complete their victory, attacked Colonel Bouquet at Royal Hanna. After a few hours' struggle, during which the English lost sixty-seven officers and men killed and wounded, they were repulsed. In this engagement, Lieutenant Prather and two privates of the Maryland troops were killed, Ensign Bell and six privates wounded and eleven missing. In another skirmish, on the 12th of November, near Loyal Hanna, Captain Evan Shelby, of Frederick county, killed with his own hand one of the greatest chiefs of the enemy.

With fifty miles of road to open across the forests, the winter rapidly approaching, and the disheartened troops beginning to desert, it was decided that it was inexpedient to proceed further in the campaign. Fortunately Captain Ware, of the Maryland troops, with a scouting party, brought in three prisoners, from whom information was obtained of the actual condition of Fort Du Quesne. They learned the weakness and distress of the French garrison, and nerved by this intelligence, General Forbes determined on making a vigorous effort to gain possession of the place ere it could be reinforced. Leaving their tents and heavy baggage at Loyal Hanna, they advanced within a few hours' march of the fort, when the French garrison, having set fire to the works, retreated down the Ohio. General Forbes took posession of the abandoned fort, caused the works to be repaired, and gave

[1] October 5, 1758.

it the name of Fort Pitt, in honor of the prime minister, assigning a garrison of four hundred and fifty men taken from the Maryland, Pennsylvania and Virginia troops for its defence.

The news of the capture of Fort Du Quesne was brought to Annapolis by Lieutenant Colonel Dagworthy on the 13th of December, filling the city with joy. As the harassed frontiers of Maryland, Virginia and Pennsylvania were now freed from the incursions of the enemy, Governor Sharpe immediately issued his proclamation, requesting the people to "offer up public prayer, praise and thanksgiving." The assembly which was in session, to testify their gratitude to the men who served in the expedition, on the 24th of December, appropriated £1,500 to be distributed in manner following; To Lieutenant Colonel Dagworthy, £30; to each captain, £16; lieutenant, £12; ensign, £9; and non-commissioned officer, £6; and the remainder to be expended in the purchase of clothing and suitable necessaries to be divided among the privates. The representatives of officers or soldiers who either died or were killed during the campaign were entitled to their proportion of the distribution.[1] But the assembly positively declined to make other appropriations for the support of the army.

General Forbes, after the capture of Fort Du Quesne, led his troops back to Philadelphia, where, worn out with sickness and the fatigues of the campaign, he died on March 13, 1759.

It was now resolved to follow up the success obtained, by a vigorous attack on Canada. The plan adopted comprised several distinct operations, all having in view the reduction of Montreal and Quebec as the final result. Stanwix was to occupy the posts from Pittsburgh to Lake Erie; Prideaux was to reduce Fort Niagara; Amherst, now commander-in-chief, was to advance to Lake Champlain; and Saunders was to support the attack on Quebec, while Wolfe was to command the army on the St. Lawrence. As success depended on joint action, Mr. Pitt, who was the soul of the whole movement, communicated his plans to the governors of the colonies, to be laid before their respective legislatures under oath of secrecy. So soon as they were received, Governor Sharpe convened the assembly and laid the matter before them, urging hearty co-operation; but that body, firm in its purpose, refused to make any appropriation unless a proportionate share of the tax was laid on the lands and revenues of the proprietary. Finding them inflexible, the governor, on the 17th of April, prorogued them with the following speech:

"After the resentment you have expressed at my endeavors to remind you of, and exhort you to, the discharge of your duty, when you seemed to have lost sight of it in the too eager and unseasonable pursuit of other objects, and after you have explicitly resolved to admit of no propositions to provide for his Majesty's service upon any other plan than that of which you had experienced the certain impracticability in the miscarriage of the same bill five times in as many successive sessions. I have not the least

[1] Bacon.

glimmering of hope, however expressive of zeal your professions have been, and interesting the occasion, that you will entertain any disposition to make amends for your former failures, and therefore have determined to put a period to this Assembly, by proroguing it to the 6th of July next."

And in a letter to Mr. Pitt he recommends that that minister devise some plan for having the dispute between the two houses investigated, and if possible, settled, as without some agreement no money-bill could be offered that would satisfy both houses.

The colonies north of Maryland did not throw difficulties in the way of raising supplies, and advanced large sums of money for the succeeding campaign. With the opening of the spring twenty thousand colonial soldiers were again in the field

But the events of this campaign, though they fill a brilliant page in colonial history, do not belong to that of Maryland. Fort Niagara was taken on the 25th of July, and this capture was followed by the surrender of all the French forts from Pittsburg to Lake Erie. On the 26th Ticonderoga was evacuated, and Crown Point five days later. At Quebec, Montcalm was beaten by Wolfe on September 13, and the city and garrison surrendered on the 17, thus virtually deciding the fate of Canada and the great question whether North America was to be English or French.

When the news reached Annapolis—which was not until November 1st—they were received with unusual demonstrations of joy. Early in the morning minute-guns were fired from the Point Battery, and at noon the militia were paraded and salutes of small arms and cannon fired. At night the city was illuminated, and bonfires blazed on every hill. The governor gave a grand ball in the council-chamber, and universal rejoicing prevailed. Similar demonstrations were made in Baltimore and the other towns, and nothing clouded the general joy save regret for the loss of the gallant Wolfe.

Thus brilliantly closed the campaign of 1759. But the conquest of Canada, though assured, was not yet comptete. Montreal was still in possession of the French, and Vaudreuil, the governor-general of the province, had established his headquarters there, thrown up fortifications, and gathered about him the remains of the forces. Amherst resolved to strike a final blow, and again called for assistance from the colonies. Sharpe, as in duty bound, convened the assembly on March 22d, 1760, and endeavored to induce them to waive, for a time at least, their old objections, and render the aid required. But the Lower House stood firm, notwithstanding the menaces of the crown, and the mutterings of discontent now heard from parliament; and in April they were again prorogued, and the governor reported his ill-success to Amherst and to Pitt, in a tone approaching despair.

Amherst, however, had abundant supplies from other sources, and his slow and systematic operations were crowned with success by the fall of Montreal on the eighth of September.

Thus ended the fierce struggle between the French and English for dominion in America, although peace was not formally declared until 1763. The attitude which the Maryland assembly—and we may say, Maryland, since there can be no doubt that the conduct of the delegates was sustained by the approval of their constituents—may appear to the superficial observer selfish and unpatriotic; but we trust that our readers will be able to judge their motives more justly. Maryland from the first saw that this was merely the old standing quarrel of four hundred years, transferred to a new arena; that it was the ancient struggle for supremacy between England and France renewed upon this side the Atlantic; and she was not deceived by the pretence that it was a matter in which the colonies were chiefly concerned, and the brunt of which they should bear. Moreover, it cannot be too often repeated, Maryland, by virtue of her exceptional charter, enjoyed privileges and independence above all the other colonies, and she was justly jealous of these rights, and suspicious of all encroachments upon them, however plausibly colored. She was jealous of the position assumed by the Upper House, which, from being a mere privy council, had now grown to consider itself an estate,[1] whereas it represented no interests but those of the proprietary, and therefore apart from him, had no distinct and individual political status.[2] And, although the charter made no provision for taxing the estates and revenues of the proprietary, yet the equity of the demand that he who had most at stake; who conferred no personal benefit whatever on the colony; neither led its troops nor guided its councils; did not even, as its feudal head, resist on its behalf all attempts at aggression in parliament; but merely drew from it his opulent revenues—should bear a reasonable share of the common burden, was so apparent, that they were resolved to insist upon it. They were not to be moved by the governor's appeals to waive their objections for the present, in view of the urgency of the case. They knew that encroachments upon popular liberties usually come in the form of merely temporary expedients to meet great emergencies; and that if they conceded the point now, it would establish a precedent that would tell fatally against them in any future attempt at resistance. They were not placed there to defend the lives and property of the settlers of Frederick county, but to uphold the rights and liberties of the people of Maryland, and despite the clamors of the frontiersmen, the objurgations of the governor, the indignation of the general, and the gathering displeasure of the crown and parliament, they triumphantly held their own. They were the first on this continent to make a firm stand against the

[1] The Senate of the United States is truly an Upper House and an estate, since it represents one element of the Federal Government—the States in their sovereign capacities as co-equal members of the Federation; while the House represents the other element—the people of the States in their individual capacities.

[2] This character of the Upper House was very apparent in this contest. The Delegates passed a supply bill whenever called upon—passed eight or more during the whole war—but always containing the condition that the proprietary's estates should be taxed, thus throwing the onus of rejecting them upon the Upper House. The Upper House was *compelled* to reject them, having no independent power of its own to go beyond the proprietary's instructions.

encroachments of power, to offer a bold front to the omnipotence of parliament, and to insist that legislation should be on principles of equity and justice as well as precedent and prerogative. In this contest they learned their inherent strength, and entered boldly upon that path which led to independence.

On May 6th, 1760, Governor Sharpe issued his proclamation, commending to the benevolence and charity of the good people of Maryland "their distressed fellow subjects of the town of Boston, who were suffering by the great fire which broke out in that town on the 20th of March, and destroyed one hundred and seventy-four dwelling houses, and as many warehouses, shops, and other buildings to the value of £100,000." To this appeal, the people responded liberally, as will be seen by the following returns made to the governor:

Counties.	*Amounts.* £	*s.*	*d.*
Baltimore	192	13	8¾
Anne Arundel	228	10	3
Calvert	58	16	3¾
Somerset	137	17	3½
Prince George's	191	7	10
Cecil	79	0	0
Charles	173	2	8
Dorchester	123	16	3
Queen Anne's	143	1	0
St. Mary's	178	16	3
Kent	115	8	3
Talbot	233	15	5
Worcester	73	4	6
Frederick	75	6	5½
Total	2,004	16	11½

On October 25, George II. died, and England, after forty-six years, had again an English-born sovereign. The news was received in Maryland in December, and on January 22, 1761, the governor formally proclaimed the succession of George III., and the event was celebrated with great rejoicings.

The contest which commenced in America between England and France, was ended by a treaty signed at Paris on the 10th of February, 1763. And as there appeared to be safety for settlers west of the mountains, emigration began to move over those hitherto impassable barriers of civilization. These encroachments roused Pontiac, a sagacious Ottawa chief, who went secretly from tribe to tribe among the Indians, and obtained their solemn pledges to a confederation, whose object was the expulsion of the English from all the posts and settlements on the frontier. So adroitly were their plans matured, that the commanders of the western forts had no suspicion of the conspiracy until it was ripe and the first blow had been struck in June, 1763. Their plan was that the border settlements were to be invaded during harvest, the men, corn, and cattle to be destroyed, and the outposts to be reduced by famine, by cutting off their supplies. Pursuant to these plans, the Indians massacred traders whom they had invited among them, and seized their property; and large scalping parties advanced to the frontiers of Maryland, Pennsylvania, and Virginia, marking their way with blood and devastation. The most remote outposts were attacked about the same time, and within a fortnight all those west of Oswego, except Niagara, Fort Pitt and Detroit, fell into their hands. The whole country west of Fort Frederick became the prey of the savages, who burned barns and houses, surprised and massacred the settlers in the fields or asleep in their dwellings. "Another tempest has arisen upon our frontiers," Washington wrote to a friend, "and the alarm spreads wider than ever. In short, the inhabitants are so apprehensive of danger that no families remain above the Conecocheague road, and many are gone below. The harvests are, in a manner, lost, and the distresses of the settlements are evident and manifold."

The inhabitants of Frederick town did their best to relieve the unhappy fugitives, a large part of whom were women and children, who had lost their all, and crowded their streets in a state of destitute misery. Their immediate necessities were relieved by food and shelter, and a considerable sum for their relief was subscribed throughout the province. An interesting contemporary account of the state of things in and about Frederick is given in the following letter, published in the *Gazette:*

"*Frederick Town, July 19th, 1763.*

"Every day, for some time past, has offered the melancholy scene of poor distressed families driving downwards through this town, with their effects, who have deserted their plantations, for fear of falling into the cruel hands of our savage enemies, now daily seen in the woods. And never was panic more general or forcible than that of the back inhabitants, whose terrors at this time exceed what followed on the defeat of General Braddock when the frontiers lay open to the incursions of both French and Indians. Whilst Conecocheague settlement stands firm, we shall think ourselves in some sort of security from their insults here. But should the inhabitants there give way, you would soon see your city and the lower counties crowded with objects of compassion, as the flight would, in that case, become general. Numbers of those who have betaken themselves to forts, as well as those who have actually fled, have entirely lost their crops, or turned in their own cattle and hogs to devour the produce, in hopes of finding them again in better condition, should it hereafter appear safe for them to return. The season has been remarkably fine, and the harvest in general afforded the most promising appearance of plenty and goodness, that has been known for many years. But alas! how dismal an alteration of the prospect! Many who expected to have sold and supplied the necessities of others, now want for themselves, and see their warmest hopes defeated, the fruits of their honest industry snatched from them by the merciless attacks of these bloodthirsty barbarians, whose treatment of such unhappy wretches as fall into their hands, is accompanied with circumstances of infernal fury, too horrid and shocking for human nature to dwell upon, even in imagination. We were so sensible of the importance of Conococheague settlement, both as a bulwark and supply to this neighborhood, that on repeated notice of their growing distress, Captain Butler, on Wednesday last, called the Town Company together, who appeared under arms on the court-house green with great unanimity. Just as the drum beat to arms we had the agreeable satisfaction of seeing a wagon sent up by his Excellency (whose tender care for the security of the Province raised sentiments of the highest gratitude in the breast of every one present) loaded with powder and lead. Articles of the greatest importance, at this critical juncture, when the whole country had been drained of those necessary articles by the diligence of our Indian traders, who had bought up the whole for the supply of our enemies, to be returned, as we have dearly experienced, in death and desolation upon us. A subscription was then set on foot and cheerfully entered into, in consequence of which twenty stout young men immediately enlisted under Mr. Peter Grosh, to march immediately to the assistance of the back inhabitants, and with other volunteers already there raised, to cover the reapers, in hopes of securing the crops. Had not the Governor's supply arrived so seasonably it was doubted whether the whole Town could have furnished ammunition sufficient for that small party, half of which marched backwards in high spirits on Thursday, and the remainder on Friday morning. And on Sunday subscriptions were taken in the several congregations in Town for sending up further assistance. On Sunday afternoon we had the pleasure of seeing Mr. Michael Cresap arrive in Town with mokosins on his legs, taken from an Indian whom he killed and scalped, being one of those who shot down Mr. Welder, the circumstances of whose much lamented murder, and the success of Col. Cresap's family, you no doubt have received from other hands. Money has been cheerfully contributed in our town towards the support of the men to be added to Col. Cresap's present force, as we look upon the preservation of the Old Town to be of great importance to us, and a proper check to the progress of the savages; but notwithstanding our present efforts to keep the enemy at a distance, and thereby shelter the whole province, our inhabitants are poor, our men dispersed, and without a detachment from below, it is to be feared we must give way, and the inundation break upon the lower counties."

In consequence of these outrages, the governor convened the assembly on the 4th of October, 1763, and further provision was made for the protection of the frontiers. The commissioners of the loan office having £2,120 still unexpended of the several sums appropriated by the act of 1756, were directed to pay to Daniel and Michael Cresap, John Walker, Nathan Friggs, William Young, Abraham Richardson and Ezekiel Johnson £50 for the scalp of an Indian taken by them in July, and the same amount to James Davis, of Virginia, who in August, with a party of frontiersmen, had pursued a party of Indians from Cape Capon on the south side of the Potomac to George's creek in Maryland, where they overtook the savages, killing one, and rescuing James Coniston and his wife, whom they were carrying off as prisoners. The rest of the money was appropriated for Indian scalps or prisoners at the rate of £50 for each.

Fort Pitt was in the meantime surrounded and cut off from all communition with the interior. In July, General Amherst directed Col. Bouquet to proceed with five hundred men to reinforce it and drive back the savages. At Bushy Run, Bouquet's command was attacked by Indians on the 5th of August, and the fight continued all day without decisive result. On the next day the contest was renewed, and the Indians were put to flight. Four days later Bouquet reached Fort Pitt.

Hearing that Colonel Bouquet desired reinforcements to enable him to pursue the enemy beyond the Ohio, Captain William McClellan organized a body of "forty-three brave woodsmen, besides officers, all of them well equipped with good rifles, and most of them born and bred on the frontiers of Frederick county," and marched them from Frederick town on October 3d, 1764, to Fort Pitt, to serve without pay.

CHAPTER XVII.

The treaty of Paris (February 10, 1763,) gave to Great Britain all the territory east of the Mississippi, from the Gulf of Mexico to Hudson's Bay, and to the American colonies peace with their savage enemies along the western borders, who had for nearly a century made them the scenes of pillage, devastation and murder. In their joy and exultation we cannot wonder that the colonists believed that a brighter day was about to dawn, and that a future of happiness and prosperity was opening before them. Patriotic and loyal addresses were sent to the king, and public sentiments of gratitude were offered; yet, in the midst of all their happiness and hope lay the *amarum aliquid*—the drop of bitterness, which was in time to turn all the sweetness to gall. The triumphs of the English arms were to bear evil fruit for them, as the policy which the statesmen of the mother-country had long been maturing was to be more fully developed and carried out with a rigor far exceeding any former oppression.

The main objects of the parliamentary measures which followed the peace of 1763, were to relieve the financial embarrassments of Great Britain, and to punish the colonies for the reluctance and insubordination they had shown in meeting her demands. The manner in which the royal requisitions had been canvassed in the provincial legislatures, and particularly in that of Maryland, had exhibited a growing spirit of freedom in the colonial governments which was by no means pleasing to that of the mother-country, and which it was now resolved to repress, before it should be too late. To understand the means by which it was proposed to accomplish these objects, we must glance at the existing relations between England and the colonies.

It had long been the avowed right, as well as the policy of England, to keep to herself the colonial trade; and many acts of parliament had been framed with this view. The Navigation Act of 1651 has been generally supposed to have been the beginning of that system which had for its object the suppression of the colonial carrying trade; but this is an error. Long before this period, in consequence of the heavy duties and impositions levied by the crown, the southern planters sent their tobacco to Holland, to the considerable detriment of English revenue and commerce. To counteract this an order was issued by the king in council "that no tobacco or other productions of the colonies should thenceforth be carried into any foreign ports, until they were first landed in England and the duties paid." This was the beginning of a system of commercial monopoly which continued until the American revolution.

This order, however, was not rigidly enforced; and as Holland was reaping a rich harvest from this lucrative trade, the government proposed to put a stop to it by the more stringent act of 1651, by which the trade with the colonies, as well as with other countries, was restricted to English-built ships, owned by Englishmen or English colonial subjects, with an exception, however, in the case of such articles of merchandise as should be imported directly from the original place of their growth or manufacture, in Europe only. The Act 12, Car. ii, directed that sugars, tobacco, cotton, wool, indigo, ginger, fustic and other dye-woods should only be carried to England, Ireland or the principality of Wales, or to other British plantations. Not content with thus restricting the colonial *export* trade to the mother-country, Parliament, in 1663, limited the *import* trade in the same manner, by declaring that "no commodity of the growth or manufacture of Europe, shall be imported into any of the king's plantations, which are or shall be in Asia, Africa or America, but what shall have been shipped in England, Wales, or town of Berwick, and in English-built shipping, etc., whereof the master and three-fourths of the mariners are English, and carried *directly* thence to the said plantations," etc. Vessels so navigated were, however, allowed to take salt from any part in Europe to the fisheries of New England, Newfoundland, and also wines from Madeira and the Azores, and provisions from Scotland to the plantations.

To the monopoly of their foreign trade, the inter-colonial trade, hitherto free and unincumbered, was now, by the act of 1672, made to succumb. By this act certain colonial products, transported from one colony to another were subjected to duties. White sugars were to pay five shillings, and brown sugars one shilling and six pence, per hundred; tobacco and indigo, one penny, and cotton wool a halfpenny per pound.

These acts, which restrained the colonists from seeking the most lucrative market for their products, and receiving in exchange the articles they most needed, without the excessive charges of a circuitous route by the way of England, were deemed highly injurious, and were considered by the people of Maryland a violation of their chartered rights. No colony had a higher claim for commercial privileges and exemptions than the colony of Maryland, and none was more familiar with taxation not sanctioned by their assent. By the terms of their charter all commodities were permitted to be imported into the province, except such as were specially prohibited, upon payment of the ordinary customs. The colonists were permitted to export from it all articles whatsoever, of its growth or produce, to any of the ports of England or Ireland, subject only to the customs and impositions paid in similar cases by the inhabitants of England; and if they did not deem it proper there to dispose of them, they might store them, and within one year computed from the time of unlading, they were permitted to re-ship and export them to any part of the English dominions, or of the dominions of any foreign power in amity with England, subject, as upon their import, only to the customs paid in similar cases by the people of England. Full and absolute power was given to the proprietary to establish ports of entry and discharge for the commerce of the province, and to invest them with such rights and privileges as he deemed expedient. The proprietary, by the assent of the colony, was permitted to impose customs upon the exports and imports of the province, and was entitled to the avails of those customs to the exclusion of the crown; and the kings of England, by the express covenant of the 20th article, were prohibited "from imposing or causing to be imposed, any impositions, customs, or other taxations, quotas or contributions whatsoever, upon the persons or property of the inhabitants being within the province; or upon any merchandise whatsoever within the province, or whilst being laden or unladen in its ports."

This fundamental principle of exemption from the taxation of England, was not only established by the express words of the charter, but had been the uninterrupted practice of the colony from the first settlement. By that instrument the king renounced, for himself and his successors, all right to tax Maryland, transferring that power to the proprietary, who, however, was to exercise it only "by the advice and assent of the freemen, or a majority of them;" and that every possible security might be thrown around this right, it was expressly declared by the law of the province, in 1650, "That no subsidies, aids, customs, taxes, or impositions, shall hereafter be laid, assessed, levied or imposed, upon the freemen of the province, or on their merchandise, goods, or chattels, without the consent and approbation of the freemen, their deputies, or a majority of them, first had and declared in a general assembly of the province."

This act was confirmed among the laws of 1676, and the same principle constantly extended by every act of the assembly down to the revolution. The vigilance with which the assemblies guarded this right, and their constant assertion of it against everything which even indirectly tended to its infringement, gave it the character of an imprescriptible privilege. The encroachments upon their exemptions by the trade-acts, were, after many solemn protests, very reluctantly submitted to; and their acquiescence in them was owing to the circumstances of the times, and not to their relinquishment of the exemption.

"The navigation act had for a time operated very oppressively upon Maryland. Its inhabitants, devoted almost exclusively to planting, had no shipping of their own, and relied entirely upon others for the exportation of their produce. It appears from their revenue acts and their other Assembly transactions, that the Dutch, at the passage of this act, were the principal carriers of the trade of the province. These being excluded, it required the operation of the act for some time, so to enlarge the shipping of England, as to give the colonists the same facilities of transportation, which they had previously enjoyed, when the shipping of the whole world was open to them. Being speedily followed by the acts relative to the export of the enumerated commodities, it soon involved the proprietary in difficulties with the crown.' One of these enumerated articles was *Tobacco*, which was the principal, if not the sole export of the colony; and these acts in effect reached their whole commerce. The proprietary's situation would not permit him to take the broad ground of entire exemption under his charter; but he maintained, that his subjects were not bound to export their tobacco to England or Ireland, or to give bond for that purpose, if they paid the duty. The collectors were soon drawn into very angry contests with him, in which they were sustained by the crown; and the proprietary was warned to look to it, lest he might be stripped of his charter. These dissensions continued in some degree, until the Protestant revolution in 1689, when the proprietary was stripped of his government by his own subjects; and his very defence of the commerce of his colony against the oppressions of the crown collectors, was made a substantive charge against him by his own people. Thus, by the excitement of the moment, the colonists themselves were ranged on the side of the restrictive system. From that period it was rivetted upon the colony, and its general validity does not seem to have been questioned. Acknowledged and sustained by the colony, as predicated upon *a mere power to regulate commerce*, it was considered as the limit of the supremacy of England, and was distinguished from *the power of internal taxation for the purpose of revenue*."[1]

While the merchants of England were thus securing a monopoly of the products of the colonists, the manufacturers were no less eager to secure to themselves a monopoly of their consumption. For many years after their first settlement the colonists were too much occupied in cultivating their lands to engage in manufactures. Indeed, as late as 1767, the Lower House, in a message to the governor, representing the necessity of manufacturing for themselves state "what is very generally known, that nothing has been set up in this province which deserves the name of a manufactory. It is true, that several families make some of their coarse clothing within themselves, but in so few instances as not to deserve notice, and that without any encouragement from public or private subscriptions, except the small bounty lately paid by the county courts upon a few pieces of linen. Your Excellency may well report, from your own sight and knowledge, that the inhabitants of the province, from the first to the lowest rank, are generally clothed in British manufactures." The colonists were content to exchange the products of their farms, as well as their fish and lumber, for the manufacturers of England and other countries. No sooner, however, did they commence to manufacture for themselves than the jealousy of the English manufacturers was excited. In 1699 parliament placed the first restriction on colonial manufactures by enacting "that no wool, yarn or woollen manufactures of their American plantations should be shipped there, or even laden, in order to be transported from thence to any place whatever." And the House of Commons in 1719 further declared "that the erecting manufactories in the colonies tended to lessen their dependence upon Great Britain."

The next complaint was from the hatters in London, who represented to parliament that great quantities of hats were made in New England, and exported to Spain, Portugal, and the British West India Islands, thereby injuring their business. Through their influence an act was passed not only to prevent the exportation of hats from the colonies to foreign countries, and their transportation from one plantation to another, but to restrain, to a certain extent, the

[1] McMahon, p. 166.

manufacture in the colonies. In 1732, hats were prohibited from being shipped, or even laden upon a cart, or other vehicle, with an intent to be exported to any other plantation, or place whatever. No hatter in the colonies was allowed to employ more than two apprentices at once, nor to make hats, unless he had served as an apprentice to the trade seven years; and no negro was permitted to work at the business.

The complaint of the London hatters was followed by one from the West India sugar-planters, and this was promptly heard. By an Act of Parliament of the 6th, of George II., in 1733, a duty of sixpence per gallon was imposed upon all foreign molasses imported into the colonies; and in case of forfeiture, one-third part went to the king for the use of the colony where the forfeiture was made, one-third to the governor, and one-third to the informer.

England had now fully established the monopoly she desired, as the trade of the province in every valuable import or export, was conducted exclusively with England, and in English vessels. Tobacco was still the principal export of the colony, and the chief source of its wealth, although the province at this period exported wheat, lumber, corn, flour, pig and bar iron, skins and furs. The total value of her exports, exclusive of tobacco, was estimated, in 1749, at £16,000; and 1761, £80,000 currency. Her imports were drawn almost exclusively from England, upon which she depended, owing to the restrictions on her trade, for nearly everything, excepting her food-supply. The value of her English imports was estimated, in 1756, at £150,000 annually; and in 1761, at £160,000. Besides these, the province carried on a small trade with the New England colonies in bread-stuffs, and imported salt from the Portuguese Islands, and a small quantity of wine from Madeira. In 1748, her trade employed 200 vessels of 12,000 tons burthen; in 1756, 180 vessels of 10,000 tons; but in 1761, in consequence of the French war, it had decreased to 30 vessels, of 1,300 tons burthen, in the aggregate employing 200 men. Tobacco being the principal trade of Maryland and Virginia, these two colonies in 1731, exported about 60,000 hogsheads of 600 pounds each. In 1740, the estimated exports of this article had risen to about 30,000 hogsheads, of about 900 pounds. In 1761, the Governor and Council of Maryland reported to the Board of Trade that there were annually about 28,000 hogsheads shipped from the province to England, valued at £140,000.

To the general retardation of manufactures in the province there was one exception, and that was the production of iron. Even before 1719, there were iron works in Maryland, but they appear to have suspended operations for want of encouragement, as in that year we find the assembly passing "An Act for the encouragement of an Iron Manufacture within the Province." Similar acts were passed in 1732, 1736, and 1750, by which time an extensive trade had grown up, for we find that in 1749 there were eight furnaces and nine forges in active operation. The quantity of iron annually manufactured in them, as estimated by the governor and council in 1761, was 2,500 tons of pig, and 600 tons of bar. In 1750, the manufacture of iron in the colonies (principally Maryland and Pennsylvania) had become an important industry, and to check the danger of rivalry, a committee, of which Charles Townshend was chairman, reported a bill which permitted the importation of pig or bar iron duty free, but forbade, under a penalty of two hundred pounds, and declared to be "nuisances," the erection of mills for slitting or rolling iron, or plating forges to work with a tilt hammer, or furnaces for making steel. Maryland and Pennsylvania denounced this act as an infringement of their rights as English subjects. To the English manufacturers it was objectionable so far as it encouraged the importation of the raw material; and, to appease them, such importation was limited to the port of London. The most odious clause in the law was that requiring a return of existing mills, the number of which was never to be increased; and it was only by a small majority that a proposition for the destruction of every slitting mill was defeated. The enactment of this law excited the indignation of the American people, and deepened their hatred of the tyranny which oppressed them.

To prevent competition on other articles, duties were imposed, while the colonial ports afforded a free market for British produce and British manufactures. And to enforce strict obedience to these laws of trade, the penalties for their breach were made recoverable in any court of record or admiralty in the colony where the offence should be committed, or in any vice-admiralty court appointed by the crown over all America "at the election of the informer or prosecutor." This act (4 George III., Chap. XV.) threatening to deprive the colonists of the cherished right of trial by jury, and to subject them to a judicial tribunal out of their own colony, necessarily increased the causes of discontent already general, and the destruction of their lucrative commerce with the West Indies, with other restraints as rigid and injurious in their effects, nearly produced an open rupture.

But though the system of monopoly proved as prejudicial to those who bore its restraints, as it was profitable to those for whose benefit they were imposed, it was yet professedly for the regulation of trade, and not for the acquisition of revenue. Though regarded by some colonies as a violation of their rights, by others as arbitrary and oppressive, by all as impolitic and detrimental to their interests, it had for its sole object the extension of British trade, the increase of British manufactures;—if counteracted in its effects, its existence was yet tolerated; if not strictly obeyed, it was not openly violated; if not admitted as a right, it was not resisted as a wrong. But a distinction was then drawn, which was never suffered to be done away—the limits of parliamentary power were then set never to be extended. The powers of *internal* regulation and self government, had never been surrendered—the valued right of *internal* taxation was yet untouched.[1] Though Governor Sharpe, as early as 1754, had again and again urged the taxation of the colonies by parliament[2] yet a scheme to draw revenue from the colonies by direct parliamentary taxation was not seriously contemplated. Near the

[1] *Address of T. H. Hagner;* 1837.

[2] Bancroft, iv., pp. 167, 221, 249, 267.

close of the seventeenth century, this idea had been started, but it was not then relished even by the people of England. It received at the time a refutation of distinguishing clearness, argument and force, upon the ground then taken and ever after maintained, that taxation and representation are inseparable—that as the colonies were not represented in, neither could they be taxed by parliament, without their consent. The sentiments of the people of Maryland at that very period, are fully expressed in a letter written by Mr. Nicholson, then governor of Maryland, in August 1698, to the Council of Trade in England. "I have observed," says he, "that a great many people, in all these provinces and colonies, especially in those under proprietaries, and the two others under Connecticut and Rhode Island, think that no law of England ought to be in force and binding upon them without their consent; for they foolishly say, they have no representatives sent from themselves to the parliament of England; and they look upon all laws made in England that put any restraint upon them, as great hardships."[1]

The war with France, of 1754, re-animated the proposition to tax the colonies; and as the statesmen of England had entered upon the task of legislating for the colonies, they found this work so congenial to their tastes, that the very opposition their measures awakened served to confirm them in their course.

Governor Sharpe, in his devotion to the crown and the proprietary, continued to urge upon Cæcilius Calvert, secretary of the province, in London, the necessity of parliament "raising a fund in the several provinces by a poll-tax," or by imports, "or by a stamp duty;"[2] officers in every colony clamored for the same object; and Lord Halifax, in July, 1755, insisted with the ministry on a "general system to ease the mother country of the great and heavy expenses with which it of late years was burdened." It was accordingly resolved "to raise funds for American affairs by a stamp duty, and a duty on products of the West Indies imported into the continental colonies." A tax upon "stamped paper" was likewise suggested, which was to be "so diffused as to be in a manner insensible." These projects were pressed upon Pitt immediately upon his accession to the ministry, but he "scorned to take an unjust and ungenerous advantage" of the colonies. Though the war with France prevented its immediate prosecution, yet measures of taxation were not abandoned by the English press or people. The debt of the English government, at the close of the war, amounted in the aggregate to one hundred and forty millions of pounds sterling, of which seventy millions were borrowed. For relief from the burden of debt, of which all classes complained, it was authoritatively announced that it was "just and necessary that a revenue be raised in his majesty's dominions in America for defraying the expenses of defending, protecting, and securing the same."

[1] Chalmers, p. 412.

[2] Letter, dated September 15, 1754.

Before anything definite was effected, however, a change took place in the ministry; and after some difficulty, in April, 1763, a new cabinet was formed. George Grenville took the place of Bute at the head of the treasury and the exchequer; the Earl of Egremont and Lord Halifax became the two Secretaries of State; and Charles Jenkinson, the able and indefatigable Secretary of Bute, was retained under Grenville as principal Secretary of the Treasury.

Immediately upon the formation of this ministry, Grenville, as Lord of the Treasury, renewed the attempt for the passage of a revenue bill, "extending the stamp duties to the colonies." On the 9th of March, 1764, he read in the House of Commons a series of resolutions declaring the intention of the government to raise a revenue in America by a duty on stamped paper; announcing, however, that final action on the question would be delayed, with a view of allowing the colonists an opportunity of suggesting other modes of laying a tax. The king on proroguing parliament, on the 19th of April, gave a hearty approval to what he characterized as "the wise regulations which had been established to augment the public revenues, to unite the interests of the most distant possessions of the crown, and to encourage and secure their commerce with Great Britain." In pursuance of the declaratory resolves, the herald of the famous Stamp Act, Lord Halifax, on the 11th of August, 1764, addressed a letter to Governor Sharpe, in which he said that "the House of Commons having, in the last session of parliament, come to a resolution by which it is declared, that towards defraying, protecting and securing the British colonies and plantations in America, it may be proper to charge certain stamp duties in the said colonies and plantations, it is his majesty's pleasure that you should transmit to me, without delay, a list of all instruments made use of in public transactions, law proceedings, grants, conveyances, securities of land or money, within your government, with proper and sufficient descriptions of the same, in order that if parliament should think proper to pursue the intention of the aforesaid resolutions, they may thereby be enabled to carry it into execution, in the most effectual and least burthensome manner."

The intelligence of the intention to impose a direct internal tax on the colonies, awakened the most serious apprehensions among the American people. The principle now asserted by the English government was in direct conflict with the chartered powers of the province of Maryland,[1] secured by the express and solemn pledge of the crown, and with the established rights of the whole people of America, guaranteed them as British subjects, sanctioned by use for more than a century, and hallowed and revered by the fondest associations. In America the subject was discussed in public meetings, and by the press and people everywhere. In all British America union of feeling began to spring up; and as the meshes of tyranny were drawn closer and closer, and escape seemed impossible, the resolute made ready to abide the issue, and the gauntlet of defiance was thrown at the feet of the king and

[1] *Charter of Maryland*, § 22.

his ministers. "Liberty" was the watchword in every mouth, and the energy it imparts to a nation's genius had inspired the gifted to advocate its claims.[1]

But in spite of the strongest representations of its impolicy, and the most convincing proof of its unconstitutionality, the Stamp Act passed; and on the 22d of March, 1765, received the royal assent. It provided that all bills, bonds, leases, notes, ship's papers, insurance policies, and legal documents, to be valid in the courts, must be written on stamped paper, which was to be sold by public officers at prices that constituted a tax.

In America, the announcement of the passage of the Stamp Act aroused a strong spirit of indignation and determined resistance to its mandates. Public assemblies put forth protestations the most eloquent, resolves the most determined, in opposition, while the merchants of the larger cities, whose patriotism preferred the public weal to private emolument, entered into engagements not to import goods from England until the act should be repeated; from one end of the continent to the other, the love of civil liberty strengthened the nerve and animated the hearts of the colonists. The citizens of Maryland displayed a most patriotic spirit, and to their resolves and individual associations, the action of the province was for a time necessarily confined. She could not express through the assembly her opposition to this measure before its passage, as the power to convene the assembly resided wholly with the governor, and it had been prevented by repeated prorogations from November, 1763, until the 23d of September, 1765, six months after the imposition of the Stamp Act.

In the meantime, however, there were other indications of public feeling, which fore-ran the proceedings of the assembly, in showing the detestation in which the measure was held by the people of Maryland. The Maryland *Gazette*, the solitary newspaper in the province, was an admirable reflector of public sentiment, and being conducted with great impartiality, its columns were open to a free and temperate discussion of the important topics of the day. The course of the paper itself was one of determined hostility to the measure. The first intimation of the British government to tax the colonies was communicated in its number of May 17th, 1764; and on April 18th, 1765, it announced in the following terms the intention to suspend its publication, if the accounts, which had just been received, of the probable passage of the Stamp Act should prove true; the announcement being inclosed in "reversed rules," the typographical symbol of woe:

"☞This *Gazette*, No. 1041, begins the twenty-first year of its publication; but, alas! must soon droop and expire, at least for some time, if the melancholy and alarming account we have just heard from the northward prove true, that an act of Parliament is shortly to take place, laying a heavy and insupportable Stamp Duty on all AMERICAN GAZETTES, &c., &c."

[1] The opposers of the measures of the administration were termed Whigs, Patriots and Sons of Liberty; and the supporters of the administration were called Loyalists, Tories and Friends of Government.

It thus conveys the intelligence of its actual passage:

"Friday evening last, between 9 and 10 o'clock, we had a very smart thunder gust, which struck a house in one part of the town, and a tree in another. But we were more *thunderstruck* last Monday, on the arrival of Capt. Joseph Richardson, in the ship *Pitt*, in six weeks from the Downs, with a certain account of the *stamp act* being absolutely passed."

The English ministry selected as stamp-distributor for Maryland, Mr. Zachariah Hood, a native of the province, and a merchant of Annapolis, who was in England at the time. His appointment was announced in a letter from London to a gentlemen, published (August 22d, 1765) about the time of his arrival. Among the many other promotions of officers in the colonies it remarks:

"We are credibly informed that Z——h H——d, late a sojourning merchant of the City of Annapolis, in Maryland, but at present Z——h H——d, Esq., at St. James's, has, for his many eminent services to his king and country during the late war, got the commission of Distributor of Stamps in that province. This gentleman's conduct is highly approved of here, by all court-cringing politicians; since he is supposed to have wisely considered that if his country must be *stamped*, the blow would be easier borne from a native, than a foreigner, who might not be acquainted with their manners and institutions."

In conclusion, the letter adds:

"It gives too many here pleasure to find, that let them make what laws they please to cramp your trade and destroy your freedom, there are not wanting sycophants enough of your own country to sue for commissions to put those very laws in execution among their nearest relations and friends. Oh! degeneracy of antient BRITONS! AMERICA! how art thou fallen! when even thy own offspring, who have been nurtured with all the tenderness of maternal affection, are base enough to solicit thy oppressors to make them the instruments of thy destruction. From the conduct of your Americans now in England, we doubt not but Mr H——d, will be highly applauded among you by all those patriots who set out with the old man's maxim:

"'Get place and wealth, if possible, with grace,
If not, by any means, get wealth and place.'

"There are too many of these mercenary wretches in all countries; but as yours is an infant one, take the advice of an old experienced Briton, prevent the growth of their power by nipping it in the bud; and instead of allowing them to stamp you legally, crush them forcibly, whenever they attempt to invade your rights, or interrupt your quiet. Let all who breathe the Spirit of Liberty, act as Addison makes Cato say of Cæsar to his little senate of Utica, and join in the prayer:

"'May the man forever be accursed,
Who owes his greatness to his country's ruin.'"

Such was the state of feeling when Hood, the stamp distributor, arrived in Annapolis. As the law was not to take effect until the 1st of November, he was directed by Mr. Charles Lowndes, one of his Majesty's Lords Commissioners of the Treasury, to appoint, with the assistance of the governor, "in every town and place in the province, proper distributors, with stamps for all demands." The governor was also directed to give his "attention to the detection of all frauds in this branch of his majesty's revenues."

Opposition to the stamp duties was not confined to legislative resolutions and declarations. Meetings were held in every part of the country, and in bold and decided language were expressed, not only detestation of the act, but an unalterable determination that it should never be carried into effect. In some of the colonies the indignation broke out into acts of violence against the persons and property of its supporters. In Annapolis, Mr. Hood, while engaged in preparing for the reception of the stamps, was grossly insulted. At first the indignation of the people was wreaked upon his effigy alone. The following is the account of the affair as published in the *Gazette* of August 29th, 1765:

"Monday morning last, a considerable number of people, *asserters of British American privileges*, met here to show their detestation of, and abhorrence to, some late tremendous attacks on liberty; and their dislike to a certain late arrived officer, *a native of this province*. They curiously dressed up the figure of a man, which they placed on a one-horse cart, malefactor-like, with some sheets of his paper in his hands before his face. In this manner, they paraded through the streets of the town till noon, the bells at the same time tolling a solemn knell, when they proceeded to the Hill; and after giving it the Mosaic law at the whipping-post, placed it in the pillory, from whence they took it, and hung it to a gibbet erected for that purpose, and then set fire to a tar barrel underneath, till it fell into the barrel. By the many significant nods of the head, while in the cart, it may be said to have gone off very penitently."

He was honored in the same significant manner at Baltimore, on the 28th of August, at Elk Ridge on the 29th, and in the same month at Frederick and other towns of the province.

These proceedings were prompted by men of the highest position and character, but as they did not seem to deter Mr. Hood in his preparations for the distribution of his stamps, it was determined to express the public feeling in a manner not to be misunderstood. Accordingly, on the 2d of September a mob gathered in Annapolis, and proceeding to his house levelled it to the ground. Several other persons who were obnoxious to the people, were insulted, and in some instances assaulted. Hood then fled to New York for safety.

Governor Sharpe, in a letter to the Earl of Halifax, dated Annapolis, September 5th, gives the following particulars of Hood's reception in Maryland:

"My Lord:

"I am sorry to have such a reason for troubling Your Lordship, but it is my Duty to inform you that the Proceedings of a great Number of the People in this Province since the Person said to be appointed Distributor of the Stamps for Maryland arrived here gives me so much room to apprehend they will endeavor to prevent the Stamp Act having its intended effect. Your Lordship will, I presume, long before this can reach you, have received an account of the late riotous Proceedings of the Populace at Boston & other Places in the Northern Colonies on account of that New Act of Parliament, and will not therefore I suppose be surprized at receiving similar accounts from other Parts of North

America, nor at my telling your Lordship that the Inhabitants of this Province instigated by the Example of the New England People, or actuated by the same spirit, were not satisfied with expressing their Indignation against their Countryman, Mr. Hood, the Distributor, by hanging or burning him in Effigie, but having in the night of the second Instant assembled to the Number of three or four hundred in or near this Place, pulled down a house which he was repairing for the reception of a Cargo of Goods that he had, it seems, imported for sale. Being very uneasy & much terrified at the contemptuous Treatment he had since his Return from England met with from his former acquaintance, & the violent Proceedings of the Populace (who really are not to be restrained on this occasion without a Military Force.) Mr. Hood intimated to me that if I thought his Resigning the Office would reconcile his Countrymen to him, & should advise him to take that step he would even do so; but as I could not take upon myself to give him such advice, and both he and his relations doubted whether he could, while the Ferment continued, be safe in mine or any other House in the Province, he has retired for a few Weeks to New York. To what lengths People who have made such a beginning may go to render the act of Parliament ineffectual, I cannot tell, but am very apprehensive that if the Stamp paper was to arrive here & be landed at this time it would not be in my power to preserve it from being burnt, as there is no place of Security here wherein it might be lodged, & the Militia is composed of such Persons as are by no means proper to be appointed a Guard over it. If, therefore, a vessel should arrive here soon with the Paper I shall caution the Master of her against landing it, and advise him either to lye off at a distance from the Shore, or return to the Men-of-Wars' Station in Virginia untill the People shew a better Disposition, or I have the satisfaction to receive from Your Lordship some Instruction about it."[1]

Upon the retirement of the stamp distributor to New York, Governor Sharpe gave him the following letter of introduction to General Gage:

"*Annapolis, 6th Sept., 1765.*

"Your Excellency will, I hope, excuse the liberty I am now taking, in making known and introducing to you Mr. Hood, the person by whom this will be presented to you, when you know my motive for doing so. Happening to be in London at the time when the Act of Parliament for laying a Stamp Duty in these colonies was passed, some friends of his were pleased to recommend him for the office of distributor of stamps within this Province, which he, not apprehending that the holding such office would render him more obnoxious to his countrymen than any other officer under the crown, was glad to accept; but on his arrival in the Province, about a fortnight ago, he was treated with contempt by many of his former acquaintances, and hath since been so much terrified by the proceedings of a mob in this place, who met last Monday night and pulled down an uninhabitated house of which he had taken a lease and was about to repair, that he does not think it safe for him at present to remain here, though I offered him the protection of my own house; but is advised by his friends to keep out of the way of insults till the popular clamor and resentment of his countrymen shall abate. If therefore he should resolve to leave the Province and repair to New York, I flatter myself your Excellency will give him your countenance and protection while he may choose to stay there. As so great an outcry has been made in these parts of his Majesty's dominions against the Stamp Act, that there is reason to apprehend the people in general will endeavor to oppose or obstruct the execution of the Act. I am afraid that an attempt will be made to burn the stamped paper as soon as it arrives here, nor do I think it will in such case be in my power to prevent it, unless your Excellency can order a detachment of the king's troops hither to guard it, and to assist in suppressing any insurrection which might happen."

[1] London Public Record Office, America and West Indies, No. 197.

As soon as Hood's arrival at the King's Arms Tavern became known to the Sons of Liberty in New York, "a design was formed to force a resignation from him, which he escaped, the moment before it was to be put in execution, by retiring into the fort." But the guns of the fort and its garrison did not divert the Sons of Liberty from their object, for a large number of them visited him, and on the 28th of November, 1765, compelled him to resign. In return for this discomfiture of "the first and last stamp distributor of Maryland," the Sons of Liberty of Baltimore, through Thomas Chase, William Lux, D. Chamier, Robert Alexander, and Robert Adair, sent to the Sons of Liberty in New York, a formal letter of thanks.[1]

The annexed letter, descriptive of the transaction in New York, was published in the Maryland *Gazette* January 30, 1766:

"*New York, December 5th, 1765.*

"To the Printer:

"SIR—The following account of the proceedings of the Sons of Liberty, since your last, is desired to be inserted in your next paper:

"After the honorable resignation of Peter De Lancey, jr., Esq., as mentioned in your last paper, the same free, patriotic spirit, to which future ages will be indebted for the preservation of the rights and liberties of the English dominions in America, suggested to many of the inhabitants of this city (whose hearts are the most susceptible of its impressions, and whose hands have been ever ready to execute its dictates), that while the holding of any office for executing any part of the odious Stamp Act, was not permitted even to persons of the most respectable characters and families, belonging to this place, the Stamp officers belonging to any other place in his Majesty's dominions in America, ought not here to find protection from the just resentment of our brethren, actuated by the same principles of liberty as ourselves; and as it was known that Mr. Zachariah Hood, appointed Stamp Officer for Maryland, had fled from thence, and taken sanctuary in Fort George in this City, which Governor Colden (for the protection of himself, or of Mr. Hood or the stamps, though it does not appear that he had ever any directions about them,) had strongly fortified. But on the arrival of his Excellency, Sir Henry Moore, Baronet, our Governor, those fortifications being all rendered unnecessary (by removal of the stamps to imprisonment in the City Hall, and the Lieutenant Governor and Mr. Hood to Flushing, on Nassau Island, or Long Island), the Fort, which lately menaced destruction to the City, was soon dismantled of its military furniture, and was no longer supposed to be in the hands of an enemy to America and British liberty. As Mr. Hood had, by his flight, deprived his country of that justice it had a right to demand of him—the resignation of an office calculated to enslave them—it was determined by the Freemen of this place that he should not do it here, or not be allowed to remain among us, but sent back to the place from whence he came. In pursuance of this resolution, a sufficient number of resolutions immediately appeared, and on Thursday last put it in execution. To prevent an escape or notice, and to find out the place of his concealment, small parties were sent before, and others followed successively, both by land and water. The first party having discovered Mr. Hood's lodging (for it had not been judged safe for him to remain at the house of the Lieutenant Governor), gave notice to the rest, amounting then to near fifty, who surrounded the house, some of the company entered, and civilly, though resolutely told him their business. He was much surprised—endeavored to excuse his conduct and

[1] Dawson's *Sons of Liberty in New York*, p. 73.

desired liberty to relate his case, and read the letters he had wrote to reconcile himself to his incensed country. The liberty was granted. He said some considerable service that he had done or designed his country, together with his long absence from it and his friends, on his late return from England to Maryland, had given him expectations of the most agreeable and endearing reception, and the pleasing views of a genteel subsistence for life. But that on his arrival he was every way so totally disappointed that he was really an object of compassion rather than resentment. That he was obliged to leave all his affairs in the greatest confusion, and fly for the preservation of his life. That his absence had occasioned great losses, and that his life was still in danger should he offer to return. That he had been in a state of continual painful anxiety ever since his arrival in America, that even his enemies might pity; that he had made offers of all that could reasonably be expected from him in order to reconcile him to his country, but without effect; that he had offered to resign his office on the only conditions that he thought he could with honor and justice to those who had been his securities; and he read several letters to prove the truth of what he said, and would have read more, but the company, though they treated him with as much tenderness as the cause would admit, insisted upon his making an absolute resignation. He stipulated a long time for some conditions, particularly, that his declaration upon honor, like Mr. De Lancey's, might be accepted without an oath; and that he might be allowed to hold his office, if his countrymen should hereafter desire it, but neither of these requests could be granted. He was told that Mr. De Lancey's ready and honorable resignation, and being in the midst of his friends and relations, respect to whom would be as a security for his conduct, entitled him to such indulgence, which could not be claimed by a man who was a stranger here, a fugitive from the justice of his country; a stamp man, obstinate in holding, till compelled to resign. He was told that the people in Maryland, having an absolute right to freedom, it was determined by the company that he should absolutely renounce a commission that gave him a pretence to enslave them. And it was hoped on a like occasion the Marylanders would do as much for their brethren of the other colonies; and unless he gave up his commission forever, and declared it upon oath, he would be delivered into the hands of an exasperated multitude, and conveyed with labels signifying his office and designs, till he was delivered into the hands of his own countrymen. About 8 o'clock P. M. he determined on an absolute and final resignation, declaring he had no desire or design to act in the office, and only wanted to give it up in an honorable way. He accordingly signed a paper for that purpose on the spot, and the company being about this time augmented to about 100, set out from Flushing on horseback and in carriages in regular order, Mr. Hood, with another gentleman in a chair, in the centre, and went about five miles to Jamaica, where he read the paper before a magistrate, and solemnly made oath to the matters therein contained. The following is an exact copy:

"'As I have found, *upon mature deliberation*, the Act of Parliament imposing certain stamp duties in America, to be replete with ruin to the constitution of Great Britain and the American colonies, and therefore odious and detestable to all his Majesty's free and loyal subjects in his American dominions; and have unhappily for me accepted the office of distributor of Stamps for the Province of Maryland, while I was lately in England, which has, to my great mortification, drawn upon me the hatred of the whole continent, and being unwilling to remain any longer at enmity with liberty and the good of mankind, I do hereby, with the *utmost cheerfulness* and willingness, promise to resign the said office of distributor of stamps, and do without any equivocation or mental reservation, solemnly declare, that I never will, directly or indirectly, either by myself or any other person, serve in the said office; nor in any way or manner contribute to the execution of the Stamp Act either in Maryland, or in any other part of his Majesty's Territories in America, and ardently hope, and with that this last act and deed will excuse me in the opinion of my countrymen for my former conduct.

"'Given under my hand, at Flushing, on Nassau Island, in the Province of New York, this 28th day of November, in the year of cur Lord, one thousand seven hundred and sixty-five, in the presence of a number of gentlemen inhabitants of the City of New York, aforesaid.

"'ZACH. HOOD.

"'Sworn before me the date above written.

"'SAMUEL SMITH, *Justice*.'"

"He then thanked the company for their politeness and humanity, and behaved with great prudence, but shewed every sign of grief at his situation, said he should have been happy if his countrymen had shewed him the same humanity, but above all things wished to be on good terms with them.

"He was complimented and huzza'd, and invited to an entertainment, but excused himself, and said he was in such a frame of body and mind that he should be unhappy in company. He was then, according to promise, conducted in a carriage to his lodgings. Many constitutional toasts were drunk by the company, and the night was conducted with great good humour and joy.

"N. B.—Mr. Hood was, by the company, assured of the future good will of the people of the Province, and that he might safely appear in any part of it. The next day the company set out for this city, (except those who lived on Long Island) in several divisions, carrying the flag of Liberty, with the words, 'Liberty,' 'Property' 'and no Stamps;' and arrived without any accident or damage to any one."

In a short time the stamped paper arrived in H. M. Sloop of War *Hawke*, Captain Browne; but there being no person authorized to receive it in the absence of Mr. Hood, and no place of security in the province where it could be lodged, the Governor directed the commander of the man-of-war to keep it on board until he could receive instructions from the ministry concerning its disposition. In the meantime the governor received the following letter from Lord Conway:

"*St. James, 24th October, 1765.*

"*Sir:* It is with the greatest concern that His Majesty learns the disturbances which have arisen in some of the North American Colonies. If this evil should spread to the Government of Maryland, where you preside, the utmost exertion of your prudence will be necessary so as justly to temper your conduct between that caution and coolness which the delicacy of such a situation may demand, on one hand, and the vigor necessary to suppress outrage and violence on the other. It is impossible, at this distance, to assist you by any particular or positive instruction, because you will find yourself necessarily obliged to take your resolution as particular circumstances and emergencies may require.

"His Majesty and the servants he honors with his confidence, cannot but lament the ill-advised intemperance shewn already in some of the Provinces, by taking up a conduct which can in no way contribute to the removal of any real grievances they might labor under, but may tend to obstruct and impede the exertion of his Majesty's benevolent attention to the ease and comfort, as well as the welfare of all his people.

"It is hoped and expected that this want of confidence in the justice and tenderness of the mother country, and this open resistance to its authority can only have found place among the lower and more ignorant of the people. The better, and wiser part of the colonies will know that decency and submission may prevail, not only to redress grievances, but to obtain grace and favor; while the outrage of a public violence can expect nothing but severity and chastisement. These sentiments you and all his Majesty's servants, from a sense of your duty to, and love of your country, will endeavor to excite and encourage. You will, in a particular manner, call upon them not to render their case desperate. You will, in the strongest colors, represent to them the dreadful consequences that must inevitably attend the forcible and violent resistance to Acts of the British Parliament, and the scene of misery and calamity to themselves, and of mutual weakness and distraction to both countries, inseparable from such a conduct.

"If by lenient and persuasive methods, you can contribute to restore that Peace and tranquillity to the Provinces, on which their welfare and happiness depend, you will do a most acceptable and essential service to your country. But having taken every step which the utmost prudence and lenity can dictate, in compassion to the folly and ignorance of some misguided people, you will not, on the other hand fail to use your utmost power for the repelling all acts of outrage and violence, and to provide for the maintenance of peace and good order in the Province, by such a timely exertion of force as the occasion may require; for which purpose you will make the proper application to General Gage, or Lord Colville, Commander of His Majesty's land and naval forces in America. For, however unwillingly His Majesty may consent to the exertion of such powers as may endanger the safety of a single subject, yet can he not permit his own dignity, and the authority of the British Legislature to be trampled on by force and violence, and in avowed contempt of all order, duty, and decorum.

"If the subject is aggrieved, he knows in what manner, legally and constitutionally, to apply for relief; but it is not suitable either to the safety or dignity of the British Empire, that any individuals under the pretence of redressing grievances, should presume to violate the public peace. I am, with great truth and regard,

"Sir, your most obedient and humble servant,

"H. S. CONWAY."

The reply of Governor Sharpe to this letter, dated February 12th, 1766, apprised the secretary that his majesty's subjects in the colony of Maryland preferred their own powers of defence even to his tender mercies. He assured the secretary, that although the disturbances in the province had not mounted as high as in some of the other colonies, he believed that this was owing entirely to the early and precipitate flight of the stamp distributor, and to his own prudent policy in preventing the landing of the stamp paper; and that had Mr. Hood attempted to execute his office, it would not have been in his power to protect him.

"Had I not been convinced, (says he in conclusion) that it would be impossible, without a considerable military force, to carry the act of parliament into execution here, while it was opposed so violently in other colonies, I should have called upon Mr. Hood to execute his office, and have promised to support him in discharge of his duty; but after the proceedings of the people of New York, in the presence of General Gage and a body of his majesty's forces, I presume that nothing more could be expected from me under such circumstances, than to preserve peace and good order in the province until I could receive his majesty's instructions."[1]

[1] In a letter to General Gage, dated September 23, 1765, the governor denied the report that the attorney general (Edmund Key) participated in the late riot. He also denied that the sheriff was in sympathy with the rioters, but admitted that the mob came to his house, compelled him to give them a bottle of wine, and forced him to accompany them to an adjoining house, where he escaped and returned home. In conclusion, he adds: "What your Excellency had probably heard about an officer belonging to his majesty's sloop, the *Hornet*, being very ill-used at a public house here a few nights after the mob had assembled and pulled down Mr. Hood's house, was too true; but the gentleman is, I hope, by this time pretty well recovered, as he was in a fair way when he left this place about a fortnight ago. The occasion of it was an unlucky dispute, about their prowess, into which a passenger the officer had with him and one Mr. Hammond had fallen, about midnight, in a large company, at a public

While public feeling was thus agitated, the governor, to convince the bers of the assembly of his desire to gratify them, called them together. members required no time for discussion or deliberation, as to the cours should pursue, for the matters that would come before them had thoroughly discussed by the press and people. They had been fully en ened on the subject of their rights and liberties, and were firmly resol oppose every violation of them. In some instances, to prevent all po misapprehension, the members were specially instructed by their constit The instructions given by "the free-holders and freemen of Anne Ar county" to their representatives, show the spirit then universally preva These instructions to Messrs. Brice T. B. Worthington, William Ham Henry Hall and Thomas Johnson, of the House of Delegates, are as fol

"GENTLEMEN—The shock received by America, and our Province in particula some late *unconstitutional measures* pursued by the British Parliament, in derogat we conceive, of our *ancient inherent Rights and Privileges*, as *Freemen* and *liege Sul* the Crown of Great Britain, requires us to be exceedingly circumspect with regard LIBERTIES, and early to remonstrate to you, our Representatives in Assembly con in support of our RIGHTS thereto, giving you at the same time some few instru which we entreat you will specially attend to and punctually observe.

"By the *unalterable Law of Nature* we look upon ourselves to be Freemen: Prov seemingly averse to the *miseries of slavery* hath placed us in the happy estate of *Fr* and we are conscious to ourselves that we have in no wise forfeited or departed w *natural Right* thereto. By the *Common Law* of *Great Britain*, the *Law of our Lan* declaratory in this respect of the *law of nature*, and consequently of the Liberty Subject, we look upon ourselves also to be FREEMEN; equally free with our *Subjects*, resident *within* the *realm* of Great Britain: And we trust we shall be esteen by our Sovereign and the world, until it can be rationally shown that *mere inhabit* America, or anywhere else, *within the Dominions of the Crown* of Great Britain, bu *out the land* thereof, is sufficient of itself to strip an ENGLISHMAN or his POSTER their natural and civil BIRTHRIGHT—we mean their FREEDOM. On this Freedom subject asserted by us, dependeth, in our opinions, the necessity of his *assenting* by or his *representatives* to Laws, in order to his being bound thereby; and from such ariseth, as we take it, the *obligation* of all *human laws*. How, then, in point of NA or CIVIL Law, are we rightly chargeable, or liable to be burdened by the STAMP attempted to be imposed upon us by the Mother-Country? Have we assented to *sonally* or *representatively?* If we have not, which is notorious to the world, the Mi *virtual representation*, adduced argumentatively, in support of the TAX on us, is fant and frivolous. Can the Parliament by the *fiction* of a *virtual representation* impose o on us, *without our* assent, they may also another, and so on, *ad infinitum*. We can where the line is to be drawn. And each *new law* so imposed on us may pave the some *new tax;* each *new tax*, to some *new oppression;*—oppression (unresisted) lead direct and open path to *bondage;* and that to the immediate privation and utter d

house, which they agreed to decide by a bout at boxing, in which Mr. Hammond was, it seems, defeated and obliged to leave the company; whereupon, there was an outcry (supposed to have been raised by some who had been concerned in Mr. Hood's affair) through the town, that he had been killed by the officers, who, when the mob was thereby brought together, had really like to have been murdered h upon that supposition; but, as every gen in town expressed their abhorrence of th rage as soon as it was known, nobody to acknowledge themselves the actors, an few that they had been even present; there been any mob raised or the least v committed here since that night."

tion of *Liberty*, of *Property*, and of *all* that is dear to us. The *inconveniencies* therefore, arising on the supposition of the Parliament having any such power, as that of laying *Taxes* on us without our *assent*, vested in it, is, in our opinion, no very inconclusive argument to the being and existence of such a power, in the *Legislature* of any *State* whatsoever, much more of that of Great Britain, which glories in the FREEDOM of its SUBJECTS.

"By the *Constitutional Laws* of our Mother-Country, the *birthright* of every English subject, and consequently of us Americans, liege subjects also of the Crown; it is ordained and enacted, '*That no aid, prize, tax, tallage, &c., shall be taken or levied without the good will and the assent of the Freemen of the Land.*' And by the CHARTER of our PROVINCE, it is expressly granted, 'That the king, his heirs and successors, shall at no time hereafter, set or make, or cause to be set, any *imposition*, *custom*, or other *taxation*, rate or contribution whatsoever, in or upon the *dwellers* and *inhabitants* of the aforesaid Province, for their lands, tenements, goods or chattels, within the said Province, or to be laden or unladen within any the Ports or Harbors of the said Province;' And it is charged and commanded, that the above declaration be henceforward, from time to time, received and allowed in all his Courts, and before all the Judges of the King, his heirs and *successors*, for a sufficient and lawful *discharge*, *payment* and *acquittance*. And all *officers* and *ministers of the King*, his heirs and *successors* are enjoined, upon pain of high displeasure of the crown, that they do not presume, at any time, to attempt any thing to the contrary of the premises, or that they do in any sort *withstand the same*; but that be at all times aiding and assisting, as is fitting unto the Proprietor of our Province, and to the *inhabitants*, and merchants thereof, their servants, ministers, factors and assigns, in *the full use* and *fruition of the benefit* of this *Charter*. And by another paragraph in the same *Charter*, the *privilege* of *legislation* is expressly *confined* to the proprietor and the *Freemen* of our *Province*. The words of it are as follows: 'And we do grant free, full and absolute power, unto the proprietor and his heirs, for the good and happy government of the said Province, to ordain, make, enact, and under his and their seals, to publish any *laws* whatsoever, appertaining either unto the public State of the said Province, or unto the private *utility* of particular persons, according unto their best discretions, *of and with the advice, assent and approbation* of the *Freemen of the said Province*, or the greater part of them, or of their *Delegates or Deputies*, whom for the enacting of the said *Laws*, when, and as often as need shall require, we will that the Proprietor and his heirs, shall assemble in such sort and form, as to him or them shall seem best, &c.'

"Hence the foundation of our claim to be affected by *no law*, or *burdened with any kind of tax*, but what is laid on us by *assent* of our *Representatives*, in Assembly convened, agreeable with the *fundamental laws of the Constitution of our Mother Country;*—our rights and privileges as Englishmen, declared and confirmed *by our Charter;*—and the *uninterrupted usages and practice* of our *Province*, from its first settlement to the present time. *And we unanimously protest* against our being *charged* in any other *manner*, and by any other *powers* whatsoever; And we do request of you, our Representatives, that this, our *Protest*, may be entered, and stand recorded, in your journal, among the *proceedings* of your House; if it may regularly be done.

"As *subjects* of the *Crown* of Great Britain, bearing, all of us, *true and faithful allegiance* to our *Sovereign;* we supplicate his most gracious *protection;* and as we conceive ourselves to stand in *equal* relation to him, with our *fellow-subjects*, residing *within* the *Realm* of Great Britain, altho' we are so far distant therefrom; we therefore humbly hope an *equal* share of his countenance and favor with them. We most submissively *pray* of him also, the *redress* of *our grievances*, which are *numerous* and *great*, and in particular, the *Repeal*, or even the *suspension* of the *operation* of the *Stamp Act* among us, until the *Legality* of imposing the same on the COLONIES, be fairly discussed between his American and British Subjects.

"And to the end that we may have your best and most effectual services rendered us, in all and singular the premises, whereon we have largely remonstrated to you; and may also hope to obtain speedy and suitable *redress* of our *grievances*, from the Crown, with the *Repeal*, or even the *suspension* of the operation of the Stamp-Act among us; WE ENJOIN and REQUIRE YOU, to use your earnest *endeavors*,—

"I. That our *essential inherent rights, and constitutional privileges*, derived to us as *British subjects*, from the clear fountain of the British laws—declared and confirmed to us by our *Charter*—and the *usages* and *customs* of our *Province*, be clearly and distinctly expressed and asserted by you in General Assembly; and in proper stile and mode (which we submit to the judgment and discretion of your Honorable House), be entered also on your Journal, among your RESOLVES.

"II. That a *Committee* be appointed early in the Session by your House, and furnished with due instructions, to attend at the *Congress* to be held at New York, the first day of next month, there to meet the commissioners from the other Provinces on the continent; agreeable with the proposal in the *Massachusetts* circular letter, in order to confer on the circumstances of *our Country*, and join in an humble and dutiful petition to his *Majesty* for *relief* from the *Stamp-Act*, with its numerous train of complicated *evils;* and for *redress* of all other of our *grievances*.

"III. We recommend it to you (as in gratitude we are bound) to move in your House for a proper address of *thanks* to be presented to General CONWAY, and Colonel ISAAC BARRE, those *worthy patriots*, and *distinguished asserters* of *British and American* liberty.

"Other matters unconnected with the above, and which may happen to fall under your consideration, in the course of the session of Assembly, we leave totally to your skill and management; and doubt not but you will acquaint yourselves of the trusts reposed in you, with the usual satisfaction to yourselves, your country and us, your constituents."

As the assembly had not an opportunity at an earlier period of declaring their hostility to the Stamp Act, at the first moment of their assembling they took into consideration the two letters referred to which had been received from Massachusetts. The first letter, dated June 13th, 1764, from Messrs. James Otis, Thomas Cushing, Oxenbridge Thacher, Thomas Gray, and Edward Sheaffe, a committee appointed by the House of Representatives of Massachusetts, declared that "the House of Representatives of his majesty's province of the Massachusetts Bay, at the session of the General Assembly, in May last, being informed of the late Act of Parliament, relating to the sugar trade with foreign colonies, and the resolutions of the House of Commons, relating to the stamp duties and other taxes proposed to be laid on the British colonies; were humbly of opinion, that those measures have a tendency to deprive the colonists of some of their most essential rights, as British subjects, and as men, particularly the right of assessing their own taxes, and being free from any impositions, but such as they consent to by themselves or representatives.

"Our agent informs us, that in a conference he had with Mr. Grenville on these subjects, he was told that the ministry were desirous of consulting the ease, the quiet, and good will of the colonies.

"Such expressions induce us to hope that there is nothing punitive in these measures, and that humble, dutiful remonstrances may yet have their effect. But if, while these things are thus publicly handled, no claim is made, no remonstrance is preferred on the part of the colonies, such silence must be interpreted a tacit cession of their rights, and an humble acquiescence under all their burdens.

"This House has wrote fully upon this subject to the agent of this province, and directed him to remonstrate against these measures, and to endeavor a repeal of said act; and if possible, to prevent the imposition of any further duties and taxes on the colonies; for this purpose they were desirous of the united assistance of the several colonies, in a petition against such formidable attacks on what they conceive to be the inseparable rights of British subjects; and that the agents of the several colonies might be directed by the representatives of the people on the continent of North America, to unite in the most serious remonstrance against measures so destructive of the liberty, the commerce, and property of the colonists, and in their tendency so pernicious to the real interests of Great Britain."

The second letter from the Speaker of the House of Representatives of Massachusetts, dated Boston, June 8th, 1765, proposed a "meeting, as soon as may be, of committees from the House of Representatives or Burgesses of the several British colonies on this continent, to consult together on the present circumstances of the colonies, and the difficulties to which they are, and must be reduced, by the operation of the acts of parliament for levying duties and taxes on the colonies; and to consider of a general, and united, dutiful, loyal, and humble representation of their condition, to his majesty and the parliament, and to implore relief." In conclusion, the House of Representatives of Massachusetts, aware of the importance and necessity of unity of action and sentiment among the colonies, on a subject so vital to all, declared in this letter that it was expedient that a congress composed of delegates from all the colonies should be held at New York, on the first Tuesday of October, 1765, and that they had appointed three persons to attend, and requested Maryland to appoint similar delegates.

Before proceeding with other business, on motion of Colonel Edward Tilghman, of Queen Anne's county, the House "resolved" to take the letters which had been laid before them "into consideration on the morrow morning," September 24th. On the following morning, this was the first subject that engaged their attention. As public sentiment had already been heard in determined hostility to the act, the request of the Massachusetts Assembly met with no opposition, and it only remained for them to appoint the delegates. The House, at this time, was graced by men of large ability, genius, learning and practical sense. Here several of the patriots, who had discussed the rights of freemen in their localities, met for the first time. Samuel Chase stood in this body the foremost speaker and champion of liberty. His "energies," says McMahon, "quickened all that he touched, and his abilities illustrated all that he examined. Just arrived to manhood, he already gave promise of that happy combination of talents, for which he was afterwards eminent beyond the reach of rivalry, when all eyes were turned

SAMUEL CHASE.

upon him, to acknowledge the profound lawyer, the eloquent advocate, the resistless orator of the people, and the unrivalled leader of deliberative assemblies. Honored by his fellow-citizens, even at this early period, with a seat in the legislature, he was already conspicuous, at the age of twenty-four, as the champion of colonial liberties. He, himself, has characterized these proceedings in the following energetic language, which is extracted from an indignant reply to an attack made upon him by the municipal authorities of Annapolis, in a publication, after the repeal of the Stamp Act, relative to the city affairs, in which he was described as 'a busy, restless incendiary, a ring-leader of mobs, a foul-mouthed and inflaming son of discord and faction, and a promoter of the lawless excesses of the multitude.' 'Was it a mob (he replies), who destroyed, in effigy, our stamp distributor? Was it a mob who assembled here from the different counties, and indignantly opened the public offices? Whatever vanity may whisper in your ears, or that pride and arrogance may suggest, which are natural to despicable tools of power, emerged from obscurity and basking in proprietary sunshine, you must confess them to be your superiors, men of reputation and merit, who are mentioned with respect, while you are named with contempt, pointed out and hissed at, as *fruges consumere nati.* I admit that I was one of those who committed to the flames, in effigy, the stamp distributor of this province, and who openly disputed the parliamentary right to tax the colonies; while you skulked in your houses, some of you asserting the parliamentary right, and esteeming the stamp act a beneficial law. Others of you meanly grumbled in your corners, nor daring to speak out your sentiments.'

"Thrown into the midst of an age calculated to uprouse, even in vehemence and harshness, the bold and indignant spirit of a freeman, Mr. Chase was assailed, in the very outset of his career, by the courtly adherents of the royal cause, with whom his boldness was faction, and his vehemence arrogance. In his encounters with such as these, he disdained all reserve, and gave no quarter. '*Seeming,*' he learned to despise; and there never was a man, who could say with Hamlet, more justly than Mr. Chase, '*I know not seems.*' What he felt, he expressed; and, what he expressed, came stamped with all the vigor of his mind, and the uncompromising energy of his character —if his manner was a fault, it leaned to virtue's side. It is not for my feeble pen to portray his virtues and abilities—they are registered in the nation's history; and there is no true American, to whom his name, recorded on the imperishable roll of American Independence, does not bring back the grateful recollection of his services. He was a son of Maryland, and when will she have his like again?"[1]

John Hanson, Jr., was afterwards President of the Continental Congress, Wm. Smallwood, Commander of the Maryland Line, and Thomas Johnson, the first Constitutional Governor of Maryland. John Hall, George Plater, James Hollyday, and Thomas Cresap were pillars of the revolution, and appear prominently in the subsequent career of the province.

The House unanimously concurred in the proposition of Massachusetts, and appointed Colonel Edward Tilghman, of Queen Anne's, William Murdock, of Prince George's, and Thomas Ringgold, of Kent, delegates to the General Congress to be held in New York. The Upper House and the governor approved and sanctioned the measure, as well as the appropriation of £500, to meet their expenses. Messrs. James Hollyday, of Queen Anne's, Thomas Johnson, of Anne Arundel, Edmund Key, of St. Mary's, John Goldsborough, of Talbot, John Hammond, of Anne Arundel, Daniel Wolstenholme, of St. Mary's, and John Hanson, Jr., of Charles, were then appointed a committee to draft instructions for the delegates. On the 25th, Mr. James Hollyday, on behalf of the committee, reported the instructions, which directed the delegates to repair to the congress, "there to join in a general and united, dutiful, loyal, and humble representation to his Majesty and the British Parliament, of the circumstances and condition of the British colonies; and to pray relief from the burdens and restraints lately laid upon

[1] McMahon, pp. 339-340.

their trade and commerce, and especially from the taxes imposed by the Stamp Act, whereby they are deprived, in some instances, of that invaluable privilege of Englishmen and British subjects, trials by juries; and to take care that such representation should humbly and decently, but expressly, contain an assertion of the right of the colonists, to be exempt from all and every taxations and impositions upon their persons and property, to which they do not consent in a legislative way, either by themselves, or their representatives freely chosen and appointed."

Having thus speedily and efficiently endorsed the proposition of a general congress, they now determined by explicit legislative action to declare the principles upon which their colonial rights were founded. And to dispel all doubts, if any such existed, as to the cordial concurrence of Maryland with the other colonies, the following committee was "appointed to draw up resolves, declarative of the constitutional rights and privileges of the freemen of the province:" William Murdock, of Prince George's; Edward Tilghman, of Queen Anne's; Thomas Ringgold, of Kent; Samuel Chase, of Annapolis; Samuel Wilson, of Somerset; D. Wolstenholme, of St. Mary's; John Goldsborough, of Talbot; John Hammond, of Anne Arundel; Henry Hollyday, of Talbot; Charles Grahame, of Calvert; James Hollyday, of Queen Anne's; Thomas Johnson, of Anne Arundel; Edmund Key, of St. Mary's, and Brice T. B. Worthington, of Anne Arundel.

On the 28th, Mr. Murdock, from the committee, brought into the House the following declarations, which from their dignified tone and the unanimity with which they were adopted, form one of the proudest pages of Maryland's history:

"I. *Resolved, unanimously*, That the first adventurers and settlers of this province of Maryland brought with them and transmitted to their posterity, and all other his Majesty's subjects, since inhabiting in this province, all the liberties, privileges, franchises, and immunities, that at any time have been held, enjoyed, and possessed, by the people of Great Britain.

"II. *Resolved, unanimously*, That it was granted by Magna Charta, and other the good laws and statutes of England, and confirmed by the petition and bill of rights, that the subject should not be compelled to contribute to any tax, tallage, aid, or other like charges not set by common consent of parliament.

"III. *Resolved, unanimously*, That by a royal charter, granted by his Majesty, king Charles I., the eighth year of his reign and in the year of our Lord one thousand six hundred thirty and two, to Cecilius, then Lord Baltimore, it was, for the encouragement of people to transport themselves and families into this province, amongst other things, covenanted and granted by his said Majesty for himself, his heirs, and successors, as followeth:

"And we will also, and of our more special grace, for us, our heirs and successors, we do strictly enjoin, constitute, ordain and command, that the province shall be of our allegiance, and that all and singular the subjects and liege people of us, our heirs and successors, transported into the said province, and the children of them, and of such as shall descend from them, there already born, or hereafter to be born, be, and shall be denizens and lieges of us, our heirs, and successors, of our kingdom of England and Ireland, and be in all things held, treated, reputed and esteemed, as the liege faithful people of us, our heirs, and successors, born within our kingdom of England, and likewise any lands, tenements, revenues, services, and other hereditaments whatsoever, within our kingdom of England, and other our dominions, may inherit, or otherwise purchase, receive, take, have, hold, buy and possess, and them may occupy and enjoy, give, sell, alien, and bequeath, as likewise, all liberties, franchises and privileges, of this our kingdom of England, freely, quietly, and peaceably, have and possess, occupy and enjoy, as our liege people, born, or to be born, within our said kingdom of England, without the let, molestation, vexation, trouble, or grievance of us, our heirs and successors, any statute, acts, ordinance, or provision to the contrary thereof, notwithstanding.

"And further, our pleasure is, and by these presents, for us, our heirs and successors, we do covenant and grant, to and with the said now Lord Baltimore, his heirs and assigns, that we, our heirs and successors, shall at no time hereafter, set or make, or cause to be set, any imposition, custom, or other taxation, rate, or contribution whatsoever, in or upon the dwellers and inhabitants of the aforesaid province, for their lands, tenements, goods or chattels, within the said province, or in or upon any goods or merchandises, within the said province, or to be laden and unladen within any of the ports or harbors of the said province: And our pleasure is, and for us, our heirs, and successors, we charge and command, that this our declaration shall be henceforward, from time to time, received and allowed in all our courts, and before all the judges of us, our heirs and successors, for a sufficient and lawful discharge, payment and acquittance: commanding all and singular our officers and ministers of us, our heirs and successors, and enjoining them upon pain of our high displeasure, that they do not presume, at any time, to attempt any thing to the contrary of the premises, or that they do in any sort withstand the same; but that they be at all times aiding and assisting, as it is fitting, unto the said now Lord Baltimore, and his heirs, and to the inhabitants and merchants of Maryland aforesaid, their servants, ministers, factors, and assigns, in the full use and fruition of the benefit of this our charter.

"IV. *Resolved*, That it is the *unanimous* opinion of this house, that the said charter is declaratory of the constitutional rights and privileges of the freemen of this province.

"V. *Resolved unanimously*, That trials by juries are the grand bulwark of liberty, the undoubted birth-right of every Englishman, and consequently of every British subject in America; and that the erecting other jurisdictions for the trial of matters of fact, is unconstitutional, and renders the subject insecure in his liberty and property.

"VI. *Resolved*, That it is the *unanimous* opinion of this house, that it cannot, with any truth or propriety, be said, that the freemen of this province of Maryland, are represented in the British parliament.

"VII. *Resolved, unanimously*, That his Majesty's liege people of this ancient province, have always enjoyed the right of being governed by laws to which they themselves have consented, in the articles of taxes and internal polity; and that the same hath never been forfeited, or any other way yielded up, but hath been constantly recognized by the king and people of Great Britain.

"VIII. *Resolved*, That it is the *unanimous* opinion of this house, that the representatives of the freemen of this province, in their legislative capacity, together with the other part of the legislature, have the sole right to lay taxes and impositions on the inhabitants of this province, or their property and effects; and that the laying, imposing, levying or collecting, any tax on or from the inhabitants of Maryland, under colour of any other authority, is unconstitutional, and a direct violation of the rights of the freemen of this province."

Having thus asserted the liberties and immunities of English subjects to be their undoubted birth-right, these patriotic men declined to enter upon the consideration of any other business, and therefore requested the governor to give them "a short recess of a few weeks." The request was granted, and the assembly was prorogued until the 1st of November following. Before the prorogation, the governor, in a message to the House, stated that probably the stamped paper destined for the province would "arrive here before I shall have an opportunity of advising with you again; and the master of the vessel who may have charge thereof, will desire me to give orders for its being landed and lodged in a place of security, especially as the person appointed to distribute the stamps here, has, I understand, left the province. I should be glad to know how you would advise me to act on such occasion." The House took into consideration the message, and appointed Mr. James Hollyday, John Hammond, Col. Edward Tilghman, Thomas Johnson, William Murdock, Daniel Wolstenholme, Thomas Ringgold, Samuel Chase, Henry Hollyday, William Allen and John Goldsborough, a committee to draft a reply. In a short time they prepared an address to the governor, in which they said, "we should think ourselves extremely happy were we in circumstances to advise your Excellency on so new a subject; but it being a matter of importance, and such as we do not think ourselves at liberty to advise in, without the instructions of our constituents, which we cannot now obtain, we hope your Excellency will think us excusable for declining to offer you any advice upon the occasion." After the adoption of the address, the assembly, on the 28th of September, adjourned to the 1st of November.

The public mind now turned to the first Continental Congress, which assembled in the City Hall, at New York, on the 7th of October, 1765. The congress consisted of twenty-eight delegates, representing Massachusetts, Rhode Island, Connecticut, New York, New Jersey, Pennsylvania, Delaware, Maryland, and South Carolina. Virginia, New Hampshire, Georgia, and North Carolina, though sympathizing with the movement, did not send delegates. The congress organized by the choice of Timothy Ruggles as chairman, and John Cotton, clerk. On the second day of the session, it took into consideration the rights, privileges, and grievances of "the British-American Colonists;" and, after a session of eighteen days, it put forth a Declaration of Rights and Grievances, a memorial to the House of Lords, a petition to the House of Commons, and an address to the king.[1]

On the 25th of October, the congress adjourned, and at the November (27th) session of the assembly the Maryland delegates submitted to that body an account of their expenses and a statement of their proceedings. After a full and careful examination they were unanimously approved; and the Speaker of the House directed, by its unanimous vote, to present its thanks to the delegates for the able manner in which they had discharged their duties, which he did in the following words:

"The House have perused and fully considered the whole proceedings of the Congress, lately held at New York, which you have laid before them; and as a testimony that they highly approve of the manner in which you have executed the great trust reposed in you

[1] William Murdock was on the committee on the Address to the King, and Colonel Edward Tilghman on the Memorial to the House of Lords.

The *MARYLAND* GAZETTE.

E X P I R I N G:

In Hopes of a Resurrection to LIFE again.

[XXIst Year.] THURSDAY, *October* 10, 1765. [N°. 1066.]

WE are sorry, heartily sorry, to acquaint the Public in general, and our good Customers in particular, That this GAZETTE will not any longer be Published [for some Time] for Reasons already given, which cannot but be known. It is true, it might have liv'd Three more Weeks, before that Dooms-Day, the dreadful First of *November*; but as this Week's Paper [N°. 1066.] compleats the Year with all our old Customers, as well as finishes the Seven Years PARTNERSHIP in it, between the *PRINTERS*; and that dismal Day being near at Hand, it ceases Now.

☞ A Paper by Way of POSTSCRIPT, SUPPLEMENT, or APPENDIX, to this GAZETTE, is design'd to be Printed each Week, (without any Charge to the Customers) in order to Publish some Advertisements, *&c. &c.*) until the above Time.

BOSTON, *September* 23.

NEWPORT, *September* 23.

HARTFORD, *September* 25.

PHILADELPHIA, *October* 3.

in every respect, they have unanimously resolved that the thanks of this House should be given you, and it is with great pleasure I now do it, as I am sensible that the conduct that has given such satisfaction to the members of this House will permit the approbation of all the well-wishers to this country, when the whole affair shall, at a proper season, be communicated to them."

The columns of the Maryland *Gazette* being still crowded with publications attesting the rights of the colonies and the necessity of their maintenance, to show its detestation of the Stamp Act, on the 10th of October the paper was put into mourning, and headed with a funeral manifesto.

Shortly after this, on the 31st of October, Mr. Green issued his "third and last supplement to the Maryland *Gazette*, of the tenth instant," and announced "that as by means of a late . . . Act of Parliament, a stoppage is put to the publication of all gazettes, papers of public intelligence, and advertisers, after this date, except on such intolerable and burthensome terms as cannot *at present* be complied with here, of course this must now cease and determine. . . . This paper has never had occasion to appear in deep mourning, since the death of our late good king until now." The "supplement" was now in deep mourning, with a skull and cross-bones (representing the stamp) on the right hand corner of the front page, with the following impressive words in deep black type: "The Times are DREADFUL, DISMAL, DOLEFUL, DOLOROUS and DOLLAR-LESS."

On the 10th of December, 1765, the editor announces in "an apparition of the late Maryland *Gazette*, which is not dead but only sleepeth," that "Captain Brown, in one of his Majesty's sloops of war, is arrived here with fetters forged in England for the good people of this province; but they are not landed." He also says "we have received information from Frederick county, that at the last court there, the magistrates taking into consideration the bad consequences that would attend a stop being put to the ordinary course of justice, if any notice was taken of the Stamp Act (which had never been legally transmitted to them), they in a very full court, *unanimously resolved and ordered*, that all the business and process of that court should be transacted in the usual manner *without stamps*, and that such proceedings should be good and valid. The clerk of the court, apprehending damage to himself if he made any entry, or issued any process without stamped paper, refused to comply with the order of the court; upon which the court ordered him to be committed to prison for contempt. He then submitted and was discharged, and proceeded on business as formerly."[1]

[1] On the 5th of September, the following card appeared in the *Gazette*:

"*To Messrs. Green and Rind:*

"GENTLEMEN—I am informed that the Stamp law takes place the first day of November next. I, therefore, hereby give notice to all officers whatever that may be appointed by virtue of that most grievous and unconstitutional Act (to prevent them trouble), that I will pay no tax whatever but what is laid upon me by my representatives. I am, gentlemen,

"Your humble servant,

"BENJAMIN WELSH."

Ships were cleared from the several ports of the province without stamps.

The decision of the court was celebrated in Frederick town on the 30th of November, in a manner most characteristic of the times. The following amusing description of it is published in the Maryland *Gazette* of 16th December, 1765:

"THE STAMP ACT having received a mortal wound by the hands of justice, on Saturday last gave up the ghost, to the great joy of the inhabitants of Frederick County. The lifeless body lay exposed to public ignominy till yesterday, when it was thought proper, for preventing infection from its stench, to bury it in the following manner:

"The SONS OF LIBERTY assembled at the house of Mr. *Samuel Swearingen*, in the Afternoon, and the coffin was taken up exactly at 3 o'clock.

Form of the Funeral.

"1. The colors of the Town Company.

"2. Drums.

"3. The banner displayed, with this inscription in large characters: CONSTITUTIONAL LIBERTY ASSERTED BY THE MAGISTRATES OF FREDERICK COUNTY 22D NOVEMBER, 1765.

"4. The cap of Liberty mounted on a staff, with the several following inscriptions: MAGNA CHARTA. CHARTER OF MARYLAND. TRIALS BY JURIES RESTORED. OPPRESSION REMOVED. LIBERTY AND LOYALTY.

"5. Conductors.

"6. The coffin, with this inscription on the lid, THE STAMP ACT, EXPIRED OF A MORTAL STAB RECEIVED FROM THE GENIUS OF LIBERTY IN FREDERICK County Court, 23d November, 1765—Aged 22 days. On the ends, sides, and ledges of the coffin appeared several inscriptions, which were altogether deposited in the ground, as appendages to the Stamp Act, viz.: Tyranny—Villenage—Military Execution—Soldiers quartered on private houses—Court of Vice-Admiralty—Guarda de Costa's to prevent corruption in North Americans from a Redundancy of Spanish dollars—Britons employed in fastening chains on the necks of British Subjects—Fines—Imprisonment—Ruin—Desolation—Slavery taking possession of America, in order to extend her dominion over Great Britain.

"7. Z—— H——, Esq., as sole mourner, carried in an open chariot—His countenance pale and dejected—his dress disorderly, unsuitable to his rank, and betraying great inward distraction of mind, and his tottering situation (being scarce able to keep his seat) demonstrated the weakness to which he was reduced, and plainly indicated the melancholy catastrophe which shortly ensued.

"8. Sons of Liberty, two and two.

"During the whole procession, which marched thro' the principal streets till it arrived at the gallows erected on the Court House Green, the bells continued ringing; and on every huzza by the crowd, or loud laugh of female spectators, Z—— H——, Esq.; was observed to nod, or drop his head into his bosom, in token of the utmost sorrow and confusion.

"On their arrival at the gallows, under which the grave was dug, the drums ceasing, and proclamation made for silence, Z—— H——, Esq., was observed to be struck with such astonishment, that tho' he seemed to demand audience by a weak motion of his head, he was not able to utter word, and his features were fixed as death. Being asked whether he had anything to say, he made no answer, but a paper appearing in his bosom, was taken out; and it being demanded whether that paper contained the substance of what he had to say on the occasion, he continued silent, but was seen to make a faint nod of approbation.

"The paper, which was ordered to be read, contained the following words, and appears to have been composed by him by way of funeral oration or lamentation over the body of that beloved act, which had engrossed his whole mind and affections. 'GOOD PEOPLE—for countrymen I dare not call you—having forfeited all claim or title to that appellation—wonder not at my hesitation of speech, or my sighs and groans on this sad occasion. The powers of utterance being, in a great measure, taken from me by the sight of that mournful object! Cursed be the day, that direful day, in which my eyes beheld the fatal catastrophe of the beloved of my soul! May the 23d *November* be struck out of the Calendar, and never be reckoned in the future Annals of time! And shall a record appear, to eternize the downfall of my beloved, naked and unadorned with the beautiful Stamp which ought to have been annexed by my influence? Can I possibly survive the dreadful thought! And must all my hopes perish, my schemes for advancing my fortune at the expense of my country be blasted, and public emolument triumph over private gain? Shall Maryland freely export her wheat and corn, and find out markets for her flour and provisions without my participation in the fruits of the toil and sweat of her laborious Sons? Shall the press continue free, and exist only to publish my disgraces, and instill notions of constitutional rights and liberties into the minds of North Americans? Shall the Power of taxing the poor (who are chiefly involved in the duties of the Stamp Act) by imposing an arbitrary price on stamped paper, be wrested from me; and instead of lording it over my countrymen, must I need be reduced to the state of an exile, a fugitive and a vagabond on the face of the earth? Forbid it, all ye black infernal powers, of tyranny, avarice and oppression! For to you have I devoted myself! But, soft! Your powers are enervated and your dominion blasted by the bold Sons of Liberty, before whom I now stand! Pardon, good people, this last testimony of my affection to the deceased. For her I despised country, humanity, friendship, kindred, and all the ties of honor, nature, gratitude and honesty. For her was every motive of justice, benevolence, pity, and compassion banished from my breast. For her could I have sacrificed the good of the public, the happiness of individuals, and (encircled in her embraces) have smiled at the curses of the poor, the tears of the orphan, the cries of the widow, the groans of the oppressed; and, without one pang of remorse, have viewed the land of my birth gnashing her teeth under the load of bondage, whilst I enjoyed the sunshine of ministerial influence. and decked myself in the spoils of the wretched and unfortunate! Dear object of my warmest wishes! thou art now expired under the hand of Justice! The same spirit animated us both, and the cold grasp of fate is now upon me! My faculties, sink together with thee, and death freezes my stagnating fluids! Let me be buried together with thee, and one grave receive our breathless remains! I hope, Good People, you will not refuse this last request of a dying person. And, Oh! Oh! Oh!'

"No sooner had the person appointed to read it come to the Oh! Oh! &c., than Z—— H——, Esq., was seen to sink suddenly down, and tumble out of the Chariot, his body becoming instantaneously cold and stiff, so violent an assault had grief made on all his vital faculties, and left him a lifeless figure scarce resembling humanity. As he was falling, a Son of Liberty, with a voice like thunder, cried out—Let him die like a dog. A loud huzza and ruff of the drums immediately followed, and, according to his own request, his corpse was deposited in the earth together with that of his beloved.

"The grave being filled up, and acclamations repeated, the company marched in their former order, with colors, banner, &c., to the house of Mr. Samuel Swearingen, where an elegant supper was prepared, and a ball given to the ladies, who made a brilliant appearance on the occasion. Many loyal and patriotic toasts were drank, and the whole concluded with the utmost decorum."

At a meeting of the freemen of Talbot county held on the 25th of November, they manifested the highest indignation, and adopted the following preamble and resolutions:

"The Freemen of Talbot County, assembled at the Court House of the said county, do in the most solemn manner declare to the world:

"That they bear faith and true allegiance to his Majesty, King George the Third.

"That they are most affectionately and zealously attached to his Royal person and family, and are fully determined, to the utmost of their power, to maintain and support his Crown and dignity, and the succession as by law established, and do, with the greatest cheerfulness, submit to his government according to the known and just principle of the British Constitution, and do unanimously RESOLVE:

"*First*, That under the Royal Charter granted to this Province, they and their Ancestors have long enjoyed, and they think themselves still entitled to enjoy all the Rights and Privileges of British subjects.

"*Secondly*, That they consider the trial by jury, and the privilege of being taxed only with their own consent, given by their legal Representatives in Assembly, as the principal foundation, the main source of all their Liberties.

"*Thirdly*, That by the Act of Parliament lately passed, for raising Stamp Duties in America (should it take Place), both those invaluable privileges, enjoyed in their full extent by their fellow-subjects in Great Britain, would be torn from them, and that therefore the same is in their opinion unconstitutional, invasive of their just rights, and tending to excite disaffection in the breast of every American subject.

"*Fourthly*, That they will, at the risk of their lives and fortunes, endeavor, by all lawful ways and means, to preserve and transmit to their posterity, their rights and liberties, in as full and ample manner as they received the same from their Ancestors; and will not, by any act of theirs, countenance or encourage the execution or effect of the said Stamp Act.

"*Fifthly*, That they will detest, abhor, and hold in the utmost contempt, all and every person or persons, who shall meanly accept of any employment or office relating to the Stamp Act, or shall take any shelter or advantage from the same, and all and every Stamp-pimp, informer, or favorer of the said Act, and that they will have no communication with any such person, nor speak to them on any occasion, except it be to upbraid them with their business.

"And in testimony of this their fixed and unalterable resolution, they have this day erected a GIBBET twenty feet high, before the Court-House door, and hung in chains thereon, the effigy of a Stamp informer, there to remain *in terrorem* till the STAMP ACT shall be repealed.

"After the above declaration publicly read and assented to by every person present, the effigy hung up, etc., the gentlemen of the County adjourned to a Tavern, where the King, the Royal family, and other loyal healths were drunk, every thing concluding with the utmost decency and good order."

The pens of patriotic Marylanders, in opposition to the Stamp Act, during the year 1765, were not confined to newspaper publications. The "Considerations on the propriety of imposing taxes on the British Colonies, for the purpose of raising a revenue by Acts of Parliament," by Daniel Dulany, can never be forgotten. The Messrs. Dulany, father and son, were the most distinguished lawyers and statesmen in America, and not surpassed in ability by any of the crown lawyers in the House of Commons. Mr. Pinkney, himself the wonder of his age, who saw but the setting splendor of the talents of

DANIEL DULANY.

the younger Dulany, is reported, says McMahon, to have said of him, "that even amongst such men as Fox, Pitt and Sheridan, he had not found his superior."[1]

[1] Daniel Dulany the elder, the father of the distinguished person alluded to in connection with the discussion on the stamp tax, was as conspicuous amongst cotemporaries as his most accomplished son, and enjoyed a reputation in the province surpassed only by that of the latter. He came into the province from England when about eighteen years of age, and was admitted to the bar of the provincial court in 1710; and from that period his career was one of uninterrupted honor and usefulness. For nearly forty years, he held the first place in the confidence of the proprietary and the affections of the people. During that period, he filled the various offices of alderman, city counciliman and recorder of Annapolis, attorney general, judge of the admiralty, commissary general, agent and receiver general and councillor of the province, the latter of which he held under the successive administrations of Governors Bladen, Ogle and Sharpe. He was also, for several years, a member of the Lower House from Anne Arundel county and Annapolis, in which capacity he was distinguished as the leader of the country party, in the controversy about the extension of the English statutes. After a long and lingering illness, he died, at Annapolis, Wednesday, December 5, 1753, in the sixty-eighth year of his age.

Daniel Dulany the greater, was the son of Daniel Dulany, above named, and Rebecca, his second wife, the daughter of Colonel Walter Smith, of Calvert county. He was born at Annapolis, July 19, 1721; was educated at Eton and at Clare Hall, Cambridge, England; was entered of the Temple; and, returning to

"He admitted that the colonies were subordinate to the supreme national council; that the British parliament had the unquestionable right to legislate on the trade of the colonies; that trade may frequently be most properly regulated by duties on imports and exports: that parliament is itself to determine what regulations are most proper; and that if they should produce an incidental revenue, they are not, therefore, unwarrantable.

"But in reply to the arguments of the crown lawyers, and the ministerial defenders of the Stamp Act, he argued, with minute and elaborate learning, that the late regulations for the colonies were not just, because the Commons of England, in which the Americans were neither actually nor virtually represented, had no right, by the common law or the British constitution, to give and grant the property of the Commons in America; that they were rightfully void, as their validity rested only on the power of those who framed them to carry them into effect; that they were not lenient, the taxes imposed being excessive and unequal; that they were not politic, as Great Britain, by the acts of trade, had all

America, was admitted to the bar of Maryland in 1747. He married Rebecca, daughter of Benjamin Tasker, of Annapolis, and died in Baltimore on the 19th of March, 1797. His remains are buried in St. Paul's cemetery, at the corner of Lombard and Fremont streets, Baltimore. His monument bears the following inscription: "In memory of the Hon. Daniel Dulany, Esq., barrister-at-law, who, with great integrity and honor for many years, discharged the important appointment of commissary general, Secretary of Maryland, and one of the Proprietary Council. In private life, he was beloved, and died regretted, March 19, 1797, aged 75 years and 8 months. Rebecca, his wife, daughter of the late Benjamin Tasker, Esq., of Annapolis, caused this tomb to be erected." The children of Daniel Dulany were: Daniel, who d. s. p.; Rebecca Ann, who married, and had one daughter, who d. s. p.; and Benjamin, who married Elizabeth French, from whom are numerous descendants. Mr. McMahon says: "For many years before the downfall of the Proprietary Government, he stood confessedly without a rival in this colony, as a lawyer, a scholar and an orator; and we may safely hazard the assertion that, in the high and varied accomplishments which constitute these, he has had amongst the sons of Maryland but one equal and no superior. We may admit that tradition is a magnifier, and that men seen through its medium and the obscurity of half a century, like objects in a misty morning, loom largely in the distance. Yet, with regard to Mr. Dulany, there is no room for such illusion. '*You may tell Hercules by his foot*,' says the proverb; and this truth is as just, when applied to the proportions of the mind, as to those of the body. The legal arguments and opinions of Mr. Dulany, which yet remain to us, bear the impress of abilities too commanding, and of learning too profound, to admit of question. Had we but these fragments, like the remains of splendor which linger around some of the ruins of antiquity, they would be enough for admiration. Yet they fall very far short of furnishing just conceptions of the character and accomplishments of his mind. We have higher attestations of these, in the testimony of cotemporaries. For many years before the Revolution, he was regarded as an *oracle* of the law. It was the constant practice of the courts of the province, to submit to his opinion every question of difficulty which came before them; and so infallible were his opinions considered, that he who hoped to reverse them was regarded 'as hoping against hope.' Nor was his professional reputation limited to the colony. I have been credibly informed, that he was occasionally consulted from England upon questions of magnitude: and that in the southern counties of Virginia adjacent to Maryland, it was not unfrequent to withdraw questions from their courts and even from the Chancellor of England, to submit them to his award. Thus unrivalled in professional learning, according to the representations of his cotemporaries, he added to it all the power of the orator, the accomplishments of the scholar, the graces of the person, and the suavity of the gentleman. Mr. Pinkney, himself the wonder of his age, who saw but the setting splendor of Mr. Dulany's talents, is reputed to have said of him, 'that even amongst such men as Fox, Pitt, and Sheridan, he had not found his superior.'

"Whatever were the errors of his course during the Revolution, I have never heard them ascribed, either to opposition to the rights of America, or to a servile submission to the views of the ministry: and I have been credibly informed, that he adhered, throughout life, to the principles advanced by him in opposition to the Stamp Act. The conjecture may be hazarded, that had he not been thrown into collision with the leaders of the Revolution in this State, by the proclamation controversy, and thus involved in discussion with them, which excited high resentment on both sides, and kept him at a distance from them until the Revolution began, he would, most probably, have been found by their side, in support of the measures which led to it."—McMahon, i., pp. 355-7.

from the colonies before, and could but drive them to observe the strictest maxims of frugality, and to establish manufactures of leather, cotton, wool and flax; that they were not consistent with charters, which were the original compacts between the first emigrants to America and the crown; that they were against all precedents of the previous legislation of the British parliament; that they were equally against the precedents of legislations for Ireland, which was as subject to Great Britain as were the colonies; that they were against the judgment of former British ministers, whose requisitions for revenue were uniformly transmitted to the colonies to tax themselves."[1]

"There may be a time," this patriotic statesman added, "when redress may be obtained. Till then, I shall recommend a legal, orderly, and prudent resentment to be expressed in a zealous and vigorous industry. A garment of linsey-woolsey, when made the distinction of patriotism, is more honorable than the plumes and the diadem of an emperor without it. Let the manufacture of America be the symbol of dignity and the body of virtue, and it will soon break the fetters of distress."[2]

In the midst of the discussion, and on the day (Nov. 1st, 1765,) on which the Stamp Act went into operation, the General Assembly met in Annapolis. On the second day of the session the "committee of grievances and courts of justice," composed of Walter Dulany, of Annapolis, John Hammond, of Anne Arundel, William Murdock, of Prince George's, Colonel Edward Tilghman, of Queen Anne's, Colonel Nicholas Hyland, of Cecil, and Fielder Gantt, of Frederick, were instructed "to inspect the form of the oaths of office, that have been, and now are usually taken by the several magistrates, and if the following clause be not inserted in the said oath," it was declared and resolved to be necessary: "To do equal law and right to all the king's subjects, rich and poor; and not to delay any person of common right, for the letters of the king, the Lord Proprietary, or of any other, or for any other cause; but if any such letters come to them, they shall proceed to do the law, the same letters notwithstanding." The House also unanimously resolved:

"That this province is not under the circumstances of a conquered country; that if it were, the present Christian inhabitants thereof would be in the circumstances, not of the conquered, but of the conquerors, it being a colony of the English nation, encouraged by the crown to transplant themselves hither, for the sake of improving and enlarging its dominions; which, by the blessing of God upon their endeavors, at their own expense and labor, has been in a great measure obtained: And it is *unanimously resolved*, that whoever shall advance, that his majesty's subjects, by such their endeavors and success, have forfeited any part of their English liberties, are not well-wishers to the country, and mistake its happy constitution.

"*Resolved also*, That if there be any pretence of conquest, it can be only supposed against the native Indian infidels; which supposition cannot be admitted, because the Christain inhabitants purchased great part of the land they at first took up from the Indians, as well as from the Lord Proprietary, and have ever since continued in an amicable course of trade with them; except some partial outrages and skirmishes, which never amounted to a general war, much less to a general conquest, the Indians yet enjoy-

[1] Bancroft, vol. v., p. 326.

[2] Dulany's pamphlet was published October 14, 1765.

ing their rights and privileges of treaties and trade with the English, of whom we yet frequently purchase their rights of such lands as we take up, as well as of the Lord Proprietary.

"*Resolved also*, That this Province hath always hitherto had the common law, and such general statutes of England, as are securitative of the rights and liberties of the subject, and such acts of assembly as were made in the Province to suit its particular constitution, as the rule and standard of its government and judicature; such statutes and Acts of Assembly being subject to the like rules of common law, or equitable construction as are used by the Judges in construing State statutes in England; which happy rules have, by his Majesty and his royal ancestors, and also by his Lordship, and his noble ancestors, or some of them, been hitherto approved, by having the commissions of judicature, to include directions of that nature to the several judicial magistrates; unless those words have at any time been casually or carelessly omitted by the officers in this province, that drew such commissions.

"*Resolved*, That the levying and taking the sum of twelve pence sterling per hogshead by the right honorable the Lord Proprietary of this Province, on all tobacco exported out of the same, under pretence and color of the act of 1704, is not warranted by law."

Captain James Hawker of his majesty's ship *Sardoine*, while anchored at New Castle, Delaware, informed Governor Sharpe that he had on board of his vessel the stamped paper for New Jersey and Pennsylvania, and a portion for Maryland; but not having a place of safety to land it, begged directions for its disposal. The governor applied to the Lower House for advice, and they informed him that they were extremely sorry they could not comply with his request as it was "not agreeable to the sentiments of their constituents to give him any advice upon the subject." A few days after this, on the 13th of December, they rebuked the governor for his delay in convening them at a period when they were desirous to unite with their fellow citizens in the other colonies, in the preservation of their rights. Their "address" clearly displays their talents and patriotism. "We are truly concerned" they say "that the duty we owe to our constituents, lays us under the indispensable necessity of observing, that every power lodged in the hands of government is there entrusted by the constitution, to be exercised for the common good. To this end hath your Excellency, as supreme magistrate, the power of convening and proroguing; which, we need not remark, according to the bill of rights, confirmed at the happy revolution, ought, for redress of all grievances, and for amending, strengthening, and preserving of laws, to be held frequently. The unhappy prevalence of the small-pox, from the month of March to that of September last, rendered a convention of assembly within that time impracticable; but we are ignorant of any reasons that could occasion the long intervention from November, 1763, to last March; within which time circumstances of a peculiar nature required a meeting of assembly, which was prevented by prorogation. It is incumbent on us, as the representatives of a free people, to remonstrate against that measure; especially, as it prevailed at a time so very critical to the rights of America; at a time when the good people of this province ardently wished for an opportunity to express, by their representatives in assembly, their sense of a scheme then entertained by the

British House of Commons, of imposing stamp duties on the colonies; and for want of which, their involuntary silence on a subject so interesting and important, has been construed by a late political writer of Great Britain, as an acquiescence in that intended project."

In conclusion, they say: "If we should be now silent, at some future time, when it may be the unhappiness of this province to be under the government of a gentleman less favorable in his inclinations to the interest of America than yourself, the occasion, which has laid us under the disagreeable necessity of troubling your Excellency with this assertion of our rights, might be made use of as a precedent for promoting measures prejudicial to the rights and privileges of the good people of this province."

In consequence of the ravages of the small pox (one of the members of the assembly having died with it), the governor, on the 20th of December, prorogued the assembly until the first Monday in March, 1766.[1]

The opposition against the government was now organized into a compact and enterprising party, strengthening itself throughout the province, and making itself known by its influence over the action of representatives in the assembly. In Maryland, its more aggressive members, under the name of "Sons of Liberty"—a phrase used by Barré, in his celebrated speech in parliament, in February, 1765,—by a series of bold and defiant attacks upon the government of the province, at a very early period increased their power, and steadily sapped the reverence for British law and legislative authority. In October, the Sons of Liberty of Frederick county formed an organization under the leadership of Colonel Thomas Cresap, and in December, about three or four hundred of them, "armed with guns and tomahawks," assembled at Frederick town, and threatened "to march down in companies to Annapolis, in order to settle the disputes betwixt the two Houses of Assembly."[2]

[1] On the 4th of November, 1765, Mr. Hugh Hamersley, of Sergeant's Inn, London, was appointed by Frederick, Lord Baltimore, Secretary of the Province, in consequence of the death of Cecilius Calvert, uncle of Lord Baltimore, and late Secretary of Maryland, resident in London.

[2] Dr. David Ross, in his deposition, submitted to the assembly, said that about the 27th or 29th of October, a "writing addressed to the Lower House of Assembly," was circulated in Frederick county for signatures, which was in substance as follows: "It expressed a satisfaction of the conduct of the Lower House, in opposing the Stamp Act, and intimated a reliance that they would endeavor, like the renowned, true, ancient Roman Senate, to suppress any future attempts to deprive them of their liberty; it also expressed, that the signers were informed, that a very large unjust claim in tobacco, was made against the public, by particular gentlemen in Annapolis [alluding to the governor and his council, who insisted on the collection of the twelve pence per hogshead on tobacco exported under the Act of 1804, and which the Lower House, since 1739, had constantly and ineffectually declared that his Lordship had no right to collect], preventing the payment of other just claims, and desiring that if the said unjust and dishonorable claim should still be insisted upon, the Lower House would give speedy intelligence, in order that the signers might come down and cause justice to take place." These threats produced considerable excitement in Annapolis, as it was rumored at one time that some of the "Sons" were already at Elk Ridge, on their march to the capital. The governor became alarmed, and immediately summoned his council together, and laid the whole matter before them.—See *House Journal*, December 11, 1765.

These associations of citizens, under the style of Sons of Liberty, were organized in all parts of the province. On the 24th of February, 1766, a large number of the most prominent citizens of Baltimore assembled at the market-house, and organized an association for the avowed purpose of removing the cause of the partial suspension of public affairs, by compelling the officers at Annapolis to transact business without stamped paper. They adjourned to meet at the seat of government on the 1st of March ensuing, and at the same time invited the Sons of Liberty of the other counties to be present and co-operate with them. In the meantime, they notified the public officers of their coming, and advised them to be in readiness to receive them.[1]

At the appointed time the Sons of Liberty of Baltimore and Anne Arundel counties were personally present, and those of Kent by deputy. Upon their organization, application by petition was made to the chief justice of the provincial court, the secretary of the province, the commissary general, and the judges of the land office, requiring them, on pain of compulsion, to open their respective offices on the 31st of March, or earlier, if a majority of the supreme courts of the northern colonies should proceed in their business before that period. The answers they received were not entirely satisfactory; and the Sons of Liberty, after requesting the attendance of the other organizations, adjourned to meet at Annapolis on the day assigned for the officers to proceed with their business. That day arrived, and they were at their post. They repaired in a body to the provincial court, to enforce their petition. It was at first peremptorily refused, but it was again earnestly insisted upon, and demanded by "the Sons of Liberty, with united hearts and voices;" and yielding the urgency of the demand, after receiving a written indemnification, the provincial court passed the following order, which was at once acceded to by the public officers, conformably to the petition, and the detested Stamp Act was, in Maryland, forever *null and void:* "It is by the court here ordered that the clerk of this court, from henceforth, issue all manner of process, file all pleadings, give copies, and transact all business whatsoever, in his office, for which application shall be made to him, by any inhabitant of this province, as usual, *without stamped paper.*"

On March 11, 1766, the Sons of Liberty, of Cecil county, adopted the following resolutions:

"We, the free denizens and liege subjects of Great Britain, residing in the county of Cecil and in the Province of Maryland, being duly sensible of the inestimable blessings of your happy constitution (the benefits of which we derived from our birth, and by the

[1] One of these very polite notifications is preserved in the Council Records. It runs thus:

"Sir, the shutting up of the public offices, and thereby impeding Justice, being of the greatest consequence to the community, the Sons of Liberty have resolved to assemble at the city of Annapolis, on Friday, the 28th inst., in order to obtain that Justice which has been so long withheld; and of this you are to take notice, and be at home to receive them. Hereof fail not at your —— Your obedient servants,

"SONS OF LIBERTY."

tenor of our conduct have never forfeited), cannot but be affected with the deepest sentiments of sorrow and concern at the present alarming conjuncture, so eminently threatening our dearest rights and most invaluable privileges.

"To prevent, as much as in us lieth, this approaching destruction of our civil liberties, as well as to testify to all succeeding ages our just abhorrence and detestation of slavery, and that we dare, by all lawful means to maintain our birth-rights, the subscribers hereof, with hearts inviolably attached to the person and family of our present most gracious sovereign, GEORGE THE THIRD, and attached with the firmest principles of fidelity and loyalty to his crown and government, have thought proper to join and concur in the following resolves:

"*First*—That the Freemen of this colony, are, and ever have been since their first emigration from Great Britain, entitled to all the liberties, franchises and privileges, of the free subjects of Great Britain.

"*Secondly*—That the imposition of internal taxes on this colony by the British Parliament, or any other authority whatever, except that of the House of Delegates in this Province; and the depriving the inhabitants thereof, of the benefit of trials by juries, by the extension of the jurisdiction of the Courts of Admiralty, is contrary to the spirit of the English constitution, destructive of our just rights and privileges, and tending to the slavery and ruin of us and our posterity.

"*Thirdly*—That the late Act of Parliament, commonly called the Stamp Act (being an express violation of MAGNA CHARTA, contrary to the Declaration of Rights, and the spirit of the Common Law), is unjust, illegal, and unconstitutional.

"*Fourthly and lastly*—We do hereby promise and agree, cheerfully and cordially to unite with all our fellow-subjects and countrymen, throughout the whole extended Empire of British America, in every just and lawful measure, to maintain our rights and privileges.

"Signed, by order of the committee of correspondence, by Joseph Earle, Secretary, Cecil County, March 11th, 1766."

Though the frequent colonial remonstrances to the mother country had been treated with scorn, and petition after petition had been refused a hearing, parliament viewed with no small concern the representations by their own merchants and manfactures of the effect of the Stamp Act on their cherished trade, and could but regard with serious alarm the official accounts of provincial affairs which were now pouring into England. The Rockingham administration had come into power in July, 1765, and as it was free from the odium which attached to the Grenville ministry for having devised this system of taxation, the repeal of the law was recommended upon the very grounds which had prompted its imposition. Accordingly, early in the year, a bill was introduced into parliament to repeal the Stamp Act, and speedily passing, was signed by the king on the 18th of March, 1765. As a salve to the wounded pride of the British government, thus compelled to retrace its steps, and to recede from the exercise of a power so boldly claimed, its repeal was preceded by an act declaratory of full power and authority in the king and parliament "to bind the colonies in all cases whatsoever," and the colonial resolves, asserting that the sole and exclusive right of taxation resided in the Provincial Assemblies, were declared derogatory to the authority of parliament, inconsistent with the dependence of the colonies upon the crown, and null and void.

The repeal of the Stamp Act was received in Maryland with unbounded joy, and the people expressed their gratification in every form that could be devised, town vying with town, and county with county in patriotic demonstrations. There was a general jubilee as for a great deliverance. On the receipt of the news in Annapolis on the 22d of May, both Houses of the Legislature then in session, adjourned to the council chamber, "where loyal and patriotic toasts were drunk, the guns at the dock at the same time firing," amid other demonstrations of joy. The 4th of June being the king's birthday, was celebrated in Annapolis with the firing of guns, punch-drinking and other festivities, and in the evening with a general illumination of the city. In all sections of the province subscriptions were made for the erection of a monument and statue to William Pitt "for the universal services done to this province and continent, and to the lovers of liberty in general." In November, 1766, the House of Delegates, "taking into their most serious consideration, the noble and spirited conduct of the Right Honorable William Pitt, now Earl of Chatham, and the Right Honorable Charles Pratt, Lord Camden, late Lord Chief Justice of the Common Pleas, and now Lord High Chancellor of England, in defending and supporting the rights and liberties of their fellow-subjects in general," "to transmit to posterity their grateful sentiments of the inflexible integrity, and conspicuous abilities of these shining ornaments of their country, and as a monument of their virtue" and "a lasting testimony of the gratitude of the freemen of Maryland," unanimously decreed, that a marble statue of Chatham should be erected in the city of Annapolis, and a portrait of Lord Camden, by some eminent hand, should be placed in the provincial court. Messrs. Thomas Ringgold, Thomas Johnson, Daniel Wolstenholme, John Hall, Charles Grahame, John Hanson, Jr., William Murdock and Samuel Chase brought in a bill to carry the resolutions into effect, which was passed by the Lower House but was rejected in the Upper, owing to the differences existing between the two branches of the assembly. At the same time they *unanimously resolved*, "That the most grateful thanks, and sincere acknowledgments of this House be presented by Mr. Garth[1] to the Right Honorable the Earl of Chesterfield, the Right Honorable Lord Shelbourne, Secretary Conway, General Howard, Col. Barré, Sir George Saville, Alderman Beckford, and any others of the lords and commons, Mr. Garth may think have acted the like glorious part of defending through principle the just rights of the colonists; and that they be assured, their honor shall never be tarnished, or their dignity be lessened, but their memories will be endeared by their benevolence and regard to British America." The assembly, "impressed

GEORGE III.

[1] This Mr. Charles Garth was a member of Parliament, and the agent of the province in London.

with a just sense of his majesty's tender and affectionate regard for these colonies, manifested by his ready and cheerful assent to a repeal of the oppressive American Stamp Act" on the 6th of December, 1766, adopted the following address to the king, and transmitted it to the Lord Proprietary with the request to present it to his majesty:

"THE HUMBLE ADDRESS OF THE UPPER HOUSE OF ASSEMBLY OF THE PROVINCE OF MARYLAND.

"To the King's most excellent Majesty:

"*Most Gracious Sovereign:* We, your Majesty's most dutiful and loyal subjects, the Upper House of Assembly of the Province of Maryland, beg leave to present our unfeigned thanks for the recent and signal instance of your Royal Attention to the welfare of your Majesty's American Colonies.

"When we contemplate and compare their late distressed condition and dismal prospect with their present situation, we admire the wisdom and justice of your Majesty's councils, to which they are indebted for the happy change; and our hearts are filled with gratitude to the best of Sovereigns, for an event so highly interesting, not only to your American, but also to your British subjects, the welfare of these colonies and that of your European dominions being absolutely inseparable.

"We take the liberty to assure your Majesty, that we shall, by our conduct on all occasions, endeavor to give continual proof of our zeal, loyalty, and respect to your Majesty and the Parliament of Great Britain; with the greatest fervor we implore of Heaven that the tranquillity now restored throughout these Provinces, the affectionate regard of Great Britain towards her Colonies and their attachment to her may be perpetual, and that your Majesty may long live to enjoy the pleasure it must afford you, to see all your subjects throughout your extensive dominions perfectly happy under your mild, equal, and auspicious government.

"BENJ. TASKER, *President.*

"*6 December, 1766.*"

Previous to the meeting of the assembly, "a meeting of the gentlemen and freeholders of Queen's town, Queen Anne's county, was held on the 6th of June, for the purpose of sharing in the general exultation over the repeal of the Stamp Act." These proceedings are thus described:

"The citizens met at the house of Thomas Baker, and proceeded from thence to the green, before the court house, where a hole was dug in the ground and the emblems of DISCORD deposited therein. A pillar was erected on the spot, amid the joyful shouts of the assembled crowd and booming of cannon, upon the sides of which was the following inscription:

"'Underneath the foot hereof lieth buried in oblivion *Discord*, And by the friends of liberty of Queen Anne's county this pillar is dedicated to *Concord*, In memory of the restoration of union, mutual affection and tranquility to Great Britain and her colonies, under the auspices of their good King, George the Third, By the friends to American Freedom, but more particularly by the virtuous influence of the great guardian of the rights of mankind, William Pitt, The great preserver of English liberty, Lord Camden, and the present worthy and patriotic ministry.' The company then returned to Mr. Baker's, where an elegant entertainment was prepared; after which the followng toasts were drunk, with the discharge of cannon.

"1. The King. 2. Queen. 3. Prince of Wales and all the Royal family. 4. Perpetual union and harmony between Great Britain and her colonies, under the auspicious government of the illustrious house of Hanover. 5. May the submission of America to the mother country be ever compatible with her constitutional liberty. 6. The House of Lords. 7. The House of Commons. 8. Mr. Pitt. 9. Lord Camden. 10. Col. Barré. 11. General Howard. 12. The Governor and Prosperity of Maryland. 13. The Virginia Assembly. 14. The man that first proposed the Congress of New York. 15. All the gentlemen of the Congress, except those that refused to sign. 16. Daniel Dulany, Esq. 17. John Dickinson, Esq. 18. The London Committee of Merchants. 19. The Navy and Army. 20. Trade and Navigation. 21. Number 105 in the House of Lords. 22. Number 250 in the House of Commons. 23. All true hearts and sound bottoms.

"The company then returned to the Pillar and drank the health, &c., of Pitt and Concord. After which they passed unanimously the following resolution: 'That they think it their duty (as they have not the means of directly addressing the Throne) to declare to the world, with hearts full of the warmest duty and affection, their unshaken and inviolable attachment and loyalty to their lawful, rightful, most good and gracious sovereign George the Third, and gratitude for his royal and beneficent attention to the complaints of his subjects on the continent of America in relieving them from the confusion and distress which must inevitably have attended the execution of the Stamp Act, and most solemnly to join in the ardent prayer which cannot but flow from the hearts of every American, that there may not, to the latest period of time, be wanting a Prince of his most illustrious house to adorn the Imperial Crown of Great Britain, and extend the royal beneficence to all his loyal subjects however remote.' In the evening the day's celebration was concluded with the illumination of the town."

On the 27th of June, Governor Sharpe wrote to General Conway that "tranquillity and good order is now perfectly restored here, and the late distractions will, I hope, soon be forgotten. The resentment some time ago expressed against the person that was appointed to distribute the stamped paper here, is entirely subsided, and he now resides and carries on business in this place to as great extent and advantage as he did before his appointment."

Secretary Conway, in his circular letter of March 31, to the governor, said that the king and parliament "seemed disposed not only to *forgive* but to *forget* those most unjustifiable marks of an undutiful disposition too frequent in the late transactions of the colonies;" but at the same time required them strongly to recommend to the assemblies to make full and ample compensation to those who had suffered "for their deference to the Act of the British Legislature." In November, this letter and a set of resolutions of the House of Commons were laid before the assembly, who complied with the royal recommendation by voting an appropriation to Arme Gaither as a compensation for his house, that was torn down by the mob on the night of September 2, 1765, while occupied by Hood; and also compensation to Wight Miles for the loss of his tools, which were in the house. The governor, in a letter to Lord Shelburne, dated December 9, 1766, says, "the sufferers were entirely satisfied."[1]

[1] Hood was rewarded by the British government with a commissionership at Turk's Island. He died at St. George's, Bermuda, on the 4th of May, 1780, where he had gone for the recovery of his health.

Thus the first act of the drama had closed with a triumph for the colonies. But it was impossible that the matter could end here. The pride of England had received a rebuke: her authority had been resisted, and that in a quarter from which she could least patiently brook it. Not all the loyal toasts, fervent protestations of devotion, and humble phraseology of the addresses could deafen English ears or blind their eyes to the true meaning of the shouts and bonfires which rang and blazed through the province. The son had not only dared to question the father's authority, but had plucked the rod from his hand and broken it before his face. Policy might demand temporary acquiescence, but the forward child must be brought back to obedience.

Only such enlightened and far-reaching minds as those of Pitt, Camden, Burke, and a few others, could grasp the idea of a transatlantic England: could understand that "Englishmen" meant men of a certain race, speech, mode of thought and feeling, and not those alone who dwelt within certain geographical boundaries, and were governed by acts of parliament. Yet this conception was innate and instinctive in the minds of the colonists: they felt themselves Englishmen in every fibre; heirs of all the history, all the traditions, and all the free spirit of their race, their love of liberty and revolt against tyranny: Englishmen, too, who had deserved well of England, by enlarging its dominions, fighting its battles, and augmenting its wealth and dignity. They felt themselves to be, in courage, in intelligence, in patriotism, no whit inferior to their brethren in the old home, whose only claim to superiority rested on the fact that they had done none of these things; and it was an exasperating injustice to them to be treated as conquered enemies or an inferior race—men whose claims to justice were to be held subordinate to insular interests; who had somehow forfeited their rights as freemen, their share in the common law and the Great Charter, by having planted and defended the flag of England beyond the seas.

Yet the position of England was not altogether unreasonable. While it is true that the war which established English supremacy in North America was really the collision of concurrent ambitions, and an episode in the rivalry of four hundred years, yet it cannot be denied that in material and immediate interests the colonies reaped a far greater benefit than the mother-country. To the Englishman the conquest of Canada meant triumph and flattered pride; to the colonists it meant peace, prosperity and abundance; while to the frontiersman it meant comfort, instead of desolation, security instead of incessant fear, a smiling home instead of blazing rafters, life instead of death. While the colonists had done their full share of the fighting, the burden of expense fell upon England; and it seemed intolerable to ministers like Grenville and Townshend, accustomed to figure up a budget and lay a tax by a simple Act of Parliament, that the contributions of the colonies could only be obtained by requests, always sharply canvassed, and sometimes squarely refused by the colonial legislatures. The principles of equity involved seemed not so clear when urged from another hemisphere; and the letter of charters granted by Stuarts to their favorites, was of small account in their eyes. As for the remedy of colonial representation, the practical difficulties were too great; and even had they not existed, a colonist sitting, voting, and urging the rights of his constituents in the British Parliament, would have been to the English mind, as to the Hebrew, a Gibeonite entering the Holy of Holies and opening the Ark of the Covenant.

The problem was urgent: though difficult, it was not insoluble; and events were now steadily bearing it to a solution which neither party at that time desired, but which some already descried as a possible contingency of the future.

END OF VOLUME I.

www.ingramcontent.com/pod-product-compliance
Lightning Source LLC
Chambersburg PA
CBHW021823220426
43663CB00005B/110

* 9 7 8 1 4 4 6 0 1 7 8 9 0 *